A SOURCEBOOK ON
PLANNING LAW IN IRELAND

To Heide, Roger and Tim
(Philip O'Sullivan)

To Colin
(Katharine Shephard)

A SOURCEBOOK ON
PLANNING LAW
IN
IRELAND

by

PHILIP O'SULLIVAN   and   KATHARINE SHEPHERD
Senior Counsel   *Barrister-at-Law*

PROFESSIONAL BOOKS LIMITED
1984

Published in 1984 by
Professional Books Limited,
Milton Trading Estate, Abingdon, Oxon.
Typeset by Oxford Publishing Services, Oxford
and printed in Great Britain by
Billing & Sons Ltd, Worcester

ISBN: 0-86205-090-1

PHILIP O'SULLIVAN AND KATHARINE SHEPHERD
1984

PREFACE

Despite the existence of a number of other publications in the field we believe that the increasing complexity of Irish planning law justifies an up-to-date source book bringing together in one place all Irish legal material which may be required by any practitioner in the planning field. We hope that this book will be of assistance not only to lawyers of both branches of the profession but also to town planners, architects, engineers, local authority officials, lecturers, associations of professional bodies concerned with promoting or advising on the promotion of development or with the protection of the environment, and indeed to any other individual or organisation requiring knowledge of any aspect of Irish planning law.

We decided that there was need for such a book almost three years ago. We feel this decision has been amply justified not only by the new legislation which has since come on to the statute book but also by the ever increasing volume of planning decisions which have been delivered by the Irish courts. These decisions are the least accessible to the non-legal practitioner: yet they can be of crucial importance. For this reason we have sought to include reference to, and in the vast majority of cases, excerpts from all written judgments delivered before the 31st December, 1983. In addition the book contains the four Acts (1963, 1976, 1982 and 1983) together with all regulations made thereunder.

The book makes available to the general reader for the first time the circular produced by the Department of Environment addressed to local authorities entitled 'Development Control: Advice and Guidelines'. This circular contains a statement of the policy of the Department in regard to various planning matters and should be of particular use to anyone making application for planning permission.

Undoubtedly there will be many more significant planning decisions in the future and most probably further important legislation. In the light of this we have agreed with our publisher that the book will be updated by supplements and, if necessary, further editions.

We acknowledge the permission of the Controller of the Stationery Office for permission to reprint the Acts and Regulations, of the Incorporated Council of Law Reporting for permission to reproduce extracts from the Irish Reports, of the Department of Justice to reprint extracts from unreported judgments and of the Editor of the Irish Law Reports Monthly for permission to reprint extracts from that publication. We would also like to thank the Minister for the Environment for permission to reproduce the circular on development control referred to above.

No practising barrister can function adequately, let alone publish a book, without drawing on a pool of knowledge which is contributed to by colleagues in the Law Library and which according to our tradition we make freely available to one another. We gratefully acknowledge our debt to our colleagues in this regard.

We would also like to offer particular thanks to our colleagues, Ernan P. De Blaghd, Barrister-at-Law for help with proof reading and preparation of the Index and to Mrs. Jennifer Aston and Miss Finola O'Sullivan for their assistance in obtaining unreported judgments and Miss Karen McCabe for photocopying and general help. Philip O'Sullivan would also like to thank Marie Swan for her painstaking and prompt typing of his portion of the manuscript.

Philip O'Sullivan

Katharine Shepherd
The Law Library
Four Courts
Dublin 7.
31st December, 1983

CONTENTS

TABLE OF STATUTES

TABLE OF STATUTORY INSTRUMENTS

TABLE OF CASES

Chapter 1

PLANNING AUTHORITIES

INTRODUCTION

Under the Planning Acts planning authorities[1] are constituted protectors of the environment. In this capacity their functions may be analysed broadly into four separate divisions, namely, (a) they prepare and revise development plans[2]; (b) they make decisions on individual applications for planning permissions[3]; (c) they are given extensive powers by way of enforcement proceedings in Court[4] and (d) they are given a variety of further powers designed to (1) ensure the effectiveness of the above[5], (2) protect specific amenities in a way not appropriate for inclusion in development plans[6] and (3) enable them to develop or ensure the development of community facilities.[7]

The enforcement and planning-decision functions of planning authorities are dealt with in separate chapters: this chapter will deal with their remaining functions.

DEVELOPMENT PLAN

Apart from exercising jurisdiction on planning applications the main way in which planning authorities attain the objectives of the planning code is in making and reviewing[8] the Development Plan. This comprises a statement which may be illustrated by maps.[9] The code lays down certain planning objectives which must be dealt with in the development plan[10] and once a development plan is duly implemented the planning authority is itself bound[11] by its provisions. The plan must be reviewed at least once every five years when the planning authority may make any variations in the existing plan or may make a new development plan.[12] In

---

[1] Defined at s.2(2) of the Act of 1963.
[2] Part II of the Act of 1963.
[3] Ss. 26 and 27.
[4] See chs. 2–3 and 5, *post*.
[5] See p. 26, *post*.
[6] See p. 18, *post*.
[7] Part VII of the Act of 1963, especially s. 77.
[8] Ss. 19(1) and 20(1) of the Act of 1963. See also s. 2(7)(a).
[9] S. 19(2) of the Act of 1963.
[10] There may be one or several plans: see sub-s. (5).
[11] See S. 26(1) and S. 26(3) of the Act of 1963 (as substituted by S. 39 of the Act of 1976). Compare *State (Pine Valley Developments Limited)* v. *Dublin County Council* (p. 207, *post*).
[12] S. 20 of the Act of 1963.

State (Abenglen Properties Ltd.) v. *Dublin Corporation* D'Arcy J. at first instance[13] held that the 1980 Development Plan made by Dublin Corporation was a new plan in itself and was not a variation of the earlier plan. The effect of Section 2(7)(*a*) of the Act of 1963 should be noted. This sub-section applies to many sections in the code where there is a reference to the provisions of the development plan. Most importantly by Section 26(1) when a planning authority is considering a planning application they must have regard to, inter alia, the provisions of the development plan. Section 2(7)(*a*) provides in effect that the planning authority shall have regard to the draft provisions.

Section 21 of the Act of 1963 (as amended) provides a fairly elaborate scheme for the publication of proposed variations in a development plan. A published notice must state that a copy of the draft may be inspected at a stated place and at stated times, that objections or representations made within this period will be taken into account before the making of the variations and that any ratepayer making objection has a right to make his case before a person or persons appointed by the planning authority.

The effect of these provisions was significantly curtailed as a result of *Finn* v. *Bray Urban District Council*.[14] In that case Butler J. held that if as a result of public objection variations were made to the draft revisions of the development plan the whole statutory scheme had to be gone through again so that the draft review as varied ought to have been again published and opportunity given to the public to make further objections or representations. In the result planning authorities tended merely to go through the motions of considering objections or representations but declined to introduce them into the draft review in order to avoid the possibility of an endless system.

It has been stated that the planning authority is bound by the provisions of its own plan. The position is as follows: in the Act of 1963 by Section 26(3)(*a*) the planning authority was prohibited from granting planning permission for a development which would contravene materially the development plan, save with the consent of the Minister for Local Government. The Act of 1976 substituted an entirely new Section 26(3) which now provides that the planning authority may grant such a permission provided that notice of their intention so to do is published in a daily newspaper circulating in the area, copies of the notice are given to the applicant and any person submitting an objection in writing, any objection or representation received within 21 days after the first publication of the notice shall be considered, and the proposal is approved by a resolution passed by the authority requiring that a decision to grant permission be made. Such a resolution must be carried by at least one-third of the total number of the members of the planning authority. Further provisions are made to deal with the situation where a 'section 4' motion[15] is passed directing the manager to grant permission in a specific case where the manager considers that the proposal would constitute a material contravention of the provisions of the development plan.

Under the Act of 1963 a planning authority had no jurisdiction to grant permission for a development which would involve a material contravention of the

---

[13] This decision is also noteworthy as indicating the scope of a planning authority's jursidiction to alter a proposal by the imposition of conditions. On appeal the case turned on the jurisdictional aspect in *certiorari* cases (see p. 316, *post*).
[14] [1974] I.R. 169.
[15] S. 4 of the City and County (Amendment) Act, 1955.

development plan save with the consent of the Minister. The Supreme Court decided in *State (Pine Valley Developments Ltd.)* v. *Dublin County Council*[16] that the Minister himself had no power to grant permission for such a development unless he was requested so to do by the planning authority. This decision caused consternation as it invalidated a great number of long standing planning permissions in reliance upon which people had carried out development or purchased property. In the result the Oireachtas supervened with section 6 of the Act of 1982 which at sub-section 1 provided that planning permissions in this category should not be regarded as ever having been invalid.

In *Short* v. *Dublin County Council*[17] McMahon J. held that reservation of lands for a particular purpose referred to in Rule 11 is not the same as the general zoning objectives provided for by Section 19(3) of the 1963 Act. In the context of Rule 11 the reservation of lands for a particular purpose means only the setting apart of these lands for a purpose distinct from the purpose for which the other land in the area is zoned. This decision was upheld in the Supreme Court.

It is worth noting that by Section 22(1) of the 1963 Act a planning authority has a duty to take such steps as may be necessary for securing the objectives which are contained in the provisions of the development plan. It is also noteworthy that the Minister for the Environment may require a planning authority to make specified variations in the development plan:[18] he may also give planning authorities general instructions in relation to the preparation of development plans,[19] and also policy directives in relation to planning and development generally.[20]

FURTHER POWERS OF PLANNING AUTHORITIES

Perhaps the best known of these powers is that conferred by Section 42 of the Act of 1963 whereby a planning authority can make a special amenity area order. Such an Order must be confirmed by the Minister. To date no Order has been so confirmed although the three Dublin local authorities have made them. Within the area of a special amenity area order a conservation order can be made relating to flora or fauna which shall have special value or interest.

Planning authorities have powers to make orders protecting hedges, trees, plants, and controlling noise, litter and advertisements.[21]

The Planning Acts appear to envisage a somewhat more active role for planning authorities as developers in their own right than has happened in practice. Whilst it has been held that there is no specific power of acquisition contained in the

---

[16] See p. 310.
[17] See pp. 423 ff. for the *Short* case and compare *Holiday Motor Inns Limited* v. *Dublin County Council* (see 441) which also considered Rule 11. In that case McWilliam J. held that the Rule 11 exclusion did not apply to a road which was practically complete at the date of service of the notice to treat although the lands on which it was constructed would have been 'reserved . . . for a particular purpose' in the development plan. The decision in the Supreme Court in the *Short* case was delivered by O'Higgins C.J. (Henchy, Hederman JJ. concurring) on 13th May 1983, see [1983] I.L.R.M. 377.
[18] S. 22(3).
[19] S. 23.
[20] S. 7 of the Act of 1982 and compare S. 31 of the Act of 1976. (The Minister consults with the Board and the Board makes submissions to the Minister). Useful circulars have been issued to planning authorities by the Minister.
[21] Part V of the Act of 1963 deals generally with amenities.

Planning Acts themselves,[22] the Acts do confer a significant range of powers enabling a planning authority to deal in land in one way or another for planning purposes[23] and of course the acquisition powers already existing can be used for planning purposes as well. Despite this planning authorities appear to have been somewhat reluctant developers in their own right. Planning authorities have power to appropriate land in their ownership to planning purposes, they may dispose of land for planning purposes,[24] they have powers to create and extinguish public rights-of-way,[25] powers to lay cables, pipelines, etc. over private property[26] and in Section 77 several detailed powers of development in their own right. These developments are such as may not be attractive to a private developer such as the renewal of obsolete areas, the preservation of a view and the provision of sites for a number of specified kinds of development.

ANCILLARY POWERS

Planning authorities have a number of support powers to enable them to carry out their functions. They may encourage tourist and planning studies;[28] they may enter lands,[29] the Minister may pass building regulations,[30] planning authorities enter specific agreements regarding specific lands[31] and there are a number of provisions specifying the duties of the public, vis-à-vis planning authorities, for example, imposing a duty on the public to give them specified information.[32]

THE REGISTER

Planning authorities are obliged to keep planning registers[33] in which all relevant planning information is to be recorded. They are also obliged to publish weekly lists[34] of planning decisions.

CONSTITUTIONALITY OF THE PLANNING ACTS

A challenge to the constitutional validity of several provisions of the Act of 1963 was made in the *Central Development Association Limited and Others* v. *the Attorney General*.[35] Judgment was delivered by Kenny J. on 6th October, 1969 rejecting the plaintiff's claims on all counts. This judgment is of more interest to the constitutional lawyer rather than the planning lawyer. However, the recent decision of the Supreme Court in *Blake and Others* v. *the Attorney General*[36] has cast a fresh light on some of the dicta.

One of the points made by the plaintiffs in the *Central Dublin* case was that

---

[22] *Leinster Importing Company Limited* v. *Dublin County Council* (p. 43 and *Movie News Limited* v. *Galway County Council* (p. 44).
[23] Especially in S. 7 and Part VII of the Act of 1963 generally.
[24] S. 24 of the Act of 1963.
[25] S. 76 of the Act of 1963.
[26] S. 85 of the Act of 1963.
[27] S. 14(2)(*b*).
[28] S. 15.
[29] S. 83.
[30] S. 86. Draft building regulations have been circulated by the Department of the Environment.
[31] S. 38.
[32] S. 9.
[33] S. 8.
[34] Regulation 24 of Statutory Instrument No. 65 of 1977.
[35] 109 ILTR 19.
[36] [1981] ILRM 34.

sections 19, 20 and 21 of the Act of 1963 requiring planning authorities to make and review development plans would mean that private property could be devalued as a result. The judge accepted this proposition but held that it was not an unjust attack on property rights remarking (at page 35 of a 59-page judgment) 'If this argument were correct, many owners of houses would have been entitled to be paid compensation when the Rent Restrictions Act, 1946 was passed'. Earlier he had remarked that no one had ever suggested that the Rent Restrictions Acts or the Landlord and Tenant Acts were unconstitutional.

In delivering the judgment of the Supreme Court in the *Blake* case O'Higgins C.J. held that the restrictions of the property rights of one group of citizens for the benefit of another implemented by Part II of the Act of 1960 without compensation to the landlords constituted 'an unjust attack on the property rights of landlords of controlled dwellings and are therefore contrary to the provisions of Article 40.3.2. of the Constitution'. Reaching this conclusion O'Higgins C.J. laid particular emphasis on the fact that ascertainment of the basic rent was beyond review. The provisions of the development plan are, on the other hand, reviewed every five years. Moreover the public or any affected individual has a right of objection to a proposed development plan.

The constitutionality of the Act of 1976 was unsuccessfully challenged on a handful of points in *Finnegan* v. *An Bord Pleanala*:[37] an appeal to the Supreme Court was also unsuccessful.

LOCAL GOVERNMENT (PLANNING AND DEVELOPMENT) ACT, 1963

AN ACT TO MAKE PROVISION, IN THE INTERESTS OF THE COMMON GOOD, FOR THE PROPER PLANNING AND DEVELOPMENT OF CITIES, TOWNS AND OTHER AREAS, WHETHER URBAN OR RURAL (INCLUDING THE PRESERVATION AND IMPROVEMENT OF THE AMENITIES THEREOF), TO MAKE CERTAIN PROVISIONS WITH RESPECT TO ACQUISITION OF LAND, TO REPEAL THE TOWN AND REGIONAL PLANNING ACTS, 1934 AND 1939, AND CERTAIN OTHER ENACTMENTS AND TO MAKE PROVISIONS FOR OTHER MATTERS CONNECTED WITH THE MATTERS AFORESAID. [*7th August, 1963*]

BE IT ENACTED BY THE OIREACHTAS AS FOLLOWS:–

PART I

PRELIMINARY AND GENERAL

1. – (1) This Act may be cited as the Local Government (Planning and Development) Act, 1963.

(2) This Act shall come into operation as follows:

---

[37] See p. 49.

(*a*) this section shall come into operation on the passing of this Act,

(*b*) sections 86, 87 and 88 and subsection (5) of section 92 shall come into operation on the day fixed for that purpose by the Minister for Local Government by order,[38]

(*c*) if an order is made under paragraph (a) of subsection (3) of this section, the rest of this Act shall come into operation on the day appointed by that order,[39]

(*d*) if an order is not made under paragraph (a) of subsection (3) of this section, the rest of this Act shall come into operation in an area on the day appointed with respect to that area by order made under paragraph (b) of that subsection.

(3) The Minister for Local Government –

(*a*) may by order appoint a day[39] to be the day appointed under this Act, or

(*b*) may by orders appoint two or more different days to be, with respect to different areas respectively, the days appointed under this Act.

2. – (1) In this Act, save where the context otherwise requires –

'The Act of 1919' means the Acquisition of Land (Assessment of Compensation) Act, 1919;

'the Act of 1934' means the Town and Regional Planning Act, 1934 (repealed by this Act);

'advertisement' means any word, letter, model, balloon, kite, poster, notice, device or representation employed for the purpose of advertisement, announcement or direction;

'advertisement structure' means any structure which is a hoarding, scaffold, framework, pole, standard, device or sign (whether illuminated or not) and which is used or intended for use for exhibiting advertisements;

'agriculture' includes horticulture, fruit growing, seed growing, dairy farming, the breeding and keeping of livestock (including any creature kept for the production of food, wool, skins or fur, or for the purpose of its use in the farming of land), the use of land as grazing land, meadow land, osier land, market gardens and nursery grounds, the use of land for turbary, and the use of land for woodlands where that use is ancillary to the farming of land for other agricultural purposes, and 'agricultural' shall be construed accordingly;

'alteration' includes any plastering or painting which materially alters the external appearance of a structure so as to render such appearance inconsistent with the character of the structure or of neighbouring structures;

'appointed day'[39] means –

(*a*) if a day is appointed under paragraph (a) of subsection (3) of section 1 of this Act, that day, and

(*b*) if a day is not appointed under that paragraph, the day appointed under paragraph (*b*) of that subsection with respect to the relevant area;

'building regulations'[38] has the meaning assigned to it by section 86;

'car park' has the same meaning as in section 101 of the Road Traffic Act, 1961;

'development' has the meaning assigned to it by section 3, and 'develop' shall be construed accordingly;

[38] No such Order has been made. Draft Building Regulations have been circulated by the Department of the Environment.

[39] The 'appointed day' is the 1st October, 1964 for the whole country.

'development plan' has the meaning appropriate in accordance with subsection (9) of section 19;

'exempted development' has the meaning specified in section 4;

'exhibit', in relation to an advertisement, includes affix, inscribe, print, paint and otherwise delineate;

'fence' includes a hoarding or similar structure;

'functions' includes powers and duties;

'land' includes any structure and any land covered with water (whether inland or coastal) and, in relation to the acquisition of land, includes any interest or right in or over land (including an interest or right granted by or held from the authority acquiring the land);

'local authority' means a local authority for the purposes of the Local Government Act, 1941;

'the Minister' means the Minister for Local Government;[40]

'non-municipal town' means a place (not being a county borough, borough, urban district or town in which the Towns Improvement (Ireland) Act, 1854, is in operation) which is designated a town in the report of the census of population taken in the year 1956;

'obsolete area' means an area consisting of land (in this definition referred to as the principal land) which, in the opinion of the planning authority, is badly laid out or the development of which has, in their opinion, become obsolete, together with such land contiguous or adjacent to the principal land as, in the opinion of the planning authority, is necessary for the satisfactory development or user of the principal land;

'owner', in relation to land, means, a person, other than a mortgagee not in possession, who, whether in his own right or as trustee or agent for any other person, is entitled to receive the rack rent of the land or, where the land is not let at a rack rent, would be so entitled if it were so let;

'prescribed' means prescribed by regulations made by the Minister;

'public place' means any street, road, seashore or other place to which the public have access whether as of right or by permission and whether subject to or free of charge;

'public road' has the same meaning as in the Road Traffic Act, 1961;

'the register' means the register kept under section 8;

'reserved function' means –

    (*a*) with respect to the council of a county or an elective body for the purposes of the County Management Acts, 1940 to 1955, a reserved function for the purposes of the County Management Acts, 1940 to 1955,

    (*b*) with respect to the corporation of a county borough, a reserved function for the purposes of the Acts relating to the management of the county borough;

'road' has the same meaning as in the Road Traffic Act, 1961;

'scheduled town' means –

    (*a*) any town specified in Part I of the First Schedule to this Act, or

    (*b*) any non-municipal town specified in Part II of that Schedule;

'seashore' has the same meaning as in the Foreshore Act, 1933;

'special amenity area order' means an order confirmed under section 43;

[40] Now the Minister for the Environment.

'statutory undertaker' means a person authorised by a British or Saorstát Éireann statute or an Act of the Oireachtas or an order having statutory force to construct, work, or carry on a railway, canal, inland navigation, dock, harbour, gas, electricity, or other public undertaking;

'structure' means any building, erection, structure, excavation, or other thing constructed, erected, or made on, in, or under any land, or any part of a structure so defined, and, where the context so admits, includes the land on, in, or under which the structure is situate;

'unauthorised structure' means –

    (*a*) in relation to a structure in an area in relation to which a resolution under section 26 of the Act of 1934 was passed, a structure other than –

        (i) a structure in existence when that resolution was passed,

        (ii) a structure for which there was a general or special permission under that Act, being a permission which has not been revoked,

        (iii) a structure the construction, erection or making of which was the subject of a permission for development granted under section 26 of this Act, being a permission which has not been revoked, or which exists as a result of the carrying out on or after the appointed day of exempted development,

        (iv) a structure for the retention of which a permission was granted under section 27 of this Act, being a permission which has not been revoked,

        (v) a structure which, immediately before the appointed day, had the protection afforded by section 15 of the Act of 1934, or

    (*b*) in relation to a structure in any other area, a structure other than –

        (i) a structure in existence on the commencement of the appointed day, or

        (ii) a structure the construction, erection or making of which was the subject of a permission for development granted under section 26 of this Act, being a permission which has not been revoked, or which exists as a result of the carrying out on or after the appointed day of exempted development;

'unauthorised use' means, in relation to land, use commenced on or after the appointed day, the change in use being a material change and being development other than development the subject of a permission granted under section 26 of this Act or exempted development;

'use', in relation to land, does not include the use of the land by the carrying out of any works thereon;[41]

'works' includes any act or operation of construction, excavation, demolition, extension, alteration, repair or renewal.

    (2) In this Act 'planning authority' means –

    (*a*) in the case of a county exclusive of any borough or urban district therein, the council of the county,

    (*b*) in the case of a county or other borough, the corporation of the borough, and

    (*c*) in the case of an urban district, the council of the district,

and references to the area of the planning authority shall be construed accordingly.

    (3) A reference in this Act to contravention of a provision includes, where

---

[41] *In re Viscount Securities, Viscount Securities Limited* v. *Dublin County Council* (p. 453).

appropriate, a reference to refusal or failure to comply with that provision.

(4) Any reference in this Act to performance of functions includes, with respect to powers, a reference to exercise of powers.

(5) Any reference in this Act to any other enactment shall, except so far as the context otherwise requires, be construed as a reference to that enactment, as amended by or under any other enactment including this Act.

(6)(*a*) A town specified in Part II of the First Schedule to this Act shall be taken for the purposes of this Act as comprising the area declared by the council of the county in which the town is situate to be comprised therein for those purposes.

(*b*) Declaration of any such area shall be a reserved function.

(*c*) A declaration made under this subsection may be amended by the council of a county by whom it was made and the making of any such amendment shall be a reserved function.[42]

(7) In subsection (1) of section 22, subsection (1) of section 26, subsection (1) of section 27, subsection (2) of section 30, subsection (2) of section 31, subsection (2) of section 32, subsection (2) of section 33, subsection (2) of section 35, subsection (3) of section 36 and subsection (3) of section 37 of this Act –

(*a*) the references to the provisions of the development plan shall, until that plan is made, be construed as references to the provisions which the planning authority consider will be included in that plan;[43]

(*b*) the references to the provisions of any special amenity area order relating to the area of the planning authority shall be construed as including references to any provisions which the planning authority consider will be included in a special amenity area order relating to their area.

(8) The Minister may by order vary the First Schedule to this Act by addition or deletion, but, where any such order is proposed to be made, a draft thereof shall be laid before each House of the Oireachtas and the order shall not be made until a resolution approving of the draft has been passed by each such House.

6. – (1) A planning authority shall have all such powers of examination, investigation and survey as may be necessary for the performance of their function in relation to this Act or to any other Act under which they have functions affected by the performance of their functions under this Act.

(2) In particular and without prejudice to the generality thereof, subsection (1) of this section shall be construed as conferring powers to make –

(*a*) examinations of tourist potential, interest and need,

(*b*) land use surveys,

(*c*) traffic, sociological and demographic surveys.

7. – (1) Where a notice or copy of an order is required or authorised by this Act or any order or regulation made thereunder to be served on or given to a person, it shall be addressed to him and shall be served on or given to him in some one of the following ways:[44]

---

[42] Para. (*c*) added by S. 43(1)(*a*) of the Act of 1976.
[43] A Planning Authority is accordingly authorised to have regard to the draft development plan.
[44] See *Freeney* v. *Bray Urban District Council* (p. 291). Compare S. 22 or the Act of 1976 for posting *appeals*.

(*a*) where it is addressed to him by name, by delivering it to him;

(*b*) by leaving it at the address at which he ordinarily resides or, in a case in which an address for service has been furnished, at that address;

(*c*) by sending it by post in a prepaid registered letter addressed to him at the address at which he ordinarily resides or, in a case in which an address for service has been furnished, at that address;

(*d*) where the address at which he ordinarily resides cannot be ascertained by reasonable inquiry and the notice or copy is so required or authorised to be given or served in respect of any land or premises, by delivering it to some person over sixteen years of age resident or employed on such land or premises or by affixing it in a conspicuous position on or near such land or premises.

(2) Where a notice or copy of an order is required by this Act or any order or regulation made thereunder to be served on or given to the owner or to the occupier of any land or premises and the name of the owner or of the occupier (as the case may be) cannot be ascertained by reasonable inquiry, it may be addressed to 'the owner' or 'the occupier' (as the case may require) without naming him.

(3) For the purposes of this section, a company registered under the Companies Acts, 1908 to 1959, shall be deemed to be ordinarily resident at its registered office, and every other body corporate and every unincorporated body shall be deemed to be ordinarily resident at its principal office or place of business.

(4) Where a notice or copy of an order is served on or given to a person by affixing it under paragraph (*d*) of subsection (1) of this section, a copy of the notice or order shall, within two weeks thereafter, be published in at least one newspaper circulating in the area in which the person is last known to have resided.

(5) A person who, at any time during the period of three months after a notice is affixed under paragraph (*d*) of subsection (1) of this section, removes, damages or defaces the notice without lawful authority shall be guilty of an offence and shall be liable on summary conviction thereof to a fine not exceeding ten pounds.

(6) Where the Minister is satisfied that reasonable grounds exist for dispensing with the serving or giving under this Act or under any order or regulation made thereunder of a notice or copy of an order and that dispensing with the serving or giving of the notice or copy will not cause injury or wrong, he may dispense with the serving or giving of the notice or copy and every such dispensation shall have effect according to the tenor thereof.

(7) A dispensation under the foregoing subsection may be given either before or after the time when the notice or copy would, but for the dispensation, be required to be served or given and either before or after the doing of any act to which the notice or copy would, but for the dispensation, be a condition precedent.

8. – (1) A planning authority shall keep a register (in this Act referred to as the register) for the purposes of this Act in respect of all land within their area affected by this Act, and shall make all such entries and corrections therein as may from time to time be appropriate in accordance with this Act and any regulations made thereunder.

(2) The register shall incorporate a map for enabling a person to trace any entry in the register.

(3) The register shall be kept at the offices of the planning authority and shall be available for inspection during office hours.

(4)(*a*) A document purporting to be a copy of an entry in the register and to be certified by an officer of the planning authority as a correct copy shall be *prima facie* evidence of the entry and it shall not be necessary to prove the signature of such officer or that he was in fact such officer.

(*b*) Evidence of an entry in the register may be given by production of a copy thereof certified pursuant to this subsection and it shall not be necessary to produce the register itself.

(*c*) Where application is made to a planning authority for a copy under this section, the copy shall be issued to the applicant on payment by him to the planning authority of the prescribed fee[45] in respect of each entry.

9. – (1) A planning authority may, for any purpose arising in relation to their functions under this Act, by notice in writing require the occupier of any structure or other land or any person receiving, whether for himself or for another, rent out of any structure or other land to state in writing to such authority, within a specified time not les than fourteen days after being so required, particulars of the estate, interest, or right by virtue of which he occupies such structure or other land or receives such rent (as the case may be), and the name and address (so far as they are known to him) of every person who to his knowledge has any estate or interest in or right over or in respect of such structure or other land.

(2) Every person who is required under this section to state in writing any matter or thing to a planning authority and either fails so to state such matter or thing within the time appointed under this section or, when so stating any such matter or thing, makes any statement in writing which is to his knowledge false or misleading in a material respect, shall be guilty of an offence under this section and shall be liable on summary conviction to a fine not exceeding twenty pounds.

10. – (1) The Minister may make regulations for prescribing any matter referred to in this Act as prescribed or to be prescribed or in relation to any matter referred to in this Act as the subject of regulations.

(2) Every regulation made under this Act shall be laid before each House of the Oireachtas as soon as may be after it is made and, if a resolution annulling the regulation is passed by either such House within the next twenty-one days on which that House has sat after the regulation is laid before it, the regulation shall be annulled accordingly but without prejudice to the validity of anything previously done thereunder.

11. – The enactments mentioned in the Second Schedule to this Act are hereby repealed to the extent specified in the third column of that Schedule.

PART II

FINANCIAL PROVISIONS

12. – The expenses incurred by the Minister in the administration of this Act shall, to such extent as may be sanctioned by the Minister for Finance, be defrayed out of moneys provided by the Oireachtas.

[45]The words 'the prescribed fee' replaced 'a fee for ten shillings' by S. 12 of the Act of 1982.

13. – Expenses under this Act of a planning authority who are the council of a county shall be charged on the county (exclusive of every borough and urban district therein).

14. – (1) A planning authority may assist any of the bodies and persons specified in subsection (2) of this section by helping the body or person in money or kind or by the provision of services or facilities (including the services of staff).

(2) The bodies and persons referred to in subsection (1) of this section are:

    (*a*) a local development association,

    (*b*) a company under the Companies Acts, 1908 to 1959, having as one of its objects the object of providing amenities and facilities at tourist resorts and developing tourist traffic at or to such resorts,

    (*c*) a body or person concerned, with respect to the area of the planning authority, in the preservation or development of amenities (including the preservation of flora and fauna and of buildings, caves, sites, features and objects of artistic, architectural, archaeological, geological or historical interest) or in the carrying out of works of local improvement (including parking places) or maintenance of amenities,

    (*cc*) a body or person providing homes or shelters for stray or unwanted dogs and cats,[46]

    (*d*) in case the planning authority are the council of a county, the commissioners of a town in the county having commissioners.

(3) Assisting under this section shall be a reserved function.

15. – (1) A planning authority may, within such limits and on such conditions as may be fixed by the Minister from time to time, contribute to the funds of any body which provides for training and research in relation to town and regional planning.

(2) Contributing under this section shall be a reserved function.

16. – (1) Two or more planning authorities may make and carry out an agreement for sharing the cost of performing all or any of their functions under this Act and, where an agreement has been made under this subsection, the planning authorities concerned may terminate it at any time if they so agree.

(2) Where the Minister is satisfied that a planning authority propose to perform in their area a function under this Act wholly or partially in the interests of the area of, or at the request of, another planning authority (being a planning authority) whose area is contiguous with the area of the first-mentioned planning authority), the other planning authority shall defray the cost of the performance of the function to such extent as may be agreed upon between the authorities or, in default of agreement, as may be determined by the Minister.

(3) The making of an agreement under this section shall be a reserved function.

17. – Where a sum is due under this Act to any person by a planning authority and, at the same time, another sum under this Act is due by that person to that authority, the former sum may be set off against the latter either, as may be appropriate, in whole or in part.

---

[46] Added by S. 43(1)(*d*) of the Act of 1976.

18. – (1) Where an appeal is made to the Minister under this Act or under any order under this Act against a decision of a planning authority –

(*a*) the Minister, if he so thinks proper and irrespective of the result of the appeal, may direct the planning authority to pay –

    (i) to the appellant, such sum as the Minister, in his absolute discretion, specifies as compensation to the appellant for the expense occasioned to him in relation to the appeal,

    (ii) to the Minister, such sum as, in his absolute discretion, he specifies as compensation to him towards the expense incurred by him in relation to the hearing of the appeal;

(*b*) if, but only if, the appeal fails, the Minister, if he so thinks proper, may direct the appellant to pay –

    (i) to the planning authority, such sum as the Minister, in his absolute discretion, specifies as compensation to the planning authority for the expense occasioned to them in relation to the appeal,

    (ii) to the Minister, such sum as, in his absolute discretion, he specifies as compensation to him towards the expense incurred by him in relation to the hearing of the appeal.

(2) Any sum directed under this section to be paid shall, in default of being paid, be recoverable as a simple contract debt in any court of competent jurisdiction.

PART III

DEVELOPMENT PLANS

19. – (1) Every planning authority shall, within the period of three years beginning on the appointed day (or such longer period as the Minister may in any particular case allow), make a plan indicating development objectives for their area.[47]

(2) A development plan shall consist of a written statement and a plan indicating the development objectives for the area in question, including objectives –

(*a*) with respect to county boroughs, boroughs, urban districts and scheduled towns –

    (i) for the use solely or primarily (as may be indicated in the development plan) of particular areas for particular purposes[47] (whether residential, commercial, industrial, agricultural or otherwise),

    (ii) for securing the greater convenience and safety of road users and pedestrians by the provision of parking places or road improvements or otherwise,

    (iii) for development and renewal of obsolete areas,

    (iv) for preserving, improving and extending amenities;

(*b*) with respect to other areas –

    (i) for development and renewal of obsolete areas,

    (ii) for preserving, improving and extending amenities,

---

[47] See judgment of McMahon J. (High Court) in *Short* v. *Dublin County Council* (p. 424). 'Particular purpose' in this sub-s. does not have the same meaning as in Rule 11 (a) of the rules for assessing compensation.

(iii) for the provision of new water supplies and sewerage services and the extension of existing such supplies and services.

(3) Without prejudice to the foregoing subsection and subsection (5) of this section, a development plan may indicate the objectives for any of the purposes mentioned in the Third Schedule to this Act and, with respect to areas other than county boroughs, boroughs, urban districts and scheduled towns, objectives for the use solely or primarily (as may be indicated in the development plan) of particular areas for particular purposes (whether residential, commercial, industrial, agricultural or otherwise).

(4) Where a planning authority propose to include in a development plan any development objective the responsibility for the effecting of which would fall on another local authority, the planning authority shall not include that objective in the plan save after consultation with the other local authority.

(5) A planning authority may make either –

    (*a*) one development plan, being a plan in relation to the whole of their area and all the subparagraphs in paragraph (*a*) and, where appropriate, paragraph (*b*) of subsection (2) of this section, or

    (*b*) two or more development plans, each plan being a plan in relation to the whole of their area and some one or more of those subparagraphs or to a part of their area and all or some one or more of those subparagraphs.

(6)(*a*) The making of an application to the Minister for the allowance of such a longer period as is referred to in subsection (1) of this section shall be a reserved function.

    (*b*) Where a planning authority have applied to the Minister for the allowance of such a longer period as is referred to in subsection (1) of this section, they shall cause notice of the application to be published in at least one newspaper circulating in their area and in the *Iris Oifigiúil.*

    (*c*) A notice under the foregoing paragraph -

        (i) shall specify the longer period applied for, and

        (ii) shall state that objections with respect to the application made to the Minister within a specified period of not less than one month will be taken into consideration before the grant of the application (and such objections shall be taken into consideration accordingly).

(7) The making of a development plan or any variations of any such plan shall be a reserved function.

(8) Regulations may make provision with respect to the making available for purchase by the public of printed copies of development plans and extracts therefrom.

(9)(*a*) Any reference in this Act to a development plan shall be construed as a reference to a plan under subsection (1) of this section (subject to any variations thereof).

    (*b*) In this Act 'the development plan' means the plan or plans under subsection (1) of this section of the relevant planning authority (subject to any variations thereof).

20. – (1) Where a planning authority have made a development plan, they shall, from time to time as occasion may require and at least once in every five years after the date of making of the plan, review the plan and make in it any variations (whether by way of alteration, addition or deletion) which they consider proper, or make a new development plan.

(1A) The Minister may extend (either in relation to planning authorities generally or in a particular case) the period during which a planning authority may comply with the requirements of subsection (1) of this section.[48]

(2) Where a planning authority have completed the discharge of their obligations under section 19 of this Act by making two or more plans as provided for by paragraph (*b*) of subsection (5) of that section, the periods of five years referred to in subsection (1) of this section shall run from the date of making the last of such plans.

21. – (1) Where a planning authority have prepared a draft of a proposed development plan or of proposed variations of a development plan –
- (*a*) they shall send copies of the prescribed documents to the prescribed authorities,
- (*b*) they shall cause notice of the preparation of the draft to be published in the *Iris Oifigiúil* and in at least one newspaper circulating in their area,
- (*c*) where the draft includes any provision relating to any structure or internal fixture or feature proposed to be preserved because of its artistic, historic or architectural interest, they shall serve notice (which shall incorporate particulars of the provision) of the preparation of the draft on the owner and on the occupier of the structure concerned,[49]
- (*d*) where the draft includes any provision relating to the preservation of a public right of way, they shall serve notice (which shall incorporate particulars of the provision and a map indicating the right of way) of the preparation of the draft on the owner and on the occupier of the land.

(2) A notice under the foregoing subsection shall state –
- (*a*) that a copy of the draft may be inspected at a stated place and at stated times during a stated period of not less than three months (and the copy shall be kept available for inspection accordingly), and
- (*b*) that objections or representations[50] with respect to the draft made to the planning authority within the said period will be taken into consideration before the making of the plan or variations (and any such objections or representations shall be taken into consideration accordingly), and
- (*c*) that any ratepayer making objection with respect to the draft may include in his objection a request to be afforded an opportunity to state his case before a person or persons appointed by the planning authority (and such opportunity shall be afforded to such objector and his statement shall be considered together with his objection),

and, in the case of a notice served pursuant to paragraph (*d*) of subsection (1) of this section, the notice shall also state that the draft includes provision relating to the preservation of the public right of way and that there is a right of appeal to the Circuit Court in relation to such provision.

---

[48] Added by S. 43(1)(*f*) of the Act of 1976.
[49] Substituted by S. 43(1)(*g*) of the Act of 1976.
[50] See *Finn* v. *Bray U.D.C.* (p. 39).

(3) Any person may, before the expiration of the twenty-one days next following the period stated pursuant to paragraph (*a*) of subsection (2) of this section, appeal to the Circuit Court against the inclusion in the proposed plan or variations of any such provision as is referred to in paragraph (*d*) of subsection (1) of this section, and the Court, if satisfied that no public right of way subsists, shall so declare and the provision shall accordingly not be included.

(4) Where a planning authority make a development plan or variations of any such plan, they shall cause a notice of the making to be published in the *Iris Oifigiúil* and in at least one newspaper circulating in their area.

(5) A notice under the foregoing subsection shall state that a copy of the plan or variations is available for inspection at a stated place and at stated times (and the copy shall be kept available for inspection accordingly).

(6)(*a*) A document purporting to be a copy of the development plan or of a part thereof and to be certified by an officer of a planning authority as a correct copy shall be *prima facie* evidence of the plan or part, and it shall not be necessary to prove the signature of such officer or that he was in fact such officer.

(*b*) Evidence of a development plan or any part thereof may be given by production of a copy thereof certified pursuant to this subsection and it shall not be necessary to produce the plan itself.

(*c*) Where application is made to a planning authority for a copy under this section, the copy shall be issued to the applicant on payment by him to the planning authority of such fee as they may fix not exceeding the reasonable cost of making the copy.

21A. – (1) Where a planning authority have prepared a draft of a proposed development plan or of proposed variations of a development plan and, after complying with the requirements of subsections (1) and (2) of section 21 of this Act, it appears to the authority that the draft should be amended, subject to subsection (2) of this section they may amend the draft and make the development plan or variations accordingly.[51]

(2) In case the proposed amendment would, if made, be a material alteration of the draft concerned, the planning authority shall cause notice of the proposed amendment to be published in the *Iris Oifigiúil* and in at least one newspaper circulating in their area, and having complied with the requirements of subsection (3) and, where appropriate, a requirement of subsection (4) of this section, and having taken into account any representations, they may, as they shall think fit, make the proposed plan or proposed variation, as the case may be, with or without the proposed amendment or with such other amendment (not being an amendment providing for the preservation of a structure or public right of way) as, having regard to the particular circumstances, they consider appropriate.

(3) A notice under the foregoing subsection shall state that –

(*a*) a copy of the proposed amendment of the draft may be inspected at a stated place and at stated times during a stated period of not less than one month (and the copy shall be kept available for inspection accordingly), and

---

[51] This provision (inserted by S. 37 of the Act of 1976) avoids the dilemma highlighted in *Finn v. Bray U.D.C.*

(*b*) written representations with respect to the proposed amendment of the draft made to the planning authority within the said period will be taken into consideration before the making of any amendment (and any such representations shall be taken into consideration accordingly).

(4)(*a*) Where the proposed amendment includes any provision to preserve any structure because of its artistic, historic or architectural interest, the planning authority shall, in addition to complying with the requirements of subsection (2) of this section, serve a notice incorporating particulars of the provision on the owner and on the occupier of the structure.

(*b*) Where the proposed amendment includes any provision to preserve a public right of way, the planning authority shall, in addition to complying with the requirements of the said subsection (2), serve a copy of the notice incorporating particulars of the provision and a map indicating the right of way on the owner and on the occupier of the land.

(5) Any person may, before the expiration of twenty-one days next following the period stated pursuant to paragraph (*a*) of subsection (3) of this section, appeal to the Circuit Court against the inclusion in the proposed amendment of any such provision as is referred to in subsection (4)(*b*) of this section, and the Court, if satisfied that no public right of way subsists, shall so declare and the provision shall accordingly not be included.

22. – (1) It shall be the duty of a planning authority to take such steps as may be necessary for securing the objectives which are contained in the provisions of the development plan.

(2) The Minister may require the development plans of two or more planning authorities to be co-ordinated in respect of matters and in a manner specified by him and thereupon –

(*a*) the authorities shall comply with the requisition, and

(*b*) any dispute between them arising out of any matters inserted or to be inserted in a development plan shall be determined by the Minister.

(3) The Minister may require a planning authority to vary the development plan in respect of matters and in a manner specified by him and thereupon it shall be the duty of the authority to comply with the requisition.

(4) Subsection (3) of this section shall have effect subject to the proviso that where the planning authority, as a result of considering pursuant to paragraph (*b*) of subsection (2) of section 21 of this Act any objection or representation, decide, with the consent of the Minister, that the proposed variations should be altered in any respect, they may make the variations subject to that alteration.

(5) Where under this section the Minister requires a planning authority to vary the development plan, pending compliance by them with the requisition it shall be the duty of the authority to have regard to the requisition in the performance of their functions under this Act.[52]

23. – The Minister may, as and when he thinks fit, prepare and publish, for the use and guidance of planning authorities and other persons interested, general instructions in relation to the preparation of development plans, together with

---

[52] Added by S. 43(1)(*h*) of the Act of 1976.

model forms of development plans and of provisions and clauses usually inserted in such plans.

PART V

AMENITIES

42. – [53](1) When it appears to the planning authority that by reason of –

(a) its outstanding natural beauty,

(b) its special recreational value, or

(c) a need for nature conservation,

an area should be declared under this section to be an area of special amenity, they may by order do so and the order may state the objective of the planning authority in relation to the preservation or enhancement of the character or special features of the area including objectives for the prevention or limitation of development in the area.[54]

(1A) The Minister may, if he considers it necessary, direct a planning authority to make an order under this section in relation to an area specified in the direction and may, if he thinks fit, require that objectives specified in the direction be included by the planning authority in their order in respect of matters and in a manner so specified and in case the Minister gives a direction under this subsection the planning authority concerned shall comply with the direction and an order made pursuant to a direction under this subsection shall be revoked or varied only with the consent of the Minister.

(2) An order under this section shall come into operation on being confirmed,[54] whether with or without modification, under the next section.

(3) Where the functional areas of two planning authorities are contiguous, either authority may, with the consent of the other, make an order under this section in respect of an area in or partly in the functional area of the other.

(4) Any order under this section for the time being in force may be revoked or varied by a subsequent order under this section.

(5) A planning authority shall, from time to time and at least once in every period of five years, review any order made by them under this section and for the time being in force (excepting any order merely revoking a previous order) for the purpose of deciding whether it is desirable to revoke or amend the order.

(6) The making of an order under this section shall be a reserved function.

43. – (1) As soon as may be after they have made an order under section 42 of this Act, a planning authority shall publish in one or more newspapers circulating in the area to which the order relates a notice –

(a) stating the fact of the order having been made and describing the area to which it relates,

(b) naming a place where a copy of the order and of any map referred to therein may be seen during office hours,

(c) specifying the period (not being less than one month) within and the manner in which objections to the order may be made to the planning authority,

---

[53] Sub-ss. (1) and (1A) substituted by S. 40(a) of the Act of 1976.

[54] Whilst a number of special amenity area orders have been made by the Dublin Metropolitan Planning Authorities none has been confirmed.

(*d*) specifying that the order requires confirmation by the Minister and that, where any objection are duly made to the order and are not withdrawn, a public local inquiry will be held and the objections will be considered before the order is confirmed.

(2) As soon as may be after the said period for making objections has expired, the planning authority may submit the order made under section 42 of this Act to the Minister for confirmation, and, when making any such submission, they shall also submit to the Minister any objections to the order which have been duly made and have not been withdrawn.

(3) If no such objection as aforesaid is duly made, or if all such objections so made are withdrawn, the Minister may by order confirm the order made under section 42 of this Act with or without modifications or refuse to confirm it; but in any other case he shall, before confirming, cause a public local inquiry to be held and shall consider any objections not withdrawn and the report of the person who held the inquiry, and may then by order confirm the order with or without modifications or refuse to confirm it.

(4) Every order made under this section by the Minister shall be laid before each House of the Oireachtas as soon as may be after it is made and, if a resolution annulling the order is passed by either such House within the next subsequent twenty-one days on which that House has sat after the order is laid before it, the order shall be annulled accordingly but without prejudice to the validity of anything previously done thereunder.

(5) Any reference in this Act to a special amenity area order shall be construed as a reference to an order confirmed under this section.

44. – (1) If it appears to the planning authority that it is expedient in the interests of amenity that any hedge should be removed or altered, the planning authority may serve on the owner and on the occupier of the land on which the hedge is situate a notice requiring the carrying out of such removal or alteration and, in the case of a removal, any replacement appearing to the planning authority to be suitable.

(2) Where a notice is served under this section, any person may, at any time before the day (not being earlier than one month after such service) specified in that behalf in the notice, appeal to the Minister against the notice.

(3) Where an appeal is brought under this section from a notice, the Minister may confirm the notice with or without modifications or annul the notice.

(4) A notice under this section (other than a notice which is annulled) shall take effect –

(*a*) in case no appeal against it is taken or every appeal against it is withdrawn before the expiration of the period for taking an appeal – on the expiration of the period for taking an appeal,

(*b*) in case an appeal or appeals is or are taken against it and the appeal or appeals is or are not withdrawn during the period for taking an appeal – when every appeal not so withdrawn has been either withdrawn or determined.

(5) If within the period specified in a notice under this section, or within such extended period as the planning authority may allow, the removal or alteration required by the notice has not been effected, the planning authority may enter on the land on which the hedge is situate and may effect such removal or alteration and any replacement specified in the notice.

(6) Where a notice under this section is complied with, the planning authority shall pay to the person complying with the notice the expenses reasonably incurred by him in carrying out the removal or alteration and any replacement specified in the notice.

(7) Particulars of a notice served under this section shall be entered in the register.

45. – (1) If it appears to the planning authority that it is expedient in the interests of amenity to make provision for the preservation of any tree, trees, group of trees or woodlands, they may for that purpose make an order with respect to any such tree, trees, group of trees or woodlands as may be specified in the order; and, in particular, provision may be made by any such order –

(*a*) for prohibiting (subject to any exemptions for which provision may be made by the order) the cutting down, topping, lopping or wilful destruction of trees except with the consent of the planning authority, and for enabling that authority to give their consent subject to conditions;

(*b*) for applying, in relation to any consent under the order, and to applications therefor, any of the provisions of Part IV of this Act relating to permission to develop land, and to applications for such permission, subject to such adaptations and modifications as may be specified in the order.

(2) Any person who has suffered damage in consequence of any refusal of consent required under an order under this section, or of any grant of any such consent subject to conditions, shall, if he makes a claim on the planning authority within the time and in the manner specified by the order, be entitled to recover from such authority compensation in respect of the damage, but –

(*a*) where the order declares that, as respects any tree, trees or group of trees not comprised in woodlands, the tree, trees or group is or are of special amenity value or special interest no compensation shall be payable in relation to the tree, trees or group.

(*b*) where the order declares that, as respects any trees comprised in woodlands, a condition comprising a requirement to replant is an essential condition for attachment in the interests of amenity to any consent given under the order no compensation shall be payable in relation to such a condition attached to any such consent.

(3) Any order under this section may be revoked or varied by a subsequent order under this section.

(4) Where a planning authority make an order under this section, they shall serve a notice of the making of the order and a copy of the order on every person who is the owner or occupier of any land affected by the order, and on any other person then known to them to be entitled to fell any tree, trees, group of trees or woodlands to which the order relates.

(5) Any person on whom a notice and a copy of an order is served under this section may, at any time before the day specified in that behalf in the notice (not being earlier than one month after such service), appeal to the Minister against the order.

(6) Where an appeal is brought under this section against an order, the Minister may confirm the order with or without modifications or annul the order.

(7) Without prejudice to any other exemption for which provision may be made

by an order under this section, no such order shall apply to the cutting down, topping or lopping of trees which are dying or dead or have become dangerous or the cutting down, topping or lopping of any trees in compliance with any obligation imposed by or under any statute or so far as may be necessary for the prevention or abatement of a nuisance.

(8) If any person contravenes the provisions of an order under this section (other than an order which has been annulled), he shall be guilty of an offence and shall be liable on summary conviction to a fine not exceeding two hundred pounds.

(9) Particulars of an order under this section shall be entered in the register.

(10) Any reference in this Act to a tree preservation order shall be construed as a reference to an order under this section (other than an order which has been annulled).

46.[55] – (1) If it appears to the planning authority, after consultation with the prescribed authorities, that it is expedient in the interests of amenity to make provision to preserve from extinction or otherwise protect any flora or fauna in an area, or part of an area, to which a special amenity area order relates, being flora or fauna which are of special amenity value or special interest, they may make an order prohibiting (subject to any exemptions for which provision may be made by the order) the taking, killing or destroying of such flora or fauna.
. . .[56]

(3) Any order under this section may be revoked or varied by a subsequent order under this section.

(4) Where a planning authority make an order under this section, they shall cause a notice stating the effect of the order and stating the right of appeal under the next subsection to be published in at least one newspaper circulating in the area to which the order relates.

(5) Any person may, at any time before the expiration of one month after the publication of a notice under the foregoing sub-section, appeal to the Minister against the order to which the notice relates.

(6) Where an appeal is brought under this section against an order, the Minister may confirm the order with or without modifications or annul the order.
. . .[56]

(8) If any person contravenes the provisions of an order under this section (other than an order which has been annulled), he shall be guilty of an offence and shall be liable on summary conviction to a fine not exceeding two hundred pounds.

(9) Particulars of an order under this section shall be entered in the register.
. . .[56]

(11) Any reference in this Act to a conservation order shall be construed as a reference to an order under this section (other than an order which has been annulled).

47. – (1) A planning authority may enter into an agreement with any person having the necessary power in that behalf for the creation, by dedication by that person, of a public right of way over land.

[55] Sub-s. (1) substituted by S. 40(*b*) of the Act of 1976. S. 45 of the same Act repealed Sub-ss. (2), (7) and (10).
[56] Sub-ss. (2), (7) and (10) have been repealed by S. 45 of the Local Government (Planning and Development) Act, 1976.

(2) An agreement made under this section shall be on such terms as to payment or otherwise as may be specified in the agreement, and may, if it is so agreed, provide for limitations or conditions affecting the public right of way.

(3) Where an agreement has been made under this section, it shall be the duty of the planning authority to take all necessary steps for securing that the creation of the public right of way is effected in accordance with the agreement.

(4) Particulars of an agreement made under this section shall be entered in the register.

48. – (1) Where it appears to the planning authority that there is need for a public right of way over any land, the planning authority may by order create a public right of way over the land.

(2) Where a planning authority make an order under this section, they shall serve a notice of the making of the order and a copy of the order on every person who is the owner or occupier of any land over which the order creates a public right of way and on any person who in their opinion will be affected by the creation of the public right of way.

(3) Any person on whom a notice and a copy of an order is served under this section may, at any time before the day specified in that behalf in the notice (not being earlier than one month after such service), appeal to the Minister against the order.

(4) Where an appeal is brought under this section against an order, the Minister may confirm the order with or without modifications or annul the order.

(5) An order under this section (other than an order which is annulled) shall take effect –

   (*a*) in case no appeal against it is taken or every appeal against it is withdrawn before the expiration of the period for taking an appeal – on the expiration of the period for taking an appeal,

   (*b*) in case an appeal or appeals is or are taken against it and the appeal or appeals is or are not withdrawn during the period for taking an appeal – when every appeal not so withdrawn has been either withdrawn or determined.

(6) Particulars of a right of way created under this section shall be entered in the register.

49. – (1) Where a public right of way is created pursuant to this Act or a provision relating to its preservation is included in the development plan, the way shall be maintained by the planning authority.

(2)(*a*) Where a right of way is required by this section to be maintained by the planning authority, a person shall not damage or obstruct the way, or hinder or interfere with the exercise of the right of way.

   (*b*) A person who contravenes this subsection shall be guilty of an offence and shall be liable on summary conviction to a fine not exceeding one hundred pounds; and if in the case of a continuing offence the contravention is continued after conviction, he shall be guilty of a further offence and liable on summary conviction to a fine not exceeding twenty pounds for each day on which the contravention is so continued.

   (*c*) In a prosecution for an offence under this subsection in relation to a right of way with respect to which a provision for its preservation is included in the development plan, it shall not be necessary for the prosecution to show, and it shall be assumed until the contrary is shown by the defendant, that the right of way subsists.

(3) Where, in the case of a right of way required by this section to be maintained by the planning authority, the way is damaged or obstructed by any person, the planning authority maintaining the right of way may repair the damage or remove the obstruction, and the expenses incurred by them in the repair or removal shall be paid to them by the said person and, in default of being so paid, shall be recoverable from him as a simple contract debt in any court of competent jurisdiction.

(4) A planning authority may, for the purpose of carrying out their duties under subsections (1) and (3) of this section, enter on land at all reasonable times.

50. – (1) For the purpose of preserving or enhancing the amenities or natural beauty of any land, the planning authority –

    (*a*) may plant trees, shrubs or other plants on the land,

    (*b*) assist any person or body proposing to plant trees, shrubs or other plants on the land by providing trees, shrubs or other plants or by a grant of money.

(2) The powers conferred by this section shall be exercised by an authority either on land belonging to them or, with the consent of all persons interested therein, on other land; and in relation to such other land the said powers shall include power to make arrangements whereby the planting or work is carried out, on such terms as may be provided under the arrangements, by a person other than the authority.

(3) Where the planning authority exercise their powers under the foregoing provisions of this section on land not belonging to the authority, the management of the land, so far as relates to anything done by the authority, may be undertaken either by the authority or by a person interested in the land, as may be agreed upon between the authority and the persons so interested, and on such terms as may be so agreed.

(4) Assisting under this section by a grant of money shall be a reserved function.

(5) Particulars of an agreement made under subsection (3) of this section shall be entered in the register.

51. – (1) A person shall not –

    (*a*) in any public place or in connection with any premises which adjoins any public place and to which the public are admitted, or

    (*b*) upon any other premises,

either –

        (i) by operating, or causing or suffering to be operated any wireless, loudspeaker, television, gramophone, amplifier, or similar instrument, or any machine or other appliance, or

        (ii) by any other means,

make or cause to be made, any noise or vibration which is so loud, so continuous or so repeated or of such duration or pitch or at such times as to give reasonable cause for annoyance to persons in any premises in the neighbourhood or to persons lawfully using any public place.

(2) Paragraph (*a*) of subsection (1) of this section shall not apply to any public meeting.

(3) Proceedings shall not be taken against any person for any offence under this

section in respect of premises referred to in paragraph (*b*) of subsection (1) of this section unless the annoyance is continued after the expiration of seven days from the date of the service on such person of a notice alleging annoyance, signed by not less than three persons residing or carrying on a business within the area in which the noise is heard or the vibration is felt.

(4) A person who contravenes this section shall be guilty of an offence and shall be liable on summary conviction to a fine not exceeding fifty pounds; and if in the case of a continuing offence the contravention of this section is continued after conviction, he shall be guilty of a further offence and liable on summary conviction to a fine not exceeding ten pounds for each day on which the contravention is continued.[57]

(5) Nothing in this section shall apply to noise or vibration caused –
    (*a*) by aircraft, or
    (*b*) by any statutory undertakers in the exercise of powers conferred on them
          by any statute or order or other instrument made under statute.

(6) In proceedings brought by virtue of this section in respect of noise or vibration caused in the course of a trade or business or in performing any statutory functions, it shall be a good defence for the defendant to prove that the best practicable means have been used for preventing, and for counteracting the effect of, the noise or vibration.[58]

. . .

54. – (1) If it appears to the planning authority that, having regard to the interests of public safety or amenity, an advertisement structure or advertisement in their area should be repaired or tidied, the planning authority may serve on the person having control of the advertisement structure or advertisement a notice requiring that person to repair or tidy the advertisement structure or advertisement within a specified period.

(2) If within the period specified in a notice under this section, the advertisement structure or advertisement is not repaired or tidied, the planning authority may enter on the land on which the structure is situate or the advertisement is exhibited and repair or tidy the structure or advertisement and may recover as a simple contract debt in any court of competent jurisdiction from the person having control of the structure or advertisement any expenses reasonably incurred by them in that behalf.

. . .

PART VII

Acquisition of Land, etc.[59]

74. – (1) Where –
    (*a*) land is vested in a planning authority otherwise than for the purposes of
          their functions under this Act, and
    (*b*) the planning authority are satisfied that the land should be made available
          for those purposes,

---

[57] The words from 'exceeding' added by S. 40(*c*) of the Act of 1976.
[58] Ss. 52 and 53 which dealt with litter and advertising offences respectively has been repealed by S. 19 of the Litter Act, 1982.
[59] There is no power of compulsory acquisition in the Act of 1963. (See *Movie News Limited*

the planning authority may, with the consent of the appropriate Minister, appropriate the land to any of those purposes.

(2) In subsection (1) of this section 'the appropriate Minister' means –

    (a) if the Ministerial functions relating to the land in question are vested in a single Minister other than the Minister – that Minister,

    (b) if those functions are vested in two or more Ministers (neither or none of whom is the Minister) – such one of those Ministers as has, in relation to the land, the greater or greatest concern,

    (c) in all other cases – the Minister.

(3) If, in relation to paragraph (b) of the foregoing subsection, any doubt as to which one of two or more Ministers has the greater or greatest concern, the doubt shall be determined by the Minister.

75. – (1) Any land acquired for the purposes of or appropriated under this Act by a planning authority may be sold, leased or exchanged subject to such conditions as they may consider necessary in order to secure the best use of that or other land, and any structures or works which have been, or are to be, constructed, erected, made or carried out on, in or under that or other land, or to secure the construction, erection, making or carrying out of any structures or works appearing to them to be needed for the proper planning and development of their area.

(2) The consent of the Minister shall be requisite for any sale, lease or exchange under subsection (1) of this section –

    (a) in case the price or rent, or what is obtained by the planning authority on the exchange, is not the best reasonably obtainable, or

    (b) in case the development proposed for the land would contravene materially the development plan,

but, save as aforesaid, shall not be requisite notwithstanding the provisions of any other enactment.

(3) Capital money arising from the disposal of land under subsection (1) of this section shall be applied for a capital purpose for which capital money may be properly applied.

(4)(a) Where, as respects any land acquired for the purposes of or appropriated under this Act by a planning authority, the authority consider that they will not require the use of the land for any of their functions for a particular period, the authority may grant a lease of the land for that period or any less period and the lease shall be expressed as a lease granted for the purposes of this subsection.

    (b) Neither the Landlord and Tenant Acts, 1931 and 1958, nor the Rent Restrictions Act, 1960, shall apply in relation to a lease granted as aforesaid for the purposes of this subsection.

76. – (1) A planning authority may, with the approval of the Minister, by order extinguish a public right of way, but an order made under this subsection shall be published in the prescribed manner, and if there is an objection to the order and the

v. *Galway County Council* (p. 44), and *Leinster Importing Company Limited* v. *Dublin County Council* (p. 43): however, there is power under S. 10 of the Local Government (Ireland) Act, 1898 as extended by S. 10 of the Local Government (No. 2) Act, 1960.

objection is not withdrawn, the Minister shall cause an oral hearing to be held and shall afford the person making the objection an opportunity of being heard.[60]

(2) Subsection (1) of this section does not apply to a public right of way over land acquired compulsorily by a planning authority for the purposes of this Act if the order authorising the compulsory acquisition authorised the extinguishment of such right of way.

(3) The Minister may, if he thinks fit, approve an order under this section in so far only as it relates to a part specified by him of the right of way which the order proposes to extinguish, and in case the Minister so approves such an order, the order shall be construed and have effect in accordance with the approval.[61]

77. – (1) A planning authority may develop or secure the development of land and, in particular and without prejudice to the generality of the foregoing, may –

    (*a*) secure, facilitate and control the improvement of the frontage of any public road by widening, opening, enlarging or otherwise improving,

    (*b*) develop any land in the vicinity of any road or bridge which it is proposed to improve or construct,

    (*c*) provide areas with roads and such services and works as may be needed for development,

    (*d*) provide areas of convenient shape for development,

    (*e*) secure or carry out, as respects obsolete areas, the development or renewal thereof and the provision therein of open spaces,

    (*f*) secure the preservation of any view or prospect, any structure or natural physical feature, any trees subject to a tree preservation order, any site of geological, ecological or archaeological interest or any flora or fauna subject to a conservation order.

(2) A planning authority may provide –

    (*a*) sites for the establishment or relocation of industries, businesses (including hotels, motels and guest-houses), dwellings, offices, shops, schools, churches and other community facilities and of such buildings, premises, dwellings, parks and structures as are referred to in paragraph (*b*) of this subsection,

    (*b*) factory buildings, office premises, shop premises, dwellings, amusement parks and structures for the purpose of entertainment, caravan parks, buildings for the purpose of providing accommodation, meals and refreshments, buildings for providing trade and professional services and advertisement structures, buildings or structures for the purpose of providing homes or shelters for stray or unwanted dogs and cats,[62]

    (*c*) any services which they consider ancillary to anything which is referred to in paragraphs (*a*) and (*b*) of this subsection and which they have provided,

and may maintain and manage any such site, building, premises, dwelling, park, structure or service and may make any charges which they consider reasonable in relation to the provision, maintenance or management thereof.

(3) A planning authority may, in connection with any of their functions under

---

[60] The words after 'prescribed manner, and' substituted by S. 43(1)(*i*) of the Act of 1976.
[61] Sub-s. (3) added by S. 43(1)(*j*) of the Act of 1976.
[62] The words after 'advertisement structures' added by S. 43(1)(*k*) of the Act of 1976.

this Act, make and carry out arrangements with any person or body for the development or management of land.

(4) For avoidance of doubt it is hereby declared that the powers which a planning authority may exercise pursuant to section 10 of the Local Government (No. 2) Act, 1960, with respect to compulsory acquisition for the purposes of any of their functions under this Act apply in relation to anything which is specified in subsection (1) of section 2 of this Act as being included in 'land'.

78. – Regulations made in relation to any specified cases or classes of cases of development proposed to be carried out by local authorities who are planning authorities may –

  (*a*) require the authority to give public notice in any specified manner of development which they propose to carry out,

  (*b*) require the inclusion in any such notice of an invitation for the making by interested persons of objections to the proposed development,

  (*c*) in cases where any such objection is made and is not withdrawn, require the authority to have the consent of the Minister before carrying out the proposed development.

79. – (1) 'business' in the Landlord and Tenant Act, 1931, shall include the carrying out by a planning authority of any of their functions.

(2) Subsection (1) of section 22 of the Landlord and Tenant Act, 1931, is hereby amended by the insertion after paragraph (*b*) of the following paragraph:

  (*bb*)that, such landlord being a planning authority within the meaning of the Local Government (Planning and Development) Act, 1963, such tene-ment or any part thereof is situate in an area in respect of which the development plan within the meaning of that Act indicates objectives for its development or renewal as being an obsolete area, or'.[63]

(3) Subsection (1) or section 15 of the Landlord and Tenant (Reversionary Leases) Act, 1958, is hereby amended by the addition of 'or alternatively, being a planning authority within the meaning of the Local Government (Planning and Development) Act, 1963, satisfies the Court that, in case the reversionary lease would be a lease of the whole of the land, the land or any part of the land is situate in an area in respect of which the development plan within the meaning of that Act indicates objectives for its development or renewal as being an obsolete area or that, in case the reversionary lease would be a lease of part of the land, that part or any part of that part is situate in such an area'.

. . .

PART VIII

MISCELLANEOUS

85. – (1) A planning authority may, with the consent of the owner and of the occupier of any land not forming part of a public road, place, erect or construct cables, wires and pipelines (other than waterpipes, sewers and drains), and any apparatus incidental to such cables, wires and pipelines, on, under or over such

---

[63] Now see S. 17(1)(*a*) of the Landlord and Tenant (Amendment) Act, 1980.

land, and may from time to time inspect, repair, alter or renew, or may at any time remove, any cables, wires or pipelines placed, erected or constructed under this section.

(2) A planning authority may, with the consent of the owner and of the occupier of any structure, attach to such structure any bracket or other fixture required for the carrying or support of any cable, wire or pipeline placed, erected or constructed under this section.

(3) A planning authority may erect and maintain notices indicating the position of cables, wires or pipelines placed, erected or constructed under this section and may, with the consent of the owner and of the occupier of any structure, affix such a notice to such structure.

(4) The foregoing subsections of this section shall have effect subject to the proviso that –

(*a*) a consent for the purposes of any of them shall not be unreasonably withheld,

(*b*) if the planning authority consider that such a consent has been unreasonably withheld, they may appeal to the Minister,[64]

(*c*) if the Minister determines that such a consent was unreasonably withheld, it shall be treated as having been given.

(5) The planning authority may permit the use of any cables, wires or pipelines placed, erected or constructed under this section and of any apparatus incidental to such cables, wires or pipelines subject to such conditions and charges as they consider appropriate.

. . .

FIRST SCHEDULE

TOWNS

PART I

Ardee
Balbriggan
Ballybay
Ballyshannon
Bandon
Bantry
Belturbet
Boyle
Callan
Cootehill
Droichead Nua
Edenderry
Fethard in the county of Tipperary South Riding
Gorey
Granard
Kilkee

[64] To be construed as The Board: S. 14(10) of the Act of 1976.

Lismore
Loughrea
Mountmellick
Muinebeag
Mullingar
Newcastle West
Passage West
Portlaoighise
Rathkeale
Roscommon
Tramore
Tuam

PART II

Abbeyfeale
Abbeyleix
Athenry
Bailieborough
Ballaghaderreen
Ballinrobe
Ballybofey
Ballybunion
Ballyhaunis
Banagher
Blanchardstown
Blarney
Caher
Cahersiveen
Carndonagh
Carrick-on-Shannon
Castlecomer-Donaguile
Castleisland
Castlereagh
Celbridge
Clara
Claremorris
Clifden
Clondalkin
Dingle
Donegal
Dunmanway
Ennistimon
Gort
Graiguenamanagh-Tinnahinch
Greystones-Delgany
Kanturk
Kenmare
Kildare

Killorglin
Killybegs
Kilmallock
Lucan-Doddsborough
Malahide
Maynooth
Millstreet
Mitchelstown
Moate
Monasterevin
Mountrath
Moville
Portarlington
Portlaw
Rathdrum
Rathluirc
Roscrea
Rush
Skerries
Swineford
Swords
Tallaght
Thomastown
Tullow

THIRD SCHEDULE

PURPOSES FOR WHICH OBJECTIVES MAY BE INDICATED IN DEVELOPMENT PLAN[65]

PART I

Roads and Traffic

1. Securing the greater convenience and safety of road users and pedestrians.
2. Reservation of land for roads and parking places.
3. Establishment of public rights of way.
4. Construction of new roads and alteration of existing roads.
5. Closing or diverting of existing roads.
6. Extinguishment of public and private rights of way.
7. Establishing –
   (a) the line, width, level and construction of,
   (b) the means of access to and egress from, and
   (c) the general dimensions and character of,
roads, whether new or existing.

[65] It will be recalled that S. 19(2) sets out objectives which *shall* be included in the development plan. Stated shortly these are concerned with (a); general zoning, road and parking improvements, (b) renewal of obsolete areas and amenities in urban areas and (c) in rural areas, renewal of obsolete areas, amenities and water and sewerage supplies. The development plan *may* include further objectives relating to any of the purposes set out in Schedule III. (See pp. 13 and 14).

8. Providing for works incidental to the making, improvement or landscaping of any road, including the erection of bridges, tunnels and subways and shelters, the provision of artificial lighting and seats and the planting or protecting of grass, trees and shrubs on or adjoining such road.

PART II

Structures

1. Regulating and controlling, either generally or in particular areas, all or any of the following matters –
   (a) the size, height, floor area and character of structures;
   (b) building lines, coverage and the space about dwellings and other structures;
   (c) the extent of parking places required in, on or under structures of a particular class or size or services or facilities for the parking, loading, unloading or fuelling of vehicles;
   (d) the objects which may be affixed to structures;
   (e) the purposes for and the manner in which structures may be used or occupied, including, in the case of dwellings, the letting thereof in separate tenements.
2. Regulating and controlling the design, colour and materials of structures.
3. Reserving or allocating any particular land, or all land in any particular area, for structure of a specified class or classes, or prohibiting or restricting either permanently or temporarily, the erection, construction or making of any particular class or classes of structures on any specified land.
4. Limiting the number of structures or the number of structures of a specified class which may be constructed, erected or made, on, in or under any area.
5. The removal or alteration of structures which are inconsistent with the development plan.
6. Regulating and controlling –
   (a) the disposition or layout of structures or structures of any specified class (including the reservation of reasonable open space in relation to the number, class and character of structures in any particular development proposal);
   (b) the manner in which any land is to be laid out for the purpose of development, including requirements as to road layout, landscaping, planting;
   (c) the provision of water supplies, sewers, drains and public lighting;
   (d) the provision of service roads and the location and design of means of access to roads;
   (e) the provision of facilities for parking, unloading, loading and fuelling of vehicles on any land.

PART III

Community Planning

1. Regulating the layout of areas, including density, spacing, grouping and orientation of structures in relation to roads, open spaces and other structures.
2. Determining the provision and siting of schools, churches, meeting halls and other community facilities.

3. Determining the provision and siting of sanitary services and recreational facilities.

PART IV

Amenities

1. Reserving of lands as –
   (*a*) open spaces, whether public or private (other than open spaces reserved under Part II of this Schedule or under the next paragraph),
   (*b*) caravan or camping sites.
2. Reserving, as a public park, public garden or public recreation space, land normally used as such.
3. Reserving of land for burial grounds.
4. Reserving of lands for game and bird sanctuaries.
5. Preservation of buildings of artistic, architectural or historical interest.

5A. Preservation of plasterwork, staircases, woodwork or other fixtures or features of artistic, historic or architectural interest and forming part of the interior of structures.[66]

6. Preservation of caves, sites, features and other objects of archaeological, geological or historical interest.

7. Preservation of views and prospects and of amenities of places and features of natural beauty or interest.

8. (*a*) Preservation and protection of woods.
   (*b*) Preservation and protection of trees, shrubs, plants and flowers.

9. Prohibiting, restricting or controlling, either generally or in particular places or within a specified distance of the centre line of all roads or any specified road, the erection of all or any particular forms of advertisement structure or the exhibition of all or any particular forms of advertisement.

10. Preventing, remedying or removing injury to amenities arising from the ruinous or neglected condition of any structure, or from the objectionable or neglected condition of any land attached to a structure or abutting on a public road or situate in a residential area.

11. Prohibiting, regulating or controlling the deposit or disposal of waste materials and refuse, the disposal of sewage and the pollution of rivers, lakes, ponds, gullies and the seashore.

12. Providing on derelict sites or other land facilities such as car parks, seating, playing facilities, tennis-courts, shelters, toilets and playgrounds.

13. Preservation of any existing public right of way giving access to seashore, mountain, lakeshore, riverbank, or other place of natural beauty or recreational utility.

LOCAL GOVERNMENT (PLANNING AND DEVELOPMENT) ACT, 1976

35. – The Minister may make regulations,[67]
   (*a*) providing for,
      (i)   the payment to planning authorities of prescribed fees by appli-

---

[66] Inserted by S. 43(1)(*l*) of the Act of 1976.
[67] Regulations are made under Ss. 4, 10, 19, 21, 25, 26, 46, 67, 76, 82 and 89 of the Act of

(i) the payments to planning authorities of prescribed fees by applicants for a waiver notice under section 29 of this Act,

(ii) the publication by planning authorities of specified notices with respect to applications for permission under the Principal Act to develop land or for such a waiver notice,

(b) enabling an applicant to appeal to the Board against a refusal of an approval which is required to be obtained under a condition subject to which a permission or approval is granted under the Principal Act,

(c) making such incidental, consequential, transitional or supplementary provision as may appear to him to be necessary or proper for any purpose of this Act or in consequence of, or to give full effect to, any of its provisions.

LOCAL GOVERNMENT (PLANNING AND DEVELOPMENT) ACT, 1982

7. – (1) The Minister shall, from time to time, issue such general directives as to policy in relation to planning and development as he considers necessary.[68]

(2) A planning authority and the Board shall in performing its functions have regard to any directive under this section.

(3) Nothing in this section shall be construed as enabling the Minister to exercise any power or control in relation to any particular case with which a planning authority or the Board is or may be concerned.

(4) Where the Minister gives a directive under this section, the following provisions shall apply:

(a) as soon as may be the Minister shall cause a copy of the directive to be laid before each House of the Oireachtas.

(b) the directive shall be published in the *Iris Oifigiúil*, and

(c) the Minister shall cause a copy of the directive to be sent to each planning authority and to the Board.

LOCAL GOVERNMENT (IRELAND) ACT, 1898

10.[69] – (1) A county council, for the purpose of any of their powers and duties, may acquire, purchase, take on lease or exchange, any land or any easements or

1963; Ss. 5, 20, 25, 29, 32 and 35 of the Act of 1976 and S. 11 of the Act of 1982. These regulations are (excluding commencement orders): (i) S.I. No. 65 of 1977 (general regulations); (ii) S.I. No. 231 of 1980 (licence fees for petrol and oil pumps become payable to the local as distinct from central authority); (iii) S.I. No. 154 of 1981 (the area of exempted extensions to dwelling houses increased from 18 to 25 sq. metres and porches are made exempt); (iv) S.I. No. 342 of 1982 (providing for applications for extension of the life of planning permissions and sundry amendments to the general regulations including a new provision that applications shall not be decided for 14 days after receipt); (v) S.I. No. 30 of 1983 (establishing fees for planning applications, appeals, etc.).

[68] This section replaced S. 6 of the Act of 1976 (which is repealed by S. 15(2)(a) of this Act). The difference is that planning authorities are now required to have regard to ministerial directives as well as the Board. See p. 537 for Directive.

[69] This section is the origin of most local authority acquisition powers. Its operation was extended by Ss. 10 and 11 of the Local Government (No. 2) Act, 1960 and these sections now provide ample power of compulsory acquisition for the purposes of the Planning Acts. See the *Leinster Importing* (p. 43) and *Movie News* (p. 44) cases.

rights over or in land, whether within or without their county, including rights to water, and may acquire, hire, erect, and furnish such halls, buildings, and offices as they require, whether within or without their county, and for the purpose of this section section two hundred and three of the Public Health Act, 1878, shall apply with the necessary modifications, and in particular with the modification that the advertisements mentioned in subsection two of the said section may be published in any month, and that the notice mentioned in the said subsection shall be served in the next succeeding month.

(2) A county council shall not take or use any such land, easements, or rights, without either the consent of the owner and occupier or the authority of a provisional order duly confirmed.

LOCAL GOVERNMENT (NO. 2) ACT, 1960

10.[70] – (1) Where –

(a) a local authority intend to acquire compulsorily any land, whether situate within or outside their functional area, for purposes for which they are capable of being authorised by law to acquire land compulsorily,

(b) those purposes are purposes other than the purposes of the Housing Act, 1966, or are purposes some only of which are purposes of that Act, and

(c) the local authority consider that it would be convenient to effect the acquisition under that Act,

the local authority may decide so to effect the acquisition.

(2) Where –

(a) a local authority consider that any land, whether situate within or outside their functional area, would, if acquired by them, be suitable for the provision of halls, buildings and offices for the local authority, and

(b) the local authority consider that it would be convenient to effect the acquistion under the Housing Act, 1966,

the local authority may decide so to effect the acquisition.

(3)(a) Where a local authority make a decision under subsection (1) or (2) of this section, they may be authorised to acquire the land compulsorily by means of a compulsory purchase order as provided for by section 76 of the Housing Act, 1966, and the Third Schedule thereto and for the purposes of this paragraph any reference to a housing authority in the said section 76 or the said Third Schedule shall be construed as a reference to a local authority.

(b) For the purposes of paragraph (a) of this subsection, 'the Minister', wherever that expression occurs in section 76 of the Housing Act, 1966, and the Third Schedule thereto shall be construed as referring to the appropriate Minister.

(4)(a) The provisions of sections 78, 79, subsection (1) of section 80, sections 81, 82 and 84 of the Housing Act, 1966, and the Fourth Schedule thereto, shall apply in relation to an order made by virtue of this section and any reference in the said sections and subsection and in the said Fourth Schedule as so applied to a housing authority or the Minister shall be construed as a reference as to the local authority or the appropriate Minister, respectively.

[70] As substituted by S. 86 of the Housing Act, 1966.

(*b*) The provisions of sections 3, 4, 5 and 49 of the Housing Act, 1966, are hereby extended so as to have effect for the purposes of this section, and any reference in the said sections as so extended to a housing authority or, except in the said section 5, to the Minister shall be construed as a reference to the local authority or the appropriate Minister, respectively.

(*c*) The provisions of subsection (2) of section 83 of the Housing Act, 1966, shall apply in relation to land acquired by means of an order made by virtue of this section.

(*d*) Where –

    (i) an order is made by virtue of this section, and

    (ii) there is a public right of way over the land to which the order relates or any part thereof,

the order may authorise the local authority, by order made by them after they have acquired such land or part, to extinguish the right of way.

(*e*) Where –

    (i) an order made by virtue of this section authorises the extinguishment of a public right of way, and

    (ii) apart from this paragraph, it would not be obligatory on the Minister to cause a public local inquiry to be held pursuant to the Third Schedule to the Housing Act, 1966,

it shall be obligatory on the Minister to cause the inquiry to be held save where he thinks fit not to confirm the order.

(5) A local authority may, in a case in which they have made a decision under subsection (1) of this section, be authorised to acquire land compulsorily by means of a single order made by virtue of this section irrespective of the number of the purposes for which the land is required.

(6) In this section, 'land' includes any interest or right over land granted by or held from the local authority acquiring the land.

11. – (1) In subsection (1) of section 10 of the Local Government (Ireland) Act, 1898 –

(*a*) 'A county council' shall be construed as referring to any local authority,

(*b*) 'county' shall, in both places where that word occurs without qualification, be construed as referring to the functional area of the local authority in question, and

(*c*) 'powers and duties' shall be construed as referring to all such powers, functions and duties as may at any material time stand exercisable or performable by the local authority in question.

(2) In subsection (2) of the said Section 1, 'A county council' shall be construed as referring to any local authority.

LOCAL GOVERNMENT (PLANNING AND DEVELOPMENT) REGULATIONS, 1977

The Minister for Local Government, in exercise of the powers conferred on him by sections 4, 10, 19, 21, 25, 26, 46, 67, 76, 82 and 89 of the Local Govenrment (Planning and Development) Act, 1963 (No. 28 of 1963) as amended by the Local

Government (Planning and Development) Act, 1976 (No. 20 of 1976), and by sections 5, 20, 25, 29, 32 and 35 of the Local Government (Planning and Development) Act, 1976, hereby makes the following Regulations:–

PART I

PRELIMINARY AND GENERAL

1. These Regulations may be cited as the Local Government (Planning and Development) Regulations, 1977.

2. These Regulations shall come into operation on the 15th day of March, 1977.

3. (1) In these Regulations, any reference to a Schedule, Part or article which is not otherwise identified is a reference to a Schedule, Part or article of these Regulations.

(2) In these Regulations, any reference to a sub-article or paragraph which is not otherwise identified is a reference to the sub-article or paragraph of the provision in which the reference occurs.

(3) In these Regulations –

'the Act of 1963' means the Local Government (Planning and Development) Act, 1963;

'the Act of 1976' means the Local Government (Planning and Development) Act, 1976;

'the Acts' means the Act of 1963 and the Act of 1976;

'the Board' means An Bord Pleanála;

'the Minister' means the Minister for Local Government.

(4) In these Regulations a reference to a provision of the Act of 1963 which has been amended by the Act of 1976 is a reference to such provision as so amended.

4. The Regulations mentioned in the First Schedule are hereby revoked.

PART II

DEVELOPMENT PLANS

5. The prescribed documents for the purposes of section 21 (1)(a) of the Act of 1963 shall be –

   (a) in relation to the authorities prescribed at (a) to (g) of article 6 –
      (i) a copy of the written statement comprised in any draft of a proposed development plan, or of proposed variations of a development plan, and
      (ii) a copy of the notice of the preparation of the draft published in accordance with section 21 (1)(b) of the Act of 1963;
   (b) in relation to the authority prescribed at (h) in article 6 –
      (i) a copy of the written statement comprised in any draft of a proposed development plan, or of proposed variations of a development plan, for any area which comprises or in which is included any place which is or is in an area determined to be a Gaeltacht area by order under section 2 of the Ministers and Secretaries (Amendment) Act, 1956, and
      (ii) a copy of the notice of the preparation of the draft published in

accordance with section 21 (1)(*b*) of the Act of 1963 for any such area; and

(*c*) in relation to the authorities prescribed at (*i*) *to (l)* of article 6 –

(i) a copy of the written statement comprised in any draft of a proposed development plan, or of proposed variations of a development plan,

(ii) a copy of the notice of the preparation of the draft published in accordance with section 21 (1)(*b*) of the Act of 1963, and

(iii) a copy of any plan comprised in the draft.

6. The prescribed authorities for the purposes of section 21 (1)(*a*) of the Act of 1963 shall be –

(*a*) An Chomhairle Ealaíon,

(*b*) Bord Fáilte Éireann,

(*c*) An Taisce – the National Trust for Ireland,

(*d*) The National Monuments Advisory Council,

(*e*) The Minister for Industry and Commerce,

(*f*) The Minister for Fisheries,

(*g*) The Minister for Defence,

(*h*) The Minister for the Gaeltacht,

(*i*) The Minister.

(*j*) An Bord Pleanála,

(*k*) every planning authority whose area is contiguous to the area of the planning authority which prepared the draft, and

(*l*) every local authority in the area to which the draft relates.

7. A planning authority shall make available for purchase by the public printed copies of the development plan and extracts therefrom.

8. Where application is made to a planning authority by a member of the public for a printed copy of a development plan or of an extract therefrom the copy shall be issued to the applicant on payment by him to the planning authority of such fee as they may fix not exceeding the reasonable cost of making the copy.

. . .

PART VIII

EXTINGUISHMENT OF PUBLIC RIGHTS OF WAY

58. – (1) In this Part, 'section 76 hearing' means an oral hearing held pursuant to section 76 of the Act of 1963.

(2) In this Part, 'party', in relation to a section 76 hearing, means –

(*a*) any person who made an objection to the relevant order made by a planning authority for the extinguishment of a public right of way, and

(*b*) the planning authority who made the order.

59. – (1) Where an order is made by a planning authority under section 76 of the Act of 1963 for the extinguishment of any public right of way, they shall, not less than three weeks before submitting the order to the Minister for approval –

(*a*) publish in one or more newspapers circulating in their area a notice in the form set out in Form No. 3 of the Second Schedule, describing the public right of way to which the order relates and naming a place where a copy of the order and a map indicating the public right of way may be inspected during office hours, and

(b) affix a copy of such notice in a prominent position at each end of the public right of way to which the order relates.

(2) Every notice affixed in accordance with this article shall be kept exhibited in such position for a period of not less than three weeks.

(3) A copy of the order and a map indicating the public right of way described in the order shall be kept available for inspection in accordance with the terms of the published notice.

60. – (1) Where a section 76 hearing is to be held, the Minister shall so inform each of the parties and give each party not less than seven days notice of the time and place of the opening of the hearing or such shorter notice as may be accepted by all the parties.

(2) The Minister may, at any time before the opening of a section 76 hearing, alter the time or place of the opening of the hearing and, in the event of such alteration, the Minister shall give each party not less than seven days notice of the new time or place or such shorter notice as may be accepted by all the parties.

(3) Where the parties have been informed that such a hearing is to be held and where the objection or all of the objections which caused the hearing to be arranged are withdrawn, the Minister shall give notice accordingly to the parties and shall not approve the relevant order under section 76 of the Act of 1963 until seven days after the giving of the notice.

(4) A section 76 hearing shall be conducted by a person appointed for the purpose by the Minister generally or for a particular hearing.

61. At a section 76 hearing, the person conducting the hearing shall have discretion as to the conduct of the hearing and in particular shall –

(a) conduct the hearing without undue formality,

(b) decide the order of appearance of the parties and any witnesses,

(c) permit any party to appear in person or to be represented by another person, and

(d) hear, if he thinks fit, any person who is not a party to the hearing.

62. – (1) Subject to sub-articles (2) and (3), a person conducting a section 76 hearing may adjourn or re-open any hearing or, notwithstanding that any party to the hearing has failed to attend the hearing, proceed with the hearing.

(2) Notice of the time and place of the re-opening of a section 76 hearing or resumption of such a hearing that has been adjourned indefinitely shall be given by the Minister not less than seven days before the said time unless all the parties accept shorter notice.

(3) Unless the Minister otherwise directs, a section 76 hearing shall not be re-opened after the report thereon has been submitted to the Minister.

63. If, for any reason, the person appointed is unable or fails to conduct, or to complete the conduct of, a section 76 hearing or, for any reason, is unable or fails to furnish a report on such a hearing to the Minister, the Minister may appoint another person to conduct the hearing or to conduct a new hearing.

PART IX

64. The prescribed authorities for the purposes of section 46 of the Act of 1963 (being the authorities which must be consulted by a planning authority before they make an order under that section) shall be –
  (*a*) the Minister for Fisheries,
  (*b*) the Royal Irish Academy,
  (*c*) Bord Fáilte Éireann, and
  (*d*) An Taisce – the National Trust for Ireland.

65. Each of the following bodies is hereby declared to be a public authority for the purposes of section 5 of the Act of 1976 –
  (*a*) An Chomhairle Ealaíon,
  (*b*) Bord Fáilte Éireann,
  (*c*) The National Monuments Advisory Council,
  (*d*) The Industrial Development Authority,
  (*e*) Gaeltarra Éireann,
  (*f*) The Shannon Free Airport Development Company Limited,
  (*g*) Córas Iompar Éireann, and
  (*h*) The Electricity Supply Board.

66. Form No. 4 set out in the Second Schedule, or a form substantially to the like effect, shall be the prescribed form of vesting order to be made by a planning authority in exercise of the powers conferred on them by section 25 (5) of the Act of 1976.

LOCAL GOVERNMENT (PLANNING AND DEVELOPMENT) (FEES AND AMENDMENT) REGULATIONS, 1983

PART IV

Register Fee
24. The prescribed fee for a copy of an entry in the Register shall be £5.

CASES

PUBLICATION OF DRAFT DEVELOPMENT PLAN

FINN V. BRAY URBAN DISTRICT COUNCIL
[1969] I.R. 169

The plaintiff objected to proposals contained in the draft development plan of the defendant and lodged a written objection. She was represented by Counsel at an oral hearing. Following this the Council purported to make a development plan containing a new and different provision from that objected to by the plaintiff. In this action the plaintiff contended that the amended plan should have been treated as a draft and re-published before being adopted. This contention was upheld in the High Court by Butler J. In the result, planning authorities were, naturally, reluctant to incorporate amendments into the draft thereby incurring an obligation to further publish. The situation is now catered for by section 21A (introduced by s. 37 of the Act of 1976) which allows the making of an amended development plan or amended variations following the hearing of objections.

Butler J.:

There had been no notification or publication of the Council's intention to make any amendments. In particular, the plaintiff had not been informed as to the result of her written and oral statement of objection and knew nothing of the new provision until it was included in the plan by virtue of the resolution of the 26th September. The Council, having adopted the plan on that date, arranged a further meeting for the 30th September in order to have the plan formally signed and sealed, but in the meantime the plaintiff instituted these proceedings. She obtained an interim injunction on the 28th September, and the present interlocutory injunction on the 20th October, 1967.

Shortly, her case is that Part III of the Act, taken as a whole, requires a planning authority to prepare a draft of their proposals before making a plan; to publish notice of the making of such draft and to allow objections to be made and the case in support of the objection to be stated and considered. If, as a result of objection or otherwise, the draft is amended, the planning authority cannot simply make a plan consisting of the amended draft without further publication. She contends that the amendment becomes a new draft which must be advertised and made available for inspection again, so that persons who were entitled to object to the original draft may be afforded the same opportunity to object to the proposed amendment. If this is so, the Council in the present case were not entitled to pass the resolution of the 26th September, 1967, and are not entitled to proceed with the signing and sealing of the plan. [His Lordship referred to the provisions of ss. 19–22 of the Act of 1963 which appear at pp. 13–17, *ante*, and then continued:]

Certain statutory obligations are clearly and specifically imposed on the planning authority by these sections in relation to a plan; they must make a plan within the prescribed time or any longer time allowed by the Minister; the plan must include specified objectives and may include others; they must review the plan as occasion requires and, in any event, once every five years; when the plan is made notice of the making must be published which shall include a statement that the plan is available for inspection at a stated place and at stated times. In addition, where they have prepared a draft of a proposed plan they must take the steps set out in sub-ss. 1 and 2 of section 21.

Mr. Peart submitted that the sections deal with two distinct and separate documents neither of which, he says, necessarily owes anything to the other; first, a development plan and, secondly, a draft of a proposed development plan. While the provisions in relation to the plan are mandatory in all circumstances, the obligations in relation to the draft arise only where a draft is in fact prepared. There is, he says, no obligation to prepare a draft at all and a planning authority may avoid any of the requirements of sub-ss. 1 and 2 of s. 21 by not doing so. Furthermore, he says, even where a planning authority makes a draft, they may proceed to make the plan in an entirely different form without basing it on the draft, without being bound by the draft or by any objections or submissions made under the procedure in the sub-sections, provided only that they have considered the objections and the representations and statements received and made. There is no provision enabling the planning authority to amend a draft (except in the one case to which I shall advert later) and Mr. Peart concedes that, unless his submissions are well founded, the Council in the present instance has no power to make this plan containing, as it does, a new provision of which no notice had been given.

In support of his propositions, Mr. Peart submits, first, that there is no provision in the Act which in terms directs the planning authority to prepare a draft of a proposed plan. Secondly, nowhere in the present Act or in the previous legislation, or indeed in the entire history of town-planning legislation here or in England, is there any obligation to publish the contents of a plan before it is made. Thirdly, under the Act it is mandatory to publish notice of the making of a plan *after it is made*, and to make it available for inspection and that this, coupled with the statutory obligation to review, affords adequate protection for an owner whose property may be affected, or to anyone wishing to have the plan altered. Fourthly, the purpose of sub-ss. 1 and 2 of s. 21 is not to provide a protection for interested persons and bodies, but to provide machinery for a planning authority who wish to avail of it to stimulate public interest in, and discussion of, their proposals and to test the climate of public opinion in their area without being in any way bound by the result. Mr. Peart further says that the present procedure is merely a streamlining of the procedure under the former code and that one should look at the earlier position as an aid to the correct interpretation of the present Act.

In his first submission Mr. Peart is technically correct. There is no specific directive to the planning authority to prepare a draft of their proposals as there is requiring them to make a plan. However, the provisions must be considered in context. The first consideration is that, as conceded, a plan may adversely affect private property. Hence, if there is an interpretation of the Act fairly open which ensures that before that happens an owner of property shall be given notice of the proposed plan and be enabled to object and to state his case in support of the objection, that interpretation should be adopted: see the judgment of Mr. Justice Walsh in *McDonald* v. *Bord na gCon*.[71] Again certain other persons and bodies are obviously interested in any planning proposals and may want to make representations thereon. The Act recognizes this and makes provision for it by requiring copies of the written statement of the draft to be sent to prescribed authorities. These are prescribed by the regulations made under the Act[72] (S.I. No. 219 of 1964) and include the Minister himself together with the Ministers for Industry and Commerce, and for Lands and Defence, and also Bord Fáilte Eireann, An Chomhairle Ealaion, An Taisce and others. If Mr. Peart's submissions are correct, the planning authority may make a plan containing provisions of which none of these persons or bodies would have had any notice. Even the Minister would not

---

[71] [1965] I.R. 217.
[72] Since revoked by the Local Government (Planning and Development) Regulations, 1977 (S.I. No. 65 of 1977).

have had an opportunity of indicating his views in relation thereto and would be left to his powers under sub-s. 3 of s. 22 to require variations to be made.

I do not think that Mr. Peart is correct in his interpretation of the former law. Under the earlier code the Minister had to approve of a planning scheme adopted by a planning authority after extensive publication and provision was made whereby any person affected could object direct to the Minister before he gave his approval. See Part III of the Town and Regional Planning Act, 1934, and the regulations made thereunder (S.R. & O. 1934 No. 334) and in particular Articles 9 to 19. I take Mr. Peart as being correct in describing the new procedure as a streamlining and modernization of the old. I do not think it can ever have been intended that the Minister's general powers of supervision and approval at all stages leading up to the adoption of the plan and thereafter should be so reduced that he need not know anything of it until after it has been made, particularly in view of the far greater scope and comprehension of the new Act.

I next consider the adequacy of the steps open to an interested party after the plan has been made. In the first place the obligation of the planning authority is merely to review the plan, and to make any variations which they think proper. They are not obliged to make any variations and, unless they do, they need not receive objections, or consider representations or afford a hearing. They must make the plan available for inspection, but it is only after they have decided to propose a variation that they must consider objections etc., and then only in relation to the proposed alteration and not to the plan as a whole. This is hardly an acceptable alternative to the rights conferred by sub-ss. 1 and 2 or s. 21 of the Act of 1963.

In view of all these considerations, I am of the view that the correct interpretation of Part III of the Act of 1963 is that, before making a plan, the planning authority must first prepare a draft of their proposals and must give notice of having done so and must make it available for inspection; in addition they must receive and consider objections and representations, and they must afford an objecting ratepayer the opportunity of stating his case. If any amendment is made in the draft, which amendment is a material alteration of the draft proposals, then notice of such amendment must similarly be given and like opportunities afforded. I have noted that, apart from this procedure, no power of amending the draft is conferred on the planning authority and, I think, necessarily and designedly so. I am fortified in this view by a consideration of the one instance in which a power to amend a proposal is given, namely, in sub-s. 4 of section 22. Under sub-s. 8 of that section the Minister may require a planning authority to vary a plan, and sub-s. 4 goes on to provide that 'where the planning authority, as a result of considering pursuant to paragraph (*b*) of subsection (2) of section 21 of this Act any objection or representation, decide, with the consent of the Minister, that the proposed variations should be altered in any respect, they may make the variations subject to that alteration.' It is, I think, implicit in this provision, first, that a proposal to make an alteration (and as a consequence a proposal to make a plan) must be prepared and published and, secondly, that no power to make an amendment in a draft proposal exists or is to be implied apart from this one instance.

In order that the consideration in this judgment of the earlier procedure may be complete, I should note that, under the former code, if any provision of a planning scheme was adopted which was not included in the draft scheme, the Minister might require additional notices to be published. Again, it is unlikely that it was intended to remove this valuable protection.

ACQUISITION POWER OF PLANNING AUTHORITY

LEINSTER IMPORTING COMPANY LIMITED V. DUBLIN COUNTY COUNCIL
Unreported (Judgment of McWilliam J. delivered 26th January, 1977)

Dublin County Council made a compulsory acquisition order for purposes including the provision of recreational open space and playing fields pursuant to its general obligation under the Planning Acts. The order was confirmed by the Minister for Local Government. The plaintiff challenged the validity of the order on the basis that there was no power compulsorily to acquire land for the purposes of the Planning Acts. Reliance was placed on the decision in *Movie News Limited. v. Galway County Council*[73] in which Kenny J. had found that there was no compulsory acquisition power vested in Planning Authorities in the Act of 1963. In the *Movie News* case the acquiring authority apparently did not rely on Section 10 of the 1898 Act. In the *Leinster Importing* case specific reliance was placed on Section 10 of the 1898 Act and also Section 11 of the Local Government (No. 2) Act, 1960 which amends the earlier section. McWilliam J. held that these powers conferred the necessary power of acquisition.

McWilliam J.:
. . . As I understand the case made on behalf of the plaintiff, it is that the defendant can only acquire these lands for recreational purposes in its capacity as planning authority and that, although the defendant may be both the planning authority and the local authority, its functions as local authority are quite separate and the powers available to it as local authority cannot be exercised by it when acting as planning authority, and that there is no power given to planning authority to acquire land as such. The judgment of Kenny, J., in the case of *Movie News Ltd. v. Galway Co. Co.* is very strongly relied on.

It is accepted on behalf of the defendant that section 10 of the Local Government (No. 2) Act, 1960, as substituted by section 86 of the Housing Act, 1966, does not give any power of acquisition for the purpose of the 1963 Act, but it is submitted that section 11 of the 1960 Act, by its interpretation of section 10(1) of the Local Government (Ireland) Act, 1898, does give a local authority this power. . .

[The judge then quoted relevant portions from S. 10 of the 1898 Act and S. 11 of the Local Government (No. 2) Act, 1960.[74]]

These two sections were not opened to Kenny, J., in the Galway case although he does refer in his judgment to section 10 of the 1898 Act, but merely to indicate that no reliance was placed upon it on behalf of Galway County Council.

Clause (c) of subsection (1) of section 11 of the 1960 Act could hardly be more comprehensive in its terms and I am satisfied that, on the correct interpretation of this section with section 10 of the 1898 Act, the defendant was entitled to acquire

---

[73] Unreported judgment delivered 30th March 1975.
[74] See pp. 35–7.

these lands compulsorily and that such acquisition could, under the provisions of the new section 10 of the 1960 Act, be effected under that Act.

MOVIE NEWS LIMITED V. GALWAY COUNTY COUNCIL
Unreported Judgment of Kenny J. (delivered 30th March, 1975)

The nett issue was whether the planning authority had been authorised by the Act of 1963 to acquire lands compulsorily for the purposes of that Act. It is clear that acquisition powers conferred by other Acts are sufficiently wide to enable a planning authority to acquire lands compulsorily for the purposes of the Planning Acts. S.10 of the Local Government Act, 1898 is such a section. Its extension by S.11 of the Local Government (No. 2) Act, 1960 was (subsequently) held sufficiently wide to authorise compulsory acquisition by a planning authority for its purposes. In the *Movie News* case S.11 of the Act of 1960 was not cited to the judge and the local authority disclaimed reliance on S.10 of the Act of 1898. Interestingly Kenny J. appeared to consider that the fact that this section was not referred to in the Compulsory Purchase Order meant that it could not be relied upon to justify the acquisition.[75]

In the Supreme Court the defendant sought to rely for the first time on S.10 of the Act of 1898 to justify the making of the acquisition order but was refused liberty to introduce this argument which had not been made to the High Court judge – indeed the Council had disclaimed reliance on this section in the Court below. No other argument was presented on appeal indicating an acceptance of the position as decided in the *Leinster Importing* case. The Supreme Court judgment was delivered on the 15th July, 1977 by Henchy J. (Griffin, Parke, JJ. concurring). In the course of it he observed – 'We wish to make clear, however, that we find it unnecessary to decide whether a Compulsory Purchase Order should recite each and every statutory provision under which it is made.'

Kenny J.:
The important issue which arises therefore is whether a local authority, who are a planning authority under the Planning Act 1963, have been authorised by that Act to acquire lands compulsorily for the purpose of development or for the provision of amenities under that Act. . . .

There is however nothing in the Planning Act 1963 which authorises a local authority or a planning authority to acquire lands compulsorily for the purposes of that Act. The assumption which underlies s. 77 sub s. 4 of the Planning Act 1963 that section 10 of the Local Government (No. 2) Act 1960 confers a power to acquire land compulsorily for the purposes of the Planning Act 1963 was incorrect.

Counsel for the defendants contended that the Planning Act 1963 had created an implied power of compulsory acquisition. He said that the planning authority were given power by the Planning Act 1963 to develop land and that they could not do this unless they had compulsory powers of acquisition. I do not think that it is permissible to imply that a power of compulsory acquisition has been created because a power to develop has been conferred on a local authority. Powers of compulsory acquisition must be created by reasonably clear language and are not to be inferred or implied.

[75] But see *McCoy and Other.* v. *Cork Corporation* [1934] I.R. 779 at p. 794.

Section 76 sub-section 2 of the Planning Act 1963 refers to land acquired compulsorily by a planning authority for the purposes of the Planning Act 1963 but this too is based on the assumption that a power to acquire land compulsorily for the purposes of the Planning Act 1963 exists. In my view it does not.

The defendants disclaimed any reliance on s. 10 of the Local Government Act 1898 and as that section is not referred to in the Compulsory Purchase Order it cannot be invoked[76] to justify it.

In my opinion the plaintiff's contention that the Planning Act 1963 does not confer any power to authorise a planning authority to acquire land compulsorily for the purposes of that Act is correct and section 10 of the Local Government (No. 2) Act 1960 has no application. The Compulsory Purchase Order will accordingly be quashed.

CONSTITUTIONALITY OF PLANNING ACTS

THE CENTRAL DUBLIN DEVELOPMENT ASSOCIATION LIMITED AND OTHERS V. THE ATTORNEY GENERAL (109 I.L.T.R. 69)

The plaintiffs challenged the constitutional validity of several sections of the Act of 1963. Kenny J. delivered judgment on the 6th October, 1969 dismissing all the points made by the plaintiffs. The judgment of Kenny J. is necessarily long and is available in a published report. Brief extracts only are included here.

The judgment commences with a summary of the entire Act of 1963 and then proceeded to rule that the plaintiffs had *locus standi* to challenge the validity of the Act. There is an obvious tension between community interests and private interests where environmental planning is concerned. This was recognised by the judge, who observed 'Town and Regional planning is an attempt to reconcile the exercise of property rights with the demands of the common good and Part IV defends and vindicates as far as practicable the rights of the citizens and is not an unjust attack on their property rights.'

Kenny J.:

. . . . In my view an analysis of the text of the Constitution and of the decisions on it lead to these conclusions:

(1) The right of private property is a personal right;

(2) In virtue of his rational being, man has a natural right to individual or private ownership of worldly wealth;

(3) This constitutional right consists of a bundle of rights most of which are founded in contract;

(4) The State cannot pass any law which abolishes all the bundle of rights which we call ownership or the general right to transfer, bequeath and inherit property.

(5) The exercise of these rights ought to be regulated by the principles of social justice and the State accordingly may by law restrict their exercise with a view to reconciling this with the demands of the common good.

(6) The Courts have jurisdiction to inquire whether the restriction is in accordance with the principles of social justice and whether the legislation is necessary to reconcile this exercise with the demands of the common good.

---

[76] See reservation expressed by Henchy J. quoted at p. 44.

(7) If any of the rights which together constitute our concept of ownership are abolished or restricted (as distinct from the abolition of all the rights), the absence of compensation for this restriction or abolition will make the Act which does this invalid if it is an unjust attack on property rights.

The plaintiffs accept that planning and control of buildings and land and of the use of these is required in the interests of the common good. Their principal complaint is that many of the provisions of the Act are an unjust attack on some of the rights included in the concept of ownership: they also make the charge that some of the powers given to the Minister are judicial and not limited and so cannot be validly conferred on him. . . .

In paragraph 9 it is said that as 19, 20 and 21 make it obligatory on the planning authority to make a development plan and to review it, that this is left to the arbitrary discretion of the authority and there is no right of appeal to any Court against the plan. The result of this, it is pleaded, is that some private property within the areas to which the plan relates will be substantially reduced in value. I do not think that the giving of power to a planning authority to make a development plan after they have considered and heard objections to the draft is an unjust attack on property rights. A plan of development for each city and town is necessary for the common good, someone must prepare it, and the planning authority, who have staff trained in this work, seem to me to be the best persons to do it. While the High Court can decide questions as to the meaning of the Act, this Judge at least is not qualified to make decisions on planning policy. The making of a plan will necessarily decrease the value of some property but I do not think that the Constitution requires that compensation should be paid for this as it is not an unjust attack on property rights. If this argument were correct, many owners of houses would have been entitled to be paid compensation when the Rent Restrictions Act, 1946 was passed. Complaint is also made that the authority may carry out development which is not in accord with the development plan but as they are the persons to give permission for development, it would be ridiculous that they had to apply to themselves for it. . . .

S. 31 gives the planning authority power to serve an enforcement notice (which may require work to be done) when any development has been carried out without permission or when a condition attached to that permission has been broken. S. 32 gives similar powers when a condition relating to the retention of a structure has not been observed. Under both sections the authority may enter on the lands if the work mentioned in the enforcement notice is not carried out within the specified period. The plaintiffs complain that no appeal to any Court or tribunal against an enforcement notice is given and that entry on the lands may be made without a Court Order authorising this. Both these contentions are incorrect. The High Court would have jurisdiction to declare that an enforcement notice had been served without sufficient reason or that it was invalid while s. 81 of the Act provides that if an owner refuses to allow a planning authority to enter, they cannot do so until they have obtained an order of the District Court approving the entry. These considerations dispose of the constitutional objections to ss. 31, 32, 33, 35 and 36. . . .

Paragraph 21 of the Statement of Claim lists a number of sections and subsections of the Act which are said to be unconstitutional because they confer the power to administer justice on the planning authority or on the Minister, a power which can be exercised by Judges only. The answer was that the Judicial powers given to the planning authority and the Minister were limited while the other powers were to decide administrative matters and so not an administration of justice. Before dealing with each of the impugned provisions it is necessary to say something about the difference between the administration of justice and judicial decisions in contrast to administrative awards. I have read the decisions in the *Shell Company of Australia* v. *the Federal Commissioners of Taxation* [1931] A.C. 275, *Fisher* v. *the Irish Land Commission* [1948] I.R. 3, *McDonald* v. *Bord Na gCon* [1965] I.R. 217 and the judgments given in the Privy Council in *United Engineering Workers Union* v. *Devanayagam* [1967] 2 All E.R. 367. In the last case the dissenting judgment of Lord Guest and Lord Devlin contains an outstanding analysis of the judicial power and mentions some of the features by which it may be distinguished from arbitral and administrative powers. In *McDonald* v. *Bord Na gCon* [1965] I.R. 217, I said (at p. 230/231) 'It seems to me that the administration of justice has these characteristic features:

1. A dispute or controversy as to the existence of legal rights or a violation of the law.
2. The determination or ascertainment of the rights of parties or the imposition of liabilities or the infliction of a penalty.
3. The final determination (subject to appeal) of legal rights or liabilities or the imposition of penalties.
4. The enforcement of those rights or liabilities or the imposition of a penalty by the Court or by the executive power of the State which is called in by the Court to enforce its judgment.
5. The making of an order by the Court which, as a matter of history, is an order characteristic of Courts in this country.'

In the *United Engineering Union case* [1967] 2 All E.R. the dissenting judgment points out that 'the judicial power must be exercised so as to do justice in the case that is being tried and the Judge must not allow himself to be influenced by any other consideration at all. Considerations of policy or expediency, which are permissible for the administrator, must be altogether excluded by the Judge'. While the requirements of constitutional justice oblige an administrative tribunal to act judicially, it does not follow that every tribunal which is bound to act in this way is exercising the judicial power of the State. It seems to me that many of the powers conferred on the Minister by the Act to decide appeals involve not the application of legal rules or principles but decisions on questions of policy in planning matters.

The first section attacked is s. 5 under which the Minister may decide any question as to what is or is not development or exempted development. 'Development' is defined in s. 3 and 'exempted development' in s. 4. The answer to the question as to what is development, and what is exempted development depends then upon the application of legal standards prescribed by the Act and is, therefore, an administration of justice. It is, however, in my opinion a limited power and there is a right of appeal from the Minister's decision to the High Court. 'The test as to whether a power is or is not limited in the opinion of the Court lies in the effect of the assigned power when exercised. If the exercise of the assigned powers and functions is calculated ordinarily to affect in the most profound and far reaching way the lives, liberties, fortunes or reputations of those against whom they are exercised they cannot properly be described as limited' (per Mr. Justice Kingsmill Moore in the *Solicitors Act Case* [1960] I.R. 239). I do not think that the decision as to what is or is not development or exempted development affects the fortunes of citizens in a profound way because the result of the Minister's decision is that planning permission has to be obtained. The Minister's decision does not decide finally that a particular development cannot be carried out: it decides only that permission is or is not required.

Sub-sections 3, 4, 5 and 9 of section 26 are attacked. Sub-s. (3) provides that a planning authority shall not grant permission for development in a case in which it would contravene materially the development plan or a special amenity Order without the consent of the Minister. This is not the exercise of judicial power but is an administrative decision as to whether divergence from the development plan should be permitted. Sub-s. 4 fixed the time within which a grant of permission for development is to be given: in the case of an application to the Minister under sub section 3, it is to be regarded as having been given within seven days from the receipt by the authority of the Minister's decision. As sub-section 3 is valid and as sub-section 4 fixes a time only within which permission is deemed to have been given, it is not invalid. Sub-s. 5 gives every person a right to appeal to the Minister against the decision of a planning authority on an application for permission to develop and provides that the Minister is to determine the application as if it had been made to him originally so that he is restricted to considering the proper planning and development of the area of the authority having regard to the provisions of the plan. When deciding the appeal, the Minister has not to decide it in accordance with any known legal principles or rules. In my opinion, the Minister when deciding appeals under this sub-section is not exercising judicial powers but is deciding matters of administrative policy. Sub-s. 9 provides that when the planning authority decide to grant a permission they shall grant it after the expiration of the period for the taking of an appeal if no appeal is taken but if there is an appeal the Minister shall grant it, if he allows the appeal, as soon as possible after the decision. As the Minister's decision is not the exercise of judicial power, the grant of permission cannot be the administration of justice.

Sub-ss. 4 and 6 of section 27 deal with the Minister's powers to decide an appeal under that section which deals with the granting by the authority of permission to retain an unauthorised structure which existed before the 1st of October 1964 and for which permission has not been granted under earlier Town Planning Acts. Again, the exercise by the Minister of this power to decide such an appeal is not an administration of justice for he is deciding a policy matter and he has not to apply legal rules.

Section 29 provides that when permission to develop any land has been refused by the Minister on an appeal, the owner may, in certain circumstances, serve on the authority a notice requiring them to purchase his interest in the land and they must within three months serve a notice stating whether they are or are not willing to comply with it and a copy of their notice must be sent to the Minister. If he is satisfied that the conditions mentioned in paragraphs (a) to (c) or paragraph (a) and (b) of sub-s. 1 have been fulfilled, he may confirm the purchase notice served by the person who has been refused permission. It then becomes the duty of the authority to serve a notice stating that they intend to comply with the purchase notice which is to have effect as if it were a compulsory purchase order made under s. 10 of the Local Government (No. 2) Act, 1960. The Housing Act of 1966 is now the code under which most compulsory acquisitions of property are carried out but in deciding on the constitutional validity of provisions in the Act, the Court is limited to considering it having regard to the Acts which were in force when the Act was passed. The function conferred on the Minister under sub-section 4 is to decide whether the conditions in sub-s. 1 have been fulfilled. His decision is thus not on policy but on the interpretation of the conditions in sub-s. 1 and their application to the case which he is considering. I think that this is an exercise of a limited judicial power and is saved by Article 37. . . .

FINNEGAN V. AN BORD PLEANALA AND OTHERS
(1977 No. 5503 P.) Unreported (High Court decision of McWilliam J. delivered 15th December 1978.)

The plaintiff was an objector to a proposal for an asbestos waste dump near Ovens, Co. Cork who resided four miles away. He was among a number of third party appellants against a proposal to grant planning permission and there was an oral hearing before the first named defendant. In a subsequent challenge to the validity of the grant of permission he maintained that the Act of 1976 was repugnant to the Constitution (in that it required a £10 fee for third party objectors, gave power in certain circumstances to An Bord Pleanala to deal with an appeal in the absence of the appellant and gave them discretion to refuse to grant an oral hearing of an appeal); that the Board acted contrary to constitutional and natural justice in the conduct of the instant hearing (in not considering a submission by the plaintiff dealing with a topic which had been dealt with at a previous adjourned hearing which the plaintiff was unable to attend); that the permission dealt with matters wihin the jurisdiction of the Minister for Health and for Labour and was therefore ultra vires the powers of the Planning Acts and that a permission was given to the wrong party, namely the I.D.A. rather than the development company.

In the High Court McWilliam J. rejected these arguments and in doing so stressed that the High Court was not entitled to review the decision of the planning authorities on planning grounds: it was confined to dealing with legal points.

The plaintiff in his appeal to the Supreme Court limited his case to challenging the constitutional validity of Sections 15 (the £10 deposit section), 16 (discretion to refuse an oral hearing subject to an appeal to the Minister) and 18 (power of the Board to determine a reference or appeal in the absence of the party concerned after serving notice of an intention so to do). These challenges were in turn dismissed in the Supreme Court.

McWilliam J.:

In these proceedings, the plaintiff claims declarations that the Local Government (Planning and Development) Act, 1976, is repugnant to the Constitution, that the Board acted unconstitutionally and without regard to the principles of natural justice in its conduct of the hearing of the appeals, that the permission given by the Board was ultra vires its powers under the Act in that it concerned matters within the jurisdiction of the Minister for Health and the Minister for Labour, that the grant of permission is null and void because the grant of permission was made to the Industrial Development Authority and not to Raybestos Manhattan (Ireland) Limited, who are proposing to use the site, and, in effect, that due consideration was not given by the Board to the evidence tendered to establish the danger to health arising from the proposed user.

The plaintiff, who has appeared in person, is genuinely and properly greatly perturbed about the effects of the dissemination of asbestos waste on the health of the community. He has shown an immense amount of energy and done a great deal of research in his efforts to demonstrate this and a very large proportion of the arguments he addressed to me dealt with this aspect of the case. He has also given me many legal references from Magna Carta to the present day.

I am, however, not entitled to treat this action as a re-hearing of the appeal to the Board or as an actual appeal from the decision of the Board. I have no jurisdiction in these respects. I am confined to a consideration of the constitutionality of the statute, whether the principles of constitutional or natural justice were or were not observed on the hearing of the appeal, whether there was evidence on which the Board was entitled to come to the decision which was reached, whether the matter was ultra vires the jurisdiction of the Board and whether the grant of permission was, on its face, for any reason bad.

The main grounds advanced to support the argument that the 1976 Act is unconstitutional are that this Act permits an assault on the bodily integrity of the citizen which is one of the unspecified personal rights guaranteed by Article 40 of the Constitution and that the provision for the deposit of £10 at the time of lodging an appeal offends against the provisions of Article 4 that all citizens shall be held equal before the law. The plaintiff's arguments on the first of these grounds proceed on the basis that the present system of waste disposal is dangerous to health, a question which it is not within my province to decide, that this has been permitted by the Board, and that the statute has been enacted to enable such a state of affairs to exist and is therefore unconstitutional. Assuming for the moment that the permitted method of waste disposal is dangerous to health, it appears to me that this argument might be described as inverted. The statutes were enacted to control such activities and the fact that they may not have been successful in achieving this desirable object does not make them in any way unconstitutional. If it were not for such statutes, it is possible that the dumping of this waste could be indiscriminate as appears to have been the case many years ago at Calderdale in England, a case to which the plaintiff has referred me. With regard to the second ground, I can see nothing unconstitutional in making a reasonable charge for initiating an appeal, particularly where, as here, the deposit is returnable if the citizen proceeds with his appeal. There might be some substance in the argument if the charge were put so high as to prevent all but the very wealthy from appealing but nothing of this nature is involved in a charge of £10.

Two grounds are advanced for the proposition that the proceedings were conducted in a manner contrary to the principles of natural and constitutional justice. The first is that the plaintiff was not permitted to represent the Crosshaven Community Association which was unable to arrange for another representative to be present after the first day of the hearing. I can see no substance in this objection. The plaintiff was permitted to produce any evidence and submit any arguments he wished on his own behalf and I cannot see how these could have been materially advanced by the acceptance of his appearance on behalf of this association. The second ground is that the plaintiff was not permitted to tender additional evidence to contradict or refute evidence given at an adjourned hearing and that a written submission or statement by the plaintiff for this purpose was not considered. I was referred to the case of *Kiely* v. *The Minister for Social Welfare* [1971] I.R. 21. That case was quite different from the present. There the tribunal refused to admit evidence to rebut evidence given at the hearing and produced at the last minute and without notice. In the present case the hearing was adjourned for the express purpose of hearing the additional evidence but, unfortunately, the plaintiff was not able to be present at this adjourned hearing, and, some time later, sent in a statement of evidence tending to rebut the evidence which had been given at the adjourned hearing. This statement was not considered by the tribunal and, in my opinion, it would have been more satisfactory if it had been but, if it was relevant, a statement to the same effect could have been tendered at an earlier stage in the hearing as the matters being dealt with were all of a general nature, and there must be some limitation put to the indefinite extension of the hearing of an appeal or inquiry such as this. I cannot see that there was any breach of the principles of natural or constitutional justice in the conduct of the proceedings in this respect.

The essence of this inquiry was as to the suitability of the site for the disposal of asbestos waste and the names of the parties concerned were very well publicised at an early stage and I cannot accept that there was any impropriety in granting the permission either to the Industrial Development Authority or to the Raybestos Company no matter which of them initiated the application for planning permission or which of them proposed actually to use the site, and no statutory provision has been indicated to me which makes this procedure bad.

The fact that the Minister for Labour or the Minister for Health or both of them may have powers to control the disposal of this waste material cannot make the powers given to the Board ultra vires the statute. It may be that the Minister for Health or the Minister for Labour is entitled to impose conditions as to the disposal of waste or the user of the site in addition to the conditions imposed by the Board, but this cannot in any way make the grant of permission by the Board ultra vires although such additional conditions might restrict further the operation of the waste disposal site for which the Board has granted permission.

The major part of the plaintiff's argument throughout was devoted to establishing the danger to health from asbestos fibres and dust and the difficulty or, as he argued, the impossibility, of disposing of it safely; to establishing how ineffective the conditions imposed for the operation of the site are; and to establishing that the evidence given at the hearing on his behalf and on the behalf of others shows that the use of this site in accordance with the permission given is dangerous to the health of those living in the locality. It is accepted by all parties that asbestos dust and fibres are dangerous to health when adequate controls are not provided. There is a dispute as to the adequacy of the controls which have been required. It may be that asbestos and installations like nuclear power stations should not be permitted to be used at all because it cannot be guaranteed that no danger to health will ever arise, but this is not a matter for me and was not a matter for the Board to decide. I am only concerned in this action to consider whether there was evidence upon which, if accepted, this permission could properly be granted subject to the conditions which were imposed. There was abundant evidence given to this effect and I have no jurisdiction to review the evidence and evaluate it myself. Therefore I cannot, on these grounds, take any steps to reverse the Order of the Board either by declaring it void or by quashing it or by directing any further inquiry into the matter.

Accordingly, I must dismiss the plaintiff's claim.

SUPREME COURT
(Unreported decision delivered 27th July 1979)

O'Higgins C.J. (*nem. diss.*):

As part of his claim in these proceedings the plaintiff seeks a declaration that certain provisions of the Local Government (Planning and Development) Act 1976 are repugnant to the Constitution. Originally in his statement of claim the plaintiff sought a declaration that the entire Act was so repugnant. However, having failed in the High Court and having appealed to this Court he has by his notice of appeal confined his claim to seeking a declaration that Sections 15, 16 and 18 of the Act are so repugnant.

The plaintiff was not professionally represented and conducted his appeal himself. His action is concerned with the Planning Appeal heard and determined before the Local Government (Planning and Development) Act, 1976 came into operation. The only personal interest which the plaintiff is entitled to claim in the outcome of these proceedings arises from the fact that he resides some four miles from the questioned development. Whether that propinquity gives him sufficient standing to mount an attack on the relevant statutory provisions on the ground of alleged unconstitutionality was not raised, and therefore not considered in the High Court. Because the plaintiff has not been professionally represented either in the High Court or in this court, because the question of his standing to raise the constitutional issue has not been pleaded by the defendants, and because of the urgency and gravity of the complaint against the development in question, the Court is prepared to assume, without so holding, that in the particular circumstances the plaintiff was entitled to impugn the constitutional validity of the sections in question.

The Local Government (Planning and Development) Act 1976 inter alia provides for the establishment of a Board known as An Bord Pleanála which is authorised to hear planning appeals and other matters referred to it. Such planning appeals were formerly, under the provisions of the Local Government (Planning and Development) Act 1963, determined by the Minister for Local Government. The Act also provides for certain other amendments affecting the bringing and determination of appeals. It is the plaintiff's contention that three of these amendments contained in Sections 15, 16 and 18 are repugnant to the Constitution and therefore invalid. . . .

[The Chief Justice then quoted Ss. 15, 16 and 18 and continued]

With regard to Section 15 the plaintiff contends that by the imposition of a deposit of £10 a restriction which he describes as being contrary to the democratic nature of the Constitution is imposed on persons wishing to appeal and that thereby a discrimination is made between those who have money and those who have not. In other words he submitted that this provision was repugnant to Art. 40 s. 1. In the opinion of the Court this submission is without substance. The purpose of the section is to prevent appeals or references which are without reality or substance. The amount of the deposit is not so high as to prevent genuine appeals being brought. In addition it is a deposit which is returnable when the appeal is heard, withdrawn or determined. A similar provision is made under the Electoral Acts in relation to candidates standing for Dáil and other elections. In the opinion of the Court there is no unconstitutional discrimination involved in the Section and the plaintiff's contention in this respect fails.

As to Section 16 the plaintiff contends that giving the discretion to the Board as to whether an appeal should be heard orally or otherwise is an unconstitutional interference with certain constitutional rights of citizens which he did not clearly specify. His complaint appears to have been that as such a citizen bringing a planning appeal under the 1963 Act had an absolute right to an oral hearing this change in the law was an unconstitutional deprivation of a right. In the opinion of the Court this submission is fallacious. It was open to the Oireachtas in providing for this type of appeal to alter the law in the manner provided for in the Section.

With regard to Section 18 the plaintiff did not go into detail in his submissions apart from saying that such wide powers ought not to have been given to the Board. This Section enjoys a presumption of constitutionality and it is also to be presumed that it will be operated without violating constitutional rights. While the Section gives to the Board power to determine an appeal notwithstanding the fact that it has heard no submission from the appellant it must be assumed that the notice provided for in the Section will be accompanied by an opportunity given to the appellant to put forward his case. The powers given to the Board by the Section can only be exercised under the Section after an opportunity is so afforded. Accordingly, in the opinion of the Court, this Section does not infringe the Constitution in the manner alleged.

Accordingly the submissions made by the plaintiff on this appeal impugning the constitutionality of Sections 15, 16 and 18 of the Local Government (Planning and Development) Act, 1976 fail.

ESTOPPEL AND PLANNING AUTHORITIES

DUBLIN CORPORATION V. ELIZABETH McGRATH
Unreported (decision of McMahon J. delivered 17th November 1978)

The general rule that estoppel cannot operate so as to validate an invalid exercise of statutory power has been applied to a Planning Authority in *Dublin Corporation v. Elizabeth McGrath*.[77] A representation by a planning inspector that the defendant could proceed without planning permission to build a structure which required such permission and that the inspector would look after the matter of planning permission could not bind the planning authority to grant planning permission.

McMahon J.:
This building was erected by the defendant without having obtained planning permission under the Local Government (Planning and Development) Act 1963. The District Justice accepted the evidence of the defendant's husband Patrick McGrath that he commenced this development in May 1975 and during the progress of the work he received a number of visits from an inspector from the complainants' Planning Department and the inspector assured Mr. McGrath that he could proceed with the erection of the building and that the Inspector would look after the matter of planning permission for him and that he, Mr. McGrath, believed that there would be no objection by the Planning Authority if he completed the building, which he did. The inspector involved was suspended from duty shortly afterwards and subsequently dismissed.

The District Justice decided that by reason of these misleading representations the complainants were estopped from denying that the building erected by Mr. McGrath was exempted development. He dismissed the summons and on the application of the solicitor for the complainants stated this case raising for the determination of the High Court the question of law which is stated as follows:

[77] Unreported decision of McMahon J. delivered 17th November, 1978.

'Was I correct in law in holding that the complainants qua Planning Authority were estopped from denying the representations made by their former employee'?

On the question of estoppel of a Planning Authority by representations by its officials the Court was referred to the following English authorities *Southend-on-Sea Corporation* v. *Hodgson Limited* [1961] 2 All E.R. 41; *Wells* v. *Minister of Housing* [1967] 2 All E.R. 1041; *Lever (Finance) Limited* v. *Westminster Corporation* [1970] 3 All E.R. 496. The Planning Authority was held to be estopped by a decision of an officer made within his ostensible authority. In our legislation the Planning Authority is not given the power to decide whether a particular development is or is not an exempted development. Exempted developments are defined in Section 4 of the Act of 1963 and under Section 5 of the Act any question which arises as to whether a particular development is or is not an exempted development must be referred to and decided by the Minister. There could be no question of the Inspector from the complainants' Planning Department having ostensible authority to make the representations which the District Justice found he had made. The case of *Wells* v. *Minister of Housing* [1967] 2 All E.R. 1041 was referred to in the decision of the Supreme Court. In *Greendale Building Company* v. *Dublin County Council*[78] Henchy J. said in the course of his judgment:

'The general rule is that a plea of estoppel of any kind cannot prevail as an answer to a well-founded claim that something done by a public body in breach of a statutory duty or limitation of function is ultra vires. That was held by Cassels J. in *Minister of Agriculture and Fisheries* v. *Matthews* [1950] 1 K.B. 148 by Harman J. in *Rhyl U.D.C.* v. *Rhyl Amusements Limited* [1959] 1 All E.R. 257 and in the unreported case of *Minister of Agriculture and Fisheries* v. *Hulkin*[79] (which was cited with approval by Cassels J. and Harman J. in those cases) in which Lord Greene M. R. said 'the power given to an authority under a Statute is limited to the four corners of the power given. It would entirely destroy the whole doctrine of ultra vires if it were possible for the donee of a statutory power to extend his power by creating an estoppel'. There are of course some modern cases (such as *Robertson* v. *Minister of Pensions* [1949] 1 K.B. 227) which have engrafted exceptions on the general rule so as to debar a public authority from relying on a mere irregularity of procedure which it was held they should in all fairness have overlooked. But as far as I am aware the exceptions are confined to such technicalities. 'I take the law to be' says Lord Denning M.R. in *Wells* v. *Minister of Housing and Local Government* [1967] 2 All E.R. 1041 at 1044 'that a defect in procedure can be cured and an irregularity can be waived, even by a public authority, so as to render valid that which would otherwise be invalid'. I know of no case where a public authority was held to be estopped from asserting that it had acted in breach of an express or implied prohibition or restriction of function in a Statute; see Spencer Bower and Turner 'The Law of Estoppel by Representation' 2nd Ed. pp. 132/3. The reason I believe is that it is incompatible with parliamentary democracy for the Court under the guise of estoppel or waiver or any other doctrine to set aside the will of Parliament as constitutionally embodied in a Statute.'

If the complainants had told the defendant that the building which her husband was erecting was an exempted development they would be acting ultra vires and could not be held to have estopped themselves from asserting subsequently that

[78] Reported at [1977] I.R. 256.
[79] [1950] K.B. 154.

planning permission was necessary for the development in question and accordingly, no representation by their agent could work a similar estoppel.

In so far as the representation referred to in the question of law in the Case Stated includes a representation that planning permission would be granted for the development this cannot bind the complainants to grant planning permission. Under Section 26 of the Local Government (Planning and Development) Act 1963 the complainants in dealing with an application for planning permission must consider the proper planning and development of the area of the Authority having regard to the provisions of the development plan, any special amenity area order and the other matters referred to in sub-section 2 of Section 26.

Any undertaking by the complainants to grant planning permission without complying with the provisions of Section 26 would clearly be ultra vires. The Authority could not be bound therefore by any representation of its agent to act illegally by granting planning permission in disregard of the terms of Section 26 of the Act.

Accordingly the question of law in the Case Stated must be answered in the negative. The matter is referred back to the learned District Justice.

Chapter 2

DEVELOPMENT

DEVELOPMENT

For the purposes of the Planning Acts and Regulations 'development' is divided
into two broad categories:

    (1) the carrying out of any works on, in or under land[1]

or (2) the making of any material change in the use of any structures[2] or other
       land[1]

(see Section 3 of the 1963 Act).

While the two categories may in some circumstances overlap (Finlay P. *in Re
Viscount Securities*)[3] they are more often mutually exclusive because of the artificial
meaning given to the word 'use' in relation to land by Section 2 of the 1963 Act, as
excluding 'the use of land by the carrying out of any works thereon'.[4] Thus the
construction of 288 houses on land previously used for agricultural purposes will
not amount to a change in the use of the land, although there will be development
within the first category. (see *in Re Viscount Securities*)[3] Nor, it seems, will there be
a change in the use of land where land formerly used for quarrying is used for tillage
although there is development within the first category (see *obiter dictum* of
Costello J. in *Patterson* v. *Murphy*).[5]

Some provisions of the Acts and Regulations apply to one category of development but not to the other with the result that the category into which a particular
development falls can be important. For example, Section 56 (1)(a) of the 1963 Act
excludes the payment of compensation under Section 55 where there is a refusal of
permission in respect of or including development in the second category. There is
no such exclusion in respect of the refusal of permission for development in the first
category (see *in Re Viscount Securities; Central Dublin Development Association* v.
The Attorney General).[6] The category of development may also be important when
determining whether or not a particular development is exempted. Thus Section 4
(1)(g) of the 1963 Act exempts development consisting of the carrying out of works
for specified purposes which affect the interior of the structure only but there is no

---

[1] Note 'land' includes any structure.
[2] Note 'structure' includes where the context so admits the land on, in or under which the
structure is situated.
[3] See page 453.
[4] Query whether 'thereon' includes 'therein' or 'thereunder'?
[5] See page 59.
[6] See page 453.

exemption given for a material change in the use of the structure although the change affects the interior of the structure only (see *Cork Corporation* v. *O'Connell*).[7]

THE CARRYING OUT OF ANY WORKS ON, IN OR UNDER LAND

'Works' is defined in Section 2 of the 1963 Act as *including* specified acts and operations. While the definition is extensive it is not expressed to be exhaustive which would seem to indicate that activities other than those specified may amount to development. In England it has been held that the test to be applied in determining whether or not an 'operation' amounts to development is whether or not it changes the physical character of the land.[8] There is no Irish decision on the point, but in the event of the Courts holding that the section is not exhaustive such a test might be used to identify unspecified 'works'. It should be noted, however, that in respect of the specified acts and operations the English section refers to 'the carrying out of building, engineering, mining and other operations. . . .'[9] Section 2 of the 1963 Act refers to '*any* act or operation of construction, excavation, demolition, extension, alteration, repair or renewal.' If this is to be interpreted literally it would appear that the effect on the land of the act or operation is irrelevant. It remains to be seen how literally the courts will interpret the section.

Development in the second category may arise where an existing use is intensified (see below). In *Patterson* v. *Murphy*[10] Costello J. employed the concept of intensification in respect of works as an aid to determining whether or not those works commenced before the appointed day. The case, however concerned a situation where the development in question would have fallen into the second category but for the artificial meaning given to the word 'use'. Indeed, in his subsequent decision of *Dublin County Council* v. *Tallaght Block Company Ltd.* Costello J. refers to *Patterson* v. *Murphy* as establishing that intensification of use can be a material change in use. The application of the concept of intensification amounting to development in the first category poses difficulties. When dealing with development in the first category one is not concerned with a change in works, but with the 'carrying out of works'. Once works have been commenced it is difficult to see the relevance of the intensity with which they are carried out.

THE MAKING OF ANY MATERIAL CHANGE IN THE USE OF ANY STRUCTURE OR OTHER LAND

There must be a *change* in the use of a structure or land which is *material* in planning terms for development to take place in the second category. Continuation of use does not amount to development. The 1963 Act specifies certain changes will always amount to a material change in use of a structure or land (see section 3(2) and section 3(3)). Whether other changes amount to a material change in use is a question of fact. When considering the materiality of a change regard will be had to not only the use itself but also to its effects. Thus, for example, in *Cork Corporation* v. *O'Connell*[11] the Court took into account that an amusement hall would attract

---

[7] See page 60.
[8] See *Cheshire County Council* v. *Woodward* [1962] 2 Q.B. 126.
[9] See s. 22(1) of the Town and Country Planning Act, 1971.
[10] See page 59.
[11] See page 60.

large crowds of young people into the area and in *Carrickhall Holdings Limited* v. *Dublin Corporation*[12] the Court considered *inter alia* the effect the new use would have on traffic in the area.

It is not necessary that the change be in the *type* of use being made of a structure or land. An intensification of use may also amount to development. Whether the intensification of an existing use amounts to a material change in use depends on the degree of intensification. (*Dublin County Council* v. *Tallaght Block Company Limited*;[13] *Carrickhall Holdings Limited* v. *Dublin Corporation*).

A change of use will also occur when an abandoned use is re-commenced (see *Dublin County Council* v. *Tallaght Block Company Limited*; *Cusack & McKenna* v. *Minister for Local Government*;[14] *Cork County Council* v. *Ardfert Quarry Products Limited*).[15] While it is a question of fact in every case a temporary suspension of use will not usually amount to abandonment. In determining whether a use was discontinued it is necessary to consider the evinced intention of the person who used the structure or land and any intervening use.

A use may be lost by extinguishment – i.e. when the structure or less usually the land being used perishes (see *Galway County Council* v. *Connacht Proteins Limited*).[16] Re-commencement of an extinguished use is development. Where there is an extinguishment of use the use will be extinguished for the entire planning unit and it will not be open to the user to transfer the use of the whole unit to a portion of the unit only (see *Galway County Council* v. *Connacht Proteins Limited*).

There is no Irish decision dealing with how one should identify the planning unit. In many cases it is a matter of common-sense. Problems can arise, however, where there is more than one activity being carried out in the unit of occupation. The matter has been considered in England in *Burdle* v. *Secretary of State for the Environment* [1972] 3 All E.R.

LOCAL GOVERNMENT (PLANNING AND DEVELOPMENT) ACT, 1963

3. – (1) 'Development' in this Act means, save where the context otherwise requires, the carrying out of any works[17] on, in, or under land or the making of any material change in the use[18] of any structures or other land.

(2) For the purposes of subsection (1) of this section and without prejudice to the generality thereof –

    (*a*) where any structure or other land or any tree or other object on land becomes used for the exhibition of advertisements,[19] or

    (*b*) where land becomes used for any of the following purposes:

        (i) the placing or keeping of any vans, tents or other objects, whether or not moveable and whether or not collapsible, for the purpose of caravanning or camping or the sale of goods,

---

[12] See page 65.
[13] See page 62.
[14] See page 66.
[15] See page 67.
[16] See page 70.
[17] See page 8 for definition of 'works'.
[18] See page 8 for definition of 'use'. See also *In re Viscount Securities*.
[19] See page 6 for the definition of 'advertisement'.

    (ii) the storage of caravans or tents,

    (iii) the deposit of bodies or other parts of vehicles, old metal, mining or industrial waste, builders' waste, rubble or debris,

the use of the land shall be taken as having materially changed.

(3) For the avoidance of doubt it is hereby declared that for the purposes of this section the use as two or more dwellings of any structure previously used as a single dwelling involves a material change in the use of the structure and of each part thereof which is so used.

PATTERSON V. MURPHY AND TRADING SERVICES LIMITED
The High Court (Unreported) Costello J., 4 May 1978
(Ref. No. 1977 No. 6215P)

The applicants lived near a quarry which was the property of the first-named respondent and from mid-1977 used by the second-named respondent to obtain rock for the manufacture of stones. Prior to the appointed day until 1977 the quarry had been used intermittently to obtain shale by relatively primitive means. In mid-1977 the first-named respondent through her son entered into an agreement with the second-named respondent which allowed them to work the quarry and gave them 'permission to install crusher screeners and conveyors and necessary equipment for the purpose of manufacturing stone'. The second-named respondents installed the permitted machinery and commenced intensive operations including blasting operations. The applicants instituted proceedings seeking *inter alia* an Order under section 27. The High Court held that operations were being carried out which differed materially from those being carried out on the appointed day and that planning permission was required in respect of them.

Costello J.:

The respondents' submission on the substance of the application is that, briefly put, no permission under the 1963 Act is required for what is being done in the quarry field, because the present 'development' was commenced before the 'appointed day' (which was the 1st October 1964). . . .

Turning firstly to section 27 itself it will be noted that it refers to two distinct and separate situations (a) where 'development' is being carried out without permission and (b) where an 'unauthorised use' is being made of land. For a definition of these terms it is necessary to refer back to the 1963 Act. It will then be seen that these words depend for their construction on the artificial meaning given to the word 'use' by section 2 of the 1963 Act.

The consequences of that meaning were pointed out by Mr. Justice Finlay in the *Claim of Viscount Securities* (112 I.L.T.R.17).[20] As it does not include, when used in relation to land, the carrying out of 'works' on land, and as 'works' includes any act or operation of excavation, it follows that if the user of a field is changed from say, tillage to quarrying this does not amount to a 'change of use' for the purposes of the 1963 Act. Such a change would, of course, amount to 'development' as defined by section 3; it would come within the first limb of the definition, as it would constitute the carrying out of 'works' on land. On the facts of the present case, therefore, it seems to me that because of this artificial definition it cannot be

[20] See page 453.

successfully contended that there has been an 'unauthorised use' in relation to the quarry field, and the applicant's claim under section 27 falls to be considered under subsection (1)(a) rather than under subsection (1)(b) of the section.

Considering the case, then, under the first part of subsection (1) I must be satisfied that 'development' of land being development for which a permission under Part IV of the 1963 Act is required, is being carried on before I would be justified in making a prohibition order. The respondents admit that no permission of any sort has been obtained in respect of the present operations in the quarry field, and their case is that Permission under Part IV of the 1963 Act is not required for what is now being done because under section 24(1) of the 1963 Act permission is not required for 'development' commenced before the appointed day, and the present 'development' was in fact commenced before that day. . . .

The present operations differ materially from those carried on prior to the 1st October 1964. I have reached this conclusion bearing in mind the following considerations. The *object* of the present operations is to produce a different product to that being produced in 1964. As stated in the parties' agreement, the operations are designed to manufacture stone. The 4 inch stone now being produced is different to shale; it is used for a different purpose in the building industry, and it fetches a different price. The *method of production* is different to that obtaining in and before 1964. The raw material (rock) for the end product is now obtained by means of blasting and this is done on a regular basis. Large crushing and screening plant is used to produce stones of the correct dimensions. Considerable ancillary equipment is used and a considerable labour force employed. Finally, the *scale of operations* is now a substantial one, and bears no relationship to the scale of operations carried on prior to the appointed day. In England it has been held that an intensification of use may amount to a material change of use (see *Guildford Rural District Council* v. *Fortescue* [1959] 2 Q.B. 112, 125; and *Brooks and Burton Ltd.* v. *Environment Secretary* [1977] 1 W.L.R. 1294, 1306). It seems to me that this concept is a correct one and that it applies whether the Court is considering 'development' under the second limb of the definition (i.e. material change of use) or under the first limb (i.e. the carrying out of works on land), which was commenced prior to the appointed day. So, if it appears that the scale of operations has so intensified as to render contemporary operations materially different from those carried on before the appointed day, this fact can be taken into account in considering whether what is at present being done commenced prior to the 1st October 1964.

If present-day 'development' differs materially from the 'development' being carried on prior to the 1st October 1964 I do not think that it can be said that it was commenced prior to the appointed day. This is the situation in the present case. . . I should add that if the case fell to be considered as one of 'development' arising from the making of a material change in the use of land I would have reached the same conclusion.

CORK CORPORATION V. CHRISTOPHER O'CONNELL
[1982] ILRM 505

Without obtaining planning permission the respondent opened an amusement arcade in premises previously used as a retail hardware store. When the applicant planning authority commenced proceedings against him under section 26(4) of the

1976 Act the respondent made a section 5 reference to the Planning Board on the question of whether or not the change of use was an exempted development. The Board decided that it was not and the applicant commenced section 27 proceedings against the respondent. Costello J. granted the applicant an Order pursuant to section 27 which was upheld by the Supreme Court.

Griffin J.:
. . . The principal submissions made on behalf of the defendant on the hearing of this appeal, as in the High Court, were (1) that the change of use did not constitute a material change in use, (2) that the change in use was an exempted development and therefore was not an unauthorised use, and (3) that once the plenary summons was issued pursuant to S. 5 of the Act of 1963 the jurisdiction of the Court to make an order pursuant to s. 27 was ousted. . . . This Court did not consider it necessary to call on counsel for the Corporation to reply to any of these submissions.

The making of any material change in the use of any structure is included in the definition of 'development' in s. 3 of the 1963 Act. In this case, the change of use was from that of a retail hardware shop to one of an amusement arcade – a premises in which there are 35 slot machines available for play by members of the public, these machines being coin operated. Costello J. had no doubt that this was a change of considerable materiality, and I am in complete agreement with him. This business will attract to these premises and to its precincts large crowds, mostly consisting of younger people, not only those who come to play but also those who come to watch. The numbers the defendant is confident of attracting to the premises may be gauged from the £12,000 per annum which he is prepared to pay for rent alone.

The learned trial judge held that the development was not an exempted development, and with this finding I would also agree. It is alleged that the works carried out affect only the *interior* of the structure, and therefore come within s. 4(1)(g). This might be so in respect of the actual physical works carried out, but the subsection only applies to works and does not extend to a material change of use. In the alternative, however, the defendant submits that the development is exempted development under the regulations made by the Minister (S.I. No. 65 of 1977). He says that his premises is still a shop, and that change of user from one shop to another is exempted development. While certain change of use to that of a shop is exempted development under Articles 10 and 12, these articles do not apply to this premises. In addition, in the regulations 'shop' is defined (Art. 9) as a structure used for the carrying on of any retail trade or business in which the primary purpose is the selling of goods by retail, and the definition expressly excludes a structure used as a funfair. 'Funfair' is itself defined as 'including an amusement arcade'. But even if an amusement arcade was not expressly excluded, there is in my view no way in which a premises containing 35 slot machines could be considered to be a shop.

With regard to the alleged ouster of jurisdiction of the High Court to make an order under s. 27, the issue of a plenary summons pursuant to s. 5 of the 1963 Act does not, in my opinion, operate to oust the jursdiction of the High Court. In its long title, the object of the 1976 Act is stated to be to make *better* provision in the interests of the common good for the proper planning and development of cities, towns, etc. The 1963 Act had been found to have serious procedural deficiencies where unauthorised development or use was made of premises. By s. 27 the

Legislature introduced what is a very important section into the 1976 Act, and gave a new and wide jurisdiction to the High Court to be exercised at the instance of the planning authority or any member of the public to prohibit the continuance of any unauthorised development or use of land. Because of the likely urgency of any such matter, an application to the High Court for an order under the section is made by motion, without the necessity of instituting proceedings in the normal way. This section provided the Planning Acts with much needed teeth that had theretofore been lacking. It would indeed be curious if, by merely *alleging* that development was exempted development, however unmeritorious that allegation might be, the teeth provided by that important section could be entirely removed. This is all the more so when, as in this case, the Board has already decided that the work or use is not exempted development, and where the developer has applied for planning permission subsequent to the decision of the Board. What the defendant in substance says is that, although there is already a decision of the Board which stands unless and until it is reversed on appeal, he may nevertheless by merely issuing a plenary summons in pursuance of s. 5, carry on business in the premises as if the appeal had already been determined in his favour by the High Court, and that he may not be prevented from doing so by an order made under s. 27, even though such proceedings might take a considerable time until they are finally determined. If this were so, the clear intention of the Legislature in enacting s. 27 would wholly be defeated. In my opinion, the jurisdiction of the High Court pursuant to s. 27 is not ousted by the institution of proceedings under s. 5.

DUBLIN COUNTY COUNCIL V. TALLAGHT BLOCK COMPANY LIMITED
The Supreme Court Hederman J. (*nem. diss.*) 17th May 1983
(Ref. No. 282/1981)

The appellants were in the business of manufacturing concrete blocks. In 1973 they acquired a site which had previously been used by A Company for the screening and crushing of clay and gravel between 1954 and 1960 and by B Limited in 1964 for the manufacture of concrete blocks. To enable themselves to carry on their business on the premises the appellants carried out works thereon including the laying of an additional concrete slab, the installation of a concrete mixing plant and cement silo and the fencing off of the area. In 1974 they acquired further premises which had been formerly used as a wash out area by a cement company. They carried out works on these premises including the laying of another concrete slab and the fencing off of the area. At no time had these premises been used in the production of concrete blocks. Finally they acquired further premises in 1976 upon which they carried out works from 1978 onwards. These works included the laying of a concrete slab, the construction of various buildings and the construction of a cement wall. These premises had formerly been used by C Company for the production of concrete blocks from 1956 to 1960.

At no time did the appellants obtain planning permission for the works carried out or for the change in use of the premises. While not denying that the works constituted development within the meaning of the Acts they claimed that they were exempted. In respect of use they claimed that the present use had not been commenced on or after the appointed day (1st October 1964) and therefore were not 'unauthorised'. This was rejected in the High Court and the Supreme Court.

Hederman J.:

. . . .The appellants' case is that on the appointed day (i.e. 1st October 1964) portion of the site was being used as a concrete block-making plant and they say that what they have been doing on the site does not constitute a material change in the use of the site; that any development is 'exempted development'. For this latter contention they rely on the exemptions contained in Class 16 of Part I of the Exempted Development Regulations 1967 (S.I. No. 176 of 1967) for all development up to the years 1978 to 1980 and on the exemptions contained in Class 17 of Part I of the Third Schedule of S.I. No. 65 of 1977 (Local Government (Planning and Development) Regulations 1977) for the years 1978 to 1980. Further they contend that Section 5 of the 1963 Act provides for the mandatory reference of two questions to An Bord Pleanala, namely questions arising as to what is or is not (a) development or (b) 'exempted development', the matter not having been referred to the Board under the provisions of Section 5, the Court on a Section 27 application cannot decide what is or is not 'exempted development'.

The learned trial Judge having found as a fact that no block making manufacturing or allied business had been carried out on any of the site from 1965 to 1973; held that the use of the lands on the site since 1973 has been an unauthorised use following the principles laid down in *Hartley* v. *Minister for Housing and Local Government* [1970] 1 Q.B. page 413. The Head Note in the Report correctly sets out the Court's conclusions as follows:

'Where a previous use of land had been not merely suspended for a temporary and determined period, but had ceased for a considerable time, with no evidenced intention of resuming it at any particular time, the tribunal of fact was entitled to find that the previous use had been abandoned, so that when it was resumed the resumption constituted a material change of use'.

I would respectfuly adopt this statement as being appropriate for application to the facts as found by the trial Judge in this case. It is quite clear that on the facts as found by the High Court Judge there was a material change of use on the site of the appellants for which no Planning Permission had been sought or granted. The trial Judge further held that the intensification of use can be a material change applying the principle laid down in *Brooks and Burton Limited* v. *Environment Secretary* [1977] 1 W.L.R. page 1295. On the facts in this case he held that from 1973 to 1980 there was such an intensification of use as to amount to a material change of use.

The development work carried out on the site was for the purpose of commencing a business. At the time when the works were being carried out there was no 'industrial process' being carried out on the site. Class 16 of the 1967 Regulations exempts development on lands already occupied and used by an industrial undertaker for an industrial process. In my view the trial Judge was correct in holding that it does not embrace works carried out for the purpose of setting up an industrial process. Further the trial Judge rightly held on the evidence that the development materially altered the external appearance of the premises on the site. He further held that the extending of the concrete area in 1977 and the erection of a concrete post and wire fence was an unauthorised structure within the meaning of Article 3(5)(vii)[21] of the 1967 Regulations and was not an exempted development.

---

[21] See Article 11(1)(*a*)(viii) of the Local Government (Planning and Development) Regulations 1977.

The Judge also held that the works carried out between 1978 and 1980 comprised extensions to unauthorised structures or structure the use of which was an unauthorised use, and so by virtue of the provisions of Article 11(1)(a)(viii) of the 1977 Regulations the development was not 'exempted', and in my view he was fully justified in so holding. The appellants claim under Class 17 in Part I of the Schedule of the 1967 Regulations and to Class 18 in Part I of the third Schedule to the 1977 Regulations only exempts 'storage' which is within the curtilage of an industrial building of products 'so as not to be visible from any public road contiguous or adjacent to the curtilage'. The trial Judge held that the storage of most of the appellants' products was quite clearly visible from the public road, consequently the appellants cannot claim the limited protection of this class of exemption as 'storage'. I further agree with the findings of Costello J. that 'if an occupier of land carries out development . . . . applies under Section 28 of the 1963 Act for permission to retain the unauthorised structure and is refused, then he cannot be heard to argue in proceedings instituted against him under Section 27 of the 1976 Act that permission for the development was not required'. With regard to the contention of the appellants relating to the application of Section 5 of the 1963 Act, this Court has held in the case of *Cork Corporation* v. *Christopher O'Connell* 1982 I.L.R.M. p. 525[22] per Henchy J. –

'that section 27 of the 1976 Act amounts to a summary and self-contained procedure which should not be allowed to be frustrated or protracted by the utilization of the collateral procedures allowed by Section 5 of the 1963 Act'.

And per Griffin J. –

'The jurisdiction of the High Court pursuant to Section 27 is not ousted by the institution of proceedings by Section 5'.

In this case the trial Judge held that the Court had a wide discretion under Section 27, and could if it thought fit, adjourn the Section 27 application so that an application under Section 5 could be brought or alternatively itself decide the issue. In his discretion he did not adjourn the Section 27 application but decided the issue himself in the interest of its expeditious determination. In my opinion this was a course that he was fully justified in adopting on the facts of this case and fully accords with the decision of this Court in *Cork Corporation* v. *O'Connell*.

As in this case, where a planning authority gives due notice of its intention to proceed against an occupier of lands for alleged breaches of the Planning Acts, the onus is on the occupier to avail with all reasonable speed of the provisions of Section 5 of the 1963 Act if he claims that the development complained of is 'exempted development'.

I am quite satisfied that on the facts accepted by the learned trial Judge the respondents have established that the appellants have carried out development for which a permission under Part IV of the 1963 Act was required and that an unauthorised use was and is being made of the land and that the respondents are accordingly entitled to the Orders made by the learned trial Judge.

I would accordingly dismiss the appeal.

[22] See page 60.

CARRICKHALL HOLDINGS LIMITED V. DUBLIN CORPORATION
The High Court [1983] ILRM 268

The plaintiffs were the owners of a small hotel. Upon acquiring an ordinary seven-day licence for the hotel they opened a public bar on the premises. Prior to this the hotel had a hotel licence only and there had been no public bar on the premises. The opening of the bar resulted in a substantial increase in traffic and noise in the area. The defendants sought a decision from the Planning Board on the question of whether the change of use as a hotel without a public bar to use as a hotel with a public bar was development and if so was it exempted development. The Board decided that such a change was development which was not exempted. The plaintiffs appealed the decision to the High Court. The High Court confirmed the decision of the Board. The plaintiffs have appealed to the Supreme Court.

McWilliam J.:
. . . It has been urged on behalf of the Plaintiff that the hotel licence was an ordinary publican's licence although there was a restriction preventing the installation of a public bar, and that the change to an ordinary seven day licence merely removed this restriction without altering the essential nature of the licence; the suggestion being that there is therefore no change in use. It is difficult to ascertain the effect of the long series of Licensing and Intoxicating Liquour Acts from 1833 to 1962, but it does appear that a hotel licence is an ordinary publican's licence and does not contain any restriction on sales to the public.

I have been referred to the judgments of the Supreme Court in the case of *Readymix (Eire) Ltd.* v. *Dublin County Council* delivered on 30th July 1974,[23] and to the judgment of Costello J., in *Patterson* v. *Murphy* delivered on 4th May, 1980.[24] The decision in the Readymix case did not turn on the point, but Griffin J., laid emphasis on the relevance of the very substantial increase in the volume of vehicular traffic, indicating that it was a matter which it might be appropriate to consider. Costello, J., in *Patterson* v. *Murphy* held that an increased scale of operations bearing no relation to the scale of operation previously carried on is a factor which may be taken into account when considering whether there has been a material change in use or not. He referred with approval to the case of *Brooks and Burton Ltd.* v. *Environment Secretary* [1977] 1 W.L.R. 1294, in which Lawton, L.J., said at page 1306 'We have no doubt that the intensification of use can be a material change of use. Whether it is or not depends upon the degree of intensification.'

In the present case, the evidence is conclusive that the change from a hotel licence without a public bar to an ordinary seven day licence with a public bar has changed the whole character of the business carried on in the premises and directly and for the first time cause the increase in traffic parking, noise and other unsatisfactory changes in amenities for the local residents which I have already mentioned.[25]

I am satisfied that there were ample grounds on which An Bord Pleanala could make the decision they did make and I agree with it.

---

[23] See page 198.
[24] See page 59.
[25] I.e. obstruction of the gateways of the residents and abuse by customers to the residents.

CUSACK & McKENNA V. MINISTER FOR LOCAL GOVERNMENT & DUBLIN CORPORATION
The High Court (Unreported) McWilliams J., 4 November 1980, (Ref. No. 1976 No. 5240P)

In an area zoned residential the plaintiffs commenced using a portion of premises for their solicitor's practice without obtaining planning permission for change of user. Prior to their occupation of the premises, the premises had been used first for a dentist's practice and then for residential flats. A section 5 reference was made to the Minister for Local Government on the question of whether a change of use of the premises from use as a dentist's practice to use as solicitors' offices was or was not exempted development. By decision dated the 26th August 1978 the Minister decided that the said change was development within the meaning of the 1963 Act and that it was not exempted development. The plaintiffs appealed the decision. No reference was made to the use of premises as residential flats in the pleadings of either party. McWilliam J. held that the relevant change was from dentist's surgery to residential flats and that such change was not exempted. He rejected *obiter dicta* the argument that a change from dentists' surgery to solicitors' offices was exempted.

McWilliam J.:

Permission for use for the purposes of a dentist's practice was not required by the plaintiff's predecessor in title as that practice was commenced before the appointed day for the commencement of the Act.

It is submitted on behalf of the plaintiffs that the change of use for a dentist's practice to use for a solicitor's practice is not development because it is not a material change of use within the meaning of section 3 of the 1963 Act or, alternatively, if it is development within the meaning of the Act, it is exempted development as the change from use for a dentist's practice to use for a solicitor's practice are both uses for an office and thus come within class 2 of Part IV of the Third Schedule to S.I. No. 65 of 1977 so as to be exempted under Regulation 12.

These submissions ignore the fact that, at the time of the purchase of the premises by the plaintiffs, the premises were entirely used for residential purposes, a circumstance which is emphasised on behalf of the defendants. It cannot be seriously disputed that the change from residential use to use for the purposes of solicitors' offices is a material change of use. That this is so is confirmed by the case of *Dublin Corporation* v. *Mulligan*, in which the President of the High Court delivered judgment on 6th May, 1980, although the matter there in issue concerned different aspects of the Acts.

I am of opinion that, in considering whether there has been a change of use or not, I must decide the question on the facts as they actually occurred and I am satisfied that there was a change in use from a dentist's surgery to use as a residence whether planning permission for such a change was obtained or not. I have not been referred to any authority which suggests that an unauthorised change of use must be deemed not to be a change of use merely because the change was not authorised and my view that there was a change of use which I must take into account is supported by a note, to which I have been referred, of a case of *Grillo* v. *Minister of Housing and Local Government* (1968) 208 E.G. 1201 decided in the Queen's Bench in England. The note is as follows: 'From 1951 to 1958 there was established a light industrial use. From 1958 to 1964 the landowner tried unsuccessfully to let the land for similar purposes, using it meanwhile for storage. In 1964 he recommenced light industrial use and an enforcement notice was served and was confirmed by the Minister. The owner appealed. The Divisional Court held: (1) in 1964 a change of use had occurred and it was not open to the appellant to argue that light industrial user had been kept notionally alive from 1958 to 1964 in the mind of the occupier when, in fact, the land had been used for a different purpose.'

As I have formed the opinion that the relevant change of use in this matter is the change from residential use to use for solicitors' offices, the questions considered by the Minister and pleaded on this appeal appear to be inappropriate and I will declare that there was a change of user from residential use to use for solicitors' offices in 1975 and that this was development within the meaning of the 1963 Act and was not exempted development within the meaning of that Act.

Although this disposes of the case, I feel that I should state my views on the other matters which were argued before me. I am of opinion that a change of use from use for a dentist's practice to use as solicitors' offices is a material change of use and constitutes development within the meaning of the 1963 Act. The two professions have nothing in common other than the attributes common to all professions and to hold that there is not a material change in use would, to my mind, be perverse. The professions are completely different in their training, in their skills and in their general nature.

It was strongly urged upon me that a dentist or dental surgeon must have considerable office work and that part of his premises would normally be treated as an office for the filing of records, preparation of accounts, etc., that he must have at least one secretary who might properly be described as an office worker and that these factors are sufficient to bring the use of the premises for a dentist's practice within the meaning of the expression 'use as an office for any purpose' so as to make the change of use exempted development under the provisions of section 4 of the 1963 Act or Part III of S.I. No. 65 of 1977. I do not accept this contention. The central and essential part of a dentist's premises must be the surgery and such other room or rooms as may be required for the use of the incidental dental equipment and the preparation of dental materials and neither of such rooms could reasonably be described as an office within any ordinary meaning of the term. If a dentist's surgery could be brought within any class in Part IV of the Third Schedule to the Regulations it seems to me that Class 13 is more appropriate than Class 2.

CORK COUNTY COUNCIL V. ARDFERT QUARRY PRODUCTS LIMITED AND ORS
The High Court, Murphy J., 7th December 1982
(Ref. No. 1982 No. MCA)

In March 1982 the respondents and General Portland Cement Limited began using premises for the importation, storing, distribution and bagging of cement. The previous planning history of the premises was as follows:

From 1953 to 1966 the premises were used as an animal food processing plant.

From 1966 to 1970 the premises were vacant.

From 1970 to May 1974 the premises were used for the manufacture and storage of tyres.

From May 1974 to February 1976 the premises were used for the fabrication of hydraulic equipment and for engineering purposes.

In February 1976 to 1979 the premises were used for the warehousing and distribution of various goods and materials.

From 1980 to March 1982 they were once again vacant and in March 1982 the respondents began to use the premises.

The applicants successfully sought Orders under section 27 to restrain the respondents from using the premises.

Murphy J.:

. . . It is clear in my view that the phrase 'unauthorised use' in Section 27 of the 1976 Act falls to be read in conjunction with definition of that phrase in Section 2 of the 1963 Act wherein it is defined as meaning:

> 'In relation to land, use commenced on or after the appointed day (the 1st October 1964) the change in use being a material change and being development other than development the subject of a permission granted under Section 26 of this Act or exempted development.'

It would seem to follow, therefore, that every use is an unauthorised use unless:

1. It was commenced before the appointed day or,
2. It is an immaterial change from an authorised use.
3. Being a development it is the subject matter of a permission granted under Section 26 of the 1963 Act or,
4. Being a development that it constitutes an exempted development.

It is contended on behalf of the respondents that the use made of the premises in question on the operative date constituted use as 'a general industrial building' within the meaning of Clause 9 of the Local Government (Planning and Development) Regulations, 1977 (S.I. Number 65 of 1977) and that such use was not and could not be abandoned. I reject that contention. In the *County Council of the County of Dublin* v. *Tallaght Block Company Limited*,[26] Costello J., following a decision in *Hartley* v. *Minister for Housing and Local Government* [1970] 1 Q.B. 413, held in an unreported Judgment delivered on the 4th of November 1981 that a previous use might be abandoned, and in the particular circumstances of the case under consideration by him held that such an abandonment had occurred. In his decision Mr. Justice Costello quoted with approval the head note from the decision in the Hartley case as follows:

> 'Where a previous use of land had been not merely suspended for a temporary and determined period but had ceased for a considerable time with no evinced intention of resuming it at any particular time, the tribunal of fact was entitled to find that the previous use had been abandoned, so that when it was resumed the resumption constituted a material change of use.'

In fact it is significant that in the Hartley case the duration of the non-user was from March 1961 to February 1965 a period of almost four years which is virtually identical with the period which elapsed between the cessation of the animal food processing business which ceased in the present case in 1966 and the commencement of the manufacture and storage of tyres in 1970. Having regard to that elapse

---

[26] See page 62.

of time and the absence of any satisfactory explanation therefore I must conclude that the user as of the operative date was subsequently abandoned.

If, as is the case, an authorised user may be lost or abandoned by non-user over a period of time so that the resumption of the original use itself would involve a material change *a fortiori* the commencement at that time of any other user would necessarily involve such a change.

It follows, in my view, that the use of the premises in question for the manufacture and storage of tyres; the fabrication of hydraulic equipment; and the warehousing of various goods and the present user for the distribution and bagging of cement all constituted an unauthorised use of the premises.

If, contrary to the view which I have taken, the last active use made of the premises, that is to say, the use for the warehousing of goods had been sanctioned by a planning permission granted under Section 26 of the 1963 Act or was for any other reason not an unauthorised use I would not have accepted even in those circumstances that the present use was an authorised use. Even assuming that the non-user of the premises during the fifteen months from January 1980 to March 1982 did not constitute an abandonment it would seem to me on the evidence at present available that the warehousing business constituted use as a light industrial building within the meaning of Article 9 of the Planning Regulations aforesaid whereas the present use constitutes use as a general industrial building within the meaning of the same regulations so that the transition from one to the other would not attract the exemption provided by Class 11 in Part 1 of the Third Schedule to those regulations.

Those regulations define 'light industrial buildings' as meaning (quotation of definition follows, see page 74).

In accordance with the definition of a 'general industrial building' an industrial building which is not a light industrial building (or a special industrial building) necessarily constitutes a general industrial building.

Whilst there is a serious conflict in the Affidavits as to whether the process at present carried on in the premises in question will generate dust the fact is that in the short history of the plant there has been one serious escape of dust already. Whilst the respondents have stated unequivocally that the particular incident was accidental and unlikely to be repeated (in addition to their contention that its significance was exaggerated by the applicants) it is clear that the process involves dealing with large quantities of material in dust and powder form. The respondents have emphasised the efforts which they have made and the steps which they have taken to ensure that dust will not escape in the future. Hopefully such efforts would be effective and no doubt if permission is granted by the planning authority for the particular user it will be subject to conditions which will ensure as far as practicable that this is so. In the meantime it seems to me that as a matter of law and logic that an industry of this nature is not one which in the ordinary way could be carried on in a residential area without detriment of the amenity by reason of dust and perhaps also noise. It is for that reason it seems to me that the particular user constitutes use as a general industrial building rather than as a light industrial building.

Having regard to the view which I take of the nature of the present business and the last preceeding activity it is clear that no exemption can derive from changes within the classes listed in Part 4 of the Third Schedule to the Planning Regulations by virtue of Clause 12 of those regulations.

I should add that Counsel on behalf of the respondents urged me to adjourn the hearing of this Application until an Application could be made to An Bord Pleanala for the determination of the question whether the particular development constitutes an exempted development. Whilst I accept—as did Mr. Justice Costello in the *Tallaght Block Company* case,—that the Court had jurisdiction to grant an adjournment for that purpose I took the view that it would not be an appropriate course to adopt in the present case.

GALWAY COUNTY COUNCIL V. CONNACHT PROTEINS LTD.
The High Court (Unreported) Barrington J., 28th March 1980, (Ref. No. 1979 No. 67MCA)

Planning permission was obtained by the respondents' predecessor in title for alteration of an old mill for use as an animal by-products processing plant and the premises were in fact used by them for that purpose. On the 17th October 1968 a fire occurred at the premises. The respondents continued to use the site as a rendering plant and buildings were built for that purpose without obtaining permission. The applicants brought proceedings under section 27 seeking an Order prohibiting the unauthorised use of the land.

Barrington J.:
I accept that . . . the mill was totally gutted at the time of the fire. What happened on the ground after the fire is not quite clear. What is clear is that no Planning permission was ever obtained to re-build the mill and the mill was not, in fact, re-built. It appears to me that when the mill perished, the permission to use those premises for a specific purpose perished also. It could be argued that the permission to use the mill for a specific purpose implied a permission to use outbuildings for ancillary purposes. But when the mill itself perished, it appears to me one could not imply a permission to use the outbuildings for the principal business. . . .

It is quite clear that the respondents, or Mr. McGann, have besides building this new factory on the site, also carried out, again without Planning Permission, other works on the site, and that these include at least one building or reinstated building which now stands on the site of the old mill. . . As previously indicated, I accept the evidence . . . that the mill building was completely gutted in the original fire. It follows that the respondents have not got Planning Permission for using the existing buildings or any of them for the extraction of oils and fats from slaughterhouse offals or for the manufacture of meat or bone meal.

DUBLIN COUNTY COUNCIL V. SELLWOOD QUARRIES AND ORS
[1981] ILRM 23

See p. 370 for the facts of the case.
Gannon J.:
. . . The questions for determination on this application are (a) whether or not the activities now being carried on by the respondents on these lands constitute a development of land for which permission is required under Part IV of the Local Government (Planning and Development) Act 1963 and which is being carried out without such a permission and (b) whether or not such activities are an unauthorised use of the land. . . The respondents contend that this parcel of land has been

known and worked as a quarry continuously since 1926, that there is no significant difference as to the product or methods used as between sand and gravel pits and open rock quarries, and that both are subject to the same statutory regulations. There could conceivably be circumstances in which, on a comparison of the product and methods of operation, there might be no significant difference between a gravel pit and an open rock quarry, but those circumstances do not exist in this case. The work of removal of sand and gravel can be carried on, and in this case was carried on, by relatively simple methods on a moderate scale. Because of the rock base the removal was unlikely to lower significantly the surface of the land. According to the evidence the rock cannot be removed except by blasting and would have little commercial value without crushing and screening and grading. The work involves a number of technical skills not required in the sand and gravel pits and the concentrated use of machinery and equipment which makes the work involved more akin to a factory operation than to a land operation. The drawing of sand or gravel from pits on land is a normal part of the use of land similar to drawing turf from turbary. 'Use' in relation to land requires no definition for those who live on or from land and would connote, I think, the idea of winning or taking from the land what it can yield or give with or without cultivation. The statement in relation to the word 'use' in the definition section namely Section 1(1) of the 1963 Act that 'use' in relation to land does not include the use of the land by the carrying out of any works thereon' is not a definition but a distinction necessarily made to relate to the word 'development' as defined in Section 3(1) of that Act. The word 'development' is defined as the carrying out of any works on, in or under land and does not appear to connote any idea of using land in the ordinary sense or otherwise than as a site or a structure. The expression 'unauthorised use' is defined as meaning, in relation to land, a change from the use to which it had been put prior to the 1st October 1964 of a material nature and also 'being development' that is to say, is use involving the carrying out of works on, in or under the land.

From the evidence given in this application there cannot be any doubt that the activities of the respondents in the extraction by blasting of rock for commercial purposes on these lands constitute the carrying out of works on the land and in relation to the land involves a material change of use from that to which the land was being put prior to 1st October 1964.

EXEMPTED DEVELOPMENT

Exempted development is development which may be carried out without planning permission. Development which comes within the provisions of section 4(1) of the 1963 Act as amended or within the provisions of Part III and Schedule III of the 1977 Regulations as amended are exempted. All other development requires planning permission.

Sub-section 4(1A) contains only the express restriction on the exemptions specified in sub-section 4(1). There are, however, of necessity other implied restrictions. Thus development consisting of the maintenance of an unauthorised structure is not exempted even if it affects the interior of the structure only (see *Dublin Corporation* v. *Langan*).[27] Further it is submitted that development which is exempted under sub-section 4(1) loses its exempted status where it contravenes a

---

[27] See page 100.

condition attached to a permission (see *Horne* v. *Freeney*[28]) or where it is inconsistent with a use specified in a permission.

The Minister has made Regulations pursuant to sub-section 4(2) providing that other developments are exempted in certain circumstances (see Part III and Schedule III of the Local Government (Planning and Development) Regulations 1977 as amended). The developments set out in Parts I, II and III of the Third Schedule are exempted provided the development complies with the relevant limitations and conditions specified in columns 1 and 2 and provided it does not come within any of the restrictions set out in Article 11 of the Regulations (see Articles 10 and 11).

A change of use within any of the clauses of use set out in Part IV of the Third Schedule will be exempted provided (1) it does not require the carrying out of any works which are not exempted and (2) it would not contravene a condition attached to a permission under the Acts and (3) it would not be inconsistent with any use specified as included in such permission (see Article 12(1)).

Where a group of contiguous or adjacent structures used as part of a single undertaking includes industrial buildings used for purposes falling within two or more of the classes specified in Part IV as classes 3 to 8 inclusive the two or more classes may be treated as a single use in relation to that group of structures provided the area occupied in that group by general or special industrial buildings is not increased (see Article 12(2)).

Where a use is incidental to another use specified in Part IV it will not be excluded from that use as an incident thereto merely because it is specified as a separate use in Part IV (see Article 12(3)).

If a person carries out development and then applies for retention which is refused it would appear that he cannot then argue in section 27 proceedings that it is exempted (see *Dublin County Council* v. *Tallaght Block Company Ltd.*).[29]

LOCAL GOVERNMENT (PLANNING AND DEVELOPMENT) ACT, 1963

4. – (1) The following shall be exempted developments for the purposes of this Act:

(a) development consisting of the use of any land for the purposes of agriculture or forestry (including afforestation), and development consisting of the use for any of those purposes of any building occupied together with land so used;

(b) development by the council of a county in the county health district;

(c) development by the corporation of a county or other borough in such borough;

(d) development by the council of an urban district in such district;

(e) development consisting of the carrying out by the corporation of a county or other borough or the council of a county or an urban district of any works required for the construction of a new road or the maintenance or improvement of a road;

(f) development consisting of the carrying out by any local authority or

[28] See page 101.
[29] See page 62.

statutory undertaker of any works for the purpose of inspecting, repairing, renewing, altering or removing any sewers, mains, pipes, cables, overhead wires, or other apparatus, including the breaking open of any street or other land for that purpose;

(g) development consisting of the carrying out of works for the maintenance, improvement or other alteration of any structure, being works which affect only the interior of the structure or which do not materially affect the external appearance of the structure so as to render such appearance inconsistent with the character of the structure or of neighbouring structures;[30]

(h) development consisting of the use of any structure or other land within the curtilage of a dwellinghouse for any purpose incidental to the enjoyment of the dwellinghouse as such;

(hh) development consisting of the use of land for the purposes of a casual trading area (within the meaning of the Casual Trading Act 1980);[31]

(i) development consisting of the carrying out of any of the works referred to in the Land Reclamation Act, 1949 not being works comprised in the fencing or enclosure of land which has been open to or used by the public within the ten years preceding the date on which the works are commenced;[32]

(IA) Where a planning authority in their development plan, for the purpose mentioned in paragraph 5A of Part IV of the Third Schedule to this Act, (inserted therein by section 43 of the Local Government (Planning and Development) Act, 1976), indicate objectives for the preservation of specified fixtures or features which form part of the interior of a structure specified in the development plan and which are stated in such plan to be of artistic, historic or architectural interest, then, notwithstanding subsection (1) of this section, works which involve the alteration or removal of, or which may cause injury to, any such fixture or feature shall not be exempted development for the purposes of this Act.[33]

(2)(a) The Minister may by regulations provide for any class of development being exempted development for the purposes of this Act and such provision may be either without conditions or subject to conditions and either general or confined to a particular area or place.

(b) Regulations under this subsection may, in particular and without prejudice to the generality of the foregoing paragraph, provide, in the case of structures or other land used for a purpose of any specified class, for the use thereof for any other purpose being exempted development for the purposes of this Act.

(3) References in this Act to exempted development shall be construed as references to development which is –

(a) any of the developments specified in subsection (1) of this section, or

(b) development which, having regard to any regulations under subsection (2) of this section, is exempted development for the purposes of this Act.

---

[30] Does not include a use affecting only the interior of the structure, see *Cork Corporation* v. *O'Connell* at page 60 and *Dublin Corporation* v. *Langan* at page 100.

[31] Inserted by section 7(3) of the Casual Trading Act 1980.

[32] Words from 'not being works. . .' inserted by section 43(1)(b) of 1976 Act.

[33] Inserted by section 43(1)(c) of the 1976 Act.

LOCAL GOVERNMENT (PLANNING AND DEVELOPMENT) REGULATIONS, 1977

PART III

EXEMPTED DEVELOPMENT

9. In this Part –

'betting office' means premises for the time being registered in the register of bookmaking offices kept by the Revenue Commissioners under the Betting Act, 1931 (No. 27 of 1931);

'business premises' means any structure or other land (not being an excluded premises) which is normally used for the carrying on of any professional, commercial or industrial undertaking or any structure (not being an excluded premises) which is normally used for the provision therein of services to persons;

'excluded premises' means –

(*a*) any premises used for purposes of a religious, educational, cultural, recreational or medical character,

(*b*) any hotel, guest house, inn or public house, block of flats, club, boarding house or hostel, and

(*c*) any structure which was designed for use as one or more separate dwellings, except such a structure which was used as business premises immediately before the appointed day or is so used with permission under section 26 of the Act of 1963;

'funfair' includes an amusement arcade;

'illuminated' in relation to any advertisement, sign or other advertisement structure means illuminated internally or externally by artificial lighting, directly or by reflection, for the purpose of advertisement, announcement or direction;

'industrial building' means a structure (not being a shop, or a structure in or adjacent to and belonging to a quarry or mine) used for the carrying on of any industrial process;

'light industrial building' means an industrial building (not being a special industrial building) in which the processes carried on or the machinery installed are such as could be carried on or installed in any residential area without detriment to the amenity of that area by reason of noise, vibration, smell, fumes, smoke, soot, ash, dust or grit;[34]

'general industrial building' means an industrial building which is not a light industrial building or a special industrial building;

'special industrial building' means an industrial building used for one or more of the purposes specified in classes 5, 6, 7 and 8 in Part IV of the Third Schedule;

'industrial process' means any process which is carried on in the course of trade or business other than agriculture and which is for or incidental to the making of any article or part of an article, or the altering, repairing, ornamenting, finishing, cleaning, washing, packing or canning, or adapting for sale, or breaking up or demolition of any article, including in particular the getting, dressing or treatment of minerals;

---

[34] See *Cork Corporation* v. *Ardfelt Quarries and Anor*, p. 67.

'article' means an article or substance of any description, including a vehicle, aircraft, ship or vessel;

'industrial undertaker' means a person by whom an industrial process is carried on and 'industrial undertaking' shall be construed accordingly;

'minerals' includes all minerals and substances in or under land of a kind ordinarily worked by underground or by surface working for removal but does not include turf;

'motor vehicle' means any mechanically propelled vehicle for the purposes of the Road Traffic Act, 1961 (No. 24 of 1961);

'office' includes a bank but does not include a post-office or betting office;

'painting' includes any application of colour;

'permission under the Acts' includes a permission treated as a permission granted under section 26 of the Act of 1963 by virtue of section 92 of that Act;

'repository' means a structure (excluding any land occupied therewith) where storage is the principal use and where no business is transacted other than business incidental to such storage;

'shop' means a structure used for the carrying on of any retail trade or retail business wherein the primary purpose is the selling of goods by retail and includes a structure used for the purposes of a hairdresser, undertaker or ticket agency or for the reception of goods to be washed, cleaned or repaired, or for any other purpose appropriate to a shopping area, but does not include a structure used as a funfair, garage, petrol filling station, office, or hotel or premises (other than a restaurant) licensed for the sale of intoxicating liquor for consumption on the premises;

'wholesale warehouse' means a structure where business, principally of a wholesale nature, is transacted and goods are stored or displayed but only incidentally to the transaction of that business.

10. –. (1) Subject to article 11, development of each class specified in column 1 of Part I of the Third Schedule shall be exempted development for the purposes of the Acts, provided such development complies with the limitations specified in the said column 1 in relation to that class and with the conditions specified in column 2 of the said Part I opposite the mention of that class in the said column 1.

(2) Subject to article 11, development consisting of the use of a structure or other land for the exhibition of advertisements of a class specified in column 1 of Part II of the Third Schedule shall be exempted development for the purposes of the Acts provided that –

(a) such development complies with the limitations specified in the said column 1 in relation to that class and with the conditions specified in column 2 of Part II of the said Schedule opposite the mention of that class in the said column 1, and

(b) the structure or other land on which the advertisement is exhibited shall not be used for the exhibition of any advertisement other than an advertisement of a class which is specified in column 1 of Part II of the said Schedule and which complies with the limitations specified in the said column and the conditions specified in column 2 of the said Part II in relation to that class.

(3) Subject to article 11, development consisting of the erection of any advertisement structure for the exhibition of an advertisement of any one of the classes

specified in column 1 of Part II of the Third Schedule shall be exempted development for the purposes of the Acts provided that –

> (a) the area of such advertisement structure which is used for the exhibition of an advertisement does not exceed the area specified in a condition in column 2 of Part II of the said Schedule opposite the mention of that class in the said column 1, and
>
> (b) the advertisement structure is not used for the exhibition of advertisements other than advertisements of the class to which the exemption relates.

(4) Subject to article 11, in areas other than county boroughs, boroughs, urban districts and towns specified in the First Schedule to the Act of 1963, development of each class specified in column 1 of Part III of the Third Schedule shall be exempted development for the purposes of the Acts provided that such development complies with the limitations specified in the said column 1 in relation to that class and with the conditions specified in column 2 of Part III of the said Schedule opposite the mention of that class in the said column 1.

(5) Development commenced prior to the coming into operation of these Regulations and which was exempted development for the purposes of the Acts by reason of a provision of regulations revoked by these Regulations shall, notwithstanding such revocation, continue to be exempted development for the purposes of the Acts.

11. – (1) Development to which article 10 relates shall not be exempted development for the purposes of the Acts –

> (a) if the carrying out of such development would –
>
>> (i) contravene a condition attached to a permission under the Acts or be inconsistent with any use specified in a permission under the Acts,
>>
>> (ii) consist of or comprise the formation, laying out or material widening of a means of access to a public road the metalled part of which is more than 4 metres in width,
>>
>> (iii) endanger public safety by reason of traffic hazard or any obstruction to the view of persons using any public road at or near any bend, corner, junction or intersection,
>>
>> (iv) contravene any building regulation made under section 86 of the Act of 1963 or any byelaw in force under section 41 of the Public Health (Ireland) Act, 1878, in the area in which the land to which the development relates is situated,[35]
>>
>> (v) comprise the erection, construction, extension or renewal of a building on any street so as to bring forward the building, or any part of the building, beyond the front wall of the building on either side thereof or beyond a line determined as the building line in the development plan for the area or, pending the variation of the development plan or the making of a new development plan, in the draft variation of the development plan or the draft new development plan,

---

[35] See section 87 of the 1963 Act re relaxation of building regulations. Note, however, that this section is not yet to be brought into force.

(vi) consist of or comprise the carrying out under a public road of works other than a connection to a sewer, water main, gas main or electricity supply line or cable, or any works specified in class 21 or 22 of Part I of the Third Schedule,

(vii) restrict a view or prospect of special amenity value or special interest the preservation of which is an objective of a development plan for the area in which the development is proposed or, pending the variation of the development plan or the making of a new development plan, in the draft variation of the development plan or the draft new development plan,

(viii) consist of or comprise the extension, alteration, repair or renewal of an unauthorised structure or a structure the use of which is an unauthorised use,

(ix) consist of the alteration or demolition of a building or other structure other than an alteration consisting of the painting of any previously painted part of such building or structure, where such building or structure is specified in a development plan for the area or, pending the variation of a development plan or the making of a new development plan, in the draft variation of the development plan or the draft new development plan, as a building or other structure, or one of a group of buildings, of artistic, architectural or historic interest, the preservation of which it is an objective of the planning authority to secure,

(x) consist of the alteration or demolition of a building or other structure other than an alteration consisting of the painting of any previously painted part of such building or structure, where such building or structure is specified in a development plan for the area or, pending the variation of a development plan or the making of a new development plan, in the draft variation of the development plan or the draft new development plan, as a building or other structure, or one of a group of buildings, of artistic, architectural or historic interest, the preservation of which it is the intention of the planning authority to consider in the event of an application for permission being made to alter or demolish the building or structure,

(xi) consist of the demolition or such alteration of a building as would preclude or restrict the continuation of an existing use of a building where it is an objective of the planning authority to secure that the building would remain available for such use and such objective has been included in the development plan for the area or, pending the variation of a development plan or the making of a new development plan, in the draft variation of the development plan or the draft new development plan,

(xii) consist of the fencing or enclosure of any land habitually open to or used by the public during the ten years preceding such fencing or enclosure for recreational purposes or as means of access to any seashore, mountain, lakeshore, riverbank or other place of natural beauty or recreational utility, or

(xiii) obstruct any public right of way, or

(*b*) in an area to which a special amenity area order relates, if such development would be development –

    (i) of class 1, 3, 13, 17, 18, 23 or 24 specified in column 1 of Part I of the Third Schedule,

    (ii) consisting of the use of a structure or other land for the exhibition of advertisements of class 4, 5, 8, 9, 13, 14 or 17 specified in column 1 of Part II of the said Schedule or the erection of an advertisement structure for the exhibition of any advertisement of any of the said classes or,

    (iii) of class 6, 7, 8 or 9 specified in column 1 of Part III of the said Schedule.

(2) Sub-paragraph (vii) of paragraph (*a*) of sub-article (1) shall not apply where the development consists of the construction by any electricity undertaking of an overhead line or cable not exceeding one hundred metres in length for the purpose of conducting electricity from a distribution or transmission line to any premises.

(3) Sub-paragraph (v) of paragraph (*a*) of sub-article (1) shall not apply where the development consists of the construction of a porch as described in class 6A in column 1 of Part I of the Third Schedule and which complies with the condition mentioned opposite such class in column 2 of the said Part of the said Schedule.

12. – (1) Development which consists of a change of use within any one of the classes of use specified in Part IV of the Third Schedule and which does not require the carrying out of any works, other than works which are exempted development, shall be exempted development for the purposes of the Acts provided that the development, if carried out, would not contravene a condition attached to a permission under the Acts or be inconsistent with any use specified or included in such a permission.

(2) Where a group of contiguous or adjacent structures used as parts of a single undertaking includes industrial buildings used for purposes falling within two or more of the classes specified in Part IV of the Third Schedule as classes 3 to 8, inclusive, those particular two or more classes may, in relation to that group of structures and so long as the area occupied in that group by general or by special industrial buildings is not increased, be treated as a single class for the purposes of these Regulations.

(3) A use which is ordinarily incidental to any use specified in Part IV of the Third Schedule is not excluded from that use as an incident thereto merely by reason of its being specified in the said Part of the said Schedule as a separate use.

THIRD SCHEDULE

PART I

EXEMPTED DEVELOPMENT – GENERAL

Column 1 Description of Development	Column 2 Conditions

Development within the curtilage of a dwellinghouse

CLASS 1

Any works for the provision of an extension to the rear of a dwellinghouse or the conversion for use as part of a dwellinghouse of any garage, store, shed or other similar structure attached to the rear or to the side of the dwellinghouse, where the height of any structural addition does not exceed that of the dwellinghouse and the original floor area of the dwellinghouse is not increased by more than 23 square metres.[36]

CLASS 2

The provision, as part of a central heating system of a dwellinghouse of a chimney, boiler house or oil storage tank having a capacity not exceeding 3,500 litres.

CLASS 3

The erection, construction or placing within the curtilage of a dwellinghouse of any tent, awning, shade or other object, greenhouse, garage, shed or other similar structure.

1. The height above ground level of any such structure shall not exceed, in the case of a building with a tiled or slated ridged roof, 4 metres or any other case, 3 metres.

2. The structure shall not be used for human habitation or for the keeping of pigs or poultry or for any other

---

[36] Inserted by S.I. 154 of 1981.

purpose other than a purpose incidental to the enjoyment of the dwelling-house as such.

CLASS 4

The erection of a wireless or television aerial on the roof of a dwellinghouse.

1. The height of the aerial above the roof shall not exceed 6 metres.

CLASS 5

The erection, construction or alteration within or bounding the curtilage of a dwellinghouse of a gate, railing, wooden fence or of a wall constructed of brick, stone, split blocks or other blocks with decorative finish but not of other concrete blocks or of mass concrete.

1. The height above ground level of any such structure shall not exceed 2 metres or, in the case of a wall or fence within or bounding any garden or other space in front of a dwelling-house, 1·2 metres.
2. Every wall shall be capped.

CLASS 6

The construction of any path, drain or pond or the carrying out of any landscaping works within the curtilage of a dwellinghouse.

The level of the ground shall not be altered by more than 1 metre above or below the level of the adjoining ground.

CLASS 6A

The erection or construction, outside any external door of a dwellinghouse and not less than 2 metres from any public road, of a porch, having a floor area not exceeding 2 square metres.[37]

The height above ground level of any such structure shall not exceed, in the case of a building with a tiled or slated ridged roof, 4 metres or in any other case, 3 metres.[38]

Sundry minor works

CLASS 7

The erection, construction, renewal or replacement of any gate or gateway not exceeding 2 metres in height above ground level.

CLASS 8

The plastering of any wall of concrete blocks or mass concrete and the construction, lowering, repair or replacement of –

1. The height of any such structure shall not exceed 1·2 metres above ground level or the height of the structure being repaired or replaced, whichever

[37] Inserted by S.I. 154 of 1981.
[38] Inserted by S.I. 154 of 1981.

(i) any fence (not being a hoarding or sheet metal fence), or

(ii) any wall (not being an unplastered wall of concrete blocks or mass concrete bounding a public road),

(iii) a wall constructed of split blocks or other blocks of decorative finish.

is the greater and in any event shall not exceed 2 metres above ground level.

2. Every such wall bounding a public road (other than a dry-stone wall) shall be capped.

CLASS 9

Any alteration consisting of the replastering or painting of any external part of any building or other structure.

CLASS 10

The repair or improvement of any private street, road or way, being works carried out on land within the boundary of the street, road or way, and the construction of any private footpath or paving not exceeding 3 metres in width.

Change of use

CLASS 11

Development consisting of a change of use –

(a) from use as a general or special industrial building to use as a light industrial building,[39]

(b) from use as a special industrial building to use as a general industrial building,

(c) from use as a fried fish shop, a shop for the sale of hot food for consumption off the premises, a shop for the sale of pet animals or birds, or a shop for the sale or display for sale of motor vehicles, to use as any other type of shop,

(d) from use as a public house to use

---

[39] See *Lambert* v. *Lewis & Anor*, page 102.

as a shop for any purpose other than the exceptions specified in Class 1 of Part IV of this Schedule.

Temporary structures and uses

CLASS 12

Occasional use for social or recreational purposes of any school, hall, club, art gallery, museum, library, reading room, gymnasium or any structure normally used for public worship or religious instruction.

CLASS 13

The erection, construction or placing on land on, in, or under which or on land adjoining which developments consisting of works (other than mining), is being or is about to be carried out in pursuance of a permission granted under Part IV of the Act of 1963 or as exempted development, of structures, works, plant or machinery needed temporarily in connection with that development during the period in which it is being carried out.

Such structures, works, plant or machinery shall be removed at the expiration of the period and the land shall be forthwith reinstated save to such extent as may be authorised or required by a permission under the Act of 1963.

CLASS 14

The placing or maintenance on a public road of any movable appliance licensed under section 89 of the Act of 1963.

CLASS 15

The use of premises as offices in connection with Presidential, Dáil or local elections or referenda or election for the Assembly of the European Communities.

The use shall be discontinued after a period not exceeding 30 days.

CLASS 16

The keeping or storing of not more than

1. The caravan or boat shall not be

one caravan or boat within the curtilage of a dwellinghouse.

used for the storage, display, advertisement or sale of goods or for the purposes of any business.

2. No caravan shall be kept or stored for more than nine months in any year or occupied as a dwelling while so kept or stored.

Development for industrial purposes

CLASS 17

Development of the following descriptions, carried out by an industrial undertaker on land occupied and used by such undertaker for the carrying on and for the purposes of any industrial process, or on land used as a dock, harbour or quay for the purposes of any industrial undertaking, provided that such development does not materially alter the external appearance of the premises of the undertaking –

(i) the provision, rearrangement, replacement, or maintenance of private ways or private railways, sidings or conveyors,

(ii) the provision, rearrangement or maintenance of sewers, mains, pipes, cables or other apparatus,

(iii) the installation or erection by way of addition or replacement of plant or machinery, or structures of the nature of plant or machinery, not exceeding 15 metres in height or the height of the plant, machinery or structure so replaced, whichever is the greater.

CLASS 18

Storage within the curtilage of an industrial building of raw materials, products, packing materials or fuel, or the deposit of waste, so as not to be visible from any public road contiguous or adjacent to the curtilage.

Development by statutory undertakers

CLASS 19

The carrying out by any railway undertaking of development required in connection with the movement of traffic by
rail in, on, over or under the oper-
ational land of the undertaking except –

   (i) the construction or erection of
     any railway station or bridge, or
     of any residential structure,
     office, or structure to be used for
     manufacturing or repairing work,
     which is not situate wholly within
     the interior of a railway station,
     and
  (ii) the reconstruction or alteration of
     any of the aforementioned struc-
     tures so as materially to affect the
     design or external appearance
     thereof.

CLASS 20

The carrying out by any harbour
authority of development being –
   (i) works authorised by a harbour
     works order in pursuance of sec-
     tion 134 of the Harbours Act,
     1946, which consist of the con-
     struction, reconstruction, exten-
     sion or removal of docks, graving
     docks, quays, wharves, jetties,
     piers, embankments, breakwa-
     ters, roads, viaducts, tramways,
     railways, aerodromes, (but not
     the construction and erection of
     sheds, transit sheds, transhipment
     sheds, silos, stores and other
     structures or the reconstruction or
     alteration of such excepted struc-
     tures so as materially to affect the
     design or external appearance
     thereof), or
  (ii) the cleaning, scouring, deepen-
     ing, improving or dredging of
     their harbour or the approaches

thereto or the removal of any obstruction within the limits of their harbour, and the use of land for the disposal of dredged material in accordance with an objective in the development plan for the area in which the land is situated.

CLASS 21

The carrying out –
(a) pursuant to and in accordance with a consent given by the Minister for Transport and Power under section 8 of the Gas Act, 1976 (No. 30 of 1976) by the Irish Gas Board of development consisting of the construction of underground pipelines for the transmission of gas (but not the construction or erection of any apparatus, equipment or other thing ancillary to such a pipeline save cathodic protection equipment and marker posts), or
(b) in accordance with requirements of the Minister for Transport and Power under section 40 of the Gas Act, 1976, of development consisting of the construction of an underground pipeline for the transmission of gas (but not the construction or erection of any apparatus, equipment or other thing ancillary to such a pipeline save cathodic protection equipment and marker posts), or
(c) by any gas undertaking (other than the Irish Gas Board) of development consisting of the laying underground of mains, pipes, cables or other apparatus for the purposes of the undertaking.

CLASS 22

The carrying out by any electricity

undertaking of development consisting of the laying, underground of mains, pipes, cables, or other apparatus for the purposes of the undertaking.

CLASS 23

The carrying out by any electricity undertaking of development consisting of construction of overhead transmission or distribution lines for conducting electricity at a voltage not exceeding 10 KV.

CLASS 24

The carrying out by any electricity undertaking of development for the purposes of the undertaking consisting of the erection or construction of an overhead transmission line not more than 40 metres from a position in respect of which permission for such line was granted and which otherwise complies with such permission, but not a line in respect of which a condition attached to the relevant permission imposed a contrary requirement.

CLASS 25

The carrying out by any electricity undertaking of development consisting of the erection or construction of a 10 KV unit substation having a bulk of less than 8 cubic metres above ground level.

Development for amenity or recreational purposes

CLASS 26

Development consisting of the laying out and use of land –
  (a) as a park, private open space or ornamental garden,
  (b) as a roadside shrine,
  (c) as a golf course or pitch-and-putt course, incorporating parking

space for not less than 24 cars,

(*d*) for athletics or sports where no charge is made for admission of the public to the land.

Class 27

The construction of a swimming pool (other than a covered swimming pool) in accordance with plans approved by a sanitary authority for the purposes of making a contribution under section 55 of the Local Government Act, 1955.

Miscellaneous

Class 28

Development consisting of the use of land for the placing or maintenance of tents, vans or other temporary or movable structures or objects in connection with any fair or any local event of a religious, cultural, political, recreational or sporting character.

1. The land shall not be used for any such purposes either continuously for a period exceeding 15 days or occasionally for periods exceeding in aggregate 30 days in any year.
2. On the discontinuance of such use the land shall be forthwith reinstated save to such extent as may be authorised by a permission granted under Part IV of the Act of 1963.

Class 29

The erection, placing or keeping on land of any lighthouse, beacon, buoy or other aid to navigation on water or in the air.

Class 30

The use of land as a burial ground and works incidental to the use or maintenance of any burial ground, churchyard, monument, fairgreen, market, schoolyard or showground except –

(*a*) the erection or construction of any wall, fence or gate bounding or abutting on a public road,

(*b*) the erection or construction of any building other than a stall or store, which is wholly enclosed

within a market building, or
   (c) the reconstruction or alteration of
any building other than a stall or
store which is wholly enclosed
within a market building.

CLASS 31

Works consisting of or incidental to –
   (a) the clearance of a derelict site in
accordance with any offer
accepted or requirement made by
any local authority in pursuance
of section 2 or 3 of the Derelict
Sites Act, 1961.
   (b) the carrying out of any works on
land which are in accordance
with and necessary for compliance with the terms of any
licence granted under section 34
of the Local Government (Sanitary Services) Act, 1948, but not
including the erection of any
building, hut or chalet or the construction of any road or hard-
standing,
   (c) the removal of any structure or
object or the carrying out of any
works required by a planning
authority under the provisions of
any enactment.

CLASS 32

The excavation for the purposes of
research or discovery of sites, features
and other objects of archaeological,
geological or historical interest the preservation of which is not an objective of
any development plan.

CLASS 33

The sinking of a well, drilling of a bore-
hole, erection of a pump, or construction of a pumphouse, or other
works necessary for the purpose of providing a domestic water supply or providing a group water scheme in accord-

ance with a plan or proposal approved by the Minister for the purpose of making a grant towards the cost of such works.

CLASS 34

Any drilling of excavation for the purpose of surveying land or examining the depth and nature of the subsoil.

CLASS 35

The connection of any premises to a communal television system, sewer, watermain, gas main or electricity supply line or cable, including the breaking open of any street or other land for that purpose.

CLASS 36

The demolition of a building or other structure.[39a]

PART II

EXEMPTED DEVELOPMENT – ADVERTISEMENTS

Column 1 Description of Development	Column 2 Conditions
CLASS 1 Advertisements for the purposes of announcement or direction or warning exhibited by a statutory undertaker in relation to the operation of their statutory undertaking.	
CLASS 2 Advertisements for the purposes of identification, direction or warning with respect to the land or structures on which they are exhibited.	No such advertisement shall exceed 0.3 square metres in area.

[39a] Permission may be required under the Housing Act, 1969.

CLASS 3

Advertisements, exhibited at the entrance to any premises, relating to any person, partnership or company separately carrying on a public service or a profession, business or trade at the premises.

1. No such advertisement shall exceed 0.3 square metres in area.
2.

Not more than one such advertisement, in respect of each such person, partnership or company shall be exhibited on the premises or, in the case of premises with entrances on different road frontages, one such advertisement at one entrance on each road frontage.

CLASS 4

Advertisements relating to any institution of a religious, educational, cultural, recreational or medical or similar character, any hotel, inn or public house, block of flats, club, boarding house or hostel, situated on the land on which any such advertisement is exhibited.

1. No such advertisement shall exceed 0.6 square metres in area.
2. Not more than one such advertisement shall be exhibited in respect of each such premises or, in the case of premises with entrances on different road frontages, one such advertisement on each such frontage.

CLASS 5

Advertisements exhibited on or affixed to any external face of any hotel building wholly with reference to all or any of the following matters: the business or other activity carried on and the services provided in the hotel.

1. No such advertisement shall project more than 1 metre from the face of the building to which it is affixed.
2. Where any such advertisement projects more than 5 centimetres over any public road, the advertisement shall be not less than 2 metres over the level of such road.

CLASS 6

Advertisements relating to the sale or letting of any structure or other land (not being an advertisement structure) on which they are exhibited.

1. No such advertisement shall exceed 0.6 square metres in area.

2. No such advertisement shall be exhibited for more than seven days after the sale or letting to which the advertisement relates.

3. No advertisement structure on which such advertisement is exhibited shall remain on the structure or other land

for more than seven days after the sale or letting to which the advertisement relates.

CLASS 7

Advertisements relating to the sale on or before a date specified therein of goods or livestock, and exhibited on land where such goods or livestock are situated or where such sale is held, not being land which is normally used, whether at regular intervals or otherwise, for the purpose of holding sales of goods or livestock.

1. No such advertisements shall exceed 0.6 square metres in area.

2. No such advertisement shall be exhibited for more than seven days after the date specified.

CLASS 8

Advertisements relating to the carrying out of building or similar works on the land on which they are exhibited, not being land which is normally used, whether at regular intervals or otherwise, for the purpose of carrying out such works.

1. Where only one advertisement is exhibited, such advertisement shall not exceed 3.5 square metres in area or exceed a height of 6 metres above ground level.

2. Where more than one advertisement is exhibited, no such advertisement shall exceed 0.6 square metres in area or a height of 4 metres above ground level and the total area of such advertisements shall not exceed 2 square metres.

CLASS 9

Advertisements other than advertisements specified in class 17 of this Part of this Schedule announcing any local event of a religious, educational, cultural, political, social or recreational character, and advertisements relating to any temporary matter in connection with any local event of such a character, not in either case being an event promoted or carried on for commercial purposes.

1. No such advertisement shall exceed 1.2 square metres in area.

2. No such advertisement shall be exhibited more than 2.5 metres above ground level or be glued or pasted to any structure other than an advertisement structure.

3. No such advertisement shall be exhibited for more than seven days after the conclusion of the event or matter to which it relates.

CLASS 10

Advertisements relating to any demonstration of agricultural methods or processes on the land on which the advertisements are exhibited.

1. No such advertisement shall exceed 0.6 square metres in area.

2. No such advertisement shall be exhibited for more than seven days after the date of the demonstration to which it relates.

CLASS 11

Advertisements (other than advertisements specified in class 12 of this Part of this Schedule) which are exhibited within a structure and to which there is access from inside the structure.

CLASS 12

Internally illuminated advertisements exhibited as part of any shop or other window display on business premises and advertisements affixed to the glass surface of a window of a business premises or exhibited through a window of such premises and not less than 15 centimetres from such window.

The total area of any advertisements exhibited shall not exceed one quarter of the area of the window through which the advertisements are exhibited.

CLASS 13

Advertisements (other than those specified in classes 3, 4, 11 and 12 of this Part of this Schedule) exhibited on business premises, wholly with reference to all or any of the following matters: the business or other activity carried on and the goods or services provided on those premises.

1. No part of any such advertisement shall be more than 2.5 metres in height above ground level or, where such advertisement is exhibited on or attached or affixed to any building, 4 metres in height above ground level.

2. No such advertisement shall contain or consist of any symbol, emblem, model or device exceeding 0.6 metres in height or any letter exceeding 0.3 metres in height.

3. Where such advertisement projects more than 5 centimetres over any public road, the advertisement shall not be less than 2 metres over the level of such road nor project more than 1 metre over such road.

4. The total area of such advertisements which are not exhibited on or attached or affixed to any building shall not exceed 3 square metres of which not more than 1.5 square metres shall consist of advertisements which are internally illuminated.

5. The total area of such advertisements exhibited on or attached or affixed to the front of any building shall not exceed an area equal to 0.3 square metres for every metre length of such front less the total area of any such advertisements exhibited on the premises, but not exhibited on or attached or affixed to the building.

6. The total area of such advertisements exhibited on or attached or affixed to any face of a building other than the front thereof shall not exceed 1.2 square metres and the total area of any such advertisements on such face which are internally illuminated shall not exceed 0.3 square metres.

7. Where any such advertisement consists of a circular sign and projects maore than 5 centimetres over any public road, the diameter of such sign shall not exceed 1 metre and no other such advertisement shall be exhibited on a sign projecting more than 5 centimetres over the public road.

8. Where any one or more such advertisements are exhibited on a swinging or fixed sign or other advertisement structure (other than a circular sign), projecting more than 5 centimetres from any external face of any structure, the total area of such advertisements shall not exceed 1.2 square metres and the area of any face of such advertisement structure shall not exceed 0.4 square metres.

9. No such advertisement shall cover any part of any window in any building on

which the advertisement is exhibited or to which it is attached or affixed.

CLASS 14

An advertisements in the form of a flag which is attached to a single flagstaff fixed in an upright position on the roof of a business premises, and which bears no inscription or emblem other than the name or device of a person occupying the building.

CLASS 15

Any advertisement relating to a presidential, Dáil or local election or referendum or to an election for the Assembly of the European Communities.

No such advertisement shall be exhibited for more than seven days after the date of the election or referendum to which it relates.

CLASS 16

Advertisements required to be exhibited by or under any enactment, including (but without prejudice to the generality hereof) advertisements the exhibition of which is so required as a condition of the valid exercise of any power, or proper performance of any function, given or imposed by such enactment, or for compliance with any procedure prescribed by or under any enactment.

CLASS 17

Advertisements consisting of placards, posters or bills relating to the visit of any travelling circus, funfair, carnival, show, cinema, musicians, players or other travelling entertainment.

1. No such advertisement shall exceed 1.2 square metres in area.

2. No such advertisement shall be exhibited more than 2.5 metres above ground level or be glued or pasted to any structure other than an advertisement structure.

3. No such advertisement shall be exhibited more than seven days after the visit or performance to which it relates.

CLASS 18

Any advertisement exhibited on land wholly or for the most part enclosed within a hedge, fence, wall or similar screen or structure (not being land which is a public park, public garden or other land held for the use and enjoyment of the public, or a part of a railway undertaking's enclosed land normally used for the carriage of passengers by rail) and not readily visible from land outside the enclosure wherein it is exhibited.

CLASS 19

Any advertisement exhibited within a railway station.

PART III
EXEMPTED DEVELOPMENT – RURAL

Column 1 Description of Development	Column 2 Conditions

Limited use for camping

CLASS 1

Temporary use of any land for the placing of any tent or caravan or for the mooring of any boat, barge or other vessel used for the purpose of camping.	1. Not more than one tent or caravan shall be placed within 100 metres of another tent or caravan at any time.
	2. No tent, caravan, or vessel shall remain on the land for a greater period than 10 days.
	3. No tent, caravan or vessel shall be used for the storage, display, advertisement or sale of goods or for the purposes of any business.
	4. No tent or caravan shall be placed on land within 50 metres of any public

road unless the land is enclosed by a wall, bank or hedge, or any combination thereof, having an average height of not less than 1.5 metres.

CLASS 2

Temporary use of land by a scouting organisation for a summer camp.	The land shall not be used for such purposes for any period or periods exceeding 30 days in any year.

Minor works and structures

CLASS 3

Works relating to the construction or maintenance of any gully, drain, pond, trough, pit or culvert, the widening or deepening of watercourses, the removal of obstructions from watercourses and the making or repairing of embankments.

CLASS 4

The erection of any stand or ramp for loading or unloading vehicles (excluding the erection of a ramp on a public road and any stand which projects over any paved or metalled part of a public road).	1. The height of the stand or ramp shall not exceed 1.2 metres above ground level. 2. A stand within 50 metres of a road junction shall not be situated over or adjoining a public road.

CLASS 5

The erection of any wall or fence other than a fence of sheet metal or a wall or fence within or bounding any garden or other space in front of a dwelling-house.	The height of the wall or fence shall not exceed 2 metres above ground level.

Mining

CLASS 6

The use of land for the purpose of the	1. No such structure shall remain on the

winning and working of minerals, the carrying out of works incidental thereto (other than opencast mining or surface working or the deposit of refuse or waste materials) and, in the case of land other than land situate in an area to which a special amenity area order relates, the erection or placing of structures on the land for such specific purpose.

land for a period exceeding twelve months.

2. On the discontinuance of the use of the land, or any part thereof, all structures and materials shall be removed therefrom and the surface of the land shall be forthwith reinstated or, where reinstatement is not practicable, such excavation shall be effectively fenced or otherwise protected and, in the case of land in an area to which a special amenity area order relates, a hedge, bushes or trees shall be planted so as to screen the excavation.

Agricultural buildings

CLASS 7

Works consisting of the provision, on land not less than 10 metres from any public road the metalled part of which at the nearest point is more than 4 metres in width, of a roofed structure for the housing of pigs, cattle, sheep or poultry, having a floor area not exceeding 400 square metres (whether or not by extention of an existing structure) and any ancillary provision for effluent storage.

1. No such structure shall be used for any purpose other than the purpose of agriculture.

2. No such structure for the housing of pigs, or poultry shall be situated within 100 metres of any dwelling-house save with the consent of the owner and occupier thereof.

3. No such structure within 100 metres of any public road shall exceed 7 metres in height above ground level.

4. No effluent from such structure shall be stored within 100 metres of any dwellinghouse save with the consent of the owner and occupier thereof.

CLASS 8

Works consisting of the provision, on land not less than 10 metres from any public road the metalled part of which at the nearest point is more than 4 metres in width, of roofless cubicles, open loose yards, self feed silo or silage areas, feeding aprons, asembly

1. No such structure shall be used for any purpose other than the purpose of agriculture.

2. No such structure for the housing of pigs or poultry, or for the making, storage or feeding of silage shall be

yards, milking parlours, sheep dipping units or structures for the making or storage of silage, having an aggregate floor area not exceeding 400 square metres, and any ancillary provision for effluent storage.

situated within 100 metres of any dwellinghouse save with the consent of the owner and occupier thereof.

3. No such structure within 100 metres of any public road shall exceed 7 metres in height above ground level.

4. No effluent from such structure shall be stored within 100 metres of any dwellinghouse save with the consent of the owner and occupier thereof.

CLASS 9

The construction, extension, alteration or replacement, on land not less than 10 metres from any public road the metalled part of which at the nearest point is more than 4 metres in width, of any store, barn, shed, glasshouse or other agricultural building not being of a type specified in Class 7 or 8 of this Part of this Schedule.

1. No such structure shall be used for any purpose other than the purpose of agriculture or forestry.

2. No such structure within 100 metres of any public road shall exceed 7 metres in height above ground level.

PART IV

CLASSES OF USE

CLASS 1 – Use as a shop for any purpose except as –
   (a) a fried fish shop or a shop for the sale of hot food for consumption off the premises.[40]
   (b) a shop for the sale of pet animals or birds,
   (c) a shop for the sale or display for sale of motor vehicles other than bicycles.
CLASS 2 – Use as an office for any purpose.[41]
CLASS 3 – Use as a light industrial building for any purpose.
CLASS 4 – Use as a general industrial building for any purpose.
CLASS 5 – Use for any work which is registrable under the Alkali, etc. Works Regulation Act, 1906, except a process ancillary to the getting, dressing or treatment of minerals, carried on in or adjacent to a quarry or mine; use for any of the following processes, except as aforesaid, so far as not registrable under the above Act: –
   (a) smelting, calcining, sintering or reduction of ores, minerals, concentrates or matter,
   (b) converting, reheating, annealing, hardening, melting, carburising, forging or casting of iron or other metals or alloys.

[40] See *Dublin Corporation* v. *Raso*, p. 104.
[41] See *Cusack & McKenna* v. *Minister for Local Government & Anor*, page 60.

(*c*) recovering of metal from scrap or drosses or ashes,

(*d*) galvinising

(*e*) pickling or treatment of metal in acid

(*f*) chromium plating.

CLASS 5A – Preservation of plasterwork, staircases, woodwork or other fixtures or features of artistic, historic or architectural interest and forming part of the interior of a structure.

CLASS 6 – Use for any of the following processes so far as not included in class 5 of this Part of this Schedule and except a process ancillary to the getting, dressing or treatment of minerals, carried on in or adjacent to a quarry or mine –

(*a*) burning of building bricks,

(*b*) lime burning,

(*c*) production of calcium carbide or zinc oxide,

(*d*) foaming, crushing or screening of stone or slag.

CLASS 7 – Use for any of the following purposes so far as not included in class 5 of this Part of this Schedule –

(*a*) the production or employment of cyanogen or its compounds,

(*b*) the manufacture of glass, where the sodium sulphate used exceeds 1.5 per cent of the total weight of the melt,

(*c*) the production of zinc chloride.

CLASS 8 – Use for any of the following purposes so far as not included in class 5 of this Part of this Schedule –

The distilling, refining or blending of oils, the production or employment of cellulose lacquers (except their employment in garages in connection with minor repairs), hot pitch or bitumen or pyridine; the stoving of enamelled ware; the production of amyl acetate, aromatic esters, butyric acid, caramel, hexamine, iodoform, B-naphthol, resin products (except synthetic resins, plastic moulding or extrusion compositions and plastic sheets, rods, tubes, filaments, fibres or optical components produced by casting, calendering, moulding, shaping or extrusion), salicylic acid or sulphonated organic compounds; paint and varnish manufacture (excluding mixing, milling and grinding); the production of rubber from scrap; or the manufacture of acetylene from calcium carbide for sale or for use in a further chemical process.

CLASS 9 – Use as a wholesale warehouse or enclosed repository building for any purpose.

CLASS 10 – Use as a residential club, a hotel providing sleeping accommodation, a guest house or a hostel.

CLASS 11 – Use as a structure for public worship or religious instruction; use of such structure for the social or recreational activities of the religious body using the structure; as a monastery or convent.

CLASS 12 – Use as a residential or boarding school or a residential college.

CLASS 13 – Use as a convalescent home, a maternity home, a nursing home, a sanatorium, a hospital, a health centre, a clinic, a creche, a day nursery, a dispensary, or a home or institution for the boarding, care and maintenance of children, old people, incapacitated persons or persons suffering from mental disability.

CLASS 14 – Use as an art gallery (not being a business premises), a museum, a public library or reading room, a public hall, an exhibition hall, a social centre, a community centre or a non-residential club, but not as a dance hall, music hall or concert hall.

CLASS 15 – Use as a theatre, a cinema, a music hall, a concert hall.

CLASS 16 – Use as a skating rink, or a gymnasium, or for indoor games or sports (including boxing, wrestling and bowling).

DUBLIN CORPORATION V. LANGAN
The High Court (Unreported) Gannon J., 14 May 1982
(Ref. No. 1982 No. 36 MCA)

The respondent was in possession of a single storey premises extending 35 feet from the building line and 9 feet in front of it. Without obtaining planning permission they demolished and replaced the shop front to the premises in the area in front of the building line. In addition to these works they carried out works in the back portion of the premises which in effect replaced the interior of that part of the premises. This too was done without planning permission. Subsequent to receiving a warning notice from the applicant the respondent applied for permission to retain 'replacement of shop front'. No application was made in respect of the works done in the back portion of the premises, which the respondent claimed were exempted under section 4(1)(g) of the 1963 Act.

Gannon J.:
The applicant planning authority seek orders which will prevent any part of the premises being used or being further developed. They do not ask to have the front portion removed on the grounds that the application to retain it is the subject of a pending application requiring a decision in accordance with proper planning principles and policies. The respondent submits that no planning permission is necessary, and no order can be made in relation to any portion other than the front portion which is the subject of the retention application. This submission is founded on the contention that the only work done in the part of 35 feet depth is exempted development within the terms of section 4(1)(g) of the Local Government (Planning and Development) Act 1963. It is further submitted that the new frontage of 9 feet depth and the inner portion of 35 foot depth are both different structures, the first being one to which the retention application relates and for which planning permission is required, and the second being one upon which works of maintenance, repair and improvement have been carried out internally without affecting its external appearance.

In my opinion there are not two structures, and Mr. Gallagher for the applicant is correct in his submission that there is but one structure comprising the entire premises. But in relation to the one structure the work which may be carried out on it within the meaning of the expression 'development' as defined in the 1963 Act may consist partly of exempted development and partly of development for which planning permission must previously have been obtained. The respondent admits that the work done on the portion of the premises extending 9 feet forward of the frontage line of adjoining buildings is development for which planning permission is required. That work involved the entire replacement of a similarly extended frontage of the premises purchased. The interior area of the premises purchased to the depth of 35 feet has also been completely replaced, and in my opinion the work done is not simply repair and maintenance to conform to the requirements of covenants in the lease. The filling of the basement area, the excavations, and the erection of six supporting piers indicate an adaptation capable of supporting an entirely different construction from that at present on the site. The work done on this internal area extending 35 feet back from the frontage of the building line is of the same character relative to what had been done there before as that done in the forward projecting portion extending 9 feet beyond the frontage of the building line in relation to what preceded it. Among the factors which must be taken into account in the making of decisions for granting or withholding planning permission are the design, character and appearance of the structure relative to its environment and adjoining buildings. The policy of the Planning Acts clearly is to prevent the erection and maintenance of unauthorised structures. The definition of unauthorised structures appears to indicate that permitted structures are those only which would have been permitted structures under the repealed 1934 Act and those which existed at the time of the appointed day pursuant to the 1963 Act or approved since then pursuant to the provisions of that Act. The premises of which the respondent is the occupier and owner of a leasehold interest *prima facie* appear to be an unauthorised structure and in respect thereof a development purporting to be no more than the maintenance thereof as such would not be exempted development. But in the view I take of the evidence the work done by the respondent on the entire constitutes development and exceeds the limits for exempted development within section 4 (1)(g) of the 1963 Act upon which the respondent seeks to rely.

HORNE V. FREENEY
The High Court, (Unreported) Murphy J., 7th July 1982,
(Ref. No. 1982 No. 60 MCA)

The Respondent departed from a planning permission he had obtained for the construction of an amusement arcade by substituting a steel roof for a concrete slab roof; by building an area with two rows of 15 pillars with rooms behind on the ground floor instead of an open area for dodgem cars; and by building an open area for dodgem cars on the first floor instead of toilets and other facilities. In section 27 proceedings he argued that these departures were exempted under section 4(1)(g) of the 1963 Act. This was rejected by the Court which held that a planning permission was indivisible and authorised the carrying out of all the works and not some of them only.

Murphy J.:
. . . The issue remains whether having regard to the admitted departures from the documents lodged in support of the application it can be said that the development is being 'carried out in conformity with permission granted'. *Prima facie* this question must be answered in the negative.

The Respondent contends that all the variations from the plans constituted 'the carrying out of the works to the maintenance, improvement or other alteration of any structure being works which affect only the interior of the structure' and as such constitute an exempted development by virtue of the provisions of section 4(1)(g) of the Local Government (Planning and Development) Act 1963. It is argued on behalf of the Respondent that it would be absurd to conclude that a developer was bound to adhere to plans in the first instance in the carrying out of development in those respects where he could at a later date make such changes as he thought fit without any permission being sought or obtained.

Whilst I see the force of that argument I take the view that if planning permission is indivisible: that it authorises the carrying out of the totality of the works for which approval has been granted and not some of them only. A developer cannot at his election implement a part only of the approved plans as no approval is given for the part as distinct from the whole.

Accordingly I propose to grant an injunction . . . prohibiting the carrying on of further development works.

CHRISTINE LAMBERT V. PATRICK LEWIS AND JOSEPH KIELY
The High Court Gannon J., 24 November 1982,
(Ref. No. 1982 No. 100 MCA)

The first-named Respondent occupied premises located to the rear of premises owned by the Applicant as a weekly tenant of the second-named Respondent. The letting was subject to a covenant on the part of the first-named Respondent 'to use the premises as a woodworking workshop and for no other purpose what-soever. . . .' The first-named Respondent used the premises as such without planning permission for such use. Two applications had been made on his behalf for such use, however, both applications had been refused. The second refusal was under appeal at the time of the hearing of this action.

Prior to the first-named Respondent going into occupation the premises had been used as follows:

Between 1954 and 1959   as a woodworking shop
Between 1959 and 1965   for the storage and slicing of potatoes
Between 1969 and 1971   for the storage and cutting of beef carcasses and for
                        the storage of provisions

On the 12th February 1971 the premises were let subject to a covenant 'to use premises as a store only. . .'. On the 11th May they were again let subject to a covenant 'to use the premises as a store or garage. . .'. In both instances the premises were described in the agreement as a garage. On the 6th May 1976 they were let subject to a covenant 'to use the premises as a workshop for making furniture and pictures and as a studio. . .'. They were described as a store in the agreement. On the 27th June 1977 they were let subject to a covenant 'to use the premises as a workshop. . .'. In the agreement they were described as a shed. Finally on the 26th July 1978 the first-named Respondent took the premises.

Gannon J.:
. . .For the purpose of resolving the issues in dispute on this application I find the following facts as proved, namely:

(a) that since July 1978, Mr. Lewis has been using the subject premises for the purpose of carrying on therein an industrial process;

(b) that at no time prior to the 15th March 1977 was the subject premises used as a 'light industrial building';

(c) the use to which the subject premises is being put by Mr. Lewis is a material change of use relative to the use which the subject premises had been put prior to the 1st of October 1964 and prior to the 15th of March 1977.

Because there is no existing permission granted under the Planning Acts to use the subject premises other than as an amenity contiguous or adjacent to the curtilage of a private residence in an area zoned for primarily residential use and because the occupier Mr. Lewis has made application for permissions for retention of use the onus lies on him to establish the facts from which the Court could reasonably infer that there has been no such material change of user. This he has failed to do.

The use to which Mr. Lewis puts the subject premises is a use in the course of trade or business of a nature which comes within the definition of 'industrial process' in regulation 9 of Part III of Statutory Instrument 65 of 1977. The building in which he carries on the 'industrial process' is not being used as an amenity of or for any purpose incidental to the enjoyment of any private dwelling house or residence as such to which it is contiguous or adjacent. For the purpose of the definition of 'light industrial building' in the same regulation of Part III of the Statutory Instrument 65 of 1977 the subject premises could be so described only if it be established that the process carried on therein could be carried on without detriment to the amenity of the area. On this there is a conflict of evidence which could not be resolved satisfactorily from evidence on Affidavit, but there is strong *prima facie* evidence that there is detriment to the amenity of at least one local resident who does not have a shop or business in the area. The evidence of the use to which the subject premises was put under the May 1976 letting is that it was used for approximately one year for 'making furniture and fixtures and stone sculpting'. Whether machinery, if any, was then used or not or whether it involved any detriment to the amenities of neighbouring residents is not indicated. There is no evidence to show that such use was not an 'unauthorised use' as defined in section 2 of The Local Government (Planning and Development) Act 1963. In the absence of supportive evidence on such aspects it must be assumed the user of the premises at least did not involve breach of any of the tenant's covenants in the letting agreements exhibited by Mr. Kiely the landlord in his affidavit. In my view there is not sufficient evidence to support the submission that the subject premises were, prior to 15th March 1977, lawfully being used as light industrial buildings in which an industrial process was being lawfully carried on by an industrial undertaker in the sense in which these expressions are defined in the regulations of Statutory Instrument 65 of 1977. Accordingly I accept the submissions of Mr. Meenan for the Applicant that the use to which the subject premises is being put by Mr. Lewis is a material change in the use of the structures and as such a development within the definition of that term in section 3 of the 1963 Act for which, unless exempted, planning permission is required.

For Mr. Lewis, Mr. Sweeney submits that the development is an exempted development under Part III of the regulations in Statutory Instrument 65 of 1977, by reference to article 10 and Class 11 in Part I of the Third Schedule therein. Class 11 prescribes only four types of development consisting of change of use which may be exempted as provided for in article 10 and of these only (a) and (b) could be pertinent. Mr. Sweeney seeks to rely on paragraph (a) which reads as follows:

'development consisting of a change of use:
(a) from use as a general or special industrial building to use as a light industrial building'.

He submits that this provision should be construed to include a change of a light industrial building from the carrying on therein of one type of industrial process to some other type of industrial process without involving the change of use of the building so as to make it a general or special industrial building. Apart from the fact that such construction does not clearly fall within the wording of paragraph (a) of

Class 11 of Part I of the schedule it would be inconsistent with the other provisions which involve references to Part IV of the schedule. However the most important factor is that the use from which a change is made to qualify as an exempted development under article 10 of the regulations in Statutory Instrument 65 of 1977 must not be an 'unauthorised use' as defined in section 2 of the 1963 Act. The 1977 regulations relate to structures and use of structures or land as governed by the 1963 Act prior to the coming into force of the 1977 regulations. The buildings which comprise the subject premises are buildings which, according to the affidavit of David Semple, the Applicant's architect appeared to have 'originally built, designed and utilised as garages for the houses backing on the said yard.' From the Plan exhibited to which Mr. Semple refers the buildings appear to be within the curtilage of the dwelling houses and intended for purposes incidental to the enjoyment of the dwelling houses as such. In my view any change of use from use for such purposes is an unauthorised use unless coming within the provisions for exempted development in either the 1963 Act or the regulations of Statutory Instrument 65 of 1977. The onus of establishing exemption falls on the Respondents. In my view they have failed to show that the subject premises are not being put to an unauthorised use.

DUBLIN CORPORATION V. SALVATORE RASO
The High Court (Unreported) Finaly J., 1st June 1976,
(Ref. No. 1976 No. 36SS)

The Defendant applied for and obtained permission to 'retain change of use from foodmarket to fish and chips shop at 47 Kilbarrack Road, Raheny' subject to conditions. Local residents appealed the decision to the Minister who confirmed the decision with an additional condition that 'the premises shall not be used for the permitted use between the hours of 11 pm and 8 am'. In breach of this condition the Defendants sold fish and chips outside the permitted hours. He was prosecuted and convicted under section 24 of the 1963 Act. The Defendant then obtained an Order of Mandamus requiring the District Justice to state a Case to the High Court.

Finlay P.:
. . . Under the provision of Rule 4[42] of the Local Government Planning and Development Act 1963 (Exempted Development) Regulations 1967 being S.I. Number 176 of 1967 development consisting of a change of use within any of the classes of use specified in Part IV of the Schedule to those Regulations is an exempted development. The classes of use contained in Part IV Class 1[2] are used as a shop for any purpose except as (a) a fried fish shop. The defendant contends that it was not necessary for him to have applied for any permission for a change of user in this shop except insofar as the change was to user as a fried fish shop and not as a fish and chip shop. The argument then runs that the condition with regard to opening hours could only apply in law to the hours of opening for the sale of fried fish. That the evidence before the District Justice did not prove beyond reasonable doubt that fried fish had been sold outside the permitted hours but proved only that fish and chips had been sold and that this could be a description of boiled or say smoked fish together with chips.

---

[42] See reg. 12 of the 1977 Regulations and Class 1 of Part IV of 3rd Schedule.

On this submission I have come to the following conclusions. It is in my view within the power of the Planning Authority or of the Minister on appeal to impose a condition upon the granting of a permission governing the hours of opening of a shop for the purpose as undoubtedly occurred in this case of cutting down nuisance, noise and the frequenting or gathering of people which would disturb the residential aspect of a neighbourhood. Such an object and a condition securing such an object is clearly within the planning code. It would therefore in my view have been open to the Planning Authority even if the proper application had been made for permission, (that is to say, permission only for use as a fried fish shop without any reference to chips) to have imposed a condition that the shop would not be open for the purpose of selling either fried fish or chips after 11 p.m. although on the strict interpretation of the regulations change of user from a foodstore to a store selling chips only would be an exempted development. The words 'permitted use' contained in the condition imposed in the granting of permission by the Minister on the 11th of April 1972 must be interpreted in my view as referring back to the use referred to in the decision itself which as I have indicated was used as a fried fish and chip shop. The defendant who applied for permission in that form can not in my view be heard now to assert that because the inclusion of the words 'and chips' may have been strictly unnecessary that the condition must be construed as prohibiting only the sale of fried fish but not prohibiting the sale of fried chips after 11 p.m.

I think there are very strong grounds for saying that the expression 'fish and chip' could and should be interpreted in a common sense way as having a well accepted ordinary meaning and involving fried fish and chips. If the District Justice were entitled to impose such a construction on the evidence given before him then this point would fail entirely because even the designated use contained in Part IV of the Schedule to the Regulations would have been made after the forbidden time of 11 p.m. at night. In a criminal case however I am prepared to accept for the purpose of this decision without expressly deciding it that the onus of proof on the prosecution leaves it open to some doubt as to whether the phrase 'fish and chip' must necessarily or inevitably mean fried fish. What is clear beyond any doubt however in my view is that the word 'chip' used certainly in connection with fish and referring to a food can only mean one thing and that is a fried chip of potato.

REFERENCES

When a dispute arises as to what is or is not development or exempted development Section 5 of the 1963 Act provides that the question shall be referred to and decided by the Board. Various attempts have been made to have section 27 proceedings adjourned in order to have the question of development or exempted development determined by means of a section 5 reference. It has been held that a reference to the Board is not mandatory and that the Court has a jurisdiction to adjourn the matter or to determine it itself. (See *Dublin County Council* v. *Tallaght Block Company Limited*;[43] *Cork Corporation* v. *O'Connell*)[44]

The matter will be determined in the same manner as an appeal to the Board. (See Chapter 4) Unlike an appeal, however, there is an appeal from the decision of the Board to the High Court. Such appeal must be brought within 3 months of the

[43] See page 62.
[44] See page 60.

giving of the decision or such longer period as to the Court seems fit (see section 5(2)).

LOCAL GOVERNMENT (PLANNING AND DEVELOPMENT) ACT 1963

5. – (1) If any question arises as to what, in any particular case, is or is not development or exempted development, the question shall be referred to and decided by the Board.[45]

(2) Where a decision is given under this section, an appeal to the High Court from the decision may be taken at any time within the period of three months after the giving of the decision or such longer period as the High court may in any particular case allow.

---

[45] As amended by section 14 of the 1976 Act which transferred the Minister's jurisdiction under section 5 to the Planning Board.

Chapter 3

THE NEED FOR PLANNING PERMISSION

INTRODUCTION

The requirement for planning permission is set out in Section 24 of the Act of 1963. Permission is required in respect of any development[1] unless it was commenced before 1st October, 1964, or unless it is exempt. Development without permission is an offence under the same section.[2] Section 25 of the Act of 1963 authorises the Minister to make Regulations providing for planning applications and these are now contained in Part IV of the General Regulations of 1977.[3] Section 26 of the Act of 1963, the most important section in the entire planning code, sets out *in extenso*, the powers and duties of a planning authority on receipt of a planning application and various rights of appeal from the planning decision. These sections and Regulations are set out, *in extenso*, in this chapter, which then goes on to set out excerpts from the various relevant Irish cases.

WHO MAY APPLY?

The statutory provisions distinguish between 'owner' and 'applicant'[4] and in *Frescati Estates Ltd.* v. *Walker*, the Supreme Court dealt with the question – what interest does an applicant require to have in land in order to apply for planning permission? It was held not necessary to be possessed of a legal estate in the land if the applicant has the authority of the owner or of the person who has a reasonable prospect of carrying out the development in question, but on the other hand it is not open to a person who has no interest whatsoever in land and no prospect of acquiring such an interest to make application for purposes unconnected with the objects of the Planning Acts. A second case on the point was *State (Alf-a-Bet Promotions Ltd.)* v. *Bundoran U.D.C.* where McWilliam J. decided that an application on behalf of a company which was not yet in existence, was not thereby invalidated and held that all that was required in the ordinary way was that the

---

[1] Development is defined in section 3 of the Act of 1963. Two broad categories emerge, namely, material change of use and structural works. This distinction is analysed in *Re: Viscount Securities Limited* v. *Dublin County Council*.

[2] Note amendment of section 24 (3) by section 15(1) of the Act of 1982.

[3] As amended by S.I. No. 342 of 1982.

[4] 'Owner' is defined in section 2 of the Act of 1963; 'Applicant' is nowhere defined.

[5] This distinction must now be held doubtful in the light of the obiter remarks of Henchy J. in *The State (Finglas Industrial Estates Ltd.)* v. *Dublin County Council* (see page 225) to the effect that a grant to a non-existent legal person is invalid and nothing in the Companies Act of 1963 providing for the validation of acts done before incorporation can alter this situation.

Applicant has an interest in the land and the actual identity of the Applicant is not crucial. Following a recent *obiter dictum* of Henchy J.[5] this authority must now be regarded as doubtful. In *McCabe* v. *Harding Investments Ltd.*[6] O'Higgins C.J. observed that what the planning authority (in that case) required was a general idea of the applicant's interest in the land.

WHO IS EXEMPT?

Chapter three deals generally with the question of exempted developments, which means developments which are exempted from the requirement of having permission under the Acts. It appears that Government Departments are not required to apply for planning permission. By section 84 of the 1963 Act various State Authorities including 'a member of the Government' are required only to consult with the planning authority regarding any objections that may be raised by the planning authority. This excludes the ordinary third party objector. Section 84 does not in terms exempt State Authorities, as defined therein, from the necessity of obtaining permission under section 24 of the 1963 Act, which, on the face of it, is wide enough to catch developments no matter by whom carried out. However, it appears that the intention of the Act is to exempt for example, Government Departments, from the necessity of obtaining planning permission and that is the way in which these provisions have been interpreted to date.

APPLICATION REGULATIONS

A number of cases have dealt with the results of compliance or non-compliance with the statutory provisions. Obviously the most crucial relate to the default provisions in section 26. *Dunne Ltd.* v. *Dublin County Council*[7] is an example of a case where the developer was successful in obtaining a declaration from the High Court that the failure of the planning authority to come to any decision within the two months, meant that a planning permission by default must be regarded as having issued at the end of that period. Local authorities are naturally anxious to place every obstacle in the way of such a result and have gone to considerable lengths to produce arguments to show that the application for permission in such instances was itself invalid. Accordingly, there are a number of judgments[8] dealing with the obligation of applicants to adhere to the Regulations. In *Dunne's Case* itself, the local authority sought to argue that the failure of the developer to give his full name and to comply with one or two relatively minor requirements was sufficient to invalidate the application, but this argument was rejected by Pringle J. who held that the particular requirements involved were directory only and not mandatory.

MANDATORY OR DIRECTORY?

The issue as to whether the Regulations are directory or mandatory has produced a number of fairly recent decisions[8] and no general rule to the effect either that the

---

[6] See page 195.
[7] [1974] I.R.45. The view of the Supreme Court in *The State (Abenglen)* v. *Dublin Corporation* (p. 319) appears to be that if a planning authority gives notices of any decision, even if ultra vires, within the statutory period, then there can be no question of a default permission. (See also the remarks of McCarthy J. in *Creedon* v. *Dublin Corporation,* (page 234).
[8] See page 184.

Regulations are all of them mandatory or all of them directory, can be laid down. The Courts have dealt with each case individually, so that for example, the failure of applicants to publish notices which convey a true description of the extent and nature of the development has been held fatal, whereas an appeal against a planning decision to An Bord Pleanala which complied with the appropriate regulations in every point, save that the letter intimating the appeal did not set out the grounds, has been held to be valid.

PLANNING AUTHORITY ALSO BOUND BY REGULATIONS
Another aspect of this issue has arisen in cases[9] where the planning authority has sought by letter further information from the applicants. It can be said that if an application for planning permission is bound by the Regulations, so too is the planning authority, so that a failure by the planning authority to send a genuine notice for further information will not have the effect of suspending the time, with the result that the applicant may obtain a planning permission by default unless a decision is made within the appropriate period.

WIDE POWERS OF PLANNING AUTHORITY
Once a planning authority adheres to the Regulations, however, it seems that it has very wide powers to impose conditions on the application under Section 26 of the 1963 Act. This matter came up for consideration in *State (Abenglen)* v. *Dublin Corporation*.[10] In that case the applicant for permission argued that because the effect of the conditions attaching to the grant of outline planning permission, was such as to permit a significantly different development to that which was sought, therefore the planning authority had not adjudicated on the application submitted, but on an entirely different application. D'Arcy J. in the High Court ruled against this contention, thereby implying that the powers to impose conditions will be interpreted liberally in favour of a planning authority providing it is a bona fide exercise. The case was decided on an entirely different point in the Supreme Court,[11] namely on whether the Court should exercise its discretion to grant relief in circumstances which included a failure by the applicant to appeal to Au Bord Pleanala.

In *Pine Valley Developments Ltd.* v. *Dublin County Council*, Barrington J. considered the relationship between the application for approval consequent on an outline permission and the terms of the outline permission itself. He decided that a planning authority when considering an application for approval must consider it within the context of the outline permission and may not re-open matters which were decided by the grant of the outline permission; he also decided that an approval application affecting only portion of the site covered by the outline permission was valid[12] and lastly that because there was no challenge to the validity of any decision the case was not barred by the two-month limitation period.[13] In the Supreme Court this case turned on an entirely different point, namely, the invalidity of the Minister's outline permission because the development breached

---

[9] See pages 321 ff.
[10] See page 210.
[11] See page 316.
[12] See Regulation 19(3) of S.I. No. 65 of 1977.
[13] Section 82(3A) of the 1963 Act.

the provisions of the development plan and the Minister had not been requested to
authorise this by the planning authority.[14]

INTERPRETATION

There has been a divergence of judicial opinion as to whether or not a planning
permission will be interpreted by reference only to documents (including the grant
of permission itself) on the planning file or whether the Court will have regard to
surrounding circumstances as well. In the *Readymix* case planning permission was
described as an appendage to the title of the land[15] and the Supreme Court held
that the permission was to be interpreted objectively, that is by reference only to
documents available for public scrutiny. Private understandings between individuals
who might be unavailable to give evidence when the permission fell to be interpreted
were not to be relied upon by the Court. Subsequently, however, in the same Court
in *Dun Laoghaire Corporation* v. *Frescati Estates Limited*[16] a different line
was taken. Evidence was considered concerning negotiations and applications
between the applicant and the planning authority over the years for the purpose of
interpreting the letter of application for planning permission. This approach was
also adopted by Gannon J. in *Jack Barrett (Builders) Limited.* v. *Dublin County
Council.*[17]

IMPLICATIONS OF THE GRANT

It was suggested by Kenny J. in *Moran* v. *Dublin Corporation*[18] that a grant of full
planning permission implied the availability of services for development. This topic
merited only a passing reference in that case, but is becoming one of crucial
importance especially in suburban areas where sewerage capacity may be limited.
More recently the topic has been dealt with in *State (Finglas Industrial Estates
Limited).* v. *Dublin County Council* and *Short* v. *Dublin County Council.*[19]

CONDITIONS RESERVING DETAILS FOR FURTHER
CONSIDERATION

It was suggested in *Keleghan and Others* v. *Corby and Dublin Corporation*[20] that
the imposition of a condition that details of the development be submitted to the
planning authorities for later agreement could pose serious difficulties regarding
the validity of the planning permission, so conditioned.[21]

However, a planning permission containing a similar condition was under review
in *The State (Foxrock Construction Co. Ltd.)* v. *Dublin County Council*[22] and
attracted no adverse comment on this ground.

---

[14] The Minister (and the Board presumably) is, therefore, strictly bound by the statutory
provisions. The Board may now authorise a development which breaches the relevant
development plan – see section 14(8) of the 1976 Act. Section 6 of the 1982 Act was passed
to reverse the effect of the decision in the *Pine Valley* case.
[15] Henchy J. in the *Readymix* case. See page 198.
[16] See page 197.
[17] See Appendix C.
[18] 109 I.L.T.R. 57 at 63.
[19] Page 224. Compare the High and Supreme Court decisions in *Short* v. *Dublin Council* at
page 423. Compare also the remarks of McCarthy J. in the *Creedon* case (page 234.)
[20] Page 234.
[21] Compare section 14(4) of the 1976 Act.
[22] Page 227.

PERMISSION AS RE-ZONING

In *Pine Valley Developments Ltd.* v. *Dublin County Council*, Barrington J. held that a planning authority considering an application for an approval is confined within the four walls of the outline permission granted in respect of the lands. Providing the application for approval is made well within the 'appropriate' period,[23] therefore, it would appear that the grant of an outline planning permission effectively zones the lands in question for the use granted by the outline planning permission.

An application to a planning authority which would involve a departure from the use of the land permitted by the Development Plan can be granted by them only after a somewhat elaborate publication procedure,[24] or in any event on appeal by An Bord Pleanala.[25]

In *Dublin Corporation* v. *Kevans and Others*,[26] Finlay P. pointed out that if he refused to grant an injunction restraining an unauthorised user, he would effectively be re-zoning the premises in question from residential to office use.

DURATION OF PLANNING PERMISSION

Section 2 of the Act of 1982 provides for a limit of duration of planning permissions. The introduction of the norm of five years is staggered however so that permissions granted before November of 1976 will not expire before the 31st October, 1983; those granted between the 1st November, 1976 and 31st October, 1982, will expire on the 31st October, 1987 or seven years after the date of the grant, whichever is *earlier*; and those granted after the 1st November, 1982, will normally have a five year life. These provisions are subject to two exceptions, namely under Section 3 the planning authority has a power to grant permission for a period of more than five years and secondly, if the five-year period established under Section 29 of the Act of 1976 has been extended to a date later than that provided for, the later date applies.

Provision is also made at Section 4 of the Act of 1982 for an extension of these time limits where substantial works[27] were carried out during the relevant period and for a further extension where failure to carry out the works during the extended period was due to circumstances outside the control of the developer.

Repealed portions of Section 29 of the Act of 1976 had provided for the granting of a 'development certificate' which would certify the amount of any permitted

---

[23] That is the period 5 or more years specified by section 2 of the 1982 Act as varied by section 3 or extended by section 4 of the said Act as the case may be. It seems that 'permission' does not include 'approval' (compare the definitions in the Statutory Instruments of 1977 and 1982); accordingly by section 2(1) of the 1982 Act an approval dies with the outline permission so that there is little point in applying for approval unless there is sufficient life left in the outline permission to enable at least substantial development to take place because only in such circumstances is there jurisdiction to extend the appropriate period (see section 4(1)(c)(ii) of the 1982 Act).

[24] Section 26(3)(a) of the 1963 Act.

[25] Section 14(8) of the 1976 Act.

[26] Page 371.

[27] Under the original extension provisions of section 29 of the 1976 Act now repealed, there was a general jurisdiction to extend the life of a planning permission: under the 1982 Act substantial works are a pre-requisite for such extension. 'Substantial' is not defined: it is suggested that substantial works comprise either works which show an intention of completing the scheme or alternatively, works which would be an eye-sore or otherwise contrary to good planning or development if left unfinished.

development which was complete on the expiration of the relevant planning permission; and also a 'waiver notice' waiving compliance with any condition attaching to a planning permission. Both of these have now been repealed[28] with a saver for any existing development certificates or waiver notices or applications for the same.

Finally it is worth noting that the general rule that estoppel does not apply so as to force a Statutory Authority to act beyond or outside of the scope of its powers, has been applied to planning authorities in *Dublin Corporation* v. *McGrath*.

LOCAL GOVERNMENT (PLANNING AND DEVELOPMENT) ACT, 1963

PART IV

CONTROL OF DEVELOPMENT AND OF RETENTION OF CERTAIN STRUCTURES, ETC.

24 – (1) Subject to the provisions of this Act, permission shall be required under this Part of this Act –
  (a) in respect of any development of land, being neither exempted development nor development commenced before the appointed day,[29] and
  (b) in the case of a structure which existed immediately before the appointed day and is on the commencement of that day an unauthorised structure, for the retention of the structure.

(2) A person shall not carry out any development in respect of which permission is required by subsection (1) of this section save under and in accordance with a permission granted under this Part of this Act.

(3) Any person who contravenes subsection (2) of this section shall be guilty of an offence.[30]

(4) In a prosecution for an offence under this section –
  (a) it shall not be necessary for the prosecution to show, and it shall be assumed until the contrary is shown by the defendant, that the development in question was neither exempted development nor development commenced before the appointed day.

25. – (1) The Minister shall by regulations[31] (in this Act referred to as permission regulations) provide for –
  (a) the grant of permissions for the development of land, and
  (b) the grant of permissions for the retention of structures which existed immediately before the appointed day and are on that day unauthorised structures,
and such permissions may be granted on an application in that behalf made to the

[28] S. 15 (2)(b) of the Act of 1982.
[29] But see s. 40 of the Act of 1963.
[30] By ss. 8 and 9 respectively of the Act of 1982 this offence is punishable on indictment by a fine not exceeding £10,000 or two years imprisonment or both and if tried summarily by a fine of £800 or six months imprisonment or both. See p. 325. By s. 15 (1) of the Act of 1982 all words after 'offence' were repealed. These words had set fines for the offence, continuing offences which could be imposed on summary conviction.
[31] These are S.I. No. 65 of 1977, Part IV as amended. See pp. 144 ff.

planning authority in accordance with the provisions of the regulations[32] and subject to any requirements of or made pursuant to the regulations being complied with by the applicant.

(2) Regulations under this section may, in particular and without prejudice to the generality of the foregoing subsection, make provision for –

 (*a*) applications, expressed to be outline applications, for permission for development subject to the subsequent approval[33] of the planning authority.

 (*b*) requiring any applicants to publish any specified notices[34] with respect to their applications,

 (*c*) requiring any applicants to furnish to the Minister and to any other specified persons any specified information with respect to their applications,

 (*cc*) in cases in which the development to which the application relates will, in the opinion of the relevant planning authority, cost more than an amount specified in the regulations, the furnishing to that authority of a written study of what, if any, effect the proposed development, if carried out, would have on the environment relative to the place where that development is to take place.[35]

 (*d*) requiring any applicants to submit any further information relative to their applications (including any information as to any estate or interest in or right over land),

 (*dd*) enabling planning authorities to invite an applicant to submit to them revised plans or other drawings modifying,[36] or other particulars providing for the modification of, the development to which the application relates and, in case such plans, drawings, or particulars are submitted to a planning authority in response to such an invitation, enabling the authority in deciding the application to grant a permission or an approval for the relevant development as modified by all or any of such plans, drawings, or particulars,[37]

 (*e*) requiring the production of any evidence to verify any particulars of information given by any applicants,

 (*f*) requiring planning authorities to furnish to the Minister and to any other specified persons any specified information with respect to any applications and the manner in which they have been dealt with,

 (*g*) requiring planning authorities to publish any specified notices with respect to any applications or decisions on applications.

26. – (1) Where –

 (*a*) application is made to a planning authority in accordance with permission

---

[32] The consequences of non-compliance with the regulations may or may not be fatal; contrast *Monaghan U.D.C.* v. *Alf-a-Bet Ltd.* with *State (Elm Developments Ltd.)* v. *An Bord Pleanala.* See pp. 188 and 283

[33] An approval does not extend the duration of the outline permission, but dies with it. Compare definitions of 'permission' and 'approval' in Regulation 13 of S.I. 65 of 1977.

[34] For the effect of failure to comply see pp. 183 ff.

[35] Added by s. 39(a) of the Act of 1976.

[36] In *State (Abenglen Properties Limited)* v. *Dublin Corporation* D'Arcy J. held that this was an optional power only. See p. 215.

[37] Added by s. 39(b) of the Act of 1976.

regulations for permission for the development of land or for an approval required by such regulations, and

(*b*) any requirements relating to the application of or made under such regulations are complied with,

the authority may decide to grant the permission or approval subject to or without conditions or to refuse it; and in dealing with any such application the planning authority shall be restricted to considering the proper planning and development of the area of the. authority (including the preservation and improvement of the amenities thereof), regard being had to the provisions of the development plan, the provisions of any special amenity area order relating to the said area and the matters referred to in subsection (2) of this section.

(2) Conditions under subsection (1) of this section may, without prejudice to the generality[38] of that subsection, include all or any of the following conditions:

(*a*) conditions for regulating the development or use of any land which adjoins, abuts or is adjacent to the land to be developed and which is under the control of the applicant, so far as appears to the planning authority to be expedient for the purposes of or in connection with the development authorised by the permission,

(*b*) conditions for requiring the carrying out of works (including the provision of car parks) which the planning authority consider are required for the purposes of the development authorised by the permission,

(*bb*) conditions for requiring the taking of measures to reduce or prevent –

  (i) the emission of any noise or vibration from any structure comprised in the development authorised by the permission which might give reasonable cause for annoyance either to persons in any premises in the neighbourhood of the development or to persons lawfully using any public place in that neighbourhood, or

  (ii) the intrusion of any noise or vibration which might give reasonable cause for annoyance to any person lawfully occupying any such structure.[39]

(*c*) conditions for requiring provision of open spaces,

(*d*) conditions for requiring the planting of trees, shrubs or other plants or the landscaping of structures or other land,

(*e*) conditions for requiring the giving of security for satisfactory completion of the proposed development (including maintenance until taken in charge by the local authority concerned of roads, open spaces, car parks, sewers, watermains or drains),

(*f*) conditions for requiring roads, open spaces, car parks, sewers, watermains or drains in excess of the immediate[40] needs of the proposed development,

---

[38] Whilst the jurisdiction to attach conditions to the grant of a planning permission is undoubtedly general and not limited to those set out in sub-s. (2), all conditions must be fairly related to planning and development. See *Dunne* v. *Dublin County Council* at p. 187.

[39] Added by s. 39(c) of the Act of 1976.

[40] It is understood that An Bord Pleanala has recently imposed a condition providing for a payment by the planning authority to the developer where he was required to carry out service works in excess of the immediate needs of the development. See also s. 26(7), and Regulation 25(*e*) of S. I. No. 65 of 1977.

(g) conditions for requiring contribution[41] (either in one sum or by instalments) towards any expenditure (including expenditure on the acquisition of land and expenditure consisting of a payment under subsection (7) of this section) that was incurred by any local authority in respect of works (including the provision of open spaces) which have facilitated the proposed development, being works commenced neither earlier than the 1st day of August, 1962, nor earlier than seven years before the grant of permission for the development,

(h) conditions for requiring contribution (either in one sum or by instalments) towards any expenditure (including expenditure on the acquisition of land) that is proposed to be incurred by any local authority in respect of works (including the provision of open spaces) facilitating the proposed development, subject to stipulations[42] providing for –

    (i) where the proposed works are, within a specified period, not commenced, the return of the contribution or the instalments thereof paid during that period (as may be appropriate),

    (ii) where the proposed works are, within the said period, carried out in part only or in such manner as to facilitate the proposed development to a lesser extent, the return of a proportionate part of the contribution or the instalments thereof paid during that period (as may be appropriate), and

    (iii) payment of interest on the contribution or any instalments thereof that have been paid (as may be appropriate) so long and in so far as it is or they are retained unexpended by the local authority.

(i) conditions for requiring compliance in respect of the land with any rules made by the planning authority under subsection (6) of this section,

(j) conditions for requiring the removal of any structures authorised by the permission, or the discontinuance of any use of the land so authorised, at the expiration of a specified period,[43] and the carrying out of any works required for the reinstatement of land at the expiration of that period.

(3)[44](a) In a case in which the development concerned would contravene materially the development plan or any special amenity area order, a planning authority may, notwithstanding any other provision of this Act, decide to grant permission under this section, provided that the following requirements are complied with before the decision is made, namely,

    (i) notice in the prescribed form of the intention of the planning authority to consider deciding to grant the permission shall be published in at least one daily newspaper circulating in their area.

    (ii) copies of the notice shall be given to the applicant and to any person who has submitted an objection in writing to the develop-

---

[41] An order for payment of the outstanding balance of a contribution was made by Finlay P. on the application of Athlone Urban District Council under s. 27 (2) of the Act of 1976.

[42] The power to attach such conditions is clearly subject to the itemised stipulations. It is not stated that the stipulations should be written into the conditions; a reference to the sub-paragraph would however, seem essential – see S. 26 (8).

[43] Not affected by the 'withering' provisions of the Act of 1982 – see s. 2 (2) (a)(ii) of that Act.

[44] Substituted by s. 39(d) of the Act of 1976.

ment to which the application relates,

   (iii) any objection or representation as regards the making of a decision to grant permission and which is received by the planning authority not later than twenty-one days after the first publication of the notice shall be duly considered by the authority, and

   (iv) a resolution shall be passed by the authority requiring that a decision to grant permission be made.

(b) It shall be necessary for the passing of a resolution referred to in paragraph (a) of this subsection that the number of the members of the planning authority voting in favour of the resolution exceeds one-third of the total number of the members of the planning authority, and the requirement of this paragraph is in addition to and not in substitution for any other requirement applying in relation to such a resolution.

(c) Where notice is given pursuant to section 4 of the City and County Management (Amendment) Act, 1955, of intention to propose a resolution which, if passed, would require the manager to decide to grant a permission under this section, then if the manager is of opinion that the development concerned would contravene materially the development plan or any special amenity area order, he shall within seven days of the receipt by him of the notice make an order (a copy of which shall be furnished by him to each of the signatories to the notice) requiring that the provisions of subparagraphs (i), (ii) and (iii) of paragraph (a) of this subsection shall be complied with in the particular case and the order, when made, shall operate to cause the relevant notice given pursuant to the said section 4 to be of no further effect.

(d) If a resolution referred to in paragraph (a)(iv) of this subsection is duly passed, the manager shall decide[45] to grant the relevant permission.

(4)(a) Where –

   (i) an application is made to a planning authority in accordance with permission regulations for permission under this section or for an approval required by such regulations,

   (ii) any requirements relating to the application of or made under such regulations are complied with, and

   (iii) the planning authority do not give notice[46] to the applicant of their decision within the appropriate period,

   a decision by the planning authority to grant the permission or approval shall be regarded as having been given on the last day of that period.[47]

---

[45] It is straining language to provide that a manager 'shall decide'. See discussion in Keane: 'The Law of Local Government in the Republic of Ireland' pp. 180 ff.

[46] See s. 7; also *Freeney* v. *Bray U.D.C.* at p. 291. If an ultra vires decision is notified within time there will not be a default permission. See *State (Abenglen)* v. *Dublin Corporation* (p. 319) and *Creedon* v. *Dublin Corporation* (p. 234). The 'appropriate period' for sub-s. 4(a) (i.e. two months, or two months extended by consent) should not be confused with either 'the appropriate period' for sub s. 5(a) (i.e. one month or 21 days depending who the appellant is) or 'the appropriate period' for ss. 2 and 4 of the Act of 1982 (i.e. the several specified periods during which different categories of planning permission continue to have effect). This 'appropriate period' commences to run only when any fees payable under s. 10 of the Act of 1982 is received (see s. 10 (2)(b) of the said Act). It may also be extended by s. 10 (b) of the Housing Act, 1969.

[47] For an example of where the Court held a default permission was deemed to have been

(b) In paragraph (a) of this subsection 'the appropriate period' means –

    (i) in case any notice or notices requiring the applicant to publish any notice, to give further information[48] or to produce evidence in respect of the application has or have been served by the planning authority pursuant to permission regulations within the period of two months beginning on the day of receipt by the planning authority of the application – within the period of two months beginning on the day on which the notice or notices has or have been complied with,

    (ii) in case a notice referred to in subsection (3) of this section is published in relation to the application, within the period of two months beginning on the day on which the notice is first published,[49]

    (iii) in any other case – within the period of two months beginning on the day of receipt,[50] {by the planning authority of the application.

(4A) If, but only if, before the expiration of the appropriate period within the meaning of subsection (4)(a) of this section the applicant for a permission under this section gives to the planning authority in writing his consent to the extension by them of that period, the planning authority may extend the period and in case, pursuant to the foregoing, a planning authority make an extension, subsection (4)(b) of this section shall, as regards the particular case to which the extension relates, be construed and have effect in accordance with the extension.[51]

(5)(a) Any person may, at any time before the expiration of the appropriate period, appeal to the Minister[52] against a decision of a planning authority under this section.

  (b) Where an appeal is brought under this subsection from a decision of a planning authority and is not withdrawn, the Minister[52] shall determine the application as if it had been made to him in the first instance and his decision shall operate to annul the decision of the planning authority as from the time when it was given; and the provisions of subsections (1) and (2) of this section shall apply, subject to any necessary modifications, in relation to the determination of an application by the Minister[52] on appeal under this subsection as they apply in relation to the determination under this section of an application by a planning authority.

  (c) In paragraph (a) of this subsection 'the appropriate period'[53] means –

    (i) in case the appellant is the applicant – the period of one month beginning on the day of receipt by him of the decision,

---

given see *Dunne* v. *Dublin County Council* (p. 184).

[48] But it must be a genuine request for further information. See *State (Conlan Construction Limited)* v. *Cork County Council* (p.321 and other cases there cited).

[49] Substituted by s. 39(e) of the Act of 1976.

[50] Finlay P. held in *Genport Limited* v. *Dublin Corporation* (No. 12718P of 1981, delivered 13th Jan. 1982) that an application which was made in several stages was received on the day it was finally submitted. See p. 288.

[51] Inserted by s. 39(f) of the Act of 1976.

[52] The appeal is to the Board: s.14 (9)(10) of the Act of 1976. The word 'Minister' remains unamended, however, but the appeal is to be construed as an appeal to the Board.

[53] Not to be confused with 'the appropriate period' for sub. s. 4 (a) or ss. 2 and 4 of the Act of 1982, as defined in s. 2 (5) of that Act. See also footnote 46 *ante*.

(ii) in any other case – the period of twenty-one days beginning on the day of the giving of the decision.

(6) A planning authority may make rules for regulating the manner in which advertisement structures are to be affixed to structures or other land.

(7) In a case in which a condition referred to in paragraph (*f*) of subsection (2) of this section is attached to any permission or approval granted under this section, a contribution towards such of the relevant roads, open spaces, car parks, sewers, watermains or drains as are constructed shall be made by the local authority[54] who will be responsible for their maintenance, and the contribution shall be such as may be agreed upon between that local authority and the person carrying out the works or, in default of agreement, as may be determined by the Minister.

(8) A decision given under this section and the notification of such decision shall –

> (*a*) in case the decision is made by a planning authority and is one by which any permission or approval is refused or is granted subject to conditions, comprise a statement specifying the reasons for the refusal or the imposition of conditions, and
>
> (*b*) in case the decision is made on appeal, comprise a statement specifying the reasons for the decision,

provided that where a condition imposed is a condition described in paragraph (*a*) or any subsequent paragraph of subsection (2) of this section, a reference to the paragraph of the said subsection (2) in which the condition is described shall be sufficient to meet the requirements of this subsection.[55]

> (9)(*a*) Where the planning authority decide under this section to grant a permission or approval –
>
>> (i) in case no appeal is taken against the decision, they shall make the grant[56] as soon as may be after the expiration of the period for the taking by the applicant of an appeal or, in a case to which subsection (4) of this section applies, of the period for the taking of an appeal[57] otherwise than by the applicant,
>>
>> (ii) in case an appeal or appeals is or are taken against the decision, they shall not make the grant unless as regards the appeal, or as may be appropriate, each of the appeals—
>>
>> (I) it is withdrawn, or,
>>
>> (II) it is dismissed by the Board pursuant to section 16 or 18 of the Local Government (Planning and Development) Act, 1983, or,
>>
>> (III) in relation to it a direction is given to the authority by the Board pursuant to section 19 of the said Act,
>>
>> and, in the case of the withdrawal or dismissal of an appeal, or of all such appeals as may be appropriate, they shall make the grant as soon as may be after such withdrawal or dismissal and, in the

---

[54] See *Killiney and Ballybrack Development Association Limited* v. *Minister for Local Government and Another (No. 2)* (Sup. Ct., 24th April, 1978).

[55] Substituted by s. 39 (9) of the Act of 1976.

[56] If a planning authority refuse to make the grant the applicant should seek an order of mandamus: such application is not caught by the two-month time limit laid down in s. 82 (3A) of the Act of 1963 – see Barrington J. in *State (Pine Valley Developments Limited)* v. *Dublin County Council* at p. 207.

[57] The right of a third party to appeal a default permission is preserved.

case of such a direction, they shall make the grant in accordance with the direction as soon as may be after the giving by the Board of the direction.[57a]

(b) Where the Minister decides on appeal under this section to grant a permission or approval, he shall make the grant as soon as may be after the decision.

(10)(a) Where a permission or approval is granted under this section subject to any one or more of the conditions referred to in paragraphs (e), (g) and (h) of subsection (2) of this section, the permission or approval shall be of no effect and shall be disregarded until the condition or conditions has or have been complied with.

(b) Paragraph (a) of this subsection shall not apply where a condition referred to in paragraph (g) or (h) of subsection (2) of this section requires a contribution by instalments except in respect of development which is the subject of the permission or approval and is carried out after default in paying an instalment of the contribution.

(11) A person shall not be entitled solely by reason of a permission or approval under this section to carry out any development.[58]

27. – (1) Where, with respect to a structure which existed immediately before the appointed day and which is on the commencement of that day an unauthorised structure, –

(a) application is made to the planning authority in accordance with permission regulations for permission for the retention[59] of the structure, and

(b) any requirements relating to the application of or made under such regulations are complied with,

the authority may decide to grant the permission subject to or without conditions or to refuse it; and in dealing with any such application the planning authority shall be restricted to considering the proper planning and development of the area of the authority (including the preservation and improvement of the amenities thereof), regard being had to the provisions of the development plan and the provisions of any special amenity area order relating to the said area.

(2) Conditions under subsection (1) of this section may, without prejudice to the generality of that subsection, include all or any of the following conditions:

(a) conditions for regulating the development or use of any land which adjoins, abuts or is adjacent to the structure and which is under the control of the applicant, so far as appears to the planning authority to be expedient for the purposes of or in connection with the retention of the structure,

(b) conditions for requiring the carrying out of works (including the provision of car parks) which the planning authority consider are required if the retention of the structure is to be permitted,

---

[57a] As amended by s. 20 of the Local Government (Planning and Development) Act, 1983.

[58] See for example *O'Callaghan* v. *The Commissioners of Public Works in Ireland and Others*, unreported decision of McWilliam J. delivered 4th October, 1982.

[59] Retention permission is excluded from the 'withering' provisions of the Act of 1982: see s. 2 (2)(a)(i) of that Act. The power to grant permission includes power to retain an unauthorised use: see s. 28 (1). Retention permission takes effect from the date of construction or commencement of use: see s. 28 (2).

    (c) conditions for requiring provision of space around the structure,

    (d) conditions for requiring the planting of trees, shrubs or other plants or the landscaping of the structure or other land,

    (e) conditions for requiring compliance in respect of the structure with any rules made by the planning authority under subsection (6) of section 26 of this Act,

    (f) conditions for requiring the removal[60] of the structure at the expiration of a specified period, and the carrying out of any works required for the reinstatement of land at the expiration of that period.

(3)(a) Where –

    (i) an application is made to a planning authority in accordance with permission regulations for permission under this section,

    (ii) any requirements relating to the application of or made under such regulations are complied with, and

    (iii) the planning authority do not give notice to the applicant of their decision within the appropriate period,[61]

a decision by the planning authority to grant the permission shall be regarded as having been given on the last day of that period.

    (b) In paragraph (a) of this subsection 'the appropriate period'[61] means –

    (i) in case any notice or notices requiring the applicant to publish any notice, to give further information or to produce evidence in respect of the application has or have been served by the planning authority pursuant to permission regulations within the period of two months beginning on the day of receipt by the planning authority of the application – within the period of two months beginning on the day on which the notice or notices has or have been complied with,

    (ii) in any other case, within the period of two months beginning on the day of receipt by the planning authority of the application.

(4)(a) Any person may, at any time before the expiration of the appropriate period, appeal to the Minister[62] against a decision of a planning authority under this section.

    (b) Where an appeal is brought under this subsection from a decision of a planning authority and is not withdrawn, the Minister shall determine the application as if it had been made to him in the first instance and his decision shall operate to annul the decision of the planning authority as from the time when it was given; and the provisions of subsections (1) and (2) of this section shall apply, subject to any necessary modifications, in relation to the determination of an application by the Minister on appeal under this subsection as they apply in relation to the determination under this section of an application by a planning authority.

    (c) In paragraph (a) of this subsection 'the appropriate period'[63] means –

---

[60] Not affected by the 'withering' provisions of the Act of 1982: see s. 2 (2)(a)(ii) of that Act.
[61] Not to be confused with 'the appropriate period' for sub. s. 4(a) or ss. 2 and 4 of the Act of 1982. The appropriate period will commence to run only when the planning authority is in receipt of any fee payable under s. 10 of the Act of 1982: see s. 10 (2)(b) of that Act.
[62] To be construed as the Board: s. 14 (9)(10) of the Act of 1976.
[63] Not to be confused with 'the appropriate period' for sub-s. 3(a) or ss. 2 and 4 of the Act of 1982.

> (i) in case the appellant is the applicant – the period of one month beginning on the day of receipt by him of the decision,
>
> (ii) in any other case – the period of twenty-one days beginning on the day of the giving of the decision.

(5) A decision given under this section (whether on the original application or on appeal) by which permission is refused or is granted subject to conditions, and the notification of such decision, shall comprise a statement of the reasons[54] for the refusal or the imposition of conditions.

(6)(*a*) Where the planning authority decide under this section to grant a permission –

> (i) in case no appeal is taken against the decision, they shall make the grant[64] as soon as may be after the expiration of the period for the taking by the applicant of an appeal or, in a case to which subsection (3) of this section applies, of the period for the taking of an appeal[65] otherwise than by the applicant,
>
> (ii) in case an appeal or appeals is or are taken against the decision, they shall not make the grant unless the appeal or appeals is or are withdrawn and, in that case, they shall make the grant as soon as may be after the withdrawal.

(*b*) Where the Minister decides on appeal under this section to grant a permission, he shall make the grant as soon as may be after the decision.

(7) A person shall not be entitled solely by reason of a permission under this section to retain any structure.[66]

28. – (1) The power to grant permission to develop land under this Part of this Act shall include power to grant permission for the retention on land of any structures constructed, erected or made on, in, or under the land on or after the appointed day and before the date of the application, or for the continuance of any use of land instituted on or after the appointed day and before the date of the application (whether without permission granted under this Part of this Act or in accordance with permission so granted for a limited period only); and references in this Part of this Act to permission to develop land or to carry out any development of land, and to applications for such permission, shall be construed accordingly.

(2) Any such permission as is mentioned in subsection (1) of this section may be granted so as to take effect from the date on which the structures were constructed, erected or made, or the use was instituted, or from the expiration of the said period, as the case may be.

(3) Where permission has been granted by virtue of subsection (1) of this section for the retention on land of any structures, or for the continuance of the use of land, subject to any condition, the references in subsections (1) and (3) of section 31 of this Act to any conditions subject to which permission was granted in respect of any development include references to any such condition.

(4) The power conferred by subsection (1) of this section is exercisable not only where development has been carried out without permission or where previous permission has been granted for a limited period only, but also so as to permit the

---

[64] See fn. 54, *ante*.
[65] See fn. 57, *ante*.
[66] See fn. 58, *ante*.

retention of structures or the continuance of any use of land without complying with some condition subject to which a previous permission under this Part of this Act was granted.

(5) Where permission to develop land or for the retention of a structure is granted under this Part of this Act, then, except as may be otherwise provided by the permission, the grant of permission shall enure for the benefit of the land or structure[67] and of all persons for the time being interested therein, but without prejudice to the provisions of this Part of this Act with respect to the revocation and modification of permissions granted thereunder.

(6) Where permission is granted under this Part of this Act for the construction, erection or making of a structure, the grant of permission may specify the purposes for which the structure may or may not be used, and in case such grant specifies use as a dwelling as a purpose for which the structure may be used, the permission may also be granted subject to a condition specifying that the use as a dwelling shall be restricted to use by persons of a particular class[68] or description and that provision to that effect shall be embodied in an agreement pursuant to section 38 of this Act and if no purpose is so specified, the permission shall be construed as including permission to use the structure for the purpose for which it is designed.[69]

(7)(*a*) Where permission to develop land is granted under this Part of this Act for a limited period only, nothing in this Part of this Act shall be construed as requiring permission to be obtained thereunder for the resumption,[70] at the expiration of that period, of the use of the land for the purpose for which it was normally used before the permission was granted.

(*b*) In determining for the purposes of this subsection the purposes for which land was normally used before the grant of permission, no account shall be taken of any use of the land begun in contravention of the provisions of this Part of this Act.

30. – (1) Subject to the provisions of this section, if the planning authority decide that it is expedient that any permission to develop land granted under this Part of this Act should be revoked or modified, they may, by notice served on the owner and on the occupier of the land affected and on any other person who in their opinion will be affected by the revocation or modification, revoke or modify the permission.[71]

---

[67] Henchy J. described planning permission as an 'appendage to the title to the property' in the *Readymix* case (see p. 203): planning permission is to be construed by reference to objective documentary materials: see p. 110.

[68] Most typically by restricting occupancy of a rural dwelling to the applicant and members of his family. See *Fawcett Properties Ltd.* v. *Buckingham Co. Co.* ([1961] A.C. 636). The words between 'the structure was' and 'and if no purpose is specified' substituted by s. 39(h) of the Act of 1976.

[69] See Barrington J.'s reasoning in *Galway Corporation* v. *Connaught Protein Limited* (see p. 70), and the *Readymix* case for a discussion of the 'purpose' for which a structure is designed.

[70] But for this provision the position would be doubtful. See *Hartley* v. *Minister of Housing and Local Government* [1970] 1 O.B. 413 where cessation of use amounted to abandonment of the earlier use so that resumption constituted a material change.

[71] There is no power to revoke or modify an approval: see *State (Cogley)* v. *Dublin Corporation and another* at p. 221. However, since an approval dies with the relevant outline permission, revocation of the latter renders the former ineffective.

(2) In deciding, pursuant to this section, whether it is expedient to serve a notice under this section, the planning authority shall be restricted to considering the proper planning and development of the area of the authority (including the preservation and improvement of the amenities thereof), regard being had to the provisions of the development plan and the provisions of any special amenity order relating to the said area.

(2A) A planning authority shall neither revoke nor modify a permission under this section unless there has been a change in circumstances relating to the proper planning and development of the area concerned and such change in circumstances has occurred,

(*a*) in case a notice relating to the permission is served under this section and is annulled, since the annulment of the notice,

(*b*) in case no notice is so served, since the granting of the permission.

(2B) In case a planning authority pursuant to this section revoke or modify a permission, they shall specify in their decision the change in circumstances which warranted the revocation or modification.[72]

(3) Any person on whom a notice under this section is served may, at any time before the day (not being earlier than one month after such service) specified in that behalf in the notice, appeal to the Minister[73] against the notice.

(4) Where an appeal is brought under this section against a notice, the Minister may confirm the notice with or without modifications or annul the notice, and the provisions of subsection (2) of this section shall apply, subject to any necessary modifications, in relation to the deciding of an appeal under this subsection by the Minister as they apply in relation to the making of a decision by a planning authority.

(5) The power conferred by this section to revoke or modify permission to develop land may be exercised –

(*a*) where the permission relates to the carrying out of works, at any time before those works have been commenced or, in the case of works which have been commenced and which, consequent on the making of a variation in the development plan, will contravene such plan, at any time before those works have been completed,

(*b*) where the permission relates to a change of the use of any land, at any time before the change has taken place,

but the revocation or modification of permission for the carrying out of works shall not affect so much of the works as has been previously carried out.

(6) The provisions of section 29 of this Act shall apply in relation to a notice under this section revoking permission to develop land or modifying any such permission by the imposition of conditions and which is confirmed on appeal (whether with or without modification), as they apply in relation to the refusal of an application for such permission or the grant of such an application subject to conditions, and in any such case the said section 29 shall have effect subject to the following modifications:

(i) in paragraph (*c*) of subsection (1), for 'in a case where permission to develop the land was granted as aforesaid subject to conditions' there shall be substituted 'in a case where the permission was

---

[72] Sub.-ss. (2A) and (2B) inserted by s. 39(*i*) of the Act of 1976.
[73] Construed as the Board: s. 14 (9)(10) of the Act of 1976.

modified by the imposition of conditions';

(ii) for paragraph (i) of the proviso to subsection (4) there shall be substituted the following paragraph:

|'(i) if it appears to the Minister to be expedient so to do he may, in lieu of confirming the purchase notice, cancel the notice revoking the permission or, where the notice modified the permission by the imposition of conditions, revoke or amend those conditions so far as appears to him to be required in order to enable the land to be rendered capable of reasonably beneficial use by the carrying out of the development in respect of which the permission was granted.'

(7) A notice under this section shall state the reasons for which it is given and particulars of it shall be entered in the register.

(8) The revocation or modification under this section of a permission shall be a reserved function.

38. – (1) A planning authority may enter into an agreement with any person interested in land in their area for the purpose of restricting or regulating the development or use of the land, either permanently or during such period as may be specified by the agreement, and any such agreement may contain such incidental and consequential provisions (including provisions of a financial character) as appear to the planning authority to be necessary or expedient for the purposes of the agreement.

(1A) A planning authority in entering into an agreement under this section may join with any body which is a prescribed authority for the purposes of section 21 of this Act.[74]

(2) An agreement made under this section with any person interested in land may be enforced by the planning authority or any body joined with them against persons deriving title under that person in respect of that land as if the planning authority or such body, as may be appropriate, were possessed of adjacent land and as if the agreement had been expressed to be made for the benefit of that land.

(3) Nothing in this section or in any agreement made thereunder shall be construed as restricting the exercise, in relation to land which is the subject of any such agreement, of any powers exercisable by the Minister, the Board or the planning authority under this Act so long as those powers are not exercised so as to contravene materially the provisions of the development plan, or as requiring the exercise of any such powers so as to contravene materially those provisions.

(4) Particulars of an agreement made under this section shall be entered in the register.

39. – (1) The council of a county shall not effect any development in their county health district which contravenes materially the development plan.

(2) The corporation of a county or other borough shall not effect any development in such borough which contravenes materially the development plan.

---

[74] Sub.-s (1A) inserted by s. 39(*j*) of the Act of 1976. See also s. 39(*k*) and (*l*) for further minor amendments to sub.-ss. (2) and (3).

(3) The council of an urban district shall not effect any development in such district which contravenes materially the development plan.

40. – Notwithstanding anything in this Part of this Act, permission shall not be required under this Part of this Act –
 (*a*) in the case of land which, on the appointed day, is being used temporarily for a purpose other than the purpose for which it is normally used, in respect of the resumption of the use of the land for the last-mentioned purpose;
 (*b*) in the case of land which, on the appointed day, is normally used for one purpose and is also used on occasions, whether at regular intervals or not, for any other purpose, in respect of the use of the land for that other purpose on similar occasions after the appointed day;
 (*c*) in respect of development required by a notice under section 31, 32, 33, 35 or 36 of this Act (disregarding development for which there is in fact permission under this Part of this Act).

41. – (1) A planning authority shall enter in the register:
 (*a*) particulars of any application made to them under this Part of this Act for permission for development or for retention of structures, including the name and address of the applicant, the date of receipt of the application and brief particulars of the development or retention forming the subject of the application,
 (*b*) particulars of any application made to them under this Part of this Act for approval required by permission regulations, including the name and address of the applicant, the date of receipt of the application and brief particulars of the matters forming the subject of the application,
 (*c*) the decision of the planning authority in respect of any such application and the date of the decision,
 (*d*) the date and effect of any decision on appeal of the Minister in respect of any such application,
 (*e*) particulars of any application made by them under subsection (3) of section 26 of this Act, including the date of the sending of the application and brief particulars of the development concerned.
(2) Every such entry consisting of particulars of an application shall be made within the period of seven days beginning on the day of receipt of the application.
(3) Every such entry consisting of a decision on an application shall be made within the period of seven days beginning on the day of the decision.

PART VIII

MISCELLANEOUS

81. – (1) Where (in the case of occupied land) the occuper or (in the case of unoccupied land) the owner refuses to permit the exercise of a power of entry conferred by this Act on a planning authority, the authority shall not exercise the power save pursuant to an order of the District Court approving of the entry.
(2) The following provisions shall have effect in relation to an application for an

order under this section:

(*a*) the application shall be made, on notice to the person who refused to permit the exercise of the power of entry, to the justice of the District Court having jurisdiction in the district court district in which the land or part of the land is situate,

(*b*) the application shall be granted unless the proposed entry is to be made pursuant to section 31, 32 or 33 of this Act on a structure and the said person satisfies the court in a case of non-compliance with a condition, that the condition was complied with or, in any other case, that the structure is not an unauthorised structure,

(*c*) an order made on the application may require that entry shall not be effected during a specified period of one week or less commencing on the date of the order.

(3) Any person who, by act or omission, obstructs an entry approved of by order under this section shall be guilty of an offence and shall be liable on summary conviction to a fine not exceeding twenty-five pounds; and if in the case of a continuing offence the obstruction is continued after conviction, he shall be guilty of a further offence and liable on summary conviction to a fine not exceeding five pounds for each day on which the obstruction is so continued.

. . .

83. – (1) A member of the Board or an authorised person may, subject to the provisions of this section, enter on any land at all reasonable times between the hours of 9 a.m. and 6 p.m. for any purpose connected with this Act.

(2) A member of the Board or an authorised person entering on land under this section may do thereon all things reasonably necessary for the purpose for which the entry is made and, in particular, may survey, make plans, take levels, make excavations, and examine the depth and nature of the subsoil.

(3) Before a member of the Board or an authorised person enters under this section on any land, the appropriate authority shall either obtain the consent (in the case of occupied land) of the occupier or (in the case of unoccupied land) the owner or shall give to the owner or occupier (as the case may be) not less than fourteen days' notice in writing of the intention to make the entry.

(4) A person to whom a notice of intention to enter on land has been given under this section by the appropriate authority may, not later than fourteen days after the giving of such notice, apply, on notice to such authority, to the justice of the District Court having jurisdiction in the district court district in which the land or part of the land is situate for an order prohibiting the entry, and, upon the hearing of the application, the justice may, if he so thinks proper, either wholly prohibit the entry or specify conditions to be observed by the person making the entry.

(5) Where a justice of the District Court prohibits under this section a proposed entry on land, it shall not be lawful for any person to enter under this section on the land, and where a justice of the District Court specifies under this section conditions to be observed by persons entering on land, every person who enters under this section on the land shall observe the conditions so specified.

(6) Subsections (3), (4) and (5) of this section shall not apply to entry for the purposes of Part IV of this Act and, in a case in which such entry is proposed, if the occupier (in the case of occupied land) or the owner (in the case of unoccupied land) refuses to permit the entry –

(*a*) the entry shall not be effected unless it has been authorised by an order of the justice of the District Court having jurisdiction in the district court district in which the land or part of the land is situate and, in the case of occupied land, save after at least twenty-four hours' notice of the intended entry, and of the object thereof, has been given to the occupier.

(b) an application for such an order shall be made on notice (in the case of occupied land) to the occupier or (in the case of unoccupied land) to the owner.

(7) Every person who, by act or omission, obstructs a member of the Board or an authorised person in the lawful exercise of the powers conferred by this section shall be guilty of an offence and shall be liable on summary conviction to a fine not exceeding ten pounds; and if in the case of a continuing offence the obstruction is continued after conviction, he shall be guilty of a further offence and liable on summary conviction to a fine not exceeding five pounds for each day on which the obstruction is so continued.

(8) In this section –

'authorised person' means a person who is appointed by the planning authority, the Minister or the Board to be an authorised person for the purposes of this section;

'appropriate authority' means –

(a) in a case in which the authorised person was appointed by a planning authority – that authority,

(b) in a case in which the authorised person was appointed by the Minister – the Minister, and

(c) in a case in which the authorised person was appointed by the Board – the Board.

84. – (1) Before undertaking the construction of extension of any building (not being a building which is to be constructed or extended in connection with afforestation by the State), a State authority –

(a) shall consult with the planning authority to such extent as may be determined by the Minister, and

(b) if any objections that may be raised by the planning authority are not resolved, shall (save where the construction or extension is being undertaken by the Minister) consult on the objections with the Minister.

(2) In this section 'State authority' means any authority being –

(a) a member of the Government,

(b) the Commissioners of Public Works in Ireland, or

(c) the Irish Land Commission.

. . .

86.[75] – (1) The Minister may make regulations for all or any of the matters set out in section 41 of the Public Health (Ireland) Act, 1878, and section 23 of the Public Health Acts Amendment Act, 1890 (other than paragraph (1) of the said section 41 and the last paragraph of subsection (1) of the said section 23), and accordingly no further bye-laws shall be made under those sections for any of those matters.

Regulations made under this section shall be known and in this Act are referred to as building regulations.

[75] This section, together with ss. 87 and 88 are to become operative by ministerial order made

(2) Building regulations may prescribe standards (expressed in terms of performance, types of material, methods of construction or otherwise) in relation to all or any of the matters specified in the Fifth Schedule to this Act and may prescribe different standards for buildings of different classes.

(3) Building regulations may make provision in relation to –

(*a*) testing of drains and sewers,

(*b*) taking of samples of materials to be used in the construction of buildings, or in the execution of other works.

(4)(*a*) Building regulations may be made with respect to –

(i) structural alterations or extensions of buildings, and buildings so far as affected by alterations or extensions,

(ii) buildings or parts of buildings in cases where any material change takes place in the purposes for which a building or, as the case may be, a part of a building is used, and so far as they relate to the matters mentioned in this subsection, may be made to apply to buildings erected before the date on which the regulations came into force, but, save as aforesaid, shall not apply to buildings erected before that date.

(*b*) For the purposes of this subsection, there shall be deemed to be a material change in the purpose for which a building, or part of a building, is used if –

(i) a building, or part of a building, being a building or part which was not originally constructed for occupation as a house, or which though so constructed has been appropriated to other purposes, becomes used as a house,

(ii) a building, or part of a building, being a building or part, which was originally constructed for occupation as a house by one family only, becomes occupied by two or more families, or

(iii) where regulations contain special provisions with respect to buildings used for any particular purpose, a building, or a part of a building, being a building or part not previously used for that purpose, becomes so used.

(4A) Building regulations may make provision in relation to the special needs of disabled persons.[76]

(5) Any provision contained in building regulations may be made so as to apply generally, or in an area specified in the regulations, and the regulations may

under S. 1 (2)(b) of the Act of 1963. No such order has yet been made. Draft Building regulations have been circulated by the Department of the Environment. The intention is that the Building Regulations will replace Building Bye-Laws. (See sub-s. (1)). Building Bye-Laws are passed by the Sanitary Authority under jurisdiction conferred by s. 41 of the Public Health (Ireland) Act of 1878. Where they apply, two quite separate and distinct permissions are normally required for new structures, namely, Planning Permission and Bye-Law Approval. Building Bye-Laws apply in the 'Dublin Metropolitan' area and the granting of one such permission does not necessarily imply that the other will be forthcoming: see *State (Foxrock Construction Company Limited)* v. *Dublin County Council* at p. 227. s. 87 (6) provides for a default building regulation approval if a decision is not notified within two months: by contrast, s. 52 of the Act of 1878 does not so provide. If no decision is forthcoming within two months it appears that no action can be taken by the Sanitary Authority but this is not the same as providing for a default grant of bye-law approval.

[76] Sub.-s. (4A) inserted by s. 42(d) of the Act of 1976.

contain different provisions for different areas.

(6) Planning authorities shall, in relation to building regulations, have all such functions under the Public Health (Ireland) Act, 1878 (including, in particular, section 42 thereof), as are provided by that Act for them as sanitary authorities in relation to bye-laws under section 41 of that Act.

(7) Building regulations may include such supplemental and incidental provisions as appear to the Minister to be expedient.

(8) If a person contravenes any provision contained in building regulations, he shall be guilty of an offence and shall be liable on summary conviction to a fine not exceeding one hundred pounds;[77] and if in the case of a continuing offence the contravention is continued after conviction, he shall be guilty of a further offence and shall be liable to a further fine not exceeding twenty pounds[78] for each day on which the contravention is so continued.

(9) Building regulations may provide for a combination in one document of –

    (*a*) any application required or authorised under the regulations to be made, and

    (*b*) any application for permission for development under Part IV of this Act; and for the making of such combined applications in such form and manner as may be specified in the regulations.

(10) Section 41 of the Public Health (Ireland) Act, 1878, and section 23 of the Public Health Acts Amendment Act, 1890, shall have effect as if –

    (*a*) in lieu of so much thereof as provides for the making of bye-laws with respect to the matters specified in the said section 41 (other than paragraph (1) thereof) and the said section 23 (other than the last paragraph of subsection (1) thereof), they provided for the making, subject to the provisions of the Local Government (Planning and Development) Act 1963, of regulations with respect to those matters by the Minister, and

    (*b*) the words 'Provided that no bye-law made under this section shall affect any building erected before the passing of this Act' were omitted from the said section 41.

(11) For any reference to bye-laws under section 41 of the Public Health (Ireland) Act, 1878, with respect to any matters set out in that section (other than paragraph (1) thereof) or in subsection (1) of section 23 of the Public Health Acts Amendment Act, 1890 (other than the last paragraph thereof), or to bye-laws under subsection (4) of the said section 23, which occurs in any Act or in any instrument having effect under any Act, there shall be substituted save where the context otherwise requires, a reference to building regulations.

87.[79] – (1) Subject to the provisions of this section, if the Minister, on application made in accordance with the provisions of this section, considers that the operation of any requirement in building regulations would be unreasonable in relation to the particular case to which the application relates, he may, after consultation with the planning authority, give a direction dispensing with or relaxing subject to, or without conditions, that requirement.

---

[77] Increased to £250 by s. 38 (1)(a) of the Act of 1976.
[78] Now £50 by s. 38 (2) of the Act of 1976.
[79] Not yet operative: see fn. 75, *ante*. The words 'subject to or without condition in sub.-s. (1) inserted by s. 42 (e) of the Act of 1976.

(2) If building regulations so provide as regards any requirement contained in the regulations, the power to dispense with or relax that requirement under subsection (1) of this section shall be exercisable by the planning authority (instead of by the Minister after consultation with the planning authority), but any provisions contained by virtue of this subsection in building regulations shall except applications made by local authorities and may except applications of any other description.

(3) Building regulations may provide as regards any requirements contained in the regulations that the foregoing subsections of this section shall not apply.

(4) An application under this section shall be in such form as may be prescribed by building regulations and shall contain such particulars as may be so prescribed.

(5) The application shall be made to the planning authority and, except where the power of giving the direction is exercisable by the planning authority, the planning authority shall at once transmit the application to the Minister and give notice to the applicant that it has been so transmitted.

(6) If within a period of two months beginning with the date of an application (being an application with respect to which the power of giving the direction is exercisable by the planning authority), or within such extended period as may at any time be agreed in writing between the applicant and the planning authority, the planning authority do not notify the applicant of their decision on the application, a decision by the planning authority to grant the application shall be regarded as having been given on the last day of that period.[80]

(7) An application by a local authority shall be made to the Minister.

88.[81] – (1) If a planning authority refuse an application to dispense with or relax any requirement in building regulations which they have power to dispense with or relax, or dispense with or relax such a requirement subject to a condition, the applicant may by notice in writing appeal to the Minister within one month from the date on which the planning authority notify the applicant of their decision.

(2) Where an appeal is brought under this section from a decision of a planning authority and is not withdrawn, the Minister shall determine the application as if it had been made to him in the first instance under section 87 of this Act, as amended by section 42 of the Local Government (Planning and Development) Act, 1976, and his decision shall operate to annul the decision of the planning authority as from the time when it was given; provided that this subsection shall not be construed as requiring the Minister to consult a planning authority in relation to an appeal brought under this section.

89.[82] – (1) The planning authority may grant to any person a licence to erect, construct, place, and maintain –

    (*a*) a petrol pump, oil pump, air pump or other appliance for the servicing of vehicles,

    (*b*) a vending machine,

---

[80] This provision contrasts with the situation under s. 42 of the Public Health (Ireland) Act, 1878. See fn. 75, *ante.*

[81] Not yet operative: see fn. 75 *ante.* s. 88 substituted by s. 42 (f) of the Act of 1976.

[82] Note that by s. 42 of the Gas Acts, 1976 this section does not apply to the construction or maintenance of a pipeline by the Irish Gas Board (whether for use by itself or by another person) or for a pipeline required by the Minister for Transport and Power under s. 40 (2) of the same Act.

(*c*) a town or landscape map for indicating directions or places,

(*d*) a hoarding, fence or scaffold,

(*e*) an advertisement structure,

(*f*) a cable, wire or pipeline,

(*g*) any other appliance or structure specified by the Minister by regulations[83] as suitable for being licensed under this section,

on, under, over or along a public road.

(2) A person applying for a licence under this section shall furnish to the planning authority such plans and other information concerning the position, design and capacity of the appliance or structure as the authority may require.

(3) A licence may be granted under this section by the planning authority for such period and upon such conditions as the authority may specify, and where in the opinion of the planning authority by reason of the increase or alteration of traffic on the road or of the widening of the road or of any improvement of or relating to the road, the appliance or structure causes an obstruction or becomes dangerous, the authority may by notice in writing withdraw the licence and require the licensee to remove such appliance or structure at his own expense.

(4)(*a*) Any person may, in relation to the granting, refusing, withdrawing or continuing of a licence under this section or to the conditions specified by the planning authority for such a licence, appeal to the Minister.[84]

(*b*) Where an appeal under this section is allowed, the Minister shall give such directions with respect to the withdrawing, granting or altering of a licence under this section as may be appropriate, and the planning authority shall comply therewith.

(5)(*a*) The Minister may make regulations[85] prescribing the amount of the fee to be paid to the planning authority for the grant of a licence under this section, and any such fees shall be applied by the planning authority in the manner directed by the regulations.

(*b*) Different fees may be prescribed under this subsection in respect of different appliances and structures.

(6) Nothing in this section shall be construed as affecting the application to petrol pumps of the regulations for the time being in force relating to the storage or sale of motor spirit or to authorise the use of a petrol pump otherwise than in accordance with those regulations.

(7) A person shall not be entitled solely by reason of a licence under this section to erect, construct, place or maintain on, under, over or along a public road any appliance or structure.

(8) Subject to subsection (9) of this section, any person who –

(*a*) erects, constructs, places or maintains an appliance or structure referred to in subsection (1) of this section on, under, over or along any public road without having a licence under this section so to do, or

(*b*) erects, constructs, places or maintains such an appliance or structure on, under, over or along any public road otherwise than in accordance with a licence under this section, or

(*c*) contravenes any condition subject to which a licence has been granted to

[83] See p. 154.

[84] Construed as the Board: s. 14 (9) of the Act of 1976.

[85] See p. 163.

him under this section,

shall be guilty of an offence and shall be liable on summary conviction to a fine not exceeding ten pounds;[86] and if in the case of a continuing offence the contravention is continued after conviction, he shall be guilty of a further offence and shall be liable on summary conviction to a fine not exceeding two pounds[86] for each day on which the contravention is so continued.

(9)(*a*) A planning authority may, by virtue of this subsection, themselves erect, construct, place or maintain, on, under, over or along a public road any appliance or structure referred to in subsection (1) of this section, and it shall not be necessary for them to have a licence under this section.

    (*b*) Nothing in this subsection shall be taken as empowering a planning authority to hinder the reasonable use of a public road by the public or any person entitled to use it or as empowering a planning authority to create a nuisance to the owner or occupier of premises adjacent to the public road.

(10) Where a planning authority are not the road authority for the purposes of main roads in their area, they shall not, in pursuance of this section, grant a licence in respect of any appliance or structure on, under, over or along a main road or erect, construct or place any appliance or structure on, under, over or along a main road save after consultation with the authority who are the road authority for those purposes.

90. – Nothing in this Act shall restrict, prejudice, or affect the functions of the Minister for Finance or the Commissioners of Public Works in Ireland under the National Monuments Acts, 1930 and 1954, in relation to national monuments as defined by those Acts or any particular such monuments.[87]

91. – Section 42 of the Public Health (Ireland) Act, 1878, is hereby amended by the substitution of 'two months' for 'one month' and 'such two months' for 'such month'.

92. – (1) An application for a special permission under the Act of 1934 which was under consideration by a planning authority immediately before the appointed day shall be treated for the purposes of this Act as an application for a permission under section 26 of this Act.

(2) A general or special permission granted under the Act of 1934 shall be treated for the purposes of this Act (including, in particular, sections 30, 31 and 35) as a permission granted under section 26 of this Act, and a record of such permission shall be included in the register.

(3) An appeal under section 59 of the Act of 1934 in relation to a grant or refusal of a special or general permission which was pending immediately before the appointed day shall be treated for the purposes of this Act as an appeal under section 26 of this Act, except that a direction shall not be given in relation to the appeal under paragraph (*b*) of subsection (1) of section 18 of this Act.

---

[86] Now £100 and £25 respectively by s. 8 (1) of the Act of 1982.
[87] See *O'Callaghan* v. *The Commissioners of Public Works in Ireland and Others* (unreported decision of McWilliam J. delivered 4th October, 1982).

(4) In relation to an order made under section 14 of the Town and Regional Planning (Amendment) Act, 1939, before the appointed day, that Act and the Act of 1934 shall be treated as continuing in force for the purpose of enabling effect to be given in relation to the order to the provisions contained in the said section 14.

(5)(*a*) Any bye-laws in force immediately before the operative day under section 41 of the Public Health (Ireland) Act, 1878, for any matters other than those set out in paragraph (1) of that section shall on and after that day continue to apply in relation to –

   (i) plans which, in accordance with such bye-laws, were deposited before the operative day, and

   (ii) work carried out in accordance with plans deposited before the operative day,[88] with or without departure or deviation from those plans, and

   (iii) works carried out and completed before the operative day.

(*b*) Except, as provided by the foregoing paragraph, all bye-laws in force immediately before the operative day under section 41 of the Public Health (Ireland) Act, 1878, for any matters other than those set out in paragraph (1) of that section shall be repealed on the operative day, but subsections (1) and (2) of section 21 of the Interpretation Act, 1937, shall apply in relation to the repeals effected by this paragraph as they apply in relation to the repeal of any provision in an Act of the Oireachtas.

(*c*) The amendment made by subsection (11) of section 86 of this Act in any enactment shall not apply so as to exclude from that enactment any reference to bye-laws made under section 41 of the Public Health (Ireland) Act, 1878, as in force before the operative day, or as continued in force by this subsection.

(*d*) In this subsection 'the operative day' means the day on which this subsection comes into operation.[88]

(6)(*a*) A licence under section 137 of the Cork Improvement Act, 1868, section 47 of the Dublin Corporation Act, 1890, or section 35 of the Local Government Act, 1925, in force immediately before the appointed day shall be treated for the purposes of this Act as a licence under section 89 of this Act.

(*b*) An appeal under section 35 of the Local Government Act, 1925, pending immediately before the appointed day shall be treated for the purposes of this Act as an appeal under section 89 of this Act.

(*c*) Regulations in force immediately before the appointed day under section 35 of the Local Government Act, 1925, shall continue in force as if they were regulations under section 89 of this Act and may be amended or revoked accordingly.

(*d*) Subsection (8) of section 89 of this Act shall not have effect in relation to an appliance or structure referred to in subsection (1) of that section (other than a hoarding, fence or scaffold in the county borough of Dublin or in the county borough of Cork or a petrol pump) before the expiration of the period of six months beginning on the appointed day.

[88] 'The operative day' has yet to be fixed by ministerial order to be made under s. 1 (2)(b) of the Act of 1963.

FIFTH SCHEDULE

MATTERS FOR WHICH BUILDING REGULATIONS MAY PRESCRIBE STANDARDS.

1. Preparation of sites.
2. Strength and stability.
3. Fire precautions (including resistance of structure to the outbreak and spread of fire, the protection of occupants and means of escape in the event of fire).
4. Resistance to moisture.
5. Resistance to the transmission of heat.
6. Resistance to the transmission of sound.
7. Durability.
8. Resistance to infestation.
9. Drainage.
10. Ventilation (including the provision of open space therefor).
11. Daylighting (including the provision of open space therefor).
12. Heating and artificial lighting.
13. Services, installations and ancillary equipment (including services, installations and ancillary equipment for the supply or use of gas or electricity, and the provision of such arrangements for heating and cooking as are calculated to prevent or control so far as practicable the emission of smoke or noxious gases).
14. Accommodation and ancillary equipment.
15. Access.
16. Prevention of danger and obstruction.

LOCAL GOVERNMENT (PLANNING AND DEVELOPMENT) ACT, 1976

24. – (1) Notwithstanding anything contained in the Principal Act, a planning authority in considering,

    (*a*) an application for a permission under section 26 or 27 of that Act. . . .
        shall, where they consider it appropriate, have regard to either or both of the following, namely,
           (i) the probable effect which a particular decision by them on the matter would have on any place which is not within, or on any area which is outside, their area, and
          (ii) any other consideration relating to development outside their area.[89]

. . .

29.[90] – (5) Any person who is aggrieved by the decision of a planning authority

---

[89] This section enables the planning authority to consider, for example, the national or regional employment implications of a large development.

[90] Sub-ss. (1), (2), (3), (4), (7) and (9) of this section have been repealed by s. 15 (2)(b) of the Act of 1982. These sub-sections provided for 'withering', waiver notices (which waived compliance with a condition in a planning permission) and development certificates (which certified how much of a development was complete at the date the relevant planning permission ceased to have effect). The effect of the repeal is to abolish waiver notices and development certificates subject to current appeals which remain effective. Duration of Planning Permissions is now governed by ss. 2, 3 and 4 of the Act of 1982.

on an application for a waiver notice may appeal to the Board within the period of twenty-one days, beginning on the date on which the planning authority notify the applicant of their decision.

(6) Where an appeal is brought under subsection (5) of this section, the Board may –

> (*a*) in case a waiver notice has been isued by a planning authority, confirm or annul the notice, or
>
> (*b*) in case a waiver notice has not been so issued, confirm the decision of the planning authority or issue a waiver notice.

(8) In any legal proceedings a development certificate shall be *prima facie* evidence of the facts thereby certified, and any document purporting to be a development certificate shall be admitted as evidence without proof of the signature of the person purporting to sign the certificate or that the person was an officer of the relevant planning authority, until the contrary is shown.

(10) When a planning authority grant an extension or further extension, or issue a development certificate, particulars thereof shall be recorded on the relevant entry in the register.

(11) Any person who is aggrieved by a decision of a planning authority on an application for a development certificate may appeal to the Circuit Court within six months of the date of such decision.

(12) Where an appeal is brought under subsection (11) of this section, the Court, if satisfied that the case comes within paragraph (*a*) of subsection (7) of this section and that a dispute mentioned in paragraph (*b*) of the said subsection (7) has arisen, may decide accordingly and, as may be appropriate, determine either or both of the following, the extent to which the relevant development was completed before the relevant permission under Part IV of the Principal Act ceased to have effect, or whether or not the part in dispute of the relevant development consists of the provision of things mentioned in subparagraph (ii) of the said paragraph (*b*), inform the appropriate planning authority of its decision and direct the authority to issue forthwith, if they have not already done so, an appropriate development certificate or, if a development certificate has been issued which is inappropriate having regard to the decision of the Court, transmit such certificate to the authority and direct that in lieu thereof an appropriate development certificate be issued by the authority forthwith.

(13) Where on an application by a person, the Circuit Court is satisfied that there has been unreasonable delay by a planning authority in dealing with an application for a development certificate and the Court is also satisfied in both of the respects mentioned in subsection (12) of this section, the Court may decide accordingly and make the determination mentioned in the said subsection (12) which is appropriate, inform the authority of its decision and direct the authority to issue forthwith an appropriate development certificate.

. . .

35. – The Minister may make regulations,

> (*a*) providing for,
>> (i) the payment to planning authorities of prescribed fees by applicants for a waiver notice under section 29 of this Act,
>> (ii) the publication by planning authorities of specified notices with respect to applications for permission under the Principal Act to develop land or for such a waiver notice,

(b) enabling an applicant to appeal to the Board against a refusal of an approval which is required to be obtained under a condition subject to which a permission or approval is granted under the Principal Act,

(c) making such incidental, consequential, transitional or supplementary provisions as may appear to him to be necessary or proper for any purpose of this Act or in consequence of, or to give full effect to, any of its provisions.

LOCAL GOVERNMENT (PLANNING AND DEVELOPMENT) ACT, 1982

1. – In this Act –
'the Act of 1976' means the Local Government (Planning and Development) Act, 1976;
'development certificate' means a certificate issued under section 29 of the Act of 1976;
'waiver notice' means a notice issued under section 29 of the Act of 1976.

2. – (1) Subject to subsection (2) of this section, a permission granted under Part IV of the Principal Act, whether before or after the passing of this Act, shall on the expiration of the appropriate period[92] (but without prejudice to the validity of anything done pursuant thereto prior to the expiration of that period) cease to have effect[93] as regards –

(a) in case the development to which the permission relates is not commenced during that period, the entire development, and

(b) in case such development is commenced during that period, so much thereof as is not completed within that period.

(2)(a) Subsection (1) of this section shall not apply –

(i) to any permission for the retention on land of any structure,

(ii) to any permission granted either for a limited period only or subject to a condition which is of a kind described in section 26 (2)(j) or 27 (2)(f) of the Principal Act,

(iii) to any permission which is of a class or description specified in regulations made by the Minister for the purposes of this section,

(iv) in the case of a house, shop, office or other building which itself has been completed, in relation to the provision of any structure or works included in the relevant permission and which are either necessary for or ancillary or incidental to the use of the building in accordance with that permission.

(v) in the case of a development comprising a number of buildings of which only some have been completed, in relation to the provision of roads, services and open spaces included in the relevant permission and which are necessary for or ancillary to such completed buildings.

[92] Not to be confused with 'the appropriate period' for s. 26 (4)(a)(iii) (two months unless extended by consent); s. 26 (5)(a) (one month or 21 days depending who the appellant is); s. 27 (3)(a)(iii) (two months unless extended by consent) or s. 27 (4)(a) (one month or 21 days) of the Act of 1963.
[93] This section, together with ss. 3 and 4 replaces s. 29 (1) (2) and (9) of the Act of 1976.

(*b*) Subsection (1) of this section shall not affect –
    (i) the continuance of any use, in accordance with a permission, of land,
    (ii) where a development has been completed (whether to an extent described in paragraph (*a*) of this subsection or otherwise), the obligation of any person to comply with any condition attached to the relevant permission whereby something is required either to be done or not to be done.

(3)(*a*) Where regulations under this section are proposed to be made, the Minister shall cause a draft thereof to be laid before both Houses of the Oireachtas and the regulations shall not be made until a resolution approving of the draft has been passed by each such House.

(*b*) Section 10(2) of the Principal Act shall not apply in relation to regulations made under this section.

(4) This section shall be deemed to have come into operation on the 1st day of November, 1981.

(5) In this section and in section 4 of this Act, 'the appropriate period' means –

    (*a*) in relation to any permission which was granted before the 1st day of November, 1976, the period beginning on the date of such grant and ending on the 31st day of October, 1983.

    (*b*) in relation to any permission which was or is granted not earlier than the 1st day of November, 1976, nor later than the 31st day of October, 1982 –
        (i) in case in relation to the permission a period is specified pursuant to section 3 of this Act, that period, and
        (ii) in any other case, the period ending on the day which is seven years after the date of such grant or the 31st day of October, 1987, whichever is the earlier,

    (*c*) in relation to any permission which was or is granted on or after the 1st day of November, 1982 –
        (i) in case in relation to the permission a period is specified pursuant to section 3 of this Act, that period, and
        (ii) in any other case, the period of five years beginning on the date of such grant:

Provided that where a planning authority have, before the commencement of this section, made an order under section 29 (9) of the Act of 1976 and by virtue of the order the permission to which the order relates would, if this section had not been enacted, cease to have effect on a date which is later than that on which it would, apart from this proviso, cease to have effect, then, notwithstanding the foregoing provisions of this section and section 15 of this Act, the appropriate period in relation to the permission shall end on such later date.

(6) A planning authority is exercising, in relation to a permission referred to in subsection (5)(*b*) of this section, the power conferred on them by section 3 of this Act shall not exercise the power so as to specify a period which is shorter than that which, by virtue of the said subsection (5)(*b*), would apply in relation to the permission if the power were not so exercised.

3. – Without prejudice to the powers conferred on them by Part IV of the Principal Act to grant a permission to develop land for a limited period only, in deciding to grant a permission under section 26 of the Principal Act, a planning authority or the Board, as may be appropriate, may, having regard to the nature and extent of the relevant development and any other material consideration, specify the period, being a period of more than five years, during which the permission is to have effect,[94] and in case the planning authority exercise, or refuse to exercise, the power conferred on them by this section, such exercise or refusal shall be regarded as forming part of the relevant decision of such authority under the said section 26.

4. – (1) On an application being made to them in that behalf, a planning authority shall, as regards a particular permission, extend the appropriate period, by such additional period as the authority consider requisite to enable the development to which the permission relates to be completed, if, and only if, each of the following requirements is complied with:

(b) the application is in accordance with such regulations[95] under this Act as apply to it.

(b) any requirements of, or made under, such regulations are complied with as regards the application, and

(c) the authority are satisfied in relation to the permission that –

(i) the development to which such permission relates commenced before the expiration of the appropriate period sought to be extended, and

(ii) substantial works[96] were carried out pursuant to such permission during such period, and

(iii) the development will be completed within a reasonable time.

(2) Where –

(a) an application is duly made under this section to a planning authority.

(b) any requirements of, or made under, regulations under section 11 of this Act are complied with as regards the application, and

(c) the planning authority do not give notice to the applicant of their decision as regards the application within the period of two months beginning on –

(i) in case of all the aforesaid requirements referred to in paragraph (b) of this subsection are complied with on or before the day of receipt by the planning authority of the application, that day, and

(ii) in any other case, the day on which all of the said requirements stand complied with,

---

[94] This is an important power which planning authorities should be advised by the Minister (under the power conferred on him by s. 7 (1) of the Act of 1982) to exercise in appropriate cases. Applications for large scale developments of an ongoing nature such as mining or quarrying are cases in point. It will usually be uneconomic for a quarry operator to borrow or provide the high level of capital needed if the life of the quarry is to be limited to 5 years. A finance house is unlikely to lend unless the planning permission clearly authorises the operation to continue for the necessary 15 or 20 years. An applicant should not be put to the expense, doubt or delay of an appeal if there is no good reason for limiting the grant to 5 years. The application should specify the desired period and support the period with reasons.

[95] These regulations are contained in S.I. No. 342 of 1982; see p. 165.

[96] Although substantial works are not defined it is suggested they comprise works sufficiently comprehensive to show an intention to complete, or alternatively, such as would constitute an eye-sore if left uncompleted.

subject to section 10 (2) of this Act, a decision by the planning authority to extend, or to further extend, as may be appropriate, the period, which in relation to the relevant permission is the appropriate period, by such additional period as is specified in the application shall be regarded as having been given by the planning authority on the last day of the said two month period.

(3)(*a*) Where a decision to extend an appropriate period is given under subsection (1) of this section, or, pursuant to subsection (2) of this section, such a decision is to be regarded as having been given, the planning authority shall not further extend the appropriate period, unless each of the following requirements is complied with:

    (i) an application in that behalf is made to them in accordance with such regulations under this Act as apply to it.

    (ii) any requirements of, or made under, such regulations are complied with as regards the application, and

    (iii) the authority are satisfied that the relevant development has not been completed due to circumstances beyond the control of the person carrying out the development.

(*b*) An appropriate period shall be further extended under this subsection only for such period as the relevant planning authority consider requisite to enable the relevant development to be completed.

(4) Particulars of any application made to a planning authority under this section and of the decision of the planning authority in respect of such application shall be recorded on the relevant entry in the register.

(5) Where a decision to extend, or to further extend, is given under this section, or pursuant to subsection (2) of this section, such a decision is to be regarded as having been given, section 2 of this Act shall, in relation to the permission to which the decision relates, be construed and have effect subject to and in accordance with the terms of the decision.

(6) This section shall not be construed as precluding the extension, or the further extension, of an appropriate period by reason of the fact that the period has expired.

. . .

7. – (1) The Minister shall, from time to time, issue such general directives as to policy in relation to planning and development as he considers necessary.

(2) A planning authority[97] and the Board shall in performing its functions have regard to any directive under this section.

(3) Nothing in this section shall be construed as enabling the Minister to exercise any power or control in relation to any particular case with which a planning authority or the Board is or may be concerned.

(4) Where the Minister gives a directive under this section, the following provisions shall apply:

    (*a*) as soon as may be the Minister shall cause a copy of the directive to be laid before each House of the Oireachtas,

    (*b*) the directive shall be published in the *Iris Oifigiúil*, and

    (*c*) the Minister shall cause a copy of the directive to be sent to each planning authority and to the Board.

---

[97] S. 7 replaces s. 6 of the Act of 1976 (repealed by s. 15 (2)(a) of the Act of 1982). The important change is that under the new section the Minister shall give directions to Planning Authorities as well as to the Board. See p. 537.

10. – (1) The Minister may, with the consent of the Minister for Finance, make regulations[98] providing for –

(*a*) the payment to planning authorities of prescribed fees in relation to applications for –

(i) permission under Part IV of the Principal Act,

(ii) approvals required by permission regulations,

(iii) approvals required to be obtained under a condition subject to which a permission or approval is granted under the Principal Act, or

(iv) extensions or further extensions under section 4 of this Act.

(*b*) the payment to the Board of prescribed fees in relation to appeals or references to, or determinations by, the Board,

and the regulations may provide for the payment of different fees in relation to cases of different classes or descriptions, for exemption from the payment of fees in specified circumstances, for the waiver, remission or refund (in whole or in part) of fees in specified circumstances and for the manner in which fees are to be disposed of.

(2) Where under regulations under this section a fee is payable to a planning authority by an applicant in respect of an application referred to in subsection (1)(*a*) of this section, the following provisions shall have effect:

(*a*) the application shall not be decided by the authority unless the authority is in receipt of the fee, and

(*b*) notwithstanding anything contained in section 26(4) or 27(3) of the Principal Act or in section 4 (2) of this Act, a decision of a planning authority shall not be regarded, pursuant to any of those sections, as having been given on a day which is earlier than that which is two months after the day on which the authority is in receipt of the fee, and the said sections 26(4), 27(3) and 4(2) shall be construed subject to and in accordance with the provisions of this paragraph.

(3) Where –

(*a*) under regulations under this section a fee (other than a fee referred to in subsection (6) of this section) is payable to the Board by an appellant in respect of an appeal by him to the Board, and

(*b*) the provision of the Local Government (Planning and Development) Acts, 1963 and 1976, authorising the appeal enables the appeal only to be made within, or before the expiration of, a specified period or before a specified day, that provision shall be construed as including –

(i) a requirement that the fee is to be received by the Board within, or before the expiration of that period, or before that day (or, if the fee is sent by post, not later than the third day after that period or day), and

(ii) a provision that if the fee is not so received, the appeal shall be invalid.

(4) Where under regulations under this section a fee is payable either to a planning authority or to the Board and the person by whom the fee is payable is not –

(*a*) the applicant for a permission, approval or licence, or

---

[98] These are contained in S.I. No. 30 of 1983; see p. 168.

(*b*) an appellant to the Board, or

(*c*) the person making a reference to, or a request for a determination by, the Board,

submissions or observations made, as regards the relevant application, appeal, reference or determination, by or on behalf of the person by whom such fee is payable, shall not be considered by the planning authority or the Board, as may be appropriate, if the fee has not been received by the authority or the Board.

(5) Where under regulations under this section a fee is payable to the Board by a person making a reference to, or a request for a determination by, the Board, the relevant question or matter shall not be decided or determined by the Board unless the fee is received by the Board.

(6) Where under regulations under this section fees are payable to the Board in respect of requests for oral hearings of appeals or references to the Board, such a request shall not be considered by the Board if the fee so payable in respect of the request is not received by the Board.

(7) The provisions of subsection (3) of this section are in addition to, and not in substitution for, the provisions of section 22 of the Act of 1976.

11. – (1) The Minister may make regulations[99] providing for any matter of procedure in relation to applications under section 4 of this Act and making such incidental, consequential or supplementary provision as may appear to him to be necessary or proper to give full effect to any of the provisions of sections 2, 3 or 4 of this Act.

(2) In particular and without prejudice to the generality of subsection (1) of this section, regulations under this section may –

(*a*) specify the time at which applications under section 4 of this Act may be made, the manner in which such applications shall be made and the particulars they shall contain,

(*b*) require applicants to furnish to the planning authority any specified information with respect to their applications (including any information regarding any estate or interest in or right over land),

(*c*) require applicants to submit to a planning authority any further information relative to their applications (including any information as to any such estate, interest or right),

(*d*) require the production of any evidence to verify any particulars or information given by any applicant.

(*e*) require the notification (in a prescribed manner) by planning authorities of decisions on such applications.

. . .

14. – (1) Neither section 15 nor the proviso to section 2(5) of this Act shall be construed as affecting the exercise by the Circuit Court or the Board, in relation to any application referred to in section 15(4)(b) of this Act, of any power conferred on it by section 29 of the Act of 1976.

(2) Where before the commencement of this section an application was made to a planning authority for a permission or for an approval, a decision of the authority

---

[99] These are contained in S.I. No. 342 of 1982 (see p. 165); the application must be brought within one year of the date of expiration of the 'appropriate period'. (Regulation 4).

as regards the application shall not, by reason only of the enactment of section 2 of this Act, be regarded, pursuant to section 26(4) or 27(3) of the Principal Act, as having been given.

15. – (1) In subsection (3) of section 24 of the Principal Act all the words between 'guilty of an offence' and the end of the subsection are hereby repealed.

(2) Subject to subsection (3) of this section, the following provisions of the Act of 1976 are hereby repealed:

    (*a*) sections 6, 15(1), 26(5) and 38.

    (*b*) subsections (1), (2), (3), (4), (7) and (9) of section 29.

    (*c*) 'and shall be liable on summary conviction to a fine not exceeding two hundred and fifty pounds' in section 26(4).

(3) This section, in so far as it repeals section 15(1) of the Act of 1976, shall come into operation on such day as the Minister shall fix by order.[1]

(4) Notwithstanding subsection (2) of this section –

    (*a*) any waiver notice or any development certificate shall continue in force and to have effect,

    (*b*) a planning authority may after the commencement of this section issue a waiver notice or a development certificate if, but only if, an application made to them in that behalf has been received by them before such commencement.

16. – (1) This Act may be cited as the Local Government (Planning and Development) Act, 1982.

(2) The Local Government (Planning and Development) Acts, 1963 and 1976, and this Act may be cited together as the Local Government (Planning and Development) Acts, 1963 to 1982.

(3) This Act and the Local Government (Planning and Development) Acts, 1963 and 1976, shall be construed together as one Act.

PUBLIC HEALTH (IRELAND) ACT, 1878

41. Every sanitary authority may make byelaws with respect to the following matters; (that is to say,)

(1) With respect to the level, width, and construction of new streets, and the provisions for the sewerage thereof, and the preventing of the opening thereof for public use until such byelaws have been complied with.[2]

(2) With respect to the structure, and description and quality of the substances used in the construction of new buildings for securing stability and the prevention of fires, and for purposes of health.

(3) With respect to the sites of houses, buildings, and other erections, and the

---

[1] The day fixed was 11th April, 1983 by S.I. No. 34 of 1983. Part III of S.I. No. 30 of 1983 (Local Government) (Planning and Development) (Fees and Amendment) Regulations, 1983) which deals with fees for appeals etc. to the Board came into operation on the same date. The remainder of S.I. No. 30 of 1983 came into operation on 7th March, 1983.

[2] See ss. 86–88, 92 (5) and s. 1 (2)(b) of the Act of 1963. These sections have not yet become operative. When they do the Minister for the Environment will be empowered by s. 86 (1) of the Act of 1963 to make regulations (Building Reglations) dealing with all or any of the matters listed in s. 41 of the Act of 1878 except those set out in sub-s. (1).

mode in which, and the materials with which such foundations and sites shall be made, formed, excavated, filled up, prepared, and completed for securing stability, the prevention of fires, and for purposes of health.

For the purposes of this Act –

The term 'foundations' shall mean the space immediately beneath the footings of a wall;

The term 'site' in relation to a house, building, or other erection shall mean the whole space to be occupied by such house, building, or other erection between the level of the bottom of the foundations and the level of the base of the walls:

(4) With respect to the sufficiency of the space about buildings to secure a free circulation of air, and with respect to the ventilation of buildings:

(5) With respect to the drainage of buildings, to waterclosets, earthclosets, privies, ashpits, and cesspools in connection with buildings, and to the closing of buildings or parts of buildings unfit for human habitation, and to prohibition of their use for such habitation:

And they may further provide for the observance of such byelaws by enacting therein such provisions as they think necessary as to the giving of notices, as to the deposit of plans and sections by persons intending to lay out streets or to construct buildings, as to inspection by the sanitary authority, and as to the power of such authority (subject to the provision of this Act) to remove, alter, or pull down any work begun or done in contravention of such byelaws: Provided that no byelaw made under this section shall affect any building erected before the passing of this Act. The provisions of this section and the two last preceding sections shall not apply to buildings belonging to any railway company and used for the purpose of such railway under any Act of Parliament.

42. Where a notice, plan, or description of any work is required by any byelaw made by a sanitary authority to be laid before that authority, the sanitary authority shall,[3] within two months after the same has been delivered or sent to their clerk, signify in writing their approval or disapproval of the intended work to the person proposing to execute the same; and if the work is commenced after such notice of disapproval, or before the expiration of such two months without such approval, and is in any respect not in conformity with any byelaw of the sanitary authority, the sanitary authority may cause so much of the work as has been executed to be pulled down or removed.

Where a sanitary authority incur expenses in or about the removal of any work executed contrary to any byelaw, such authority may recover in a summary manner the amount of such expenses either from the person executing the works removed or from the person causing the works to be executed, at their discretion.

Where a sanitary authority may under this section pull down or remove any work begun or executed in contravention of any byelaw, or where the beginning or the execution of the work is an offence in respect whereof the offender is liable in respect of any byelaw to a penalty, the existence of the work during its continuance in such a form and state as to be in contravention of the byelaw shall be deemed to be a continuing offence, but a penalty shall not be incurred in respect thereof after

---

[3] See footnote to this section in Vanston's *Public Health* for the position which applies if a decision is not forthcoming. Contrast with s. 87 (6) of the Act of 1963 which provides for a default bye-law approval. The time limit for dealing with Bye-Laws was originally one month but was increased to two months by s. 91 of the Act of 1963.

the expiration of one year from the day when the offence was committed or the byelaw was broken.

PUBLIC HEALTH ACTS AMENDMENT ACT, 1890

23.[4] – (1) Section one hundred and fifty-seven of the Public Health Act, 1875, shall be extended so as to empower every urban authority to make byelaws with respect to the following matters; that is to say:

The keeping waterclosets supplied with sufficient water for flushing;

The structure of floors, hearths, and staircases, and the height of rooms intended to be used for human habitation;

The paving of yards and open spaces in connexion with dwelling-houses; and

The provision in connexion with the laying out of new streets of secondary means of access where necessary for the purpose of the removal of house refuse and other matters.[5]

(2) Any byelaws under that section as above extended with regard to the drainage of buildings, and to waterclosets, earthclosets, privies, ashpits, and cesspools, in connexion with buildings, and the keeping waterclosets supplied with sufficient water for flushing, may be made so as to affect buildings erected before the times mentioned in the said section.

(3) The provisions of the said section (as amended by this Act), so far as they relate to byelaws with respect to the structure of walls and foundations of new buildings for purposes of health, and with respect to the matters mentioned in subsections (3) and (4) of the said section, and with respect to the structures of floors, the height of rooms to be used for human habitation, and to the keeping of waterclosets supplied with sufficient water for flushing, shall be extended so as to empower rural authorities to make byelaws in respect to the said matters, and to provide for the observance of such byelaws, and to enforce the same as if such powers were conferred on the rural authorities by virtue of an order of the Local Government Board made on the day when this part of this Act is adopted; and section one hundred and fifty-eight of the Public Health Act, 1875, shall also apply to any such authority, and shall be in force in every rural district where this part of this Act is adopted.

(4) Every local authority may make byelaws to prevent buildings which have been erected in accordance with byelaws made under the Public Health Acts from being altered in such a way that if at first so constructed they would have contravened the byelaws.

HOUSING ACT, 1969

10. – In case a permission is required under this Act and under Part IV of the Act of 1963 in relation to a habitable house, the application for a permission under the Act of 1963 may be made at any time and whenever the application under the Act

---

[4] This section of the Act is included because when s. 86 of the Act of 1963 becomes operative, the Minister for the Environment will be empowered by sub-s. 1 thereof to make regulations (building regulations) for all or any of the matters, inter alia, listed in s. 23 (1) of the Act of 1890 *except* those set out in the last paragraph of sub-s.1.

[5] Building bye-laws may not deal with the matters dealt with in this sentence.

of 1963 is made the following provisions shall apply:

> (a) the application under the Act of 1963 shall not be decided until an application under section 3 has been fully determined;

> (b) subject to paragraph (c), the references in section 26 (4) (b) of the Act of 1963 to the period of two months beginning on the day of receipt by the planning authority of the application shall be construed as references to the period of five weeks beginning on –

>> (i) in case no appeal is taken under section 4 – the day on which the decision is given, or is regarded as having been given, under this Act by the housing authority, and

>> (ii) in case an appeal is so taken – the day on which the appeal is withdrawn or is determined by the Minister, as may be appropriate,

> provided that, in case the day mentioned in subparagraph (i) or the day mentioned in subparagraph (ii) occurs less than two months after the receipt by the planning authority of the application, this paragraph shall not have effect;

> (c) in case a permission under this Act is refused (whether on the original application or on appeal), the application under the Act of 1963, in so far, but only in so far, as it relates to the relevant house, shall not be considered and accordingly section 26 (4) (a) of the Act of 1963 shall cease to apply in relation to the house; and

> (d) in case a permission under this Act is granted subject to conditions, the planning authority or the Minister when considering the application or the appeal, as the case may be, under the Act of 1963 shall have regard to the conditions.[6]

THE LOCAL GOVERNMENT (PLANNING AND DEVELOPMENT) REGULATIONS, 1977

[S.I. No. 65 of 1977, as amended by Local Government (Planning and Development) (Amendment) Regulations, 1982, S.I. No. 342 of 1982.]

PART IV

PERMISSION REGULATIONS

13. In this Part –

'outline application' means an application for an outline permission;

'outline permission' means a permission for development subject to the subsequent approval of the planning authority;

'permission' includes outline permission;[7]

'approval' means an approval consequent on an outline permission or an approval which is required to be obtained under a condition subject to which a permission or an approval is granted under the Acts;

---

[6] This Act does not apply in certain circumstances (see s. 9). The onus is on an applicant to satisfy the Housing Authority that the Act does not apply in his case. See *Magauran* v. *Dublin Corporation* (unreported Supreme Court judgment delivered by Henchy J. on 22nd July 1982.

[7] But not, not approval. Compare *State (Cogley)* v. *Dublin Corporation*) p. 221.

'planning application' means an application to a planning authority for a permission to develop land and includes –
  (a) an outline application
  (b) an application for an approval,
  (c) an application for permission for the retention of a structure, and
  (d) an application for permission for the continuance of any use of any structure or other land.
'the Act of 1982' means the Local Government (Planning and Development) Act, 1982;[8]
'the appropriate period' has the meaning assigned to it in section 2(5) of the Act of 1982;[8]

13A. Notwithstanding any other provision of these Regulations, an outline application may not be made in respect of the retention on land of any structure or the continuance of any use of land.[9]

14. Prior to the making of a planning application, the applicant shall publish notice of his intention to make such application either –
  (a) in a newspaper circulating in the district in which the relevant land or structure is situate, or
  (b) by the erection or by the fixing of a notice on the land or structure.

15. A notice published in a newspaper in pursuance of article 14 shall contain, as a heading, the name of the city, town or county in which the land or structure is situate and shall state –
  (a) the name of the applicant,[10]
  (b) the location of the land or the address of the structure to which the application relates (as may be appropriate),[11]
  (c) the nature and extent of the development, or[12]
  (d) where the application relates to the retention of a structure, the nature of the proposed use of the structure and the period of the proposed retention, or
  (e) where the application relates to the continuance of any use, the nature of such use.

16. (1) A notice erected or fixed for the purposes of article 14 on any land or

---

[8] Added by Article 12(a) of S.I. 342 of 1982.
[9] Reg. 13A added by Article 25 of S.I. 30 of 1983.
[10] Compare McWilliam J.'s decision in *State (Alf-a-Bet Promotions Limited)* v. *Bundoran U.D.C.* with (p. 181) with the dictum of Henchy J. in *State (Finglas Developments Limited)* v. *Dublin County Council* (p. 225).
[11] See *Crodaun Homes Limited* v. *Kildare County Council* [1983] ILRM where the issue in the Supreme Court was whether a notice which read 'Co. Kildare – 14 Bungalows at Leixlip Gate for Crodaun Homes Limited' was sufficient for the purposes of the regulations. In the High Court Barrington J. had held the notice sufficient and in the Supreme Court O'Higgins C.J. agreed with this. However, the majority (Griffin and Hederman J.J.) held it insufficient. In his judgment (with which Hederman J. concurred) Griffin J. emphasised that notice must reach all potential objectors and 'potential objectors will not therefore be confined to persons who live in the vicinity of the lands.' On the other hand O'Higgins C.J. thought '. . . that the object of these regulations is to ensure that the location of the site to be developed is to be known in particular to people in the locality.'
[12] See McMahon J. in *Keleghan and Others* v. *Corby and Another* (p. 234).

structure shall –
(*a*) be painted or inscribed, or printed and pasted, on a durable material,
(*b*) be securely erected or fixed in a conspicuous position –
      (i) on or near the main entrance to the land or structure from a public road, or
      (ii) on any other part of the land or structure adjoining the said public road,
and shall be so erected or fixed and the text shall be so painted, inscribed or printed that the notice shall be capable of being read by persons using the said public road.

(2) Where a notice erected or fixed on any land or structure for the purposes of article 14 is not erected or fixed in such position as to be readily visible from the aforesaid main entrance, the position of the notice shall be indicated on a plan accompanying the relevant planning application.

(3) A notice published on the land to which the application for permission or approval relates shall be headed 'APPLICATION TO PLANNING AUTHOR-ITY' and shall state the name of the applicant and the nature and extent of the development in respect of which it is intended to apply for a permission or an approval.

(4) A notice published on a structure to which an application for permission or an approval relates shall be headed 'APPLICATION TO PLANNING AUTHOR-ITY' and shall state the name of the applicant, the nature of the proposed develop-ment, and in the case of an application for a permission for retention of a structure, the nature of the proposed use of the structure and the period of the proposed retention.

17. A planning application shall be accompanied by[13] –
(*a*) particulars of the interest held in the land or structure by the applicant,[14] the name and address of the applicant, and
(*b*) a copy of a newspaper circulating in the area in which the land or structure is situate in which there has been published a notice in pursuance of article 15, or
(*c*) a copy of the notice erected or fixed on the land or structure in pursuance of article 16.

18. (1) A planning application for any development consisting of or mainly consisting of the carrying out of works on, in or under land or for the retention of a structure shall, in addition to the matters prescribed in article 17, be accompanied by such plans (including a site or layout plan and drawings of floor plans, elevations and sections) and such other particulars as are necessary to identify the land and to describe the works or structure to which the application relates.

(2) A planning application for any development consisting of or mainly[15]

---

[13] In *McCabe* v. *Harding Investments Limited* O'Higgins C.J. drew a distinction between regulations which prescribe what must accompany an application and those which pre-scribe what must be done prior to lodging an application, the context suggesting that non-compliance with the former category may not be fatal to the validity of the appli-cation. See p. 196.

[14] See generally *Walker* v. *Frescati Estates Limited* (p. 175), and cases mentioned in fn. 10, *ante*.

[15] See observations of Finlay P. in *Re Viscount Securities Limited* v. *Dublin County Council* (p. 457).

consisting of the making of any material change in the use of any structure or other land or the continuance of any use of any structure or other land (whether instituted without a permission granted under the Acts or in accordance with a permission so granted for a limited period only) shall, in addition to the matters prescribed in article 17, be accompanied by –

> (*a*) a statement of the existing use and the use proposed or, where appropriate, of the former use and the use proposed to be continued, together with particulars of the nature and extent of any such proposed use,
>
> (*b*)   (i) a plan or location map marked or coloured so as to identify the structure or other land to which the application relates, or
>
> (ii) where the development to which the application relates comprises the carrying out of works on, in or under the structure or other land – such plans (including a site or layout plan and drawings of floor plans, elevations and sections) and such other particulars as are necessary to identify the structure or other land to which the application relates and to describe the works proposed.

19. (1) An outline application, notwithstanding the provisions of article 18, may, in addition to the matters prescribed in article 17, be accompanied only by such plans and particulars as are necessary to identify the land to which the application relates and to enable the planning authority to determine the siting, layout or other proposals for development in respect of which a decision is sought.

(2) An application to a planning authority for an approval consequent on an outline permission shall be accompanied by such further particulars and plans as would be required under the provisions of article 18 if application for a permission were made under that article.

(3) An application for an approval consequent on an outline permission may be related to a specified part only of the development for which an outline permission was granted and separate applications may be made in respect of other parts of the said development from time to time.[16]

(4) An application for an approval which is required to be obtained under a condition subject to which a permission or an approval is granted under the Acts shall be accompanied by such plans as are necessary to describe the works or structure in respect of which the approval is sought.

(5) An outline permission shall not operate so as to authorise the carrying out of any development until –

> (*a*) an approval has been granted consequent on an application in accordance with sub-article (2), or
>
> (*b*) as respects a specified part of the development for which an outline permission was granted, an approval has been granted for such specified part consequent on an application in accordance with sub-article (2), or
>
> (*c*) a further approval has been granted in any case where the terms of an approval consequent on an application in accordance with sub-article (2), or the terms of a permission granted consequent on an application in accordance with article 18, require such further approval[17] to be

---

[16] See Barrington J.'s decision in High Court in *State (Pine Valley Developments Limited)* v. *Dublin County Council* (p. 210).

[17] Compare observations of McMahon J. in *Keleghan and Others* v. *Dublin Corporation and*

obtained.

19A. (1)[18] A planning application shall state whether the application is for a permission, an outline permission or an approval and shall, in addition to the matters prescribed in articles 17, 18 and 19, be accompanied by the following particulars –
> (*a*) a statement of the area of the land to which the application relates, and
> (*b*) where the application relates to a building or buildings –
>> (i) a statement of the number of dwellings (if any) to be provided, and
>> (ii) except in the case of an outline application for a single dwelling house or a number of such houses, a statement of the gross floor space of the building or buildings.

(2) In this article, 'gross floor space' means the area ascertained by the external measurement of the floor space on each floor of a building or buildings, disregarding any floor space provided for the parking of vehicles by persons occupying or using the building or buildings where such floor space is incidental to development to which the application primarily relates.

20. Plans, drawings and maps accompanying a planning application shall be in duplicate and shall comply with the following requirements –
> (*a*) buildings, roads, boundaries, and other features in the vicinity of the structure or other land to which the application relates shall be shown on site plans or layout plans,
> (*b*) drawings of elevations of any proposed structure shall show the main features of any buildings which would be contiguous to the proposed structure if it were erected,
> (*c*) plans and drawings of elevations and sections shall be drawn to scale, which shall be indicated thereon, and shall indicate in figures the principal dimensions (including overall height) of any proposed structure and the distances of any such structure from the boundaries of the site,
> (*d*) the north point shall be indicated on all maps and plans other than drawings of elevations and sections,
> (*e*) plans relating to works comprising reconstruction, alteration or extension of a structure shall be so marked or coloured as to distinguish between the existing structure and the works proposed,
> (*f*) plans and drawings shall indicate the name and address of the person by whom they were prepared.

21. Where a planning authority receive an application for a permission which does not comply with article 18 and is not expressed to be an outline application they may –
> (*a*) by notice in writing require the applicant or the person acting on his behalf to submit such further plans and particulars as are necessary for the

Another (p. 234) to the effect that a full permission granted on condition that details of access be agreed with the planning authority might constitute no more than an outline permission. Such a condition passed without comment, however, in *State (Foxrock Construction Limited)* v. *Dublin County Council* (p. 227).

[18] Added by article 26 of S.I. 30 of 1983.

purpose of an outline application, or

(*b*) grant an outline permission if the application appears to them sufficient for that purpose only, or[19]

(*c*) refuse a permission if it apears to them that they are adequate reasons for such decision, or

(*d*) grant a permission.

22. On receipt[20] of a planning application, a planning authority shall –

(*a*) stamp the documents with the date of their receipt, and

(*b*) send to the applicant or the person acting on his behalf an acknowledgement stating the date of receipt of the application.

23. Where –

(*a*) a period of more than two weeks has elapsed between the publication in a newspaper of a notice in accordance with article 15 and the making of the relevant planning application, or

(*b*) it appears to the planning authority that any notice published in pursuance of article 14 –

    (i) if published in a newspaper, does not comply with the provisions of article 15, or

    (ii) if erected or fixed on any land or structure, does not comply with the provisions of article 16, or

    (iii) in either case, because of its content or for any other reason, is misleading or inadequate for the information of the public, or

(*c*) it appears to the planning authority that a notice published on the land or structure has not been maintained in position for at least one month after the making of the relevant application or has been defaced or become illegible within such period,

the planning authority may require the applicant to publish such further notice in such manner, whether in a newspaper or otherwise, in such terms as they may specify and to submit to them such evidence as they may specify in relation to compliance with any such requirement.[21]

24. Notice of every planning application and of the date of its receipt shall be published by a planning authority by inclusion in a weekly list of which copies –

(*a*) shall be made available to the members of the authority in such manner as they may by resolution direct,

(*b*) shall be displayed in or at the offices of the planning authority for a period

---

[19] In *State (Fortunestown Holdings Limited)* v. *Dublin County Council* an application was made for full planning permission for a large housing development; the planning authority granted full planning permission in part and outline planning permission in part. Finlay P. held this a valid decision on general principles with the result that 'or' in s. 26 (1) and Article 21 has the effect of 'and'.

[20] See *Genport Limited* v. *Dublin Corporation* (No. 12718P of 1981) for a detailed analysis of what occurs on 'receipt' of a planning application. In the circumstances of that case an application made in several parts was only 'received' for the purpose of commencing the two-month 'appropriate period' when the final document was lodged.

[21] This was done, twice, in *State (Stanford and Others)* v. *Dun Laoghaire Corporation* (p. 215). For other reasons the decision in this case was held invalid and may have stimulated the enactment of Regulation 30A.

of not less than four weeks in a position convenient for public inspection during normal office hours, and

(c) where the planning authority by resolution so decide, may be displayed for public inspection in any other place which the planning authority considers appropriate or published in a newspaper circulating in the district, or made available to any body, group or person likely to be interested.

25. Where a planning authority receive a planning application, they shall send notice of the nature of the application and of the date of receipt of the application –

(a) where it appears to the planning authority that the land or structure is situate in an area of special amenity, whether or not an order in respect of that area has been made under section 42 of the Act of 1963, or that the development or retention of the structure would obstruct any view or prospect of special amenity value or special interest – to An Chomhairle Ealaíon, Bord Fáilte Éireann and An Taisce — the National Trust for Ireland

(b) where it appears to the planning authority that the development would obstruct or detract from the value of any tourist amenity works – to Bord Fáilte Éireann,

(c) where it appears to the planning authority that the development would be unduly close to any cave, site, feature or other object of archaeological, geological or historical interest, or would detract from the appearance of any building of artistic, architectural or historical interest, or, in either case, would obstruct any scheme for improvement of the surroundings of or any means of access to any such place, object or structure – to An Chomhairle Ealaíon, Bord Fáilte Éireann, the National Monuments Advisory Council and An Taisce – the National Trust for Ireland,

(d) where it appears to the planning authority that the development would obstruct or detract from the value of any existing or proposed development by a local authority – to such local authority,

(e) where it appears to the planning authority that if permission were granted, a condition should be attached under section 26(2)(f) of the Act of 1963 – to any local authority (other than the planning authority) which would be affected under section 26(7) of that Act.[22]

26. (1) Where a planning authority receive a planning application they may by notice in writing, require the applicant to do any one or more of the following[23]

(a) to submit such further particulars, plans, drawings or maps as may be necessary to comply with these Regulations or as they may require;

(b) to provide not more than two additional copies of any plan, drawing or map submitted;

(c) to submit any further information relative to the application (including any information as to any estate or interest in or right over land);

(d) to produce any evidence which they may reasonably require to verify any

---

[22] See fn. 40, *ante*.

[23] The request must be genuine: see Butler J. in *State (Conlon Construction Limited)* v. *Cork County Council* (p. 321) and McMahon J. in *State (N.C.E. Limited)* v. *Dublin County Council* (p. 322).

particulars or information given by the applicant in or in relation to the application.

(2) A planning authority shall not require an applicant who has complied with a requirement under sub-article (1) to submit any further particulars, plans, drawings or information save as may be reasonably necessary to clarify the matters dealt with in the applicant's response to the said requirement or to enable them to be considered or assessed.

(3) Where an applicant fails or refuses to comply with any requirement under this article within one month of such requirement, the planning authority may, if they think fit, determine the application in the absence of the particulars, plans, drawings, maps, information or evidence specified in the requirement.

27. Where a planning authority, having considered a planning application, are disposed to grant a permission or an approval subject to any modification of the development to which the application relates, they may invite the applicant to submit to them revised plans or other drawings modifying, or other particulars providing for the modification of, the said development and, in case such plans, drawings or particulars are submitted, may decide to grant a permission or an approval for the relevant development as modified by all or any such plans, drawings or particulars.[24]

28. (1) An application to a planning authority for a permission for any development to which this article applies shall, notwithstanding the provisions of article 18 or, in the case of an outline application, article 19, be acompanied by two copies of a written study of what, if any, effect the proposed development, if carried out, would have on the environment relative to the place where the development is to take place.

(2) Where a planning authority receive an application for a permission for a development which in their opinion is a development to which this article applies and the application is not accompanied by a written study as required by sub-article (1), they may, in addition to their powers under article 26, require the applicant to submit such written study.

(3) This article applies to any development –

(a) for the purposes of any trade or industry (including mining) comprising any works, apparatus or plant used for any process which would result in the emission of noise, vibration, smell, fumes, smoke, soot, ash, dust or grit or the discharge of any liquid or other effluent (whether treated or untreated) either with or without particles of matter in suspension therein, and

(b) the cost of which, including all fixed assets as defined in section 2 of the Industrial Development Act, 1969 (No. 32 of 1969)[25] may reasonably be expected to be five million pounds or more.

---

[24] This power is discretionary only: a planning authority is not obliged to exercise it if they consider a modified development acceptable. See D'Arcy J. in *State (Abenglen Properties Limited)* v. *Dublin Corporation* (p. 215).

[25] By s. 2 of this Act '"fixed assets" means machinery, plant, equipment, land, buildings, services and other works of or for an industrial undertaking;'.

29.[26] (1) Where a planning application is received by a planning authority, the following shall, during the specified period, be available for public inspection during office hours at the office of the planning authority –

(*a*) the application and any plans, drawings, maps and particulars accompanying it,

(*b*) any further particulars, plans, drawings or maps submitted by the applicant in relation to the application,

(*c*) a copy of any written study submitted in pursuance of article 28, and

(*d*) in the case of an application for an approval, the documents referred to in paragraphs (a), (b) and (c) relating to any permission or other approval to which the application relates.

(2) The specified period for the purposes of this article shall be –

(*a*) from the time of receipt of the relevant document until the application or any appeal relating thereto is determined, and

(*b*) where any permission or approval is granted, a further period until the expiration of the appropriate period under the Act of 1982 in relation to the relevant permission.

30. Form No. 1 set out in the Second Schedule shall be the prescribed form of the notice of the intention of a planning authority to consider deciding to grant a permission in a case where the development concerned would materially contravene the development plan or any special amenity area order.

30A.[27] Without prejudice to any other provision of these Regulations, a planning authority shall not decide to grant or to refuse a permission or an approval until after the expiration of a period of fourteen days[28] beginning on –

(*a*) in case the applicant has been required pursuant to article 23 to publish a further notice of the relevant application, the day on which that requirement has been complied with,

(*b*) in any other case, the day of receipt by the planning authority of the application.

31. Every notification given by a planning authority of a decision on a planning application shall specify –

(*a*) the reference number relating to the application in the register of the planning authority,

(*b*) the nature of the decision,

(*c*) the development or retention or continuance to which the decision relates,

(*d*) the date of the decision,

(*e*) in the case of a decision to grant any permission or approval for the construction, erection or making of a structure and to specify the purposes for which the structure may or may not be used – such purposes,[29]

---

[26] Substituted by Article 9 or S.I. 342 of 1982.

[27] Added by Article 10 of S.I. 342 of 1982.

[28] This regulation clears up the difficulty which occured in *State (Stanford and Others)* v. *Dun Laoghaire Corporation* (p. 215).

[29] By Section 28(*b*) if no purpose is specified the grant includes permission to use the structure for the purpose for which it is designed. See the *Readymix* case (p. 198) for a discussion of what is meant by the purpose for which a structure is designed.

(*f*) in the case of a decision to grant any permission or approval –any conditions attached thereto,

(*ff*) in the case of a decision to grant any permission – any period specified by the planning authority pursuant to section 3 of the Act of 1982 as the period during which the relevant permission is to have effect,[30]

(*g*) in the case of any decision to refuse permission or approval or to grant permission or approval subject to conditions – the reasons for such refusal or for the imposition of the conditions,

(*h*) in the case of a decision to grant any permission or approval – that the permission or approval (as may be appropriate) shall be issued on the expiration of the period for the making of an appeal if there is then no appeal before the Board, and

(*i*) that an appeal against the decision may be made to the Board by the applicant within one month from the date of receipt by the applicant of the notification or by any other person within twenty-one days of the date of the decision.

32. (1) Where a planning authority have given notice of a planning application to a body in pursuance of article 25, the authority shall notify the body of the decision of the authority in respect of the application within seven days of the making of such decision.

(2) Where any person or body (not being a body to which sub-article (1) relates) has submitted submissions or observations in writing to a planning authority in relation to a planning application, the planning authority shall, within seven days of making a decision on the application, notify such person or body of the said decision or publish notice thereof in a newspaper circulating in the district.

33. – (1)[31] Subject to sub-article (2), Form No. 2 set out in the Second Schedule, or a form substantially to the like effect, shall be the form of every notification by a planning authority of a grant of permission or an approval.

(2) Where a planning authority in deciding to grant a permission specify a period pursuant to section 3 of the Act of 1982 as the period during which the relevant permission is to have effect the form shall include a statement of the period so specified.

34. (1) A planning authority may provide forms and instructions for the convenience or information of any person intending to make a planning application.

(2) The Minister may prepare and publish model forms for the use and guidance of planning authorities in dealing with planning applications.

. . .

PART VII

LICENSING UNDER SECTION 89 OF THE ACT OF 1963

53. In this Part –

---

[30] Inserted by Article 11(*a*) of S.I. 242 of 1982.
[31] Substituted by Article 11(*b*) of S.I. 342 of 1982.

'specified appliance or structure' means an appliance or structure referred to in section 89 (1) of the Act of 1963 and includes an appliance or structure specified in article 54.

54. The following appliances and structures are hereby specified as suitable for being licensed under section 89 of the Act of 1963 –

   (*a*) a petrol, oil or other storage tank (together with any associated manhole, inlet, outlet, or pipe for connection with a pump),

   (*b*) a delivery pipe or hose attached to a petrol pump or oil pump, which is erected in a permanent position and which is not on a public road,

   (*c*) a movable pump or other appliance for dispensing any oil or oil derivative or mixture thereof,

   (*d*) a case, rack, shelf or other appliance or structure for displaying articles for the purpose of advertisement or of sale in or in connection with any adjacent business premises,

   (*e*) a lamp-post,

   (*f*) a bridge, arch, tunnel, passage or other similar structure which is used or intended for use other than by the public and which is constructed on or after the appointed day,

   (*g*) a cellar or other underground structure constructed on or after the appointed day,

   (*h*) a coin-operated machine other than a vending machine, and

   (*i*) an advertisement consisting of any symbol, emblem, model or device.

55. (1) Where a licence under section 89 of the Act of 1963 is granted by a planning authority –

   (*a*) to erect, construct, place and maintain, or

   (*b*) to maintain

a specified appliance or structure referred to in Part I or II of the Fourth Schedule, the amount of the fee to be paid to the planning authority shall, subject to the provisions of article 56, be –

   (i) where the licence is for a period of one year, the appropriate amount indicated in the second column of that Schedule opposite the reference in the first column of the Schedule to the specified appliance or structure,

   (ii) where the licence is for a period of more than one year, an amount equal to the fee for one year for each year or part of a year for which the licence is granted, and

   (iii) where the licence is for a period of less than a year, an amount equal to one tenth of the fee for one year for each month or part of a month for which the licence is granted, or one pound, whichever is the greater.

   (2) Where a licence under section 89 of the Act of 1963 is granted by a planning authority to erect, construct, place and maintain a specified appliance or structure referred to in Part III of the Fourth Schedule, the amount of the fee to be paid to the planning authority shall be the amount indicated in the second column of that Schedule and no fee shall be payable in respect of any renewal of a licence to maintain such an appliance or structure.

56. In the case of –

(a) any pump, machine or similar appliance or structure, more than one quarter of the surface area of which is used for advertising purposes,

(b) any town or landscape map more than one third of the surface area of which is used for advertising purposes, and

(c) any other appliance or structure any part of the area of which is used for advertising purposes,

the amount of the fee under article 55 shall be increased by the amount of the fee payable under that article in respect of an advertisement structure which is on a public road.

57. (1) Licence fees received by planning authorities in respect of the specified appliances and structures referred to in Part I of the Fourth Schedule shall be lodged to the[32] county fund in the case of a council of a county and to the municipal fund in the case of a corporation of a county or other borough or the council of an urban district.

(2) Licence fees received by planning authorities in respect of the specified appliances and structures referred to in Parts II and III of the Fourth Schedule shall be paid, in the case of a council of a county, into the county fund and in the case of a corporation of a county or other borough, or the council of an urban district, into the municipal fund.

PART IX

MISCELLANEOUS

64. The prescribed authorities for the purposes of section 46 of the Act of 1963 (being the authorities which must be consulted by a planning authority before they make an order under that section) shall be –

(a) the Minister for Fisheries,

(b) the Royal Irish Academy,

(c) Bord Fáilte Éireann, and

(d) An Taisce – the National Trust for Ireland.

65. Each of the following bodies is hereby declared to be a public authority for the purposes of section 5 of the Act of 1976 –

(a) An Chomhairle Ealaíon,

(b) Bord Fáilte Éireann,

(c) The National Monuments Advisory Council,

(d) The Industrial Development Authority,

(e) Gaeltarra Éireann,

(f) The Shannon Free Airport Development Company Limited,

(g) Cofas Iompar Éireann, and

(h) The Electricity Supply Board.

66. Form No. 4 set out in the Second Schedule, or a form substantially to the like effect, shall be the prescribed form of vesting order to be made by a planning

---

[32] Words after 'lodged to the' substituted by Article 2 of S.I. 231 of 1980 for 'to the Central Motor Tax Account'.

authority in exercise of the powers conferred on them by section 25(5) of the Act of 1976.

67.[33] (4) An application for a waiver notice together with any plans or drawings accompanying it shall be available for public inspection during office hours at the offices of the planning authority until the application or any appeal in relation thereto is determined.

(5) Particulars of a waiver notice issued by a planning authority or by the Board and any confirmation or annulment of a waiver notice by the Board shall be entered in the register.

Article 4

FIRST SCHEDULE

REGULATIONS REVOKED

Number and Year	Title
216 of 1964 ..	Local Government (Planning and Development) Act, 1963, (Appeals and References) Regulations, 1964
217 of 1964 ..	Local Government (Planning and Development) Act, 1963, (Compensation) Regulations, 1964.
219 of 1964 ..	Local Government (Planning and Development) Act, 1963, (Miscellaneous) Regulations, 1964.
221 of 1964 ..	Local Government (Planning and Development) Act, 1963, (Permission) Regulations, 1964.
76 of 1965 ..	Local Government (Planning and Development) Act, 1963, (Licensing) Regulations, 1965.
172 of 1966 ..	Local Government (Planning and Development) Act, 1963, (Miscellaneous and Licensing) Regulations, 1966.
154 of 1967 ..	Local Government (Planning and Development) Act, 1963, (Copies of Development Plans) Regulations, 1967.
176 of 1967 ..	Local Government (Planning and Development) Act, 1963, (Exempted Development) Regulations, 1967.
230 of 1967 ..	Local Government (Planning and Development) Act, 1963, (Miscellaneous) (Amendment) Regulations, 1967.
210 of 1968 ..	Local Government (Planning and Development) Act, 1963, (Licensing) (Amendment) Regulations, 1968.
260 of 1968 ..	Local Government (Planning and Development) Act, 1963, (Exempted Development) (Amendment) Regulations, 1968.
219 of 1976 ..	Local Government (Planning and Development) Act, 1963, (Exempted Development) (Amendment) Regulations, 1976.
226 of 1976 ..	Local Government (Planning and Development) Act, 1976, (Section 25) Regulations, 1976.

[33] S. 29 of the Act of 1976 was substantially repealed by s. 15 (2)(*b*) of the Act of 1982, the effect being to phase out waiver notices and development certificates. Regulations 67 (1), (2), and (3) and 68 were deleted by Regulation 12(*c*) and (*d*) of S.I. No. 342 of 1982.

SECOND SCHEDULE

FORM NO. 1   *Article* 30

Notice of proposed material contravention of development plan or special amenity area order.

LOCAL GOVERNMENT (PLANNING AND DEVELOPMENT) ACTS, 1963 AND 1976.

MATERIAL CONTRAVENTION

[1] { OF DEVELOPMENT PLAN FOR ....
      { OF .... SPECIAL AMENITY AREA ORDER MADE ON

....

Ref. No. in register ....

Notice is hereby given pursuant to section 26 (3) of the Local Government (Planning and Development) Act, 1963, as amended by section 39 (*d*) of the Local Government (Planning and Development) Act, 1976, that[2] ....
intend to consider deciding to grant a permission for[3] ....

....

....

at[4] ....

Such { development }   [1]   would contravene   { development plan   } [1]
     { retention   }   materially the   { special amenity area order }
referred to above. Particulars of the development proposed may be inspected at[5]

....

during office hours. Any objections or representations received not later than 21 days
after the[6] .... day of ....
will be duly considered by the planning authority.

Signed ....

County Secretary/Town Clerk[1]

Date ....

Direction for completing this form.

1. Delete words which do not apply.
2. Insert name of planning authority.
3. Indicate nature of development.
4. Indicate location of land or structure.
5. Insert name and address of office of planning authority.
6. Insert date of first publication of notice.

FORM NO. 2   *Article* 33

Notification of a grant of a permission, an outline permission or an approval.

LOCAL GOVERNMENT (PLANNING AND DEVELOPMENT) ACTS,
1963 AND 1976.

Reference No. in Register ....

Name of Planning Authority ....

....

To   ....

Address   ....

....

....

Application by or on behalf of   ....

of (address) .... on (date) ....

for $\left\{\begin{array}{l}\text{a permission}\\ \text{an outline permission}\\ \text{an approval}\end{array}\right\}$[1] for ....

.... [2]at ....

....

$\left\{\begin{array}{l}\text{A permission}\\ \text{An outline permission}\\ \text{An approval}\end{array}\right\}$[1]   has been granted for the .... [4]

described above (for use as ....)[5]

subject to the following condition(s) – ....

....

....

....

....

The outline permission is subject to further approval being obtained prior to the commencement of any part of the development.[6]

Dated this .... day of .... 19 ....

Signed ....

County Secretary/Town Clerk[1]

——————————

Directions for completing this form.

1. Delete words which do not apply.
2. Indicate nature of development.
3. Indicate location of land or structure.
4. Insert 'development' 'retention', 'change of use' or 'continuance of use'.
5. Delete if not required.
6. This clause should be deleted except where outline permission is being granted.

Notice of order extinguishing a public right of way.

LOCAL GOVERNMENT (PLANNING AND DEVELOPMENT) ACTS, 1963 AND 1976.

EXTINGUISHMENT OF PUBLIC RIGHT OF WAY.

Notice is hereby given that the ....[1]
in pursuance of section 76 of the Local Government (Planning and Development) Act, 1963, have made an order, which will be submitted to the Minister for Local Government for his approval, ordering that the public right of way described in the Schedule hereto shall be extinguished as from the date of the approval of the said order by the said Minister.

A copy of the said order and a map indicating the public right of way have been deposited at...[2]
and may be inspected there during office hours.

Any objection to the said order should be made in writing addressed to the Minister for Local Government, Custom House, Dublin 1. The Acts provide that if there is an objection to the order and the objection is not withdrawn, the Minister shall cause an oral hearing to be held and shall afford the person making the objection an opportunity of being heard.

SCHEDULE

Description of public right of way[2]

Dated this .... day of .... 19 ....
                    (Signature) ....
                                        County Secretary/Town Clerk.

Directions for completing this form.

1. Insert name of planning authority.
2. Insert reference to the place where a copy of the order and map are available for inspection.
3. Insert such description as will be sufficient to identify the public right of way to which the order relates.

FORM NO. 4   *Article* 66

Form of Vesting Order.

LOCAL GOVERNMENT (PLANNING AND DEVELOPMENT)
ACT 1976 – SECTION 25

.... (name of planning authority).

VESTING ORDER

WHEREAS development $\genfrac{}{}{0pt}{}{\text{(is being)}}{\text{(has been)}}$ [1] carried out pursuant to a permission granted

on .... under section 26 of the Local
Government (Planning and Development) Act, 1963 (Reference No. in Register

....);

[2] AND WHEREAS a condition requiring the provision or maintenance of land
as open space, being open space to which section 25 of the Local Government
(Planning and Development) Act, 1976, (hereinafter called 'the Act') applies,
was attached to the permission;

AND WHEREAS it was $\genfrac{}{}{0pt}{}{\text{(explicit)}}{\text{(implicit)}}$ [1] in the application for the permission that
land would be provided or maintained as open space, being open space to
which section 25 of the Local Government (Planning and Development) Act,
1976, (hereinafter called 'the Act') applies;

AND WHEREAS on the .... day .... , 19......,
the ....[3] (hereinafter referred to as 'the
planning authority') served on the owner of the land a written request that within a
period of .... commencing on that day he would provide, level, plant or
otherwise adapt or maintain the said land in a manner specified in the request,
being a manner which in the opinion of the planning authority would make it
suitable for the purpose for which the open space was to be provided;

AND WHEREAS the owner has failed to comply or to secure compliance with
such request within such period;

AND WHEREAS the planning authority have, in accordance with section 25(1)
of the Act, published an acquisition notice in relation to the said land and have, in
accordance with section 25(2) of the Act, served a copy of the notice on the owner
of the land within ten days of the date of publication of the said notice;

[2] AND WHEREAS no appeal has been taken under section 25(3) of the Act;
AND WHEREAS an appeal has been taken under section 25(3) of the Act
and the appeal has been withdrawn;
AND WHEREAS an appeal has been taken under section 25(3) of the Act
and the said acquisition notice has been confirmed in relation to the land
described in the Schedule hereto;

NOW THEREFORE, the planning authority, in exercise of the powers conferred on them by section 25(5) of the Act, hereby order that the land described in the
Schedule hereto, being the land to which the said acquisition notice (as confirmed)[1]
relates, and which is shown on the map attached hereto which said map has been

marked .... [4] and sealed with the seal
of the planning authority, shall, on the .... day of .... ,
19......,[5] vest in the planning authority for all the estate, term or interest for which
immediately before the date of this order the said land was held by the owner
together with all rights and liabilities which, immediately before the said date, were
enjoyed or incurred in connection therewith by the owner together with an obligation to comply with the request made under section 25(1)(c) of the Act.

SCHEDULE

Description of land[6]

The official seal of the planning authority was affixed hereto this .... day
of... , 19......, in the presence of:
.... [7]   .... [7]
.... [7]

Directions for completing this form.

1. Delete words which do not apply.
2. Delete recitals which do not apply.
3. Insert full description of planning authority.
4. The map should be sealed and marked by a heading containing a reference to
   the order e.g. 'Map referred to in order made under section 25 of the Local
   Government (Planning and Development) Act, 1976, on the .... day
   of ...., ..., by .... '.
5. The vesting date can be the date of the order or any subsequent date.
6. The quantity, description and situation of the land should be set out, with an
   appropriate reference to the manner in which the land is shown on the map.
7. The description of the persons in whose presence the seal is affixed should be
   stated e.g. 'Lord Mayor', 'Mayor', 'Chairman', 'Nominated Member', 'City
   Manager and Town Clerk', 'Manager', etc.

FOURTH SCHEDULE

LICENCE FEES IN RESPECT OF APPLIANCES AND STRUCTURES UNDER SECTION 89 OF THE ACT OF 1963

1. Appliance or Structure	2. Licence Fee	
	Where the appliance or structure is in a county borough	Where the appliance or structure is elsewhere than in a county borough
Part I Appliances and structures for servicing vehicles:		
(a) A petrol or oil pump (including any delivery hose, air pipe, water-pipe or other attachment).	£20	£10
(b) A movable pump or other appliance for dispensing any oil or oil derivative or mixture thereof.	£10	£5
(c) A delivery pipe or hose attached to a petrol or oil pump which is not on a public road.	£10	£5
(d) A petrol, oil or other storage tank (whether sub-divided or not) together with any associated manhole, inlet, outlet or pipe for connection with a pump,	£2 for each 5,000 litres capacity or part thereof	£1 for each 5,000 litres capacity or part thereof
(e) A pipe or an appliance with a pipe attachment for dispensing air or water not being a pipe or appliance attached to a petrol or oil pump for which a fee is prescribed under paragraph (a) above.	£2	£1

Part II

Other appliances and structures:

(*a*) A vending machine or other coin-operated machine (not being a weighing machine) which is on a public road.	£20
(*b*) An appliance of any type referred to in Part I of this Schedule which is not used for servicing vehicles.	£10
(*c*) A case, rack, shelf or other appliance or structure for displaying articles for the purpose of advertisement or sale in or in connection with any adjacent business premises.	£10
(*d*) An advertisement consisting of any symbol, emblem, model or device which is on a public road.	£10
(*e*) An advertisement structure which is on a public road.	£10
(*f*) A hoarding, fence or scaffold (not being a hoarding, fence or scaffold bounding a public road).	£10
(*g*) A town or landscape map on a public road.	£2
(*h*) A weighing machine on a public road.	£2
(*a*) A cable, wire or pipeline (not being a cable for conducting electricity for domestic or agricultural purposes or a drain or waterpipe).	£5 per 800 metres length or part thereof.

Part III

Other structures:

(*a*) A bridge, arch, tunnel, passage or other similar structure used or intended for use other than by the public and constructed on or after the appointed day.	£10
(*b*) A cellar or other underground structure constructed on or after the appointed day.	£10
(*c*) A lamp-post.	£5
(*d*) A cable for conducting electricity for domestic or agricultural purposes.	£5

LOCAL GOVERNMENT (PLANNING AND DEVELOPMENT) (AMENDMENT) REGULATIONS, 1982
[S.I. No. 342 of 1982]

The Minister for the Environment, in exercise of the powers conferred on him by section 10 of the Local Government (Planning and Development) Act, 1963 (No. 28 of 1963), and by section 25 of that Act as amended by the Local Government (Planning and Development) Act, 1976 (No. 20 of 1976), and by sections 20 and 35 of the Local Government (Planning and Development) Act, 1976, and by section 11 of the Local Government (Planning and Development) Act, 1982 (No. 21 of 1982), hereby makes the following Regulations:

PART I

PRELIMINARY AND GENERAL

Citation
1. (1) These Regulations may be cited as the Local Government (Planning and Development (Amendment) Regulations, 1982.

(2) These Regulations, the Local Government (Planning and Development) Regualtions, 1977 to 1980 and the Local Government (Planning and Development) (Amendment) Regulations, 1981 (S.I. No. 154 of 1981) may be cited together as the Local Government (Planning and Development) Regulations, 1977 to 1982.

Commencement
2. These Regulations shall come into operation on the lst day of December, 1982.

Interpretation
3. (1) In these Regulations, any reference to a Schedule, Part or article which is not otherwise identified is a reference to a Schedule, Part or article of these Regulations.

(2) In these Regulations, any reference to a sub-article or paragraph which is not otherwise identified is a reference to the sub-article or paragraph of the provision in which the reference occurs.

(3)(*a*) In these Regulations –
'the Act of 1982' means the Local Government (Planning and Development) Act, 1982;
'the Acts' means the Local Government (Planning and Development) Acts, 1963 to 1982;
'the appropriate period' has the meaning assigned to it in section 2(5) of the Act of 1982;
'outline permission' means a permission for development subject to the subsequent approval of the planning authority;
'permission' includes outline permission;
'approval' means an approval consequent on an outline permission or an approval which is required to be obtained under a condition subject to which a permission or an approval is granted under the Acts;[34]
'the 1977 Regulations' means the Local Government (Planning and

---

[34] See fn. 33, p. 157 *ante*. Compare Regulation 19 (5)(*c*).

Development) Regulations, 1977 (S.I. No. 65 of 1977).

(*b*) In these Regulations, any reference to a decision to extend or further extend the appropriate period as regards a particular permission shall include a reference to such a decision which is regarded as having been given by virtue of section 4(2) of the Act of 1982 and cognate expressions shall be construed accordingly.

PART II

EXTENTION OF DURATION OF PLANNING PERMISSION

Time for making application to extend or further extend appropriate period.

4. An application under section 4 of the Act of 1982 to extend or further extend the appropriate period as regards a particular permission shall be made not earlier than one year before the expiration of the appropriate period sought to be extended.

Content of application to extend appropriate period.

5. An application under section 4 of the Act of 1982 to extend the appropriate period as regards a particular permission shall be made in writing and shall contain the following particulars –

(*a*) the name and address of the applicant,

(*b*) the location of the structure or other land to which the permission relates,

(*c*) the development to which the permission relates,

(*d*) particulars of the interest held in the relevant structure or other land by the applicant,

(*e*) the date and reference number in the register of the planning authority of the permission,

(*f*) in the case of an outline permission, the date and reference number in the register of the planning authority of the subsequent approval or approvals,

(*g*) the date on which the permission will cease, or has ceased,[35] to have effect,

(*h*) the date of commencement of the development to which the permission relates,

(*i*) particulars of the substantial works carried out pursuant to the permission before the expiration of the appropriate period,

(*j*) the additional period by which the permission is sought to be extended, and

(*k*) the date on which the development is expected to be completed.

Content of application to further extend appropriate period

6. An application under section 4 of the Act of 1982 to further extend the appropriate period as regards a particular permission shall be made in writing and shall contain the particulars referred to at paragraphs (*a*) to (*h*) inclusive of article 5 and also the following particulars –

(*a*) particulars of the works (if any) carried out pursuant to the permission since the permission was extended or further extended,

[35] See s. 4 (6) of the Act of 1982.

(*b*) the period by which the permission is sought to be further extended,

(*c*) the date on which the development is expected to be completed, and

(*d*) the circumstances beyond the control of the person carrying out the development due to which the development has not been completed during the period by which the permission has been extended or further extended.

Further information

7. (1) Where a planning authority receive an application to extend or further extend an appropriate period, they may by notice in writing require the applicant to do any one or more of the following –

(*a*) to submit such information or particulars as may be necessary to comply with article 5 or article 6, as the case may require,

(*b*) to submit such further information as they may require to consider the application (including any information regarding any estate or interest in or right over land),

(*c*) to produce any evidence which they may reasonably require to verify any particulars or information given by the applicant in or in relation to the application.

(2) A planning authority shall not require an applicant who has complied with a requirement under sub-article (1) to submit any further particulars, evidence or information save as may be reasonably necessary to clarify the matters dealt with in the applicant's response to the said requirement or to enable those matters to be considered or assessed.

(3) Where an applicant fails or refuses to comply with any requirement under this article within one month of such requirement, the planning authority may, if they think fit, determine the application in the absence of the particulars, information or evidence specified in the requirement.

Notification of decision on application to extend or further extend appropriate period

8. (1) Every notification given by a planning authority of a decision on an application to extend or further extend the appropriate period as regards a particular permission shall specify –

(*a*) the reference number relating to the permission in the register of the planning authority,

(*b*) the date of the permission,

(*c*) the development to which the decision relates,

(*d*) the date of the decision,

(*e*) the nature of the decision,

(*f*) in the case of a decision to extend or further extend the appropriate period, the additional period by which that period has been extended, and

(*g*) in the case of a decision to refuse to extend or further extend the appropriate period, the reasons for such refusal.

(2) The form set out in the Schedule, or a form substantially to the like effect, shall be the form of every notification by a planning authority of a decision to extend or further extend the appropriate period as regards a permission.

Article 8

SCHEDULE

Notification of a decision to extend or further extend the appropriate period as regards a planning permission.

LOCAL GOVERNMENT (PLANNING AND DEVELOPMENT) ACTS, 1963 to 1982.

Reference No. in Register _____

Name of Planning Authority _____

To _____

Address _____

_____

_____

_____

Application by or on behalf of ....

of (address) .... on (date) ....

for *further*[1] extension of the *outline*[1] permission for _____

_____[2] at _____

_____[3] granted on____[4] Reference No. as above

A decision to *further*[1] extend the appropriate period as regards the above-mentioned *outline*[1] permission was made on (date) ....

The *outline*[1] permission will now cease to have effect on (date) ....

Dated this ....day of .... 19...............

Signed ....

County Secretary/Town Clerk[1]

Directions for completing this form

1. Delete words which do not apply.
2. Indicate nature of development.
3. Indicate location of land or structure.
4. Insert date of permission.

LOCAL GOVERNMENT (PLANNING AND DEVELOPMENT) (FEES AND AMENDMENT) REGULATIONS, 1983
(S.I. No. 30 of 1983)

The Minister for the Environment, in exercise of the powers conferred on him by sections 8, 10 and 25 of the Local Government (Planning and Development) Act, 1963 (No. 28 of 1963), as amended by the Local Government (Planning and Development) Act, 1976 (No. 20 of 1976), and the Local Government (Planning and Development) Act, 1982 (No. 21 of 1982), and by section 10 of the Local Government (Planning and Development) Act, 1982, and with the consent of the Minister for Finance as respects Parts I, II and III, hereby makes the following Regulations –

PART I

PRELIMINARY AND GENERAL

Citation

1. (1) These Regulations may be cited as the Local Government (Planning and Development) (Fees and Amendment) Regulations, 1983.

(2) These Regulations and the Local Government (Planning and Development) Regulations, 1977 to 1982 may be cited together as the Local Government (Planning and Development) Regulations, 1977 to 1983.

2. These Regulations shall come into operation as follows –

(*a*) Parts I, II and IV and the Schedule shall come into operation on the 7th day of March, 1983,

(*b*) Part III shall come into operation on the 11th day of April, 1983.

3. (1) In these Regulations, any reference to a Schedule, Part or article which is not otherwise identified is a reference to a Schedule, Part or article of these Regulations.

(2) In these Regulations, any reference to a sub-article or paragraph which is not otherwise identified is a reference to the sub-article or paragraph of the provision in which the reference occurs.

(3) In these Regulations, a reference to a provision of the Act of 1963 which has been amended by the Act of 1976 or by the Act of 1982 is a reference to such provision as so amended.

(4) In these Regulations, a reference to a provision of the Act of 1976 which has been amended by the Act of 1982 is a reference to such provision as so amended.

(5) In these Regulations –

'the Act of 1963' means the Local Government (Planning and Development) Act, 1963;

'the Act of 1976' means the Local Government (Planning and Development) Act, 1976;

'the Act of 1982' means the Local Government (Planning and Development) Act, 1982;

'the Acts' means the Act of 1963, the Act of 1976 and the Act of 1982;

'appeal' means an appeal to the Board under the Acts or any order made under the Acts;

'approval' means an approval consequent on an outline permission or an approval which is required to be obtained under a condition subject to which a permission or an approval is granted under the Acts;

'the Board' means An Bord Pleanála;

'the Minister' means the Minister for the Environment;

'minerals' includes all minerals and substances in or under land of a kind ordinarily worked by underground or by surface working for removal but does not include turf;

'oral hearing' means an oral hearing of an appeal or of a reference;

'outline application' means an application for an outline permission;

'outline permission' means a permission for development subject to the subsequent approval of the planning authority;

'permission' includes outline permission;

'planning application' means an application to a planning authority for a permission to develop land and includes –

(a) an outline application,

(b) an application for an approval,

(c) an application for permission for the retention of a structure, and

(d) an application for permission for the continuance of any use of any structure or other land;

'reference' means a reference under section 5 of the Act of 1963;

'State authority' has the meaning assigned to it by section 84 (2) of the Act of 1963;

'the 1977 Regulations' means the Local Government (Planning and Development) Regulations, 1977 (S.I. No. 65 of 1977).

PART II

FEES IN RELATION TO PLANNING APPLICATIONS ETC., TO A PLANNING AUTHORITY

4. Subject to the following provisions of this Part, a fee shall be paid to a planning authority by an applicant in respect of a planning application.

5. The amount of the fee payable under this Part shall, subject to article 6, be the amount indicated in column 2 of the Schedule opposite the mention of the relevant class of development in column 1 of the Schedule.

6. (1) Subject to sub-article (3), the amount of the fee payable under this Part shall, in the case of an application mentioned in sub-article (2), be one-quarter of the amount indicated in column 2 of the Schedule opposite the mention of the relevant class of the development in column 1 of the Schedule, or £15, whichever is the greater.

(2) The applications referred to in sub-article (1) are –

(a) an application for an approval,

(b) an application for permission for the retention of any structure or for the continuance of any use of land without complying with a condition subject to which a previous permission was granted for the development,

(c) an application for permission for the retention of any structure or for the continuance of any use of land in respect of which previous permission has been granted for a limited period only (or subject to a condition which is of a kind described in section 26(2)(j) or 27(2)(f) of the Act of 1963) and which is made not less than two months before the expiration of the previous permission,

(d) an application which relates to development which differs from development authorised by a previous permission by reason only of –

(i) a change in the type of dwelling proposed to be constructed, erected or made, or

(ii) the modification of the design or of the external appearance of a building or other structure proposed to be constructed, erected or made.

(3) This article shall have effect only where a fee under these Regulations has been paid in relation to the relevant previous permission or approval.

7. (1) Where a planning application (not being an application for an approval) is either –

    (*a*) withdrawn before a decision to grant or to refuse the relevant permission is made by the planning authority, or

    (*b*) determined by the planning authority or by the Board,

and a subsequent such application is made by or on behalf of the same applicant, the planning authority shall, subject to article 8 and article 9, refund three-quarters of the fee paid to them in respect of the subsequent application if, and only if, each of the condtiions mentioned in sub-article (2) is complied with.

(2) The conditions referred to in sub-article (1) are –

    (*a*) the authority are satisfied that the subsequent application relates to development of the same character or description as the development to which the earlier application related, and

    (*b*) a fee under these Regulations in respect of the class or classes of development to which the subsequent application relates has been paid in respect of the earlier application, and

    (*c*) the period between the withdrawal or determination of the first application and the making of the subsequent application does not exceed twelve months, and

    (*d*) the authority are satisfied that the subsequent application relates to land substantially consisting of the site or part of the site to which the earlier application related, and

    (*e*) no previous refund under this sub-article has at any time been made to the same applicant in respect of an application which related substantially to the same land and to development of the same character or description as that to which the subsequent application relates.

8. (1) A refund under article 7 shall not be made in any case where a reduced fee has been paid under article 6.

(2) The amount of a refund under article 7 shall not in any case be such as would reduce the balance of the fee in respect of an application to less than £15.

9. A refund under article 7 shall be made on a claim in that behalf made in writing to the planning authority and received by them within (but not after) the period of two months beginning on the day of the giving of the decision by the planning authority on the subsequent application.

10. (1) Subject to sub-article (2), where a planning application relates to development which is within more than one of the classes mentioned in the Schedule –

    (*a*) an amount shall be calculated in accordance with these Regulations in respect of the development which is within each such class, and

    (*b*) the aggregate of the amounts so calculated shall be taken as the amount of the fee payable in respect of the development to which the application relates.

(2) Sub-article (1) shall not have effect in relation to development comprising the provision of roads, car parks, services, open spaces or any structures or other works which are included in the planning application and are incidental to development of the class or classes to which the application primarily relates.

(3) Where a planning application referred to in sub-article (1) relates to a

building which is to contain floor space which it is proposed to use (or which is designed for use or is capable of use) for the purposes of providing common access or common services or facilities for persons occupying or using the building, the amount of such common floor space appropriate to each class of development mentioned in the Schedule shall be taken, for the purposes of the calculation referred to in sub-article (1)(*a*), to be such proportion of the common floor space as the amount of floor space coming directly with the class bears to the total amount of gross floor space in the building.

11. Where a planning application relates to development which is designed for, or capable of, or intended for, use for one of several purposes, the amount of the fee payable in respect of each of the relevant classes of development mentioned in the Schedule shall be calculated and the fee payable shall be the highest of those amounts.

12. Where a planning application includes proposals for materially different layouts or designs relating to the proposed development, the fee payable under these Regulations shall be calculated as if each proposal constituted a separate planning application.

13. Where, in respect of any class of development mentioned in the Schedule, the amount of the fee is to be calculated by reference to the site area –
   (*a*) that area shall be taken as consisting of the area of land to which the application relates, and
   (*b*) where the area referred to in paragraph (*a*) is less than the unit of measurement specified in respect of the relevant class of development or is not an exact multiple of that unit, the fraction of a unit remaining after division of the total area by the unit of measurement shall be treated, for the purposes of calculating the fee payable in respect of the application, as a complete unit.

14. Where, in respect of any class of development mentioned in the Schedule, the amount of the fee is to be calculated by reference to the area of gross floor space to be provided –
   (*a*) that area shall be ascertained by the external measurement of the floor space, on each floor of a building or buildings disregarding any floor space provided for the parking of vehicles by persons occupying or using the building or buildings where such floor space is incidental to development to which the application primarily relates, and
   (*b*) where the area referred to in paragraph (*a*) is less than the unit of measurement specified in respect of the relevant class of development or is not an exact multiple of that unit, the fraction of a unit remaining after division of the total area by the unit of measurement shall be treated, for the purposes of calculating the fee payable in respect of the application, as a complete unit.

15. (1) Subject to sub-articles (2), (3) and (4), a fee of £10 shall be paid to a planning authority by a person making submissions or observations to the authority as regards a planning application.

(2) Sub-article (1) shall not apply where the person by or on whose behalf submissions are made is –

(*a*) the applicant for the permission or approval, or

(*b*) a body referred to in article 21.

(3) Where a fee has been paid under this article by or on behalf of a person or body of persons making submissions or observations as regards a particular application, a fee shall not be payable in respect of any further submissions or observations made by or on behalf of the same person or body of persons as regards that application.

(4) A fee shall not be payable under this article in respect of any objection or representation made to a planning authority pursuant to section 26(3) of the Act of 1963 in relation to the intention of the authority to consider deciding to grant a permission for a development which would contravene materially the development plan or any special amenity areas relating to the area of the authority.

16. (1) A fee shall be paid to a planning authority by an applicant in respect of an application under section 4 of the Act of 1982 for an extension or a further extension as regards a particular permission of the appropriate period within the meaning of section 2(5) of that Act.

(2) The amount of the fee payable under this article shall be one-tenth of the amount of the fee which would be payable under these Regulations in respect of an application for permission for the development to which the permission referred to in sub-article (1) relates, or £15, whichever is the greater.

17. (1) Notwithstanding any other provision of these Regulations, a planning authority shall have an absolute discretion to refund (in whole or in part) such amount of the fee payable in respect of a particular planning application as exceeds £15 where they are satisfied that the payment in full of the fee would not be just and reasonable having regard to any of the following –

(*a*) the limited extent of the development,

(*b*) the limited cost of the development,

(*c*) the fee payable in respect of an application for any other development of a similar character, extent or description.

(2) A decision under sub-article (1) shall contain a statement specifying the reasons for the decision.

(3) Within seven days of the making of a decision under sub-article (1), a copy of the decision shall be transmitted to the Minister.

SCHEDULE
FEES FOR PLANNING APPLICATIONS

PART I

INTERPRETATION

1. For the purpose of this Schedule, a dwelling, building or other structure or thing may be provided by –

(*a*) the carrying out of works,

(*b*) the making of a material change in the use of a structure,

(*c*) the retention on land of a structure already constructed, erected or made,

or
(*d*) the continuance of a use of any structure,
and 'provision' shall be construed accordingly.

2. At references 5 and 6 of column 1 of this Schedule, 'use of land' shall include the continuance of a use of land and the carrying out of works, or the retention of structures, on in or under the relevant land, which are incidental to the use.

PART II

SCALE OF FEES FOR PLANNING APPLICATIONS

Column 1 Class of Development	Column 2 Amount of Fee
1. The provision of dwellings.	£30 for each dwelling.
2. (*a*) Any works for the carrying out of maintenance, improvement or other alteration of an existing dwelling (including any works for the provision of an extension or the conversion for use as part of the dwelling of any garage, store, shed or other structure).	£15
(*b*) Any other works, including the erection of structures, within the curtilage of an existing dwelling, for purposes ancillary to the enjoyment of the dwelling as such.	£15
(*c*) The erection, construction or alteration within or bounding the curtilage of an existing dwelling of gates, railings, fences, walls or other means of enclosure.	£15
3. The provision of any building or other structure for the purposes of agriculture.	(i) In the case of a building, £40, or £1.75 for each square metre of gross floor space to be provided in excess of 400 square metres, whichever is the greater. (ii) In the case of any other structure, £40.
4. The provision of a building other than a building coming within class 1, 2 or 3.	£40, or £1.75 for each square metre of gross floor space to be provided, whichever is the greater.
5. The use of land for – (*a*) the winning and working of minerals, (*b*) the deposit of refuse or waste.	£250, or £25 for each 0.1 hectare of site area, whichever is the greater.

Column 1 Class of Development	Column 2 Amount of Fee
6. The use of land for – (a) the keeping or placing of any tents, caravans or other structures (whether or not moveable of collapsible) for the purpose of caravanning or camping or the sale of goods, (b) the parking of vehicles, (c) the open storage of vehicles or other objects.	£40, or £25 for each 0.1 hectare of site area, whichever is the greater.
7. The provision of, in or under land of plant or machinery, or of a tank or other structure (other than a building) for storage purposes.	£100, or £25 for each 0.1 hectare of site area, whichever is the greater.
8. The provision of a petrol filling station.	£100
9. The provision of an advertisement structure or the use of an existing structure or other land for the exhibition of advertisements.	£40, or £10 for each square metre, or part thereof, of advertising space to be provided, whichever is the greater.
10. The provision of overhead transmission or distribution lines for conducting electricity.	£40, or £25 per 1,000 metres, length, or part thereof, whichever is the greater.
11. Development not coming within any of the foregoing classes.	£40, or £5 for each 0.1 hectare of site area, whichever is the greater.

CASES

WHO MAY APPLY FOR PERMISSION?

FRESCATI ESTATES LTD. V. MARIE WALKER
([1975] I.R. 177)

The plaintiff sought to establish that a person could apply for permission to develop land in respect of which he or she had no interest whatsoever, either existing or prospective. In seeking to establish this principle, emphasis was placed on the fact that whereas 'owner' is defined in Section 2 of the 1963 Act, this term is not used of the party making an application for planning permission in the regulations which refer at all times to 'applicants' which by inference includes a wider category. 'Applicant' is not defined.

The defendant was the honorary secretary of a local voluntary association which wished to preserve Frescati House, historically associated with the life of Lord Edward Fitzgerald, which was part of the plaintiff company's property in Blackrock in respect of which they had submitted several applications for development which included demolition of the house. The defendant in turn, made her own application for planning permission which was inconsistent with the plaintiff's proposals and which involved the protection of the house. The defendant had no interest in the plaintiff's lands and no prospect of acquiring such an interest. In these circumstances the plaintiff brought proceedings seeking injunctions restraining the defendant from proceeding with her application for planning permission and directing her to withdraw it. In the High Court Kenny J. accepted the argument that 'applicant' is a wider term than 'owner' and refused the injunction. The plaintiff appealed to the Supreme Court which also accepted that the choice of the word 'applicant' indicated that the person seeking planning permission did not require to have a legal estate or interest in the property,[36] but went on to insist that the category of such persons was to be restricted, having regard to the general objects of the Act and also in consideration of the mechanisms put in train by the making of an application.

High Court
Kenny J.:

. . . I am convinced that the defendant applied for this permission as part of the campaign to prevent the plaintiffs from carrying out any development of the property, and that she has no intention or hope of acquiring any estate of any kind in the property or of developing it. . .

The question which has to be decided on this application is whether a person may apply for and obtain planning permission in respect of property in which she has no estate or proprietary interest of any kind and in which she has no hope of getting an estate or interest. This is a question of far-reaching importance to almost everyone in our community. . . .

Regulations under s. 25 of the Act of 1963 were made by the Minister. They are called the Local Government (Planning and Development) Act, 1963, (Permission) Regulations, 1964. Article 3 of the regulations provides, so far as it is relevant: 'An application to a planning authority for a permission for the development of land . . . shall be accompanied by (a) particulars of the interest held in the land . . . by the applicant, the name and address of the applicant, and . . . .' Counsel for the plaintiffs has argued that the Act of 1963 and the regulations show that an applicant for planning permission must have some estate or right in the land.

Although the Act of 1963 contains a very wide definition of the word 'owners', the person who makes the application for planning permission is throughout the Act described as 'the applicant', and there is nothing in the Act which suggests that the person applying for permission must have an estate or proprietary interest or right in the land. If a purposive interpretation of the Act is adopted, it seems to me that a person with no estate or proprietary interest or right may wish to find out, before he enters into a contract to acquire any interest in the land, whether he will get planning permission; and this may have been the type of case which the National Parliament or the draftsman had in mind. In my opinion, the Act of 1963 does not require that the applicant for permission for development should have any estate or proprietary interest or right in the land to which the application relates.

Article 3 of the regulations seems to me to require the applicant to state whether she has any estate or interest in the land: it does not make it a preliminary condition

---

[36] In *McCabe* v. *Harding Investments Limited* O'Higgins C.J. observed that the planning authority in that case sought 'a general idea of the applicant's interest or estate in the lands and a precise legal definition of what it is'. (p. 196).

for an application. Article 7 (which provides that where development of land would contravene a development plan made by the planning authority, an outline application made 'by the owner of such land may, if he so wishes, indicate in writing the type and extent of development proposed') disposes of any argument based on the regulations because it shows that 'an applicant' (a term used throughout the regulations) is a wider term than 'owner'. The regulations show that the 'applicant' and the 'owner' are not necessarily the same person.

In my view the argument that an applicant for planning permission must have an estate or propriety interest or right in the land to which the application relates is incorrect, and the plaintiffs have no prospect of success in this action. Therefore, the application for injunction fails. . . .

Supreme Court

Henchy J.: (Fitzgerald C.J.; Walsh, Budd, Griffin JJ. concurring).
The substantive question in this case may be put shortly. Is a person who has no legal estate or interest in a property entitled to apply under the Local Government (Planning and Development) Act, 1963, for permission to develop the property?

The plaintiffs are the owners in fee simple of the property in question. Not alone has the defendant no legal estate or interest in it but the trial judge found as a fact that 'she has no intention or hope of acquiring any estate of any kind in the property or of developing it.' The plaintiffs' application for permission to develop it having been refused, they claimed compensation of £1,309,972 under s. 55 of the Act of 1963. So as to avoid liability for the compensation claimed, the planning authority gave the plaintiffs an undertaking on the 4th October, 1973, to grant development permission subject to certain conditions. The matter would no doubt have proceeded to a satisfactory conclusion – at least from the plaintiffs' standpoint – were it not for the intervention of the defendant who, by letters dated the 30th August and the 8th October, 1973, applied for outline planning permission to develop the property in a manner quite inconsistent with the way the plaintiffs wished to develop it. On the 28th November, 1973, the planning authority notified the grant of the outline planning permission sought by the defendant, notwithstanding the fact (now found by the trial judge) that she had no intention or hope of acquiring any estate of any kind in the property or of developing it, and that her application was made merely as part of a campaign to prevent the plaintiffs from carrying out any development of the property.

The plaintiffs lodged an appeal to the Minister against the permission notified to the defendant and, since they contend that the defendant's planning application is a nullity, they seek in the present proceedings an injunction to restrain the defendant's application and a mandatory injunction ordering her to withdraw it. The matter came before Mr. Justice Kenny as an application for those injunctions in interlocutory form. Rejecting the submission that the defendant's application was void because she has no estate or proprietary interest or right in the land, he refused the application for the interlocutory injunction. Hence the present appeal by the plaintiffs.

Counsel for the defendant puts her case in broad and forthright terms. Conceding that his client has no special standing by virtue of any legal estate or interest, actual or prospective, in the property, he bases her claim to be entitled to apply for development permission entirely on the fact that the provisions of the Act dealing with applications for development permission (in particular, ss. 25 and 26) refer to an *applicant* and not, as in the case of certain other provisions of the Act, to an *owner* (which is specially defined in s. 2) or *occupier*.

For my part I have no difficulty in accepting that the choice of the word *applicant* and the deliberate avoidance of the use of any word or expression to suggest that the person seeking permission should have any legal estate or interest in the property show that the legislature did not intend that possession of such estate or interest by the person applying was to be necessary. The trial judge so held and I would respectfully agree.

The sweep of the argument of counsel for the defendant, however, carries with it the further submission that because no limiting qualifications are laid down by the relevant sections for an applicant, *anyone* can be an applicant for development permission. An applicant may not be debarred, the argument runs, not alone because he has no legal estate or interest in the property but also irrespective of the genuineness or otherwise of the proposed development, or whether the applicant is acting in good faith or not, or whether those with a legal estate or interest know or approve of the application, or whether other (and possibly conflicting) applications have been made or are pending. There is nothing in the Act, it is said in effect, to debar a pauper from making an application for permission for a multi-million pound development of a property which he has only read about in a newspaper.

Support for those far-reaching propositions is said to be found in the fact that development permission (except as may be otherwise provided by the permission) enures for the benefit of the property and of all persons for the time being interested therein (s. 28, sub-s. 5); so unless and until the person who has got a permission acquires the necessary interest, the permission remains merely a paper or potential benefit annexed to the land. If more than one such permission are granted, and even if they are granted without the knowledge or approval of the owner or occupier, it is argued that no harm is done to anyone because none of those permissions can be put into effect except by a person who has an interest in the property. So, it is said, the purposes of the Act of 1963 are not frustrated or diverted if applications for development permission are open to all and sundry.

That the proposition that virtually anyone may apply for permission to develop a particular property could lead to strange incongruities was shown by instances raised in the course of the argument. However, it is a matter of principle that a statute – particularly a statute like the present one which makes substantial inroads on pre-existing rights – should not be construed as intending to confer unqualified and indiscriminate rights on people generally in respect of another's property such as the right to avail themselves of the legal processes of a planning application so as to gratify what may be merely an idle or perverse whim. The long title of this Act proclaims its purpose to be '. . . to make provision in the interests of the common good, for the proper planning and development of cities, towns and other areas. . . .' The powers given by the Act must be read as being exercisable in the interests of the common good and the Courts should lean against a construction which would make the exercise of such powers available to an individual for the purpose of advancing a purely personal motive at the expense of the general purpose of the Act.

Apart from the irreconcilability with the general principle of the proposition put forward on behalf of the defendant, a number of specific provisions of the Act clearly show its unsoundness. For the sake of brevity I shall confine myself to a selection of those provisions for the purpose of showing that the operation of the Act requires that an applicant for permission must have a particular degree of standing.

When an application for development permission under Part IV of the Act is made, it puts in train a scheme of inquiry, investigation and hearing leading to a quasi-judicial determination. Much of the necessary procedure is laid down by regulations made pursuant to the Act, but these I ignore in determining the scope of the Act. As Lord Diplock said in the context of another Act : – 'It is legitimate to use the Act as an aid to the construction of the Regulations. To do the converse is to put the cart before the horse' – *Lawson* v. *Fox*.[37]

Section 25, sub-s. 1, of the Act of 1963 requires the Minister to make permission regulations and enacts that permission shall be granted on application being made in accordance with the regulations and subject to the requirements of the regulations. Sub-section 2 of that section proceeds to set out what the regulations may require from applicants. The regulations may require any applicants 'to furnish to the Minister and to any other specified persons any specified information with respect to their applications' (para. c) and 'to submit any further information relative to their applications' (including any information as to any estate or interest in or right over land)' and 'the production of any evidence to verify any particulars of information given by any applicants' – see paras. (d) and (e).

Since applications cannot be successful unless they comply with the requirements of the regulations (s. 25, sub-s. 1), the legislature must be credited with the intention of delineating the range of eligible applicants by the extent of the permitted requirements. Thus, a total stranger to the property, who has no liaison with those interested in it, could scarcely have been envisaged as a successful applicant, for normally he could not furnish the specified information (including any estate or interest in or right over the land) or produce evidence to verify particulars given as to such information.

Furthermore, when we turn to s. 9, sub-s. 1, of the Act of 1963 we find that a planning authority may, for any purpose arising in relation to their functions under the Act, require the occupier or the person receiving the rent to state in writing within a specified period particulars of the estate, interest or right by virtue of which he is an occupier or receives the rent and the name and address (so far as they are known to him) of every person who to his knowledge has any estate or interest in or right over or in respect of the property. Sub-section 2 of that section makes it an offence punishable on summary conviction with a fine not exceeding £20 for a person from whom such information is required to fail to state it within the time specified, or to make a statement in writing which is to his knowledge false or misleading in a material respect.

The effect of s. 9 is that when an application for permission to develop is made, the planning authority, in order to carry out their functions under the Act, may find it necessary to serve on the occupier or the person receiving the rent the notice referred to in sub-s. 1 of the section; if the person so served does not comply with the notice in the way specified in sub-s. 2, he will become liable to the sanction of the criminal law. If, as counsel for the defendant contends, applications for development permission may be made in multiplicity and indiscriminately by persons at large, obligations would be cast on occupiers of or persons receiving rent

[37] [1974] A.C.803, 809.

out of property and failure to comply with those obligations would subject such people to a fine with a liability to imprisonment in default of payment. The fundamental rule that a statute must be construed so as to keep its operation within the ambit of the broad purpose of the Act rules out such an interpretation; otherwise it would be possible for persons, by means of frivolous or perverse applications, to cause the imposition of duties and liabilities which would be wholly unnecessary for the operation of the Act in the interests of the common good.

Section 83 of the Act of 1963 provides an equally cogent reason why the Act does not envisage persons unconnected with any real interest in property or its development being allowed to apply for development permission. That section provides that an authorised person (*i.e.,* a person so authorised for the purposes of the section by the planning authority or the Minister) may enter, subject to an order of the District Court prohibiting or restricting the entry, on any land for any purpose connected with the Act and may do all things reasonably necessary for the purpose for which the entry is made and, in particular, may survey, make plans, take levels, make excavations, and examine the depth and nature of the subsoil. If the Act had to be read as allowing that degree of intrusion at the behest of *any* individual who chooses to make a development application in respect of another person's property, the constitutionality of the statute would be very much in question.

The inequities and anomalies that would follow if there is to be an unrestricted right to apply for permission to develop another persons's property is shown by the terms of many provisions of the Act. For example, since the planning authority must investigate and deal with each application with sufficient care to ensure that their decision will have due regard to the development plan required by Part III of the Act, a group of people making multiple applications in respect of properties in which they have no legal interest, and which they have no intention or hope of developing, could put such a strain on the resources of the planning authority as to stifle the operation of the Act in delay and confusion. Since s. 41 requires particulars of all applications for development permission to be entered on the register (which s. 8 requires the planning authority to keep), and since s. 28, sub-s. 5, provides that a grant of permission willl normally enure for the benefit of the property and all persons interested in it, the register (which incorporates documents by reference) would become encumbered with bulk and detail if applications without restriction were allowed, and consequently might prove confusing or misleading for those who would be required to consult it.

If there need never be a connexion between the applicant and those who have a legal estate or interest in the property, the period for appealing against the decision of the planning authority would be, for the applicant, one month from the *receipt* of the decision, but for others (who, if the argument on behalf of the defendant is correct, could include those with a legal estate or interest) it would be 21 days from the day of the *giving* of the decision (s. 18, sub-s. 5) – thus giving preferential treatment to someone who may be merely a meddlesome interloper. It is no answer to this complaint to say that a grant or refusal of an application for development permission cannot prejudice a subsequent application. As I have shown, the mere making of an application by a person with no legal interest can operate to the detriment of the owner or occupier. And in any case, I find nothing in the scheme of the Act that would allow interfering, if well-intentioned, outsiders to intrude into the rights of those with a legal interest to the extent of lumbering the property with unwanted grants or refusals of permission, thus cluttering the title.

To sum up, while the intention of the Act is that persons with no legal interest (such as would-be purchasers) may apply for development permission, the operation of the Act within the scope of its objects and the limits of constitutional requirements would be exceeded if the word 'applicant' in the relevant sections is not given a restricted connotation. The extent of that restriction must be determined by the need to avoid unnecessary or vexatious applications, with consequent intrusions into property rights and demands on the statutory functions of planning authorities beyond what could reasonably be said to be required, in the interests of the common good, for proper planning and development.

Applying that criterion, I consider that an application for development permission, to be valid, must be made either by or with the approval of a person who is able to assert sufficient legal estate or interest to enable him to carry out the proposed developments or so much of the proposed development as relates to the property in question. There will thus be sufficient privity between the applicant (if he is not a person entitled) and the person entitled to enable the applicant to be treated, for practical purposes, a person entitled.

As for the present case, the defendant's application was invalid and should not have been entertained for she had no legal estate or interest in the property and her application was made without the knowledge or approval of the plaintiffs who, as the owners of the fee simple, are the only persons who would be legally competent to carry out the development for which the defendant sought permission. . . .

STATE (Alf-a-Bet Promotions Ltd.) V. BUNDORAN U.D.C.
(112 I.L.T.R. 9)

Application was made by architects on the 26th February, 1974, for change of use of premises in the centre of Bundoran Town to amusement arcade 'for Messrs. Alf-a-Bet Ltd., Secretary, Jim Gorman'. Although four individuals including Jim Gorman had agreed before this to purchase the relevant premises and to form a company to be called 'Alf-a-Bet Promotions Ltd.', no such company as either of the two referred to was in existence on the date of the application and it was not until October, 1976, that Alf-a-Bet Promotions Ltd. was formed. The local planning authority did nothing within the two months following receipt of this application (save to send a notice of further particulars to the vendor of the land which the trial judge held inoperative to suspend the two-month period from running), but subsequently wrote to the applicants requiring them to submit a proper application.

At the end of 1976 the company commenced altering the premises and the planning authority moved for an injunction to restrain the new alterations, some of which included development for which permission had been sought in February, 1974. The applicants contended that they had planning permission by default and brought these proceedings for a declaration to that effect. It was held in the High Court by McWilliam J. that except in unusual circumstances the actual identity of the applicant is not material to the making of an application for planning permission, and that provided the application was made by a person with an interest in the matter, the mere fact that a company was named which had not been formed or was inaccurately or incorrectly described would not of itself render the application invalid. This decision must now be regarded as of doubtful authority following a strong *obiter dictum* of Henchy J.[38] Again, the Supreme Court held in *State (N.C.E.) Ltd. v. Dublin County Council* that the use by a well-known supermarketing company of the name of an associate company in a planning application notice was a ruse to mislead the public and that therefore the application was invalid. The only record of this decision, delivered ex tempore on the 14th May, 1980 is the notebook of the Registrar of the Supreme Court.

McWilliam J.

. . .The next contention on behalf of the Council causes me more difficulty. There was no company called Alf-a-Bet Limited, so no notice could be sent to it. On the other hand, Mr. Jim Gorman's name and address were given and he was named as secretary and the application was made by architects whose address and telephone number were on the letter of application and who would, undoubtedly, have been well known to the Council's officials. The letter of application did state that the premises had been purchased from Mr. Irvine Hamilton but this seems hardly a sufficient reason for sending the notice to him and it is hard to understand why the notice was not sent to the Architects or to Gorman or to both. I cannot accept that this notice was, in itself, sufficient, but so soon as the mistake was appreciated, and without any further delay, a new notice was sent to Gorman and the Council relies very strongly on the decision in the Norfolk County Council case. This was a case in which a council employee inadvertently notified an applicant that he had been granted permission when he had, in fact, been refused it by the Council. The applicant then made a token commencement of the development and the Council moved to stop it. There was no detriment to the applicant and the Court held that the Council was not bound by the mistaken notice and could rely on the actual decision refusing permission. That case was different from the present, in which there has been no decision other than a notional decision due to no step having been taken by the Council within the requisite time. At the same time, I think the principles with regard to mistake and absence of detriment are applicable. But this does not end the matter. Mr. Gorman and his associates ignored the letters of 3rd May and 11th June, 1974, and having already got a certificate for a gaming licence, went ahead with the development in accordance with the plans. Subsequently the main interest in the venture appears to have been acquired by John Coyle and the Company was formed at the end of October, 1976. Until this time no further step seems to have been taken by either party other than the annual applications for gaming licences until the end of 1976 when an extensive structural development not included in the original application was commenced by the Company although no application for permission appears to have been made until 7th January, 1977, and the Council moved immediately and obtained an injunction to restrain it. This

[38] This decision is now of doubtful authority following a strong *obiter dictum* to the opposite effect by Henchy J. in *State (Finglas Industrial Estates Limited) v. Dublin County Council* (p. 224), where he said 'on top of everything, the Minister's permission was granted to developers who had no existence, for they did not become incorporated until April 1981. Were the latter point the only issue in this appeal, I fear that I would hold that the Minister's permission was invalid for having been granted to a non-existent legal person. I do not think that any provisions in the Companies Act, 1963, validating acts done before incorporation, can detract from the fact that it is inherent in the Planning Code that the planning authority and the public shall have an opportunity of vetting the planning application in the light of, amongst aother matters, the identity of a named and legally existing applicant. However, this is not the main issue in this appeal.'

development is the subject-matter of the second application before me. This re-activated the original application for permission and the Architects wrote requiring a grant of permission for it on the grounds of default under Section 26 (9)(a)(i). This was refused.

Under all these circumstances, I am of opinion that the Council having made a mistake and having been made aware of it, should have taken some steps to ascertain what was going on and not relied merely on the letters of 3rd May and 11th June, 1974. Accordingly, I am satisfied that the Council is not entitled to rely on this ground either.

On the question of the Company's right to an Order of Mandamus, I do not see how the original application can be affected by the fact that there is an application for a further development of part of the premises, the subject-matter of the original application. The argument on behalf of the Council that the section does not direct the Council to grant permission may be technically correct but, on the view I have taken of the case to the Company is entitled either to a declaration that a decision by the Council to grant the permission is to be regarded as having been given on 27th April, 1974, or to an Order of Mandamus. In my view, if a decision to grant permission is regarded as having been given, the Council is bound to grant the permission and I will make the Order sought.

. . .

IMPERATIVE REGULATIONS AND DIRECTORY REGULATIONS

Considerable judicial attention has been paid to the question whether the regulations which govern the making of an application for planning permission or the submission of an appeal are imperative in the sense that non-observance renders void everything which follows or whether they are directory merely so that non-observance will not be fatal the validity of what follows.

The first in time of the Irish cases to deal with this question was *Frank Dunne Developments Limited* v. *Dublin County Council* ([1974] I.R.45). An application made in the name of 'F. Dunne', failed to state the interest owned by the applicant in the lands, or to give 'the area and the city, town or county' as a heading in the newspaper advertisement. Pringle J. held that the failure to comply exactly with the specified requirements did not invalidate the application and the requirements were directory only. Some 10 years later the Supreme Court in *Monaghan U.D.C.* v. *Alf-a-Bet Promotions Limited* cast doubt upon this decision but did not overrule it in terms. However, the Court held in the *Monaghan U.D.C.* case that the regulations regarding publication were imperative and that failure to comply would render void all subsequent proceedings. Specific advertance was made by Henchy J. to the *de minimis* rule, which would allow an exception for merely technical or minimal non-observance.

An example of a fatal failure to comply with these requirements is *State (N.C.E.)* v. *Dublin County Council* (unreported judgment of McMahon J. delivered 4th December, 1979; *ex tempore* judgment of the Supreme Court delivered 14th May, 1980). In that case the Supreme Court held that an application made by a subsidiary company in respect of land which was owned by its parent was not an application under the regulations which required the applicant to state its interest in the lands. The applicant had in fact no interest in the lands and the subsequent proceedings were void. This decision runs counter to the earlier decision of McWilliam J. in *State (Alf-a-Bet Promotions Limited)* v. *Bundoran U.D.C.* where the Judge held that an application in the name of a company yet to be formed was a sufficient compliance with the regulations.

In *State (Toft)* v. *Galway Corporation* the Supreme Court refused to make a *Certiorari* Order in favour of a neighbour quashing a planning permission where the only point was that the planning application was made in the name of Spirits Rum Co. Ltd., instead of the true name which was Rum Spirits Ltd. The evidence showed that the plaintiff was or ought to have been well aware of the identity of the applicant company and that his purpose was merely to prevent a competitor opening up business nearby.

Finally, in *State (Walshe)* v. *An Bord Pleanala* Keane J. held that the failure of a third party appellant to include the grounds of his appeal with his letter to An Bord Pleanala did not invalidate the appeal itself. The requirement that the appeal should state the grounds was directory merely having regard to the general objects of the regulations. This decision was subsequently endorsed by the Supreme Court in *State (Elm Developments Limited)* v. *An Bord Pleanala.*

The position therefore is that the Court will have regard to the purposes for which the regulations were imposed and presumably to the degree of divergence from the specific requirements in any case. The Court may also have regard to the conduct of the party seeking to challenge the validity of any decision. It seems sufficiently clear that breach of any of the requirements dealing with publicity is likely to invalidate the ensuing proceedings. In *McCabe* v. *Harding Investments Limited* O'Higgins C.J. made a distinction between regulations providing what must accompany an application and those which provide what must be done before an application is lodged.

THE REGULATIONS – MANDATORY OR DIRECTORY

FRANK DUNNE LTD. V. DUBLIN COUNTY COUNCIL
([1974] I.R. 45)

A planning application marked 'urgent' was handed in personally to the planning authority on Friday, 8th August, 1969. The applicant subsequently received an acknowledgement stating the application was received on 11th. By letter dated the 10th October, 1969, the planning authority wrote to the applicant requiring further information. An issue arose as to when the application was received the applicant contending that it was received on the 8th August, that the letter of the 10th October was outside the two-month period and that planning permission by default should be granted. The planning authority countered with an allegation that the application did not comply with the regulations in several relatively minor respects. Judge Pringle found as a fact that the application was received by an official of the planning authority on the 8th August, the evidence being that it was personally handed in on that day and that therefore the letter of the 10th October was out of time and that a default planning permission should be granted. He also held that the several minor departures from the regulations did not invalidate the application because the regulations were directory only and not imperative, as contended for by the planning authority.

This judgment is also interesting because of a subsidiary argument by the applicant that a condition directed to ensure that adequate sound insulation provisions would be provided in the houses (which were near Dublin Airport) was *ultra vires* the powers of the planning authority notwithstanding the general power under Section 26(1) of the 1963 Act to attach conditions to a planning permission. This contention was upheld by the trial judge who decided with some doubt that the particular condition was not sufficiently connected with the planning and development of the area or with the preservation or improvement of the amenities thereof to be a valid exercise of the power. Although in the 1976 Act, there is specific jurisdiction to impose conditions relating to noise, the dicta in this judgement are of relevance when considering the ambit of Section 26(1) of the 1963 Act.

Pringle J.:
. . . It appears that there is no general rule as to when a statutory enactment is imperative and when it is merely directory. As Lord Campbell said in *Liverpool Borough Bank* v. *Turner*[39] 'No universal rule can be laid down for the construction of statutes as to whether mandatory enactments shall be considered directory only or obligatory, with an implied nullification for disobedience. It is the duty of Courts of justice to try to get at the real intention of the legislature, by carefully attending to the whole scope of the statute to be construed.' It appears to be clear that some provisions in an enactment may be imperative and others merely directory.

The non-compliance with the regulations relied upon by the defendants is as follows. First, that the application did not contain particulars of the interest held in the land by the applicant in accordance with Article 3 (*a*) of the Regulations. The letter of application stated that it was made 'on behalf of Frank Dunne Limited, 5 Tara Street, Dublin 2, who has purchased the land coloured green. . .' Undoubtedly this did not indicate what particular interest the plaintiffs had purchased; for instance, whether it was a freehold or a leasehold interest. I must confess that I have had some difficulty in understanding what was the object of this requirement as, apparently, a person may apply for planning permission even if he has no interest in the land; I cannot see how it is of any importance for the planning authority to know whether the applicant has any interest or, if he has an interest, to know what is the nature of his interest. In my opinion this requirement is directory only and a failure to state particulars of the interest does not invalidate the application.

The second alleged failure to comply with the regulations is that the notice published in the Irish Press did not contain 'as a heading' the names of 'the area and the city, town, or county, in which the land' is situate in accordance with Article 9, sub-article 4(a), of the Regulations. This notice was as follows 'CO. DUBLIN – (*in large letters*] Permission to build ten houses, Carrick Hill Portmarnock, F. Dunne.' The heading 'Co. Dublin' does show the county in which the lands are situate and the body of the notice shows the area which is Carrick Hill, Portmarnock. The purpose of these requirements for the notice would appear to me to be that the public may be notified of the particular area in which the lands are situate, and in my opinion this notice is effective for this purpose and the requirements that the area should be contained in the notice 'as a heading' is merely directory and not imperative. There is another point taken about this notice, and that is that the name of the applicant is stated to be 'F. Dunne' and not 'Frank Dunne Limited.' The application for permission was made by Mr. Frank Dunne on behalf of the company and the defendants' postcard, acknowledging receipt of the notice, was

---

[39] (1861) 30 L.J.Ch. 379.

addressed to him; and in the subsequent documents served by the defendants the applicant is stated to be 'Frank Dunne.' In my opinion, the regulation was complied with although it was not stated that the applicant was applying on behalf of an undisclosed principal, namely, the company.

The last objection to the application was that the plans which accompanied it did not comply with Article 8, sub-article 1(c) and (d), of the Regulations as they did not indicate the scale upon which they were drawn and as the north point was not indicated thereon. Article 4, sub-article 1, deals with the furnishing of plans with the application and it provides that they should contain 'such other particulars as are necessary to identify the land. . .' I consider that the requirements in regard to the plans are inserted in order that the lands may be readily identifiable, and that the requirements in regard to scale and north point are merely directory and not imperative.

The effect of s. 26, sub-s. 4(a)(i) and (ii), of the Act of 1963 is that, in order that the section should apply, the application must be made in accordance with permission regulations and that any requirements relating to the application of or made under such regulations must be complied with. As I am of opinion, as already stated, that, insofar as the application in this case did not comply with the precise requirements of the regulations, these requirements were merely directory and not imperative, and that therefore the application was not invalidated by any defect therein. I think it follows that the application was made in accordance with the Regulations of 1964 and that the requirements of the Regulations were complied with, that the conditions precedent were fulfilled and that the plaintiffs are therefore entitled to the first three declarations asked for in the statement of claim. However, they are not entitled to any damages as they could either have treated the subsequent purported permission as a nullity and proceed with their work accordingly, or they could have proceeded immediately after the 8th October, 1969, to have this purported permission quashed by certiorari.

This is sufficient to conclude the matter, but I have been asked to express my views also on the plaintiffs' alternative claim. The order made by the defendants, dated the 17th December, 1969, purporting to grant planning permission contained the following conditions which the plaintiffs say are invalid, as being ultra vires the powers of the defendants:–

'2. That Messrs. Frank Dunne Ltd. and their successors and/or any subsequent developers must notify all purchasers or tenants, that the Department of Transport and Power have stated that aircraft noise will be significant in the area of the proposed development.

3. That the following modifications be carried out to the houses in construction:

    (a) All external walls shall be 11 inch cavity walling, both leaves being of 4½ inches solid concrete or stone.

    (b) That roof spaces shall be completely insulated at ceiling joist level with fibre-glass mineral wool or equivalent material.

    (c) Double glazing shall be fitted in all windows.

    (d) All external doors shall be solid, i.e. without glazed panels.

    (e) Only one open fire shall be provided in any house.

    (f) Permanent ventilation, as required in Building Bye-Laws approval No. 75 shall in so far as it is possible be provided as permitted in paragraph 5(B)(2) of that Bye-Law.'

Section 26, sub-s. 1, of the Act of 1963 provides that 'the authority may decide to grant the permission or approval subject to or without conditions or to refuse it; and in dealing with any such application the planning authority shall be restricted to considering the proper planning and development of the area of the authority (including the preservation and improvement of the amenities thereof), regard being had to the provisions of the development plan, the provisions of any special amenity area order relating to the said area and the matters referred to in subsection (2) of this section.'

Sub-section 2 of s. 26 provides that 'conditions under subsection (1) of this section may, without prejudice to the generality of that subsection, include all or any of the following conditions. . .'. There then follow ten sub-paragraphs dealing with various types of condition which may be imposed.

As regards condition 2 mentioned above, the reason stated in the notification of the decision is as follows:

'The local authority has been advised by the Department of Transport and Power by letter dated 12 March 1968 that aircraft noise will be significant in the area of the proposed development.' In my opinion this condition can have no relation to the planning and development of the area and is an unreasonable restriction which the defendants had no power to impose, and indeed the validity of this condition was not seriously pressed by Mr. Finlay.

As regards condition 3, the reason given for this is 'to provide sound insulation in houses against aircraft noise' – not, it is to be noted, as in the case of condition 4 which is stated to be made 'in the interests of the proper planning and development of the area'. However, I do not think the fact that the latter was not given as the reason for imposing the condition precludes the defendants from justifying their power to do so on the ground suggested by Mr. Finlay, which is that it was imposed in order to preserve or improve the amenities of the area. Mr. McCarthy, in answer to this contention says that the modifications required in the houses by this condition do nothing to preserve the amenities of the area, and that there is no such thing as an amenity of silence of open land. Mr. Finlay relied on *Fawcett Properties Ltd.* v. *Buckingham County Council*[40] in which the Court considered a permission to develop which had been given subject to a condition that the occupation of the houses for which permission was granted should be limited to persons who were, or had been, employed in agriculture. Apart from the fact that the relevant English Act entitled the planning authority to make 'such conditions as they think fit', differing in this respect from our Act, the condition was held to be valid because it was imposed in pursuance of the planning authorities' policy that houses should not be erected in the area (which was a 'green belt') unless they were used in connection with the use of adjoining land for agriculture or similar purposes. With some doubt, I consider that this condition is also invalid, as it is not sufficiently connected with the planning and development of the area, or the preservation or improvement of the amenities thereof. The requirements of this condition would seem to me to be more appropriately dealt with by building regulations which can be made by the Minister under s. 86 of the Act of 1963.

I will make the orders asked for at (1), (2), and (3) of the statement of claim but I will make no order on the other claims, except that I will declare the plaintiffs entitled to their costs.

---

[40] [1960] 3 W.L.R. 503.

MONAGHAN U.D.C. V. ALF-A-BET PROMOTIONS LTD.
(Unreported Supreme Court judgments delivered on the
24th March, 1980)

O'Higgins C.J.:
. . . The material facts are as follows: On the 26th April, 1977, the respondents received from the appellants an application for permission pursuant to the Act of 1963 for the change of user of premises at The Diamond, Monaghan. This application was accompanied by an extract from the Northern Standard, a local newspaper, as proof of compliance with Article 14 of the Local Government (Planning and Development) Regulations, 1977. This extract was of a notice stating that the appellants were applying for planning permission to the Monaghan County Council in respect of alterations and improvements at their premises at The Diamond, Monaghan. On the 26th April, 1977 the Town Clerk on behalf of the respondents wrote to the appellants indicating that they should publish a notice of their intention to apply to the respondents for planning permission. The letter indicated that the respondents and not the Monaghan County Council was the proper body to which to apply for planning permission. On the 28th April, 1977 the appellants published the appropriate notice and on the 11th May sent an extract to the respondents. On the 24th June 1977 the respondents refused the permission sought and on the 28th June 1977 notice of this refusal was given to the appellants. In these circumstances if the application received by the Urban District Council on the 26th April 1977 was in order and no notice envisaged by sub-section (4)(b)(iii) of Section 26 of the 1963 Act was served by the respondents the two-month period would have expired before the appellants were notified of the refusal – the appropriate dates being the 26th April 1977 and the 26th June 1977. The appellants' case is to this effect and they submit that as notification of refusal was not given until the 28th April 1977 after the two-month period had expired, sub-section (4)(a) of Section 26 of the 1963 Act operated in their favour and a decision to grant permission or approval must be deemed to have been given.

The question to be considered is whether the application received by the respondents on the 26th April was in fact in order. In accordance with sub-section (4)(*a*) already quoted, this application was required to be 'in accordance with permission regulations'. These regulations are contained in Part IV of S.I. 65 of 1977. Article 14 of these regulations provides for the publication of the notice. Article 15 provides that this notice shall contain as a heading the name of the city, town or county in which the land or structure is situate and 'shall state' other particulars including the nature and extent of the development. It is conceded that the notice published in the Northern Star was not headed as required nor did it contain the particulars required by Article 15. Mr. Browne on behalf of the appellants submitted that these requirements in Article 15 were directory merely and not imperative. He relied on the decision of Pringle J. in *Dunne Limited* v. *Dublin County Council* [1974] I.R. 45. This decision relates to the former regulations and to provisions which differ materially from the requirements of Article 15. I do not accept that what is laid down in the regulations which apply in this case can be regarded as directory merely. It seems to me that the wording of Article 15 is mandatory and that the requirements set out in the article are imperative. I have, therefore, come to the conclusion that the applicants failed to make an application to the planning authority, the Urban District Council, in accordance with the permission regulations which applied and that accordingly the notice received by the respondents on the 26th April, 1977, not being in accordance with these regulations, was a nullity. In my view, therefore, the contention put forward by the appellants on this appeal fails and I would dismiss this appeal.

Henchy J.:
. . . In my opinion the applicants failed to comply with the Regulations in at least one vital respect. Art. 15 of the Regulations required the notice in the newspaper to state, inter alia, 'the nature and extent of the development'. This it failed to do. Considering that one of the primary objects of the published notice – if not the primary object – is to enable interested members of the public to ascertain whether they have reason to object to the proposed development, the efficacy of the notice in this case was negatived by the omission from it of any indication of the real nature or extent of the proposed development. No member of the public could have been expected to glean from the general words 'alterations and improvements' that the development permission sought was for what we now know it to have been, namely, the conversion of what had been a drapery shop in the town of Monaghan into a betting office and amusement arcade. The publication of such a veiled and misleading notice was a substantial and flagrant breach of the statutory requirement that the application be in accordance with the Regulations.

In *Dunne Ltd.* v. *Dublin County Council* [1974] I.R. 45 Pringle J. gave consideration to circumstances in which the statutorily required compliance with planning regulations similar to those under consideration in the present case might be overlooked by the Courts. I do not feel called upon to express an opinion as to whether the non-compliances in that case were properly ignored as merely trivial departures from what the regulations in question mandated as being necessary, or whether such non-compliances would be excused in circumstances other than those peculiar to that case. I do, however, feel it pertinent to express the opinion that when the 1963 Act prescribed certain procedures as necessary to be observed for the purpose of getting a development permission, which may affect radically the rights or amenities of others and may substantially benefit or enrich the grantee of the permission, compliance with the prescribed procedures should be treated as a condition precedent to the issue of the permission. In such circumstances, what the legislature has, either immediately in the Act or mediately in the Regulations, nominated as being obligatory may not be depreciated to the level of a mere direction except on the application of the *de minimis* rule. In other words, what the legislature has prescribed, or allowed to be prescribed, in such circumstances as necessary should be treated by the courts as nothing short of necessary, and any deviation from the requirements must, before it can be overlooked, be shown, by the person seeking to have it excused, to be so trivial, or so technical, or so peripheral, or otherwise so insubstantial that, on the principle that it is the spirit rather than the letter of the law that matters, prescribed obligation has been substantially and therefore adequately, complied with.[41]

The combination of s. 26 of the 1963 Act and articles 14 and 15 of the Regulations makes it clear that it was part of the expressed legislative intent that, in a case such as this, development permission should not issue by default unless the notice

---

[41] This passage was explicitly relied upon by Hamilton J. in *McCabe* v. *Harding Investments Limited* (p. 195).

published in 'a newspaper circulating in the district in which the relevant land or structure is situate' has specified, amongst other things, the nature and extent of the development asked for. Every member of the public in the district in which the premises in question is situate has an interest in seeing that undesirable development will not be permitted. The environmental character of a district is the legitimate concern of, at least, all who live or work there. It is unfortunate that the wide choice of newspaper publication allowed may lead on occasion to development permission being granted before persons vitally affected are even aware that it has been applied for. Many people would hold that the permitted modes of notification to the public of planning applications are unfairly inadequate and merit amendment. It is difficult to rebut such a complaint when one realises how easily the present system allows even the most assiduous watcher of the property or of the newspapers to miss the notification of the appalication.

Be that as it may, when notification of the application is chosen to be made in a newspaper, one of the primary purposes of the notification is defeated if the notice does not, at least in fair and general terms, state the nature and extent of the proposed development. Whether the unilluminating words used in this case ('alterations and reconstruction') were chosen deliberately for their vagueness, or casually through inattention to the stated requirements of the Regulations, they were so wanting in compliance with the spirit and purpose of the Act and Regulations that the published notice, and therefore the application must be deemed to have been nullified. The planning authority were therefore entitled to treat the application as a nullity, and there was no obligation on them to point out to the applicant that the published notice was defective.

The precise extent to which a published notice must comply with the requirements specified in the Regulations must depend on the circumstances of the particular case. Consequently, notwithstanding decisions such as *Dunne Ltd.* v. *Dublin County Council*, it should not be assumed that defects in a published notice, such as the wrong name of the applicant, or an inaccurate or incomplete description of the premises or of its location, or a failure to state the existing use of the premises, will necessarily be overlooked.[42] Such powers as have been given to planning authorities, tribunals or the courts to operate or review the operation of the planning laws should be exercised in such a way that the statutory intent in its essence will not be defeated,[43] intentionally or unintentionally, by omissions, ambiguities, misstatements or other defaults in the purported compliance with the prescribed procedures.

Since the published notice in this case was defective to the extent that it nullified the application, I would dismiss this appeal and uphold the injunction granted by McMahon J.

Griffin J.:

Under Article 17 the planning application must be accompanied by a copy of the newspaper in which there has been published a notice in pursuance of Article 15. If, therefore, a notice published does not comply with the provisions of Article 15, there cannot be compliance with the provisions of Article 17. In the present case,

---

[42] See judgment of the same Court in *Cordaun Holdings Limited* v. *Kildare County Council* (p. 146).

[43] Compare the remarks of McCarthy J. in *Creedon* v. *Dublin Corporation* (p. 234).

the notice published in the Northern Standard in purported compliance with Article 15 did not in fact comply with that Article in two respects namely:
(1) it did not contain, as a heading, the name of the town in which the land or structure is situate; and
(2) It did not contain the nature and extent of the development.

Notwithstanding these defects in the published notice, it was contended on behalf of the applicants that the notice was nevertheless a valid notice as the permission regulations with which there had not been compliance were, it was alleged, merely directory and not mandatory or imperative. As authority for this proposition, the applicants relied on a decision of Mr. Justice Pringle in *Dunne Ltd.* v. *Dublin County Council*, [1974] I.R. 45. In that case, the application was in the name of Frank Dunne Ltd. whilst the publication in the newspaper was in the name of F. Dunne. In addition, the applicants failed to state in the application what interest they had in the land. Again, the regulations in force at that time required that the publication in the newspaper should contain 'as a heading' the names of 'the area and the city, town or county in which the land is situate'. It was held by Mr. Justice Pringle that these failures to comply with the regulations did not invalidate the application, as the respective regulations were not mandatory or imperative but merely directory.

Whilst it is not necessary for the purpose of this appeal to express any opinion on the question as to whether the imperfections in that case invalidated the planning application, I respectfully disagree with the learned trial Judge in that case that the relevant regulation in respect of the interest of the applicant in the land is merely directory, or that the failure to state correctly the name of the applicant or the failure to include in the notice published, as a heading, the name of the city, town or county is necessarily merely directory. In fairness to the trial Judge, when the case was heard (in 1970) it was quite usual for persons who had no interest whatever in land to apply for planning permission in the belief that an interest was not necessary, and this was one of the factors which led the trial Judge to the conclusion that the relevant regulations were directory. That practice and belief continued until the decision of this Court in *Frescati Estates* v. *Walker* [1975] I.R. 177.

It is a well established rule of construction that the ordinary sense of words used in a statute or in regulations made thereunder is primarily to be adhered to; that requirements in public statutes which are for the public benefit are to be taken to be mandatory or imperative; and that provisions which on the face of them appear to be mandatory or imperative cannot without strong reason be held to be directory. In its ordinary sense *shall* is to be construed as mandatory or imperative. This is the word which is used in Articles 14 and 15 and therefore the requirements should ordinarily be held to be mandatory unless the failure to comply with them was not substantial.

Apart, however, from the ordinary rules of construction there are, in my view, compelling reasons why the regulations should be held to be mandatory and not directory. The long title to both the Act of 1963 and the Act of 1976 commences with the following:

'An Act to make better provision, in the interests of the common good, in relation to the proper planning and development of cities, towns and other areas, whether urban or rural'. . .

The purpose of the Acts therefore is to ensure proper planning and development, not in the interests of the developer, but in the interests of the common good. The primary purpose of the requirements of Article 14 and 15 in relation to the notice in newspapers is to ensure that adequate notice is given to members of the public, who may be interested in the environment or who may be affected by the proposed development, that permission is sought in respect of that development, so as to enable them to make such representations or objections as they may consider proper. It is with that object in view that Article 15 required that the notice should contain, as a heading, the name of the city or town or county, and should also contain the name of the applicant, the address of the structure to which the application relates and the nature and extent of the development. In the present case, the stated reasons for refusal of the permission were that the use of the premises as an amusement arcade and betting office would be incompatible with the existing pattern of use in the important urban space in the central area of Monaghan town occupied by The Diamond; that the development would be ser-iously injurious to the amenities of the area and contrary to proper planning and development, and that the proposal would be seriously injurious to the amenities of the area of The Diamond and would depreciate the value of property in the vicinity. It was therefore vital that interested persons should have been given adequate notice of the fact that the application was in respect of a change of use, and that the nature and extent of the development should have been stated in the advertisement.

The respects in which it is alleged that the notice published in the Northern Standard did not comply with Article 15 were: (1) (although this was not strongly pressed) that it did not contain, as a heading, the name of the town of Monaghan; and, (2) that it did not state the nature and extent of the development, this being the main argument of the Council. As to the first, there was no heading on the notices published in the newspaper, other than the words 'planning notice'. The requirement that the name of the city, town or county should appear as a heading on the notice is, in my opinion, of importance and the reason for this requirement is clear. These notices usually appear in a lengthy column in the daily newspapers under the heading 'planning application', and the purpose of this provision is to ensure that persons examining this list may have their attention directed to those in which they are interested, without the necessity of having to read through the entire of the notice published in the list. If there was no such provision in Article 15, a person interested in watching town planning applications in his own area could quite easily miss or overlook a notice in respect of development in his area. With regard to the second respect in which it is alleged that the published notice did not comply with Article 15, the notice stated that the planning permission sought was 'for extensions and improvements of a premises at The Diamond, Monaghan'. In my view, by no stretch of the imagination could this description bring home to anyone reading it the fact that the nature and the extent of the development was a change of use from a drapery shop to a betting office and amusement arcade. In my opinion, the requirement of Article 15(c) that the published notice shall state the nature and extent of the development is mandatory, and the Council were entitled to take the stand that, in that respect, the requirements of Article 15(c) had not been complied with.

As compliance with the regulations is necessary under Section 26(4)(a)(ii) of the Act of 1963, the applicants cannot acquire planning permission by default. The user by the applicants of the premises as an amusement arcade was therefore an unauthorised use of the land. Mr. Justice McMahon was accordingly empowered, pursuant to Section 27(1) of the Act of 1976, to prohibit the applicants, its servants, agents or licencees from continuing the development or unauthorised use of the premises at The Diamond, Monaghan.

I should like to add one final word in respect of the publication of notices in compliance with the permission regulations. In *Readymix (Eire) Limited. v. Dublin County Council*,[44] in relation to planning applications I said that the planning authority were meant only to be watchdogs and not blood-hounds. It seems to me that the same words are appropropriate in relation to members of the public in so far as notices published under Articles 14 and 15 are concerned. Although the intention of the Acts and the regulations is that wide publicity should be given to these notices, in practice it is frequently the case that this is not so. Thus, notices are published in a newspaper circulating in the district with the lowest possible circulation; they are couched in such terms as are calculated, if not to mislead, to give as little information as possible; and generally are published in such a manner as is likely to escape being noticed by members of the public. These practices are repugnant to the spirit, if not always the letter, of the Acts and are to be discouraged. Planning and development have become such an important feature of modern life that the Acts and the regulations should be strictly applied by planning authorities and the courts.

I would affirm the order made by Mr. Justice McMahon in the High Court and dismiss this appeal.

STATE (TOFT) V. GALWAY CORPORATION
([1981] I.L.R.M. 439)

This case is an example of the application of the *de minimis* rule referred to by Henchy J. in his judgment in *Monaghan U.D.C.* v. *Alf-a-Bet Ltd.* In *Toft*'s case the Supreme Court refused an application to invalidate a planning permission where the application was made in the name of Spirits Rum Company Limited instead of Rum Spirits Limited. This was a genuine error which did not confuse or mislead Mr. Toft.

O'Higgins C.J.:

. . . It follows that the appellant could have been under no misapprehension as to the real identity of the true owners of the premises.

On the 1st February, 1980, the appellant obtained in the High Court from Mr. Justice D'Arcy a conditional order of *certiorari* directed to the Galway Corporation to send before the High Court for the purpose of being quashed its Order granting planning permission dated the 16th August, 1977. Prior to the obtaining of this Order the applicant sought and was granted an extension of time for the making of the necessary application. The conditional order of *certiorari* was granted on the affidavit of the appellant's solicitor who deposed to the fact that he had on that day made a search in the company's office and had discovered that the company named as Spirit Rum Company Limited in the said Order did not exist. The Solicitor's Affidavit contained the submission that on this account the provisions of Regulation 17 of the Planning Regulations, to the effect that every planning application shall be accompanied by particulars of the Applicant's interest in the land or structure the subject matter of the application, had not been observed. Cause was duly shown on behalf of Galway Corporation and the facts and circumstances to which I have already adverted were established. Mr. Justice Costello who heard the motion brought by the Applicant to have the Conditional Order made absolute, discharged this Conditional Order on the cause shown. Against his decision this appeal has been brought.

In his Report to this Court as to his reasons for dismissing the appellant's Motion and discharging the Conditional Order Mr. Justice Costello states as follows:

'I concluded that the Corporation had jurisdiction to make the impugned Order. The Regulations provide that the 'Applicant' is required to publish notice of his intention to make the application (Regulation 14 and Regulation 15), and that the Planning Application is to be accompanied by the name and address of the 'Applicant' (Regulation 17) but the mistake made in the Applicant's name in the notices and in the application did not, in my opinion, deprive the Corporation of jurisdiction in relation to the application. 'Rum Spirit Limited' had authorised the making of an application under the Act of 1963 and the Corporation had before it an application on which it was required to adjudicate. It is true that the application was brought in the name of a non-existent company, but it was not a non-existent application. It is possible that certain errors in applications might be such as to vitiate the entire proceedings under the Section and deprive the planning authority of jurisdiction but it seems to me that the mistake made in the present case did neither. The Corporation had before it an 'application' which it was empowered to consider and upon which it could adjudicate. The Corporation had power to correct the error by amending its Order so as to show the company's correct name, and Section 8 of the Act of 1963 acknowledged the right of the Corporation to make 'corrections' in its planning register.'

I think these are sound reasons and justify the decision of the learned trial Judge. I would, however, go further. *Certiorari* is at all times a discretionary remedy. In exercising a discretion as to whether the remedy should be granted regard should be had not only to the harm which the Applicant for the remedy alleges but also to his conduct. It is said with justification that *certiorari* issues *ex debito justitiae* where an aggrieved or complaining person can point to his legal rights being affected by the order or decision sought to be annulled. In such circumstances a court will be more concerned with dealing with the irregularity than with the conduct of the prosecutor. In this case, however, the appellant can only point to the inconvenience or disadvantage to him of a similar business to his own being opened in adjoining premises. He can point to no legal right of his being infringed by the Order made by the Galway Corporation. In addition it is quite clear, in my view, that his application for *certiorari* was only one of many attempts which he has made since 1977 to prevent a business competitor opening up nearby. The Order he sought to have quashed was made on the 16th August, 1977. He cannot have been unaware in view of subsequent events that a mistake had been made in naming the holding company. Nevertheless he did not seek *certiorari* until February, 1980. I am not satisfied that this delay was or could be excused. In my view, therefore, even if the genuine error made in the planning application had led to some technical non-observance of the regulations I do not think this is a case in which *certiorari* should issue.

In my view, this appeal should be dismissed. I think, however, that this Court should direct the Galway Corporation to exercise its powers under Section 8 of the Local Government (Planning and Development) Act, 1963, to correct the entry in the Planning Register by substituting for the name Spirits Rum Company Limited the name Rum Spirits Limited.

There is one other matter which I think ought to be mentioned. I note that in seeking the Conditional Order the applicant sought and was granted an extension of time. This was done, I assume, because it was thought that Order 81, Rule 10 applied to the Order in question. I do not think it does. The provisions of this rule, in my view, apply only to Orders made by the District Court or the Circuit Court. I do not think that any time limit applies in this case except such as would be considered reasonable and appropriate in the exercise of the discretion which I have mentioned.

McCABE V. HARDING INVESTMENTS LTD.
(Unreported Judgments of Supreme Court, 27th October, 1982)

A similar point arose in *John McCabe* v. *Harding Investments Limited* (1982) No. 182P: Judgment of Hamilton J. delivered on the 1st March, 1982, affirmed in the Supreme Court.

The plaintiff challenged the validity of a planning permission granted to the defendant. At the time of the application the defendant had a contract to purchase the fee simple in the subject lands. Article 17(a) of the 1977 Regulations requires an application for planning permission to be accompanied by (inter alia) particulars of the interest held in the land by the applicant. The defendant stated that it was the owner of the freehold interest in the subject site, whereas in fact it was merely entitled to a conveyance thereof pursuant to the contract which had not yet been completed. Both Courts applied the *de minimis* rule enunciated by Henchy J. in the *Monaghan Urban District Council* case. Hamilton J. said in the course of his judgment: 'I am further satisfied that there was no intention on behalf of the defendants to mislead either the Planning Authority or An Bord Pleanala and that there was compliance on the part of the defendants with the requirements of Article 17(a) of the relevant Regulations. If there was not actual compliance I am satisfied that any deviations from the requirements of the Article were so trivial, so technical and so insubstantial that, in the words of Mr. Justice Henchy, the prescribed obligation has been substantially and therefore adequately complied with.'

In the Supreme Court the Chief Justice made the point that Regulation 17(*a*) was designed so that the planning authority would be given a general idea of the applicant's interest in the lands, the concern being to establish that the applicant should have an interest in the lands. This article (together with Articles 18, 19 and 20) deal with what are to *accompany* an application and may be distinguished from other Articles prescribing what must be done prior to lodging an application. The information given by the applicant wa snot substantially inaccurate, wrong or misleading and accordingly the *de minimis* rule could be applied.

O'Higgins C.J. (Hederman J. concurring)[45]
In Dublin it appears that applications for planning permission are required to be

---

[45] Henchy J. delivered a separate judgment also dismissing the appeal.

made on a form issued by the Dublin Corporation as the planning authority. This form provides that the particulars referred to in Regulation 17(a) are to be given by filling a blank space at paragraph 10 opposte the requirement: 'State applicant's legal interest or estate in site (i.e. freehold, leasehold etc.). From this it would appear that what the planning authority seek is a general idea of the applicant's interest or estate in the lands and not a precise legal definition of what it is. The concern of the planning authority is that the applicant should have an interest in the lands sought to be developed. Further, it is to be noted that Regulation 17 (and also Regulations 18, 19 and 20) deal with what is to accompany the application made to the planning authority. In this respect these regulations differ from Regulations 14, 15 and 16 which refer to what the applicant is required to do prior to applying for planning permission. These particular Regulations cater for and deal with the interest of the general public in an intended development. In this case no question raises as to compliance by the defendants with the provisions of the Reglations affecting the general public. The plaintiff's complaint is that the defendants in dealing with paragraph 10 in the application form inserted the word 'freehold' as descriptive of their then interest in the site. The plaintiff asserts that this did not accord with the factual situation which obtained on the 6th April 1981, when the application form was completed, and that accordingly the provisions of Regulation 17(a) were not complied with. On this ground the plaintiff claims that the application was not made in compliance with what was essential to a valid application and that accordingly the permission granted to the defendants was null and void. The net question, therefore, is whether the information given by the defendants at paragraph 10 in the application form was so inaccurate, wrong and misleading as to constitute a failure to give particulars of the defendants' interest in the site and a breach of the statutory requirement imposed upon them by Regulation 17(a). I have come to the conclusion that it was not, for two reasons.

In the first place it seems to me that a general description of the defendants' interest in the lands at the time as being 'freehold' was neither inaccurate, wrong or misleading. The defendants were the purchasers of the site under a valid and subsisting contrat by which they were purchasing the fee simple interest for £300,000. They were willing purchasers and at the date of the application had already paid £200,000 of the purchase money, the balance being withheld merely for the completion of conveyancing steps already agreed to by the vendors. In these circumstances the defendants clearly had a beneficial interest in the site, certainly to the extent of the purchase money paid, which, as they were purchasers of the fee simple, could fairly be described as a freehold interest.

In the second place it seems to me that even if the description given of the defendants' interest lacked accuracy or particularity, which I do not accept, the divergence from accuracy and particularity was so insignificant and trivial as proper to be ignored. In this respect I regard as applicable the words of Henchy J. in dealing with the application of the *de minimis* rule to these permission regulations. He said in *Monaghan Urban District Council* v. *Alf-a-Bet Promotions Limited* as follows:

> In other words, what the legislature has prescribed, or allowed to be prescribed, in such circumstances as necessary should be treated by the courts as nothing short of necessary, and any deviation from the requirements must, before it can be overlooked, be shown, by the person seeking to have it excused, to be so trivial, or so technical, or so peripheral, or otherwise so insubstantial that, on the

principle that it is the spirit rather than the letter of the law that matters, the prescribed obligation has been substantially and therefore adequately, complied with.

In my view, these words apply in the circumstances of this case. Even if the description of freehold wanted in accuracy, I believe what was lacking was so technical and insubstantial as proper to be ignored.

I have come to the conclusion that the claim made by the plaintiff in these proceedings lacks reality and is without foundation. It is admittedly made for the sole purpose of seeking to deprive the defendants of the benefit of the planning permission which they obtained both from the Planning Authority and An Bord Pleanala. However justifiable the plaintiff's annoyance at this development may have been or still is, it cannot excuse the mounting of an action which cannot succeed and which is therefore vexatious. In the circumstances and on the facts the continuance of this action would constitute an injustice to the defendants. In my view, the learned trial Judge was correct in the Order which he made dismissing the plaintiff's claim.

I would dismiss this appeal.

INTERPRETING A PLANNING PERMISSION

A planning permission is an appendage to the title[46] of land, it enures for the benefit of the land and of all persons for the time being interested therein[47] and will be interpreted by reference to the documents required by the Regulations for constituting the application and grant of permission, for example, the newspaper advertisement, the letter of application, any accompanying plans and particulars, formal grant of permission and any conditions attached thereto.[48]

There has been a divergence of judicial opinion as to whether or not a planning permission will be interpreted by reference only to these documents or whether the Court can have regard to the surrounding circumstances as well. The earlier view expressed in the *Readymix* case[48] was that private understandings between or interpretations by individuals concerned is irrelevant to the interpretation of a planning permission which must be interpreted objectively by reference only to the documents referred to. The planning permission may fall to be interpreted many years after it has been granted and the individuals may not be available to give evidence.

More recently the Supreme Court in *Dun Laoghaire Corporation* v. *Frescati Estates Limited*[49] adopted a different line. In that case a question arose as to whether a reference to the intended 'retention' by the applicant of Frescati House in the letter of application for planning permission was incorporated into the subsequent conditioned grant of permission so as to impose on the developer an obligation not only to demolish this house but in fact to restore it. Both High and Supreme Courts held that there was no such obligation. In trying the issue, however, the Supreme Court requested further evidence of the relationship and

[46] This phrase is used by Henchy J. in the *Readymix* case (see p. 203): compare his observation in the *Frescati* case that a multiplicity of planning decisions could result in 'cluttering the title'.
[47] See s. 28 (5) of the Act of 1963.
[48] See the *Readymix* case at pp. 203–4.
[49] Judgment delivered ex tempore on 21st December, 1982: this case is not to be confused with *Frescati Estates Ltd.* v. *Walker* dealt with at p. 175 .

negotiation between the parties over the years in order to elucidate the context in which the undertaking to 'retain' had arisen. This approach was also adopted by Gannon J. and the Supreme Court in *Jack Barrett (Builders) Limited* v. *Dublin County Council.*[50]

One of the points decided by Barrington J. in the High Court decision in *The State (Pine Valley Developments Limited)* v. *Dublin County Council*[51] was that on an application for approval consequent upon the grant of outline planning permission the planning authority was confined within the four walls of the outline permission and were not therefore entitled to make a decision on the application for approval which was inconsistent with the existence with the grant of outline permission.

READYMIX (EIRE) V. DUBLIN COUNTY COUNCIL AND MINISTER FOR LOCAL GOVERNMENT
(Unreported High Court Judgment of Pringle J. delivered 12th August, 1970: Unreported Supreme Court Judgments delivered 30th July, 1974)

The central question in this case was whether a grant of permission for the replacement of a conventional concrete plant was sufficiently wide to permit the introduction of a considerably expanded Readymix operation. Dublin County

[50] Unreported judgment delivered 2nd May, 1979 and 28th July, 1983. (See p. 544). There have been a number of cases involving the interpretation of conditions attaching to specific planning permissions where no written judgments have been delivered. In two of these *Hayes* v. *Clare County Council* (1981: 114: S.S. and *Clifford* v. *Limerick Corporation* (1982: 272: S.S.) decided respectively by Gannon and Barrington J.J., section 56 (1)(g) of the Act of 1963 fell to be considered. In each case permission was refused on the grounds that the proposed development would interfere with scenic amenities in the area. The precise wording of Sub-s. (g) was not used in either case but in each case the Judge held that the reason for the refusal was the same as the reason set out at sub-s. (g) notwithstanding the fact that the same words were not used. Accordingly payment of compensation was excluded. The Judges in these cases went behind the actual words to the meaning of the condition.

Again in three cases brought by Athlone Urban District Council under section 27 of the Act of 1976 for the purpose of recovering monies due as contributions towards the provision of car parks by the local authority which facilitated the developments in question Finlay P. decided (on 6th December, 1982) that the monies were recoverable. The evidence showed that the local authority had spent sums significantly in excess of all monies collected under similar conditions attaching to implemented planning permissions that this had been spent on car parking facilities within the seven years prior to the relevant decision. This order was made notwithstanding the fact that the wording of the relevant conditions was somewhat vague referring as they did in the alternative to past or future works. The President took into account the fact that by s. 42 of the Act of 1976 any challenge to the validity of the relevant condition was barred as the two-month period therein referred to had long since elapsed.

St. Anne's Estates Limited v. *Dublin Corporation and Dublin County Council* was decided by D'Arcy J. in June 1978. By s. 56 (1)(c)(i) and the Third Schedule, Part 2, No. 6(c) of the Act of 1963 a condition 'regulating or controlling the provision of . . . water supplies, sewers, drains . . .' which attaches to a planning permission operates to exclude the payment of compensation under s. 55. In this case the planning authority had imposed a condition on the grant of planning permission which required that the developer provide a culvert for the River Poddle which was bigger than that needed by the development in question and which facilitated to the development of stream. It as held by D'Arcy J. that this was not a condition within the sub-section and accordingly compensation was not excluded.

[51] Judgment delivered 27th May 1981.

Council as planning authority granted the permission but when it appeared that the developer sought to set up a Readymix type operation involving several visits by specially designed lorries each day, the planning authority took the view that this would constitute a material change of use itself requiring permission and when the developer refused to accept this and indicated an intention to proceed the County Council referred the issue to the Minister under Section 5 of the 1963 Act. Proceedings were then brought by the developer seeking, inter alia, an injunction to restrain the parties from dealing with the Section 5 reference on the grounds that no question had arisen because the proposed user was within the permission granted which was to be construed as permitting a Readymix type operation.

Apart from dealing with this central issue the judgments indicate the criteria by which a planning permission must be interpreted. The situation is that the permission must stand independently as a public document and if it incorporates other documents (such as plans and particulars lodged) it should be construed by reference to these and to the newspaper or other notice. It must not, however, be construed by reference to any informal understanding which may have been shared by individuals processing the application. The judges who delivered written judgments in the case were equally divided in their actual interpretation as to whether or not the plans lodged in this case disclosed an intention that the development was for a Readymix type operation. They were, however, at one with regard to the principles to be applied.

Pringle J. at first instance held that the plans lodged did disclose a Readymix type operation, that the grant of permission did not specify (or limit) use for any particular purpose and that therefore Section 28 (6) of the 1963 Act applied which meant that the developer was entitled to use the structure for the purpose for which it was designed. The word 'designed' in this context was to be construed in a wide sense meaning 'intended' as distinct from limiting the use to any particular architectural design. Therefore there was no question for reference to the Minister.

In the Supreme Court Budd J. held that the plans did specify a particular user, namely replacement of an existing concrete and block making plant. This was radically different to a Readymix type plan which was not authorised by the grant. Accordingly there was an issue to be referred to the Minister under Section 5 and the plaintiff was refused his injunction. Griffin J. in the Supreme Court came to the same conclusion and also held that the newspaper notice failed to comply with the publication requirements to give notice of the 'nature and extent' of the proposed development if this development was for the Readymix type operation. Judge Henchy delivering a minority judgment came to the conclusion that the plans did show a purpose for which the plant was to be used, but in his case he concluded that the purpose was for the production of concrete without any limitations to any one kind of production so that Readymix production was authorised.

In the result the developer failed to get his injunction.

High Court

Pringle J.:

. . . I am satisfied that an inspection of the plans lodged should have disclosed to the qualified officers of the planning authority that the new structures were intended to be used for the production of ready-mix concrete and not for the purpose of making concrete blocks or bricks and that therefore the replacement plant for which permission was granted was not the same as the existing plant. If there was any doubt about this the County Council could have asked for further clarification of the plans, but they did not do so.

I am not satisfied that the grant of permission specified the purposes for which the structures might be used. It certainly did not expressly do so, and, even if the words 'Proposed replacement of existing concrete Plant' could be interpreted as implying that the new plant was only to be used for the same purposes as the plant which it was replacing, which I doubt, the fact that the grant stated in condition 1 that the development was to be carried out and completed strictly in accordance with the plans and specifications (which I take it referred to the new plant layout) lodged with the application, which as I have indicated showed that the user proposed was different from the former user, would negative any such implication.

As in my opinion no purpose for which the structures might be used was specified in the grant of permission it follows in accordance with Section 28(6) of the Act that the permission must be construed as including permission to use the structures for the purpose for which they were designed. I have already quoted the views of the Court of Appeal in England in the case of *Wilson* v. *West Sussex County Council*[52] as to the meaning of the word 'designed'. In the case of *Belmont Farm Ltd.* v. *Minister of Housing and Local Government and Another* 60 L.G.R. 319 decided by the Queen's Bench Division in the previous year, but not apparently referred to in *Wilson's* case, Lord Parker (with whose Judgment Mr. Justices Winn and Brabin concurred), dealing with the words 'designed for the purposes of agriculture' said 'There are three views as it seems to me as to what the word 'designed' there means. The appellants through Mr. Hawser to whom the Court is indebted for his argument, say that 'designed' means no more than 'intended for', in other words that when the structure is placed on the land it must be intended for the purposes of agriculture. The other extreme view is that it all depends upon the original design of the architect who designed or the manufacturer who made it and it depends on what he intended it for. The third and intermediate view, and the one which I think is right, is that you look at the structure at the time of its erection and ask 'Is this designed for the purpose of agriculture in the sense of its physical appearance and layout?' Lord Parker then refers to Section 18(3) of the English Act of 1947 which corresponds with Section 28(6) of our Act and says 'There I think undoubtedly it cannot merely mean for the purpose for which it is intended by the 'original erector'.

Whichever view one takes of the meaning of the word 'designed', and I must say I prefer Lord Parker's view, it seems to me that the proposed new structures for the erection of which permission was granted in this case were designed to be used for the purpose of producing ready-mix concrete. They were clearly intended by the plaintiffs to be used for that purpose and this intention was shown on the plans, so that a qualified person looking at the plans would say 'This is a plan for a ready-mix concrete plant'.

It follows that in my opinion the grant of permission in this case must be construed as including permission to use the structures for the purpose of producing ready-mix concrete and dealing with it in the manner proposed by the plaintiffs and, if this involves a material change in use of the structures, so as to amount to 'development', this has been permitted by the planning authority who cannot

[52] [1963] 2 Q.B. 764.

derogate from this permission and therefore no question has arisen for reference to the Minister under Section 5 of the Act.

Supreme Court

Budd J.:

There was a certain amount of argument as to whether or not the Court was bound to consider not only the actual grant but also the terms of the application and the plans lodged therewith but it would appear to me that the correct view with regard to this is to be found in *Wilson* v. *West Sussex County Council* 1963 2 Q.B. 764 which the learned trial judge actually referred to which decided that regard must be had to certain facts regarding the nature of the application, its construction and accompanying documents. In the first place it would appear to me that the application for permission did specify the purpose for which the structures were to be used. . . .

. . .It would appear that the experts examining the plans on behalf of the first named defendants were at first misled, or at least under a misapprehension, with regard to the nature of the intentions of the applicant and as to what these plans and documents really portrayed with the result that the first named defendants did not properly appreciate that there was a point arising which required to be decided with regard to whether or not the development was 'development' within the meaning of the statute and that the result of a tentative decision in the matter also required to be further considered, which explains their lack of activity. Now, however, that the position is more fully and clearly understood, the first named defendants have come to the conclusion that a question does arise for determination and the next question is as to what their rights are in the circumstances that have arisen. These particular rights, they claim, are to be found under the provisions of the Local Government (Planning and Development) Act, 1963, hereinafter referred to as 'the Act', the relevant sections of which I next refer to.

'Development' in this Act means, save where the context otherwise requires, the carrying out of any work on, in, or under land or the making of any material change in the use of any structures or other land. This definition is wide and would seem, on the face of it, to cover the carrying out of work such as the plaintiffs have in mind or the making of the material changes they have in mind in the use of any structures or of the land. Under the provisions of section 5 subsection (1), a very important subsection in the circumstances of this case, it is provided that 'if any question arises as to what, in any particular case, is or is not development or exempted development, the question shall be referred to and decided by the Minister.' It would seem quite clear that a question has arisen as to whether or not the new structures are or are not development and the section is mandatory that such a question shall be referred to and decided by the Minister.

Finally, I refer to the provisions of section 28 subsection (6) of the Act which provides 'Where permission is granted under this part of this Act for the construction, erection or making of a structure, the grant of permission may specify the purposes for which the structure may be used; and if no purpose is so specified, the permission shall be construed as including permission to use the structure for the purpose for which it is designed'.

Having regard, however, to the views which I have expressed as to the true construction of the grant of permission to the effect that it did specify the purpose for which the structures were to be used, it would seem to me that there is a question to be decided by the Minister as to whether or not the proposed structures as are depicted in the plans constitute development within the meaning of the Act or not. Accordingly I would refuse to make the declaration sought at paragraphs 1, 2 3 and 4 of the general endorsement of claim and the injunctions sought at paragraphs 5 and 6 of the said general endorsement of claim and I would allow this appeal.

Henchy J.:
However, behind the facade of the development application was concealed a scheme of things of which the Co. Co. were totally unaware. Prior to the application, McGurk had executed an agreement with the plaintiffs granting them an option to purchase his concrete-making premises for £20,000. Collateral with this agreement was an oral agreement that McGurk would apply for development permission to replace the existing plant. The intention was that when development permission was granted, the plaintiffs would exercise the option to purchase, thus stepping into McGurk's shoes and thereby becoming free to use the development permission granted to him, not for the purpose of manufacturing concrete products on the site but for the distribution by lorry from the site of 'readymix' concrete, i.e. concrete the constituents of which are assembled on the site in the required proportions and then churned in the drum of a specially designed lorry on its way to where the mixed concrete is to be used.

While it was McGurk who signed the application, it was an official of the plaintiff company who composed it. The reality of the situation was that McGurk was only an ostensible applicant. The permission was not being sought to enable McGurk to continue his existing business with a modernised plant. All the indications are that the plaintiffs intended that by making the application in McGurk's name and in the form in which it was made, a permission would issue in terms which, when they had exercised their option to purchase, would entitle them to operate the modernised plant for the preparation and distribution of readymix concrete.

When the permission issued to McGurk, the plaintiffs were satisfied that this end had been achieved, so they took up their option to purchase and the property was conveyed to them. They then carried out the permitted modernisation and proceeded to produce and distribute readymix concrete. This resulted in a flow of the plaintiffs' specially designed vehicles, with their revolving drums for churning the concrete, coming and going on the roads leading to the site. Occupiers of neighbouring property complained – and the Co. Co. officials agreed with them – that the use of the site for the production and distribution of readymix concrete was not within the scope of the permission granted. The plaintiffs firmly contended that it was, and refused to desist from such use.

In an effort to resolve the dispute, the defendants decided to refer the matter to the Minister for Local Government under s. 5 of the Local Government (Planning and Development) Act, 1963. That section allows a question to be referred to the Minister to decide in a particular case what is or is not development or exempted development for the purposes of the Act. The plaintiffs, asserting that no such question had arisen for the Minister's decision, instituted the present proceedings seeking declarations and injunctions which would have the effect of validating their present operations on the site and debarring the Minister from making a ruling under s. 5. In the High Court Pringle J. held with the plaintiffs and granted the declarations and injunctions sought. The Minister, who has been perpetually injuncted from proceeding under s. 5, has not appealed from the order made by Pringle J., but the Co. Co. have. The essence of their case is that the production of readymix concrete is outside the scope of the permission granted.

There is no doubt but that the replacement plant referred to in McGurk's application came within the definition of development in s. 3(1) of the 1963 Act and so required permission under s. 24(2).

When a permission issues in a case such as this, it enures for the benefit not alone of the person to whom it issues but also for the benefit of anyone who acquires an interest in the property: s. 28(5). A proper record of the permission is therefore necessary. This is provided for by s. 8, which prescribes that a planning authority shall keep a register of all land in their area affected by the Act. This register is the statutorily designated source of authoritative information as to what is covered by a permission. The Act does not in terms make the register the conclusive or exclusive record of the nature and extent of a permission, but the scheme of the Act indicates that anybody who acts on the basis of the correctness of the particulars in the register is entitled to do so. Where the permission recorded in the register is self-contained, it will not be permissible to go outside it in construing it. But where the permission incorporates other documents, it is the combined effort of the permission and such documents that must be looked at in determining the proper scope of the permission. Thus, because in the present case the permission incorporated by reference the application for permission together with the plans lodged with it, it is agreed that the decision so notified must be construed by reference not only to its direct contents but also to the application and the plans lodged.

Since the permission notified to an applicant and entered in the register is a public document, it must be construed objectively as such, and not in the light of subjective considerations special to the applicant or those responsible for the grant of the permission. Because the permission is an appendage to the title to the property, it may possibly not arise for interpretation until the property has passed into the hands of those who have no knowledge of any special circumstances in which it was granted. Since s. 24(4) of the Act allows the production by a defendant of the permission to be a good defence in a prosecution for carrying out without permission development for which permission is required, it would be contrary to the fundamentals of justice as well as the canons of statutory interpretation to hold that a permission could have variable meanings, depending on whether special circumstances known only to certain persons are brought to light or not. As Lord Reid said in reference to a permission granted under the English Planning Acts: 'Of course extrinsic evidence may be required to identify a thing or place referred to, but that is a very different thing from using evidence of facts which were known to the maker of the document but which are not common knowledge to alter or qualify the apparent meaning of words or phrases used in such a document. Members of the public, entitled to rely on a public document, surely ought not to be subject to the risk of its apparent meaning being altered by the introduction of such evidence': *Slough Estates* v. *Slough Borough Council* (No. 2) 1971 A.C. 958, at p. 962.

I must reject, therefore, the submission made by counsel for the Co. Co. that the permission in question here, incorporating as it does the application and the plans lodged with it, should be construed as having merely the meaning or effect given to it or reasonably capable of having been given to it by the Co. Co. officials who dealt with the application. The permission, like all public documents, must stand on its own and be construed objectively by the Court as if those involved in its creation were not available to give evidence.

The case against both the Minister and the Co. Co., it seems to me, hinges on the answer to be given to the question is the production of readymix concrete within the scope of the permission granted?

S. 28(6) of the Act stipulates that where a structure is permitted without specifying a purpose for which it may be used 'the permission shall be construed as including permission to use the structure for the purposes for which it is designed.' Since a permission with this statutory extension may possibly not arise for interpretation until the property has passed to a purchaser or other lawful user who may have no knowledge of special circumstances known only to those privy to the grant of the permission, it must have been the intention of the legislature that the statutory extension must, with the rest of the permission, be construed objectively, as is the case with all public documents, particularly public documents of title. Otherwise, the efficacy of the statutorily extended permission as a defence to a prosecution for an offence under s. 24(2) would depend on whether the defendant had or had not special knowledge.

The use for which the structure in the present case is designed must be determined, therefore, by a reading, in their ordinary connotation, of the application, the plans of the existing and proposed plants, and the permission itself.

I am of the opinion that the permission, with its incorporated documents, specified a purpose for which the structure was to be used, namely, the production of concrete. If the plaintiffs or any subsequent owners of the property were prosecuted under s. 24(2) for using the structure for any other purpose, in breach of s. 24(1), it would not be a good defence to produce this permission, as it might be under s. 24(4)(b) if no purpose had been specified in the permission.

The permission might have specified with greater particularity the purpose or purposes for which the structure may be used, but I find it impossible to say that it specified no purpose. It seems to me that the documents constituting the permission show that application was made and permission granted for the erection of a modern structure for the purpose of producing concrete. The Co. Co. could have narrowed that purpose, by delimiting the method of production, so as to exclude readymix concrete. But they did not do so. In my opinion the permission specified the purpose, no less than did the permission to erect an 'agricultural cottage' in *Wilson* v. *West Sussex Co. Co.* 1963 2 Q.B. 764.

I would therefore hold that the use by the plaintiffs of the plant for the production of readymix concrete is within the permission granted.

If I am incorrect in deciding that this is not a case where no purpose for which the structure may be used has been specified in the permission, the statutorily implied term that the structure may be used for the purpose for which it is designed would, in my judgment, equally authorise the use of the structure for the production of readymix concrete. Pringle J. in his judgment refers to the possible meanings to be attributed to the word 'designed' in s. 28(5) as exemplified in the judgments in *Wilson* v. *West Sussex Co. Co.* 1963 2 Q. B. 764 and *Belmont Farm Ltd.* v. *Minister of Housing and Local Government* 60 L.G.R. 319. I do not consider it necessary to choose between those meanings, for like Pringle J., I think that, whichever meaning is given to the word, it cannot be said that the permitted structure was not 'designed' for the production of readymix concrete.

Applications for development permissions, it would seem, are not always characterised by good faith or forthrightness. A favourable view of the application in this case might justify it as being a successfully uncommunicative ploy on the part of the plaintiffs. An unfavourable view might hold it to have been devious and misleading almost to the point of sharp practice. Whatever be the correct view, the fact appears to be that a permission has been granted by the planning authority to an extent not intended by them. This is unfortunate, but the experience may provide a cautionary lesson for future cases.

The Local Government (Planning and Development) Act, 1963 (Permission) Regulations, 1964, lay down in considerable detail the procedure for making and dealing with an application for a permission of this kind. Apart from the specific matters which the applicant must notify, Article 11 of the Regulations empowers the planning authority to seek such further documents or information relative to the application as they think necessary, and the planning authority have power to refuse the application if their requirements under the Article are not met within one month. Pertinent inquiries, therefore, by the Co. Co. in the present case would have brought to light the specific use to which the proposed structures were to be put. The type of non-disclosure that occurred in this case is easily avoidable by planning authorities.

Finally, as to the form of a permission. Since it will be appurtenant to the title to the land, and therefore may have to be construed by persons such as purchasers who may be strangers to the circumstances in which it was granted, it is desirable that it should be clear and specific in its terms and, as far as possible, be self-contained, so as not to incorporate unnecessarily documents such as letters of application which may be loosely or ambiguously worded.

I would dismiss the appeal.

Griffin J.:
In construing the grant of permission it is conceded by all parties that, on the authority of *Wilson* v. *West Sussex County Council* [1963] 2 W.L.R. 669 it is proper and indeed necessary to refer not only to the terms of the grant of permission but also to the terms of the application for permission for development and the documents and plans lodged with the Planning Authority. In the present case, these documents included the notice published in the Irish Press on the 28th June, 1969, James McGurk's letter of the 27th June, 1969, and the plans sent to the County Council with that letter.

When any development of land is proposed, it is of fundamental importance that the proposal should be brought to the attention of the public and in particular to that of the residents of the neighbourhood in which the development is to take place. Any person likely to be affected by the development can then inspect the documents, and although not entitled to object to the grant of permission by the Planning Authority, such person can appeal to the Minister against the decision of the Planning Authority. Regulation 9(4) of the Local Government (Planning and Development) Act, 1963 (Permission) Regulations 1964 (S.I. No. 221 of 1964) requires that the notice published in the newspaper should contain (inter alia) 'the extent and nature of the development in respect of which it is intended to apply for a permission or an approval'. This was not complied with in the present case and it appears to me that any person who would see the notice in the Irish Press in the terms 'Approval sought for *replacement concrete plant* at Newtownpark Avenue, Blackrock, for J. McGurk' (the italics are mine) would be unlikely to have any conception of the intention of the plaintiffs even if he inspected the documents and the plans lodged.

In the notice of application or in the plans submitted with it there is no express indication whatever that the application is in respect of a readymix plant. The plaintiffs' technical manager in his evidence (Question 358) stated that the application was so obviously a readymix plant that it could not be interpreted as anything else. His attitude was that the plans were lodged with the planning department of the local authority whose officials should have seen that the plant proposed was a readymix plant. The documents and plans were examined by three experienced engineers on behalf of the County Council, none of whom was able to interpret the plans as being in respect of a readymix plant. It would have been a very simple matter for the plaintiffs, in drafting the documents in the name of James McGurk, to have stated that the plant proposed was a readymix plant. It seems to me that every significant external feature which might have indicated to any person examining the documents and plans that the plant proposed to be erected was a readymix plant was omitted from the documents and plans either intentionally or inadvertently, and that it would be unreasonable to expect the officials of the County Council to interpret the documents and plans in any other way than the one in which they in fact interpreted them, i.e. as being for what I have referred to as a conventional concrete plant in which concrete is manufactured on the premises. In my view, the criticism of these officials made during the hearing in the High Court and on this appeal was not justified. At the time of the making of the present application, the planning department of the County Council dealt with over 2,000 applications per annum (this figure having considerably increased in the meantime). The plaintiffs' attitude was that it was the duty of the officials of the County Council to endeavour to ascertain exactly the intention of the plaintiffs and the purpose for which the applicants intended the structures to be used and that it was not the duty or the obligation of the applicant to show precisely what was the applicant's intention. I agree with the submission of Mr. Cooke, counsel for the County Council, that this approach is entirely wrong and that the function of the officials of the County Council is that of watchdogs not bloodhounds.

In my opinion, the grant of permission, when read in conjunction with the documents and plans lodged with the County Council, did specify the purpose for which the structures were to be used, that is for the manufacture, on the premises, of concrete as theretofore carried on by James McGurk. In the readymix method, some, but not all, of the processes of the manufacture of concrete are carried on on the premises but the dry mix is not turned into concrete on the premises. When the structures for which a grant of permission was made are used as a readymix plant they are not, in my view, 'concrete plant' within the meaning of the permission granted. In my judgment, a question does arise as to whether the plaintiffs have made any material change in the use of the structures or the land and this question was properly referred to the Minister by the County Council for decision by him under and in pursuance of the provisions of section 5 of the 1963 Act. . . .

THE STATE (PINE VALLEY DEVELOPMENTS LTD.) V. DUBLIN COUNTY COUNCIL
(Judgment of Barrington J., unreported, delivered 27th May, 1981; for Supreme Court Judgment see [1982] I.L.R.M. 169)

Outline planning permission was granted for industrial development on appeal by the Minister on 10th March, 1977, subject only to one condition relating to a contribution towards the local authority in respect of water supply and sewage facilities. On 16th July, 1980 the applicants applied to the local authority for approval consequent on the grant of this outline planning permission and the planning authority notified an intention to refuse for five reasons which included that the land was zoned for agricultural purposes which were inconsistent with the development proposed, that pipe sewage services were not available, that the proposed development would for that reason be premature, that there was unsatisfactory access and parking arrangements and that the site of application for approval was different to the site covered by the grant of outline permission. The first four reasons were identical to the reasons originally given by the planning authority for refusing to grant outline planning permission. This refusal was of course, overruled by the Ministerial grant. Barrington J. held that the planning authority on the approval application was confined within the four walls of the outline permission and this applied notwithstanding that such a grant would be in breach of its own development plan by which in the normal case a planning authority is bound. The judge also held that because the approval site differed from the site of the outline permission only in the sense that the part differs from the whole the approval was a valid approval consequent on the outline permission and the planning authority did not have power to refuse the application for this reason.

Finally, this case dealt with Section 42 (3A) of the 1976 Act, which imposes a two-month limitation period on the bringing of legal proceedings questioning the validity of a planning decision. These proceedings were instituted after the lapse of the two-month period. The proceedings were mandamus proceedings. The Judge distinguished between certiorari and mandamus and indicated that if the present proceedings were certiorari proceedings or prohibition proceedings they would be statute barred because the bar is on any proceedings 'questioning' the validity of a planning permission or approval. The applicants had contended successfully however that they were not questioning anything – they were merely demonstrating that the planning authority had failed to adjudicate and were therefore requiring a mandatory order directing them to grant planning permission by default.

Barrington J.:
. . . To deal with the first point first, common sense would appear to me to indicate that a planning authority considering an application for an approval is confined within the four walls of the outline permission granted in respect of the same lands. Mr. Walsh has submitted that there is a certain analogy between the procedure for an outline planning permission and the procedure for a declaration under section 15 of the Intoxicating Liquor Act, 1960. Both procedures are designed to save the applicant from unnecessary and wasteful expenditure. In the one case the applicant is saved the expense of having to build his public house before he discovers whether the Court will issue a certificate in respect of it or not. In the second case the

developer is saved the expense of spending perhaps several thousand pounds on preparing elaborate plans for the construction of an office block only to discover that the planning authority will not permit the building of an office block on that particular site at all. It appears to me that the purpose of the outline planning procedure is to enable the developer to discover whether a particular development is, in principle, acceptable to the planning authority. This whole procedure would be defeated if, at the approval stage, the planning authority could re-open the question of whether the development is acceptable in principle.

Section 24 of the Local Government (Planning and Development) Act, 1963 provides that, subject to the exceptions therein set out, permission shall be required for any development of land. No one is permitted to carry out any development of land in respect of which permission is required except in accordance with a permission granted under the Act. Section 25 of the Act provides that the Minister may, by regulations, provide for the grant of permission for the development of land and make provision for applications 'expressed to be outline applications' for permission to develop subject to the subsequent approval of the planning authority.

The Local Government (Planning and Development) Regulations 1977 (S.I. No. 65 of 1977), and in particular Articles 17 and 18 of these Regulations provide the machinery for applying for planning permissions.

. . . (*The judge referred in detail to these regulations*) . . .

It therefore appears that the Planning Act and the Regulations contemplate:

1. A full permission in respect of which detailed plans must be lodged and on foot of which, if granted, development may immediately commence.
2. An outline planning permission in which the applicant seeks approval in principle for the proposed development which, if granted, does not authorise the commencement of development until the applicant has obtained an approval.
3. An approval which is the detailed approval by the Planning Authority of the development permitted in principle under the outline permission and which authorises the developer to commence development.

It therefore apears that an outline permission followed by an approval is equivalent to a full permission. It therefore appears to me that a developer, having got his outline permission, has gone a certain length of the road and that when he applies subsequently for an approval the Planning Authority is only concerned with the detail whereby the developer proposes to complete the development already approved in principle by the Planning Authority.

It appears to me to follow from this that the outline permission sets the parameters within which the planning authority must consider the application for an approval and that it is not open to the planning authority, at the approval stage, to re-open matters which have already been permitted under the general terms of the outline permission.

Surprisingly enough there does not appear to be any case specifically deciding this point but the point appears to me to be obvious and this may explain the reason why it has not previously been raised.

The 1963 edition of Blundell and Dobry on 'Town and Country Planning' dealing with the corresponding provisions of the English legislation has, at page 112, under the heading of 'Binding Character of Outline Permission' the following passage:

'If planning permission has been granted on the basis that it is an outline permission under Regulation 5(2) of the Town and Country Planning General Development Order 1950, and further approval of the local Planning Authority is required only in respect of matters reserved in the permission (id est details of siting and design or external appearance of the building or the means of access) before development is commenced, the local planning authority cannot re-open the matter by refusing approval for reasons not relating to reserved matters, such as the land is not allocated for residential development or that the proposal conflicts with the local authority's intention regarding residential development . . . . It follows that an outline permission, however general the terms in which it is expressed, is as much a planning permission as one granted on fullest information; the only matters requiring the subsequent approval are those specifically reserved in the permission and the planning authority are committed by the permission to allowing the development in some form or other. Planning authorities should not grant permission in this form unless they are in possession of sufficient information to assess the merits of what is proposed, and the permission when granted should fix the main lines of the development.'

Mr. Smyth, who appeared for the planning authority in the present case, advanced the ingenious argument that the planning authority, unlike the Minister, is bound by the development plan and, in considering the application for approval, is restricted, in accordance with section 26 sub-section 1 of the 1963 Act to considering the proper planning and development of the area. He submits that notwithstanding the grant by the Minister of an outline permission the planning authority, at the approval stage, must reject the application for the approval if they consider that the development in principle violates the development plan or is contrary to the proper planning and development of the area. I cannot accept this submission. It appears to me that under the provisions of section 26 the Minister was, in effect, the Appeal Court from the planning authority and that if the Minister has granted an outline permission, that decision is binding on the planning authority and it is not open to the planning authority to reconsider whether the development is acceptable in principle. It may, indeed, in certain circumstances, revoke the planning permission but as long as the outline planning permission stands it appears to me that the planning authority is as much bound by it as if it had granted the permission itself. Any other conclusion would, in my opinion, have chaotic consequences.

That being so it appears to me that a planning authority considering an application for approval must consider it within the parameters of the outline permission. An application within these parameters is the only application it is called upon to consider at this stage. If therefore it attempts to re-open matters decided by the outline permission it is not considering the application which is before it. In the present case it is quite clear that the planning authority attempted to reconsider matters which had been decided by the Minister when he granted the outline permission. It appears to me therefore that they failed to consider the only application which was before them which was an application for an approval within the parameters of the Minister's outline permission.

In view of the conclusion I have just reached it may not be necessary to consider whether the fifth reason given by the planning authority for refusing the approval is a valid one. In the notification of a decision to refuse the planning authority puts that reason in the following words:

'The site of this application is different from the site the subject of outline permission granted by the Minister on appeal and hence cannot be regarded as an application for approval. The treatment of the omitted portion of the site has not been sufficiently indicated.'

As previously stated the site, the subject matter of the approval application, differs only from the site the subject matter of the outline permission in the sense that the part differs from the whole. The outline permission related to a site of some 21½ acres being portion of the same 22 acres. If, therefore, the planning authority means to convey that a person who has obtained an outline planning permission cannot apply for an approval confined to part only of the site, the planning authority is clearly wrong. There is no doubt that a person who has obtained an outline permission can apply for approvals for various portions of the site as his development proceeds. Article 19 sub-article 3 of the Local Government (Planning and Development) Regulations 1977 clearly states:

'An application for an approval consequent on an outline permission may be related to a specified part only of the development for which an outline permission was granted and separate applications may be made in respect of other parts of the said development from time to time.'

It therefore appears to me that an applicant who has obtained an outline planning permission in respect of a site is entitled to apply for an approval, or a series of approvals, in relation to a part or parts of it. The planning authority must consider such an application within the parameters of the outline permission and cannot refuse it simply bcause it relates to portion of the site unless there is something in it which, if implemented, would frustrate some term of the outline permission in relation to the balance of the site. Mr. Smyth has indeed argued that the services to be supplied in the present case relate to the totality of the site and that therefore, in the circumstances of this case, it is not open to the developer to apply for an approval in respect of part of the site only. I cannot accept this. It appears to me that, for this point to be valid, it would be necessary to show that there was something in the way the services were treated in relation to the application for approval of portion of the site which would frustrate the provision of services to the balance of the site. Under these circumstances it appears to me that, if this were an application for certiorari brought within time, that the developer would be entitled to quash the planning authority's order because of the fifth reason even if the other four reasons were permissible ones. This is not however, an application for certiorari and the significance of the fifth reason, in the context of the present application, is that it shows that the planning authority in effect declined to consider the application which was before it, which was an application for an approval in relation to portion of the site. . . .[53]

. . .

POWERS OF PLANNING AUTHORITY

A planning authority has wide jurisdiction to alter any particular proposal for

[53] The Supreme Court on appeal reversed the judgment of the High Court, but on quite

development by way of imposing conditions. In *State (Abenglen Properties Limited)* v. *Dublin Corporation* it was held within the power of the planning authority to impose conditions which had the effect of very radically altering the scheme in question. It was also held that the planning authority was not obliged to invite revised plans amounting to a modified application although they had discretionary power so to do. In *State (Stanford and Others)* v. *Corporation of Dun Laoghaire* it was held by the Supreme Court that in the absence of any specific regulation (at that time: see now Regulation 10 of S.I. No. 342 of 1982) requiring a planning authority to allow time after receipt of the planning application for third parties to make representations that there was an implied obligation to allow a reasonable time to elapse. In the absence of specific regulations the Court will look at the code in general and interpret any specific case in the light of the general provisions. In *State (Sweeney)* v. *Minister for the Environment and Another* it was held within the power of the planning authority to refuse planning permission on the grounds that the subject site was affected by a C.P.O. The planning authority was entitled to have regard to the reality of the situation which included their own proposal as housing authority to acquire the lands and use them for their own purposes.

In *State (Cogley)* v. *Dublin Corporation and Another* it was made clear that the power to revoke planning permission did not include power to revoke an approval and a purported revocation of approval was void and mere surplusage. However, because the approval had legal validity only within the context of an outline permission revocation of the outline permission achieved the same result. This principle is of importance in the context of S.2 of the Act of 1982 which provides for a limit of durations of planning permissions. Care should be taken that an application for approval is made well within the lifetime of the relevant outline permission as a grant of approval does not have a life of its own independent of the outline permission.

THE STATE (ABENGLEN PROPERTIES LTD.) AND DUBLIN CORPORATION
([1981] ILRM 54)

Developers applied for permission for a four-storey office block over open floor and three storeys of residential development. The planning authority granted outline permission, subject to conditions, the effect of which was to reduce the office block to two storeys with an increased residential element, a decreased office element and an overall limitation of 40 per cent use for office purposes. In Certiorari proceedings the developer claimed, inter alia, that the permission granted was for such a radically different development to the one applied for that there was a failure to adjudicate on the actual application. This should therefore be treated as having attracted an unconditioned grant of permission by default at the end of the two-month period. In the second place it was argued by the developer

different grounds, namely, that the original Minister's grant of outline permission was outside his powers and hence there was no ground on which the application for approval could follow. The Minister's powers to breach the provisions of the relevant development plan were only available when he had been requested so to do by the planning authority and since this had not happened his decision was bad. The effect of this Supreme Court decision has been removed by section 6 of the Act of 1982.

that if the planning authority was disposed to grant permission or approval for a modified version of the development applied for, then it should have invited the developer to submit revised plans amounting to a modified application under Article 27 of the Local Government (Planning and Development) Regulations, 1977. The developer also argued in this case (successfully in the High Court) that in dealing with the application the planning authority failed correctly to interpret the provisions of its own development plan and that its purported decision was for this reason void. In dealing with the case in the High Court, D'Arcy J. made it clear that in his view once the planning authority took all relevant matters into consideration and adjudicated upon the application submitted, then it was quite within its power to attach conditions to the grant which would modify the same quite significantly as in the instant case.

D'Arcy J.:
. . . On the 5th December the respondents sent to the prosecutors a notification of decision to grant outline planning permission, in respect of the premises in question. This permission was subject to three conditions, two of which are material to the matter before me. I quote:

2. 'The indicated central block for office use is to be reduced to not more than three storeys in overall height, i.e. by the omission of the two top storeys, each of the two and residential blocks to be at least double in width and floor area, with consequent reduction in the length of proposed central office block, the above modifications to the outline plans submitted to result in not more than 40 per cent of the overall floor space being in office use.

3. The development shall be so designed as to insure a minimum clearance of ten feet from the Grand Canal waterway and this area shall be reserved for amenity purposes.' . . .

For practical purposes the chief differences between the permission granted and the permission sought were threefold. Firstly, the size of the development was diminished by cutting off two storeys from the central block. Secondly, 48,000 square feet and 12,000 square feet respectively for office development and residential development had been applied for, whilst permission had been granted for only 16,000 square feet for office purposes, and 24,000 square feet for residential purposes. Thirdly, and most importantly, the permission granted imposed a limitation of 40 per cent on office user.

Before dealing with the six grounds upon which the conditional order was granted, I propose to deal with a matter which is common to all the grounds. Mr. Richard Cooke, S. C. on behalf of the respondents urged me that the remedy of certiorari did not lie in this case as the prosecutors had an alternative remedy. He relied on the *State (Vozza)* v. *District Justice O'Flynn and Judge McCarthy* and *Regina* v. *Brighton Justices Ex Parte Robinson*. Mr Gerard Lardner, S.C. for the prosecutors urged that the remedy of certiorari did lie and was appropriate. He relied on *Regina* v. *Hillingdon London Borough Council Ex Parte Royco Homes Limited*. The prosecutor had an alternative remedy namely an appeal to An Bord Pleanala. This alternative remedy was not only more convenient, it was also more appropriate than proceedings on the State Side. The reason for this is, if a prosecutor succeeds in certiorari proceedings, then two months after the making of the application for planning permission he will automatically be entitled to planning permission by default without restrictions or conditions. See Local Government

(Planning and Development) Act, 1963, Section 26. An Bord Pleanala has a far wider jurisdiction and discretion than the Courts in the matter. In former times certiorari was not granted where an alternative remedy existed. In recent times, however, a practice has grown up and been sanctioned by usage, which does not prohibit or restrict Certiorari proceedings because of the existence of an alternative remedy. Mr. Cooke suggested that the change in practice came after the decision in *The State (Vozza) and District Justice O'Flynn*. This was over 25 years ago. Were I free to decide the matter, I would accept Mr. Cooke's submission that an order absolute should not issue: I would in the exercise of a direction decide that the existence of an alternative and more appropriate remedy, debarred the prosecutor from obtaining an absolute order of certiorari. However, in view of what appears to be the accepted practice for the last 25 years I do not feel at liberty so to do. Accordingly, I must reject Mr. Cooke's argument on this point.[54]

At the date the planning application was lodged, the 7th October, 1980, the 1971 Dublin City Development Plan was in operation. Prior to the granting of the outline planning permission on the 5th December, 1980, the Dublin City Development Plan 1980 came into operation on the 20th October, 1980.[55]

The grounds on which the conditional order was made are as follows:

1. The notice of decision to grant outline planning permission does not constitute an adjudication of or notice of adjudication to show the corporation adjudicated on the applicants' planning application of the 6th October, 1980 and is ultra vires and void;

2. The notice expresses notice of adjudication of a development so radically modified as to be a wholly different character from the development for which the applicants applied for permission and is ultra vires and void;

3. The notice of decision and the adjudication of which it purports to be based do not comply with the provisions of Section 26 of the Local Government (Planning and Development) Act 1963 as amended, and Regulation 27 of the Local Government (Planning and Development) Regulations S.I. 65/1977 and the same are ultra vires unlawful and void;

4. In making the said planning determination the subject matter of the said notice the respondents proceeded on an erroneous understanding and/or interpretation of the provisions of the City Development Plan 1971 or alternatively of the said plan as varied by the City Development Plan 1980 and the said determination is bad in law and ultra vires and void;

5. In basing the said Planning Determination upon a plot ratio of 2.0. to 1.0. and a business user limitation of not more than 40 per cent the respondent proceeded on an erroneous basis and the said determination is erroneous ultra vires and void;

6. The reasons set out in the schedule of reasons for the conditions to which the said decision is subject are not valid or capable of supporting the said conditions and/or decision – full particulars of the aforesaid grounds appearing in paragraphs 6, 7, 8, 9 and 10 of the Affidavit of Mr. O'Connor.

[54] The Supreme Court refused to make the order absolute on general discretionary grounds (a view with which D'Arcy J. obviously had sympathy but felt bound by practice not to take). See p. 316.

[55] By s. 7(a) of the Act of 1963 references to the provisions of the development shall, until that plan is made, be construed as references to the provisions which the planning authority consider will be included in that plan (in other words to the draft development plan).

The arguments concerning the first three grounds were similar. I propose to take these three grounds together. Under these headings Mr. Lardner, S.C. for the prosecutors attacked the outline planning permission on two distinct grounds. Firstly, he urged that his clients had applied for outline planning permission of a certain type, that they got permission for a radically different development, in fact, a completely different development. Therefore he urged the Corporation, respondents, did not adjudicate on his client's application. Secondly Mr. Lardner urged that his clients had applied for development of a certain nature that, if the Corporation were disposed to grant permission or approval subject to modification they should have invited the prosecutors to submit to them revised plans or other drawings showing a modified development. In other words that it was mandatory in such circumstances for the respondents to put into operation the provisions of the Local Government (Planning and Development) Regulations 1977 Article 27. That Article provides:

'Where a planning authority, having considered a planning application, are disposed to grant permission or approval subject to any modification of the development to which the application relates, they may invite the applicant to submit to them revised plans or other drawings modifying, or other particulars providing for the modification of the said development and, in case such plans, drawings or particulars are submitted, may decide to grant a permission or an approval for the relevant development as modified by all or any of the plans, drawings or particulars.'

It is necessary to contrast the nature of the development for which the prosecutor sought outline planning permission, and what was authorised by the permission which was granted. In broad terms the application was for an office development four storeys over an open floor, and three storeys of residential development. The permission granted was for the same site, and was also for both office and residential development. The difference between what was sought and what was granted, was that the permission omitted the top two office storeys, increased the residential factor, decreased the office factor, and imposed 40 per cent limitation on overall use for office purposes. In considering whether the respondents made proper adjudication, I look at the evidence before me, as afforded, by the affidavits of Mr. O'Connor, Mr. O'Dea and also Mr. O'Reilly and also a lengthy and detailed memorandum from Mr. O'Dea and a Mr. Tobin to the Dublin Planning Officer, Mr. C. A. Kelly dated the 4th December, 1980. This was the day before the permission was granted. This memorandum was put in evidence by the prosecutors. These documents show, and they are not contradicted, that the respondents' officials adjudicated upon the prosecutor's application, took all relevant matters in consideration, and having done so, issued the permission of which complaint is made. This is subject to one important qualification which I will deal with when considering the fourth and fifth grounds in which the conditional order was made. When one reads the application and the permission, one relates to the other. A planning authority is entitled to attach conditions to the grant of a permission. That and no more the respondents did in this case.[56]

The respondents did not invoke the machinery provided for in the Local Govern-

---

[56] In the Supreme Court Henchy J. took the view that the conditions in this were within the powers of the planning authority. Walsh J. considered they were not.

ment (Planning and Development) Regulations 1977 Article 27. It provides that certain procedures may be availed of by the Local Authority in certain circumstances. No authority was cited to me that it was mandatory on a Planning Authority to have recourse to such procedure. In the absence of such authority my view is that the Act gave a discretionary power to the respondents. They were not obliged to operate the Article. Their failure so to do does not invalidate the permission granted in this case. . . .'

THE STATE (STANFORD AND OTHERS) V. DUN LAOGHAIRE CORPORATION AND OTHERS
(Unreported judgment of the Supreme Court delivered by Henchy J. on 20th February, 1981)

The developer applied to Dun Laoghaire Corporation for permission to reconstruct outhouses as a dwelling house on a site in Dalkey. The development involved the demolition of some of these buildings. The local authority was not satisfied with the description of the proposed development in the newspaper notice submitted, and required the developer to re-advertise with a fuller description of the proposed development. This was done in a fresh advertisement submitted to the planning authority. At the end of the two-month period commencing on the date of the re-submission of the advertisement, the planning authority decided that the address given for the premises was incorrect and required the applicant to publish yet a further advertisement, this time giving a more precise address for the development. This advertisement was published very near the expiration of the two-month period commencing on the date of receipt of the second advertisement. The planning authority regarded itself as bound to deal with the application within the two months commencing on that date and accordingly decided to grant permission for the development sought on the first business day following receipt of the third newspaper notice. In certiorari proceedings it was held, in both the High and the Supreme Court that the purported decision of the planning authority was invalid because a third party who wished to respond to the publication of the third newspaper notice would not have had time to do so before the decision was made on the application. In the absence of a specific regulation[57] requiring a planning authority in receipt of a planning application to allow reasonably sufficient time to allow third party representations or objections to be made before deciding thereupon, the Supreme Court held that there was an implied obligation on the planning authority to allow a reasonable time to elapse, and held in the instant case that one day was not sufficient.

By S.I. No. 342 of 1982 (which came into operation on 1st December 1982) Regulation 10, a planning authority is now obliged to defer a decision on a planning application for fourteen days from receipt of the application or of compliance with a notice requesting publication of a further notice under regulation 23 of the 1977 Regulations.

Henchy J.:
The requirement that a developer must give advance notice by publication of his

---

[57] This absence has now been supplied by Regulation 30 A of the 1977 Regulations inserted by Regulation 10 of the Local Government (Planning and Development) (Amendment) Regulations, 1982 which came into operation on the 1st December, 1982.

intention to make a planning application is to be found in the regulations and not in the 1963 Act. S. 26(1) of the 1963 Act requires the application to be made in accordance with the regulations. Art. 14 of the regulations stipulates that the publication of the notice of intention to apply is to take place before the making of the planning application, and it allows the publication to be in either of two ways: (a) in a newspaper circulating in the district (a requirement which is often ineffectual in its reach, because of the large number of newspapers circulating in any given district) or (b) by the erection or by the fixing of a notice on the land or structure. The developer in this case chose method (a). The notice he published was required to state the matters set out in art. 15 of the regulations.

Art. 17 of the regulations required the developer to send with his application, inter alia, a copy of the newspaper 'in which there has been published a notice in pursuance of article 15'. This the developer failed to do. The newspaper notice he sent failed, because of its inaccuracies as to both the location of the site and the nature and extent of the development, to comply with the requirements of art. 15. Art. 23 allowed the planning authority in such circumstances to require the developer to publish such further newspaper notice as they specified. Hence the second advertisement, which still did not comply with art. 15, and the third advertisement, which the planning authority finally found satisfactory.

What is the purpose of this notice which is normally expected to be published before the application for planning permission is made? Both counsel for the developer and counsel for the planning authority contend that its purpose is to enable local people who thus learn of an intended planning application to be in a position to appeal if the permission is granted. This submission, they say, is supported by the fact that neither the Act (which has been amended by the 1976 Act) nor the regulations vest in interested local residents the right to object in advance to the grant of permission.

I am unable to uphold this submission. It is true that neither the Act nor the regulations specifically give a right to interested parties to make representations or objections before a permission is granted. But the tenor of the code suggests that they are to be accorded an opportunity of making such representations or objections in writing and that the purpose of the advertisement is to give them that opportunity and thus to enable the planning authority to inform themselves of the climate of local opinion as to the permission in question.

It is difficult to see why advance notice of a planning application would have to be given to members of the public if interested persons were not to have an opportunity of taking steps in regard to the application before it is dealt with. The grant or refusal of a development permission, involves three parties: the developer, the planning authority and the public. It is to be said that the exercise of this quasi-judicial function would be flawed if the public, one of the interested parties, whose interests do not necessarily coincide with those of the planning authority, were to be denied the opportunity of yielding forth interested persons who could make representations or objections. The right of such persons to make representations or objections in writing would seem to be impliedly recognized by the regulations, for art. 32(2) provides as follows:

'Where any person or body (not being a body to which sub-article (1) relates) [namely, An Chomairle Ealaíon, Bord Fáilte Éireann and An Taisce] has submitted representations or objections in writing to a planning authority in relation to a planning application, the planning authority shall, within seven days of making a decision on the application, notify such person or body of the said decision or publish notice thereof in a newspaper circulating in the district'.

That sub-article recognizes the intervention, at the pre-decision stage, of members of the public by submitting representations or objections in writing. The only conclusion, therefore, that can be reached as to the purpose of the advertisement of the proposed application is that it is to give interested members of the public an opportunity of making such representations or objections. Without the advertisement, either in a newspaper or on the site, the public might be shut out from the decision - making process. And that is an intention that should not be imputed to a code which is aimed, as the long title of the Act shows, at ensuring, in the interests of the common good, proper planning and development.

Because a valid advertisement in accordance with the regulations is essential to a valid application, and because the purpose of the advertisement is to enable interested persons or bodies to make representations or objections in writing, the grant of development permission in this case on the day after the advertisement was published was calculated to deprive interested members of the public (such as the three prosecutors) of the opportunity of submitting representations or objections in writing. Even if a local resident were fortunate enough to spot the advertisement in the *Irish Independent* of the 13th June, and even if he wrote and posted his representations or objections in writing that night, it is unlikely that his letter would reach the planning authority's office before the permission was notified on the 14th June.

In granting development permission to the developer without giving interested persons, such as the prosecutors, a reasonable opportunity to submit written representations or objections, the planning authority breached an implied but essential precondition for the grant of a valid permission. In thus granting the permission, they acted *ultra vires*; so the permission is invalid.

What constitutes a reasonable opportunity is something that should be decided by regulations[57] made by the Minister for the Environment in exercise of the powers vested in him by the Planning Acts. So far as the present case is concerned, it is sufficient to say that in my opinion the interval of one day between the publication of the advertisement and the notification of the grant of permission was so unreasonably short that it unlawfully deprived interested persons such as the prosecutors of their rights, and thereby invalidated the permission.

I would dismiss this appeal and affirm the order of Butler J. granting an absolute order of certiorari quashing the permission.

THE STATE (PATRICK SWEENEY) V. THE MINISTER FOR THE ENVIRONMENT AND THE LIMERICK COUNTY COUNCIL
(1978: 605 S.S.: Unreported judgment of the President delivered 12th February, 1979)

The applicant applied for planning permission for lands affected by a compulsory purchase order which was due to be considered by the Minister and the application was refused on the grounds that the site formed part of the order and that the proposal for development was therefore premature pending the determination of the order by the Minister for the Environment. The prosecutor challenged the validity of this ground of refusal but his argument was rejected by the President. The prosecutor contended that a mere change of ownership was not a sufficient ground for refusal; with this proposition the President agreed but took the view that in this case the making of the compulsory purchase order indicated more than a mere change of ownership, namely a proposal by the County Council to develop the lands for housing purposes. The ground of refusal was therefore valid and it was contrary to common sense to expect a planning authority to ignore its own proposal as a housing authority. The President indicated that the purpose for giving reasons for a planning decision was to indicate to the proposer whether he had any chance of success on appeal and to enable him to arm himself for the hearing of the appeal. The statement of the reasons did not have to be set out with the precision of a Court order nor need they contain any technical words. In the instant case the proposer was at all times aware of the local authority's proposals even though these were not specifically adverted to in the grounds for the refusal. The grounds for refusal in this case did not affect the position with regard to compensation.

Finlay P.:

This is an application by the prosecutor to make absolute notwithstanding cause shown a conditional order of certiorari granted on the 1st of November 1978 directing the respondents the Limerick County Council to send before the Court for the purpose of being quashed an order made by them and dated the 22nd of September 1978 refusing to grant outline planning permission to the prosecutor for the development of land at Glin in the County of Limerick. The facts out of which this application arises are not in any dispute and are as follows.

The prosecutor on the 27th of June 1978 and by a renewed application on the 14th of August 1978 applied to the Limerick County Council who are the planning authority for the area concerned for outline planning permission for the erection of thirteen dwelling houses at Glin in the County of Limerick. By a decision, notification of which was issued on the 22nd of September 1978 the Limerick County Council refused the permission the reasons being as follows:

'The site forms part or all of an area in respect of which a compulsory purchase order has been made by the Limerick County Council. This proposal for development is therefore premature pending the determination of this Order by the Minister for the Environment.'

The grounds on which the conditional order of certiorari was granted by Mr. Justice McMahon were that the reason given in the Schedule to the notification was not a valid ground for such refusal under the Local Government (Planning and Development) Act of 1963. The affidavit, upon which the conditional Order was obtained and which is the only evidence upon this application sets out that the respondents, the Limerick County Council had purported compulsorily to acquire the lands for the purpose of the Housing Act 1966; that the prosecutor had objected to the making of that compulsory purchase order and that the Minister for the Environment on the 16th of August 1978 had ordered a public inquiry to be held concerning the making of that order.

At the time of the swearing of the affidavit, the inquiry was due to be held on the 7th of November 1978 but I have been informed by counsel and it is agreed that the matter has been adjourned by reason of the fact that in the intervening time the prosecutor in this case and the objector at the inquiry obtained an order from the

High Court directing the discovery of certain documents and the giving of certain particulars by the Limerick County Council prior to the holding of the inquiry.

Shortly the submission made on behalf of the prosecutor is that the provisions of Section 26 of the Local Government (Planning and Development) Act 1963 confine the planning authority in considering an application for permission to considerations concerning the proper planning and development of the area, and that the mere making of a compulsory acquisition order is a change of ownership only and without further detail of the purpose for which it is intended to use the lands if the order is confirmed does not indicate any question concerning the proper planning and development of the area. The prosecutor further relies upon the fact that the precise terms of the refusal does not even indicate that the compulsory acquisition order referred to is for the purpose of the Housing Acts and in particular does not set out which of the many purposes of the Housing Acts it is intended by the Limerick County Council to use the lands if they finally acquire them.

On behalf of the respondent it is urged firstly that the prosecutor being the owner of the lands and being a person upon whom the compulsory purchase order was of course served is aware of the purposes for which it was served and the statute under which and pursuant to which it was served and that that being so it is clearly a question relative to and concerning the proper planning and development of any area if a particular area of land has been acquired by the local authority for any of the purposes of the Housing Act 1966.

I am satisfied that the respondent's contention in this matter is correct.

Firstly, it is clear that having regard to the provisions of section 26 of the Local Government (Planning and Development) Act 1963 and the other provisions of that Act that the purpose of the obligation which rests upon a planning authority to set out in their notification of a refusal, reasons which have led to the decision to refuse a particular application for permission must be as follows. It is to give to the applicant such information as may be necessary and appropriate for him firstly to consider whether he has got a reasonable chance of succeeding in appealing against the decision of the planning authority and secondly to enable him to arm himself for the hearing of such an appeal. The reasons set out therefore in the Schedule to a decision of refusal under the Planning Acts need not in my view be set out with the precision of a Court order nor need they necessarily contain any particular words of a technical nature, nor refer in any formal way to any of the provisions of the Act. It is quite clear that in this case the prosecutor has been at no time in any doubt of any description as to what compulsory purchase order was referred to in this notice of refusal. Indeed, in the affidavit filed on his behalf grounding the application for a conditional order the precise purchase order made pursuant to the Housing Act 1966 is not only identified without doubt but a copy exhibited as well.

The objectives for which a local authority may acquire land compulsorily pursuant to the provisions of the Housing Act 1966 either for immediate or future use are to be found in section 55 sub-section 3 of that Act and are as follows:

A.   The repair closure or demolition of houses which are unfit or unsuitable for human habitation.

B.   The elimination of overcrowding.

C.   The provision of adequate and suitable housing accommodation for persons (including elderly or disabled persons) who in the opinion of the authority are in need of and are unable to provide such accommodation from their own resources.

D.   The provision of adequate housing accommodation to meet needs arising from the obsolescence of dwellings or the prospective increase in the population.

E.   The provision of adequate and suitable sites for building purposes.

F.   The securing of the objectives contained in a development plan under the Local Government (Planning and Development) Act 1963 for the area which comprises or includes as the case may be the functional area of the authority.

G.   The encouragement by the authority of the provision by persons of houses for owner occupation by the owner or letting.

If land is acquired for any one or more of these purposes, quite clearly the carrying into effect of that purpose either immediately or in the future affects in general terms the planning and development of an area.

It follows from this that the compulsory acquisition of land by a housing authority pursuant to the provisions of the 1966 Act is not a mere change of ownership as the prosecutor contends on this application. I would accept that a mere change of ownership is not of itself a ground for the refusal of an application for permission pursuant to the Local Government (Planning and Development) Act of 1963. Change of ownership can occur without in any way affecting either the use or development of a particular area of land within the meaning of that Act and could not therefore of itself under any circumstances constitute a ground for the refusal of an application for permission which has regard to the planning and development of the area concerned. Where however, as exists in my view in a compulsory acquisition pursuant to the provisions of the Housing Act 1966 the particular change of ownership is from the applicant to a housing authority bound under statute to make use of the land for the objectives provided for by that Act which of themselves clearly affect the planning and development of the area concerned different considerations must apply.

I accept the contention strongly urged upon me on behalf of the respondents that it does violence to common sense that a planning authority which in fact in this particular case is also the housing authority knowing that it has as a housing authority decided to acquire certain lands and decided that it requires them for one of the purposes of the Housing Act 1966 should not be expected to have regard to that decision and to the service of the compulsory purchase order following upon that decision as part of their general approach to the planning and development of a particular area. It would be equally unreal that they should give a hypothetical or academic consent to an application for outline or other permission for some other development of the same area of land on the basis either that their decision as a housing authority to acquire the land and use it for the purposes of the 1966 Act was an incorrect decision or that it was a decision which the Minister for the Environment should not confirm.

The present refusal of this application for outline planning permission is strictly upon the basis that the application is premature having regard to the service of the compulsory acquisition order and therefore of course in no way would prejudice a subsequent application were the order not to be confirmed.

It was urged upon me that the real purpose of the prosecutor in seeking to quash this refusal was to regulate or enhance his position with regard to compensation in the event of the compulsory purchase order being confirmed.

Having regard to the provisions with regard to compensation and to the amendments inserted into The Acquisition of Land (Assessment of Compensation) Act

1919 by the provisions of the Local Government (Planning and Development) Act 1963 I do not consider that there are any grounds for believing that the prosecutor's position with regard to compensation if the compulsory purchase order is confirmed will in any way be prejudiced by the issue of this refusal by the planning authority.

For these reasons I would allow the cause shown and discharge the conditional order made in this case.

THE STATE (THOMAS COGLEY) V. DUBLIN CORPORATION AND ANOTHER
([1970] I.R. 244)

The prosecutor applied for outline planning permission and was granted same by the Minister in April of 1967. In May of 1968 he applied to Dublin Corporation for an approval and by order of 18th July, 1968 the assistant City Manager decided to grant the same. Subsequently a full meeting of the councillors revoked the ministerial outline permission and purported also to revoke the decision to approve. It was contended on behalf of the prosecutor that these decisions were invalid because they were in excess of the powers of the Corporation. It was conceded on all sides that there was no power to revoke an approval. The judge held, however, that the revocation of the outline permission was valid.

Teevan J.:

From this it will be seen that the permission to develop remains the essential thing. Grants of approval are entirely subsidiary and indeed are left by the statute to be brought into operative existence by the regulations. True they are indirectly created by the statute in that it is obligatory on the Minister to make the regulations but, while the necessity for permission is made complete and inexorable by section 24, the matter of grants of approval remains inchoate and inoperable unless and until ministerial regulations bring them into effectivenes. The purpose seems to be reasonably clear. The provision of a scheme for outline applications is purely procedural and the obvious idea was to relieve intending developers of the trouble and expense of submitting completed plans which refusal of permission would render fruitless. The provision for mere outline applications in the first instance allowed for by section 25(2)(a) and implemented by Art. 5 of the Regulations, greatly eases the burden on the applicant for permission. He is absolved at the initial stage from much of the onus required by Art. 4. But grants of approval are not essential: there is nothing in the Regulations to prevent an intending developer seeking full permission straight off, in compliance with Arts. 3 and 4 in which case no question of approval would arise, or be necessary, however unlikely it might be in practice that this procedure would be adopted. In my opinion, therefore, the provision for grants of approval is no more than a procedural scheme in ease of developers. One may not develop without permission but one may develop without grant of approval save in cases where the grant of subsequent approval is made a condition of the limited form of permission known as outline permission. Take away the permission and the freedom to develop is gone. In this case the permission has been taken away by the resolution of 18 August 1968 leaving nothing for approval to operate on.

I have already referred in a general way to the authority's power to revoke permission. (*The judge here quoted from S. 30*):

It is evident from the foregoing that the corporation had power to revoke the prosecutor's permission even after a grant of approval, if at the time of revocation he had not yet commenced his permitted development. It is noteworthy too that even in a case where the planning authority decide to revoke permission after the issue of grant of approval it is only necessary under section 30 to revoke the permission; there is no need to recall the approval.

I am of opinion that the Corporation acted within their powers in revoking this permission. The result is that planning permission no longer exists for this development and in the absence of such permission the corporation have no power to issue a grant of approval for the prosecutor's proposed development and accordingly mandamus to compel them to do so cannot go. The cause shown will be allowed and the conditional order of mandamus will be discharged.

. . .

IMPLICATIONS OF THE GRANT

It was suggested by Kenny J. in *Moran* v. *Dublin Corporation*[58] that the grant of full planning permission implied the availability of service for the development. This topic merited only a passing reference in the judgment referred to but it has come up again more recently for consideration in *State (Finglas Industrial Estates Limited)* v. *Dublin County Council*. Henchy J. delivered the judgment of the Supreme Court (comprising O'Higgins C.J., Walsh, Henchy, Griffin and Hederman J.J.) on the 17th February, 1983. A ministerial permission authorised the development of over a hundred acres in Co. Dublin as a light industrial estate subject, inter alia, to a condition that the developer would pay a contribution towards the provision of public services, the amount, time and method of payment of which was to be determined by agreement or in default on appeal by the Board. No agreement was reached and the matter was referred to An Bord Pleanala which fixed a sum of £1,500 per acre payable forthwith. Pursuant to this decision the developer tendered a cheque to the planning authority for £180,750 but the planning authority refused to accept this and mandamus proceedings were brought by the developer to compel acceptance.

In the High Court McMahon J. made the order holding that the condition by necessary implication directed the Council to provide a sewerage service in the area and that they were obliged to accept the cheque. In the Supreme Court the decision went the other way. The case turned on the point that the condition itself was ultra vires since it required an amount of money to be paid to a party other than the planning authority, namely Dublin Corporation. In passing Henchy J. indicated that since the development company was not incorporated until after the ministerial grant this alone would have been sufficient to invalidate the permission. He then proceeded to give some indication of the attitude of the Supreme Court to the contention which carried the day in the High Court, namely that the attaching of a condition to a grant of planning permission requiring payment of a contribution for services imposed on the relevant local authority an obligation to provide those services. From the dicta in the case it would appear that the attaching of such a condition cannot create such a duty; it may bring into force an existing legal

[58] 109 I.L.T.R. 57.

obligation to make a connection to the sewerage system but then only it appears if there is capacity in the sewer. If, on the other hand, the sewer is already overloaded the condition may be invalid. There can be no question of imposing or creating a duty on a local sanitary authority via such a condition to provide a sewerage system where none exists. The whole matter is governed by Ss. 23 and 24 of the Public Health (Ireland) Act, 1878, and not by way of specific decisions made under the Planning Acts.

A second case on this topic is *Short* v. *Dublin County Council.*[59] In the High Court McMahon J. held that an occupier had an absolute right to connect a development to the main foul sewer and that it was not a ground of objection for the planning authority to say that the capacity of the sewer was reserved for future development. *Molloy* v. *Gray*[60] was followed.

This decision was upheld in the Supreme Court where it was also made clear that a planning authority could not refuse to connect a housing development to its main sewer if that sewer had capacity of absorbing the sewage. Furthermore a refusal on the grounds that the proposal is premature by reason of an existing deficiency in the sewerage system when such was not the case even if the spare capacity in the system was pre-empted to cater for development to be undertaken by the local authority should not have the effect of precluding the payment of compensation under S. 56(1)(*b*)(i).

The position in the light of the *Short* and *Finglas Industrial Estates Limited* cases would appear to be as follows: (a) where there is no existing sewerage system nothing in a planning permission can create an obligation on the part of the sanitary authority to provide one. If there is such an obligation it arises under the Public Health Act of 1878. This Act was not repealed by implication by anything in the Planning Acts. The effect of a condition requiring payment of a contribution towards services attaching to a planning permission in such a situation would be to assess the amount payable in the event that the sanitary authority do in fact provide a sewerage system; it does not create an obligation on them so to provide. (b) Where there is an existing system but it is full to capacity then the attaching of such a condition to a planning permission may be ultra vires as it would purport to have the effect of causing the sanitary authority to overload its sewers. This applies only where the system is full to capacity not where it is pre-booked for developments which are in the pipeline. (c) Where there is an existing system which has capacity, then occupiers of buildings have a right to connect to the system. This right arises primarily under the Public Health (Ireland) Act, 1878 and not under the Planning Acts. It seems, however, that the grant of a planning permission may confer a right to connect to the system. Per Henchy J. 'where there *are* sewers adjoining the premises in question, the granting of planning permission for the erection of those premises may bring into force an existing legal obligation of the sanitary authority to make a connection.' It is not clear precisely what is meant by this or how it will work in practice. The rights of recipients of planning permissions for occupiers of buildings and the duties of the sanitary authority and the planning authority are likely to vary according to the precise facts of each individual case.

---

[59] See [1982] I.L.R.M. 117 for a report of the High Court judgment of McMahon J. Unreported Supreme Court judgment delivered 13th May, 1983 by O'Higgins, C.J.; Henchy, Hederman JJ. concurring.

[60] 24 L.R. (Ir.) 258.

The decision in the *Short* case has recently been extended by O'Hanlon J. in *McKone Estates Limited* v. *Kildare County Council* (page 428). In the *McKone* case it was held that subject to terms and conditions to be agreed or arbitrated on in default of agreement, the owner or occupier of a premises situated outside the functional area of a sanitary authority had a *prima facie* right to connect to the sewers of that sanitary authority. The sanitary authority in question has jurisdiction to impose terms and conditions but not a right to refuse on any terms or conditions a connection to a sewer having capacity to receive. This decision is dealt with more completely in Chapter VI on Compensation.

There is a close connection between planning permission and bye-law approval. A requirement in a condition in a planning permission that details of surface water and drainage systems be submitted to the local authority can be dealt with under an application for bye-law approval. The close relationship between planning permission and bye-law approval is apparent from the judgment in *The State (Foxrock Construction Company Limited). v. Dublin County Council.*[61] Finally in *Weir* v. *Corporation of Dun Laoghaire*[62] it appeared that one of the implications of the grant of planning permission can be that if the work involved is carried out with the knowledge and approval of the planning authority and constitutes a danger to a third party who is injured thereby that the planning authority can be made liable in tort for such injury.

STATE (FINGLAS INDUSTRIAL ESTATES LTD.) V. DUBLIN CO. CO.
(Supreme Court, unreported, 19th February, 1983)

Henchy J.:

In April 1975 an application was submitted on behalf of Finglas Industrial Estates Ltd. ('the developers') to Dublin County Council ('the Council') as planning authority for permission to develop 117.5 acres at Balseskin, Finglas, Co. Dublin, as a light industrial estate. At this stage the developers did not own, nor did they have any interest in, the land in question, nor were they even incorporated as a limited company.

In June 1975 the Council refused the application for development, giving five reasons, the most important seemingly being that facilities for the disposal of piped sewage and surface water were not available and could not be provided, because the only sewer in the vicinity was in the functional area of Dublin Corporation and was already being used to full capacity.

The developers appealed to the then Minister for Local Government against that refusal. The Minister by order dated the 17 February 1977 allowed that appeal and granted the permission sought, subject to this condition:

'The developers shall pay a sum of money to the Dublin County Council and/or to Dublin Corporation, as may be appropriate as a contribution towards the provision of a public water supply and piped sewerage facilities in the area. The amount to be paid and the time and method shall be agreed between the developers and the said Council and/or the said Corporation before the development is

---

[61] Unreported judgment of Finlay P. delivered 5th February, 1980. See p. 227.
[62] Unreported Supreme Court judgment delivered 20th December, 1982 by O'Higgins, C.J. Hederman J. concurring). Griffin J. delivered a dissenting judgment. See p. 231.

commenced or failing agreement, shall be as determined by the Minister for Local Government.'

It was, to say the least of it, an unusual grant of permission. The Council had no foul sewer system within three miles of the lands and the only such system in the Finglas area was and is one maintained by Dublin Corporation, and it was said to be already overloaded. The condition attached to the Minister's permission purported to allow Dublin Corporation to become involved in the provision of the necessary sewerage facilities, but they were not even a party to the planning application or the appeal. On top of everything, the Minister's permission was granted to developers who had no existence, for they did not become incorporated until April 1981. Were the latter point the only issue in this appeal, I fear that I would hold that the Minister's permission was invalid for having been granted to a non-existent legal person. I do not think that any provisions in the Companies Act, 1963, validating acts done before incorporation, can detract from the fact that it is inherent in the planning code that both the planning authority and the public shall have an opportunity of vetting the planning application in the light of, amongst other matters, the identity of a named and legally existing applicant. However, this is not the main issue in this appeal.

Offers by the developers to meet the financial demands which were written into the condition in the Minister's permission having failed, primarily because, in the opinion of the Council, the piped sewerage facilities could not possibly be made available within the legal lifetime of the permission (apart from legal as distinct from practical difficulties), the resolution of the condition fell to be determined by the Minister for Local Government.

By this stage, however, the implementation of the Minister's permission had been overtaken by fresh legislation. His permission had been granted pursuant to the provisions of the Local Government (Planning and Development) Act, 1963. That Act was substantially amended by the Local Government (Planning and Development) Act, 1976. Among the important changes made by the latter Act was the setting up of An Bord Pleanála ('the Board'), to which were transferred most of the powers formerly exercisable by the Minister under the 1963 Act.

The developers' advisers formed the opinion that the power given to the Minister in the condition attached to his permission (i.e. to fix, in default of agreement, the amount to be paid by the developers and the time and mode of such payment) had passed to the Board. They therefore wrote to the Board asking them to carry out the assessment or adjudication that had been reserved to the Minister by the condition. The Board, after giving the developers and the Council an opportunity of making representations, issued an order on the 23 December 1980 determining that the contribution to be made by the developers was to be £1,500 per acre, and that it was to be payable forthwith to the Council as sanitary authority for the area.

The developers now considered that they were free to consummate the condition by making the payment as assessed by the Board. On the 19 January 1981 they sent by hand to the Council a letter containing a cheque for £180,750 being the amount payable in accordance with the order of the Board. But the Council would have none of it. They refused to accept either the cheque or the accompanying letter. The developers, feeling that the authority of the Board was being flouted by the Council, and that they were being thwarted in carrying out what they now considered to be an unconditional planning permission, decided to have recourse to the Courts.

On the 6 April 1981 they got a conditional order of mandamus directed to the Council commanding them to accept the cheque for £180,750, which was the amount of the financial contribution fixed by the Board. That conditional order was made absolute, notwithstanding cause shown, on the 10 July 1981, and it is from that absolute order that the present appeal has been taken. . . And as I understand the law of mandamus, a public authority, be it a planning authority or a sanitary authority, cannot be compelled by mandamus to accept money tendered to it unless there is a public duty to accept it.

This case falls outside the scope of the decision of this Court in *The State (Pine Valley Developments Ltd.)* v. *Dublin Co. Council* (1982) I.L.R.M. 169 and so is unaffected by s. 6 of the Local Government (Planning and Development) Act, 1982.

One of the curious aspects of this case which emerged during the hearing of the appeal was the assumption that the Minister's order, in so far as it required the payment of a sum of money to the sanitary authority, necessarily imposed an obligation upon that authority to supply the sewerage facilities.

The duties and obligations of sanitary authorities to permit connections to their sewers are governed by ss. 23 and 24 of the Public Health (Ireland) Act, 1878. S. 23 deals with the rights of the owners and occupiers within the district of a sanitary authority to be connected to the sewers of that sanitary authority; and s. 24 deals with the use of sewers by owners and occupiers outside that district. A glance at the extensive notes to each of these sections which appear in Vanston's *Public Health* (2nd edition) will give some idea of the complex issues which have arisen in the many cases on these sections. The numerous and sometimes conflicting judicial pronouncements on the obligations of the sanitary authority raise such questions, among others, as the adequacy of the sewerage system to carry any additional sewage – a point which is raised in the present case by the Council as an objection to the granting of planning permission. But these sections appear to deal with the right of the owner/occupier of premises to cause his drains to empty into the sewers of the sanitary authority. They therefore presuppose the existence of these sewers at a point where a connection may be made from the premises in question to the sewers. They do not appear at first sight to deal with the more knotty problem of what is to be done where there are no sewers in the locality.

When there *are* sewers adjoining the premises in question, the granting of planning permission for the erection of those premises may bring into force an existing legal obligation of the sanitary authority to make a connection. The question could well arise in such a case as the present whether the inclusion of a condition in the planning permission compelling the payment of a contribution towards the provision of sewerage facilities can lawfully be made if its effect is to impose an obligation on the sanitary authority to overload their sewers. That point has not been fully argued in the present case and therefore it is unnecessary for the Court to express any view on it.

Quite apart from that, however, there is the situation (such as arises in the present case) in which there is no sewerage system to which a connection may be made to a sewer or drain from the premises in question, and in which, in order to make any such connection possible, it would be necessary to extend the existing sewerage system to a point at which a connection could be made. If there be any legal obligation on the sanitary authority to provide a sewerage system where none exists, or to permit a connection to an existing sewerage system, it is not to be found in the planning acts. Therefore, there would not at first sight appear to be any grounds for the assumption referred to above. However, in this case the Court is not called upon to make any comprehensive ruling on that question.

For present purposes, it is sufficient to say that the condition as to financial contribution imposed by the Minister upon the developers must be construed as referring to a contribution towards the cost of providing a public water supply or piped sewerage facilities in the area only if the Council were either willing or legally bound to make such provision.

For the reasons given, I would allow the Council's appeal and discharge the order of mandamus. What the legal or practical consequences of such an order will be, I do not pause to consider. It is sufficient to say that counsel for the Council has indicated that it is sufficient for the purposes of his clients if, for the reasons underlying this judgment, the cause shown by the Council is allowed and the conditional order of mandamus discharged.

THE STATE (FOXROCK CONSTRUCTION CO. LTD.) V. DUBLIN COUNTY COUNCIL
(Unreported judgment of Finlay P. delivered 5th February, 1980)

The developers owned land which had the benefit of planning permission for eleven detached houses granted on Appeal subject to eight conditions. Subsequently they applied to Dublin County Council for bye-law Approval and received a notice of disapproval for three specified reasons. The developers contended in the High Court that none of these reasons was concerned with the Building Bye-Laws and sought an order setting aside the notice of disapproval and directing the Authority to grant them approval. The County Council admitted that they were confined to the bye-laws in dealing with the application for bye-law approval, but contended that their reasons were valid. The President held in the case of one reason for the disapproval that it was clearly not related to bye-laws and that if that were the only issue in the case, it is clear that he would have given the declaration sought. However, in the case of a second reason, he held that the reason for disapproval was valid.

The County Council also made one general contention. They submitted that even if the three stated reasons were all bad, the Court should in its discretion, refuse the reliefs claimed by the developers on the following grounds. The planning permission was conditional on the foul and surface water drainage systems and water supply being agreed with the planning authority. The conditions attaching to the notice of disapproval for bye-law it was argued, constituted the detailed requirements of the bye-law authority in regard to these matters. They therefore contended that if the specified grounds of refusal were bad, and the Court were therefore to direct the granting of bye-law approval, it would in fact be directing the granting of a bye-law approval which was directly contrary to a condition of the planning permission. With this argument, the President agreed and it appears that the effect of this decision may be that if a planning permission reserves for a subsequent occasion the agreement by the planning authority of a detailed scheme in regard to, for example, sewerage, and on the bye-law application in respect of the same development, such a scheme is elaborated, then this can be taken as the approval by the planning authority under the planning permission. It seems that the Court will interpret the meaning of any bye-law approval or disapproval by reference to planning permissions available for the same site. This is entirely logical having regard to the existence of section 86 of the 1963 Planning Act which provides for substitution of building regulations made under the Planning Act, for the Bye-Laws made under the Public Health Acts of 1878 and 1890.

Finlay P.:

. . .The agreed essential facts may thus be summarised. The prosecutors have agreed to purchase a plot of land adjoining Brighton Road, Foxrock for the purpose of developing it by building eleven detached houses on it under a contract which is subject to planning approval and building bye-law approval being obtained prior to the 31st March, 1980. A previous owner of the lands P. J. N. & Company Limited applied for planning permission and the respondents notified to them on 29th August, 1978 a decision to grant permission subject to 19 conditions. Against this decision certain objectors appealed and an oral hearing of the appeal was conducted on behalf of An Bord Pleanala in December, 1978 subsequent to which the Board on the 7th of February, 1979 decided to grant permission subject to 8 conditions.

On the 23rd October 1979 the prosecutors applied to the respondents for approval pursuant to the Building Bye-Laws for the development and by notice dated 20th December, 1979 the respondents gave notice of their disapproval for the following reasons.

1. Proposal to lay the surface water sewer outfall for the development along the Brighton Road is not acceptable.
2. That the proposal to construct the external concrete pavement above the concrete out floor (sic) is not acceptable.
3. The applications should submit an alternative surface water system drainage to the system in the neighbouring estate. Applicants should consult with the Building and Development Control Department before re-applying.'

It is agreed that the word 'out floor' in reason No. 2 is a clerical error for 'sub floor'.

The prosecutors contend that none of these reasons is concerned with any breach of, or non compliance with, the building bye-laws at present in force and made by the respondents and that accordingly as a matter of law the notice of disapproval is ultra vires the respondents who are not entitled to seek by the enforcement of its bye-law authority to amend or derogate from the decision of An Bord Pleanala granting planning permission and that they the prosecutors are entitled to an absolute order of both certiorari and mandamus.

The respondents do not dispute that as a matter of law they are confined in deciding an application for building bye-law approval to enforcement of the bye-laws, but submit that the reasons for the disapproval are in fact to secure compliance with the bye-laws and in the alternative contend that even if all or any of the reasons were held to be ultra vires that the Court should in its discretion refuse to the prosecutors both of the remedies claimed.

This alternative submission arises in the following way. Condition 5 of the permission granted by the Board reads as follows:

'The foul and surface water drainage systems and water supply to serve the proposed development shall comply with the detailed requirements of the planning authority.'

The first and third reasons given for disapproval, which I have already quoted, constitute it is submitted the detailed requirements of the respondents for the surface water drainage system. It is therefore contended that were the respondents forced by the order of the Court to grant bye-law approval over-ruling this objection they would be forced to purport to grant approval for works to be carried out in violation of a condition attached to the planning permission which would be contrary to the public interest.

I will deal first with the issue of the validity viewed in isolation of the notice of disapproval.

The bye-laws in force which are made pursuant to the Public Health (Ireland) Act, 1878 and the Public Health Acts (Amendment) Acts, 1890 and 1907 are those made by the respondents on 22nd September, 1967.

In relation to reason No. 1 the respondents rely on Rules 80 and 84 of those bye-laws.

The reality of reason No. 1 in the notice of disapproval is that it constitutes a total refusal by the respondents to permit the prosecutors' proposal to connect surface water drainage by piping it for some 400 odd metres along Brighton Road and connecting it to a main sewer near the junction of Brighton Road and Westminster Road and seeks instead to force the prosecutors to join the surface water drainage system to a sewer on land privately owned adjacent to Hainault Road. It is in short a complete re-routing of the system proposed.

I am quite satisfied that neither rule 80 which deals with detailed provisions for the paving of open space yards and incorporates a necessity to carry off the surplus water from them nor rule 84 which provides the necessity for a rainwater down pipe to discharge into a gully trap connected to either a surface water drain or a sewerage drain could on any construction be interpreted as permitting a bye-law authority as the respondents in this case candidly seek to do, to re-route an entire drainage system in the general interest of the planning and development of the area.

I am therefore satisfied that reason No. 1 is not a valid reason for disapproval.

With regard to reason No. 2 the respondents rely on Rule 14 which reads as follows:

'Every building should be so constructed as to ensure that it will not be affected adversely by moisture from adjoining earth. Every wall and pier of such building shall have a proper damp proof course of sheet lead, asphalt or other permanent material impervious to moisture laid to the full width of such wall beneath the level of the lowest timbers and at a height of not less than 6 inches above the surface of the ground adjoining such wall.'

Reason No. 2 on the evidence before me is; '(1) An attempt to secure an alteration in the relative height of the outside pavement surrounding the house and the concrete sub-floor; (2) To secure the insertion of a damp proof course in the internal dwarf walls; and (3) To secure the provision of a water-proof membrane below the concrete sub-floor.

Rule 14 contains two distinct and clearly distinguishable provisions. The first is general and wide, the second detailed and specific. I am satisfied that the second provision is clearly applicable only to outside piers and walls. From the plans submitted for approval which I have considered I am satisfied that the requirements underlying reason No. 2 are not within this specific provision. I am also however satisfied that they are requirements which could be conducive to preventing the building from being adversely affected by moisture from adjoining earth. Unless there are reasons why the first provision contained in Rule 14 should be narrowly construed it would justify disapproval for this reason.

Mr. Walsh on behalf of the prosecutors submits that it should be narrowly construed and in effect confined to a meaning dealing with the matters specifically provided in the second sub-clause. To do otherwise he argues would be to permit the bye-law authority to require a major design amendment in plans which have already received planning permission. I cannot accept this contention. In law no building development may take place even though it is the subject of a planning permission unless it also has obtained building bye-law approval where that is necessary.

There appears to me therefore to be no inconsistency in a planning authority or An Bord Pleanala confining its consideration to the proper planning and development of an area leaving such matters as the protection of a building against weather as specifically dealt with in building bye-laws to the Bye-Law Authority.[63]

I am not concerned in these applications with any dispute on the merits of the particular requirements made by the respondents but only with the question as to whether they are a prima facie attempt to secure compliance with the provision of the bye-law. I am satisfied that the disapproval based on reason No. 2 is a valid disapproval.

What is stated to be reason No. 3 is not a reason for disapproval except insofar as it amplifies reason No. 1 but is rather an indication of the procedure now to be adopted by the applicants and its validity does not arise as a separate issue. Having regard to my finding that the disapproval of the proposed drainage system is ultra vires it is necessary to deal with the alternative contention on behalf of the respondents that the proposed drainage system is in any event contrary to conditions attached to the planning permission.

It was agreed by the parties that at all material times the respondents have disapproved of a surface drainage system travelling along Brighton Road and have contended that the proper system would be one connecting up in the other direction near Hainault Road. They alleged that they implemented that view by attaching to their decision to grant planning permission condition No. 12 which reads as follows: 'That the water supply and drainage arrangements be in accordance with the requirements of the County Council', thus leaving themselves empowered to control both the route and the design features of the drainage system.

It is further agreed that the respondents submitted their views on the appropriate drainage system at the oral hearing and they contend that condition 5 imposed by the Board, so close in its effective term to condition 12 as imposed by them, must be interpreted as a decision by the Board to leave to the planning authority the right to prescribe all features of the drainage system including its route and destination.

The prosecutors on the other hand contend that if the Board intended such a large departure from their plans submitted for approval as a complete re-routing of the drainage system they would have said so by imposing an express and unambiguous condition and that I must construe 'the detailed requirements of the planning

---

[63] Query whether such a permission is a full permission or merely an outline permission. See observations of McMahon J. in *Keleghan and Others* v. *Corby and Dublin Corp.* at p. 234.

authority' mentioned in condition No. 5 as being confined to what might be described as minor questions of construction design along the route proposed in the prosecutors' plans.

On this issue I am satisfied that the contention of the respondents is correct. The reason given by the Board for imposing Condition No. 5 is 'in the interest of public health and the proper planning and development of the area'. If all the discretion intended to be left to the planning authority in relation to the drainage system concerned minor details of design and construction along a pre-determined route with a pre-determined destination some much more limited or narrower reason would appear to be appropriate.

Furthermore on the facts proved and agreed before me the Board must have been aware that the planning authority had from the beginning consistently disapproved of the route travelling along Brighton Road and were under the impression that a condition framed as was their condition 12 left them free to implement that disapproval. Had the Board decided, as the prosecutors contend, to over-rule that disapproval, they would it seems to me have done so either by imposing no condition giving to the planning authority any remaining discretion concerning the drainage system or by imposing a condition markedly different from that which the planning authority had decided to impose. I reject a contention that the insertion of the word 'detailed' before 'requirements' which is the only effective difference between the two conditions has any real significance.

I must therefore construe condition No. 5 as meaning what it appears to say namely that the planning authority may set out detailed requirements for the drainage system and that the developers who are the prosecutors must comply with them. So construing this condition it seemed to me that a building bye-law approval for the existing proposed drainage system would in the light of the planning authority's requirements be a purported approval for an unauthorised development contrary to the provisions of the Planning Acts a result which the Court should not in its discretion achieve by the grant of an order of mandamus. From that decision it follows that the prosecutors could gain no legal interest or advantage from the quashing of so much of the notice of approval as is based on reason No. 1 and I must therefore dismiss both these applications.

WEIR V. CORPORATION OF DUN LAOGHAIRE
(Supreme Court, Unreported Judgment delivered 20th December 1982)

O'Higgins C.J.: (Hederman J. concurring):
This is an appeal against the jury's verdict awarding damages to the plaintiff. The appeal rests on two submissions made by the defendants. In the first place they contend that the trial Judge ought to have withdrawn the case from the jury because there was no evidence that the interference with the roadway which caused or contributed to the plaintiff's injuries was either authorised or permitted by them. Secondly, they claim as an alternative, that the case ought to have been withdrawn from the jury because there was no evidence of negligence.

I propose to deal in the first instance with the second ground of appeal. The evidence establishes that on the Sunday morning of the accident the plaintiff who was an elderly lady was, in the company of her husband, crossing the road at Royal Marine Road, Dun Laoghaire. She was proceeding from Dun Laoghaire Church towards a new shopping centre on the far side of the road. As she neared the side to which she was proceeding she tripped, fell and suffered injuries. There was evidence that the cause of her fall was a difference in road levels of two inches or more along a line where a new lay-by for buses was being constructed. No warning of this difference in level was given and the entire roadway which was tarmacadam, appeared uniform. I am quite satisfied that on these facts it was proper that the case should have gone to the jury on the issue of negligence. The jury having found negligence I do not think that such finding can be disturbed.

As to the first ground it appears that the difference in road levels which caused or contributed to the plaintiff's fall and injuries came about in the following circumstances. A company called MEPC (Ireland) Limited sought planning permission from the defendants as the planning authority under the Local Government (Planning and Development) Act 1963 for the development of a site along Marine Road as a shopping centre. Permission was obtained from the defendants as the planning authority on the 12th December 1973 but an appeal was lodged by an objector. The appeal was decided and final planning permission granted by the Minister for Local Government on the 21st August 1973. A condition of this permission was that a bus lay-by be provided by the developers, if required by the planning authority, on Marine Road. When the building of the shopping centre was completed a firm of contractors called John Paul & Company proceeded to erect or construct a bus lay-by along Marine Road. This involved considerable interference with the roadway and adjoining footpath. The layout of this bus lay-by was agreed with the defendants. This appears from the evidence of their Assistant Borough Engineer. In addition, from his evidence it appears that the carrying out of the work was known to the defendants. From these facts it can fairly be inferred that the provision of the bus lay-by had been required by the defendants as the planning authority and that the work was carried out by John Paul & Company on behalf of the developers and with the knowledge and approval of the defendants as the planning authority.

The defendants maintain that as the highway authority under the Local Government Act of 1925 they are not to be fixed with knowledge or made liable in respect of any licence or approval which they might have or may have given as the planning authority under the Local Government (Planning and Development) Act 1963. I do not accept this submission. I am satisfied that the defendants must be held to have known and to have approved of the work undertaken by John Paul & Company. Even if the work was authorised originally by the defendants solely as the planning authority this does not mean that as the highway authority they cannot be regarded as having knowledge thereof. Whatever was done was clearly done with their knowledge and they had a responsibility to look to the safety of those using the roadway, who might thereby be exposed to danger if what was done caused risk of injury. In my view, the grounds upon which this appeal has been moved fail and this appeal should be dismissed.

Griffin J.: (Dissenting)

The facts are set out in the judgment of the Chief Justice. On those facts, the plaintiff is entitled to succeed against the person who created the danger on the highway – for danger it was to pedestrians such as the plaintiff. The work in this case was, however, not carried out by nor was the danger created by the defendants.

The defendants are the highway authority charged with the repair and maintenance of the roads (including footpaths) in Dun Laoghaire pursuant to Part III of the Local Government Act, 1925, and they are sued as such. It is well settled that, as such authority, although they are not liable to a user of the highway for injuries suffered or caused by want of repair (non-feasance), they are liable in damages for injuries suffered by such user if they or their servants, or those for whose acts they are responsible, have been negligent in doing repairs to or in interfering with the highway (misfeasance). Where the interference with the highway is done by their servants, no difficulty arises. Where the work is carried out by an independent contractor engaged by them to do the work, although they are not responsible for the casual or collateral negligence of the contractor, they are liable if their contractor fails to take reasonable precautions to protect the users of the highway from danger which, from the nature of the work, is likely to be caused to them. The authority which has undertaken the work cannot escape responsibility by delegating the performance of the duty imposed on them to the contractor.

If, therefore, in this case the defendants had undertaken the work in question, and the 2 inch difference in level had been caused by their servants or by a contractor engaged by them to carry out the work, they would be clearly liable in damages to the plaintiff. That however was not the position.

In the High Court and on the hearing of this appeal the case made on behalf of the plaintiff was that because the developers of the shopping centre obtained planning permission for the development, which included the construction of a bus lay-by on Marine Road, the lay out of which had in advance been agreed with the defendants, and because the defendants were aware that work was being carried on by the contractors engaged by the developers, the work being carried out had been 'authorised' by the defendants, and that they were liable for any negligence of such contractors in carrying out the work, and in particular in failing to warn of or guard against the danger on the highway on the occasion of the accident.

The learned trial Judge accepted this submission and ruled accordingly. In my opinion, his ruling was incorrect – so to extend the liability of a highway authority to include responsibility for the acts of a contractor engaged by a developer in doing work for which the latter had obtained planning permission, and equating this liability with that of the authority for acts of a contractor engaged by them, is in my view warranted neither by principle nor authority. Indeed, all the cases cited in the High Court and referred to in the ruling of the trial Judge were cases in which the work had been carried out to the highway by the highway authority. In this Court, counsel were unable to refer to, nor have I been able to find, any case in which liability attached to a highway authority by reason of the granting of planning permission for the work being carried out.

Although the plaintiff is entitled to be compensated in damages for the injuries suffered to her in this accident, in my judgment she is not so entitled as against the present defendants. I would accordingly allow the appeal.

. . .

CONSEQUENCES OF NON-COMPLIANCE

Only in the clearest cases will the Courts grant a default permission. In many cases non-compliance with the application regulations will result in all proceedings which follow being rendered nugatory. On the other hand the Courts have shown a marked reluctance to hold that the consequence of non-compliance with the regulations by a planning authority results in a default permission. The attitude of the Courts can be summed up in the following quotation from the judgment of the Supreme Court (O'Higgins C.J., Hederman and McCarthy J.J.) delivered by McCarthy J. on the 11th February, 1983 in *Creedon* v. *Dublin Corporation*:

'It was never the intention of the legislature that mistakes by planning or housing authorities – mis-constructions of their powers – misconception of the facts or the like – would be used as a basis for abandoning the statutory procedures and seeking to use the courts as some form of licensing or enabling authority in a field in which the legislative and executive organs of government have prime responsibility. It is not the function of the judical arm of government to aid an owner of property who, so to speak, is fortunate enough to have some innocent error made in his particular application, and so aid him as in effect, to grant him a housing permission or a planning permission which it is the express decision of the relevant authority not to grant. . . . In my view to permit such a use is not the function of the courts – there may well be cases where it can be demonstrated that there has been bad faith on the part of the authority concerned as is illustrated by the references made by O'Dalaigh C.J. in *Listowel U.D.C.* v. *McDonagh* (1968: I.R. 312), and such bad faith would not be confined by any stated limits, but, in a case such as the present where no allegations of any impropriety, ulterior motive, or anything save a mistake in law, is suggested, in my view, the necessity for the applicant to exhaust the statutory remedies is a complete answer to any claim to the discretionary asistance of the Courts.'

These observations echo those of Henchy J. in the *Monaghan U.D.C.* v. *Alf-a-Bet Promotions Limited*: 'Such powers as have been given to planning authorities, tribunals or the courts to operate or review the operation of the planning laws should be exercised in such a way that the statutory intent in its essence will not be defeated, intentionally or unintentionally, by omissions, ambiguities, misstatements or other defaults in the purported compliance with the prescribed procedures.'

KELEGHAN AND OTHERS V. CORBY AND DUBLIN CORPORATION
(111 I.L.T.R. 144)

The Sisters of the Holy Faith represented by the first named defendant applied for planning permission for what was decribed in the newspaper notice required by the regulations as 'The erection of three classrooms prefabricated extension to St. Brigid's Secondary School, Killester'. The application, in fact, included in addition a proposal to create a new access road to the grounds of the Holy Faith Secondary School through a cul-de-sac which serviced 12 houses erected under a planning permission subject to a condition that the portion of the housing estate adjoining the grounds of the Holy Faith Convent and Secondary School should be bounded by a 6 ft. wall. McMahon J. held that the newspaper notice did not give a statement of the extent and nature of the development insofar as it failed to indicate the proposed new access and that the permission was, therefore, invalidly granted.

This judgment is also of interest in that it suggests without deciding the point that a grant of permission subject to a condition that further details be submitted for agreement is also for this reason invalid if it purports to be a full planning permission, as the effect of such a condition was to preclude the public from a right of appeal in regard to the details subsequently submitted.

McMahon J.:

. . . . I am quite satisfied of one thing, that the advertisement published by the applicants, the order of nuns represented by the first defendant, Mary Hilary Corby, was entirely inadequate to put to the public who might be concerned on notice of what the permission required involved. The purpose of notice is to give members of the public who may be concerned with the development an idea whether the development looked for is the kind that may affect their interest. It appears to me that a notice of an application for permission to erect three temporary prefabricated classrooms at a secondary school where the grounds are very extensive, somewhere in excess of six acres, did not convey to the public residing in this cul-de-sac that the development might possibly include a roadway giving access to the school through the cul-de-sac. Such an access is not necessarily or normally incidental to the erection of prefabricated buildings and as far as the evidence goes, it was not provided for the service of these classrooms but for a separate reason altogether. Therefore, it appears that the public did not get proper notice of the application.

Section 26 of the Local Government (Planning and Development) Act, 1963, authorises the planning authority to decide to grant permission where an application is made to the planning authority in accordance with the permission regulations. The relevant permission regulations of 1964 require, under regulation 9, the publication of an advertisement or notice in a newspaper and, by sub-article 4(a) that notice is to contain, inter alia, a statement of the extent and nature of the development in respect of which it is intended to apply for permission.

For the reasons I have given I regard an access from this cul-de-sac to the school generally as not being within the nature or extent of an application to erect three temporary prefabricated classrooms in the school. Accordingly, for that reason in my view, the grant of permission was not validly granted.

I think it better to reserve any decision on the third point made by Mr. Gaffney, namely assuming that the application had in fact been, as it was construed by the planning authority, to include access or change of user of the land to provide access from the cul-de-sac, whether permission has been validly granted by imposing a condition that details of the access be submitted for agreement. I can see serious difficulties about that from the point of view of the planning law. A planning authority is entitled to grant permission subject to conditions requiring work to be done, but when that is done the planning permission must specify the work to be done and any person, who thinks he is prejudiced by it, can appeal because he has before him details of the work to be done, but in this case what was granted was permission for access subject to details to be submitted for agreement. The public would have no knowledge what details were in fact being agreed and no way of appealing against the details agreed on between the applicants and the planning authority. It might be that the houses in the cul-de-sac were of a particular architectural style and agreement was reached with the planning authority for the erection of a gate in complete disharmony with the buildings in the cul-de-sac. The public in the cul-de-sac ought to have a right of appeal against that.

It seems to me that what was done could only be done by way of outline planning permission. I mention this because I have serious doubts whether the thing can be done but I am prepared to decide the case on the basis of the first issue whether the application was validly granted. It is therefore unnecessary to decide the other point, whether the access is within the scope of the permission as granted. . . .

Chapter 4

APPEALS

Planning decisions may be reviewed by way of appeal to the Planning Board (or in a few instances to the Minister for the Environment) where the decision is objected to on planning grounds. An appeal may be made to the Court where the extrinsic legality of a decision of the planning authority or the Planning Board is in issue. In the case of an appeal to the Planning Board the planning merits of the decision will be reviewed. The Court is restricted to considering whether the planning authority or the Board acted within its powers and while it may declare a decision *ultra vires* and require the planning authority or the Board to reconsider the matter it cannot substitute its own decision for that of the planning authority or the Planning Board.

APPEALS TO THE PLANNING BOARD

The Board's powers derive from the Acts and must be exercised in accordance with their provisions and the principles of natural and constitutional justice.

Under the 1963 Act appeals from decisions of the planning authority were made to the Minister for Local Government (later the Minister for the Environment). Section 14 of the 1976 Act transferred most of the Minister's appellate jurisdiction to the newly created Planning Board.[1] Only in the case of appeals brought under sections 66[2] and 88[3] of the 1963 Act does the Minister retain his appellate jurisdiction.[4] The 1976 Act also gave the Planning Board appellate jurisdiction under section 25 of that Act.[5]

The vast majority of appeal dealt with by the Board are appeals made under section 26 of the 1963 Act, i.e. appeals against decisions to grant permission for development with or without conditions or to refuse permission. With this in mind the following discussion of appeals will be in the context of appeals made under section 26 with mention of other appeals being made at the end of this section.

---

[1] See page 243.
[2] See page 389.
[3] See page 130.
[4] The Minister also retained his functions under section 43 of the 1963 (confirmation of amenity orders made pursuant to section 42) and his functions under section 76 of the 1963 Act (approval of orders extinguishing public rights of way). Both sections make provision for the holding of local public enquiries to deal with objections received and not withdrawn.
[5] See page 350. The Board was also given appellate jurisdiction in respect of section 29 of the 1976 Act insofar as it relates to waiver notices. Since the coming into force of section 15(2)(b) of the 1982 Act on the 28th July 1983, no further waiver notices may be issued unless the application in their behalf was received by the planning authority prior to the 28th July 1983.

When considering whether or not to bring an appeal under section 26 it should be borne in mind that, except in the case of certain appeals against conditions only, the entire application will be reconsidered as though it had been made to the Board in the first instance and the appellant cannot restrict the Board to specific parts of the decision. (See section 26(5) of the 1963 Act;[6] section 17 of the 1976 Act[7]). Thus a refusal may be substituted for a permission or a decision which is even more objectionable to the appellant may be substituted for that of the planning authority.

Where an appeal is made against conditions only, after the coming into force of section 19 of the 1983 Act[8] and the Board is satisfied that having regard to the nature of the conditions that a redetermination of the entire application would be unwarranted it may give, at its absolute discretion, such directions to the planning authority relating to the attachment, amendment or removal of the condition(s) appealed against or of any other conditions, as it considers appropriate. (See section 19 of the 1983 Act)[9] While it may come to be the practice of the Board to deal with certain kinds of conditions in this manner, it will always be at its discretion to do so. Further the appellant cannot guarantee that the Board will restrict itself to the condition(s) against which the appeal is brought. The Board is, however, restricted to considering the matters set out in section 19(2) of the 1983 Act when exercising its powers under this section.

The form and content of the notice of appeal is dealt with in Article 36 of the 1977 Regulations.[10] *Prima facie* the article appears to be mandatory, however, in *The State (Elm Developments Limited)* v. *An Bord Pleanala* the Supreme Court held that a failure to include the grounds of appeal did not invalidate the appeal.[11] (See also *The State (Walsh)* v. *An Bord Pleanala*[12]). Prior to the coming into force of the 1983 Act if no grounds of appeal were submitted and the Board were of the opinion that the defaulting appellant was unnecessarily delaying the appeal it could serve a notice on that appellant under section 18 of the 1976 Act.[13] Such notice stated that after a specified date (not less than 7 days from the service of the notice) the Board would without further notice to the appellant determine the appeal notwithstanding that no submission (i.e. no grounds of appeal) had been made. Provided the Board did nothing to waive its rights to determine the appeal without further notice after the specified date, it could do so any time after the passing of that date. (See *The State (Genport Limited* v. *An Bord Pleanala* in which it was held that the Board had waived its rights)[14] Since the coming into force of the 1983 Act where no grounds of appeal are furnished the Board may serve a notice in accordance with section 17 of that Act.[15] If, after the expiry of the period specified

[6] See page 117.
[7] See page 246.
[8] See page 258. Section 19 came into force on the 25th October 1983.
[9] See page 258.
[10] See page 249.
[11] See page 283. Applied in *The State (Genport Limited)* v. *An Bord Pleanala*, page 288.
[12] See page 286.
[13] See page 246. Sections 18(1) and (2) were repealed on the 25th October 1983 by section 25 of the 1983 Act.
[14] See page 288.
[15] See page 257. This section came into force on the 25th October 1983. Note that it applies only to appeals made pursuant to section 26(5) of the 1963 Act.

therein the requirements of the notice have not been complied with the Board may declare the appeal withdrawn.

If having considered the grounds of appeal the Board is of the opinion that an appeal brought under section 26(5) of the 1963 Act is vexatious, frivolous or without substance or foundation or where having regard to the nature of the appeal and any previous permission or approval which in its opinion is relevant the Board is satisfied that in the particular circumstances the appeal should not be further considered by it, it may at its absolute discretion dismiss the appeal. (See section 16 of the 1983 Act)[16]

The deposit referred to in Article 36(*d*) of the 1977 Regulations has now been replaced with a fee of £30 (or in the case of an appeal by any of the bodies specified in Article 21 of the (Fees and Amendment) Regulations 1983 £15) in respect of appeals brought on or after the 11 April 1983. (See Article 18 of the (Fees and Amendment) Regulations 1983[17] and section 10 of the 1982 Act[18]). It appears that the fee need not be sent contemporaneously with the appeal. It must, however, be received by the Board within the period allowed for the making of the appeal. In the event of the fee not being received within that period the appeal shall be invalid. (See section 10(3) of the 1982 Act).

It is essential that an appeal brought under section 26 be lodged within 'the appropriate period' as defined in section 26(5)(*c*) of the 1963 Act.[19] There is no provision for any extension of this period with the result that an appeal lodged out of time is invalid. It will be seen from section 26(5)(*c*) that the applicant/appellant is favoured with a longer period within which to appeal. Further in the case of the applicant/appellant time begins to run from the giving of the decision. In the case of all other appellants time begins to run from the giving of the decision by the planning authority. It is not clear when the planning authority gives its decision. In *State (Murphy)* v. *Dublin County Council* it was held that the planning authority gives its decision on the day it posts it in accordance with section 7 of the 1963 Act.[20] This decision, however, was based on an earlier English decision which has since been distinguished and in *Freeney* v. *Bray U.D.C.* O'Hanlon J. said *obiter* that the planning authority does not give its decision until the applicant receives it.[21]

The appeal may be lodged by hand at the Board's offices or sent by post. In *The State (Connolly)* v. *The Minister for Local Government* it was held that it was sufficient to post the appeal within the 'appropriate period'.[22] It must, however, reach the Board's offices not later than three days after the expiry of the 'appropriate period'. (See section 22 of the 1976 Act)[23]

Under the 1963 Act the Minister was required to hold an oral hearing if requested to do so. (See section 82(2) of the 1963 Act)[24] After the coming into force of section 16 of the 1976 Act the holding of an oral hearing was at the

---

[16] See page 257. Note this section applies only to appeals under section 26(5) of the 1963 Act.
[17] See page 279.
[18] See page 255.
[19] See page 117.
[20] See page 9.
[21] See page 291.
[22] See page 294.
[23] See page 247.
[24] See page 252. Since amended by section 43 of the 1976 Act.

discretion of the Board unless it was directed to hold one by the Minister.[25] Since the coming into force of the 1983 Act the Board has an absolute discretion to hold an oral hearing except in the case of appeals of a class or description falling within the provisions of section 15(2) of the 1983 Act.[26] Regulations may be made under section 15(2) of the 1983 Act providing that an oral hearing shall be held in respect of appeals of a class or description specified. The Minister no longer has any power to require an oral hearing in an individual case unless he makes a regulation in respect of it.

A further fee of £30 is payable in respect of a request for an oral hearing. (See Article 23 of the (Fees and Amendment) Regulations 1983).[27] Where the Board decides not to hold an oral hearing after a request for one has been made the Board must serve a notice of its decision on the person who requested the oral hearing requiring him to make such submissions or further submissions as he thinks fit within a specified period (which must not be less than 14 days from the service of the notice). (See section 15(3) of the 1983 Act.[28] Where the Board decide to hold an oral hearing it must serve a notice in accordance with Article 44 of the 1977 Regulations informing the parties of the time and place of the oral hearing.[29]

Regardless of the method of determining the appeal documents submitted by the parties to the Board and any written submission made on the appeal to the Board will be exchanged between the parties who will be given an opportunity to comment on them. (See Articles 39–41 of the 1977 Regulations[30] and *The State (Genport Limited)* v. *An Bord Pleanala*).[31] Where the Board is of the opinion that it requires any document, particulars or other information to enable it to determine an appeal made pursuant to section 26(5) of the 1963 Act it may serve a notice on any party to the appeal or any other person who has made submissions or observations to the Board in respect of the appeal requiring them to submit such documents, particulars or other information as may be specified within a period to be specified in the notice of not less than 14 days from the service of the notice. The notice must further state that in the event of a failure to comply with the notice the Board may without further notice dismiss or otherwise determine the appeal. It may do so after the expiration of the period specified in the notice after having considered the response (if any) to the notice. (See section 18 of the 1983 Act)[32]

Where no oral hearing is to be held the matter will be determined by the Board on the basis of the documents, observations, submissions, particulars or other information submitted to it together with a site inspection. The inspection will be carried out by an inspector appointed by the Board for the purpose. The inspector must make a written report of his inspection which shall include a recommendation which the Board must consider in coming to its decision although it is not bound to accept it. (See section 23 of the 1976 Act)[33]

---

[25] See page 245. Section 16 was repealed by section 25 of the 1983 Act on the 25th October 1983. See now section 15 of the 1983 Act which came into force on the 25th October 1983.

[26] See page 256.

[27] See page 280. Part III of the Regulations dealing with appeals came into force on the 11th April 1983.

[28] See page 257.

[29] See page 251.

[30] See page 250.

[31] See page 288.

[32] See page 257. This section came into force on the 25th October 1983 and applies to appeals made pursuant to section 26 (5) of the 1963 Act only.

[33] See page 248.

Where an appeal is to be determined after the holding of an oral hearing the Board will appoint an inspector to hold the hearing and report on it. (See section 23 of the 1976 Act) The procedure at the hearing is dealt with in section 82 of the 1963 Act[34] and in Article 45 of the 1977 Regulations.[35] It is usual for the parties to be represented. The order of appearance will be decided by the inspector. Each party will be given an opportunity to comment on each of the other parties' case. At the close of the evidence and submissions of the parties the inspector will usually hear third party objectors. (See *Law* v. *The Minister for Local Government* on his duty to do so.)[36] Any third party, other than one of the bodies specified in Article 21 of the (Fees and Amendment) Regulations 1983, who wishes to make a submission or observation must pay a fee of £10.[37] The bodies specified in Article 21 may make submissions or observations without payment of a fee.[38] A third party who is liable to pay a fee may be allowed to make his submissions and observations at the oral hearing without having paid the fee, but these will not be considered by the Board unless and until the fee has been paid. (See section 10 of the 1982 Act)[39]

Though it is rarely if ever done, the inspector has the power to hear evidence on oath and he may require any person he considers necessary to attend the hearing as a witness. (See section 82(6) of the 1963 Act).[40] The inspector may if he wishes make an inspection of the site. (See section 82(5) of the 1963 Act)[41] If he does so he must include an account of his inspection in his report to the Board. (See section 23 of the 1976 Act)[42]

Once the oral hearing is completed the inspector will make a written report to the Board. As well as including an account of any site inspection made the report must include a fair and accurate account of the submission made and the evidence adduced together with a recommendation. (See section 23 of the 1976 Act; *Geraghty* v. *The Minister for Local Government*;[43] *Killiney and Ballybrack Development Association* v. *The Minister for Local Government*)[44]

In coming to its decision the Board must consider the inspector's report including the recommendation contained therein. (See section 23 of the 1976 Act) It is clear that the Board is not bound by the recommendation. Further it was held by Walsh J. (Budd J. concurring) in *Geraghty* v. *The Minister for Local Government* that the Minister to whose functions the Board has succeeded was not bound by findings of fact made by the inspector, but could make other findings of fact provided they were supportable on the evidence and material properly before him. (but cf. Henchy J.) If the Board requires further elucidation on anything contained in the report they may obtain this from the inspector. (See Gannon J. in *Geraghty* v. *The Minister for Local Government*). Where, however, new facts or matters of probative value arise the parties must be informed and given an opportunity to deal with

[34] See page 252.
[35] See page 251.
[36] See page 295.
[37] See page 280.
[38] See page 280.
[39] See page 255.
[40] See page 253.
[41] See page 253. Note, however, *Killiney and Ballybrack Development Association* v. *The Minister for Local Government*.
[42] See page 248.
[43] See page 298.
[44] See page 303.

them. Prior to the coming into force of the 1976 Act it is clear that a further oral hearing had to be held to deal with any new matters. (See *Geraghty* v. *The Minister for Local Government*). Under the 1963 Act it was mandatory on the Minister to hold an oral hearing once requested to do so and it was not open to him to deal with some matters by way of oral hearing and others by way of documentary submissions. Unlike the Minister the Board has always enjoyed some discretion on whether to hold an oral hearing. It has yet to be decided if having exercised its discretion to hold an oral hearing in the first instance it is bound to deal with all matters by way of oral hearing. The position might differ in respect of those appeals in which it has a discretion and those in which it does not.

In addition to the above matters the Board may also consider matters other than those raised by the parties. In particular it may consider matters related to the proper planning and development of the planning authority's area and the matters set out in section 24(2) of the 1963 Act.[45] It must, however, give the parties an opportunity to deal with them. (See section 17 of the 1976 Act) It may also consider the probable effect that a particular decision would have on any place outside the area of the planning authority and any other consideration relating to the development outside the planning authority's area. (See section 24 of the 1976 Act)[46] It appears that the Board may also seek advice of a technical nature in order to qualify itself to make the decision. (See Henchy J. and Gannon J. in *Geraghty* v. *The Minister for Local Government*)[47]

The Board must not delegate its duty to make the decision. The decision must be made by the Board and the Board alone.

The costs of the appeal are dealt with in section 19 of the 1976 Act.[48] Note that the costs do not depend upon the result of the appeal.

Where the Board is of the opinion that an appeal or reference or an application to which an appeal is related has been abandoned it may serve a notice pursuant to section 5 of the 1982 Act informing the appellant or applicant that it is of such opinion and giving him or her an opportunity to make submissions as to why such appeal or reference or application should not be declared withdrawn. After the expiry of the period specified in the notice and after considering such submissions as it has received it may declare the appeal reference of application withdrawn. (See section 5 of the 1982 Act)[49]

OTHER APPEALS

Appeals may also be brought against the decisions of the planning authority under the following sections:
(1) *to the Planning Board*
Under the 1963 Act

---

[45] The Board is restricted to considering matters relating to proper planning and development. Thus in an appeal from a refusal of permission for retention the Board cannot consider whether the unauthorised structure should be demolished. See *The State (Fitzgerald)* v. *An Bord Pleanala*, page 547.

[46] See page 248.

[47] See page 298.

[48] See page 246.

[49] See page 254.

Section 27[50]	retention of structures unauthorised on the 1st October 1964
Section 30[51]	revocation or modification of permission
Section 36[52]	removal or alteration of a structure
Section 37[53]	discontinuance of a use or imposition of a condition on a use
Section 44[54]	removal or alteration of hedges
Section 45[55]	tree preservation orders
Section 46[56]	conservation orders
Section 48[57]	compulsory creation of rights of way
Section 85[58]	refusal of consent to erect or construct cables, wires, pipelines etc.
Section 89[59]	licences for petrol pumps, etc. on public roads

Under the 1976 Act

Section 25[60]	acquisition of land to be provided as or maintained as open space

(2) to the Minister
Under the 1963 Act

Section 43[61]	amenity orders
Section 66[62]	compensation in relation to direction under the Act of 1934
Section 76[63]	extinguishment of a public right of way
Section 88[64]	relaxation of building regulations

LOCAL GOVERNMENT (PLANNING AND DEVELOPMENT) ACT, 1976

14. – (1) An appeal under a relevant section of the Principal Act shall, in lieu of being brought to the Minister, be brought to the Board and if it is not withdrawn, be decided by the Board, and –

(*a*) in case the appeal relates to an application, notice or order, the application, notice or order shall be determined or confirmed or annulled (as the case may be) accordingly, and

(*b*) in case the appeal relates to a licence under section 89 of the Principal Act, such directions shall be given with respect to the withdrawing or granting or altering of the licence as may be appropriate.

[50] See page 119.
[51] See page 122.
[52] See page 333.
[53] See page 334.
[54] See page 19.
[55] See page 20.
[56] See page 21.
[57] See page 22.
[58] See page 27.
[59] See page 130.
[60] See page 350.
[61] See page 18.
[62] See page 389.
[63] See page 25.
[64] See page 130.

(2) Any question as to what, in any particular case, is or is not development or exempted development shall, in lieu of being referred to and decided by the Minister under section 5 (1) of the Principal Act, be referred to and be decided by the Board.

(3) In case a condition referred to in subsection (2)(*f*) of section 26 of the Principal Act is attached to a permission or approval granted under that section and there is not agreement in relation to the contribution required by subsection (7) of the said section 26 to be made by a local authority, the matter shall, in lieu of being determined by the Minister under the said subsection (7), be referred to the Board which shall determine the amount of the contribution.

(4) In case there is attached to a permission or approval granted under section 26 of the Principal Act a condition which provides that a contribution or other matter is to be agreed between the planning authority and the person to whom the permission or approval is granted and that in default of agreement the contribution or other matter is to be determined by the Minister, the condition shall be construed as providing that in default of agreement the contribution or other matter is to be determined by the Board.

(5) The functions of the Minister under section 29 of the Principal Act are hereby transferred to the Board and without prejudice to the generality of subsection (9) of this section the references in the said section 29 to the Minister shall each be construed as referring to the Board.

(6) Any question or dispute whether a new structure would or does replace substantially within the meaning of section 56 of the Principal Act a demolished or destroyed structure shall, in lieu of being determined by the Minister, be determined by the Board.

(7) For the purposes of the foregoing subsections of this section, the Principal Act (as amended by this Act) shall, with any necessary modifications, apply to the following, namely –

   (*a*) the bringing of an appeal to the Board,
   (*b*) the making of a reference to the Board,
   (*c*) a decision of the Board on an appeal,
   (*d*) the confirmation or annulment (as the case may be) by the Board of the notice or order to which an appeal relates,
   (*e*) the determination of a question or dispute by the Board to which a reference under section 5 (1) of the Principal Act relates,
   (*f*) the determination by the Board of a disagreement, question or dispute to which section 26 (7) or section 56 (3) of the Principal Act relates,
   (*g*) the confirmation of a purchase notice served on a planning authority under section 29 of the Principal Act,
   (*h*) the compliance with directions given by the Board in relation to an appeal relating to a licence under section 89 of the Principal Act, and
   (*i*) the determination by the Board of a contribution or other matter to be determined by the Board by virtue of sub-section (4) of this section,

as, immediately before the appropriate day, it applied to whichever of the following is appropriate, namely, the bringing or making of a corresponding appeal or reference to the Minister under the Principal Act, a decision of the Minister on such an appeal, the confirmation or annulment or determination by the Minister of a notice, order, question or dispute relating to such an appeal or reference, the determination by the Minister of a disagreement, question or dispute to which the said section 26(7) or 56(3) relates, the confirmation by the Minister of a purchase notice, the compliance with directions given by the Minister in relation to an appeal relating to a licence under the said section 89 or the determination by the Minister of a contribution or other matter pursuant to a condition mentioned in the said subsection (4).

(8) The Board may in determining an appeal under section 26 or 27 of the Principal Act decide to grant a permission or approval even if the proposed development contravenes materially the development plan or any special amenity area order relating to the area of the planning authority to whose decision the appeal relates.

(9) Wherever the Principal Act refers to the Minister in relation to –

    (*a*) an appeal under a relevant section,

    (*b*) a reference under section 5 (1) of the Principal Act,

    (*c*) a determination of a disagreement, question or dispute to which section 26 (7) or section 56 (3) of the Principal Act relates,

    (*d*) a decision on an appeal under a relevant section,

    (*e*) a determination pursuant to section 85 of the Principal Act as to whether a consent was unreasonably withheld,

    (*f*) a determination, confirmation or annulment (as the case may be) of the notice or order, question or dispute to which an appeal under a relevant section or a reference mentioned in paragraph (*b*) of this subsection relates,

    (*g*) a requirement requiring applicants or planning authorities to furnish to the Minister any specified information, or

    (*h*) any word cognate to appeal, reference, decision, determination, confirmation or annulment,

that Act, other than section 18 thereof, shall be construed as referring to the Board.

(10) In this section 'a relevant section' means a section which is section 26, 27, 30, 33, 36, 37, 44, 45, 46, 48, 85 or 89 of the Principal Act.

15. – (1) *A deposit of £10 shall be lodged with the Board by an appellant with his appeal and any appeal to the Board which is not accompanied by such deposit shall be invalid.*

(2) As soon as may be after an appeal to the Board is either withdrawn or determined, subject to section 18 (3) of this Act, the Board shall return the deposit to the appellant.[65]

16.[66] – *Except where a direction is given by the Minister under this section, the Board shall have an absolute discretion to hold an oral hearing of any reference or appeal to the Board.*

(2) *Where the Board is requested to hold an oral hearing of a reference or appeal and decides to determine the reference or appeal without an oral hearing, the Board –*

    (*a*) *shall serve notice of its decision on the person who requested such hearing, and*

[65] Section 15(1) was repealed by section 15(3) of the 1982 Act which came into force on the 11th April 1983. See now Part III of the Local Government (Planning and Development) (Fees and Amendements) Regulations 1983.

[66] Section 16 was repealed by section 25 of the 1983 Act. See now section 15 of the 1983 Act which came into force on the 25th October 1983.

(b) shall not proceed to determine the reference or appeal until after the expiration of the period mentioned in subsection (3) of this section.

(3) Any person on whom a notice is served under subsection (2) of this section, other than a person on whom there has also been served a notice under section 18 of this Act relating to the relevant reference or appeal, may, at any time before the expiration of fourteen days beginning on the day on which the notice under the said subsection (2) is served, apply in writing to the Minister for a direction under this section as regards the relevant reference or appeal.

(4) In case an application is made under subsection (3) of this section to the Minister, unless the Board decides to hold an oral hearing of the relevant reference or appeal, it shall not determine such reference or appeal pending the decision of the Minister on the application.

(5) The Minister may direct the Board to hold an oral hearing of any reference or appeal to the Board and any such direction shall be complied with by the Board.

17. – The Board in deciding a reference or appeal may take into account matters other than those raised by the parties to the reference or appeal if the matters either relate to the proper planning and development of the area of the relevant planning authority or are matters to which by virtue of section 24(2) of this Act the Board may have regard, provided that the matters are brought to the notice of those parties and they are accorded an opportunity of making observations thereon to the Board or, in the case of an oral hearing, the person conducting the hearing.[67]

18.[68] – (1) *Where the Board is of opinion that a reference or appeal is vexatious or is being unnecessarily delayed by any party, the Board may serve a notice on the party stating that it will, at a time after the day specified in the notice (being a day which is not less than seven days after the service of the notice) without further notice to the party, determine the reference or appeal to which the notice relates, and that the reference or appeal may be so determined by the Board notwithstanding the fact that no submission has been made to the Board by the party in relation to the reference or appeal.*[69]

(2) Where a notice has been served under this section the Board may, at any time after the day specified in the notice, without further notice to the party on whom the notice was served, determine the reference or appeal, and the reference or appeal may be so determined by the Board notwithstanding the fact that no submission has been made to the Board by such party in relation to the reference or appeal.[68]

(3) In case the Board in determining an appeal is of opinion that the appeal is vexatious, the Board may direct that the deposit lodged in relation to the appeal shall be forfeited to the Board.

19. – (1) Subject to subsection (2) of this section, where there is an appeal to the Board against a decision of a planning authority –

(a) the Board, if it so thinks proper and irrespective of the result of the appeal, may direct the planning authority to pay –
(i) to the appellant, such sum as the Board, in its absolute discretion, specifies as compensation to the appellant for the expense occasioned to him in relation to the appeal,

[67] See *The State (Genport Limited)* v. *An Bord Pleanala*.
[68] Section 18(1) and (2) were repealed by section 25 of the 1983 Act. See now sections 16 and 17 of the 1983 Act which came into force on the 25th October 1983.
[69] See *The State (Genport Limited)* v. *An Bord Pleanala*.

     (ii) to the Board, such sum as the Board, in its absolute discretion, specifies as compensation to the Board towards the expense incurred by the Board in relation to the hearing of the appeal,

     (iii) to the Board, such sum as the Board, in its absolute discretion, specifies as compensation to the Board towards the expense incurred by the Board in relation to the hearing of the appeal.

(*b*) in case the decision of the planning authority is confirmed on appeal, or where the decision is varied on appeal, if the Board in determining the appeal does not accede in substance to the appellant's grounds of appeal, the Board, if it so thinks proper, may direct the appellant to pay –

     (i) to the planning authority, such sum as the Board, in its absolute discretion, specifies as compensation to the planning authority for the expense occasioned to them in relation to the appeal,

     (ii) to any of the other parties to the appeal, such sum as the Board, in its absolute discretion, specifies as compensation to the party for the expense occasioned to him in relation to the appeal,

(2) A direction to pay any sum exceeding £200 shall be given by the Board under subsection (1) of this section only after consultation with the Minister.[70]

(3) Any sum directed under this section to be paid shall, in default of being paid, be recoverable as a simple contract debt in any court of competent jurisdiction.

20. – (1) The Minister may make regulations providing for any matter of procedure in relation to references or appeals to the Board.[71]

(2) Regulations shall be made under this section providing for any oral hearing by the Board of a reference or appeal being conducted by a person appointed for that purpose by the Board.[72]

(3) The Minister may make regulations enabling the Board when considering an appeal under section 26 or 27 of the Principal Act to invite an applicant and to enable an applicant so invited to submit to the Board revised plans or other drawings modifying, other particulars providing for the modification of, the development to which the appeal relates.[73]

(4) In case plans, drawings or particulars mentioned in subsection (3) of this section are submitted to the Board by virtue of regulations made under that subsection, the Board may in deciding the appeal grant a permission or an approval for the relevant development as modified by all or any of such plans, drawings or particulars.

21. – (3) For the purpose of enabling the Board to perform its functions on and from the appropriate day, the Board may, as an interim measure, make arrangements for the supply to the Board by the Minister of any services required by the Board pending the making by the Board of sufficient appointments pursuant to section 10 of this Act and the Minister may supply and the Board may avail of services for which arrangements are made under this subsection. [Subsections (1) and (2) deal with the transition of power to the Board from the Minister and are not reprinted.]

[70] As amended by section 21(2) of the 1983 Act which came into force on the 25th October 1983.

[71] See the Local Government (Planning and Development) Regulations 1977–1983.

[72] See Article 44 of the 1977 Regulations.

[73] See Article 42 of the 1977 Regulations.

22. – (1) Where a provision of this Act authorising an appeal (other than an appeal to a court) enables the appeal only to be made within a specified period, the appeal, if sent by post, shall be received not later than the third day after that period and any appeal so sent which is not so received shall be invalid as not being made in time.

(2) Where a provision of the Principal Act authorising an appeal (other than an appeal to a court) enables the appeal only to be made within, or before the expiration of, a specified period or before a specified day, that provision shall be construed as including –

  (*a*) a requirement that the appeal is, if sent by post, to be received not later than the third day after that period or day, and

  (*b*) a provision that any appeal so sent which is not so received shall be invalid as not being made in time.

23. – Where in connection with either the performance by the Minister of any of the functions assigned to him under the Local Government (Planning and Development) Acts, 1963 and 1976, or the performance by the Board of its functions an inspection is carried out or an oral hearing is conducted on behalf of the Minister or the Board, as the case may be, by a person appointed for the purpose by the Minister or the Board, the person so appointed shall make to the Minister or the Board, as may be appropriate, a written report on the inspection or hearing, as the case may be, and shall include in his report a recommendation relating to the matter with which the inspection or hearing was concerned, and the Minister or the Board, as may by appropriate, shall, before determining the matter in relation to which the inspection was carried out or the hearing was conducted, consider the report (including any recommendation contained therein).[74]

24. – (1) Notwithstanding anything contained in the Principal Act, a planning authority in considering,

  (*a*) an application for a permission under section 26 or 27 of that Act,

  (*b*) whether or not it is expedient to serve a notice under section 30, 31, 32, 33 of 35 of that Act,

  (*c*) whether or not to serve a notice under section 36 or 37 of that Act.

shall, where they consider it appropriate, have regard to either or both of the following, namely,

      (i) the probable effect which a particular decision by them on the matter would have on any place which is not within, or on any area which is outside, their area, and

      (ii) any other consideration relating to development outside their area.

(2) Notwithstanding anything contained in the Principal Act, the Board in considering an appeal brought under section 26, 27, 30, 33, 36 or 37 of that Act shall, where it considers it appropriate, have regard to either or both of the following namely,

  (*a*) the probable effect which a particular decision by it on the matter would have on any place which is not within, or on any area which is outside, the area of the relevant planning authority, and

[74] See *Killiney and Ballybrack Development Association v. The Minister for Local Government.*

(*b*) any other consideration relating to development outside the area of that authority.

LOCAL GOVERNMENT (PLANNING AND DEVELOPMENT) REGULATIONS, 1977

PART V

APPEALS AND REFERENCES TO THE BOARD

35. – (1) In this Part –

'appeal' means an appeal to the Board under the Acts or any order made under the Acts;

'reference' means a reference under section 5 of the Act of 1963;

'oral hearing' means an oral hearing of an appeal or of a reference.

(2) In this Part, a party to an appeal means –

(*a*) the appellant,

(*b*) the planning authority against whose decision an appeal is made,

(*c*) the applicant for any permission, approval, licence or waiver notice in relation to which an appeal is made by another person (other than a person acting on behalf of the appellant),

(*d*) any person served or issued by a planning authority with a notice or order, or copy thereof, under section 30, 33, 36, 37, 44, 45 or 48 of the Act of 1963 or section 25 of the Act of 1976, in relation to which an appeal is made by another persons.

(3) In this Part, a party to a reference means –

(*a*) the person making the reference,

(*b*) the planning authority for the area in which the land or structure to which the particular reference relates is situated,

(*c*) any other person with whom the question to which the particular reference relates has arisen.

(4) In this Part, 'planning application' has the same meaning as in Part IV.

36. An appeal shall –

(*a*) be made in writing,

(*b*) state the subject matter of the appeal,

(*c*) state the grounds of appeal, and

(*d*) be accompanied by a deposit of £10 as required by section 15 of the Act of 1976.[75]

37. A reference shall –

(*a*) be made in writing,

(*b*) state the question that has arisen, and

(*c*) state the name and address of the person with whom the question has arisen.

---

[75] The £10 fee has been replaced with the fees set out in Part III of the Local Government (Planning and Development) (Fees and Amendments) Regulations 1983. See section 10 of the 1982 Act.

38. On receipt of an appeal or reference from a person, the Board shall give a copy thereof to each other party to the appeal or reference.

39. – (1) Where a decision of a planning authority on a planning application has given rise to an appeal to the Board, the planning authority shall submit to the Board the application and any drawings, maps, particulars, information, evidence or written study received or obtained by them from the applicant, together with such other documents or information in their possession or procurement as the Board may require.

(2) A party to an appeal (other than a planning authority) or to a reference shall give to the Board any document or information in his possession or procurement which the Board consider necessary for the purpose of determining the appeal or reference.

(3) Where a person neglects or refuses to give to the Board any such document or information within such period as may at any time be specified by the Board, the Board may determine the appeal or reference without the document or information.

(4) A copy of any document relevant to an appeal or reference which is given to the Board by any party shall be given by the Board to each party not already possessed of a copy of such document, or shall be made available for inspection at the offices of the Board or at the offices of the planning authority or at such other convenient place as the Board may specify and each party not already possessed of a copy of the document shall be informed that it is so available for inspection.

40. A person to whom a copy of an appeal or reference has been given under article 38 may, within such period as may at any time be specified by the Board, make in writing to the Board such observations on the appeal or reference as he thinks fit and a copy of such observations shall be given by the Board to each other party to the appeal or reference or, where a number of persons have made the appeal or reference jointly, to any one of such persons.

41. The Board may require any party to an appeal or reference to give such public notice in relation thereto as the Board may specify and, in particular, may require such notice to be given by publication in a newspaper circulating in the district in which is situate the land or structure to which the appeal or reference is related.

42. The Board may, when considering an appeal under section 26 or 27 of the Act of 1963, invite the applicant for any permission or approval in relation to which the appeal is made to submit to the Board, in duplicate, revised plans or other drawings modifying, or other particulars providing for the modification of, the development to which the appeal relates and an applicant so invited may submit such plans or drawings to the Board.

43. (1) The Board shall have the same powers under these Regulations in relation to an appeal arising out of a decision on a planning application as are conferred by these Regulations on a planning authority in relation to such application.

(2) The Board may arrange for the carrying out of inspections in relation to appeals or references by persons appointed for that purpose by the Board either generally or for a particular appeal or reference or for appeals or references of a particular class (including appeals or references relating to land in the area of a particular planning authority).

44. – (1) A party to an appeal or reference may request an oral hearing of the appeal or reference and any such request shall be made in writing to the Board.

(2) A request for an oral hearing may be withdrawn at any time.

(3) Where the Board decide, or is directed by the Minister,[76] to hold an oral hearing, the Board shall inform each of the parties to the appeal or reference and shall give each party not less than seven days notice of the time and place of the opening of the oral hearing or such shorter notice as may be accepted by all the parties to the appeal or reference.

(4) The Board may, at any time before the opening of an oral hearing, alter the time or place of the opening of the hearing and, in the event of such alteration, the Board shall give each party not less than seven days notice of the new time and place or such shorter notice as may be accepted by all the parties to the appeal or reference.

(5) Where the parties to an appeal or reference have been informed that an oral hearing is to be held and where, following the withdrawal of a request for an oral hearing, or a decision by the Board, the appeal or reference falls to be determined without an oral hearing, the Board shall give notice accordingly to the parties and shall not determine the appeal or reference until seven days after the date of the giving of the notice or such longer period as the Board may specify in the notice.

(6) An oral hearing shall be conducted by the Board or by a person appointed for that purpose by the Board generally or for a particular appeal or reference or for appeals or references of a particular class (including appeals or references relating to land in the area of a particular planning authority).

45. The Board or other person conducting an oral hearing shall have discretion as to the conduct of the hearing and in particular shall –

(*a*) conduct the hearing without undue formality,

(*b*) decide the order of appearance of the parties,

(*c*) permit any party to appear in person or to be represented by another person, and

(*d*) hear, if they think fit, any person who is not a party to the appeal or reference.[77]

46. (1) Subject to sub-articles (2) and (3), the Board or other person conducting an oral hearing may adjourn or re-open any hearing or, notwithstanding that any party has failed to attend a hearing, proceed with the hearing.

(2) Notice of the time and place of the re-opening of an oral hearing or resumption of an oral hearing that has been adjourned indefinitely shall be given by the Board to each of the parties to the appeal or reference not less than seven days before the said time unless all such parties accept shorter notice.

(3) Unless the Board consider it expedient to do so and so direct, an oral hearing shall not be re-opened after the report thereon has been submitted to the Board.

47. If, for any reason, the person appointed is unable or fails to conduct, or to complete the conduct of, an oral hearing or, for any reason, is unable or fails to furnish a report on an oral hearing to the Board, the Board may appoint another person to conduct the oral hearing or to conduct a new oral hearing.

[76] Note that the Minister may no longer direct the Board to hold a hearing. See section 15 of the 1983 Act. Note also section 23 of the 1983 Act.

[77] See *Law* v. *The Minister for Local Government* on the inspector's duty to do so.

48. Every notification given by the Board of a decision on an appeal relating to a planning application shall specify –

(*a*) the reference number relating to the relevant application in the register of the planning authority,

(*b*) the nature of the decision,

(*c*) the development or retention or continuance to which the decision relates,

(*d*) the date of the decision,

(*e*) in the case of a decision to grant any permission or approval for the construction, erection or making of a structure and to specify the purposes for which the structure may or may not be used – such purposes,

(*f*) in the case of a decision to grant any permission or approval –
any conditions attached thereto, and

shall state or be accompanied by a statement of the reasons for the decision (including, in the case of any decision to grant permission or approval subject to conditions, the reasons for the imposition of the conditions).

. . .

LOCAL GOVERNMENT (PLANNING AND DEVELOPMENT) ACT, 1963

82. – (1)[78] Regulations may provide for any matters of procedure in relation to appeals to the Minister under section 88 of this Act or in relation to any section 76 hearing.

(2)[79] Regulations shall be made under this section providing –

(*a*) for oral hearing of any such appeal to the Minister in respect of which oral hearing is requested by the appellant,

(*b*) for any such oral hearing or any section 76 hearing being conducted by a person appointed for that purpose by the Minister.

(3) Where a question of law arises on any reference or appeal or section 76 hearing, the question may be referred to the High Court for decision by it by,

(*a*) in the case of a reference or appeal, other than an appeal to the Minister under section 88 of this Act, the Board,

(*b*) in the case of an appeal to the Minister under section 88 of this Act or a section 76 hearing, the Minister.

(3A) A person shall not by prohibition, *certiorari* or in any other legal proceedings whatsoever question the validity of –

(*a*) a decision of a planning authority on an application for a permission or approval under Part IV of the Principal Act,

(*b*) a decision of the Board on any appeal or on any reference,

(*c*) a decision of the Minister on any appeal,
unless the proceedings are instituted within the period of two months commencing on the date on which the decision is given.

(4) A person conducting an oral hearing of any reference or appeal may require

---

[78] See the Local Government (Planning and Development) Regulations Part VIII for regulations in respect of appeals under section 76. Section 88 has not yet been brought into force.

[79] See The Local Government (Planning and Development) Regulations 1977, Part V.

any officer of a planning authority to give to him any information in relation to the reference or appeal which he reasonably requires for the purposes of the reference or appeal, and it shall be the duty of the officer to comply with the requirement.

(5) (*a*) A person conducting an oral hearing of any reference or appeal may visit and inspect any land to which the reference or appeal relates.

(*b*) Any person who obstructs the exercise of the power conferred by this subsection shall be guilty of an offence and shall be liable on summary conviction to a fine not exceeding £100.[80]

(6) A person conducting an oral hearing of any reference or appeal may take evidence on oath and for that purpose may administer oaths, and a person giving evidence at any such hearing shall be entitled to the same immunities and privileges as if he were a witness before the High Court.

(7)(*a*) Subject to the following paragraph, a person conducting an oral hearing of any reference or appeal may, by giving notice in that behalf in writing to any person, require that person to attend at such time and place as is specified in the notice to give evidence in relation to any matter in question at the hearing or to produce any books, deeds, contracts, accounts, vouchers, maps, plans or other documents in his possession, custody or control which relate to any such matter.

(*b*) The following provisions shall have effect for the purposes of the foregoing paragraph:

(i) it shall not be necessary for a person to attend in compliance with a notice at a place more than ten miles from his ordinary place of residence unless such sum as will cover the reasonable and necessary expenses of the attendance have been paid or tendered to him;

(ii) the planning authority shall, at the request of the person conducting the oral hearing, pay or tender to any person whose attendance is required such sum as the person conducting the hearing considers will cover the reasonable and necessary expenses of the attendance;

(iii) any person who in compliance with a notice has attended at any place shall, save in so far as the reasonable and necessary expenses of the attendance have already been paid to him, be paid those expenses by the planning authority, and those expenses, save as aforesaid, shall, in default of being so paid, be recoverable as a simple contract debt in any court of competent jurisdiction;

(iv) every person to whom a notice has been given who refuses or wilfully neglects to attend in accordance with the notice or who wilfully alters, suppresses, conceals or destroys any document to which the notice relates or who, having so attended, refuses to give evidence or refuses or wilfully fails to produce any document to which the notice relates shall be guilty of an offence and shall be liable on summary conviction to a fine not £100.[80]

(8) Subsections (4) to (7) of this section shall apply, with any necessary modifica-

---

[80] As amended by section 8 of the 1982 Act.

tions, in relation to a person conducting a section 76 hearing.

(9)[80] In subsections (3) to (7) of this section –

'appeal', except where the context otherwise requires, means an appeal to the Minister under section 88 of this Act or an appeal to the Board;

'reference' means a reference under section 5 of this Act to the Board;

'section 76 hearing' means a hearing held pursuant to section 76 of this Act, as amended by section 43(1) of the Local Government (Planning and Development) Act, 1976.

LOCAL GOVERNMENT (PLANNING AND DEVELOPMENT) ACT, 1982

5. – (1) Where the Board is of opinion that a reference or appeal to the Board, or an application for permission or approval to which such an appeal relates, has been abandoned, the Board may serve on the person who made the reference, appeal or application, as may be appropriate, a notice stating that fact and requiring that person, within a period specified in the notice (being a period of not less than fourteen days beginning on the date of service of the notice) to make to the Board, a submission in writing as to why the reference, appeal or application, as the case may be, should not be regarded as having been withdrawn.

(2) Where a notice has been served under subsection 1 of this section the Board may, at any time after the expiration of the period specified in the notice, and after considering the submission (if any) made to the Board pursuant to the notice, declare –

> (i) in case the notice refers to a reference, that the reference shall be regarded as having been withdrawn.
>
> (ii) in case the notice refers to an application described in subsection (1) of this section, that the application shall be regarded as having been withdrawn, and
>
> (iii) in case the notice refers to an appeal to the Board, that the appeal shall be regarded as having been withdrawn.

(3) Where pursuant to this section the Board declares that an application described in subsection (1) of this section is to be regarded as having been withdrawn, the following provisions shall apply as regards the application:

> (*a*) any appeal in relation to the application shall be regarded as having been withdrawn and accordingly shal not be determined by the Board, and
>
> (*b*) notwithstanding any previous decision under section 26 or 27 of the Principal Act by a planning authority as regards the application, no permission or approval shall be granted under either of those sections by the authority on foot of the application.

(4) Where the Board makes a declaration under this section, notwithstanding section 15 (2) of the Act of 1976, the Board may, if it thinks fit, direct that the deposit lodged in relation to the relevant appeal, or in relation to any appeal to which the relevant application relates, as may be appropriate, shall be forfeited to the Board.

6. – (1) A permission or approval granted on appeal under Part IV of the Principal Act prior to the 15th day of March, 1977, shall not be, and shall not be regarded as ever having been, invalid by reason only of the fact that the development concerned contravened, or would contravene, materially the development plan relating to the area of the planning authority to whose decision the appeal related.

(2) If, because of any or all of its provisions, subsection (1) of this section, would, but for this subsection, conflict with a constitutional right of any person, the provisions of that subsection shall be subject to such limitation as is necessary to secure that they do not so conflict but shall be otherwise of full force and effect.

10. – (1) The Minister may, with the consent of the Minister for Finance, make regulations providing for –

(*a*) the payment to planning authorities of prescribed fees in relation to applications for –

> (i) permission under Part IV of the Principal Act,
>
> (ii) approvals required by permission regulations,
>
> (iii) approvals required to be obtained under a condition subject to which a permission or approval is granted under the Principal Act, or
>
> (iv) extensions or further extensions under section 4 of this Act,

(*b*) the payment to the Board of prescribed fees in relation to appeals or references to, or determinations by, the Board,

and the regulations may provide for the payment of different fees in relation to cases of different classes or descriptions, for exemption from the payment of fees in specified circumstances, for the waiver, remission or refund (in whole or in part) of fees in specified circumstances and for the manner in which fees are to be disposed of.[81]

(2) Where under regulations under this section a fee is payable to a planning authority by an applicant in respect of an application referred to in subsection (1)(*a*) of this section, the following provisions shall have effect:

(*a*) the application shall not be decided by the authority unless the authority is in receipt of the fee, and

(*b*) notwithstanding anything contained in section 26(4) or 27(3) of the Principal Act or in section 4(2) of this Act, a decision of a planning authority shall not be regarded, pursuant to any of those sections, as having been given on a day which is earlier than that which is two months after the day on which the authority is in receipt of the fee, and the said sections 26(4), 27(3) and 4(2) shall be construed subject to and in accordance with the provisions of this paragraph.

(3) Where –

(*a*) under regulations under this section a fee (other than a fee referred to in subsection (6) of this section) is payable to the Board by an appellant in respect of an appeal by him to the Board, and

(*b*) the provision of the Local Government (Planning and Development) Acts, 1963 and 1976, authorising the appeal enables the appeal only to be made within, or before the expiration of, a specified period or before a specified day, that provision shall be construed as including –

> (i) a requirement that the fee is to be received by the Board within,

---

[81] See The Local Government (Planning and Development) (Fees and Amendment) Regulations 1983.

or before the expiration of, that period, or before that day (or, if the fee is sent by post, not later than the third day after that period or day), and

(ii) a provision that if the fee is not so received, the appeal shall be invalid.

(4) Where under regulations under this section a fee is payable either to a planning authority or to the Board and the person by whom the fee is payable is not –

(*a*) the applicant for a permission, approval or licence, or

(*b*) an appellant to the Board, or

(*c*) the person making a reference to, or a request for a determination by, the Board,

submissions or observations made, as regards the relevant application, appeal, reference or determination, by or on behalf of the person by whom such fee is payable, shall not be considered by the planning authority or the Board, as may be appropriate, if the fee has not been received by the authority or the Board.

(5) Where under regulations under this section a fee is payable to the Board by a person making a reference to, or a request for a determinaiton by, the Board, the relevant question or matter shall not be decided or determined by the Board unless the fee is received by the Board.

(6) Where under regulations under this section fees are payable to the Board in respect of requests for oral hearings of appeals or references to the Board, such a request shall not be considered by the Board if the fee so payable in respect of the request is not received by the Board.

(7) The provisions of subsection (3) of this section are in addition to, and not in substitution for, the provisions of section 22 of the Act of 1976.

LOCAL GOVERNMENT (PLANNING AND DEVELOPMENT) ACT, 1983

14. – (1) It shall not be lawful to communicate with the chairman or with an ordinary member for the purpose of influencing improperly his consideration of an appeal, reference, or other matter with which the Board is concerned or a decision of the Board as regards any such matter.

(2) If the chairman or an ordinary member becomes of opinion that a communication is in contravention of subsection (1) of this section, it shall be his duty not to entertain the communication further.

15. – (1) The Board shall have an absolute discretion to hold an oral hearing of any reference or appeal to the Board which is not a reference or appeal to which subsection (2) of this section applies.

(2)(*a*) This subsection applies to any reference or appeal to the Board which is of a class or description which may, for the time being, be prescribed for the purposes of this subsection.

(*b*) Regulations made for the purposes of this subsection may include provisions requiring the Board to hold, either generally or in such cases as may be specified in the regulations, oral hearings of references or appeals which are of a class or description so specified.

(3) Where the Board is requested to hold an oral hearing of a reference or appeal (other than a reference or appeal to which subsection (2) of this section applies) and decides to determine the reference or appeal without an oral hearing, the following provisions shall apply:

(*a*) the Board shall serve notice of its decision on the person who requested such hearing and the notice shall require that person to make, within a period specified in the notice (being a period of not less than fourteen days beginning on the date of service of the notice), to the Board in writing such submissions or further submissions (if any) as he thinks fit in relation to the reference or appeal, and

(*b*) the Board shall not proceed to determine the reference or appeal until after the expiration of the period so specified.

16. – Subject to subsection (2) of this section, the Board shall in the following circumstances have an absolute discretion to dismiss an appeal brought under section 26 (5) of the Principal Act –

(*a*) where, having considered the grounds of appeal, the Board is of opinion that the appeal is vexatious, frivolous or without substance or foundation, or

(*b*) where, having regard to –

(i) the nature of the appeal (including any question which in the Board's opinion is raised by the appeal), and

(ii) any previous permission or approval which in its opinion is relevant,

the Board is satisfied that in the particular circumstances the appeal should not be further considered by it.

(2) The exercise by the Board of the power conferred on it by subsection (1) of this section shall be subject to the restriction imposed on the Board by section 26 (1) of the Principal Act as applied by section 14 of the Act of 1976.

17. – (1) Where an appeal is made to the Board and the grounds of appeal are not stated in writing, the Board may serve on the appellant a notice –

(*a*) requiring him, within a period specified in the notice (being a period of not less than fourteen days beginning on the date of service of the notice) to submit to the Board a written statement of his grounds of appeal, and

(*b*) stating that, in default of compliance with the requirements of the notice, the Board will, after the period so specified and without further notice to the person, pursuant to this section declare that the appeal shall be regarded as having been withdrawn.

(2) Where a notice has been served under subsection (1) of this section, the Board may, having considered the response (if any) to the notice, at any time after the expiration of the period specified in the notice and without further notice to the party on whom the notice has been so served, if they so think fit declare that the appeal to which the notice relates shall be regarded as having been withdrawn.

18. – (1) Where the Board is of the opinion that any document, particulars or other information is necessary for the purpose of enabling it to determine an appeal brought under section 26 (5) of the Principal Act, the Board may serve on any person who is a party to the appeal, or on any other person who has made

submissions or observations to the Board as regards the appeal, a notice under this
section –

> (a) requiring that person, within a period specified in the notice (being a
> period of not less than fourteen days beginning on the date of service of
> the notice) to submit to the Board such document, particulars or other
> information (which document, particulars or other information shall be
> specified in the notice), and
> (b) stating that, in default of compliance with the requirements of the notice,
> the Board will, after the period so specified and without further notice
> to the person, pursuant to this section dismiss or otherwise determine
> the appeal.

(2) Where a notice has been served under subsection (1) of this section, the
Board, at any time after the expiration of the period specified in the
notice, may, having considered the response (if any) to the notice,
without further notice to the person on whom the notice has been so
served dismiss or otherwise determine the appeal.

19. – (1) Where –

> (a) an appeal is brought under section 26 (5) of the Principal Act from a
> decision of a planning authority to grant a permission or approval, and
> (b) the appeal relates only to a condition or conditions subject to which the
> decision was made, and
> (c) the Board is satisfied, having regard to the nature of the condition or
> conditions, that the determination by the Board of the relevant applica-
> tion as if it had been made to it in the first instance would not be
> warranted,

subject to compliance by the Board with subsection (2) of this section when
considering the appeal, the Board may, in its absolute discretion, give to the
relevant planning authority such directions as it considers appropriate relating to
the attachment, amendment or removal by that authority either of the condition or
conditions to which the appeal relates or of other conditions.

(2) In exercising the power conferred on it by subsection (1) of this section, apart
from considering the condition or conditions to which the relevant appeal relates,
the Board shall be restricted to considering the proper planning and development
of the area of the relevant planning authority (including the preservation and
improvement of the amenities thereof), regard being had to the provisions of the
development plan, the provisions of any special amenity area order relating to the
said area, the terms of any previous permission considered by the Board to be
relevant, the matters referred to in section 26 (2) of the Principal Act and the
matters referred to in section 24 (2) of the Act of 1976.

22. – (1) Section 26 (5)(b) of the Principal Act, as amended by section 14 (9) of
the Act of 1976, shall be construed and have effect subject to sections 16, 18 and 19
of this Act, and the other provisions relating to appeals to the Board of the Local
Government (Planning and Development) Acts, 1963 to 1982, shall be construed
and have effect subject to section 17 of this Act.

(2) Nothing in section 17 or 18 of this Act shall be construed as affecting any
power conferred on the Board by or under any enactment other than those
sections.

23. – (1) Nothing in this Act shall be construed as enabling the Minister to exercise any power or control in relation to any particular case with which the Board is or may be concerned.

(2) The reference to this Act in subsection (1) of this section shall not be construed as including a reference to section 7 of the Local Government (Planning and Development) Act, 1982.

24. Nothing in this Act shall be construed as interrupting or otherwise affecting the continued existence of the Board or the performance by it of any of its functions.

26. – (1) This Act may be cited as the Local Government (Planning and Development) Act, 1983.

(2) The Local Government (Planning and Development) Acts, 1963 to 1982, and this Act may be cited together as the Local Government (Planning and Development) Acts, 1963 to 1983.

(3) This Act shall come into operation on such day or days as the Minister may fix by order, either generally or with reference to any particular purpose or provision, and different days may be so fixed for different purposes and different provisions of this Act.[82]

(4) This Act and the Local Government (Planning and Development) Acts, 1963 to 1982, shall be construed together as one Act.

THE PLANNING BOARD

LOCAL GOVERNMENT (PLANNING AND DEVELOPMENT) ACT, 1976

AN ACT TO MAKE BETTER PROVISION, IN THE INTERESTS OF THE COMMON GOOD, IN RELATION TO THE PROPER PLANNING AND DEVELOPMENT OF CITIES, TOWNS AND OTHER AREAS, WHETHER URBAN OR RURAL, AND, FOR THAT PURPOSE, TO ESTABLISH A BODY TO BE KNOWN AS AN BORD PLEANALA AND TO DEFINE ITS FUNCTIONS AND TO AMEND AND EXTEND THE LOCAL GOVERNMENT (PLANNING AND DEVELOPMENT) ACT, 1963, AND TO PROVIDE FOR OTHER MATTERS CONNECTED WITH THE MATTERS AFORESAID.
[*5th July, 1976*]

BE IT ENACTED BY THE OIREACHTAS AS FOLLOWS:

1. – In this Act –
'the appropriate day' means the day on which section 14 of this Act comes into operation;
'the Board' has the meaning assigned to it by section 3 of this Act;

---

[82] See S.I. No. 284 of 1983. Sections 1, 2, 5 (except (11), (12), (13), (14) and (15)), 7(except subsections (8), (9), (10), (11) and (12)), 9, 24, and 26 and section 25 insofar as it repeals articles 1, 25, 26, 27 and 28 of the Schedule to the 1976 Act came into force on the 7th October 1983. Sections 15, 16, 17, 18, 19, 20, 21 and 22 and section 25 insofar as it repeals section 16, 18(1) and 18(2) of the 1976 Act came into force on the 25th October 1983.

'company' except in section 34 (4), means a company within the meaning of section 2 of the Companies Act, 1963, or a company incorporated outside the State;

'the establishment day' means the day appointed to be the establishment day for the purposes of this Act by order of the Minister under section 2 of this Act;

'judicial office' means an office, being the office of Chief Justice, President of the High Court, ordinary judge of the Supreme Court or ordinary judge of the High Court;

'manager' means a manager within the meaning of section 1 of the City and County Management (Amendment) Act, 1955;

'the Principal Act' means the Local Government (Planning and Development) Act, 1963;

'shares' includes stock and 'share capital' shall be construed accordingly.

2. – The Minister may by order appoint a day to be the establishment day for the purposes of this Act.

3. – (1) On the establishment day there shall be established a body to be known as An Bord Pleanála (in this Act referred to as the Board) to perform the functions assigned to it by this Act.[83]

. . .

5. – (1) The Board shall, so far as may in the opinion of the Board be necessary for the performance of its functions, keep itself informed of the policies and objectives for the time being of the Minister, planning authorities and any other body which is a public authority whose functions have, or may have, a bearing on the proper planning and development (including the preservation and development of amenities) of cities, towns or other areas, whether urban or rural.

(2) In this section 'public authority' means any Minister of State not being the Minister, the Commissioners of Public Works in Ireland, the Irish Land Commission, a harbour authority within the meaning of section 2 of the Harbours Act, 1946, and any other body established by or under statute which is for the time being declared, by regulation made by the Minister, to be a public authority for the purposes of this section.[84]

. . .

7. – There may, subject to such conditions, if any, as the Minister thinks proper, be paid to the Board in each financial year out of moneys provided by the Oireachtas a grant or grants of such amount or amounts as the Minister, with the consent of the Minister for Finance and after consultation with the Board in relation to its programme of expenditure for that year, may fix.

8. – (1) The Board shall keep in such form as may be approved by the Minister, after consultation with the Minister for Finance, all proper and usual accounts of all moneys received or expended by it.

(2) Accounts kept in pursuance of this section shall be submitted by the Board to the Comptroller and Auditor General for audit at such times as the Minister shall

---

[83] It is anticipated that insofar as section 25 of the 1983 Act repeals subs. (2) it will come into force early in 1984 and for this reason subs. (2) has not been reprinted.

[84] Section 6 was repealed by section 15 of the 1982 Act which came into force on the 28th July 1983.

direct and, when audited by him, shall, together with the report of the Comptroller and Auditor General thereon, be presented to the Minister who shall cause copies to be laid before each House of the Oireachtas.

9. – (1) The Board shall, not later than the 30th day of September in each year, make a report to the Minister of its proceedings during the preceding year and the Minister shall cause copies of the report to be laid before each House of the Oireachtas.

(2) The Board shall supply the Minister with such information relating to the performance of its functions as he shall from time to time request.

10. – (1) The Board shall appoint such and so many persons to be employees of the Board as the Board, subject to the approval of the Minister given with consent of the Minister for the Public Service as to the number and kind of such employees, from time to time thinks proper.[85]

(2) The Board may employ a person in a part-time capacity to be remunerated by the payment of fees of such amounts as the Board may, with the approval of the Minister given with the consent of the Minister for the Public Service, from time to time determine.

(3) An employee of the Board shall hold his employment on such terms and conditions as the Board, subject to the approval of the Minister, from time to time determines.

(4) There shall be paid by the Board to its employees out of moneys at its disposal such remuneration and allowances as the Board, subject to the approval of the Minister, with the consent of the Minister for the Public Service, from time to time determines.

11.[86] – (1) As soon as conveniently may be after the establishment day, the Board shall prepare and submit to the Minister for his approval, a scheme or schemes for the granting of pensions, gratuities and other allowances on retirement or death to or in respect of such wholetime employees of the Board as it may think fit.

(2) The Board may at any time, prepare and submit to the Minister, a scheme amending a scheme under this section.

(3) Where a scheme is submitted to the Minister pursuant to this section, the Minister may, with the concurrence of the Minister for the Public Service, approve the scheme without modification or with such modification (whether by way of addition, omission or variation) as the Minister shall, with such concurrence, think proper.

(4) A scheme submitted to the Minister under this section shall, if approved of by the Minister with the concurrence of the Minister for the Public Service, be carried out by the Board in accordance with its terms.

(5) A scheme submitted and approved of under this section shall fix the time and conditions of retirement for all persons to or in respect of whom pensions, gratuities or other allowances are payable under the scheme, and different times and conditions may be fixed in respect of different classes of persons.

[85] As amended by section 21 of the 1983 Act.
[86] See also section 9 of the 1983 Act which deals with the superannuation of members of the Board.

(6) If any dispute arises as to the claim of any person to, or the amount of, any pension, gratuity or other allowance payable in pursuance of a scheme under this section, such dispute shall be submitted to the Minister who shall refer it to the Minister for the Public Service, whose decision shall be final.

(7) Every scheme submitted and approved of under this section shall be laid before each House of the Oireachtas as soon as may be after it is approved of and if either House within the next twenty-one days on which that House has sat after the scheme is laid before it, passes a resolution annulling the scheme, the scheme shall be annulled accordingly, but without prejudice to the validity of anything previously done thereunder.

12.[87] – (1) Where a person who is an employee of the Board is nominated as a member of Seanad Éireann or for election to either House of the Oireachtas or becomes a member of a local authority, he shall stand seconded from employment by the Board and shall not be paid by, or be entitled to receive from, the Board any remuneration or allowances –

    (*a*) in case he is nominated as a member of Seanad Éireann, in respect of the period commencing on his acceptance of the nomination and ending when he ceases to be a member of that House,

    (*b*) in case he is nominated for election to either such House, in respect of the period commencing on his nomination and ending when he ceases to be a member of that House or fails to be elected or withdraws his candidature, as may be appropriate,

    (*c*) in case he becomes a member of a local authority, in respect of the period commencing on his becoming a member of the local authority and ending when he ceases to be a member of that authority.

(2) A person who is for the time being entitled under the Standing Orders of either House of the Oireachtas to sit therein shall, while so entitled, be disqualified from becoming an employee of the Board.

(3) A person who is for the time being a member of a local authority shall, while holding office as such member, be disqualified from becoming an employee of the Board.

13. – (1) The Board may from time to time engage such consultants or advisers as it may consider necessary for the discharge of its functions and any fees due to a consultant or adviser engaged pursuant to this section shall be paid by the Board out of moneys at its disposal.

(2) Any person may notify the Board in writing of his willingness to be engaged by the Board as a consultant or adviser pursuant to this section and such person when so notifying the Board shall give to the Board particulars of his qualifications and experience.

(3) The Board shall maintain a list of the persons who duly give to the Board a notification pursuant to subsection (2) of this section.

(4) The Board shall, in engaging a consultant or adviser under this section, have regard to the list maintained under subsection (3) of this section, but the foregoing provisions of this subsection shall not be construed as precluding the Board from

---

[87] See section 5(10) and (13) of the 1983 Act deals with membership of either House of the Oireachtas or of a local authority of the Chairman of the Board. Section 6(7) and (10) of the 1983 Act deals with membership of either House of the Oireachtas or of a local authority of an ordinary member of the Board.

engaging as a consultant or adviser a person whose name is not on the said list.

(5) The Board shall include in each report made under section 9 of this Act a statement of the names of the persons (if any) engaged pursuant to this section during the year to which the report relates.

. . .

32. – (1) It shall be the duty of a person to whom this section applies to give to the relevant body a declaration in the prescribed form,[88] signed by him and containing particulars of every interest of his which is an interest to which this section applies and for so long as he continues to be a person to whom this section applies it shall be his duty where there is a change regarding an interest particulars of which are contained in the declaration or where he acquires any other interest to which this section applies, to give to the relevant body a fresh such declaration.

(2)(*a*) This section applies to the following persons, namely:
  (i) a member of the Board,
  (ii) a member of a planning authority,
  (iii) an employee of the Board or any other person,
    (I) whose services are availed of by the Board, and
    (II) who is of a class, description or grade prescribed for the purposes of this section,
  (iv) an officer of a planning authority who is the holder of an office which is of a class, description or grade so prescribed.

(*b*) This section applies to the following interests, namely:
  (i) any estate or interest which a person to whom this section applies has, in case the person is a member or officer of a planning authority, in land situated in the area of the relevant authority, and in any other case, in any land
  (ii) any business of dealing in or developing land in which such a person is engaged or employed and any such business carried on by a company or other body of which he, or any nominee of his, is a member.
  (iii) any profession, business or occupation in which such a person is engaged, whether on his own behalf or otherwise, and which relates to dealing in or developing land.

(3) A person to whom this section applies and who has an interest to which this section applies shall be regarded as complying with the requirements of subsection (1) of this section if, and only if, he gives to the relevant body a declaration mentioned in that subsection within the period of twenty-eight days beginning –
  (*a*) in case the person is such a person on the commencement of this section, on such commencement,
  (*b*) in case the person becomes such a person after the commencement of this section, on the day on which he becomes such a person,
  (*c*) in case there is a change regarding an interest particulars of which are contained in a declaration already given by the person or where the person acquires any other interest to which this section applies, on the day on which the change occurs or the other such interest is acquired.

(4) For the purposes of this section, a person to whom this section applies shall be

---

[88] See Articles 69 and 70 and Forms 5 and 6 in the Second Schedule to the Local Government (Planning and Development) Regulations 1977.

regarded as having an estate or interest in land if he, or any nominee of his, is a member of a company or other body which has an estate or interest in the land.

(5) For the purpose of this section, a person shall not be regarded as having an interest to which this section applies if the interest is so remote or insignificant that it cannot reasonably be regarded as likely to influence a person in considering or discussing, or in voting on, any question with respect to any matter arising or coming before the Board or authority, as may be appropriate, or in performing any function in relation to any such matter.

(6) Where a person to whom this section applies has an interest to which this section applies by reason only of the beneficial ownership of shares in a company or other body by him or by his nominee and the total nominal value of those shares does not exceed the lesser of –

(*a*) five hundred pounds, or

(*b*) one-hundredth part of the total nominal value of either the issued share capital of the company or body or, where that capital is issued in shares of more than one class, the issued share capital of the class or classes of shares in which he has an interest,

subsection (1) of this section shall not have effect in relation to that interest.

(7) The Board and each planning authority shall for the purposes of this section keep a register (which register is in this section referred to as the register of interests) and shall enter therein the particulars contained in declarations given to the Board or the authority, as the case may be, pursuant to this section. The register of interests shall be kept at the offices of the Board or the planning authority, as the case may be, and shall be available for public inspection during office hours.

(8) Where a person ceases to be a person to whom this section applies, any particulars entered in the register of interests as a result of a declaration being given by the person to the relevant body pursuant to this section shall be removed, as soon as may be after the expiration of the period of five years beginning on the day on which the person ceases to be such a person, from the said register by that body.

(9) Subject to subsection (10) of this section, a person who fails to comply with subsection (1) of this section or who, when purporting to comply with the requirements of the said subsection (1), gives particulars which are false or which to his knowledge are misleading in a material respect, shall be guilty of an offence and shall be liable on summary conviction to a fine not exceeding eight hundred pounds or at the discretion of the court, to imprisonment for a term not exceeding six months, or to both the fine and the imprisonment.[89]

(10) In any proceedings for an offence under this section it shall be a defence for the defendant to prove that at the relevant time he believed, in good faith and upon reasonable grounds, that –

(*a*) the relevant particulars were true,

(*b*) there was no matter as regards which he was then required to make a declaration under subsection (1) of this section, or

(*c*) that the matter in relation to which the offence is alleged was not one as regards which he was so required to make such declaration.

(11)(*a*) For the purposes of this section and section 33 of this Act,

(i) a manager shall be deemed to be an officer of every planning authority for which he is manager,

---

[89] As amended by section 8(2) of the 1982 Act.

(ii) an assistant county manager for a county shall be deemed to be an officer of every planning authority in the county, and

(iii) an officer of a planning authority who, by virtue of an arrangement or agreement entered into under any enactment, is performing duties under another planning authority, shall be deemed to be also an officer of the other authority.

(*b*) In this section the 'relevant body' means,

(i) in case a person to whom this section applies is either a member or employee of the Board, or other person whose services are availed of by the Board, the Board, and

(ii) in case such a person is either a member or officer of a planning authority, the authority.

33. – (1) Where a member of the Board has a pecuniary or other beneficial interest in, or which is material to, any appeal, contribution, question or dispute which falls to be decided or determined by the Board, he shall comply with the following requirements:

(*a*) he shall disclose to the Board the nature of his interest,

(*b*) he shall take no part in the discussion or consideration of the matter,

(*c*) he shall not vote or otherwise act as a member of the Board in relation to the matter, and

(*d*) he shall neither influence nor seek to influence a decision of the Board as regards the matter.

(2) Where, at a meeting of a planning authority or of any committee of a planning authority, a resolution, motion, question or other matter is proposed or otherwise arises either pursuant to, or as regards the performance by the authority of a function under, the Local Government (Planning and Development) Acts, 1963 and 1976, or in relation to the acquisition or disposal by the authority of land under or for the purposes of those Acts or any other enactment, a member of the authority or committee present at the meeting shall, if he has a pecuniary or other beneficial interest in, or which is material to, the matter –

(*a*) at the meeting, and before discussion or consideration of the matter commences, disclose the nature of his interest,

(*b*) withdraw from the meeting for so long as the matter is being discussed or considered,

and accordingly, he shall take no part in the discussion or consideration of the matter and shall refrain from voting in relation to it.

(3) A member of a planning authority or of any committee of a planning authority who has a pecuniary or other beneficial interest in, or which is material to, a matter arising either pursuant to, or as regards the performance by the authority of a function under, the Local Government (Planning and Development) Acts, 1963 and 1976, or in relation to the acquisition or disposal by the authority of land under or for the purposes of those Acts or any other enactment, shall neither influence nor seek to influence a decision of the authority as regards the matter.

(4) Where the manager of a planning authority has a pecuniary or other beneficial interest in, or which is material to, any matter which arises or comes before the authority either pursuant to, or as regards the performance by the authority of a function under, the Local Government (Planning and development) Acts, 1963 and 1976, or in relation to the acquisition or disposal by the authority of land under or for the purposes of those Acts or any other enactment, he shall, as soon as may be,

disclose to the members of the planning authority the nature of his interest.

(5)(*a*) Where an employee of the Board or any other person whose services are availed of by the Board has a pecuniary or other beneficial interest in, or which is material to, any appeal, contribution, question or dispute which falls to be decided or determined by the Board, he shall comply with the following requirements:

    (i) he shall neither influence nor seek to influence a decision of the Board as regards the matter, and

    (ii) in case, as such employee or other person, he is concerned with the matter, he shall disclose to the Board the nature of his interest and comply with any directions the Board may give him in relation to the matter.

(*b*) Where an officer of a planning authority, not being the manager, has a pecuniary or other beneficial interest in, or which is material to, any matter which arises or comes before the authority, either pursuant to, or as regards the performance by the authority of a function under, the Local Government (Planning and Development) Acts, 1963 and 1976, or in relation to the acquisition or disposal of land by the authority under or for the purposes of those Acts or any other enactment, he shall comply with the following requirements:

    (i) he shall neither influence nor seek to influence a decision of the authority as regards the matter, and

    (ii) in case, as such officer, he is concerned with the matter, he shall disclose to the manager of the authority the nature of his interest and comply with any directions the manager may give him in relation to the matter.

(6) For the purposes of this section but without prejudice to the generality of any of the foregoing subsections hereof, a person shall be regarded as having a beneficial interest if –

(*a*) he or his spouse, or any nominee of his or of his spouse, is a member of a company or any other body which has a beneficial interest in, or which is material to, a resolution, motion, question or other matter mentioned in the foregoing subsections of this section,

(*b*) he or his spouse is in partnership with or is in the employment of a person who has a beneficial interest in, or which is material to, such a resolution, motion, question or other matter,

(*c*) he or his spouse is a party to any arrangement or agreement (whether or not enforceable) concerning land to which such a resolution, motion, question or other matter relates,

(*d*) his spouse has a beneficial interest in, or which is material to, such a resolution, motion, question or other matter.

(7) For the purposes of this section, a person shall not be regarded as having a beneficial interest in, or which is material to, any resolution, motion, question or other matter by reason only of an interest of his or of any company or of any other body or person mentioned in subsection (6) of this section which is so remote or insignificant that it cannot reasonably be regarded as likely to influence a person in considering or discussing, or in voting on, any question with respect to the matter, or in performing any function in relation to that matter.

(8) Where a person has a beneficial interest mentioned in subsections (1), (2),

(3), (4) or (5) of this section by reason only of the beneficial ownership of shares in a company or other body by him or by his spouse and the total nominal value of those shares does not exceed the lesser of –

   (*a*) five hundred pounds, or
   (*b*) one-hundredth part of the total nominal value of either the issued share capital of the company or body or, where that capital is issued in shares of more than one class, the issued share capital of the class of shares in which he has an interest,

none of those subsections shall have effect in relation to that beneficial interest.

(9) Where at a meeting described in subsection (2) of this section a disclosure is made under that subsection, particulars of the disclosure and of any subsequent withdrawal from the meeting pursuant to the said subsection shall be recorded in the minutes of the meeting.

(10) Subject to subsection (11) of this section, a person who contravenes or fails to comply with a requiremet of this section shall be guilty of an offence and shall be liable on summary conviction to a fine not exceeding eight hundred pounds or, at the discretion of the court, to imprisonment for a term not exceeding six months, or to both the fine and the imprisonment.[90]

(11) In any proceedings for an offence under this section it shall be a defence for the defendant to prove that at the time of the alleged offence he did not know and had no reason to believe that a matter in which, or in relation to which, he had a beneficial interest had arisen or had come before, or was being considered by, the Board or the relevant planning authority or committee, as may be appropriate, or that the beneficial interest to which the alleged offence relates was one in relation to which a requirement of this section applied.

34. – (1) Proceedings for an offence under section 32 or 33 of this Act shall not be instituted except by or with the consent of the Director of Public Prosecutions.

(2) Where a person is convicted of an offence under section 32 or 33 of this Act, the following provisions shall have effect:

   (*a*) the person shall be disqualified for being a member of the Board,
   (*b*) in case the person is a member of the Board, he shall on such conviction accordingly cease to be a member of the Board,
   (*c*) in case the person is a member of a planning authority or a member of any committee of a planning authority, he shall on such conviction cease to be a member of the authority or the committee, as may be appropriate,
   (*d*) in case the person is a member of both a planning authority and any one or more such committees, he shall so cease to be a member of both the authority and every such committee, and
   (*e*) in case the person by virtue of this subsection ceases to be a member of a planning authority or any such committee, he shall be disqualified for being a member of the authority or committee during the period which, but for the cessation of his membership of the authority or committee under this section, would be the remainder of his term.

(3) In case a person contravenes or fails to comply with a requirement of section 32 or 33 of this Act, or acts as a member of the Board, a planning authority or committee of a planning authority while disqualified for membership by virtue of

[90] As amended by section 8(2) of the 1982 Act.

this section, the fact of such contravention or failure or of his so acting, as the case may be, shall not invalidate any act or proceeding of the Board, authority or committee.

(4) Where any body which is a company within the meaning of section 155 of the Companies Act, 1963, is deemed under that section to be a subsidiary of another or to be another such company's holding company, a person who is a member of the first-mentioned such company shall, for the purposes of sections 32 and 33 of this Act be deemed also to be a member of the other company.

LOCAL GOVERNMENT (PLANNING AND DEVELOPMENT) REGULATIONS 1977

69. – (1) The following classes, descriptions and grades of employees of the Board and other persons are hereby prescribed for the purposes of section 32 of the Act of 1976 –

(a) every employee of the Board, other than an employee the qualifications for whose employment are not wholly or in part professional or technical and the maximum remuneration for whose employment is less than the maximum remuneration for the office of Executive Officer in the Civil Service, and

(b) every officer of the Minister who, pursuant to arrangements made under section 21(3) of the Act of 1976, is engaged wholly or mainly in duties relating to appeals, contributions, questions or disputes which fall to be determined by the Board or in duties relating to the functions of the Board under section 29 of the Act of 1963, but excluding the holder of any office the qualifications for which are not wholly or in part professional or technical and the maximum remuneration for which is less than the maximum remuneration for the office of Executive Officer, and

(c) every other person employed by the Minister in a part-time capacity and remunerated by the payment of fees who, pursuant to arrangements made under section 21(3) of the Act of 1976, is engaged in duties relating to appeals, contributions, questions or disputes which fall to be determined by the Board or in duties relating to the functions of the Board under section 29 of 1963.

(2) The following classes, descriptions and grades of offices under a planning authority are hereby prescribed for the purposes of section 32 of the Act of 1976 –

(a) the offices of County Manager, City Manager and Town Clerk, Dublin City Manager and Town Clerk and Dublin County Manager, Assistant County Manager, Assistant City and County Manager (Dublin), Assistant City Manager (Cork), County Secretary and Town Clerk;

(b) the offices of County Engineer, City Engineer, Borough Engineer and Town Engineer;

(c) the offices of Planning Officer, Deputy Planning Officer, Senior Planning Assistant, Planning Assistant Grade I, Development Control Assistant Grade I, Planning Assistant Grade II, Chief Planning Assistant, Chief Assistant County Engineer (Planning) and Planning Assistant; and

(d) any other office under a planning authority the holder of which is assigned duties which relate to the performance of any functions of a planning authority under the Acts.

70. – (1) Form No. 5 as set out in the Second Schedule shall be the prescribed form of a declaration to be given to the Board under section 32 of the Act of 1976.

(2) Form No. 6 as set out in the Second Schedule shall be the prescribed form of a declaration to be given to a planning authority under section 32 of the Act of 1976.

SECOND SCHEDULE

FORM No. 5   *Article* 70

Declaration to An Bord Pleanála of estate or interest.

LOCAL GOVERNMENT (PLANNING AND DEVELOPMENT) ACT, 1976 – SECTION 32

I, ... , hereby give to An Bord Pleanála the following declaration of interests in compliance with the requirements of section 32 of the Local Government (Planning and Development) Act, 1976:–

(*a*) Particulars* of any estate or interest which I have in any land:–

....

....

(*b*) Particulars of any business of dealing in or developing land in which I am engaged or employed and of any such business carried on by a company or other body of which I, or any nominee of mine, is a member:–

....

....

(*c*) Particulars of any profession, business or occupation in which I am engaged, whether on my own behalf or otherwise, and which relates to dealing in or developing land:–

....

....

I hereby declare that the foregoing is a true and complete declaration of every interest of mine which is an interest to which section 32 of the Local Government (Planning and Development) Act, 1976, applies.

Signature ....

Date ....

*Including the area of the planning authority in which the land is situate.

FORM No. 6   *Article* 70

Declaration to planning authority of estate or interest.

LOCAL GOVERNMENT (PLANNING AND DEVELOPMENT) ACT, 1976 – SECTION 32

I, ... , hereby give to the planning authority
{ of which I am a member   } *
{ under which I hold the office of .... }   the following

declaration of interests in compliance with the requirements of section 32 of the Local Government (Planning and Development) Act, 1976:–

(*a*) Particulars of any estate or interest which I have in land situated in the area of the planning authority:–

....

....

(*b*) Particulars of any business of dealing in or developing land in which I am engaged or employed and of any such business carried on by a company or other body of which I, or any nominee of mine, is a member:–

....

....

(*c*) Particulars of any profession, business or occupation in which I am engaged, whether on my own behalf or otherwise, and which relates to dealing in or developing land:–

....

....

I hereby declare that the foregoing is a true and complete declaration of every interest of mine which is an interest to which section 32 of the Local Government (Planning and Development) Act, 1976, applies.

Signature ....

Date ....

*Delete words which do not apply.

LOCAL GOVERNMENT (PLANNING AND DEVELOPMENT) ACT, 1983

AN ACT TO AMEND AND EXTEND THE LOCAL GOVERNMENT (PLANNING AND DEVELOPMENT) ACTS, 1963 TO 1982 [*20th July, 1983*]

BE IT ENACTED BY THE OIREACHTAS AS FOLLOWS:

1. – In this Act –
'the Assembly' means the Assembly of the European Communities;
'the Act of 1977' means the European Assembly Elections Act, 1977;
'chairman' means, save where the context otherwise requires, the chairman of the Board and 'chairmanship' shall be construed accordingly;
'deputy chairman', except in section 8 (1) of this Act, means the deputy chairman of the Board and 'deputy chairmanship' shall be construed accordingly;
'ordinary member' means a member of the Board other than the chairman.

2. – (1) The Board shall continue to be a body corporate with perpetual succes-

sion and a seal and power to sue and be sued in its corporate name and to acquire, hold and dispose of land.

(2) The seal of the Board shall be authenticated by the signature of the chairman or of some other member, or of an employee of the Board or of a person whose services are availed of by the Board by virtue of section 21 (3) of the Act of 1976, authorised by the Board to act in that behalf.

(3) Judicial notice shall continue to be taken of the seal of the Board and every document purporting to be an instrument made by the Board and to be sealed with the seal (purporting to be authenticated in accordance with subsection (2) of this section) of the Board shall be received in evidence and be deemed to be such instrument without proof unless the contrary is shown.

(4) A person who immediately before the passing of this Act held the office either of chairman or of an ordinary member shall, subject to section 3 (2) of the Act of 1976 and to section 10 of this Act, continue to hold that office.

3. – On and from the commencement of this section the Board shall consist of a chairman and five other members.

4. – (1)(*a*) It shall be the duty of the Board to ensure that appeals, references and other matters with which it is concerned are disposed of as expeditiously as may be and, for that purpose to take all such steps as are open to it to ensure that, in so far as is practicable, there are no avoidable delays at any stage in the consideration of such appeals, references and other matters.

(*b*) The Board shall conduct, at such intervals as it thinks fit or the Minister directs, reviews of its organisation and of the systems and procedures used by it in relation to appeals, references and other matters with which it is concerned.

(*c*) Where the Minister gives a direction under this section, the Board shall report to the Minister the results of the review conducted pursuant to the direction and shall comply with any directive which the Minister may, after consultation with the Board as regards such results, give in relation to all or any of the matters which were the subject of the review.

(2) The Board may make submissions to the Minister as regards any matter pertaining to its functions.

(3) The Minister may consult with the Board as regards any matter pertaining to the performance of –

(*a*) the functions of the Board, or

(*b*) the functions assigned to the Minister by or under the Local Government (Planning and Development) Acts, 1963 to 1983, or by any other enactment or by an order, regulation or other instrument thereunder.

(4)(*a*) The provisions of subsection (1) of this section are without prejudice to the provisions specified in paragraph (b) of this subsection.

(*b*) The provisions referred to in paragraph (*a*) of this subsection are –

(i) the provisions of the Local Government (Planning and Development) Acts, 1963 to 1983, or of any regulations made thereunder which relate to the performance by the Board of its functions,

(ii) the provisions of any other enactment, order, regulation or other instrument thereunder which so relates.

5. – (1) The chairman shall be appointed by the Government.

(2) There shall be a committee (in this section subsequently referred to as 'the committee') consisting of –

(*a*) the President of the High Court,

(*b*) the Chairman of the County Councils General Council,

(*c*) the Chief Engineering Adviser of the Department of the Environment,

(*d*) the Chairman of the Council of An Taisce – the National Trust for Ireland,

(*e*) the President of the Construction Industry Federation, and

(*f*) the President of the Executive Council of the Irish Congress of Trade Unions.

(3) Where –

(*a*) any of the persons aforesaid signifies at any time his unwillingness or inability to act for any period as a member of the committee,
or

(*b*) any of the persons aforesaid is through ill-health or otherwise unable so to act for any period,

the Minister may, when making a request under subsection (7) of this section, appoint another person to be a member of the committee in his place and such person shall remain a member of the committee until such time as the selection by the committee pursuant to the request is made.

(4) Where the Minister makes a request under subsection (7) of this section and at the time of making the request any of the offices aforesaid is vacant, the Minister may appoint a person to be a member of the committee and such person shall remain a member of the committee until such time as the selection by the committee pursuant to the request is made.

(5) Where pursuant to subsection (3) or (4) of this section the Minister appoints a person to be a member of the committee, he shall, as soon as may be, cause a notice of the appointment to be published in the *Irish Oifigiúil.*

(6)(*a*) The Minister may by order amend subsection (2) of this section.

(*b*) The Minister may by order amend or revoke an order under this subsection (including an order under this paragraph).

(*c*) Where an order under this subsection is proposed to be made, the Minister shall cause a draft thereof to be laid before both Houses of the Oireachtas and the order shall not be made until a resolution approving of the draft has been passed by each such House.

(*d*) Where an order under this subsection is for the time being in force, subsection (2) of this section shall be construed and have effect subject to the terms of the order.

(7)(*a*) The committee shall, whenever so requested by the Minister, select three candidates, or if in the opinion of the committee there is not a sufficient number of suitable applicants, such lesser number of candidates as the committee shall determine, for appointment to be the chairman and shall inform the Minister of the names of the candidates, or, as may be appropriate, the name of the candidate, selected and of the reasons why, in the opinion of the committee, they are or he is suitable for such appointment.

(*b*) In selecting candidates the committee shall have regard to the special knowledge and experience and other qualifications or personal qualities which the committee consider appropriate to enable a person effectively to perform the functions of the chairman.

(8) Except in the case of a reappointment under subsection (12) of this section, the Government shall not appoint a person to be the chairman unless the person was amongst those, or, where appropriate, was the candidate, selected by the committee pursuant to a request under subsection (7) of this section in relation to that appointment but –

(*a*) if the committee is unable to select any suitable candidate pursuant to a particular request under the said subsection (7), or

(*b*) if the Government decide not to appoint to be the chairman any of the candidates, or, where appropriate, the candidate, selected by the committee pursuant to a particular such request,
then either –

(*c*) the Government shall appoint a person to be the chairman who was amongst those, or, where appropriate, was the candidate, selected by the committee pursuant to a previous such request (if any) in relation to that appointment, or

(*d*) the Minister shall make a further such request to the committee and the Government shall appoint to be the chairman a person who was amongst those, or, where appropriate, was the candidate, selected by the committee pursuant to that request or pursuant to another such request made in relation to that appointment.

(9)[91] The Minister may make regulations as regards –

(*a*) the publication of notice that a request has been received by the committee under subsection (7) of this section,

(*b*) applications for selection by the committee,

(*c*) any other matter which the Minister considers expedient for the purposes of this section.

(10) A person who is, for the time being –

(*a*) entitled under the Standing Orders of either House of the Oireachtas to sit therein,

(*b*) a representative in the Assembly,

(*c*) a member of a local authority,
shall be disqualified for being appointed as the chairman.

(11) The chairman shall be appointed in a wholetime capacity and shall not at any time during his term of office hold any other office or employment in respect of which emoluments are payable.

(12) Subject to the provisions of this section, the chairman shall hold office for a term of seven years and may be reappointed by the Government for a second or subsequent term of office: Provided that a person shall not be reappointed under this subsection unless, at the time of his reappointment, he is or was the outgoing chairman of the Board.

(13)(*a*) The chairman may resign his chairmanship by letter addressed to the Minister and the resignation shall take effect as on and from the date of the receipt of the letter by the Minister.

(*b*) The chairman shall vacate the office of chairman on attaining the age of sixty-five years.

---

[91] See S.I. 285 of 1983.

(c) A person shall cease to be the chairman if he –
    (i) is nominated either as a member of Seanad Éireann or for election to either House of the Oireachtas,
    (ii) is either nominated for election to the Assembly or appointed under section 15 of the Act of 1977 to be a representative in the Assembly,
    (iii) becomes a member of a local authority.
(14)(a) There shall be paid by the Board to the chairman the same salary as is paid to a judge of the High Court.
  (b) Subject to the provisions of this section, the chairman shall hold office on such terms and conditions (including terms relating to allowances for expenses) as the Minister, with the consent of the Minister for the Public Service, determines.
(15) The chairman may be removed from office by the Government if he has become incapable through ill-health of effectively performing his duties, or if he has committed stated misbehaviour, or if his removal appears to the Government to be necessary for the effective performance by the Board of its functions, and in case the chairman is removed from office under this subsection, the Government shall cause to be laid before each House of the Oireachtas a statement in writing of the reasons for the removal.

6. – (1) It shall be the function of the chairman, or, where he is not available or where the office of chairman is vacant, of the deputy chairman –
  (a) to ensure the efficient discharge of the business of the Board, and
  (b) to arrange the distribution of the business of the Board among its members.
(2) Where the chairman is of opinion that the conduct of an ordinary members has been such as to bring the Board into disrepute or has been prejudicial to the effective performance by the Board of all or any one or more of its functions, he may in his absolute discretion –
  (a) require the member of the Board to attend for interview and there interview the member privately and inform him of such opinion, or
  (b) where he considers it appropriate to do so, otherwise investigate the matter and, if he considers it appropriate so to do, report to the Minister the result of the investigation.

7. – (1) The Minister may prescribe[92] –
  (a) for the purposes of paragraph (a) of subsection (2) of this section any two or more organisations which in his opinion are representative of persons whose professions or occupations relate to physical planning and development,
  (b) for the purposes of paragraph (b) of the said subsection (2) any two or more organisations which in his opinion are representative of persons concerned with the protection and preservation of the environment and of amenities,
  (c) for the purposes of paragraph (c) of the said subsection (2) any two or more organisations which in his opinion are concerned with the promo-

[92] See S.I. 285 of 1983.

tion of economic or other development or are representative of either or both of the following, namely, persons carrying on the business of developing land or persons employed or engaged in or otherwise connected with the construction industry,

(*d*) for the purposes of paragraph (d) of the said subsection (2) any two or more organisations which in his opinion are, in relation to the community, concerned with the promotion of social, economic or general interests.

(2) Subject to section 12 (4) of this Act, the ordinary members shall be appointed by the Minister as follows:

(*a*) one shall be so appointed from among persons selected by organisations which for the time being stand prescribed for the purposes of this paragraph by the Minister;

(*b*) one shall be so appointed from among persons selected by organisations which for the time being stand prescribed for the purposes of this paragraph by the Minister;

(*c*) one shall be so appointed from among persons selected by organisations which for the time being stand prescribed for the purposes of this paragraph by the Minister;

(*d*) one shall be so appointed from among persons selected by organisations which for the time being stand prescribed for the purposes of this paragraph by the Minister;

(*e*) one shall be so appointed from among the officers of the Minister who are established civil servants for the purposes of the Civil Service Regulation Act, 1956.

(3) An organisation prescribed for the purposes of paragraph (*a*), (*b*), (*c*) or (*d*) of subsection (2) of this section shall, whenever so requsted by the Minister, select such number of candidates (not being less than two) as the Minister may specify for appointment as an ordinary member and shall inform the Minister of the names of the candidates selected and of the reasons why, in the opinion of the organisation, they are suitable for such appointment.

(4) Except in the case of an appointment pursuant to paragraph (*e*) of subsection (2) of this section or of a re-appointment under subsection (9) of this section and subject to section 12 (4) of this Act, the Minister shall not appoint a person to be an ordinary member unless the person was amongst those selected pursuant to a request under subsection (3) of this section in relation to that appointment, but –

(*a*) if all of the appropriate organisations refuse or fail to select any candidate pursuant to a particular request under the said subsection (3), or

(*b*) if the Minister decides not to appoint as an ordinary member any of the candidates selected by such organisations pursuant to a particular request under that subsection,
then either –

(*c*) the Minister shall appoint as an ordinary member a person who was amongst those selected by such an organisation pursuant to a previous request (if any) under that subsection in relation to that appointment, or

(*d*) the Minister shall make a further such request and shall appoint as an ordinary member a person who was amongst those selected pursuant to that request or pursuant to another such request made in relation to that appointment.

(5) Where a request is made pursuant to subsection (3) of this section, failure or refusal by the organisation of whom the request is made to select the number of candidates specified in the request shall not preclude the appointment as an ordinary member of a person who was selected in relation to that appointment either by the aforesaid organisation or by any other organisation.

(6) The Minister may make regulations as regards –

   (*a*) the period within which the Minister is to be informed in accordance with subsection (3) of this section,

   (*b*) any other matter which the Minister considers expedient for the purposes of this section.

(7) A person who is for the time being –

   (*a*) entitled under the Standing Orders of either House of the Oireachtas to sit therein,

   (*b*) a representative in the Assembly,

   (*c*) a member of a local authority,

shall be disqualified for being appointed to be an ordinary member.

(8) Each of the ordinary members shall be appointed in a wholetime capacity and shall not at any time during his term of office hold any other office or employment in respect of which emoluments are payable.

(9) Subject to the provisions of section 12 (4)(*b*) of this Act, an ordinary member shall hold office for such term (not exceeding five years) as shall be specified by the Minister when appointing him to office and may be re-appointed by the Minister for a second or subsequent term of office: Provided that a person shall not be re-appointed under this subsection unless, at the time of his re-appointment, he is or was an outgoing member of the Board.

(10)(*a*) An ordinary member may resign his membership by letter addressed to the Minister and the resignation shall take effect as on and from the date of the receipt of the letter by the Minister.

   (*b*) A person shall vacate the office of ordinary member on attaining the age of sixty-five years.

   (*c*) A person shall cease to be an ordinary member if he –

      (i) is nominated either as a member of Seanad Éireann or for election to either House of the Oireachtas,

      (ii) is either nominated for election to the Assembly or appointed under section 15 of the Act of 1977 to be a representative in the Assembly,

      (iii) becomes a member of a local authority.

(11)(*a*) There shall be paid by the Board to each ordinary member such remuneration and allowances for expenses as the Minister, with the consent of the Minister for the Public Service, determines.

   (*b*) Subject to the provisions of this section, an ordinary member shall hold office on such terms and conditions as the Minister, with the consent of the Minister for the Public Service, determines.

(12) An ordinary member may be removed from office by the Minister if he has become incapable through ill-health of effectively performing his duties, or if he has committed stated misbehaviour, or if his removal appears to the Minister to be necessary for the effective performance by the Board of its functions, and in case an ordinary member is removed from office under this subsection, the Minister shall cause to be laid before each House of the Oireachtas a statement in writing of the reasons for the removal.

8. – (1) The Minister shall appoint from amongst the ordinary members a person to be the deputy chairman of the Board and such appointment shall be for such period as shall be specified in the appointment.

(2) If at any time the deputy chairman ceases to be an ordinary member of the board, he shall thereupon cease to be deputy chairman.

(3) The deputy chairman shall, in addition to his remuneration as an ordinary member, be paid by the Board such additional remuneration (if any) as the Minister, with the consent of the Minister for the Public Service, determines.

(4) The deputy chairman may resign his deputy chairmanship by letter addressed to the Minister and the resignation shall take effect as on and from the date of the receipt of the letter by the Minister.

9.[93] – (1) The Minister may with the concurrence of the Minister for the Public Service –

> (*a*) make a scheme or schemes for the granting of pensions, gratuities or other allowances to or in respect of the chairman and ordinary members ceasing to hold office,
>
> (*b*) make a scheme or schemes for the granting of gratuities to or in respect of persons ceasing to hold office by virtue of section 10 of this Act.

(2) A scheme under this section may provide that the termination of the appointment of the chairman or of an ordinary member during that person's term of office shall not preclude the award to him under the scheme of a pension, gratuity or other allowance.

(3) The Minister may, with the concurrence of the Minister for the Public Service, amend a scheme made by him under this section.

(4) If any dispute arises as to the claim of any person to, or the amount of, any pension, gratuity, or allowance payable in pursuance of a scheme under this section, such dispute shall be submitted to the Minister who shall refer it to the Minister for the Public Service, whose decision shall be final.

(5) A scheme under this section shall be carried out by the Board in accordance with its terms.

(6) No pension, gratuity or other allowance shall be granted by the Board to or in respect of any person referred to in subsection (1) of this section ceasing to hold office otherwise than in accordance with a scheme under this section.

(7) Notwithstanding section 25 of this Act, the scheme made by the Minister under Article 28 of the Schedule to the Act of 1976, shall continue in force and may be amended as if made under this section.

(8) Every scheme made under this section shall be laid before each House of the Oireachtas as soon as may be after it is made and if either such House, within the next twenty-one days on which that House has sat after the scheme is laid before it, passes a resolution annulling the scheme, the scheme shall be annulled accordingly, but without prejudice to the validity of anything previously done thereunder.

10. – (1) The person who, immediately before the commencement of this subsection, held the office of chairman of the Board, shall, on such commencement, cease to be chairman.

(2) Every person who, immediately before the commencement of this subsection was an ordinary member of the Board, shall, on such commencement, cease to be such ordinary member.

---

[93] See also section 11 of the 1976 Act in respect of superannuation of employees of the Board.

11. – (1) The Board shall hold such and so many meetings as may be necessary for the performance of its functions.

(2) The chairman and each ordinary member at a meeting of the Board shall have a vote.

(3) At a meeting of the Board –

    (*a*) the chairman shall, if present, be chairman of the meeting,

    (*b*) if and for so long as the chairman is not present, or if the office of chairman is vacant, the deputy chairman shall, if present, be chairman of the meeting,

    (*c*) if and for so long as neither the chairman nor the deputy chairman is present, or if the chairman is not present or if the office of chairman is vacant, and in either case, the office of deputy chairman is vacant, the ordinary members who are present shall choose one of their number to be chairman of the meeting.

(4) Every question at a meeting of the Board shall be determined by a majority of votes of the members present and, in the event that voting is equally divided, the person who is chairman of the meeting shall have a casting vote.

(5)(*a*) Subject to the Local Government (Planning and Development) Acts, 1963 to 1983, and to any regulations made thereunder, and subject also to any other enactment or order, regulation or other instrument thereunder, which regulates or otherwise affects the procedure of the Board, the Board shall regulate its own procedure and business.

    (*b*) The Minister may require the Board to keep him informed of the arrangements made under this subsection for the regulation of its procedure and business.

(6)(*a*) Subject to paragraphs (*b*) and (*c*) of this subsection, the Board may perform or exercise any of its functions through or by any member of the Board or other person who, in either case, has been duly authorised by the Board in that behalf.

    (*b*) Paragraph (*a*) of this subsection shall be construed as enabling a member of the Board finally to determine a particular case if, and only if, the case to which an authorisation under that paragraph relates has been considered at a meeting of the Board prior to the giving of the authorisation.

    (*c*) Paragraph (*a*) of this subsection shall not be construed as enabling the Board to authorise a person who is not a member of the Board finally to determine any particular case with which the Board is concerned.

12. – (1) The quorum for a meeting of the Board shall be three.

(2) Subject to subsection (1) of this section, the Board may act notwithstanding a vacancy in the chairmanship, the deputy chairmanship or among the ordinary members.

(3) Where a vacancy occurs in the chairmanship, deputy chairmanship or among the ordinary members, the Minister shall, as soon as may be, take steps to fill the vacancy.

(4)(*a*) Where, owing to the illness of the chairman or of an ordinary member, or for any other reason, a sufficient number of members of the Board is not available to enable the Board effectively to perform its functions, the Minister may, as an interim measure, appoint from among the officers referred to in section 7 (2)(*e*) of this Act, one or more persons to be an ordinary member.

(*b*) A person shall not be appointed to be an ordinary member under this subsection for a term in excess of twelve months.

13. – (1) No person shall, without the consent of the Board (which may be given to the person, subject to or without conditions, as regards any information, as regards particular information or as regards information of a particular class or description) disclose –

(*a*) any information obtained by him while serving as a member or employee of, or consultant or adviser to, the Board or as a person whose services are availed of by the Board by virtue of section 21 (3) of the Act of 1976,

(*b*) any information so obtained relative to the business of the Board or to the performance of its functions.

(2) A person who contravenes subsection (1) of this section shall be guilty of an offence and shall be liable on summary conviction to a fine not exceeding £800.

(3) Nothing in subsection (1) of this section shall prevent –

(*a*) disclosure of information in a report made to the Board or in a report made by or on behalf of the Board to the Minister,

(*b*) disclosure of information by any person in the course of and in accordance with the duties of his office.

LOCAL GOVERNMENT (PLANNING AND DEVELOPMENT) (FEES AND AMENDMENT) REGULATIONS 1983

PART III
FEES FOR APPEALS ETC., TO THE BOARD

Fee for appeals
18. Subject to article 21, a person making an appeal to the Board shall pay to the Board a fee of £30.

Fee for reference
19. Subject to article 21, a person making a reference to the Board shall pay to the Board a fee of £30.

Fee in relation to requests for determinations
20. (1) Subject to article 21, a person making a request to the Board for a determination to which this article applies shall pay to the Board a fee of £30.

(2) This article applies to a request for a determination by the Board in relation to –

(a) a contribution or other matter which, pursuant to a condition attached to a permission or an approval, is to be agreed between a planning authority and another person and in default of agreement is to be determined by the Board;

(b) the amount of a contribution to be paid under section 26 (7) of the Act of 1963;

(c) a question or dispute to which section 56 (3) of the Act of 1963 relates.

Reduced fee payable in certain circumstances

21. Where an appeal, a reference, or a request for a determination to which article 20 applies is made to the Board by –

    (*a*) a State authority,

    (*b*) a planning authority,

    (*c*) An Chomhairle Ealaion,

    (*d*) Bord Failte Eireann,

    (*e*) An Taisce – The National Trust for Ireland,

    (*f*) The National Monuments Advisory Council,

    (*g*) The Royal Irish Academy,

the fee to be paid to the Board in respect of the appeal, reference, or request shall be £15.

Fee for submissions or observations to the Board

22. (1) Subject to sub-articles (2) and (3), a fee of £10 shall be paid to the Board by a person making submissions or observations to the Board as regards an appeal, a reference or a determination to which article 20 applies.

(2) Sub-article (1) shall not apply where the person by or on whose behalf submissions or observations are made is –

    (*a*) the appellant or person making the reference to, or request for a determination by, the Board,

    (*b*) the applicant for the permission, approval or licence in relation to which the appeal is made,

    (*c*) any person served or issued by a planning authority with a notice or order, or copy thereof, under section 30, 36, 37, 44, 45, or 48 of the Act of 1963 or section 25 of the Act of 1976, in relation to which an appeal is made by another person, or

    (*d*) a body referred to in article 21,

(3) Where a fee has been paid under this article by or on behalf of a person or body of persons making submissions or observations as regards a particular appeal, reference or determination, a fee shall not be payable in respect of any further submissions or observations made by or on behalf of the same person or body of persons as regards that appeal, reference or determination.

Fee in relation to requests for oral hearings

23. A person making a request to the Board for an oral hearing of an appeal or reference shall, in addition to the fee prescribed by article 18 or article 19, as may be appropriate, pay to the Board a fee of £30 in respect of the request.

LOCAL GOVERNMENT (PLANNING AND DEVELOPMENT) (AN BORD PLEANÁLA) REGULATIONS, 1983

PART I
PRELIMINARY AND GENERAL

1. – (1) These Regulations may be cited as the Local Government (Planning and Development) (An Bord Pleanála) Regulations, 1983.

(2) The collective citation 'the Local Government (Planning and Development) Regulations, 1977 to 1983' shall include these Regulations.

2. – (1) In these Regulations, any reference to an article which is not otherwise identified is a reference to an article of these Regulations.

(2) In these Regulations, any reference to a sub-article or paragraph which is not otherwise identified is a reference to the sub-article or paragraph of the provision in which the reference occurs.

(3) In these Regulations:–

'the Act of 1983' means the Local Government (Planning and Development) Act, 1983;

'chairman' means the chairman of An Bord Pleanála;

'the committee' means the committee referred to in section 5 of the Act of 1983;

'the Minister' means the Minister for the Environment.

PART II

CHAIRMAN

3. – Whenever a request is made to the committee under section 5(7) of the Act of 1983 for the selection of candidates for appointment to be the chairman –

  (*a*) the committee shall meet on a day and at a time and place determined by the President of the High Court who shall cause to be communicated to the other members of the committee the day, time and place of the meeting, and

  (*b*) the committee shall, before selecting candidates for appointment to the office of chairman pursuant to the request, cause an advertisement to be published inviting applications for appointment to such office.

(2) An advertisement published pursuant to paragraph (*b*) shall specify a period of not less than twenty-one days for the making of applications and any applicatioan which is not received by the committee within the period so specified shall be invalid.

4. Application shall include a *curriculum vitae* and particulars of the special knowledge and experience and other qualifications and personal qualities which the applicant considers relevant to the application.

5. Where the committee receive an application they may require the applicant to submit within a period of not more than twenty-one days such further particulars as they may require (including any evidence which the committee may reasonably require to verify any particulars given by the applicant in or in relation to his application).

6. – (1) Where the committee consider it necessary for the purposes of selecting candidates they may, subject to sub-article (2), invite applicants to attend for interview.

(2) Where the committee decide to invite applicants to attend for interview pursuant to sub-article (1), the committee may in their absolute discretion, having examined the information contained in the applications in the context of the matters referred to in section 5(7)(*b*) of the Act of 1983, invite to attend for interview only those applicants who appear to them to be likely to be suitable to be considered for selection as candidates for appointment to the office of chairman.

7. Applicants who do not attend for interview or who do not furnish such particulars or evidence as may be requested pursuant to article 5 shall not be entitled to further consideration by the committee for selection as candidates for appointment to the office of chairman.

8. – (1) The committee shall hold such meetings as may be necessary for the performance of its functions.

(2) The quorum for a meeting of the committee shall be four.

(3) The President of the High Court shall preside at meetings of the committee at which he is present.

(4) If the President of the High Court is not present at a meeting of the committee, a member of the committee selected by the committee shall preside at the meeting.

(5) Every question at a meeting of the committee shall be determined by a majority of votes of the members present.

9. Subject to the provisions of article 8 the committee shall regulate its own procedure.

10. An officer of the Minister designated by the Secretary of the Department of the Environment shall act as secretary to the committee.

PART III

ORDINARY MEMBERS

11. The prescribed organisations for the purposes of section 7(2)(a) of the Act of 1983 shall be –
    (a) The Irish Planning Institute Limited,
    (b) The Royal Town Planning Institute, Irish Branch – Southern Section,
    (c) The Institution of Engineers of Ireland,
    (d) The Society of Chartered Surveyors in the Republic of Ireland, and
    (e) The Royal Institute of the Architects of Ireland.

12. The prescribed organisations for the purposes of section 7(2)(b) of the Act of 1983 shall be –
    (a) An Taisce – the National Trust for Ireland,
    (b) Bord Fáilte Éireann,
    (c) The Heritage Trust,
    (d) The Royal Irish Academy, and
    (e) The County and City Managers' Association.

13. The prescribed organisations for the purposes of section 7(2)(c) of the Act of 1983 shall be –
    (a) The Construction Industry Federation,
    (b) The Irish Congress of Trade Unions,
    (c) The Industrial Development Authority,
    (d) The Confederation of Irish Industry, and
    (e) The Association of Chambers of Commerce of Ireland.

14. The prescribed organisations for the purpose of section 7(2)(*d*) of the Act of 1983 shall be –
  (*a*) Aontacht Cumann Riartha Aitreabhthoiri (A.C.R.C.),
  (*b*) The National Association of Tenants' Organisations,
  (*c*) The National Youth Council of Ireland,
  (*d*) The Irish Farmers' Association,
  (*e*) The Irish Creamery Milk Suppliers' Association,
  (*f*) The Irish Countrywomen's Association, and
  (*g*) The Council for the Status of Women.

15. Where a request is made to a prescribed organisation pursuant to section 7(3) of the Act of 1983 the organisation shall, before the expiration of two months commencing on the day on which the request is made, inform the Minister of the names of the candidates selected and of the reasons why, in the opinion of the organisation, they are suitable for such appointment and shall send to the Minister a *curriculum vitae* in relation to each candidate together with a written consent of each candidate to his selection in accordance with the request.

16. Where a request is made to a prescribed organisation pursuant to section 7(3) of the Act of 1983 the organisation shall select two candidates for appointment as ordinary members of An Bord Pleanála.

CASES

THE STATE (ELM DEVELOPMENTS LTD.) V. AN BORD PLEANALA
[1981] I.L.R.M. 108

The prosecutor sought an Order of *Prohibition* to prevent the Board from determining an appeal where the appellant did not include his grounds of appeal in his initial letter of appeal. The High Court refused to grant an absolute Order. An appeal to the Supreme Court was dismissed. Henchy J. observed that having regard to Section 17 of the 1976 Act (which entitles the Board in dealing with a reference or appeal to take into account matters other than those raised by the parties) the Board is entitled to treat the grounds lodged with the appeal as merely interim or provisional grounds. Even if the appeal contains a full statement of the grounds of appeal, therefore, that statement is not conclusive as to the grounds that may be considered on the hearing of the appeal. The grounds of the appeal are not to be equated with the pleadings in Court proceedings. They do not or cannot circumscribe or identify the issues on which the appeal will be decided. Accordingly the Board's practice of informing an appellant who has not stated his grounds that his appeal will not be entertained unless he submits them is a correct evaluation of the role of the grounds of appeal in the statutory scheme.

Henchy J.:
. . . In this case, one E. Power ('The appellant') wrote to the Board on the 28th February, 1980. The letter stated that on behalf of local residents and himself he wished to appeal against the grant of permission. The letter was accompanied by a deposit of £10. In every respect except one, the letter was unquestionably a valid

appeal. The single questionable feature was that the letter did not state the grounds of appeal. Instead, what the appellant put in the letter was: 'Full particulars of the extent and nature of our appeal will be submitted to you shortly when the residents have examined the implications of this decision in detail'.

Because of the failure of the appellant to state the grounds of appeal in the letter, the developer has claimed that the 'appeal' is a nullity and that the Board has no jurisdiction to hear it. To bring his point home, he sought and obtained a conditional order of prohibition against the Board, under which the Board would be debarred from hearing the appeal. But D'Arcy J. refused to make absolute the conditional order. He held that the requirement that the written appeal should state the grounds of appeal is directory rather than mandatory, and that, accordingly, the Board was entitled in the circumstnces to overlook the non-compliance with it. Keane, J., in *The State (Walsh)* v. *An Bord Pleanala*, a case in which the facts were indistinguishable from those of the present case, reached the same conclusion. The sole question in this appeal by the developer against the order of D'Arcy J. is whether that conclusion is correct.

Whether a provision in a statute or a statutory instrument, which on the face of it is obligatory (for example, by the use of the word 'shall'), should be treated by the courts as truly mandatory or merely directory depends on the statutory scheme by the provision in question. If the requirement which has not been observed may fairly be said to be an integral and indispensable part of the statutory intendment, the courts will hold it to be truly mandatory, and will not excuse a departure from it. But if, on the other hand, what is apparently a requirement is in essence merely a direction which is not of the substance of the aim and scheme of the statute, non-compliance may be excused.

An example of a truly mandatory provision is to be found in the decision of this Court in *Monaghan U.D.C.* v. *Alf-a-Bet Promotions Ltd.* The developer in that case was seeking development permission which would allow him to convert a drapery shop in the town of Monaghan into a betting office and amusement arcade. The relevant planning regulations required that a notice published by the developer in a newspaper of this intention to apply for development permission should state, *inter alia*, 'the nature and extent of the development'. The notice published by the developer in that case referred only to 'alterations and improvements'. By no stretch of interpretation could that be said to be indicative of the nature and extent of the proposed development. The Court considered that the inclusion in the notice in a newspaper of information as to the nature and extent of the proposed development was vital to the proper operation of the statutory scheme for the grant of development permission. The veiled and misleading notice that was published was held to be a non-compliance with that mandatory provision and it could not, therefore, be excused. . . .

The present case is the antithesis of that case. In that case it was the developer who was seeking to have the departure from the statutory requirements excused. In that case the notice in the newspaper, so far from informing the public of 'the nature and extent' of the proposed development, concealed that information behind the general and undescriptive words 'alterations and improvements'. Local residents or local business people to whom a betting office and amusement arcade would be anathema might well have been led by the notice to think that all that was proposed was a refurbished drapery premises. Whether intentionally or inadvertently, the notice was calculated to lure interested parties into abandoning their opportunity of making representations against the grant of the permission. In the circumstances, it would have been a travesty of the statutory scheme of development control if the requirement which was departed from had been held to be merely directory.

Here it is a local resident, acting for himself and other local residents, who is said to have been inexcusably at fault in not conforming to the Regulations. His letter to the Board stated that they wished to appeal and requested an oral hearing. That was an appeal in writing, as was required. The letter adequately stated the subject matter of the appeal, as was required. It was accompanied by a deposit of £10, as was required. It departed from the requirements of the Regulations only in not stating the grounds of appeal. But it undertook to submit those grounds shortly when the residents had an opportunity of examining the implications of the decision in detail.

The decision of a planning authority to grant a development permission, while not necessarily final, will become final if an appeal is not lodged within the time fixed by the Act. Since an extension of that time is not provided for, the requirement as to time is mandatory, so that a departure from it cannot be excused. The requirement that the appeal be in writing is so obviously basic to the institution of an appeal that it too must be considered mandatory. So also must the requirement that the written appeal state the subject matter of the appeal, for the absence of such identification could lead to administrative confusion. The lodgment of a deposit of £10 with the appeal (perhaps not necessarily physically or contemporaneously with the appeal) would also seem to be an essential part of the statutory scheme, so as to discourage frivolous, delaying or otherwise worthless appeals.

The requirement that the appeal should state the grounds of appeal seems to me to rest on different considerations. Even when the appeal contains a full statement of the grounds of appeal, that statement is not conclusive as to the grounds that will be considered on the hearing of the appeal. That is because s. 17 of the 1976 Act says this:

'The Board in deciding a reference or appeal may take into account matters other than those raised by the parties to the reference or appeal if the matters either relate to the proper planning and development of the area of the relevant planning authority or are matters to which by virtue of section 24(2) of this Act the Board may have regard, provided that the matters are brought to the notice of those parties and they are accorded an opportunity of making observations thereon to the Board or, in the case of an oral hearing, the person conducting the hearing'.

The effect of that provision is that the Board may always treat the grounds lodged with the appeal as merely interim or provisional grounds. Even if the objector in this case had lodged a set of grounds of appeal with his appeal, the Board would be entitled to entertain further or other grounds, at any stage up to the determination of the appeal, provided those further or other grounds relate to the proper planning and development of the area, or are matters to which by virtue of s. 24 (2) of the 1976 Act the Board may have regard, and provided the developer is given an opportunity of making observations thereon.

Because of that, the grounds of appeal required to be stated in the appeal are not to be equated with pleadings in court proceedings, or with a notice of appeal from one court to a superior court. They cannot circumscribe or identify the issues on which the appeal will be decided. The Board (or the person holding the oral hearing, if there is one) may go outside them. They cannot be treated with any confidence by the developer as indicative of the scope of the case he will have to meet on the hearing of the appeal. I deduce that the primary purpose of the requirement of stating grounds of appeal in a case such as this is to inform the Board as to the primary matters relied on, so that the procedure for the disposition of the appeal may be decided on. Whether that deduction be correct or not, I am satisfied that the grounds of appeal required are essentially informative. To hold that they must be given as part of, or contemporaneously with, the notice of appeal, would be to attribute a conclusiveness to them which the statute clearly shows they cannot have. I consider that the Board's practice of informing an appellant in a case such as this, who has not stated grounds in his appeal, that his appeal will not be entertained unless he submits grounds of appeal, is a correct evaluation of the place that grounds of appeal take in the statutory scheme. It would be unduly legalistic, and unfair, if laymen who may have no skill in such matters but who may be vitally affected by the permission which they wish to appeal against, were to be shut out from appealing merely because their notice of appeal did not state their grounds of appeal, particularly when those grounds of appeal can never be anything more than an opening salvo in the appellate battle. In such circumstances, the requirement of stating the grounds of appeal is essentially informative and directory, and therefore not mandatory. When the appellant in this case furnished grounds of appeal within a few weeks of his appeal to the satisfaction of the Board, it did not lie in the mouth of the developer to say that he had been in any way wrong-footed or damnified, or that the spirit or purpose of the Acts or Regulations had been breached. In seeking an order of Prohibition against the Board, he is endeavouring to benefit from what is no more than a technical breach of a Regulation, which breach has been put right by the appellant and has been therefore rightly overlooked by the Board in the interests of justice.

THE STATE (WALSH) V. AN BORD PLEANALA
The High Court (Unreported) Keane J., 19 November 1980
(Ref. No. 328SS)

The prosecutor obtained a decision to grant permission for the change of use of premises from an amusement arcade to a gaming arcade. Within the time allowed for appealing the Board received a notice of appeal from a Third Party in the following terms:

'I wish to appeal against the decision of Bundoran U.D.C. to grant planning permission to Robert Walsh for a licensed amusement centre at Main Street on behalf of the people I represented in the objection to the U.D.C. in the application.'

The prosecutor sought and obtained a conditional order of prohibition debarring the Board from hearing or determining the appeal on the ground that the notice was an invalid notice of appeal because it failed to state the grounds of appeal. On a motion to have the order made absolute the High Court held that the absence of grounds of appeal did not invalidate the notice of appeal.

Keane J.:
The case depends on the construction of Article 36 of the Local Government (Planning and Development) Regulations 1977 (S.I. No. 65 of 1977) which is in the following terms:

[Quotation of the article follows][94]

It is conceded on behalf of the respondents that the notice does not state the grounds of appeal as required by article 36(c) and it is submitted on behalf of the prosecutor that this failure is fatal to the validity of the notice and deprives the respondents of any jurisdiction to hear and determine the appeal purportedly made thereby.

The language of Article 36 is undoubtedly mandatory; but that by no means concludes the matter. The law has for long recognised a distinction between those parts of an enactment which may properly be regarded as imperative and those which are merely directory. The distinction – and its consequences were thus explained by Lord Penzance in *Howard and ors* v. *Bodington* (1876/77) 2 P.D. 203 at p. 210:

'Now the distinction between matters that are directory and matters that are imperative is well known to us all in the common language of the Court at Westminster. . . a thing has been ordered by the legislature to be done. What is the consequence if it is not done? In the case of statutes that are said to be imperative, the Courts have decided that if it was not done the whole things fails, and the proceedings that follow upon it are all void. On the other hand, when the Courts hold a provision to be mandatory or directory, they say that, although such provision may not have been complied with, the subsequent proceedings do not fail.'

It is clear from the unreported judgment of the Supreme Court in *Monaghan U.D.C.* v. *Alf-a-Bet Promotions* (Judgments delivered 24th March 1980) that in applying this principle to the legislation under consideration the Courts must have regard to the purpose of the Acts and the Regulations. (See in particular the judgment of Mr. Justice Griffin at pp. 10/11).

There is no provision in the Local Government (Planning and Development) Acts 1963 and 1976, for an extension of time in cases where a notice of appeal against a decision of the planning authority is late. In the case of what is normally described as a 'third party appeal', the time limit is 21 days. It is well known that such appeals are frequently lodged by persons who are not lawyers and have no particular familiarity with the legislation in question. It is indeed obvious that the legislature envisaged that this would be so, since article 45 of the Regulations provides that, where an oral hearing of an appeal takes place, it is to be conducted 'without undue formality'. One must credit the legislature with having envisaged that notices of appeal would not infrequently be lodged by persons who through haste, inadvertance or lack of knowledge did not specify any grounds. If Article 36(c) is to be construed as imperative, it would follow that all such appeals were void. In the case of a major development with serious implications for the environment, it would mean that the decision of the planning authority would have to stand without any opportunity being given to interested parties to canvass its desirability either in written submissions or at an oral hearing.

By contrast, the position of the other parties to the appeal is not seriously affected by the failure of the appellant to comply with Article 36(c). In paragraph 4 of his affadavit, Mr. O'Buachalla says that the practice of the respondents in such circumstances is to write to the appellant drawing his attention to the provision of Article 36 and seeking a statement and details of grounds relied upon by the

[94] See page 249.

appellant as the grounds of his appeal. They also warn the appellant that unless this statement is received without delay, they will be obliged to proceed with the determination of the appeal.[95] Plainly, the determination of the appeal in the absence of any grounds in support of it being advanced on behalf of the appellant could only be of advantage to the other parties. It is equally obvious that if such grounds are furnished, albeit belatedly, the respondents would, in accordance with principles of natural justice and constitutional justice, be required to furnish those grounds to the other parties and afford them an opportunity of dealing with them. The other parties to the appeal would, accordingly not be adversely affected if the appropriate procedure is followed by the respondents; and I have no reason to suppose that the respondents would not follow that procedure. Any failure by them to do so would, in any event, be inevitably remedied by the High Court.

I think it is accordingly clear that, if one is to give effect to the purpose of the Acts of 1963 and 1976 and the Regulations, article 36(*c*) must be construed as directory rather than imperative.[96]

THE STATE (GENPORT LIMITED) V. AN BORD PLEANALA
[1983] I.L.R.M. 12

The prosecutor, through his architects, lodged an appeal against a decision of the planning authority to refuse permission for retention of various extensions to a hotel. The appeal failed to state the grounds of appeal but stated that these would be furnished in due course. The respondents wrote to the architects requiring a statement of the grounds of appeal without delay. No reply was made by the prosecutor or his architects to this letter and on the 14 July 1981 the respondents wrote to the architects in the following terms:

'A Chara,
I have been asked by An Bord Pleanala to refer to the above-mentioned appeal and in particular to your letter of the 22nd June of 1981 in which you indicated that it was intended to make a further submission to the Board about the appeal. If you wish any such submissions to be taken into account by the Board in its consideration of the appeal, please forward it to the Board within 14 days from the date of this letter otherwise the Board will be obliged to determine the appeal on the basis of the information available to it.'

No reply was forthcoming within the 14 day period, however, shortly afterward the architects wrote to the Board stating that the grounds of appeal were to be withheld as there were still third party objections being received. The Board replied to this letter stating that they had received the letter and that the contents thereof had been noted. The Board continued to forward objections from third parties as they were received. Each of these was accompanied by a letter in the following form:

Enclosed for your information is a copy of correspondence received from (blank) about the above-mentioned appeal but it is not necessary for you to furnish any comments on the correspondence you may do so if you wish. Any such comments

---

[95] See now section 17 of the 1983 Act.
[96] See also *The State (Elm Developments Limited)* v. *An Bord Pleanala*.

should be forwarded at an early date if you wish to have them taken into consideration when the appeal is being determined.'

The prosecutor did not reply to any of this correspondence nor were the grounds of appeal ever furnished. On the 4th November 1981 the Board made a decision to refuse permission. The prosecutor brought Certiorari proceedings. In granting the Order the Court held that the Board may not determine an appeal in the absence of representations from the appellant if it has unequivocally called upon it to make such representations and it has failed to do so.

Finlay P.

. . . On these facts, I have come to the conclusion that the following legal propositions arise.

1. Having regard to the decision of the Supreme Court in *The State (Elm Developments) v. An Bord Pleanala*[97] delivered on the 23rd day of February 1981 and unreported I am satisfied that the Notice of Appeal served in this case was a valid Notice of Appeal notwithstanding the absence of grounds delivered with or immediately after it. No contention was made before me by either of the parties to any other effect.

2. I am satisfied that as a matter of general law An Bord Pleanála carrying out a quasi-judicial function would have an obligation to take reasonable steps to ensure that every party interested in any application before it should be aware of the submissions or representations made by any other party; should have a reasonable opportunity of replying to them; should have a general reasonable opportunity of making representations to the Board.

3. Those general obligations of the Board arising from the requirements of natural justice are indeed to be found implemented in part at least by Sections 17 and 18 respectively of the Act of 1976. Section 17 permits the Board in deciding an appeal to take into account matters other than those raised by the parties to the appeal provided that the matters are brought to the notice of those parties and they are accorded an opportunity of making observation thereon to the Board. Under Section 18 where the Board is of opinion that an appeal is vexatious or unnecessarily delayed by any party it may serve a notice on the party stating that it will at a time after the day specified in the notice which being a day which is not less than 7 days after the service of the notice without further notice to any party determine the appeal notwithstanding the fact that no submission has been made to the Board by the party in relation to it.[98]

Section 17 applies only to matters other than those raised by parties to the appeal and parties to the appeal as defined in Regulation 35 of the Local Government (Planning and Development) Regulations 1977 S.I. No. 65 of 1977 in effect include the appellant, the Planning Authority and person who had objected to the application for permission who would accordingly have been served with notice of the order made by the Planning Authority.

4. I am quite satisfied that the letter written on behalf of the Board on the 14th of July 1981 which I have already quoted was a complete compliance by them with

[97] See page 283.

[98] Section 18(1) and (2) was repealed by section 25 of the 1983 Act. See now sections 16 and 17 of the 1983 Act.

the requirements of Section 18 of the Act of 1976 and that if they had, as they indicated they would, proceeded 14 days after the date of that letter to determine the appeal (and that would of course have been at a period prior to the 6th August 1981) that their decision could not validly be challenged in any court. I am also satisfied that the form of letter which they sent to the prosecutor's architects with each of the objections and letters which they received concerning this appeal was insofar as the parties communicating to the Board were persons other than parties to the appeal within the meaning of the Regulation an adequate and complete compliance with the provisions of Section 17 of the Act. Insofar as there is no section specifically providing the method by which the Board shall discharge their general obligation to give a reasonable opportunity to an appellant such as this prosecutor to deal with representations made by the other parties to the appeal, I am satisfied that the letters were an adequate discharge of that obligation.

5. It seems to me that having regard to the fact that the onus of proof was clearly on the prosecutor not by reason of the fact that they were appellants but rather by reason of the fact that they were applicants for permission, it seems to me that the course indicated by them in their letter of the 6th August 1981 whereby they would make no submissions at all not even stating their grounds of appeal until after they had heard all that was being said against their application by other parties was quite unusual and wholly unjustifiable. I find it very difficult to believe that a careful Town Planner who gave any thought to the procedure which was necessary on an appeal such as this where no oral hearing was sought, should not have realised this was a most unusual and in a general sense unfair procedure to seek to adopt and should have ensured before relying on a simple letter stating without even asking for permission so to do that this was the course being adopted on behalf of the appellant that the Board was agreeable to such an unusual course.

6. With some hesitation, however, I conclude that the reply to the letter of the 6th August 1981 merely noting its contents and not raising on behalf of the Board any objection to the proposal or intention stated in it coupled with the sending for a considerable period after that time of objections and communications and inviting the making of observations by the appellant on them could be construed as a waiver by the Board of the right which they undoubtedly had after a period of 14 days from the 14th of July 1981 to determine the appeal without further reference to the appellants.

7. In general, the determination of a matter as important as an appeal against a refusal for planning permission should not be concluded in the total absence of representations on behalf of the appellant unless he has unequivocally been called upon to make such representations and has failed to do so. The possibility of an injustice having occurred in this case due to what I would consider to be the unusual and unreasonable attitude of the appellant but to some slight extent contributed to by the further communication sent by the Board to the architects is sufficiently real to drive me to the conclusion that I should quash the order and decision made in this case. It seems to me that the Board should, bearing in mind the entire of the correspondence and communications between the parties before finally deciding the appeal on the 4th of November, have written a letter in similar terms to that which they sent on the 14th of July 1981.

In these circumstances, I am satisfied that the decision should be quashed and that the Board should be directed to enter continuances and to proceed anew to determine this appeal.

FREENEY V. BRAY UDC
[1982] I.L.R.M. 29

The plaintiff sought *inter alia* a declaration that he had a default permission because the defendant had failed to give notice of their decision to refuse permission within the time allowed for the giving of that decision by section 26 of the 1963 Act.

O'Hanlon J.:

Having regard to the conclusion I have arrived at in the earlier part of this judgment it does not appear to be strictly necessary to go on and consider the third question, which asks whether notice should be regarded as having been given for the purposes of the Acts when the registered packet was handed in for posting to the post office. As the matter may go further however, it may be helpful if I express my views in relations to this Act, 1937, sec. 18 of which provides as follows:

'Where an Act of the Oireachtas or an instrument made wholly or partly under any such Act authorises or requires a document to be served by post, whether the word 'serve' or any of the words 'give', 'deliver', or 'send' or any other word is used, then unless the contrary intention apears the service of such document may be effected by properly addressing, prepaying (where requisite), and posting a letter containing such document, and in such case the service of such document shall, unless the contrary is proved be deemed to have been effected at the time at which such letter would be delivered in the ordinary course of post.'

A situation not unlike that which has arisen in the present case was considered by O'Keeffe P., in the case of *The State (Murphy)* v. *The Dublin County Council*, [1970] I.R. 253. The learned President took the view that the provisions of sec. 18 of the Interpretation Act, 1937, were not involved in the resolution of the issue concerning the point of time at which the respondents gave notice of their decision to the prosecutor, and he concluded that the respondents had given the prosecutor notice of their decision by posting the notice on a particular day in a prepaid registered letter addressed to the prosecutor's agent, as authorised by s. 7 sub-s. 1 of the Act of 1963.

The *ratio decidendi* appears in the closing paragraph of his judgment, which reads as follows (p. 258):

'It seems to me that one must consider in each case what the legislature intended. In the case of the Act of 1963 the legislature obviously intended that the planning authority should arrive at a decision without undue delay, and should give notice of the decision to the applicant. The planning authority was to be required to do its part within the appropriate period by dispatching notice of its decision, but the time of receipt of the notice seems not to be of importance. I think that the notice was given when it was sent by registered post in the manner prescribed by the Act, namely, on the 10th January, 1969. There is no reference to 'service' of the notice in sub-s. 4 of s. 26 of the Act of 1963 to bring into operation the second limb of s. 18 of the Interpretation Act, 1937. For this reason I think that the prosecutor's submission is incorrect, and that the cause shown should be allowed.'

The case of *Moody* v. *Godstone R.D.C.* [1966] 1 W.L.R. 1085 on which the learned President appears to have placed some reliance in reaching those conclusions has since been distinguished (in rather critical terms) in the later cases of *Thomas Bishop Ltd.* v. *Helmville Ltd.* [1972] 1 A.E.R. 365 and *Maltglade Ltd.* v. *St. Albans Rural District Council* [1972] 3 A.E.R. 129.

I would interpret the statute in a manner different from the learned President. Sec. 26 (4) (a) deals with the situation which is to arise where the planning authority 'do not give notice to the applicant of their decision within the appropriate period'. Sec. 7 provides that where a notice or copy of an order is required or authorised by the Act to be served on or given to a person, it shall be addressed to him and 'shall be served on or given to him in one of the following ways:

(a) where it is addressed to him by name, by delivering it to him;

(b) by leaving it at the address at which he ordinarily resides or, in a case in which an address for service has been furnished, at that address;

(c) by sending it by post, in a prepaid registered letter addressed to him at the address at which he ordinarily resides or, in a case in which an address for service has been furnished, at that address;

(d) where the address at which he ordinarily resides cannot be ascertained by reasonable inquiry and the notice or copy is so required or authorised to be given or served in respect of any land or premises, by delivering it to some person over sixteen years of age, resident or employed on such land or premises or by affixing it in a conspicuous position on or near such land or premises.'

If one leaves out of consideration for the moment, the method prescribed at '(c)', which was the method adopted in the present case, it will be seen that utilisation of any of the other methods of giving notice under the Act, which are permitted by the section, involve either personal delivery of the notice to applicant or delivery of it at the address where he normally resides, or at an address he has given for purposes of service, or by delivering it physically at the land to which the application relates or affixing it conspicuously at or near the said land. Under these provisions time continues to run against the planning authority until the notice has been physically delivered to or brought to the notice of the applicant or left at some premises where it may reasonably be regarded as having come into his possession and control.

If the decision in *Murphy* is to be followed it would achieve a much more favourable result for the planning authority, since the aplicant would be bound by notice from the moment it was posted to him by registered letter, even though, by reason of a postal strike, or loss in course of post, (eventualities which have not been so uncommon in recent years), or some other cause, the letter might never reach him or any address with which he was associated, or might only do so after a long interval of time. In the case of an applicant who failed to see a notice conspicuously displayed in his premises, or who failed to collect it from his own address, or whose agent failed to deliver it to him after it had been left at his premises, responsibility for his ignorance of the existence of the notice may be fairly regarded as resting on his own shoulders rather than on those of the planning authority, but in the case of an applicant to whom notice is sent by post and who never receives it, he is a completely innocent party and the consequences of the mishap should fall on the planning authority who have elected to use this means of communication, rather than on him.

I am of opinion that the provisions of sec. 7. of the Act, read in conjunction with sec. 26 (4)(a)(b) indicate an intention on the part of the Legislature that planning applications were to be dealt with as matters of some urgency and that there was to be an obligation on the planning authorities to communicate their decision to applicants within a strict limit of time; and further that it was intended that notice of decisions should reach applicants either personally or at their premises within the period described by the Act as 'the appropriate period'.

The Interpretation Act, 1937, sec. 18, is in ease of the sender of such statutory notice, since it raises a presumption in his favour that the notice has reached the applicant at the time when it would have been delivered to him in due course of post. The onus is thereby shifted to an applicant who asserts that the notice was not given by the planning authority within the statutory period, but if the service was by registered post and he can show that it did not, in fact, reach him within the 'appropriate period', then I am of opinion that the planning authority must suffer the consequences of resorting to this method of service rather than the more conclusive methods of personal service or service at the premises to which the application relates, or where the applicant resides, or at the address for service which he has given.

The alternative interpretation of the statute which is suggested by the judgment in the *Murphy* decision appears to me to introduce an element of considerable uncertainty into the legal position of the parties, which is illustrated by the circumstances of the present case, and which is unlikely to have been intended by the Legislature when enacting the relevant sections in their present form. Was the registered letter 'posted when it was given in to the post office during the 'Hours of Business', but after the time given as 'Latest Time for posting' for registered letters? In the case of an unregistered letter, should it be regarded as having been 'posted' when put into a post box, although it is clear from the 'times of posting' that it will not be collected until the following day?

In the present case I would incline to the view that the registered letter should be regarded as having been 'posted' when it was handed in to the post office, properly stamped, and accepted by the person in charge of the post office, even though the time was later than the time given as the latest time for posting for that particular day. The Post Office authorities had charge of the letter from that time forward and had accepted certain responsibilities for it as a registered postal packet, even though it could proceed no further on its journey to the person to whom it was addressed until the following day. I would hope, however, that notice was not given for the purposes of the Acts until the 25th September, 1979, at the earliest – a date clearly outside the five-week period prescribed by the relevant statutory provisions.

I am also of opinion that receipt of notice is a matter of considerable importance for an applicant for planning permission. A contract for the sale of the property may be held up awaiting the decision, or a developer may be waiting anxiously to enter into a building contract at the earliest possible moment if his project is approved. Any delay in such cases may be fraught with disastrous consequences for the persons concerned. For these reasons I am of opinion that it was intended by the Oireachtas that the planning authorities should be bound strictly by the time limits imposed by the Acts.

There remains the problem of the time limit for bringing proceedings, which is dealt with specifically by the Local Government (Planning and Development) Act, 1976, (No. 20 of 1976) amending section 82 of the Act of 1963 by substituting three new subsections for subsections (1), (2) and (3) of that section. The new subsection (3A) reads as follows:

> '(3A) A person shall not be prohibition, certiorari or in any other legal proceedings whatsoever question the validity of – (a) a decision of a planning authority on an application for a permission or approval under Part IV of the Principal Act, (b) a decision of the Board on any appeala or on any reference, (c) a decision of the Minister on any appeal, unless the proceedings are instituted within the period of two months commencing on the date on which the decision is given'.

This provision has already been considered recently by Barrington J. in the case of *The State (Pine Valley Developments Limited)* v. *Dublin Co. Council*, (27th May, 1981 – unreported). The application for planning approval is that case was dated the 16th July, 1980, and the decision to refuse approval was dated the 15th September, 1980. Proceedings were commenced on the 8th December, 1980, (outside the two-month limitation period, referred to), seeking an Order of Mandamus commanding the Dublin County Council to grant planning approval. It was held that the Planning Authority had not, in fact, considered and decided on the application which was submitted to them, but had sought to revive matters which had already been concluded on the application for outline permission. On this basis it was further held that at the end of the relevant two-month period they should be regarded as having given on the last day of that period. If, subsequent to that date, the defendant made an order refusing permission, there would exist two conflicting decisions of the same planning authority, and in such circumstances the earlier one must, in my opinion prevail. In other words, the applicant is entitled to rely on the earlier decision deemed by force of the statute to have been given, and to act on the faith of that decision, without having to institute proceedings to challenge the validity of the later decision.

The plaintiff has, in my opinion, taken the correct course in the present proceedings, in seeking relief in the form of a declaratory order as to the legal position which arises by virtue of the alleged failure of the defendant to give notice of its decision in relation to his planning application within the appropriate period. I agree with the statement of Barrington J. in the *Pine Valley* case that, 'at the expiration of the relevant period a decision to grant the approval is to be regarded as having come into existence by operation of law. . .'. Accordingly, no further act or decision on the part of the planning authority is then needed to entitle the applicant to proceed with his development, and it is, in my opinion, inappropriate to seek relief by way of Mandamus against the authority to compel it to make or give a decision in favour of an applicant, when it is already deemed to have done so by act and operation of law.

THE STATE (CONNOLLY) V. THE MINISTER FOR LOCAL GOVERNMENT
The High Court (Unreported) Butler J., 13 November 1968,
(Ref. No. 1968 No. 201SS)

The applicant wished to appeal a decision of the Dublin Corporation.He posted his appeal on the final day for appealing. The letter reached the Minister's office on the following day. The Minister treated the appeal as late and therefore invalid. The applicant sought an Order of Mandamus compelling the Minister to accept the appeal. The Court held that it was sufficient to post the appeal within the time allowed by section 26.

Butler J.:

. . . I have had more difficulty in deciding whether an appeal must be communicated to the Minister within the time limited by the Act or whether it is sufficient if it is posted within that time. I was surprised to learn that this point had not been decided previously either in relation to planning or to any similar statutory notices. The only decisions to which counsel were able to refer by way of analogy were those concerning the acceptance by post of an offer in commercial transactions. I have considered these cases and in particular *Henthorn* v. *Fraser* (1892) 2 Ch. 27 in which a large number of earlier decisions are referred to and considered. I think the principles therein stated may be considered as having a wider application than to purely commercial transactions and might be stated thus: where a tentative or inchoate situation has been created by the action of one party and a fixed time is ordained within which that situation can be altered by the action of another party and where by reason of general usage or of the relations between the parties, that other party's action may take the form of a letter or document transmitted through the post, all that is required is that the letter or document be posted within the time so limited. This general principle is of course subject to modification as to the manner and place of posting in particular cases.

The principle so stated applies to the present case. On the 3rd April Dublin Corporation gave outline permission which was provisional until 23rd April when, if no appeal were taken, it would have become final. Within that time any objector could alter the position and prevent the Corporation's decision from becoming final by appealing to the Minister and so making the matter subject to further consideration and decision. This appeal had to be in writing and, as I have already indicated, could be transmitted through the post. If the principles which I have suggested be correct, Mr. Connolly's appeal was complete and in time when the notice of appeal was posted on 23rd April.

This approach and reasoning would not, of course, apply were it provided that the appeal should be received by the Minister within the appointed time.[99]

LAW V. MINISTER FOR LOCAL GOVERNMENT & TRADITIONAL HOMES LTD.
The High Court (Unreported) Deale J., 9 May 1974
(Ref. No. 1973 No. 113P)

After an oral hearing at which the plaintiff was an objector, the presiding inspector submitted a report to the first-named defendant in which he recommended that soakage tests should be carried out and that if these proved satisfactory outline permission should be granted to the second-named defendants. This report was not made available to the plaintiff. The tests were carried out without his knowledge and he was not informed of their result. On the basis of the inspector's report and

[99] See section 22 of the 1976 Act which requires receipt of appeals sent by post no later than 3 days after the expiration of the 'appropriate period' as defined in section 26(5) of the 1963 Act.

the engineer's report on the tests, the first-named defendant granted outline permission to the second-named defendant to build 27 houses on a site in Shankill. The plaintiff sought to have the permission set aside on the ground that it had been granted upon evidence not in the inspector's report which he had not been given an opportunity to controvert. The defendants objected that the plaintiff was not entitled to sue because (1) he was not a party to the hearing, and (2) the right to enforce provisions of the planning legislation was vested exclusively in the planning authority and it was not for him to seek to correct injustice or infringements of legal rights arising from errors of procedure. The Court held that the plaintiff had a right to sue and set aside the decision of the Minister.

Deale J.:

It is, of course, clear beyond yea or nay that within Article 2(2)[1] the plaintiff is not or was not a party. But that does not in my opinion, mean that he cannot maintain this action. To test his right to sue, one must look far beyond Article 2(2) and at the realities of the plaintiff's position in connection with the planning application, the appeal, and in this Court.

The plaintiff began by opposing the action for planning permission by letter of 17th December 1969, along with a number of fellow residents in the area of the proposed development. That application was refused by the Dublin County Council and the second-named defendants appealed. On the appeal hearing the plaintiff appeared, along with a Mr. Knaggs for all 23 residents and objected to the granting of the permission. The Inspector in exercise of his powers and duty under Article 18(d)[1a] of the Regulations heard both Mr. Knaggs and the plaintiff and received from both written submissions on their objection, which concerned the unsuitability of septic tank drainage at this place. I mention the Inspector's duty because, in my opinion the Inspector had a duty as well as a discretion to hear those whose interest required that they should be heard as a matter of natural justice, for the Inspector was in a quasi-judicial position; or to put it in another way, it was his duty when exercising his discretion to do so judicially as far as possible. And the objection raised by Mr. Knaggs and the plaintiff was the sole matter which weighed with the inspector and made him defer his recommendation to grant planning permission. He said that, subject to satisfactory percolation tests of the soil, planning permission should be granted for housing development on the portion of the site concerned.

So, the plaintiff took an active part in the whole affair from the very start; he entered into contention with the second-named defendants at the appeal hearing; he succeeded by his contentions in preventing the granting of the permission; and he had an interest as a nearby occupier in conducting these activities. His position at the hearing in my opinion was almost indistinguishable from that of a defendant in a civil proceeding who enters into contention with the plaintiff and succeeds either in preventing the plaintiff from recovering in the action-or succeeds in having the plaintiff's remedy postponed. The only difference between a defendant's position and Mr. Law's is that in the civil action the plaintiff's remedy would be against Mr. Law, whereas in the hearing by the inspector the second-named defendant's remedy would be against the Dublin County Council.

---

[1] See now Article 35 of the 1977 Regulations.
[1a] See now Article 45(d) of the 1977 Regulations.

If the submission by Mr. Liston and Mr. Walsh on the plaintiff's absence of *locus standi* is correct, then notwithstanding that the plaintiff had a real interest in the appeal hearing and was allowed by the inspector as a matter of law to litigate that interest, he cannot come to this Court to seek to have his legal rights preserved or declared. And what is the reason for this prohibition on Mr. Law? Only the definition of the word 'party' in S.I. 216/1964. There is no other basis for the submission. But I have already said that in this Court the Statutory Instrument has been left behind. Here, we are concerned with the substance of Mr. Law's position, and not its shadowy form as found in the Statutory Instrument. The reality in my opinion, is that Mr. Law's legal right to litigate the matters he complains of cannot be taken away by something to be found in a statutory instrument which applies only to a quasi-judicial proceeding.

Mr. Walsh argued that the infirmity of Mr. Law's position is illustrated by the total absence in the Statutory Instrument of any right of a non-party to be given notice of dates or places of the hearing; and by his inability, not being a party, to cause the hearing to take place, or to advance it in any way, if the appellant should decide not to proceed. Mr. Walsh used the word 'parasitic' by way of analogy of Mr. Law's position, inasmuch as if the appellant had dropped the appeal Mr. Law would have had no standing whatever and would have been without remedy. This, of course, is true but in my opinion it would not have worked any detriment to Mr. Law if the appeal had been dropped, for in that case the refusal would have been confirmed, in effect, which is what he wanted. And if the application been originally granted instead of refused when Mr. Law could have appealed and would have been the controlling party in the appeal, and in no way disadvantages.

Mr. Sheridan pointed out that it would be absurd if the plaintiff as an objector who appealed, could have full legal rights as a party, yet have no legal rights as a party because one of the other parties appealed although he, the plaintiff, had exactly the same interest in defeating his opponent as he had had as an objector.

I am of opinion and hold that Mr. Law's participation in the events I have already set out, and his interest as a resident in preventing septic tanks from being used near his house, give him the legal right to have that interest protected in a Court of Chancery, and that he is therefore entitled to maintain this action. . . .

The second ground of objection by the defendant is that the plaintiff has no legal right to sue, for the purpose of establishing that the Minister for Local Government or the planning authority has erred in a matter of procedure, or of legal right on an appeal hearing – or as Mr. Walsh and Mr. Liston put it, has no right to act as watchdog for the public in seeking correction, by the Courts, of injustices or infringements of legal right coming from such errors of procedure. The right to enforce provisions of the planning legislation is said to be exclusively vested in the planning authority, and the recent case of *Buckley* v. *Holland Clyde Ltd.*, (Kenny J. unreported) is relied on to support this proposition. In that case the plaintiff sought a remedy, against a building company, for what he claimed was a departure by the company from the planning permission they had received, to erect a building consisting of a block of flats. The action failed, Kenny J. holding that the planning authority could sue for such departures and that a member of the public had no such right. He followed the decision of *Simpson* v. *Edinburgh Corp. & Univ. of Edinburgh* (1960) S.C. 313.

In my opinion *Buckley* v. *Holland Clyde Ltd.* is clearly distinguishable from the present case. Here there is no question of departure from planning permission, or an attempt to enforce planning policy, as in Simpson's case. Here the plaintiff claims – and has shown – a right in law springing from the appeal hearing regulations and procedure, which he says has been infringed by a wrongful act of the first-named defendant and this has damaged him – the plaintiff – but not any outside member of the public. The plaintiff appears to me to have the same right as any other citizen to come to this Court and seek a remedy for the infringment of his legal right.

GERAGHTY V. THE MINISTER FOR LOCAL GOVERNMENT
[1976] I.R. 153

The plaintiff was refused outline permission to develop her lands and she appealed to the Minister for Local Government. An oral hearing was held by an inspector appointed by the Minister. The inspector in his report recommended refusal of permission. The report was sent to his superiors in the Department of Local Government who made suggestions about the reasons which should be given for the refusal and a suggestion that the Minister use his powers under s. 22 of the 1963 Act to require a variation of the relevant development plan. Permission was refused and the plaintiff brought these proceedings seeking a declaration that the decision was *ultra vires* and void because of the actions of the officials in the Department of Local Government. The Supreme Court granted the declaration sought.

Walsh J. (with **Budd J**. agreeing):
. . . there are certain fundamental matters or principles which are unalterable. The first is that the Minister is the deciding authority. He cannot in any way be treated simply as an authority whose function is to review the recommendations or opinions, if any such are made or offered, of the person holding or conducting the inquiry. The second is that the Minister is acting *ultra vires* if he comes to a conclusion or makes a decision which is not supportable upon the evidence or the materials properly before him. Thirdly, neither the Minister nor the person holding or conducting the inquiry can come to a conclusion of fact unless there is evidence upon which such a conclusion could be formed. Fourthly, if the person holding or conducting the inquiry should come to a conclusion of fact and should express it, the Minister is not bound to come to the same conclusion of fact and is quite free to form a contrary conclusion if there is evidence and materials properly before him from which he could come to such a conclusion. Fifthly, to enable the Minister to come to any decision, the person holding or conducting the inquiry must transmit to the Minister a report which fairly and accurately informs the Minister of the substance of the evidence and the arguments for and against the issues raised at the inquiry by those represented at the inquiry.

Ordinarily, the Minister can only look at what is in the report.[2] He cannot avail himself of other testimony, expert or otherwise, or of other material from within his department or elsewhere without informing the persons concerned and giving them an opportunity to deal with that evidence or material. It may well be that in practice the person holding or conducting the inquiry, in most if not all cases, will be an expert – an engineer, an architect or person of some such qualifications – but the Act does not require that such a person should be the only one to hold or

---

[2] See section 17 and 24 of the 1976 Act.

conduct such an inquiry. No doubt, in any such case, the inquiry must necessarily benefit from being held or conducted by a person of such expert knowledge; but that does not entitle the Minister to permit his own responsibility and statutory duty to make a decision to be partly or wholly laid upon or undertaken by some other person. . . .

In cases such as the present where the inquiry falls within the terms of s. 82 sub-s. 2 of the Act of 1963, the procedure laid down is procedure by way of oral hearing.[3] It appears to me that the effect of that is that all materials, evidence, submissions and observations going to the merits of the particular subject matter of the inquiry must be laid open for examination at an oral hearing, and nowhere else. If such matters should come to light or arise for consideration only after the termination of the oral hearing then there is provision for a further oral hearing made by article 16[4] of the Regulations of 1964. Such further oral hearing, according to the Regulations requires the consent of the Minister before it can be undertaken.[5] It is not necessary here to consider in what circumstances a Minister could validly refuse such further oral hearing, but it is clear that, if he should do so, he cannot then base any part of his decision upon materials which would have been laid before and examined at the oral hearing if he had consented to such a hearing.

In the present case the procedure prescribed by s. 82 sub-s. 2 of the Act of 1963 was not followed in that certain materials, which were put before the defendant and which were taken into account by him in arriving at his decision, were materials of a type which could properly only have been put forward for consideration and examination at an oral hearing and they were not raised or put forward at an oral hearing. The facts of this case have been so fully set out by the learned trial judge that it is unnecessary for me to detail the history of the particular events which led to the making of the defendant's decision. It is sufficient to say that the evidence as found by the learned trial judge, discloses that the defendant's decision was *ultra vires* because it took into account such materials. These materials should have been subject to the scrutiny and examination of an oral hearing and, if that had been done, the defendant would have received from the person conducting the inquiry a report containing an adequate and unbiased record of the material presented and one which would fairly and accurately inform him of the substance of the respective arguments which were made by the protagonists at such hearing.

In my view, the Minister is not bound by the findings of fact of the person conducting the inquiry, if such person chooses to make findings of fact; but the Minister can only make such findings of fact as are sustainable on the evidence put before him. If the Oireachtas had intended the Minister to be bound by the findings of fact of such person, it could quite easily have said so by saying that the Minister's decision should be based upon the findings of the person holding or conducting the inquiry. It did not do so. If it is sought to construe the Minister's powers as being essentially based upon being bound by the findings of fact of the person conducting the inquiry, the question is immediately raised as to whether he is bound by the primary facts and is free to draw different inferences from the facts or whether that

---

[3] Under the 1976 Act the Board was given a discretion to hold an oral hearing unless directed to hold on by the Minister. Since the coming into force of section 15 of the 1983 Act on the 25th October 1983, the Board has an absolute discretion to hold an oral hearing unless the appeal (or reference) is of a class or description coming within section 15(2) of the 1983 Act.
[4] See now Article 46 of the 1977 Regulations.
[5] See now Article 46(3) of the 1977 Regulations.

is also a matter for the person conducting the inquiry. In other words such a situation would put the Minister in a somewhat similar position to that of this Court in hearing workmen's compensation cases. In my view, the wording of the Act of 1963, which refers expressly to a report as distinct from findings, makes it clear that the Minister not merely makes the final decision but also decides all the necessary constituent elements which go to make up the final decision. This may well be regarded as an unsatisfactory way of dealing with the matter but that is a matter for the Oireachtas.

Henchy J.:

. . . .The only guide in the Act of 1966[6] to the respective functions and powers of the Minister and the inspector is what is obliquely indicated by the statement in article 5 of the Third Schedule to that Act that when an objection to the making of a compulsory purchase is duly made, the Minister shall not (save in special cases) confirm the compulsory purchase order 'until he has caused to be held a public local inquiry into such objection and until he has considered such objection and the report of the person who held the inquiry. . .'. From this brief statement it was deduced in *Murphy's Case* that it was for the inspector merely to make a report of what took place at the inquiry. Section 82, sub-s. 2 of the Act of 1963, with which we are concerned here, points to a different conclusion. It makes very clear that when an oral hearing is requested, there *shall* be an *oral hearing* of the appeal;[7] such oral hearing shall be conducted by a person appointed for that purpose by the Minister; the appointed person shall furnish to the Minister a report *on* (not *of*) the oral hearing; and the Minister shall consider that report before he gives his decision.

Therefore, it is clear that the appointed person is no mere recorder for the Minister of what took place at the oral hearing. If that was what he was expected to be, the section would have merely required him to furnish a report *of* (not *on*) the oral hearing. A report on the oral hearing imports an accurate, but not necessarily exhaustive, account of what was presented at the oral hearing in the way of evidence and submissions; the appointed person's finding of fact; together with such observations, inferences, submissions and recommendations as he thinks proper to put forward and which arise out of the evidence and submissions or out of any visit and inspection he may have made under the power given to him to do so by s. 82, sub-s. 5(a) of the Act of 1963. An accurate and reasonable account of what took place at the hearing is necessary – of the evidence, to support the findings of fact, and of the submissions to make clear the parties' attitudes and to identify the points of law and, in particular to enable the Minister to see if there is a point of law which he might wish to refer to the High Court under s. 82, sub-s. 3 of the Act of 1963.

It is inherent in the scheme for hearing the appeal that the facts shall be found by the appointed person. He, and not the Minister, will have seen and heard the witnesses and from that it should be inferred that the legislature intended, in order to preserve constitutionally guaranteed standards of fair and just procedure, that,

---

[6] The Housing Act 1966.
[7] See now section 15 of the 1983 Act, which makes the holding of oral hearings a matter at the discretion of the Board, unless they are of a prescribed class or description within the meaning of section 15(2).

where an oral hearing is provided for, conflicts of fact will not be resolved by a person who learns of the evidence only at second hand from a report and whose conclusions might conflict with those of the person who saw and heard the witnesses. Furthermore, s. 82, sub-s. 2(c) of the Act of 1963, in prescribing merely for 'consideration by the Minister of the report before he gives his decision' indicates that, while the decision on the appeal is reserved for the Minister, his function in regard to the report is to consider it before he gives his decision.

For these reasons I conclude that the appointed person *must* include in his report a fair and accurate summary of the evidence and submissions together with his findings of fact, and that he *may* include observations, inferences, submissions and recommendations limited to what took place at the hearing. Only the findings of fact are binding on the Minister, and while the decision to allow or disallow the appeal is reserved solely for the Minister, he cannot make that decision until he has considered the report. . . .

As a layman, he may be lacking in the necessary understanding and appreciation of those matters or of the technical considerations underlying the application, so the exercise of his powers must be deemed to include a right to inform himself by expert opinion, whether from experts within his Department or from outside experts, as to the nature and scope of the application, as to his discretion in the matter, and as to the implications, within the context of the Act and having regard to decisions in other cases, of the grant or refusal of the permission. But the Minister may not allow himself to be informed, under the guise of expert advice or otherwise, as to factual matters not dealt with in the report which might be capable of augmenting, affirming or diminishing the degree of factual proof found by the appointed person in the report. Were the Minister to do so, he would be violating the assurance of an oral hearing given to the parties by s. 82, sub-s. 2 for there would then be only a partly-oral hearing. Furthermore, since in deciding the appeal the Minister is acting in a quasi-judicial capacity, he must not act in disregard of natural justice, so if new facts or probative material in relation to the appeal are brought to his notice he should not take them into reckoning for the purpose of the appeal until the parties have had an opportunity of dealing with them at an oral hearing, and until the appointed person has reported on them. Article 16[8] of the Regulations of 1964 provides for such a further oral hearing to be held with the consent of the Minister.

Gannon J. (Griffin J. affirming):
 . . . The fact that the legislature requires the Minister on an appeal from the planning authority to deal with an appeal by an applicant in the same manner as if the application had been made to him in the first instance is an indication that the legislature does not intend that the Minister should give effect on such an appeal to a course which would have been available to him under s. 22 of the Act of 1963.

Before making his decision, the Minister must consider the evidence and facts reported to him by his inspector for the purpose of drawing therefrom the inferences upon which he, the Minister, may make his decision. Insofar as the Minister may find it necessary, when considering the report, to obtain elucidation on any aspect thereof, he may do so by enquiry of the inspector but limited to the matter

---

[8] See now Article 46 of the 1977 Regulations.

before him in the report. When considering the report the Minister may find it necessary to consult the High Court on a point of law and is authorised by s. 82, sub-s. 3 of the Act to do so. He may also find it necessary to consult a legal adviser, or a planning adviser to obtain technical assistance or advice of some other nature to assist him in the making of his determination. Enquiry by the Minister in relation to the report should not seek or invite advice or recommendations on matters outside the scope of the report or on matters extraneous to or not pertinent to the subject matter of the particular oral hearing. His enquiry should be made only to the inspector, save on matters of such technical nature as might properly necessitate consulting an expert such as a lawyer or planning expert. If the Minister should find it necessary to have the assistance of a planning expert upon his consideration of the inspector's report, he might consider an officer of the planning section of his Department an appropriate planning expert to give him such assistance. But a person so chosen by the Minister for expert advice of that nature in such circumstances would be acting as a personal adviser to the Minister because of his particular skill and not because he happens to be an officer of a particular section of the Department. Needless to say, an officer of the Department who might have given evidence before the inspector on the oral hearing should not be referred to or consulted by the Minister after the hearing.

The Minister may not seek or have regard to a further opinion of any other expert chosen by him or tendered to him after the report has been made in addition to or in substitution for the expert evidence obtained at the enquiry and referred to in the report. The only purpose of, and circumstances for having, additional expert assistance of any sort is to qualify the Minister to make the determination which he alone must make on the evidence and the material presented to him in the report on the enquiry and then only after he has considered the report. In seeking such advice or technical assistance, the Minister may not delegate to such adviser the function of making the decision which it is the Minister's duty to make on the appeal. The Minister may not invite the inspector or any other person to make for the Minister the decision required of him under the duty imposed on him by the statute. In the discharge of this duty the Minister is not exercising his executive powers, nor are the officers of his department entitled to intervene in or interfere with the communications between the Minister and the person appointed by him to conduct the oral hearing: see *Murphy* v. *Corporation of Dublin*.[9]

Prima facie, the matters and factors which would be appropriate for the consideration of the Minister in the exercise of his executive functions under s. 22 of the Act of 1963 would not be pertinent or relevant for the consideration at the oral hearing. If such matters should appear to be relevant for consideration by the Minister, they should be raised and dealt with at the oral hearing before the inspector but should not otherwise be introduced into the report on the hearings: see Article 9 of the Regulations of 1964.[10] The introduction otherwise of extraneous matter of that nature into the report or into the consideration of the Minister as a factor for his determination on an appeal to him, would render his determination invalid.

---

[9] See [1972] I.R. 215.

[10] There is no equivalent regulation in the 1977 Regulations. See however, section 24 of the 1976 Act.

KILLINEY AND BALLYBRACK DEVELOPMENT ASSOCIATION V. MINISTER FOR LOCAL GOVERNMENT AND TEMPLEFINN ESTATES LTD.
(1974) 112 I.L.T.R. 69

The plaintiff sought to have a grant of planning permission for a housing development made by the first-named defendant to the second-named defendant set aside *inter alia* because the report of the inspector who presided over the oral hearing of the appeal included matters which could not validly be included and where the Minister did not state reasons for his decision the Court must presume that the Minister acted upon that evidence unless it was proved otherwise. The Court held that the report did include matters which could not validly be included and quashed the decision.

[*N.B.* This decision must be read in the light of subsequent Act of 1976 and in particular in the light of section 23 and Regulation 42 of the 1977 Regulations.]

Finlay J.:
The power of the Courts to interfere with the decision of persons or bodies which are not ordinarily considered to be Courts of Justice has been clearly set out by Lord Justice Atkin in the case of *Rex* v. *The Electricity Commissioners ex parte London Electricity Joint Committee Company* [1924] 1 KB 171. In the course of his judgment he there said that

> 'the operation of the writs (of prohibition and certiorari) has extended to control the proceedings of bodies which do not claim to be and would not be recognised as Courts of Justice. Whenever any body of persons having legal authority to determine questions affecting the rights of subjects and having the duty to act judicially, act in excess of their legal authority, they are subject to the controlling jurisdiction of the King's Bench Division exercised in these writs.'

This general statement of the position was cited with approval by Lord Reid in the case of *Ridge* v. *Baldwin* reported at 1964 Appeal Cases at page 40. I find these authorities persuasive but I also find in the case of *Murphy* v. *The Corporation of Dublin* reported in 1972 Irish Reports at page 215 a clear expression of view by the Supreme Court as to the control which the Courts are bound to exercise over proceedings so close in type and character to the decision of a Minister under the Local Government (Planning and Development) Act 1963 as to be in my view a binding precedent upon me in relation to this case. . . .

The procedure provided by the Housing Acts for the determination by the Minister for Local Government of objections to the making of a compulsory purchase order are similar to the extent of almost being identical to the provisions for the determination by him of a planning appeal including of course the direction for the holding of a public oral hearing and the report of an inspector to the Minister who upon receiving such report is the deciding authority. At page 238 of the judgment of Mr. Justice Walsh in *Murphy* v. *Dublin Corporation* the following passage occurs:

> 'In this context it is necessary to examine the precise function of the inspector in this role. By statute the Minister is the one who has to decide the matter – not the inspector. In doing so, the Minister must act judicially and within the bounds

of constitutional justice. No direct assistance is obtainable from the statute as to the precise functions of the inspector or of his powers. It is clear, however, that in so far as the conduct of the inquiry is concerned he is acting as recorder for the Minister. He may regulate the procedure within the permissible limits of the inquiry over which he presides. In as much as he is there for the purpose of reporting the Minister, the inspector's function is to convey to the Minister, if not a *verbatim* account of the entire of the proceedings before him, at least a fair and accurate account of what transpired and one which gives accurately to the Minister the evidence and the submissions of each party because it is upon this material that the Minister must make his decision and on no other. The inspector has no advisory function nor has he any function to arrive at a preliminary judgment which may or may not be confirmed or varied by the Minister. If the inspector's report takes the form of a document, then it must contain an account of all the essentials of the proceedings over which he presided. In my view, it is no part of his function to arrive at any conclusion. If the Minister is influenced in his decision by the opinions of the inspector or the conclusions of the inspector, the Minister's decision will be open to review. It may be quashed and set aside if shown to be based on materials other than those disclosed at the public hearing. . .'.

I can find no distinction in principle between this procedure under the Housing Acts and the procedure under the Planning Acts. Each concerns and vitally affects the property rights of citizens, each is a decision imposed upon a Minister of State who does not himself hold the inquiry. Each provides for an inquiry, however, to be held by a person nominated by him with a duty to report to him. Although the Planning Act and Regulations made under it do provide powers for the inspector it cannot be said on my reading of them that they define his precise functions nor is there any suggestion that he has any advisory function.[11]

I therefore conclude that the test which I must apply to the issues in this case is the test laid down by Mr. Justice Walsh in the portion of his judgment which I have just above quoted.

Arising out of those principles the main challenge on the facts revealed by the report of Mr. Cassidy the person directed to hold the oral hearing in this case is two-fold. Firstly it is asserted on behalf of the plaintiff that there was no evidence contained in the report of the public hearing to support a view that the development proposed would not, by reason of the demand it made upon existing sewerage facilities and the inadequacy of those facilities cause pollution on the sea-shore at Killiney and it is argued that without a finding based on such evidence that pollution would not be caused the Minister could not make a valid decision under the Planning Acts to grant permission.

Secondly it is asserted that in two particular instances the report of Mr. Cassidy contains a reference to facts and evidence which was not presented at the oral hearing and that therefore in the words of Mr. Justice Walsh's decison the Minister's decision must be presumed to have been based on materials other than those disclosed at the public hearing.

With regard to the first of these contentions it is important to emphasise that I cannot be concerned with the weight of evidence produced, either for or against any particular issue arising at the inquiry, nor am I concerned with whether I would

[11] See section 23 of the 1976 Act at page 248.

decide upon such evidence the issues in the way which the Minister has apparently decided them. A review of the Minister's decision based upon an inquiry as to whether there was evidence to support it seems to me to be in principle indistinguishable from the review by an Appellate Court of the decision of a jury directed to the question as to whether there was evidence upon which the jury could reach its verdict. It is necessary therefore only to seek in the report of Mr. Cassidy, the accuracy of which is not challenged, evidence upon which the Minister could conclude that the development for which permission was being sought could be carried out without polluting the adjoining area. . .

The contention that the report includes material other than that disclosed at the public hearing upon which the Minister must be presumed to have acted, is directed towards two specific portions of the report. The first is to be found at the very end of page thirty-eight and reads as follows: 'It has been clearly accepted at the oral hearing that the works are over-loaded. It has also been suggested that new provisions for sewerage disposal is imminent. I have discussed this (with) our own sanitary inspectors and indeed have made inquiries with the relevant local authority. There is no doubt that the works are now coping with a vastly greater load than that originally envisaged.' It is submitted on behalf of the plaintiffs that this constitutes the relating by the inspector of the result of some discussion he had outside the public oral hearing with some official or officials of a local authority and that it is within the definition of material other than that disclosed at the public hearing. This contention may be technically correct but a consideration of the phrase somewhat carefully used by Mr. Cassidy at this part of his report, would indicate that he has not really conveyed to the Minister what the result of his discussions with the relevant local authority were nor can it be said to constitute any fact or recital of a fact upon which the Minister might act or which might influence his opinion. Conceivably it is open to the construction of containing some sort of implied corroboration of what Mr. Gibbons had given evidence about at the public hearing but I think this is a rather far-fetched interpretation of this particular paragraph of this report.

The second main portion of the report immediately following at page thirty-nine of which the plaintiff complains is however in a different category. That reads as follows 'On the other hand I have recently and carefully walked along the line of the stream and the river and the fore-shore on the eastern side of the old railway culvert for a distance of about half a mile or so and can state that I have seen no clear evidence of raw human excreta present. I should stress, however, that I am speaking from a comparatively unqualified point of view. Both the stream and the river do indicate substantial discolouration and there is certainly in the river evidence of floating matter but a reasonably close visual examination indicates that this appears to be organic debris from the bottom of the river which has broken off and is floating down stream. This matter is easily dispersed when hit with stones. A somewhat more disturbing element which was noticed on the shore-line was the presence of numerous remnants of sanitary towels. I should state that they were not in an objectionable state and it is probable that they had been washed up on the shore-line possibly from the out-fall at sea having been immersed possibly for a substantial period in the sea water, they are relatively innocuous nevertheless they are a matter for some substantial concern.' This undoubtedly constitutes a statement of fact by Mr. Cassidy of the result of a visual observation by him of the area in respect of which the issue with regard to pollution and sewerage arose. There is no indication in the report that the fact of the visit nor the observations or results of the observations made by Mr. Cassidy were disclosed by him at the public hearing and *prima facie* this falls within the definition of material not disclosed at the hearing.

Its relevance and importance to any decision which the Minister had to make with regard to this question of pollution arises from the fact that Professor Fitzgerald a witness called on behalf of the plaintiff, is recorded at page twenty-one of the report as having stated in evidence that there were signs of sewerage rubbish etc. along the beach and that there were also signs of raw sewerage. Mr. Jones on the other hand, in a portion of his evidence . . . stated that on a number of visits there was no sign of raw sewerage. A situation had thus arisen in the reported evidence that there was a direct conflict of fact in regard to this question and it is possible to construe the account given by Mr. Cassidy of the result of his own visit and observations in the area as corroborating the evidence of Mr. Jones and aiding in the contradiction of the evidence of Professor Fitzgerald.

Counsel for the defendants contend that there is a direct statutory power in the person directed to hold the oral hearing to visit the site in respect of which the planning permission is sought and that this must be taken to be a statutory endorsement of his right having so visited it to report the result of that visit to the Minister.

This right of inspection is provided by section 82 sub-section 5 of the Act. . . [section quoted][12]

It appears to me quite reasonable and logical that the section should be construed as providing a right of inspection for the person holding the oral hearing so that he would be in a position fully and clearly to understand the evidence which was being given before him and appreciate the nature of the submissions being made and thus faithfully and accurately report on both those matters to the Minister. It seems to me further as I have indicated necessary to construe it in this way and with this purpose only so as to ensure that the decision of the Minister will be one reached by him acting within the bounds of constitutional justice. If it were to be construed as the defendants contend then the Minister in considering the report of a visual inspection would be acting on what is in fact evidence not disclosed at the oral hearing and which the party concerned had no opportunity to refute or challenge.

It is further contended on behalf of the defendants that even if there is not a special statutory protection for the report of Mr. Cassidy of the result of his visual inspection of the adjoining lands that the terms of that report the observations made by him and his conclusions are of minimal or neutral evidential value. I am prepared to accept that it is not a strongly worded report nor does it urge upon the Minister any particular view with regard to the conflict of evidence arising in the other parts of the report on this issue of pollution. As I have already indicated however, in the particular context of the report where there was direct clash of evidence between two of the witnesses called as to whether raw sewerage was to be found or seen on the fore-shore and on the adjoining area and a factual account by Mr. Cassidy of what he saw and did not see on the occasion of his visit is capable of influencing the Minister.

As I have indicated at the outset of my judgment, it was contended on behalf of

[12] See page 253.

the plaintiff that if evidence not disclosed at the public hearing was included in the material before the Minister then because of the absence of any reasons in the decision of the Minister indicating upon what evidence he relied and upon what evidence he did not rely that the Court must interfere and set aside the decision of the Minister. I accept this in this particular instance as a sound submission of law. Again I find the position of the Court asked to review the decision of the Minister in this case as being similar in this context to the function of an Appellate Court asked to review the decision of a jury. It is clear beyond dispute that if for example, in a criminal or civil case there has been admitted before a jury evidence which the Appellate Court holds to be inadmissible and if that evidence was capable of being acted upon by the jury the Court must set aside its verdict. I see no reason why a different principle can apply to the review of the decision of the Minister carrying out a function of a judicial nature in this case and accordingly I conclude that the inclusion of this account by Mr. Cassidy in his report of the result of his visual inspection of the area adjoining the land be developed is fatal to the validity of the decision of the Minister.

FINNEGAN V. AN BORD PLEANALA AND IDA AND RAYBESTOS MANHATTAN (IRE) LTD.
The Supreme Court (Unreported) O'Higgins C.J., 27 July 1979)
Ref. No. 30–1979)

The plaintiff sought a declaration that sections 15, 16 and 18 of the 1976 Act were unconstitutional. [See page 49 for excerpts.]

APPEALS TO THE COURT
The High Court has supervisory jurisdiction over the planning authority and the planning board and may grant relief by means of State-side Orders and Declarations where they purport to act outside their jurisdiction or refuse to do that which they are legally required to do.

Where an Order of *Certiorari* or Prohibition is sought or it is otherwise sought to question a decision of the planning authority for permission or approval under Part IV of the 1963 Act or a decision of the Boad or any appeal or reference or the Minister on any appeal the proceedings must be instituted within two months of the giving of the decision. (See section 82(3A) as inserted by Section 42(3A) of the 1976 Act). Proceedings other than *Certiorari* or Prohibition may be instituted outside the two month period provided they do not question the validity of the decision.

In *The State (Pine Valley Developments Limited)* v. *Dublin County Council*[13] the prosecutor obtained an absolute Order of Mandamus outside the two month period commanding the respondent to grant an approval on foot of an outline permission granted by the Minister by arguing that the proceedings did not question the validity of the planning authority's decision to refuse approval but merely sought to require them to provide evidence of a default permission. In the Supreme Court it was held that no question of a default permission could arise in the particular circumstances of the case, but the Minister's decision could be impugned outside the two month period because at the time the decision was made section 82 (3A) had not yet come into force. It was not necessary for the Court to consider the

[13] See page 309.

validity of the prosecutor's argument that the Mandamus proceedings did not question the validity of the planning authority's decision to refuse approval.

In *Freeney* v. *Bray Urban District Council* it was held *inter alia* that the plaintiff was not questioning the validity of the defendant's decison to refuse permission by seeking declarations that he had a default permission and that the notice to refuse permission was null and void, with the result that the proceedings could succeed outside the two month period. In the course of his judgment O'Hanlon J. further held that declaratory proceedings were appropriate rather than Mandamus proceedings where it was claimed that the plaintiff had a default permission. This was on the ground that it was unnecessary for the planning authority to do anything further. This, however, ignores the fact that the grant of permission is a two-step process and all the applicant gets by default is a decision to grant permission. It is still necessary for the planning authority to make an actual grant under section 26(9) of the 1963 Act. It is submitted that even assuming the applicant has obtained all other necessary permission he is not entitled to proceed with his development until he has a grant under section 26(9) of the 1963 Act. For this reason it may be necessary to bring Mandamus proceedings to compel the planning authority to make the grant. (See also *Alf-a-Bet Promotions Limited* v. *Bundoran UDC*[14])

Where it applies section 82(3A) is a complete bar and the invalidity of a decision cannot be relied upon in defence outside – the two month period nor will the Court consider the validity of the decision in deciding to exercise its discretion to grant or withhold Mandamus. (See the High Court, *The State (Finglas Industrial Estates Limited* v. *Dublin County Council*[15])

Section 82 (3A) does not apply to decisions made by the Board otherwise than on appeal or reference. Thus a decision by the Board fixing the amount of contribution payable under a condition attached to a planning permission may be questioned outside the two month period. (See The Supreme Court, *The State (Finglas Industrial Estates Limited)* v. *Dublin County Council*)

In deciding how to exercise its discretion the Court will look at all the circumstances of the case including the reasons for which the Order is sought. (See *The State (Toft)* v. *Galway Corporation*;[16] *The State (Abenglen Properties Limited)* v. *Dublin Corporation)*[17] the conduct of the applicant including delay in pursuing the State Side Order (See *The State (Conlon Construction Limited)* v. *Cork County Council*;[18] *The State (Toft)* v. *Galway Corporation*[19]) the availability of an alternative remedy and its adequacy (See *The State (Abenglen Properties Limited)* v. *Dublin Corporation*[20] *The State (NCE)* v. *Dublin County Council*[21]) and the harm which has been suffered by the applicant (See *The State (Abenglen Properties Limited)* v. *Dublin Corporation*;[22] *The State (Toft)* v. *Galway Corporation.*[23] Where the Order sought will not achieve the object of the applicant in seeking it no Order will be made (see *The State (Abenglen Properties Limited)* v. *Dublin Corporation).*[24] nor

[14] See page 181.
[15] See page 313.
[16] See page 316.
[17] See page 316.
[18] See page 321.
[19] See page 316.
[20] See page 316.
[21] See page 322.
[22] See page 316.
[23] See page 316.
[24] See page 316.

will an Order be made where another equally or more effective or beneficial remedy exists (see *The State (Abenglen Properties Ltd.*) v. *Dublin Corporation*). Once the applicant has elected to pursue another remedy he will not usually be allowed to change his mind and seek a State-Side Order. In *The State (NCE)* v. *Dublin County Council*[25] however, it was held that the applicant could bring Mandamus proceedings although he had appealed to the Board because at the time he appealed he was unaware of his right to Mandamus and the appeal was not an equally beneficial remedy.

APPEALS TO THE COURT

STATE (PINE VALLEY DEVELOPMENTS LIMITED) V. DUBLIN COUNTY COUNCIL
The High Court (Unreported), Barrington J., 27 May 1981 (Ref. No. 1980 No. 55 SS)
The Supreme Court [1982] I.L.R.M. 196

The Minister granted outline permission to the prosecutors which contravened the Development Plan on an appeal from a refusal of full permission from the respondents. At no time was the Minister asked to give his consent to the planning authority contravening the Development Plan. When the prosecutor later sought approval the respondents refused for the same reasons they had refused the original application together with one further reason. The prosecutor sought an Order for Mandamus commanding the respondents to grant approval. Barrington J. granted the Order in the High Court which Order the respondents appealed. It was not indicated to the High Court Judge that Section 42 (3A) of the 1976 Act was not in force at the time the Minister made his decision. The Supreme Court refused to make an Order on the grounds that the Minister could not on his own motion grant permission which contravened the Development Plan.

As a result of the decision given in the Supreme Court of the Local Government (Planning and Development) Act 1982 was enacted to validate permissions granted by the Minister in contravention of the development plan.

Barrington J.:
. . . The decision in the present case was given on the 15th of September 1980. The present proceedings were not instituted until the 8th December 1980. If the present proceedings were *certiorari* proceeding or prohibition proceedings it is clear that section 42 sub-section 3A would be a complete answer. These proceedings however, are mandamus proceedings. The problem is what relevance the provision that a person may not 'question' the validity of a planning permission or approval 'in any other legal proceedings whatsoever' has for the present application. Mr. Smyth draws an analogy with s. 78 of the Housing Act 1966. He submits that Mr. Walsh is questioning the validity of the decision of the planning authority dated the 15th of September 1980. That order is there and must be presumed to be valid until the contrary is shown, and the contrary, he submits can not now be shown.

Mr. Walsh, however, submits that he is not questioning the validity of the decision of the 15th September 1980 explaining his proceedings do not do so expressly, or by implication. He says that he is showing that the planning authority did not consider his applicaion for approval within the four walls of the outline

[25] See page 322.

permission. As this application was the only application before them he is showing that they did not consider his application at all. He submits that it might be possible to have shown this in a number of ways and by different kinds of evidence. He has shown it by reference to the terms of the notification of a decision to refuse dated the 15th September 1980. Once he shows that he has placed an application before the planning authority and that the planning authority did not consider and decide on that application within two months from the date on which it was lodged then, Mr. Walsh claims, he is carried by section 26 sub-section 4 of the 1963 Act which provides that a decision by the planning authority to grant the approval shall be regarded as having been given on the last day of that period. The application in the present case was lodged on the 16th July 1980 but was never considered or decided by the planning authority. Therefore at the expiration of the relevant period a decision to grant the approval is to be regarded as having come into existence at the expiration of the relevant period. This decision comes into existence by operation of law and the only purpose of the present proceedings is to direct the planning authority to provide evidence of the decision which the law regards as having come into existence.

I have found both these submissions forceful and have had difficulty in making up my mind between them. On the whole I prefer Mr. Walsh's submission.

Mr. Smyth has argued that the effect of such a conclusion would, in many cases, be to deprive innocent people of their right of appeal against a planning decision as they might not know of its existence until too late. But it appears to me that this risk exists in every case in which the Statute deems a permission or an approval to have been granted because of some failure or default on the part of the planning authority. The applicant for permission cannot be blamed for this and he is entitled to such rights as the statute confers upon him.

In all the circumstances I disallow the cause shown and direct that an absolute order of mandamus issue.

In the Supreme Court
Henchy J.:

. . . I unreservedly reject the contention put forward on behalf of the developers that the Minister, when hearing an appeal from the refusal of a permission, had power, of his own motion and in the absence of a request therefor from the planning authority, to grant the permission even though it materially contravened the plan. It is true that such a power was granted to An Bord Pleanala by s. 14 (8) of the 1976 Act, but it was never given, either expressly or implicitly, to the Minister. . . . By granting the outline permission, the Minister violated an essential part of the plan, and he did so by disregarding the conditions precedent to a permitted material contravention of the plan, ignoring the rights of the planning authority and of those who were entitled to get notices and to be heard before such a material contravention could take place . . . .

The outline planning permission granted by the Minister in this case was clearly *ultra vires* and therefore a nullity. Counsel for the developer has contended, however, that even if that be so, there is now an absolute statutory bar on any attempt to question the validity of the Minister's decision in any legal proceedings. The source of this submission is s. 82 (3A) of the 1963 Act which provides that (quotation of the section follows):[26]

[26] See page 252.

This limited ouster of judicial intervention was not contained in the original Act of 1963. It was interpolated by s. 42 of the 1976 Act. The 1976 Act, however, came into operation piecemeal by statutory instruments which the Minister was allowed to make by s. 46 (3) of the 1976 Act; and s. 42 of the 1976 Act did not come into operation until the 15 March 1977 (by S.I. No. 56 of 1977). The result was that the Minister's grant of outline planning permission on the 10 March 1977 was made before s. 82 (3A) had come into operation. In consequence, its nullity for having been made *ultra vires* was not subject to the time bar introduced by s. 82 (3A). The latter subsection was clearly intended to apply only to cases where an aggrieved person had the full period of two months in which to question the Minister's decision. I deem it to be a fundamental rule of judicial interpretation that when a statutory provision purports to oust, after a specified period, the jurisdiction of the courts to question the validity of a decision which up to then would have been open to question in the courts, the purported ouster will not have effect unless the exclusionary provision was in operation when the decision in question was made. The ouster of jurisdiction aimed at by s. 82 (3A) was intended to remove at the end of two months the risk that the grant of permission could be questioned in the courts at any time, thus enabling duly granted development to be retarded by delaying tactics in the courts long after the grant of permission had been made. S. 82 (3A), therefore, partakes of the characteristics of a statute of limitations. Apart from the facts that the courts should be reluctant to surrender their inherent right to enter on a question of the validity of what are *prima facie* justifiable matters, it would be a wrong and unjust method of statutory interpretation to attribute to the legislature the intention that a developer could rely on s. 82 (3A) so as to get the benefit of a demonstrably void decision when the full period of two months allowed for questioning it was not open to him – not open for the simple reason that s. 82 (3A) did not become operative until after the decision had been made.

I would hold, therefore, that in the special circumstance of this case the developer cannot use s. 82 (3A) to shield what was plainly a void outline planning permission from being questioned in the courts.

The present appeal is from an order of the High Court granting an absolute order of mandamus commanding the planning authority to grant full planning permission to the developers in implementation of the outline planning permission granted by the Minister. Because, for the reasons I have adduced, that decision of the Minister was not given immunity from being questioned by s. 82 (3A) of the 1963 Act; because its validity has in fact been questioned by the planning authority in these proceedings; and because it now appears that the decision was *ultra vires* and therefore a nullity, the grant of an order of mandamus to implement a ministerial decision which was clearly devoid of validity would not be a proper exercise of the Court's jurisdiction. . . .

Finally, I should deal with the submission of counsel for the developer that, because the planning authority did not within 'the appropriate period' deal with the application to implement the outline permission granted by the Minister, the application should be deemed to have been granted under s. 26 (4) of the 1963 Act. The short answer to this submission is that permission by default under s. 26 (4) (even if the application was made in compliance with the relevant regulations) cannot be held to have been given if it would contravene s. 26 read as a whole. Here it undoubtedly would, particularly s. 26 (3). An order of mandamus in a case such as this is discretionary, and it would be a wrongful exercise of the court's discretion to issue such an order when its effect would be to violate both the spirit and the letter of the statute.

Walsh J. (Hederman J. concurring):

. . . Because of the fact that the statute gave the Minister a particular jurisdiction with reference to any such application to contravene the development plan by the planning authority but was silent with regard to any power to do so on his own initiative on appeal where no such application had been made I am satisfied that the statute never contemplated and cannot be construed as meaning that the Minister had such a power. . . . As was pointed out in the decision of this Court in *Murphy* v. *The Minister for Local Government*, the Minister as such appellate tribunal is not exercising any of the executive functions of the State but is simply exercising statutory functions conferred upon a *persona designata*. He has no function in the matter outside those either expressly or by necessary implication conferred on him by the statute. In my opinion there is nothing in the statute which can be found to substantiate the view that such power was expressly or by necessary implication conferred upon the Minister. I am satisfied that the outline planning permission granted by the Minister was made without jurisdiction in so far as it permitted contraventions of the development plan and was therefore *ultra vires* and of no legal effect.

The present proceedings were brought for the purpose of obtaining an order from the Court to compel the planning authority to grant planning permission in conformity with the outline planning permission granted by the Minister. Notwithstanding the order of the Minister the provisions of section 26 (3) of the Act of 1963 still bind the planning authority and they are not entitled to grant any planning permission which would materially contravene the development plan in the absence of a permission to that effect granted by the Minister upon application made by them. As no such application was made and as no valid permission to that effect was ever granted by the Minister the planning authority cannot be compelled to violate the provisions of the Act.

The prosecutors have sought to rely upon the default procedure provided for by section 26, subsection (4) of the Act of 1963. . . The present application, in as much as it is an application for a permission which the planning authority has no statutory or other power to grant because to do so would amount to a contravention of their own development plan, is clearly not within the subsection. In my view, the default procedure does not operate to produce an effect which is equivalent to the granting of permission in a case where the application is itself for something which is prohibited by the statute. The principle of the decision of this Court in *Monaghan U.D.C.* v. *Alf-a-Bet Promotions Ltd* is relevant in the present context. An order of mandamus cannot issue to compel the planning authority in the present case to consider an application to do something which would be illegal if done.

It is further argued on behalf of the prosecutors that the planning authority should have moved by way of certiorari or otherwise to quash the Minister's decision as one made without jurisdiction. The argument goes on then to submit that in a case where no such move was made within the time limited by the Act of 1963, namely two months, that the order stands. It is correct that the ruling of the Minister stands, but it stands as it is. If it is one which is *ultra vires* and therefore void on that account it cannot be relied upon as a ground for seeking to compel any other person or body to do something which is illegal.

THE STATE (FINGLAS INDUSTRIAL ESTATES LIMITED) V. DUBLIN COUNTY COUNCIL
The High Court (Unreported) McMahon J., 10 July 1981
(Ref. No. 1981 No. 166SS)
The Supreme Court (Unreported) Henchy J., 17 February 1983 (Ref. No. 1981 No. 228)

On appeal to the Minister the Prosecutors obtained permission for a light industrial estate subject to *inter alia* the following condition:

'The developers shall pay a sum of money to the Dublin County Council and/or to Dublin Corporation, as may be appropriate as a contribution towards the provision of a public water supply and piped sewerage facilities in the area. The amount to be paid and the time and method shall be agreed between the developers and the said Council and/or the said Corporation before the development is commenced or failing agreement, shall be as determined by the Minister for Local Government.'

The land was located within the area of the respondents, but the only foul sewer system in the area was maintained by the Dublin Corporation. The amount payable was determined by the Board who had succeeded to the Minister's function. The respondents refused to accept a cheque tendered in the amount payable. The prosecutors obtained an order of Mandamus in the High Court directing the respondents to accept the cheque. This decision was appealed to the Supreme Court who allowed the appeal and discharged the Order.

In the High Court
McMahon J.:
. . . In answer to the objection that the developer's interest in the land was misstated and to the County Council objections to the validity of the Minister's order generally the developers relied on section 42 of the Local Government (Planning and Development) Act 1976. That section substitutes for section 82 sub-section (3) of the principal Act the following sub-section:
[quotation of section follows][27]
It was submitted for the Council that this limitation on the right to question the validity of an Order applied only to proceedings brought for that purpose and did not preclude a defendant or respondent from relying on the invalidity as a defence. The sub-section it was said barred a challenge to validity as a sword but not as a shield.
The sub-section does not in terms distinguish between reliance on invalidity in attack and in defence and when regard is had to the purpose of the sub-section no distinction is in my view justified. Very large investments in property are made in reliance on orders granting permission and new developments such as office blocks are normally sold by the developers to pension funds or insurance companies

[27] See page 252.

shortly after completion.

It is necessary that the validity of a planning permission should not be allowed to be called in question even if only by way of defence many years alter. In my view the sub-section must be given its literal meaning and it prevents invalidity being raised by any party in any legal proceedings which have not been commenced within the period of two months. Counsel for the developers referred to the decision of the Court of Appeal in *Reg.* v. *Environment Secretary Ex. P. Ostler* (1977) 1 Q.B. 122. In that case a schedule to the Highways Act 1959 provided that a person aggrieved by certain orders and schemes could apply to the High Court to question the validity thereof within six weeks but subject thereto such a scheme or order should not be questioned in any legal proceedings whatever. The Court of Appeal applied the decision of the House of Lords in *Smith* v. *East Elloe R.D.C.* (1956) A.C. 736 and upheld the ouster of jurisdiction. The Court distinguished the decision of the House of Lords in the *Anisminic* v. *Foreign Compensation Commission* (1969) 2 A.C. 147 that a statutory provision that a determination of a tribunal could not be called in question in any Court did not include a decision which was a nullity on three principle grounds (see the judgment of Lord Denning M.R. at p. 135). In the *Anisminic* case the Act ousted the jurisdiction of the Court altogether but in the *East Elloe* case the Court had jurisdiction to consider the validity of an Order so long as the proceedings were brought within six weeks. In the *Anisminic* case the House of Lords was considering a determination by the Foreign Compensation Commission which was a judicial body. In *East Elloe* the order challenged was very much in the nature of an administrative decision in which the public interest played an important part. Finally in the *Anisminic* case the House of Lords had to consider the actual determination of the tribunal whereas in the *East Elloe* case it was the process by which the decision was reached which was impugned. The order of the Minister in the present case resembles the order in the *East Elloe* case as an administrative decision involving the public interest. The misstatement of the applicant's interest in the land is a defect in procedure the substance of the Order being *intra vires* the powers of the Minister. In my view sub-section (3A) precludes a challenge to the validity of the Minister's order based on a defect in procedure and the question whether an order which is *ultra vires* in a matter of substance can be challenged after 2 months does not arise.

I am satisfied that it is not now open to the County Council to challenge the validity of the Minister's Order on the grounds that the application for planning permission wrongly stated that the lands were the property of the developers.

Finally it was submitted for the County Council that if the validity of the Minister's Order was not now open to challenge nevertheless the validity was a matter which the Court could take into consideration in the exercise of the very wide discretion which the Courts undoubtedly possess in granting or withholding mandamus and the court should refuse to enforce the order because of its original invalidity. In my view if the Court were to act in this way it would be doing what sub-section (3A) says is not to be done that is permitting the validity or the order to be questioned after the expiry of the period of two months. Furthermore I do not think that the County Council's complaints of procedural defects have any merits the Council having failed to avail of the opportunity to question the validity of the order within the period of two months.

Accordingly the Conditional Order will be made absolute. . . .

In the Supreme Court
Henchy J.:

The arguments in this appeal have ranged over a wide field, but in my opinion the essential issue is whether an order of mandamus should have been made compelling the Council to accept the cheque tendered. While this question (or its ramifications) does not appear to have been explored in the High Court, I think it is so crucial to this case, and possibly to others, that it cannot be ignored.

Counsel for the developers have proceeded on the basis that the Board's order of the 23 December 1980 could not be questioned as to its validity. This belief was reached because s. 82 (3A) of the 1963 Act (as inserted by s. 42 of the 1976 Act) provided as follows:

'A person shall not by prohibition, *certiorari* or in any other legal proceedings whatsoever question the validity of –

  (a) a decision of a planning authority for permission or approval under Part IV of the Principal Act [i.e. the 1963 Act],
  (b) a decision of the Board on any appeal or on any reference,
  (c) a decision of the Minister on any appeal, unless the proceedings are instituted within the period of two months commencing on the date on which the decision was given'.

It is common case that the Council did not question the validity of the Board's order within two months after it was made. But does the two-months period of limitation apply to the order? I think not. It did not come under (a), for it was not a decision of a planning authority as statutorily defined; it did not come under (b), for it was not a decision of the Board on any appeal or reference (which latter term is statutorily limited to questions as to what is or is not development or exempted development); and it plainly was not a decision of a Minister on any appeal, but was only a matter included in a condition attached to such a decision. I am satisfied, therefore, that the two-months time bar on questioning the validity of the Board's order does not apply and that it is open to the Council to argue that that order was invalid.

For my part, I consider that the Board's order was and is a nullity. The power of the Minister to attach the condition requiring the developers to pay a sum of money before the permission became effective was inserted by the Minister in purported exercise of the power vested in him under s. 26 of the 1963 Act. If there could be a transfer to the Board of the assessment or arbitration power given to the Minister under the condition as a *persona designata*, that transfer would have taken place under s. 14 (4) of the 1976 act, which is in the following terms:

'In case there is attached to a permission or approval granted under s. 26 of the Principal Act a condition which provides that a contribution or other matter is to be agreed between the planning authority and the person to whom the permission or approval is granted and that in default of agreement the contribution or other matter is to be determined by the Minister, the condition shall be construed as providing that in default of agreement the contribution or other matter is to be determined by the Board'.

It is to be noted that the type of condition envisaged by this subsection is one that required agreement between the developer and the planning authority. In other words, it is the type of agreement that could have been inserted as a condition by the Council as planning authority if they had granted the permission. But the Minister, in purported exercise of his appellate jurisdiction, provided for a payment 'to the Dublin County Council and/or to Dublin Corporation'. If the Council had granted permission subject to such a condition they would have been acting ultra vires, for the statute does not provide for a condition as to payment to another planning authority, either primarily or in the alternative. Since the Council as planning authority had no power to do so under s. 26, the Minister in exercising his appellate jurisdiction was no less bereft of such a power.

S. 14 (4) of the 1976 Act must be read as referring to a permission validly containing a condition as to a contribution as between the developer and the relevant planning authority, and as the Minister's condition introduced without authority a possible contribution to a third party, i.e. the Dublin Corporation, it is to be said that s. 14 (4) does not apply to it, so that the Board had no power to fix the contribution.

But even if the contrary were held to be the case, namely that the Board had power under s. 26 (4) to fix the amount, the time and the method of payment, it would have to be held that the effect of their order was merely to determine the nature and extent of the financial duty that fell on the developers as the condition for getting development permission. The developers were then entitled to tender the required amount; and this they did. However, I fail to see how mandamus could issue to compel the Council to accept the amount tendered. The developers might have had other remedies open to them, such as a declaratory action as to their rights, or a claim for a mandatory injunction, but I have heard no valid argument advanced to show that there was a public duty, at common law or under statute, on the Council to accept the cheque tendered by the developers. And as I understand the law of mandamus, a public authority, be it a planning authority or a sanitary authority, cannot be compelled by mandamus to accept money tendered to it unless there is a public duty to accept it.

THE STATE (TOFT) V. GALWAY CORPORATION
The Supreme Court (Unreported) O'Higgins C.J., 30 July 1981,
(Ref. No. 153–80)

In an application for planning permission the applicant was decribed in error as Spirits Rum Company Limited. The correct name of the applicant was Rum Spirit Limited. The respondents granted permission to the applicant as decribed in the application. The appellant sought to have the grant quashed on the ground that it was made to a non-existent company. He obtained a condition order but the Court refused to make the order absolute. On appeal to the Supreme Court. The Court dismissed the appeal. See the extract from **O'Higgins C.J.**'s judgment given in chapter 3 (page 193).

THE STATE (ABENGLEN PROPERTIES LTD.) V. DUBLIN
CORPORATION
[1982] I.L.R.M. 590

In an appeal against an Absolute Order of *certiorari* granted by the High Court quashing a planning decision of the appellants it was contended by the appellants that *certiorari* should not lie because the respondents were entitled to appeal to the

Board which could deal with all their contentions. See page 211 for a fuller statement of the facts of the case.

O'Higgins CJ.:

(*Certiorari*'s) purpose is to supervise the exercise of jurisdiction by such bodies or tribunals and to control any usurpation or action in excess of jurisdiction. It is not available to correct errors or to review decisions or to make the High Court a court of appeal from the decisions complained of. In addition it remains a discretionary remedy. This discretion remains unfettered where the applicant for the relief had no real interest in the proceedings and is not a person aggrieved by the decision (e.g. see *State (Doyle)* v. *Carr* 1970 I.R. 87; *State (Toft)* v. *Galway Corporation* (Supreme Court 30/7/1981). Where, however, such applicant has been affected or penalised and is an aggrieved person, it is commonly said that certiorari issues *ex debito justitiae*. This should not be taken as meaning that a discretion does not remain in the High Court as to whether to give the relief or to refuse it. There may be exceptional and rare cases where a criminal conviction has been recorded otherwise than in due course of law and the matter cannot be set right except by certiorari. In such circumstances the discretion may be exercisable only in favour of quashing (see *The State (Vozza)* v. *O'Flynn and McCarthy* 1957 I.R. 227). In the vast majority of cases, however, a person whose legal rights have been infringed may be awarded *certiorari ex debito justitiae* if he can establish any of the recognised grounds for quashing; but the Court retains a discretion to refuse his application if his conduct has been such as to disentitle him to relief or, I may add, if the relief is not necessary for the protection of those rights.

For the Court to act otherwise, almost as of course, once an irregularity or defect is established in the impugned proceedings would be to debase this great remedy.

The question immediately arises, as to the effect on the exercise of the Court's discretion, of the existence of a right of appeal or an alternative remedy. It is well established that the existence of such ought not to prevent the Court from acting. It seems to me to be a question of justice. The Court ought to take into account all the circumstances of the case, including the purpose for which *certiorari* has been sought, the adequacy of the alternative remedy and of course, the conduct of the applicant. If the decision impugned is made without jurisdiction or in breach of natural justice then, normally, the existence of a right of appeal or of a failure to avail of such, should be immaterial. Again, if an appeal can only deal with the merits and not with the question of jurisdiction involved, the existence of such ought not to be a ground for refusing relief. Other than these, there may be cases where the decision exhibits an error of law and a perfectly simple appeal can rectify the complaint or where, under administrative legislation, adequate appeal machinery, particularly suitable for dealing with errors in the application of the code in question, exists. In such cases while retaining always the power to quash, the Court should be slow to do so, unless satisfied that, for some particular reason, the appeal or alternative remedy is not adequate.

In this case the appellants contend and submit as their primary ground of appeal that there was available to the respondents adequate appeal facilities under the Planning Acts, and that their failure to avail of such and the reasons for such failure, warrants the refusal of *certiorari*, even if sufficient grounds for granting such relief exists. This is an important submission and deserves very careful consideration.

As already indicated the respondents' argument with the appellants' planning officers related to the proper interpretation of paragraph 3.4.20 of the Dublin City Development Plan 1980. Once this Plan applied, as was apparently the case, the appellants, as the planning authority were bound by the provisions. The planning officers decided that the paragraph in question required the appellants to impose a 40 per cent limit on office development as a condition for the development of the site. The respondents contended that these officers were wrong in this interpretation and that their error resulted in the appellants, as the planning authority, failing to consider the application for development in a proper manner or on a proper basis and led to the granting of outline permission for a development that had never been applied for. It was in these circumstances that certiorari was applied for.

If instead of applying to the High Court the respondents had appealed to An Bord Pleanala would they have suffered or been at a loss in any way? I think no. The site could not, in any event, be developed without permission. Accordingly, the respondents had either to act on the permission which they had obtained or seek to have it altered or, alternatively to apply afresh for permission for another development. By appealing to An Bord Pleanala they were in the position that their original application would be considered *de novo*, by the appeal board. That board would hear all the arguments and submissions for allowing the full development sought and was free to consider the whole proposal on its merits. Further – and this is very important – this appeal board was not bound to confine the development within the limits prescribed by the Dublin City Plan. Accordingly, An Bord Pleanala could waive the 40 per cent restriction if it thought proper so to do or, alternatively, could state a case to the High Court on the proper interpretation of the paragraph in question. I find it hard to conceive a more effective means of dealing with the respondents' complaints against the planning authority. On such appeal their point of view could be vindicated if it deserved vindication and, meanwhile, and pending such appeal, their rights could in no way be affected.

We know that the respondents did not appeal. Instead, they waited until the two months from the decision had almost expired and then applied for certiorari. In doing so they turned their backs on the appeal machinery which the Legislature had provided and deprived possible objectors from being heard in relation to any suggested alteration of the planning authority's decision. The purpose of their application for certiorari was not, primarily to correct a grievance which they had suffered, as a result of a process alleged to have been without legal authority, but to avail of the alleged irregularity to obtain a benefit not contemplated by the planning code. It is clear that if the planning authority's decision were declared a nullity the respondents would seek a declaration that they had secured a default permission under Section 26(4) and all opposition to the original development would have been silenced. I do not find it necessary to express a view as to whether this subsection would operate in such circumstances. It is sufficient to say that the object and purpose of this application was to by-pass the scrutiny of planning proposals provided by the Planning Acts and thereby to frustrate their operation in this instance.

In my view, having regard to the existence of an adequate appeal procedure, to the conduct and motives of the respondents and to all the circumstances of this particular case, the High Court should, in the exercise of its discretion, have refused to make absolute the Conditional Order of *Certiorari*.

Henchy J.:

. . . Where an inferior court or a tribunal errs within jurisdiction without recording that error on the face of the record, certiorari does not lie. It is only when in such cases there is the extra flaw that the court ot tribunal acted in disregard of the requirements of natural justice that certiorari will issue. In the present case, there is no suggestion that the Corporation, in dealing with this application, acted in disregard of any of the regulations of natural justice. They went wrong in law, if at all, in answering legal questions within their jurisdiction, and they did not reproduce any such legal error on the face of the record of their decision. Consequently, in my view, they did not leave themselves open to certiorari in respect of their decision.

However, even if I am incorrect in the conclusion that certiorari does not lie in this case for the reason I have given, there are two further reasons why, in my opinion, certiorari should not issue to quash the decision of the Corporation.

The first reason is this. If it could be held that the Corporation acted in this case in excess of jurisdiction, the grant of certiorari would necessarily be a matter of discretion; for no, or no particular, benefit would accrue to Abenglen by the granting of the order. Their counsel has frankly admitted that the only purpose for which they have sought to quash the Corporation's decision is so that they may lay claim to a grant of development permission by default (under s. 26 (4)(*a*) of the 1963 Act) to the extent applied for (that is, without the conditions attaching to the permission granted), on the ground that the Corporation, not having dealt within jurisdiction with the application, should be deemed not to have given any decision for the purpose of s. 26 (4)(*a*). Because of that, it is contended Abenglen are entitled to say that they should be regarded as having been given by default the permission applied for, on the last day of 'the appropriate period' (as that expression is defined in s. 26 (4)(*b*) of the 1963 Act).

I am bound to say that I find this process of reasoning totally unacceptable. It is a syllogism resting on the premises that no decision was given by the Corporation. But that is palpably not so. Even if it were to be held that the decision given was one reached in excess of jurisdiction, it was nevertheless a decision – a decision of which notice was given within the appropriate period (in compliance with s. 26 (4)(*a*)(iii) and unless and until invalidated by a court decision it retains the status of a decision for the purpose of s. 26 (4). S. 26 (4) is designed to enable an applicant to be deemed to have got permission by default when, regardless of whether the planning authority have or have not made a decision within the appropriate period, they have failed to give him *notice* of their decision within the appropriate period (see s. 26 (4)(*a*)(3). The section has no application to a case such as the present, where there was no violation of the requirements of natural justice and where notice of the decision (which was in the prescribed form and bore no characteristic of illegality or lack of jurisdiction on its face) was given within the appropriate period. Such a decision, even if defective because of a latent overstepping of jurisdiction, is and remains a decision both for the purpose of s. 26 (4) and for the purpose of certiorari proceedings, until the High Court, or this court on appeal, in the due exercise of its discretion quashes it. But whether or not it be thus struck down as an invalid decision, it would be incompetent for Abenglen to contend that (in the words of s. 26 (4)(*a*)(iii) 'the planning authority (did) not give notice to the applicant of their decision within the appropriate period'. Since the ability to make such a contention successfully is the only reason for bringing these certiorari proceedings, an absolute order of certiorari would be worthless to Abenglen.

In such circumstances, the grant of certiorari is a matter of discretion, and it does not seem to me that it would be a proper exercise of the Court's discretion to grant certiorari when the sole purpose of the quashing is the attainment of an object which is legally unattainable. That being the position here, even if the Corporation made a decision which they had not the required jurisdiction to make, Abenglen, on their own admission as to the reason for bringing the application for certiorari, have no standing to have that decision quashed. . . .

The second reason why I would refuse to quash the corporation's decision, even if it was made in excess of jurisdiction, is that the correct procedure for the correction of the legal errors complained of lay in an appeal to the Board. The statutory scheme for making applications for development permission to the relevant planning authority – giving prior notice, as prescribed, to the public and complying with the requirements of the regulations; allowing interested parties to make representations by way of objection or otherwise; requiring the planning authority to deal with the application within a given time and according to pre-cribed standards; requiring that the decision shall contain prescribed essentials; allowing an appeal from the planning authority's decision to the Board, who may hold oral hearings, who are not bound to comply with the development plan (s. 14 (8) of the 1976 Act), and who may refer a question of law to the High Court (s. 82 (3) of the 1963 Act); and the fact that the Board's decision is put beyond the reach of certiorari or other legal proceedings questioning its validity unless such proceed-ings are brought within two months of the giving of the Board's decision (s. 82 (3A) of the 1963 Act) – these and other features of the Acts envisage the operation of a self-contained administrative code, with resort to the Courts only in exceptional circumstances. The present case does not seem to me to exhibit the exceptional circumstances for which the intervention of the Courts was intended. On the contrary, certiorari proceedings would appear to be singularly inapt for the resolu-tion of the questions raised by Abenglen. Certiorari proceedings, based as they are on affidavit evidence can result only in a stark and comparatively unilluminating decision to quash or not to quash; whereas an appeal to the Board would have allowed all relevant matters to be explored (if necessary, in an oral hearing, with the aid of experts in the field of planning), thus allowing an authoritative practice and procedure, aided, if necessary, by reference to the High Court of a question of law.

Because of the technicality of the objections raised by Abenglen, because their resolution might require oral evidence, because the resulting decision would prob-ably govern other cases, past, present or future, I would, in the exercise of my discretion, refuse certiorari, on the ground that Abenglen should have pursued the appellate procedure that was open to them under the Acts. . . .

I pause to stress that the primary reason why I would refuse certiorari in this case is because the alleged errors of law were not made in excess of jurisdiction and do not appear on the face of the record of the Corporation's decision. I am merely explaining why I would exercise my discretion against Abenglen in the event of the Court deciding that certiorari lies as a matter of discretion.

Walsh J.:
. . . An order of *certiorari* quashing the decisions made by the planning authority

would be of no benefit to the prosecutors. While the Court could make such an order in the present case the Court in its discretion could refuse to do so where it would not confer any benefit upon the prosecutors. In the present case, . . . , the quashing of the order would not give the prosecutors the advantage of the default procedure which is what the prosecutors sought to achieve in the proceedings. In the result, in my view, the correct procedure is that the applicants should apply anew to the planning authority as they have allowed the time for appeal to the appeals tribunal to expire . . .

During the course of the argument the parties canvassed the question of whether or not the prosecutors were entitled to seek an order of *certiorari* when there was available an alternative remedy in the form of an appeal which was not availed of. There is no doubt that the existence of alternative remedies is not a bar to the making of an order of *certiorari*. The court in its discretion may refuse to make such an order when the alternative remedy has been invoked and is pending. However, a court ought never to exercise its discretion by refusing to quash a bad order when its continued existence is capable of producing damaging legal effects. A court's discretion cannot in justice be exercised to produce or permit a punitive or damaging result to be visited upon an applicant as a mark of the court's disapproval or displeasure when such result flows from or is dependent upon an order bad in law even when the applicant by his conduct or otherwise has contributed to the making of such an order. Such conduct can be dealt with in deciding the question of costs.

THE STATE (CONLON CONSTRUCTION LIMITED) V. CORK COUNTY COUNCIL
The High Court (Unreported) Butler J., 31 July 1975
(Ref. No. 1975 No. 313SS)

Butler J.:

. . . It is clear that mandamus is an appropriate remedy at the suit of an applicant for planning permission where the planning authority refuses to make a grant which they are required to make under sub-section 9 of section 26 . . .

An order of mandamus is made like all State-side orders in the nature of former prerogative writs to secure that rights are protected, justice done and injustice prevented where no equally effective remedy exists. The making of the order within the discretion of the Court. The Court must consider all the circumstances of the case including the conduct of the parties and, unless coerced by the manifest requirements of justice to exercise the discretion to make the order, may refuse it on judicial grounds. Where mandamus is sought to secure a right the right must be promptly claimed and the claim pursued vigorously without being abandoned. Among well recognised grounds for refusing the remedy is delay on the part of the applicant in pursuing the claim and the abandonment of the claim in favour of alternative remedies. Where such delay and abandonment was deliberate because the claimant may have thought such a course to be in his better interests he cannot repent his decision and ask for the discretion of the Court to be exercised in his favour by the making of the order.

The facts of this case which I have outlined above clearly show a delay between June 1973 and February 1975 occasioned by the applicant's choice to pursue successive alternative courses of conduct. Had any of these alternatives resulted in a grant were prepared to accept they would have achieved the desirable end of getting, if not what they wanted, what they were prepared to settle for and at the same time remaining on good terms with the planning authority.

It is only when those efforts failed that they fell back on a claim to a right to a planning permission based on a technicality. Furthermore, on the evidence before me it is a case where planning permission might have been properly refused on sound planning grounds. To my mind and for these reasons the application for mandamus should be refused.

STATE (N.C.E. LIMITED) V. DUBLIN COUNTY COUNCIL
The High Court (Unreported) McMahon J., 4 December 1979
(Ref. No. 1979 No. 344SS)

The respondents received an application from the prosecutor on the 1st December 1979 seeking an approval. On the 11th of April the respondents made a decision to refuse approval. The prosecutor appealed to the Board. Subsequent to the lodging of the appeal the prosecutor was advised that a letter which had been sent to them on the 26th of January 1979 was not a valid request for further information and that they therefore had a default permission, the respondent having failed to give their decision within the two month period specified in Section 26 of the 1963 Act. The prosecutor sought an order of Mandamus requiring the respondent to grant approval. The respondents submitted *inter alia* that the prosecutor could not seek an order of Mandamus once they appealed. This argument was rejected.

McMahon J.:
Mr. Cooke on behalf of the Council submitted that by appealing to An Bord Pleanala the developer had adopted an alternative remedy and was not entitled to pursue the remedy of Mandamus. I am satisfied that the developer was not aware of his right to Mandamus when the course of appealing to An Bord Pleanala was adopted. In my opinion that appeal can not be regarded as an alternative remedy to Mandamus. In the view I take of the letter of the 26th January 1979 the developer was entitled to a grant of permission from the Council on the expiry of two months from the receipt of the developer's application. All the developer was entitled to obtain from An Bord Pleanala was a decision on the merits of the application. It cannot be said therefore that the appeal to An Bord Pleanala was another remedy equally beneficial convenient and effective as an order of Mandamus.

Chapter 5

ENFORCEMENT OF PLANNING CONTROL

PROSECUTIONS UNDER SECTION 24 OF THE 1963 ACT

Any person who carries out development which requires permission under section 24(1) of the 1963 Act without obtaining such permission is guilty of an offence. (See section 24(3) of the 1963[1] Act as amended by section 8(3) and (4) of the 1982 Act[2])

Where the development concerned consists of the carrying out of works the person who carries out the works commits the offence. Where the development concerned consists of a material change of use it appears that not only the person who made the initial change commits an offence but an offence is also committed by any other person who continues the use. While there is no decision of the Superior Courts available on the point the District Courts have accepted the argument that every day an unauthorised use continues a new offence is committed.

Prior to the coming into force of the 1982 Act[3] the offence was of a summary nature. Since no time limit was nominated in the Act within which proceedings had to be commenced section 10(4) of the Petty Sessions (Ireland) Act 1851 applied and complaint had to be made within six months of the commission of the offence. On the 1st November 1976 section 30 of the 1976 Act[4] came into force. This section limits alternative time periods within which summary proceedings must be commenced. From the 1st November 1976 proceedings must be commenced within six months of the date on which the offence is committed *or* within three months from the date on which evidence sufficient to justify proceedings comes to the knowledge of the person instituting the proceedings. The sufficiency of such evidence is to be judged by the person who brings the proceedings. (See section 30(*b*)) Proceedings cannot be brought later than five years after the offence is committed. It has been suggested by Walsh J. in his book *Planning and Development Law* that the period may always be extended to five years by finding a prosecutor who knew nothing of the offence for four years and nine months.[5]

Since the coming into force of the 1982 Act an offence under section 24(3) is an indictable offence which may in limited circumstances be tried summarily. (See section 8(3)[6] and section 9 of the 1982 Act)[7]

---

[1] Section 24 is quoted at page 324.
[2] See page 325.
[3] With the exception of that part of section 15 of the 1982 Act which repealed section 15(1) of the 1976 Act, the 1982 Act came into force on the 28th July 1982.
[4] See page 327.
[5] See Walsh, *Planning and Development Law*, 1st edition, page 112.
[6] See page 325.
[7] See page 326.

There is no time limit for bringing proceedings on indictment. If, however, the District Justice decides to try the offence summarily and he has the consent of the DPP and the defendant the offence becomes a summary offence and the time limits set out in section 30 apply.

The prosecution do not need to negative the existence of a permission (see section 36 of the 1976 Act)[8] nor need they prove that the development is exempted or that it was not commenced before the 1st October 1964. (See section 24(4)(*a*) of the 1963 Act) Where the defendant wishes to rely upon such matters the onus of proof is on him.

Where a person has been convicted of an offence under section 24(3) as amended and he continues the offence after conviction he will be guilty of a further offence. (See section 8(4) of the 1982 Act)[9] It appears that the offence is a continuing one and there may be repeated prosecutions. (See *Dublin Corporation* v. *Flynn)*[10] This offence may be tried summarily or on indictment. (See section 9 of the 1982 Act)[11]

LOCAL GOVERNMENT (PLANNING AND DEVELOPMENT) ACT, 1963

24. – (1) Subject to the provisions of this Act,[12] permission shall be required under this Part of this Act –

(*a*) in respect of any development of land, being neither exempted development nor development commenced before the appointed day, and

(*b*) in the case of a structure which existed immediately before the appointed day[13] and is on the commencement of that day an unauthorised structure, for the retention of the structure.

(2) A person shall not carry out any development in respect of which permission is required by subsection (1) of this section save under and in accordance with a permission granted under this Part of this Act.

(3) Any person who contravenes subsection (2) of this section shall be guilty of an offence.[14]

(4) In a prosecution for an offence under this section –

(*a*) it shall not be necessary for the prosecution to show, and it shall be assumed until the contrary is shown by the defendant, that the development in question was neither exempted development nor development commenced before the appointed day.[15]

---

[8] See page 328.
[9] See page 325.
[10] See page 345.
[11] See page 326.
[12] See section 40 of the 1963 Act which permits certain developments to be carried out without permission.
[13] The appointed day was the 1st October 1964.
[14] Subsection (3) was amended by section 15(1) of the 1982 Act.
[15] The appointed day was the 1st October 1964.

AMENDED PENALTIES FOR ENFORCEMENT SECTIONS (INCLUDING SECTION 24)

LOCAL GOVERNMENT (PLANNING AND DEVELOPMENT) ACT, 1982

8. – (1) A person convicted by the District Court of an offence for which a penalty is provided in any section of the Principal Act specified in column (2) of the Table to this section at any reference number shall, in lieu of the penalty so provided, be liable to the penalty specified in column (3) of the said Table at that reference number, and that section shall be construed and have effect accordingly.

(2)(*a*) A person convicted of an offence under subsection (9) of section 32 of the Act of 1976 shall, in lieu of so much of the penalty specified in that subsection as consists of a fine, be liable to a fine not exceeding £800, and the said subsection (9) shall be construed and have effect accordingly.

(*b*) A person convicted of an offence under subsection (10) of section 33 of the Act of 1976 shall, in lieu of so much of the penalty specified in that subsection as consists of a fine, be liable to a fine not exceeding £800, and the said subsection (10) shall be construed and have effect accordingly.

(3) A person who is guilty of an offence under section 24 (3) of the Principal Act or section 26 (4) of the Act of 1976 shall be liable, on conviction on indictment, to a fine not exceeding £10,000, or, at the discretion of the court, to imprisonment for a term not exceeding two years, or to both the fine and the imprisonment.

(4)(*a*) Where a person is convicted of an offence referred to in subsection (3) of this section and there is a continuation by him of the offence after his conviction, he shall be guilty of a further offence and shall be liable, on conviction on indictment, to a fine not exceeding £1,000 for each day on which the offence is so continued or to imprisonment for a term not exceeding two years, or to both the fine and the imprisonment.

(*b*) In any proceedings for an offence under this section in which it is alleged that there was a continuation by the defendant of an offence under subsection (3) of section 24 of the Principal Act, subsection (4) of the said section 24 shall, as regards the proceedings, apply as it applies to a prosecution for an offence under that section.

(*c*) In any proceedings for an offence under this section in which it is alleged that there was a continuation by the defendant of an offence under subsection (4) of section 26 of the Act of 1976 –

  (i) subsection (7) of the said section 26 shall, in relation to the proceedings, apply as it applies in relation to proceedings mentioned in that subsection, and

  (ii) subsection (8) of the said section 26 shall, as regards the proceedings, apply as it applies to a prosecution for an offence under that section.

(5) This section shall have effect as respects offences committed after the commencement of this section.

TABLE

Ref. No. (1)	Section of Principal Act (2)	Penalty (3)
1.	7(5), 9(2), 80(4), 82(5)(*b*) and 82(7)(*b*)(iv).	A fine not exceeding £100.
2.	31(8), as amended by section 38 of the Act of 1976, 34(6), as so amended, 37(7), as so amended and 49(2)(*b*), as so amended.	A fine not exceeding £800 and, in the case of a further offence under the section, a further fine (not exceeding in all £800), not exceeding £150 for each day during which the offence is continued.
3.	51(4), as amended by section 40(*c*) of the Act of 1976, 81(3), 83(7) and 89(8).	A fine not exceeding £100 and, in the case of a further offence under the section, a further fine (not exceeding in all £800) not exceeding £25 for each day during which the offence is continued.
4.	34(1), as amended by section 38 of the Act of 1976, 35(7), as so amended, 45(8), as so amended and 46(8), as so amended.	A fine not exceeding £800.
5.	34(5), as amended by section 38 of the Act of 1976, and 35(8), as so amended.	A fine (not exceeding in all £800) not exceeding £150 for each day during which the further offence under the section is continued.

9. – A Justice of the District Court shall have jurisdiction to try summarily an offence referred to in section 8(3) of this Act, or an offence under section 8(4) of this Act if –

(*a*) the Justice is of opinion tht the facts proved or alleged against a defendant charged with such an offence constitute a minor offence fit to be tried summarily,

(*b*) the Director of Public Prosecutions consents, and

(*c*) the defendant (on being informed by the Justice of his right to be tried by a jury) does not object to being tried summarily,

and, upon conviction under this subsection, the said defendant shall be liable –

(i) in case he is convicted of an offence so referred to, to a fine not exceeding £800, or, at the discretion of the court, to imprisonment for a term not exceeding six months, or to both the fine and the imprisonment,

(ii) in case he is convicted of an offence under the said section 8(4), to a fine (not exceeding £800 in all) not exceeding £150 for each day during which the offence is continued, or, at the discretion of the court, to imprisonment for a term not exceeding six months, or to both the fine and the imprisonment.

(2) Section 13 of the Criminal Procedure Act, 1967,[16] shall apply in relation to an offence referred to in subsection (1) of this section as if, in lieu of the penalties specified in subsection (3) of the said section 13, there were specified therein the penalty provided for by subsection (1) of this section in relation to the offence, and the reference in subsection (2)(*a*) of the said section 13 to the penalties provided for in the said subsection (3) shall be construed and have effect accordingly.

PROCEDURE

(1) **Summary Proceedings**

(a) *Prosecutions by planning authority*

LOCAL GOVERNMENT (PLANNING AND DEVELOPMENT) ACT, 1963

80. – (1) An offence under this Act may be prosecuted summarily[17] by the planning authority in whose area the offence is committed.

(2) A planning authority shall not prosecute in a case in which an offence under section 53 of this Act is alleged to have been committed in relation to an advertisement unless the advertisement is exempted development and they have decided that the advertisement would injure the amenities of their area and, in the case of an advertisement advertising a public meeting, unless the advertisment has been in position for seven days or longer after the date of the meeting.

(3) Where –

(*a*) an offence under section 46 or section 52 of this Act, or

(*b*) an offence under section 53 of this Act consisting of defacing any structure, door, gate, window, tree or post,

is alleged to have been committed, any officer of the planning authority, duly authorised by them in writing and producing, if so required, his authority, may demand the name and address of any person whom he reasonably believes to be guilty of the offence.

(4) Any person whose name and address has been demanded under the foregoing subsection and who fails to comply with the demand shall be guilty of an offence and shall be liable on summary conviction to a fine not exceeding £100.[18]

(b) *Time limits*

LOCAL GOVERNMENT (PLANNING AND DEVELOPMENT) ACT, 1976

30. – (1) Subject to subsection (2) of this section, summary proceedings to which this section applies may be commenced –

(*a*) at any time within six months from the date on which the offence was

---

[16] Section 13 of the Criminal Procedure Act, 1967 deals with the procedure to be followed where an accused pleads guilty to an indictable offence in the District Court.

[17] 'Summarily' was inserted by section 13 of the 1982 Act.

[18] As amended by section 8 of the 1982 Act.

committed, or

(*b*) at any time within three months from the date on which evidence sufficient, in the opinion of the person by whom the proceedings are instituted, to justify proceedings comes to such person's knowledge,

whichever is the later.

(2) Summary proceedings mentioned in subsection (1) of this section shall not be
instituted later than five years from the date on which the offence was committed.

(3) For the purposes of this section, a certificate signed by or on behalf of the
person instituting the proceedings as to the date on which evidence described in
subsection (1) of this section came to the knowledge of such person shall be *prima
facie* evidence thereof and in any legal proceedings a document purporting to be a
certificate issued for the purposes of this section and to be so signed shall be
deemed to be so signed and shall be admitted as evidence without proof of the
signature of the person purporting to sign the certificate, unless the contrary is
shown.

(4) Subsection (1) of this section shall have effect notwithstanding section 10 (4)
of the Petty Sessions (Ireland) Act, 1851.

(5) This section applies to the following summary proceedings, namely:

(*a*) summary proceedings pursuant to section 26 of this Act or in respect of a
contravention of section 24 (2) of the Principal Act and which are
instituted by the planning authority in whose area the offence is alleged
to have been committed,

(*b*) summary proceedings pursuant to section 32 or 33 of this Act.

(2) **Onus of Proof**

36. – In any proceedings for an offence under this Act or under the Principal
Act, it shall not be necessary to negative by evidence the existence of any permission granted under Part IV of the Principal Act and the onus of proving such
permission shall be on the person seeking to avail himself thereof.

ENFORCEMENT NOTICES

Sections 31, 32, and 35 of the 1963 make provision for the enforcement of
planning control by means of the service of notices – called enforcement notices –
which specify a breach of planning control and which may require that specified
steps be taken within a specified time to remedy the breach. Each section makes
provision for the service of an enforcement notice in different circumstances and
care must be taken to ensure that the notice is served under the correct section.
Failure to comply with the terms of an enforcement notice is an offence. Notices
under each section will be considered in turn below.

Sections 36 and 37 of the 1963 Act make provision for the service of notices
which require the alteration or removal of a structure (see section 36) or the
discontinuance of a use (see section 37). It is not a pre-condition to the service of
these notices that a breach of planning control occur. While these notices are not
enforcement notices they are similar in nature and will be considered below.

ENFORCEMENT NOTICES UNDER SECTION 31[19]

This is the appropriate notice to serve (1) where development requiring planning

---

[19] Section 31 is quoted at page 334.

permission has been carried out on or after the 1st October 1964 without permission being obtained or (2) where there has been a failure to comply with a condition attached to a planning permission. Where either of these breaches occurs the planning authority may serve a notice on the owner and the occupier of the land if they decide it is expedient to do so. They are not obliged to do so, however, unless directed to do so by the Minister. When considering the expediency of serving a notice the planning authority are restricted to considering the matters set out in section 31(2). These are the same matters they may consider when deciding whether or not to grant planning permission with the addition of one further matter in the case of non-compliance with a condition viz. the terms of the planning permission to which the condition attaches. The Minister is restricted to considering the same matters when deciding whether to direct the planning authority to serve a notice.

The notice must be served on the owner and the occupier within five years of the development being carried out or in the case of non-compliance with a condition within five years of the latest date for compliance. (See section 31(1)) In the case of development being carried out without permission it may not always be clear at what point development may be said to have 'been carried out' and thus when time begins to run. Where the development consists of works it is not clear if substantial completion is sufficient or if total completion is necessary to start time running. Where the development consists of a material change of use it may be difficult to pinpoint exactly when the material change took place particularly when it results from an intensification of use carried out over a long period of time. There is no ambiguity in the case of non-compliance with a condition. Time begins to run as soon as the latest date for compliance has passed. If the latest date for compliance is not specified in the condition the planning authority may serve a notice on the owner and occupier nominating the latest date. If the condition has not been complied with by that date the five year period for the service of an enforcement notice will begin to run once the date has passed.

Once the five year period has elapsed the planning authority are precluded from serving an enforcement notice under this section. However, the expiry of the five year period does not affect the unauthorised character of the development nor does it dispense with the necessity to comply with any condition. (See *Dublin Corporation* v. *Mulligan*[20]) The planning authority may still pursue other remedies. Thus the planning authority may institute section 27 proceedings to which no time limit applies. (See *Dublin Corporation* v. *Mulligan*) The planning authority may also serve notices under section 36 and 37 in appropriate circumstances.[21] They are unlikely to do so, however, since compensation becomes payable upon compliance with the terms of the notice. No compensation is payable in respect of compliance with the terms of an order under section 27.[22]

Service must be effected upon both the owner(s) and the occupier(s) of the land in accordance with section 7 of the 1963 Act.[23] It appears that service on one but not the other or on some but not all of the owners and occupiers is not sufficient. In England it has been held that service of the notice has to be effected on the owner and occupier on the same day. This, however, arose in circumstances where the

---

[20] See page 342.
[21] See pages 333–4 for discussion of section 36 and section 37.
[22] See below for discussion of section 27 at page 360.
[23] Section 7 is quoted at page 9.

enforcement notice came into force on a day determined by reference to the day of service of the notice with the result that it came into force on different days for the owner and the occupier if served on different days.[24]

It has been held in England that 'occupier' may include a licensee[25] although it need not necessarily do so.[26] 'Owner' is defined in section 2 of the 1963 Act.[27] If any difficulty arises the planning authority may ascertain the identity and address of any owner or occupier by serving a notice pursuant to section 9 of the 1963 Act.[28]

The minimum contents of the notice are specified in section 31(3), (4) and (5). The notice must specify

(1) the development which it is alleged has been carried out without permission or the matters in respect of which it is alleged any condition has not been complied with. Section 83 of the 1963 Act[29] allows a person authorised to do so by the planning authority to enter unto the land for any purpose connected with the Act which it is submitted includes entry on the land for the purposes of preparing an enforcement notice.

(2) The notice must specify a period at the expiration of which the notice will come into force. This period must not be less than one month after the service of the notice. (See section 31(4))

(3) The notice may and invariably does, specify steps to be taken to remedy the breach. In the event of such steps being specified the notice must limit a further time period within which the steps must be taken.

Steps may be specified requiring the land be restored to its pre-development condition or to secure compliance with the condition. Steps may not be required to be taken for any other purpose and must not be in excess of what would be required to achieve either purpose. (See section 31(3)) It has been held in England that it is open to the planning authority to require steps be taken which achieve less than restoration of the land to pre-development condition or which achieve less than full compliance with the condition.[30]

Where there is a failure to take any steps required within the time allowed other than the discontinuance of a use the planning authority may enter onto the land and carry out the steps themselves. (See section 31(5), section 81 of the 1963 Act)[31] Any expenses reasonably incurred by the planning authority in carrying out the steps may be recovered from the then owner as a simple contract debt. (See section 31(5) Where an owner or occupier incurs expenses complying with a notice or an owner pays the expenses of the planning authority incurred while carrying out the steps in respect of a development not carried out by the owner or occupier the expenses and payments are deemed to have been incurred or paid for the use and at the request of the person who carried out the development. (See section 31(6))

Failure to comply with an enforcement notice is an offence. Where there has been a failure to discontinue a use or to comply with a condition whether in respect of use or the carrying out of works an offence is committed under section 31(8).

[24] See *Banbury* v. *Hounslow L.B.C.* [1966] 2 Q.B. 204.
[25] See *Stevens* v. *London Borough of Bromley* [1972] 1 All E.R. 712.
[26] See *Munnich* v. *Godstone R.D.C.* [1966] 1 All E.R. 930.
[27] See page 6 for section 2.
[28] See page 11 for section 9.
[29] See page 126 for section 83.
[30] See *Iddenden* v. *Secretary of State for the Environment* [1972] 3 All E.R. 883.
[31] See page 125 for section 81 concerning the power of the planning authority to enter onto land.

The offence is committed by any person who uses the land or carries out works in contravention of the notice or who causes or permits such use or such works to be carried out in contravention of the notice. There is no express requirement that such person must have been served with the notice. It should be noted, however, that the particulars of every enforcement notice must be entered on the register (see section 31(1)) and it is open to any person to inspect the register to see if an enforcement notice is in force.

It is a defence to produce a valid planning permission in respect of the development. There is no onus, however, on the prosecution to disprove the existence of a valid planning permission. (See section 36 of the 1976 Act[32])

The continuation of a use or the continued carrying out of works in contravention of the notice after conviction is a further offence comitted by the person who was convicted. This further offence is a continuing offence for the repetition of which a successive prosecution may be brought. (See *Dublin Corporation* v. *Flynn*[33]) In order to secure a conviction the prosecution must prove the making and service of the enforcement notice each time and it cannot rely upon a certified copy of the original conviction to prove these matters. (See *Dublin Corporation* v. *Flynn*)

An offence is committed under section 34(1)[34] where there is a failure to carry out steps other than the discontinuance of a use within the time allowed. The offence is committed by the owner of the land on whom the notice has been served. 'Owner' in this context does not include an agent actually receiving the rack rent. (See section 34(4)) Where this person ceased to be the owner before the time for compliance with the notice has expired he may have his successor in title brought before the court. (See section 34(2) If he can show that the failure to carry out the steps was wholly or partially attributable to his successor, his successor may be convicted. In order to avoid conviction himself he must show that he took all reasonable steps to secure compliance with the notice. (See section 34(3) A further offence is committed by a person who has been convicted if he does not as soon as practicable do everything in his power to secure compliance with the notice. This offence is of a continuing nature and there may be repeated prosecutions. (See *Dublin Corporation* v. *Flynn*) It is an offence to obstruct or interfere with an owner taking any steps required to comply with a notice and a further offence to continue the obstruction. An occupier of the land will not be guilty of the offence unless he was first served with written notice of the owner intention to carry out the steps. (See section 34(6) and 34(7))

It would appear that compliance with the terms of the notice does not discharge the notice and it will remain in force indefinitely unless it is withdrawn by the planning authority under section 28 of the 1976 Act.[35]

ENFORCEMENT NOTICES UNDER SECTION 32[36]

This is the appropriate notice to serve where there has been a failure to comply with a condition attached to a permission for the retention of a structure. It does not apply to a condition attached to a permission for retention of a use. The planning authority are not obliged to serve a notice but they may do so if they

---

[32] See page 328 for section 36.
[33] See page 345.
[34] See page 337 for section 34.
[35] See page 342 for section 28.
[36] Section 32 is quoted at page 336.

consider it expedient. There is no provision for the Minister to require the planning authority to serve a notice under this section as there is in the case of notices under section 31. Thus the service of a notice under this section is at the absolute discretion of the planning authority. When deciding whether to serve a notice under this section the planning authority are restricted to considering the matters set out in section 32(2). It should be noted that they may consider the terms of *any* planning permission and it would appear that they are not restricted to considering the terms of the planning permission to which the condition attaches.

The same rules as to service of the notice apply to service of a notice under section 32 as apply to the service of a notice under section 31. (See above)

The notice must specify the matters in respect of which it is alleged that any condition has not been complied with and it must specify a period at the expiry of which the notice will come into effect. This period must not be less than one month after service of the notice. (See section 32(4)) The notice may specify steps to be taken in order to secure compliance with the condition and in particular may specify the steps set out in section 32(3). Care must be taken to ensure that the steps are clear and unambiguous and that they do not exceed what is necessary to ensure compliance with the condition.

In the event of a failure to carry out the specified steps within the time allowed the planning authority may enter onto the structure and carry out the steps themselves and recover any expenses reasonably incurred from the then owner of the land. Failure to comply with the terms of the notice is an offence under section 34. For a consideration of offences under section 34 see Enforcement Notices Under Section 31.[37]

ENFORCEMENT NOTICES UNDER SECTION 35[38]

This is an appropriate notice to serve where planning permission has been obtained and the development has been commenced on foot of that permission but it is not being carried out or it has not been carried out in conformity with the permission. There is no time limit within which notices under section 35 must be served. It is not clear whether the planning authority can serve a notice under this section where there has been a failure to comply with a condition and thereby avoid the five year limitation period or whether it is confined to serving a notice under section 31 or section 32 as appropriate.

The planning authority may serve a notice if they consider it expedient to do so and shall serve a notice if directed to do so by the Minister. When considering whether it is expedient to serve a notice or in the case of the Minister whether to direct that a notice be served, only those matters set out in section 35(2) may be considered. Note that *any* permission granted may be considered. The notice may be served on the person who commenced the development *or* on any person who has carried out or is carrying out the development. It is for the planning authority to decide who should be served. For consideration of the service and contents of the notice see above under notices served under section 31. In the event of a failure to carry out any steps required within the time allowed the planning authority may enter onto the land, carry out the steps and recover any expenses reasonably

---

[37] See page 334.
[38] Section 35 is quoted at page 338.

incurred in that behalf from the person on whom the notice was served. Failure to take the steps required within the time allowed is an offence under section 35(7) committed by the person on whom the notice was served. Where that person fails to do everything within his power to secure compliance with the notice as soon as practicable after conviction he is guilty of a further offence under section 35(8). This is an offence of a continuing nature and repeated prosecution may be brought. (See *Dublin Corporation* v. *Flynn*)[39]

ENFORCEMENT NOTICES UNDER SECTION 36[40]

A notice may be served under this section when the planning authority decide in the interests of proper planning and development that a structure should be removed or altered. In coming to that decision the planning authority are restricted to considering the matters set out in section 36(3). The notice may be served in respect of an authorised development at any time or in respect of an unauthorised development any time five years after the construction, erection or making of the structure. (See section 36(2))

Service must be effected on the owner and occupier of the structure and on any other person who in the opinion of the planning authority will be affected by it. The notice may require the removal or alteration of the structure and where removal is required it may require any replacement which appears suitable to the planning authority be provided. (See section 36(2)) The notice must specify a period within which the removal or alteration or replacement must be effected in the event of the notice coming into force. The notice must also specify a time of not less than one month from service of the notice within which an appeal to the Board may be brought. (See section 36(4)) Any person may appeal within that period. In the event of no appeal being brought or any appeals brought being withdrawn within the period for appealing the notice will take effect on the expiration of tht period. (See section 36(6)(a)) In the event of an appeal being brought and not withdrawn or withdrawn after the expiration the time for bringing appeal the notice will come into effect when every appeal is withdrawn or when and if the Board decides to confirm the notice. Appeals are dealt with in Chapter 4.

In the event of a failure to comply with the notice within the time allowed the planning authority may enter on the structure and effect the removal, alteration or replacement as specified.

In the event of compliance with the notice the planning authority must pay the expenses reasonably incurred by the person complying less the value of any salvage.

Where a notice is confirmed on appeal whether with or without modification it will be treated as a refusal of an application for permission to develop land for the purposes of section 29 of the 1963 Act.[41] Thus a Purchase Notice under section 29 may be served on the planning authority if the notice makes the land incapable of reasonably beneficial use in its existing state and the land cannot be rendered capable of reasonably beneficial use in its existing state and the land cannot be rendered capable of reasonably beneficial use by carrying out any other develop-

---

[39] See page 345.
[40] Section 36 is quoted at page 339.
[41] See page 393 and Chapter 6.

ment for which permission has been granted or for which the planning authority has undertaken to grant permission.

Where there is no duty on the planning authority under section 29 compensation may be payable under section 60. (See Chapter 6)

Notices under this section are rarely if ever served.

ENFORCEMENT NOTICES UNDER SECTION 37[42]

A notice under this section may be served by the planning authority if it decides that in the interest of the proper planning and development that a use should be discontinued or conditions should be imposed on the continuation of a use. (See section 37(1) and 37(3)) The notice may be served at any time in respect of an authorised use. In respect of an unauthorised use a notice may be served only in relation to a use commenced on or after the 1st October 1964 and only after five years from its commencement have elapsed. (See section 37(2)) The service and contents of the notice are similar to those required by section 36 notices. (See above and section 37(1), (4)) As with notices under section 36 an appeal may be brought to the Board from the service of a notice. (See section 37(5), (6))

An offence is committed by any person who contravenes a notice or who causes or permits a notice to be contravened and a further offence of a continuing nature is committed if the contravention is continued after conviction. (See section 37(7) and *Dublin Corporation* v. *Flynn*)[43]

Section 29 as modified by section 37(9) applies to notices confirmed on appeal (whether with or without modifications). Where there is no duty imposed on the planning authority to acquire an interest in the land by section 29 as applied by section 37(8); compensation may be payable under section 61. (See Chapter 6)

LOCAL GOVERNMENT (PLANNING AND DEVELOPMENT) ACT, 1963

31. – (1)(*a*) Where any development of land, being neither exempted development nor development commenced before the appointed day, has been
carried out after the appointed day[44] without the grant of permission
required in that behalf under this Part of this Act, or any condition
subject to which such permission was granted in respect of any development has not been complied with, the planning authority within five
years of such development being carried out, or, in case of non-
compliance with a condition, within five years after the appropriate
date, may, if they decide that it is expedient so to do, and shall, if they
are directed by the Minister so to do serve on the owner and on the
occupier of the land a notice under this section.

(*b*) In the foregoing paragraph 'the appropriate date' means, in relation to a
condition, the date specified in the condition (or in default of being
specified in the condition, specified by notice served by the planning
authority on the owner and on the occupier of the land) as the latest date
for compliance with the condition.

---

[42] Section 37 is quoted at page 340.
[43] See page 345.
[44] The appointed day is the 1st October 1964.

(2) The planning authority, in deciding whether it is expedient to serve a notice under paragraph (*a*) of subsection (1) of this section, and the Minister, in deciding whether he will direct the planning authority to serve such a notice, shall be restricted to considering the proper planning and development of the area of the authority (including the preservation and improvement of the amenities thereof), regard being had to the provisions of the development plan, the provisions of any special amenity area order relating to the said area and, in a case of non-compliance with a condition, the terms of the permission.[45]

(3) Any notice served under paragraph (*a*) of subsection (1) of this section (hereafter in this section, referred to as an enforcement notice) shall specify the development which is alleged to have been carried out without the grant of such permission as aforesaid or, as the case may be, the matters in respect of which it is alleged that any such condition as aforesaid has not been complied with, and may require such steps as may be specified in the notice to be taken within such period as may be so specified for restoring the land to its condition before the development took place, or for securing compliance with the condition, as the case may be; and, in particular, any such notice may, for the purpose aforesaid, require the removal or alteration of any structures, the discontinuance of any use of land, or the carrying out on land of any works.

(4) An enforcement notice shall take effect at the expiration of such period (not being less than one month after the service thereof) as may be specified therein.

(5) If within the period specified in an enforcement notice, or within such extended period as the planning authority may allow, any steps required by the notice to be taken (other than the discontinuance of any use of land) have not been taken, the planning authority may enter on the land[46] and take such steps, and may recover as a simple contract debt in any court of competent jurisdiction from the person who is then the owner of the land any expenses reasonably incurred by them in that behalf.

(6) Any expenses incurred by the owner or occupier of any land for the purpose of complying with an enforcement notice in respect of any development, and any sums paid by the owner of any land under the foregoing subsection in respect of the expenses of the planning authority in taking steps required to be taken by such a notice, shall be deemed to be incurred or paid for the use and at the request of the person by whom the development was carried out.

(7) An enforcement notice may be served whether or not there has been a prosecution under section 24 of this Act in relation to the relevant development.

(8) Where, by virtue of an enforcement notice, any use of land is required to be discontinued, or any condition is required to be complied with in respect of any use of land or in respect of the carrying out of any works thereon, then, if any person, without the grant of permission in that behalf under this Part of this Act, uses the land or causes or permits the land to be used, or carries out or causes or permits to be carried out those works, in contravention of the notice, he shall be guilty of an offence and liable on summary conviction to a fine not exceeding eight hundred pounds,[47] and if the use or carrying out of works in contravention of the notice is continued after the conviction, he shall be guilty of a further offence and liable on

---

[45] The planning authority and the Minister may also consider the matters set out in section 24 of the 1976 Act.

[46] See section 81 at page 12ɔ concerning entry onto the land by the planning authority.

[47] As amended by section 8(1) of the 1982 Act.

summary conviction to a fine (not exceeding in all £800)[48] not exceeding £150 for each day on which such use or carrying out of works is so continued.

(9) Nothing in this Part of this Act shall be construed as requiring permission to be obtained thereunder for the use of any land for the purpose for which it could lawfully have been used under this Part of this Act if the development in respect of which an enforcement notice is served had not been carried out.

(10) Particulars of an enforcement notice shall be entered in the register.[49]

32. – (1)(a) Where any condition subject to which a permission for the retention of a structure was granted under this Part of this Act has not been complied with, the planning authority may within five years after the appropriate date, if they decide that it is expedient so to do, serve on the owner and on the occupier of the structure a notice under this section.

(b) In the foregoing paragraph 'the appropriate date' means, in relation to a condition, the date specified in the condition (or, in default of being specified in the condition, specified by notice served by the planning authority on the owner and on the occupier of the structure) as the latest date for compliance with the condition.

(2) In deciding, pursuant to this section, whether it is expedient to serve a notice under paragraph (a) of subsection (1) of this section, the planning authority shall be restricted to considering the proper planning and development of the area of the authority (including the preservation and improvement of the amenities thereof), regard being had to the provisions of the development plan, the provisions of any special amenity area order relating to the said area and the terms of any permission granted.[50]

(3) Any notice served under paragraph (a) of subsection (1) of this section (hereafter in this section referred to as an enforcement notice) shall specify the matters in respect of which it is alleged that any such condition as aforesaid had not been complied with, and may require such steps as may be specified in the notice to be taken within such period as may be so specified for compliance with the condition; and, in particular, any such notice may, for the purpose aforesaid, require the removal of the structure or require all or any of the following:

(a) the alteration of the structure,

(b) the carrying out of works (including the provision of car parks) which the planning authority consider are required if the retention of the structure is to be permitted,

(c) the provision of space around the structure,

(d) the planting of trees, shrubs or other plans or the landscaping of the structure or other land.

(4) An enforcement notice shall take effect at the expiration of such period (not being less than one month after the service thereof) as may be specified therein.

(5) If within the period specified in an enforcement notice, or within such extended period as the planning authority may allow, any steps required by the notice to be taken have not been taken, the planning authority may enter on the structure and take those steps, and may recover as a simple contract debt in any

---

[48] As amended by section 8(1) of the 1982 Act.

[49] See section 28 of the 1976 Act in respect of the withdrawal of the notice and cancellation of entries on the register.

[50] See section 24 of the 1976 Act for additional matters to which the planning authority may have regard.

court of competent jurisdiction from the person who is then the owner of the structure any expenses reasonably incurred by them in that behalf.

(6) Particulars of an enforcement notice shall be entered in the register.[51],[52]

. . .

34. – (1) Subject to the provisions of this section, where an enforcement notice (other than a notice which has been annulled) has been served under any of the last three preceding sections on the person who was, when the notice was served on him, the owner of the land to which the enforcement notice relates and within the period specified in the enforcement notice, or within such extended period as the planning authority may allow, any steps required by the enforcement notice to be taken (other than the discontinuance of any use of land) have not been taken, that person shall be guilty of an offence and shall be liable on summary conviction to a fine not exceeding eight hundred pounds.[53]

(2) If a person against whom proceedings are brought under this section has at some time before the end of the said period specified in the enforcement notice for compliance with the notice (or of such extended period as the planning authority may allow for compliance with the notice) ceased to be the owner of the land, he shall, upon complaint duly made by him and on giving to the prosecution not less than three clear days' notice of his intention, be entitled to have the person who then became the owner of the land brought before the court in the proceedings.

(3) If, after it has been proved that any steps required by the enforcement notice have not been taken as aforesaid, the original defendant proves that the failure to take the steps was attributable in whole or in part to the default of the said other person, that other person may be convicted of the offence and, if the original defendant further proves that he took all reasonable steps to secure compliance with the enforcement notice, he shall be acquitted of the offence.

(4) For the purposes of subsection (1) and (2) of this section, a person who, apart from this subsection, would be the owner of land by reason of receiving rent shall, if he receives the rent as agent for another person, be regarded as not being such owner.

(5) If after a person is convicted under the foregoing provisions of this section he does not as soon as practicable do everything in his power to secure compliance with the enforcement notice, he shall be guilty of a further offence and shall be liable on summary conviction to a fine (not exceeding in all £800) not exceeding £150 for each day following his first conviction on which any of the requirements of the enforcement notice (other than the discontinuance of any use of land) remain unfulfilled.[53]

(6) If the owner of any land is obstructed or interfered with in taking steps required to be taken by an enforcement notice under any of the last three preceding sections, the person obstructing or interfering shall be guilty of an offence and shall be liable on summary conviction to a fine not exceeding eight hundred pounds; and if in the case of a continuing offence the obstruction or interference is continued

---

[51] See section 28 of the 1976 Act in respect of the withdrawal of notices and the cancellation of entries on the register.

[52] Section 33 dealt with the Enforcement of planning control in respect of structures which were unauthorised on the commencement of the 1st day of October, 1964. The time within which notices could be served under this section expired in 1969.

[53] As amended by section 8(1) of the 1982 Act.

after conviction, he shall be guilty of a further offence and liable on summary conviction to a fine (not exceeding in all £800) not exceeding £150 pounds for each day on which the obstruction or interference is so continued.[53]

(7) Subsection (6) of this section shall not apply where the person obstructing or interfering is the occupier of the land unless the owner has given to him not less than fourteen days' notice in writing of the intention to take the steps.

35. – (1) Where any development authorised by a permission granted under this Part of this Act has been commenced but has not been or is not being carried out in conformity with such permission, the planning authority may, if they consider it expedient so to do, and shall, if they are directed so to do by the Minister, serve a notice under this section.

(2) The planning authority, in deciding whether it is expedient to serve a notice under this section, and the Minister, in deciding whether he will direct the planning authority to serve such a notice, shall be restricted to considering the proper planning and development of the area of the authority (including the preservation and improvement of the amenities thereof), regard being had to the provisions of the development plan, the provisions of any special amenity area order relating to the said area[54] and the terms of any permission granted.

(3) A notice under this section may be served on –
  (a) the person who commenced the development, or
  (b) any other person who has carried out or is carrying out development authorised by the permission,
as the planning authority may decide.

(4) Any notice served under this section (hereafter in this section referred to as an enforcement notice) may require such steps as may be specified in the notice to be taken within such period as may be so specified for securing the carrying out of the development in conformity with the permission and, in particular, any such notice may, for the purpose aforesaid, require the removal or alteration of any structures, the discontinuance of any use of land or the carrying out on land of any works.

(5) An enforcement notice shall take effect at the expiration of such period (not being less than one month after the service thereof) as may be specified therein.

(6) If within the period specified in an enforcement notice, or within such extended period as the planning authority may allow, any steps required by the notice to be taken have not been taken, the planning authority may enter on the land and take such steps[55] and may recover as a simple contract debt in any court of competent jurisdiction from the person on whom the notice was served any expenses reasonably incurred by them in that behalf.

(7) Where an enforcement notice has been served on a person and within the period specified therein, or within such extended period as the planning authority may allow, any steps required by the notice to be taken have not been taken, that person shall be guilty of an offence and shall be liable on summary conviction to a fine not exceeding eight hundred pounds.[56]

[54] See section 24 of the 1976 Act for additional matters which the planning authority may consider.
[55] See section 81 of the 1963 Act in respect of the powers of the planning authority to enter onto land.
[56] As amended by section 8(1) of the 1982 Act.

(8) If after a person is convicted under this section he does not as soon as practicable do everything in his power to secure compliance with the enforcement notice, he shall be guilty of a further offence and shall be liable on summary conviction to a fine (not exceeding in all £800) not exceeding £150 for each day following his first conviction on which any of the requirements of the enforcement notice remain unfulfilled.[56]

(9) Particulars of an enforcement notice shall be entered in the register.[57]

36. – (1) If the planning authority decide that any structure should be removed or altered, the planning authority may serve a notice, requiring the carrying out of such removal or alteration and, in the case of a removal, any replacement appearing to the planning authority to be suitable, on the owner and on the occupier of the structure and on any other person who in their opinion will be affected by the notice.

(2) Subsection (1) of this section shall not apply in relation to an unauthorised structure unless –

(*a*) it is a structure which existed immediately before the appointed day and was on the commencement of that day an unauthorised structure and the notice under this section is served after the expiration of five years from the appointed day[58], or

(*b*) it is a structure constructed, erected or made on or after the appointed day[58] and the notice under this section is served after the expiration of five years from its having been constructed, erected or made.

(3) In deciding pursuant to this section that a structure should be removed or altered, the planning authority shall be restricted to considering the proper planning and development of the area of the authority (including the preservation and improvement of the amenities thereof), regard being had to the provisions of the development plan and the provisions of any special amenity area order relating to the said area.[59]

(4) Where a notice is served under this section, any person may, at any time before the day (not being earlier than one month after such service) specified in that behalf in the notice, appeal to the Board against the notice.

(5) Where an appeal is brought under this section against a notice, the Board may confirm the notice with or without modifications or annul the notice, and the provisions of subsection (3) of this section shall apply, subject to any necessary modifications, in relation to the deciding of an appeal under this subsection by the Board as they apply in relation to the making of a decision by the planning authority.[60]

(6) A notice under this section (other than a notice which is annulled) shall take effect –

(*a*) in case no appeal against it is taken or every appeal against it is withdrawn before the expiration of the period for taking an appeal – on the expiration of the period for taking an appeal.

---

[57] See section 28 of the 1976 Act in respect of the withdrawal of notices and the cancellation of entries in the register.

[58] 1st October 1964.

[59] See section 24 of the 1976 Act for additional matters which the planning authority may consider.

[60] Section 14 of the 1976 Act transferred the Minister's powers to the Board.

(*b*) in case an appeal or appeals is or are taken against it and the appeal or appeals is or are not withdrawn during the period for taking an appeal – when every appeal not so withdrawn has been either withdrawn or determined.

(7) If within the period specified in a notice under this section, or within such extended period as the planning authority may allow, the removal or alteration required by the notice has not been effected, the planning authority may enter on the structure and may effect such removal or alteration and any replacement specified in the notice.[61]

(8) Where a notice under this section is complied with, the planning authority shall pay to the person complying with the notice the expenses reasonably incurred by him in carrying out the removal or alteration and any replacement specified in the notice, less the value of any salvageable materials.[62]

(9) The provisions of section 29 of this Act shall apply in relation to a notice which is served under this section and which is confirmed on appeal (whether with or without modification) as they apply in relation to the refusal of an application for permission to develop land, in any any such case the said section 29 shall have effect subject to the following modifications:

(i) paragraph (*c*) of subsection (1) shall be disregarded;

(ii) for paragraph (i) of the proviso to subsection (4) there shall be substituted the following paragraph:

'(i) if it appears to the Minister to be expedient so to do he may, in lieu of conforming the purchase notice, cancel the notice requiring removal or alteration.'

(10) Particulars of a notice served under this section shall be entered in the register.[63]

37. – (1) If the planning authority decide, as respects any use of land, that –

(*a*) the use should be discontinued, or

(*b*) any conditions should be imposed on the continuance thereof,

the planning authority may serve a notice, requiring discontinuance of that use or imposing those conditions, on the owner and on the occupier of the land and on any other person who in their opinion will be affected by the notice.

(2) Subsection (1) of this section shall not apply in relation to an unauthorised use unless it is a use commenced on or after the appointed day and the notice under this section is served after the expiration of five years from its having been commenced.

(3) In deciding, pursuant to this section, that any use should be discontinued or any conditions should be imposed, the planning authority shall be restricted to considering the proper planning and development of the area of the authority (including the preservation and improvement of the amenities thereof), regard being had to the provisions of the development plan and the provisions of any special amenity area order relating to the said area.[64]

---

[61] See section 81 at page 125 in respect of the planning authority's power of entry onto the land.

[62] See section 60 of the 1963 Act in respect of compensation which may be payable.

[63] See section 28 of the 1976 Act in respect of the withdrawal of notices and the cancellation of entries on the register.

[64] See section 24 of the 1976 Act for additional matters which the planning authority may consider.

(4) Where a notice is served under this section, any person may, at any time before the day (not being earlier than one month after such service) specified in that behalf in the notice, appeal to the Board against the notice.[65]

(5) Where an appeal is brought under this section against a notice, the Board may confirm the notice with or without modifications or annul the notice, and the provisions of subsection (3) of this section shall apply, subject to any necessary modifications, in relation to the deciding of an appeal under this subsection by the Board as they apply in relation to the making of a decision by the planning authority.[65]

(6) A notice under this section (other than a notice which is annulled) shall take effect –

(*a*) in case no appeal against it is taken or every appeal against it is withdrawn before the expiration of the period for taking an appeal – on the expiration of the period for taking an appeal,

(*b*) in case an appeal or appeals is or are taken against it and the appeal or appeals is or are not withdrawn during the period for taking an appeal – when every appeal not so withdrawn has been either withdrawn or determined.

(7) Where, by virtue of a notice under this section, the use of land for any purpose is required to be discontinued, or any conditions are imposed on the continuance thereof, then, if any person uses the land for that purpose or, as the case may be, uses land for that purpose in contravention of those conditions, or causes or permits the land to be so used, he shall be guilty of an offence and liable on summary conviction to a fine not exceeding eight hundred pounds, and if such use is continued after the conviction, he shall be guilty of a further offence and liable on summary conviction to a fine (not exceeding in all £800) not exceeding £150 for each day on which such use is so continued.[66]

(8) The provisions of section 29 of this Act shall apply in relation to a notice which is served under this section requiring discontinuance of use of land, or imposing conditions on such use, which is confirmed on appeal (whether with or without modifications), as they apply in relation to the refusal of an application for permission to use land or the grant of such an application subject to conditions, and in any such case the said section 29 shall have effect subject to the following modifications:

(i) for paragraph (*a*) of subsection (1) there shall be substituted the following paragraph:

'(*a*) that the land has become incapable of reasonably beneficial use on account of the required discontinuance or the imposed conditions (as the case may be)';

(ii) Paragraph (*c*) of subsection (1) shall be disregarded;

(iii) for paragraph (i) of the proviso to subsection (4) there shall be substituted the following paragraph:

'(i) if it appears to the Board to be expedient so to do he may, in lieu of confirming the purchase notice, cancel the notice requiring discontinuance or imposing conditions.'

[65] Section 14 of the 1976 Act transferred the Minister's appellate functions under this section to the Board.

[66] As amended by section 8(1) of the 1982 Act.

(9) Particulars of a notice served under this section shall be entered in the register.[67,68]

LOCAL GOVERNMENT (PLANNING AND DEVELOPMENT) ACT, 1976

28. – (1) Where a planning authority serve a notice mentioned in section 30, 31, 32, 35, 36, 37 or 44 of the Principal Act they may by notice in writing withdraw the notice.

(2) Where a notice is withdrawn pursuant to this section by a planning authority, the fact that the notice was withdrawn shall be recorded by the authority in the register.

CASES

DUBLIN CORPORATION V. MULLIGAN
The High Court. Finlay P., 6 May 1980 (Ref. No. 1980 No. 16 MCA)

In 1972 the respondent purchased premises which had been used as a residence by his predecessor in title and which were located in an area zoned exclusively for residential use. He began to practise as a solicitor in the basement portion of the premises shortly afterwards and retained the remainder of the premises as his residence. He made no attempt to hide the fact that he was using the basement portion for his practice. The unauthorised use came to the attention of the applicants in May 1978. On the 19th December 1978 a warning notice was served on him. In March 1979 the respondent vacated the residential portion of the premises and began to use the whole of the premises for his practice. On the 31st March 1980 he was served with section 27 proceedings. When the matter came on for hearing he did not dispute the applicant's right to an Order in respect of the portion of the premises other than the basement. In respect of the basement portion of the premises he argued that an order could not be made since the use had continued for a period in excess of five years or in the alternative if an order could be made it should not be made because of the lapse of time. The Court held that, in the circumstances of this case, the respondent had acquired a vested interest in continuing to use the basement for his practice by reason of the lapse of time between the commencement of the use and the commencement of the proceedings. See, however, *Dublin Corporation* v. *Kevans*[69] and *Dublin Corporation* v. *Garland.*[70]

Finlay P.:
. . . The respondent made two submissions to me.

The first was that by reason of the fact that the unauthorised use had commenced in February 1973 and had therefore continued for a period in excess of 5 years at the time of the making of this application that having regard to the provisions in particular of Section 31 of the Local Government (Planning and Development) Act

---

[67] See section 28 of the 1976 Act in respect of the withdrawal of notices and the cancellation of entries on the register.
[68] See section 61 of the 1963 Act in respect of compensation which may be payable.
[69] See page 371.
[70] See page 374.

1963 and to the general construction of the Acts of 1963 and 1976 that the Court has not got jurisdiction now to make an order under Section 27 in respect of that unauthorised use.

In the alternative the respondent submits that even if there is a discretion in the Court to make an order under Section 27 in respect of use which commenced in February 1973 that having regard to that lapse of time and to the other facts of this case that the Court should not exercise its discretion in favour of granting an order.

I have dealt with the submission made firstly by the respondent in a case of the *Dublin County Council* v. *Matra Investments Ltd*[71] and although that was not a reserved judgment Counsel were able to provide for me a transcript of my judgment which I had approved as being accurate. In that case I came to the conclusion that there were no grounds as a matter of interpretation for implying into Section 27 of the Act of 1976 the time limit created by Section 31 of the Act of 1963. Section 31 of the Act of 1963 is a section providing for the enforcement of planning control decisions creating in short a machinery for the service of notices and upon due service of them and the provision of a time for compliance than alternative remedies consisting in part of the carrying out of works by the planning authority and the recovery of the cost of them as a simple contract debt and also providing for the commission by the person who disobeys a valid enforcement notice of a criminal offence punishable by a fine not exceeding £100[72] and in the case of continuance a further offence liable to a fine not exceeding £20[73] for each day of the continuance. The entire of the provisions of the Section and the powers thereby vested in a planning authority are subject under sub-section (1)(*a*) to the restriction that the development which was unauthorised or the failure to comply with a condition in a grant of permission shall have occurred within five years of the service of the enforcement notice. There is not contained in any other provision of the Planning and Development Acts 1963 or 1976 any general provision that a development or use which is unauthorised shall after the continuance of 5 years without enforcement or proceedings by the planning authority become lawful or authorised. All that is contained in Section 31 of the Act of 1963 is a condition similarly repeated in Section 30 of the Act of 1976 limiting a particular power of enforcement to a period of 5 years from the unlawful development or the non-compliance with a condition.

As I indicated in my decision in the *Dublin County Council* v. *Matra Investments Ltd.* from which I see no reason after further submissions to depart. Section 27 of the Act of 1976 is an entirely new section in this planning code and gives to the Court an entirely new power not hitherto provided. There is nothing contained in section 27 nor in any other section of the Act of 1976 in any way restricting the time during which a planning authority or other interested person may apply to the Court under that section for an order. Had the legislature in 1976 intended to imply into Section 27 of that Act a time limit similar to that contained in Section 31 of the Act of 1963 it seems to me an inescapable conclusion that they would have expressly done so. It was further submitted to me however on this issue by Counsel for the respondent that I should interpret Section 31 of the Act of 1963 as making in the particular instance of this case an unauthorised change of use which had

---

[71] See page 374.
[72] Now not exceeding £800. See section 8 of the 1982 Act.
[73] Now not exceeding £150 per day to a maximum of £800. See section 8 of the 1982 Act.

occurred more than 5 years before the institution of proceedings into an authorised change of use losing its unlawful and unauthorised character. I can find no warrant for so construing Section 31 of the Act of 1963. There are, particularly in relation to summary criminal offences, a great number of instances in our statute law where the institution of proceedings in relation to such an offence is limited in time and where after the lapse of that time in the absence of the institution of proceedings a person who may have committed such an offence is immune from prosecution. That does not it seems to me, in any way alter the unlawful nature of the act first committed. In the same way I can see no ground for holding that the restriction imposed by Section 31 of the Act of 1963 upon the institution of enforcement proceedings under that Section to a period of 5 years from the unlawful development in any way makes the development lawful.

In my view therefore there is jurisdiction in the Court if in its discretion it thinks it so should do to make an order under Section 27 in respect of any unauthorised use or unlawful development no matter what lapse of time has occurred since it first commenced or was created.

As I indicated in my decision in the *Dublin County Council* v. *Matra Investments Ltd.* however it seems to me that the length of time between the commencement of an unauthorised use or the making of an unlawful development and the time when application is made to the Court under Section 27 must always remain one of, but not the only material factor in regard to the exercise by the Court of its discretion as to whether to make or not to make an order under Section 27.

If the applicant to the Court could be said to be guilty of laches and delay quite clearly as in any other proceedings seeking an injunction he might and should be disentitled to relief. I am not satisfied that in this case it can be said that the applicants have been guilty of laches and delay because whereas it is clear that it was possible for any person to have ascertained that these premises had commenced to be used as an office in February 1973 there is no evidence before me that the planning officials were actually aware of it until some time in 1978. I accept the contention made on behalf of the applicants that difficulties in assembling proof of the user of the premises at the date of the commencement and coming into operation of the Act of 1963 were considerable and that there were grounds for the delay from May 1978 up to the present.

To the question however of the relevance and importance of the lapse of time between the commencement of an unauthorised use and an application to the Court under Section 27 there appears to me to be another aspect other than laches or delay on the part of the applicant. That is, the position in which the respondent finds himself even though he may have originally committed a breach of the Planning Acts if after a very considerable number of years without any attempt on the part of any person to enforce those Acts he suddenly faces an order under Section 27. Section 31 of the Act of 1963 and Section 30 of the Act of 1976 appear to me to be relevant to the consideration of the Court in this way and in this way only. The legislature in those two Sections imposed on a different form of consequential enforcement proceedings in effect a time limit of 5 years. This must, it seems to me, be construed as an acceptance by the legislature that with regard to those particular forms of enforcement it would be unjust that a person after the lapse of 5 years should face the relevant Court proceedings. . .

In these particular circumstances applicable to this case I am satisfied that by reason of the lapse of time since the commencement of the change of this user before the institution of these proceedings that I, at my discretion, should refuse to the applicants an order in regard to the basement of the premises. This decision, however, should not be construed as being equivalent to a decision that this user has now become lawful or authorised or to the effect that any successor in title from the purchaser would of necessity be immune from the making of an order under Section 27 were he to use the basement of the premises for office use.

I am satisfied that the respondent has behaved incorrectly notwithstanding the warning notice of 1978 which he should fully have understood and his legal position which I must assume he particularly understood in extending his solicitors practice into a residential portion of the premises, as he admits he did, in March 1979. His conduct in so doing must reduce to some extent his merits in relation to the length of time which it is now appropriate that he should be given to make alternative arrangements and to cease using the portion of the premises other than the basement as a solicitor's office.

I accordingly will make an order directing that the respondent should discontinue the use of so much of the premises exclusive of the basement for any purpose other than residential purposes within three months from this date.

DUBLIN CORPORATION V. FRANCIS FLYNN
[1980] I.R. 357, Henchy J.

The respondent built a factory-warehouse without obtaining planning permission. In 1973 he was served with an enforcement notice requiring him to remove the building within a specified time. The respondent failed to comply with the notice and in June 1973 he was convicted under section 34(1) of the 1963 Act. Following conviction he continued to fail to remove the building thereby committing an offence under section 34(5) of the 1963 Act. He was prosecuted, convicted and fined four times under section 34(5) between 1973 and 1976. In 1978 he was again prosecuted under section 34(5). At the hearing the defendant raised the defence for the first time that no evidence had been given to prove the enforcement notice or its service. The prosecution had, however, put in evidence a certified copy of the conviction in June 1973 in which it was recited that the enforcement notice had been served on the defendant in February 1973. The prosecution argued that this established that the District Justice who made the conviction had found as a matter of fact that the enforcement notice had been validly served on the defendant and that the issue of service was now *res judicata* and further that the defendant was estopped from raising the point by reason of his failure to do so at any of the previous prosecutions. The defendant was convicted for a fifth time, however the District Justice stated a case to the High Court on the question of whether he was bound to convict on the evidence before him and whether the prosecution had to prove the making and service of the enforcement notice. At the hearing in the High Court the Court raised a further question of whether section 34(5) creates a continuing offence or a single non-continuing offence.

The High Court held that the District Justice had not been bound to convict on the evidence before it; that it was not necessary to prove the making and service of the enforcement notice but it was necessary to prove the contents thereof; and that the offence created by section 34(5) was non-continuing. It was held by the Supreme Court that the offence was a continuing offence and that it was necessary for the prosecution to prove the making and the service of the enforcement notice.

Henchy J.:

. . . In the High Court the judge reached the conclusion that an offence under s. 34(5) of the Act is not a continuing offence – just as, admittedly, an offence under s. 34(1) of the Act is not a continuing one. His rationale in coming to that conclusion derives from the absence from s. 34(5) of any specific nomination of the offence as a continuing one. He thought it significant that whereas Parliament, having in s. 24(2) made it an offence to carry out development of land without the required permission, provided in s. 24(3) of the Act that 'if in the case of a continuing offence the contravention is continued after conviction', there is to be a further offence, no similar express nomination of the offence as a continuing one is to be found in the text of s. 34(5). Because of the absence of any use of the expression 'continuing offence' in s. 34(5), the judge felt bound to conclude that an offence under s. 34(5) was not intended to be a continuing offence.

I fear I am unable to reach the same conclusion. Whether a statute has made an act or default a continuing offence, meriting repeated prosecutions, depends not on the use of a special verbal formula but on whether the statutory provision properly interpreted indicates an intention to that effect. It is not necessary that the offence be expressly designated a continuing offence. It will usually be sufficient if (as is the case in s. 34(5)) a penalty is provided for each day on which the prohibited act or default takes place. It is true that in s. 24(3) Parliament both designated the contravention a continuing offence and provided for a recurring penalty for each day's contravention. But a continuing offence would have been none the less created of the express nomination of a continuing offence had been omitted from s. 24(3) – as it has been, not alone from s. 34(5), but also from other sections, such as s. 31(8) and s. 35(8) of the Act and s. 26(5) of the amending Act of 1976.

The judge considered that an offence under s. 34(5) is a 'once and for all offence'. I do not think so. The characteristic of such an offence is the fixing of a single penalty for a single or composite act or default. That is not what s. 34(5) has done. It has laid down a fine not exceeding £50[74] for each day, following the accused's first conviction, on which he is in default of any of the specified requirements of the enforcement notice. Such an offence is necessarily a continuing one; it is committed afresh on each day on which the accused is in default; and a conviction must impose a fine for each day of default: see *Westropp* v. *Commissioners of Public Works* (1896) 2 I.R. 93 and *Tyrrell* v. *Bray U.D.C.* (1957) I.R. 127.

If s. 34(5) created only a single offence, the penalty for a massive and continued breach of planning requirements would be only a single fine of a maximum size scarcely sufficient to deter the breach. I do not think the wording of s. 34(5) permits the attribution of such an intention to Parliament.

Support for the conclusion that s. 34(5) has created a continuing offence, for the repetition of which successive prosecutions will lie, is to be found in the fact that the corresponding provision in the English planning code has also been interpreted to that effect: see *R.* v. *Chertsey Justices, ex p. Franks* (1961) 2 Q.B. 152 and *St. Alban's District Council* v. *Harper (Norman) Autosales* 1977 76 LGR 300.

I would reverse the decision under appeal to the extent that it held that only a single prosecution may be brought under s. 34(5) and that accordingly this prosecution does not lie.

---

[74] Now not exceeding £150 per day to a maximum of £800. See section 8 of the 1982 Act.

The questions in the case stated.

. . . With regard to the making, the contents and the service of the enforcement notice, the prosecution relied on the certified copy of the conviction in June 1973 under s. 34(1). That certified copy, which was put in evidence by the prosecution in the District Court on the hearing of the present charge under s. 34(5), recited that it was served on the defendant on the 21 February 1973. It was urged on behalf of the prosecution that this showed conclusively that due service had been found by the District Justice in that prosecution; that this finding had been accepted by the defendant in the four subsequent prosecutions; and that, this issue being *res judicata* the defendant is now estopped from contending to the contrary.

It is true that there are dicta to be found in cases such as *Ager* v. *Gates* (1934) 32 L.G.R. 223 and *Munnich* v. *Godstone R.D.C.* (1966) 1 All E.R. 930, 936 suggesting that an issue found against an accused in an earlier prosecution may not be questioned by him in a later prosecution. But later decisions have rejected that approach: see, for example, *Hailsham R.D.C.* v. *Moran* (1966) 64 L.G.R. 367, where it was held that an accused was not precluded from challenging the validity of an enforcement notice under the English Planning code notwithstanding that in a previous prosecution he had been convicted of failing to comply with it.

What is being urged on behalf of the prosecution in this case is that because it was necessarily found in an earlier prosecution of the defendant that the enforcement notice had been duly served on him and was valid, those issues should stand conclusively determined as a matter of *res judicata*. I consider that to be an insupportable proposition. In the criminal law the conclusive determination in an earlier prosecution of *issues* (as distinct from *verdicts*, which are impressed with conclusiveness under the rules of *autrefois convict* or *autrefois acquit*) arises, if at all, for benefit of an accused. Whether issue estoppel should be given recognition in the criminal law has given rise to conflicting opinions in courts of the highest authority in England, the United States and Australia. Those cases are referred to in *D.P.P.* v. *Humphrys* (1976) 2 All E.R. 497 in which the House of Lords rejected the existence of issue estoppel in the criminal law.

It is not necessary in this case to make a ruling as to whether the total rejection of issue estoppel made in *D.P.P.* v. *Humphrys* should be followed in this State, for in that case (and in the cases referred to therein, with the exception of *R.* v. *Hogan* (1974) Q.B. 398) the question of issue estoppel arose only at the invocation of the defence in respect of issues decided in a previous prosecution in favour of the accused. Here it is being raised against the accused.

Under the rubric 'May issue estoppel be used against the accused?' Spencer Bower and Turner on *The Doctrine of Res Judicata* (1969) 2nd edn. p. 287–8 gives this reply:

Estoppels are in their nature reciprocal, and if it is to be accepted that the prosecution may be precluded by issue estoppel based upon an earlier verdict from making a fresh accusation against the accused on a different charge, because of a fundamental inconsistency between such a charge and the formal verdict, can the prosecution be denied resort to the same course as a means of convicting a prisoner in later proceedings where the formal verdict is shown to be inconsistent with his innocence? No-one has yet contended that this should be the result of the application of issue estoppel to criminal proceedings'.

For this opinion that issue estoppel has never been claimed for the prosecution, there is the support of a dictum of Lord Devlin to the same effect in *Connelly* v. *D.P.P.* (1964) A.C. 1254 at 1346. Even if it is not quite correct that there is no such precedent, I am satisfied that it would be contrary to principle to allow a prosecution to prove certain issues by giving evidence that they were determined against the accused in an earlier prosecution. The determination of those issues against the accused in the previous prosecution may be insupportable for being wrong in law or not in accordance with the true facts. There is no valid reason why a determination of that kind should be stamped with finality and immutability. It may have been reached in default of appearance by the accused; or, even if he did appear, because of ignorance or inadvertence or bad advice the appropriate submissions may not have been made; or the tribunal in the earlier case may simply have gone wrong. It would be contrary to the fundamentals of criminal justice if an accused, because of an estoppel of the kind suggested, were to be debarred from showing in a later trial that the earlier determination of a particular issue was wrong. For one reason or another he may have been prepared to allow the earlier determination to go against him, but there are no reasons of justice why he should be bound to accept that determination for the purposes of a later trial. For example, to avoid undue publicity, or to get the matter disposed of quickly, or for some other reason he may have been prepared to accept a wrong decision in an earlier prosecution to the effect that he had committed an act of assault or had driven a motor car dangerously; but that is no reason why, if a death ensues from the event in question and he is later charged with murder or with the statutory offence of dangerous driving causing death, the earlier determination as to assault or driving should not only relieve the prosecution of proof in that respect but also make it incompetent for him to attempt to disprove the correctness of the earlier determination. Estoppel in such circumstances, because it would deprive the accused of the opportunity of making what might be a good defence, would be repugnant to the fair administration of justice. A decision to this effect was given by Gannon J. in *The State (Brady)* v. *McGrath* (25 May 1979, unreported).

In my judgment, in this or in any other criminal charge, the prosecution is not relieved of the onus of proof in regard to necessary issues by showing that those issues were expressly or impliedly decided against the accused in earlier proceedings. It is of the essence of a criminal trial that it be unitary and self-contained, to the extent that proof of the ingredients of the offence may not be established as a result of a dispersal of the issues between the court of trial and another tribunal. Evidence of a previous conviction, whether given as an ingredient of or as an element in the charge, or given pursuant to a special statutory permission, does no more than provide conclusive proof of that conviction. As to the issues that were decided against the accused in the earlier trial, the conviction does not operate to foreclose those issues in the subsequent trial.

The opposite of that was thought to be the law by Lawson J. in *R.* v. *Hogan* [1974] Q.B. 398, but his opinion was emphatically rejected by the House of Lords in *D.P.P.* v. *Humphrys* [1976] 2 All E.R. 497 . . . .

The real objection to the ruling given by Lawson J. in *R.* v. *Hogan* is summed up in a sentence in the speech of Lord Salmon in *D.P.P.* v. *Humphrys* (at p. 529):

'On a charge of murder the onus lies on the prosecution to prove its case, not by technical doctrine but by evidence, and the jury's duty is to decide the case on the evidence called before them, which might be quite different from the evidence adduced in the previous trial'.

In my judgment, that is a correct statement of the law, whatever be the charge and whether the trial be before a jury or a summary one.

I would answer the questions put in the case stated by holding that in order to secure a conviction, it was necessary for the prosecution to prove the due making and service of the enforcement order. Because this evidence was not adduced, the defendant was entitled to a dismiss.

SECTION 25 – ENFORCEMENT OF OPEN SPACES[75]

Section 25 of the 1976 Act provides a procedure whereby a planning authority may acquire land for public open space where the owner fails to provide or maintain such land as public open space as required by a permission granted under section 26 of the 1963 Act.

The requirement to provide and maintain public open space may arise in two ways:

(1) as a result of a condition being attached to the permission requiring the provision or maintenance of land as open space being land which is not described as private open space or in terms indicating that it is not intended that the public have unrestricted resort to it. (See Section 25(1)(b)(i) and (10))

or

(2) where it was explicit or implicit in the application for permission that land not described in the application as private open space or in terms indicating that it was not intended that the public were to have unrestricted resort to it would be provided as open space. (See Section 25(1)(b) (ii) and (10)).

The imposition of a condition requiring land be provided or maintained as public open space does not preclude an obligation arising under (2) to provide or maintain further public open space at another part of the site. (See *Dublin County Council* v. *Brennan*[76])

Where provision or maintenance of public open space is required under a permission granted pursuant to section 26 of the 1963 Act the planning authority may serve a notice on the owner[77] of the land anytime after the development commences requiring him to provide, level, plant or otherwise adapt or maintain land in a manner specified so as to make it suitable for the purpose for which the open space is to be provided. The request must limit a period of not less than two months commencing on the date of the request within which the terms of the request must be complied with. In the event of the owner failing to comply with or failing to secure compliance with the request the planning authority may if they think fit publish a notice – known as an acquisition notice – in a newspaper circulating in the district. Such notice must indicate that the planning authority intend to acquire the land and limit a time within which appeals may be made to the Board against their decision to acquire the land. A copy of the acquisition notice must be served on the owner of the land in accordance with section 7 of the 1963 Act not later than 10 days after publication of the notice.[78]

---

[75] Section 25 is quoted at page 350.
[76] See page 355.
[77] 'Owner' is defined in section 2 which is quoted at page 7.
[78] Section 7 is quoted at page 9.

Any person who for the time being has an interest in the land it is intended to acquire may appeal to the Board within the time allowed. There is no provision for extension of the time for appeals. The Board may having considered any appeals annul the notice or confirm it with or without modification. (See section 25(4))

If no appeal is made or if such appeals as are made are withdrawn or if the notice is confirmed on appeal the planning authority may make an Order in accordance with Form 4 of the 1977 Regulations vesting the land in itself. It will take the land for the same interest as was enjoyed by the owner immediately prior to acquisition subject to the same rights and liabilities as he enjoyed or incurred immediately prior to acquisition. The planning authority is obliged to comply with the requirements of its own request served on the owner.

No compensation is payable in respect of the acquisition unless it is shown by or on behalf of the owner that an amount equal to the value of the land to which the permission relates has not been recovered as a result of the development nor will such amount be recovered as a result of the development by disposing of the remaining land in the future. The value of the land is determined by reference to its value at the date of the application for permission. No regard shall be had to its value other than as open space and deduction must be made in respect of the cost of carrying out the works required to comply with the request made by the planning authority.[79]

LOCAL GOVERNMENT (PLANNING AND DEVELOPMENT) ACT, 1976

25. – (1) Where –

(a) development is being or has been carried out pursuant to a permission under section 26 of the Principal Act, and

(b)　　(i) a condition requiring the provision or maintenance of land as open space, being open space to which this section applies, was attached to the permission, or

　　(ii) it was either explicit or implicit in the application for the said permission that land would be provided or maintained as such open space, and

(c) the planning authority have served on the owner of the land a written request that, within a period specified in the request (being a period of not less than two months commencing on the date of the request), he will provide, level, plant or otherwise adapt or maintain such land in a manner so specified, being a manner which in their opinion would make it suitable for the purpose for which the open space was to be provided, and

(d) the owner fails to comply or to secure compliance with such request within the period so specified,

the planning authority may, if they think fit, publish in a newspaper circulating in the district a notice (subsequently in this section referred to as an acquisition notice) of their intention to acquire the land by order under this section and the acquisition notice shall specify a period (being a period of not less than two months commencing on the date on which the notice is published) within which an appeal may be made under this section.

(2) Where a planning authority publish an acquisition notice, they shall serve a copy of the notice on the owner of the land to which the notice relates not later than ten days after the date of the publication.

(3) Any person for the time being having an interest in the land to which an acquisition notice relates may within the period specified in the notice appeal –

    (*a*) in case the appeal is made before the appropriate day, to the Minister,

    (*b*) in case the appeal is made on or after the appropriate day, to the Board.

(4) Where an appeal is brought under this section, the Minister or the Board, as may be appropriate, may –

    (*a*) annul the acquisition notice to which the appeal relates, or

    (*b*) confirm the acquisition notice, with or without modification, in respect of all or such part of the relevant land as the Minister or the Board considers reasonable.

(5) In case a planning authority publish an acquisition notice and either –

    (*a*) the period for appealing against the notice has expired and no appeal has been taken, or

    (*b*) an appeal has been taken against the notice and the appeal has been withdrawn or the notice has been confirmed whether unconditionally or subject to modifications,

the planning authority may make an order in the prescribed form which order shall be expressed and shall operate to vest the land to which the acquisition notice, or, where appropriate, the acquisition notice as confirmed, relates in the planning authority on a specified date for all the estate, term or interest for which immediately before the date of the order the said land was held by the owner together with all rights and liabilities which, immediately before the said date, were enjoyed or incurred in connection therewith by the owner together with an obligation to comply with the request made under paragraph (*c*) of subsection (1) of this section.

(6) Where a planning authority have acquired by an order under this section land which is subject, either alone or in conjunciton with other land, to a purchase annuity, payment in lieu of rent, or other annual sum (not being merely a rent under a contract of tenancy) payable to the Irish Land Commission or to the Commissioners of Public Works in Ireland, the authority shall become and be liable, as from the date on which the land is vested in them by the vesting order, for the payment to the Irish Land Commission or to the Commissioners of Public Works in Ireland as the case may be, of the annual sum or such portion thereof as shall be apportioned by the Irish Land Commission or by the Commissioners of Public Works in Ireland, as the case may be, on the land as if the land had been transferred to the authority by the owner thereof on that date.

(7) When a planning authority make an order under this section in relation to any land, they shall send the order to the registering authority under the Registration of Title Act, 1964, and thereupon the registering authority shall cause the planning authority to be registered as owner of the land in accordance with the order.

(8) Where a claim is made for compensation in respect of land to which an order under this section relates and the matter falls to be determined by arbitration in pursuance of section 68 of the Principal Act, the following provision shall apply:

(*a*) unless it is shown by or on behalf of the owner that an amount equal to the value of the land to which the relevant permission under section 26 of the Principal Act relates, being that value at the time when the application for the permission was made, as a result of the development has not been recovered and as a further such result will not in the future be recoverable by disposing of the land which is land to which the permission relates and which is not land to which the order relates, the arbitrator shall make a nil award, and

(*b*) in the assessment of the value of the land to which the order relates, no regard shall be had to its value for use other than as open space and a deduction shall be made in respect of the cost of carrying out such works as may be necessary to comply with the request made pursuant to paragraph (*c*) of subsection (1) of this section.

(9) A planning authority shall enter in the register –

(*a*) particulars of any acquisition notice published by them,

(*b*) the date and effect of any decision on appeal in relation to such notice,

(*c*) particulars of any order made under this section,

and every such entry shall be made within the period of seven days commencing on the day of publication, receipt of notification of the decision or the making of the order, as may be appropriate.

(10) This section applies to any form of open space (whether referred to as open space or by any other description in the relevant application for a permission or in a condition attached to the relevant permission) being land which is not described in the said application or condition either as private open space or in terms indicating that it is not intended that members of the public are to have resort thereto without restriction.

LOCAL GOVERNMENT (PLANNING AND DEVELOPMENT) REGULATIONS 1977

66. Form No. 4 set out in the Second Schedule, or a form substantially to the like effect, shall be the prescribed form of voting order to be made by a planning authority in exercise of the powers conferred on them by section 25(5) of the Act of 1976.

SECOND SCHEDULE

FORM NO. 4   *Article 66*

Form of Vesting Order

LOCAL GOVERNMENT (PLANNING AND DEVELOPMENT) ACT, 1976 – SECTION 25

.... (name of planning authority).

VESTING ORDER

WHEREAS development $\frac{\text{(is being)}}{\text{(has been)}}$ [1]carried out pursuant to a permission

granted on .... under section 26 of the Local Government (Planning and Development) Act, 1963 (Reference No. in Register ....);

[2] AND WHEREAS a condition requiring the provision or maintenance of land as open space, being open space to which section 25 of the Local Government (Planning and Development) Act, 1976, (hereinafter called 'the Act') applies, was attached to the permission;

AND WHEREAS it was $\frac{\text{(explicit)}}{\text{(implicit)}}$[1] in the application for the permission

that land would be provided or maintained as open space, being open space to which section 25 of the Local Government (Planning and Development) Act, 1976, (hereinafter called 'the Act') applies;

AND WHEREAS on the .... day ...., 19 ...., the .... [3] (hereinafter referred to as 'the planning authority') served on the owner of the land a written request that within a period of .... commencing on that day he would provide, level, plant or otherwise adapt or maintain the said land in a manner specified in the request, being a manner which in the opinion of the planning authority would make it suitable for the purpose for which the open space was to be provided;

AND WHEREAS the owner has failed to comply or to secure compliance with such request within such period;

AND WHEREAS the planning authority have, in accordance with section 25(1) of the Act, published an acquisition notice in relation to the said land and have, in accordance with section 25(2) of the Act, served a copy of the notice on the owner of the land within ten days of the date of publication of the said notice;

[2] AND WHEREAS no appeal has been taken under section 25(3) of the Act;

AND WHEREAS an appeal has been taken under section 25(3) of the Act and the appeal has been withdrawn;

AND WHEREAS an appeal has been taken under section 25(3) of the Act and the said acquisition notice has been confirmed in relation to the land decribed in the Schedule hereto;

NOW THEREFORE, the planning authority, in exercise of the powers conferred on them by section 25(5) of the Act, hereby order that the land described in the Schedule hereto, being the land to which the said acquisition notice (as confirmed)[1] relates, and which is shown on the map attached hereto which said map has been marked...[4] and sealed with the seal of the planning authority, shall, on the .... day of ...., 19.....,[5] vest in the planning authority for all the estate, term or interest for which immediately before the date of this order the said land was held by the owner together with all rights and liabilities which, immediately before the said date, were enjoyed or incurred in connection therewith by the owner together with an obligation to comply with the request made under section 25(1) (c) of the Act.

SCHEDULE
Description of land[6]

The official seal of the planning authority was affixed hereto this ....
day of .... , 19......., in the presence of:
....[7]   ....[7]
....[7]

Directions for completing this form

1. Delete words which do not apply.
2. Delete recitals which do not apply.
3. Insert full description of planning authority.
4. The map should be sealed and marked by a heading containing a reference to the order e.g. 'Map referred to in order made under section 25 of the Local Government (Planning and Development) Act, 1976, on the .... day of ...., 19........., by ....'.
5. The vesting date can be the date of the order or any subsequent date.
6. The quantity, description and situation of the land should be set out, with an appropriate reference to the manner in which the land is shown on the map.
7. The description of the persons in whose presence the seal is affixed should be stated e.g. 'Lord Mayor', 'Mayor', 'Chairman', 'Nominated Member', 'City Manager and Town Clerk', 'Manager', etc.

DUBLIN COUNTY COUNCIL V. BRENNAN AND MCGOWAN
LIMITED AND ANOR
The High Court (Unreported) Barron J., 7th February 1983,
(Ref. No. 1982 No. 2 MCA)

The respondents made an outline application for permission to develop a site at Kilnamanagh, Tallaght as a residential community. Outline permission was granted on the 5th July 1971. It was provided in the permission that full permission be obtained within one year. This was not done with the result that the outline permission lapsed. Another application was made on the 11th August 1972 in which full permission was sought. Permission was granted for development in accordance with the plans and particulars lodged and subject to various conditions, including conditions requiring the provision of public open space. In Section 27 proceedings a dispute arose as to whether or not the respondents were requested to develop an area of 9½ acres on the site as public open space. This area was described in a report accompanying the planning application as a reserved area and as open green space on the site plan. On a construction of the report the Court held that the area was public open space to which section 25 applied.

Barron J.:
. . . A fundamental question of law has also arisen and it is that question which I have been asked to deal with as a preliminary issue.

The question relates to the nature of the obligations, if any, imposed on the respondents in relation to an area of 9½ acres on the north-eastern boundary of the site.

The applicant maintains that this area was to be landscaped and to be provided as an amenity for the residential community. The respondents contend that it was a reserved area, by which they mean that they were not obliged to develop it in any particular way and in support of this argument point to the fact that it was similarly designated in the application for outline permission. They further submit that the full permission did not refer to this area either by permitting its development or by imposing any condition in respect of it. The respondents' contention in effect is that so far as this area is concerned it is not the subject matter of any planning permission.

The report accompanying the application for permission contained a number of provisions which are material to the present issue. They are as follows:
2. Location
 The site is located between Greenhills Road and Belgard Road and is bounded on the North by a proposed new motorway reservation and on the south by an industrial zoning line in Tallaght. See location map to scale 6 inches equals 1 mile.
The application refers only to this site even though land ownership extends beyond these boundaries.
7. Proposed site use.
 The proposed site use is residential and community services for the development of a residential community.
9. Site Area.

The combined site area is 222.52 acres approximately, including reserved area at north east corner of site.
15. Planning Considerations. Public open areas.
Allocation of 4.13 acres per two hundred and fifty houses for public open space. This open area has been so located that the major portion is centrally placed in the development, with minor portions stretching into the housing groups, giving adjacent recreation facilities to all the housing clusters. A landscape architect is being retained for the design and development of the public open areas and proposals will be submitted to the Planning Authority for approval at a later date.
16. Summary of Amenity areas.
Public open space 24.83 acres. School site Number 1 14.375 acres School site Number 2 7 acres, Shopping centre, public house, and community buildings 6.50 acres, Service station 1.75 acres, reserved open space 9.50 acres.

The site layout map distinguishes between public open space and open green area. (References to the former include underneath on each occasion where the words are inserted the word 'landscaped'.) No such addition occurs under the words 'open green area'.

A review of these matters indicates that the application was drawing a distinction between public open space which it was intended to landscape and green open area which it was not intended to landscape. What was not indicated was what the applicant intended to do with this latter area. It was clearly part of the site and as such its use was to be either residential or for community services. Since it was included in paragraph 16 of the report as an amenity area, it was clearly being put forward as available for such use. It may well have been that the respondents were not fully alive to the distinction. For example in paragraph 15 of the report the landscape architect being retained by the respondents was being retained for the design and development not apparently of the public open spaces but of the public open areas.

What has given rise to the present issue is in large part the conduct of the parties since the planning permission was granted. The proposed new roads to the north and north-east of the site are still proposed roads. There is no actual boundary between the proposed carriageways on the site and the present appearance and use of the land reserved for such new roads and the green open area is roughly the same.

So far as the public open spaces are concerned, it is common case that the applicant has agreed to take over these areas from the respondents and has agreed to develop them in the manner required by the planning permission for payment of the sum of £40,000. Unfortunately, the deed of transfer has never been executed because the map to be annexed thereto has not yet been agreed. This is unfortunate because it gives rise to uncertainty as to the exact meaning of the agreement which the parties made in relation to landscaping.

Two distinct questions have been argued. The first is whether or not the green open area is open space within the meaning of Section 25 of the Local Government (Planning and Development) Act 1976 and to which the provisions of that Section apply; the second is the extent, if any, to which the green open area is controlled by the planning permission granted on the 5th March 1973. If it is open space within the meaning of Section 25 in the sense that the provisions of that Section apply to it, then it follows that it is subject to the planning permission and the question then remaining is, in what manner and to what extent?

The applicant submits that the open green area is open space within the meaning of Section 25 because it is not described as private open space and, because it is referred to in the report accompanying the application for planning permission as being an amenity area, it is explicit in the application for such permission that that area would be provided as open space.

The respondents submit that, since the permission under which the development of the site was carried out has attached to it a condition requiring the provision of land as open space, the terms of Section 25(*b*)(i) have been complied with and that accordingly Section 25(*b*)(ii) is not applicable.

I do not accept this latter contention. So far as the area is designated public open space on the site layout and location plan are concerned, they are covered by Section 25 *inter alia* because a condition requiring the provision of maintenance of that land is attached to the permission. However, the green open area is different land. It is in respect of that different land that the question arises whether or not it is covered by Section 25.

This land is not described as private open space nor is it described in terms indicating that it is not intended that members of the public are to have resort thereto without restriction. On the contrary in the report accompanying the application for planning permission it is described as an amenity area for the scheme as a whole. It is therefore open space to which the section applies. Although there is no condition attached to the permission requiring it to be provided or maintained as open space, it is explicit in the application for the permission that the land would be provided as open space and at least implicit that it would be maintained as such. In my view, this land is covered by the provisions of Section 25. . . .

SECTION 26 – WARNING NOTICES[80]

The planning authority may serve a warning notice on the owner of land if it appears to it that –

(1) land is being or is likely to be developed in contravention of section 24 of the 1963 Act, or
(2) an unauthorised use is being made of land,[81] or
(3) any tree or other feature or any other thing the preservation of which is required by a condition attached to a permission for development of land may be removed or damaged.

In addition to serving a notice on the owner of the land in accordance with section 7 of the 1963 Act the planning authority may give a copy of the notice to any person who in its opinion may be concerned with the matters to which the warning notice relates. (See section 26(1)).

The contents of the notice are set out in section 26(2).

An offence is committed by any person who *knowingly* fails to comply with the requirements of a warning notice or who *knowingly* assists or permits another to

---

[80] Section 26 is quoted at page 358.
[81] It is not sufficient that it appear to the planning authority that an unauthorised use is likely to occur. A warning notice is only appropriate if the unauthorised use has commenced and is continuing.

contravene a warning notice. (See section 26(4)). The onus of proof in relation to the knowledge of the defendant rests with the prosecution except in the case of offences consisting of the removal or damage to a tree or other feature or thing. In such cases if the defendant is the owner of the land it is sufficient for the prosecution to prove the fact of the removal or damage to the tree or feature or other thing. (See section 26(4)(*a*)). A tree shall be regarded as being removed if it is cut down or otherwise wilfully destroyed. (See section 26(9)). It is a good defence for the owner to show that he took or caused to be taken reasonable steps to secure compliance with the warning notice and that he at all times acted in good faith in relation to the notice. Where the defendant is not the owner of the land to which the notice relates the onus of proof in relation to the defendant's knowledge will shift to the defendant if the prosecution prove that steps were taken to inform persons of the warning notice or to protect from damage or to preserve tree, feature or other thing to which the notice relates after service of the notice and that the alleged removal or damage by the defendant occurred after such steps had been taken. (See section 26(4)(*b*))

Where the offence concerns a development the prosecution need not show that the development concerned is not exempted nor commenced before the appointed day. (See section 26(9))

As in the case of an offence committed under section 24(3) of the 1963 Act as amended offences under section 26(7) are indictable but triable summarily in certain circumstances. (See section 8 of the 1982 Act and section 9 of the 1982 Act)[82] The same restrictions on the time within which proceedings must be commenced apply to proceedings under section 26(7). These were discussed under prosecutions under section 24 of the 1963 Act. (See above[83])

Where a person has been convicted of an offence under section 26(7) continues the offence after conviction he will be guilty of a further offence. (See section 8(4) of the 1982 Act) In the light of the provision of a daily fine it appears that the offence is of a continuing nature and that there may be repeated prosecutions. (See *Dublin Corporation* v. *Flynn*)[84] The further offence may be tried summarily or on indictment. (See section 9 of the 1982 Act)

The particulars of the warning notice must be entered on the register maintained by the planning authority. (See section 26(10))

LOCAL GOVERNMENT (PLANNING AND DEVELOPMENT) ACT, 1976

26. – (1) Where it appears to a planning authority that –

(*a*) land is being or is likely to be developed in contravention of section 24 of the Principal Act, or

(*b*) any unauthorised use is being made of land, or

(*c*) any tree or other feature (whether structural or natural) or any other thing the preservation of which is required by a condition subject to which a permission for the development of any land was granted, may be removed or damaged,

---

[82] See pages 325 and 326 respectively.
[83] See page 323.
[84] See page 345.

the planning authority may serve on the owner of the land a notice (in this section subsequently referred to as a warning notice) and may give a copy of the said notice to any other person who in their opinion may be concerned with the matters to which the notice relates.

(2) A warning notice shall refer to the land concerned and –

(*a*) in relation to any land being developed or likely to be developed, require that development thereof in contravention of section 24 of the Principal Act shall not be commenced or, if such development has been commenced, that it shall be discontinued forthwith,

(*b*) in relation to any unauthorised use of land, require that the unauthorised use shall be discontinued forthwith.

(*c*) in relation to a condition requiring the preservation of any tree, other feature or thing, require that the tree, other feature or thing, as may be appropriate, shall neither be removed nor damaged and that any reasonable steps necessary for its preservation shall be taken by the owner of the land.

and such notice shall also require the owner of the land to take adequate steps to ensure compliance with the notice and shall contain a warning that proceedings under this section may be brought by the relevant planning authority against him and any other person who fails to comply with the requirements of the notice or who assists or permits any development or use of land or the doing of any other thing in contravention thereof.

(3) In case a warning notice has been served in relation to the breach of a condition mentioned in paragraph (*c*) of subsection (2) of this section, anything done in relation to the tree, other feature or thing to which the notice relates shall if it is done with the consent in writing of the planning authority by whom the notice was served not be an offence under this section.

(4) Any person who –

(*a*) knowingly fails to comply with the requirements of a warning notice, or

(*b*) knowingly assists or permits.

(i) the carrying out by another of any development required by a warning notice not to be commenced or to be discontinued, or

(ii) the continuance by another of a use required by a warning notice to be discontinued, or

(iii) the doing by another of any other thing in contravention of a warning notice, or

(*c*) otherwise damages or removes any tree, other feature or thing to which a warning notice relates,

shall be guilty of an offence.[85,86]

(6) An enforcement notice within the meaning of section 31, 32 or 35 of the Principal Act may be served whether or not there has been a prosecution under this section.

(7) The following provisions shall apply in relation to proceedings under this section in which the offence alleged is the removal of or damage to a tree, other feature or thing to which a warning notice relates, namely –

(*a*) in case the defendant is the owner of the land to which the warning notice

[85] As amended by section 15 of the 1982 Act.
[86] Subsection (5) was deleted by section 15 of the 1982 Act.

relates,

    (i) it shall be sufficient for the prosecution to prove the fact that the tree, other feature or thing, as may be appropriate, was removed or damaged, and

    (ii) without prejudice to any other defence which may be open to him, it shall be a good defence if the defendant proves that he took, or caused to be taken, reasonable steps to secure compliance with the requirements of the warning notice and that he acted at all times in good faith in relation to the notice.

  (*b*) in any other case if, but only if, the prosecution proves that –

    (i) after the service of the warning notice steps were taken to inform persons of the existence of the notice, or to protect from damage or to preserve the tree, other feature or thing, as the case may be, with which the alleged offence is concerned, and

    (ii) the alleged removal or damage by the defendant occured after the steps referred to in subparagraph (i) of this paragraph were taken.

it shall be assumed, until the contrary is shown by the defendant, that the tree, other feature or thing was knowingly removed or damaged, as may be appropriate, by the defendant.

(8) In a prosecution for an offence under this section it shall not be necessary for the prosecution to show, and it shall be assumed until the contrary is shown by the defendant, that the development (if any) in question was neither exempted development nor development commenced before the appointed day.

(9) For the purposes of this section, a tree shall be regarded as being removed if it is cut down or otherwise wilfully destroyed.

(10) Where a warning notice is served under this section by a planning authority, particulars of the notice shall be entered by the authority in the register.

SECTION 27 – THE PLANNING INJUNCTION

This section provides for the enforcement of planning control by means of the making of Orders in the nature of injunctions by the High Court.[87]

Where development requiring permission is carried out without permission or where unauthorised use is being made of land an Order may be made under section 27(1) of the 1976 Act prohibiting the continuance of the development or use.

Where planning permission has been obtained in respect of a development and that development has been commenced but is not being or has been carried out in conformity with the permission an Order may be made under section 27(2) of the 1976 Act requiring that 'any person specified in the Order do or not do or cease to do anything which the Court considers necessary to ensure that development is carried out in conformity with the permission'. This includes the making of mandatory Orders. (See *Morris* v. *Garvey*[88])

In *Morris* v. *Garvey* it was suggested *obiter* by Henchy J. that section 27(1) empowered the Court to make prohibitory Orders only. If this is the position it has the strange result that a developer who completely ignores the necessity to obtain planning permission will be in a better position than the developer who obtains permission but does not carry out the development in conformity with it. While the

---

[87] Section 27 is quoted at page 362.
[88] See page 364.

Court may restrain both developers from carrying out any future development only the developer who had paid some heed to the requirements of the Acts and obtained permission could be ordered to undo such developments as had already been carried out. (See also *Dublin Corporation* v. *Maiden Poster Sites*[89])

Application may be made to the High Court under either sub-section by the planning authority or by any other person. Such other person need not have any interest in the land (see section 27(1); section 27(2); *Stafford* v. *Roadstone Limited*[90] nor need he show that he has suffered any damage peculiar to himself beyond the damage suffered by all members of the public when there is a breach of planning control. (See *Avenue Properties Ltd.* v. *Farrell Homes Ltd.*[91])

While any person may apply it is not mandatory on the Court to grant an order solely because a breach of planning control has been proved. (See *Stafford* v. *Roadstone Limited; Avenue Properties Ltd.* v. *Farrell Homes Ltd.*)

The Court has a discretion to grant or withhold an Order. In deciding how to exercise that discretion the Court will be influenced in some measure by the same matters which influence it in deciding to grant or withhold an injunction. (See *Avenue Properties Ltd.* v. *Farrell Homes Ltd.*) Thus acquiescence or delay may disentitle the applicant to an Order. In *Morris* v. *Garvey*, Henchy J. suggested that once a breach is proved, the Court should not refrain from making an Order unless there are exceptional circumstances. Examples of such exceptional circumstances were given in *Morris* v. *Garvey*: genuine mistake (see *Dublin County Council* v. *Sellwood Quarries Ltd.*[92] *Stafford* v. *Roadstone Limited*) acquiescence over a long period (*Dublin Corporation* v. *Mulligan*[93]) Pursuing less draconian remedies first does not constitute acquiescence (See *Dublin Corporation* v. *Kevans*[94]) triviality or technicality of the infraction; gross and disproportionate hardship (see *Avenue Properties Ltd.* v. *Farrell Homes Ltd.*) The Court may consider not only the convenience of the parties but also the convenience of the public. Thus the Court may take into account such matters as the fact that unemployment will result from the making of an Order. (See *Dublin County Council* v. *Sellwood Quarries Ltd.; Stafford* v. *Roadstone Limited* but cf. *Dublin County Council* v. *Tallaght Block Company Ltd.*[95] where an Order was made despite the fact that considerable unemployment would result)

Except in the case of development carried out without permission application may be made at any time after the development is commenced. (See *Dublin Corporation* v. *Mulligan; Dublin County Council* v. *Matra Investments Limited*[96]) In the case of development carried out without permission the application must be made before the development is completed. (See section 27(1)(a)) If, however, there is delay in bringing proceedings the Court may take this into account in deciding how to exercise its discretion and if it decides to exercise its discretion in favour of granting an Order in determining the form of that Order.

In *Dublin Corporation* v. *Mulligan* the President refused to make an Order under

[89] See page 366.
[90] See page 367.
[91] See page 368.
[92] See page 370.
[93] See page 342.
[94] See page 371.
[95] See page 373.
[96] See page 374.

section 27(1) in respect of the unauthorised use of a premises because of the hardship which would result to the respondent if after seven years without any action being taken an Order were made. He found that the respondent had acquired a vested interest in the premises and in the goodwill he enjoyed from carrying on his solicitor's practice from them and that he should be immune from an Order being made under section 27. The immunity would appear to have its basis in an estoppel which arose from the planning authority lulling the respondent in the belief that the developament would be tolerated or accepted by its inactivity. The immunity was personal to the respondent and did not authorise the development. Thus any successor in title who continued the development would be open to an Order being made against him under section 27.

In the course of his judgement in *Dublin Corporation* v. *Mulligan* the President stressed that each case must be decided on its own particular facts. In two subsequent decisions he has refused to extend a similar immunity to the respondents. It would appear that if the applicants take any action within a few years of the development commencing this will be sufficient to prevent such an immunity arising even if the remedies pursued are pursued in a dilatory fashion. (See *Dublin Corporation* v. *Kevans; Dublin Corporation* v. *Garland*[97]) Further it would appear that the respondent's interest in the premises may have to be for his own personal use. In *Dublin Corporation* v. *Kevans* the Court found that no such immunity could exist where the respondent let the offices as an investment. It would also appear that if the respondent has applied for planning permission and been refused permission the Court will not grant such an immunity. In *Dublin Corporation* v. *Garland* the President gave an Order against the respondent on the grounds that if he were to refuse to do so he would in effect be reversing or altering the decision of the planning authority a purpose for which section 27 proceedings could not be used.

Where the length of time between the commencement of the development and the bringing of proceedings is not such as to cause the Court to exercise its discretion to refrain from making an Order it may still affect the form of the order. Thus in *Dublin Corporation* v. *Kevans* and *Dublin Corporation* v. *Garland* the court gave a substantial stay on the Order to allow the respondents to make alternative arrangements.

Section 27 proceedings may be brought and determined when a section 5 reference is outstanding and the Court need not adjourn the proceedings to allow such a reference to be brought where a claim that an exempted development has taken place has been made. (See *Cork Corporation* v. *O'Connell; Dublin Council* v. *Tallaght Block Company Ltd.*)

Application must be made in accordance with Order 98A of the Rules of the Superior Courts. Unlike in the case of a common-law injunction no undertaking as to damages need be given in the case of section 27 proceedings.

LOCAL GOVERNMENT (PLANNING AND DEVELOPMENT) ACT, 1976

27. – (1) Where –

(*a*) development of land, being development for which a permission is re-

[97] See page 374.

quired under Part IV of the Principal Act, is being carried out without such a permission, or

(*b*) an unauthorised use is being made of land,

the High Court may, on the application of a planning authority or any other person, whether or not the person has an interest in the land, by order prohibit the continuance of the development or unauthorised use.

(2) Where any development authorised by a permission granted under Part IV of the Principal Act has been commenced but has not been, or is not being, carried out in conformity with the permission because of non-compliance with the requirements of a condition attached to the permission or for any other reason, the High Court may, on the application of a planning authority or any other person, whether or not that person has an interest in the land, by order require any person specified in the order to do or not to do, or to cease to do, as the case may be, anything which the Court considers necessary to ensure that the development is carried out in conformity with the permission and specifies in the order.

(3) An application to the High Court for an order under this section shall be by motion and the Court when considering the matter may make such interim or interlocutory order (if any) as it considers appropriate. The order by which an application under this section is determined may contain such terms and conditions (if any) as to the payment of costs as the Court considers appropriate.

RULES OF THE SUPERIOR COURTS (NO. 1), 1976

ORDER 98A LOCAL GOVERNMENT (PLANNING AND DEVELOPMENT ACT, 1976

1. In this Order
'the Act' means the Local Government (Planning and Development) Act 1976.
2. An application for an Order under Section 27 of 'the Act' shall be by motion on a notice to the person against whom relief is sought.
3. The notice of motion shall be entitled in the matter of 'the Act' on the application of the person bringing the application; shall state the relief sought; describe the land or development sought to be affected; shall state the name and place of residence or address for service of the person seeking relief; the date upon which it is proposed to apply to the Court for relief; and shall be filed in the Central Office.
4. Notice of the motion shall be given to the person against whom the relief is sought (the respondent); but if it shall appear to the Court that any person to whom notice has not been given ought to have or ought to have had such notice, the Court may either dismiss the application, or adjourn the hearing thereof, in order that such notice may be given, upon such terms (if any) as the Court may think fit to impose.
5. There must be at least ten days between the service of the notice and the day named therein for the hearing of the motion.
6. (a) Subject to the right of the Court to give such directions in that behalf as it considers appropriate or convenient, evidence at the hearing of a motion under Rule 2 shall be by affidavit.

(b) Any affidavit to be used in support of the motion shall be filed in the Central Office and a copy of any such affidavit shall be served with the notice., Any affidavit to be used in opposition to the application shall be filed in the Central

Office by the respondent within seven days of the service on him of the applicant's affidavit, and the respondent must within such period serve a copy of any affidavit intended to be used by him on the applicant.

7. Pending the determination of an application under Section 27 of 'the Act', the Court on the application of the applicant or the respondent, by interlocutory Order, (or if satisfied tht delay might entail irreparable or serious mischief, by interim order on application ex parte); may make any Order in the nature of an injunction; and for the detention, preservation or inspection of any property or thing; and for all or any of the purposes aforesaid may authorise any person to enter upon or into any land or building; and for all or any of the purposes aforesaid may authorise any sample to be taken or any observations to be made or experiment to be tried, which it may consider appropriate, necessary or expedient.'

MORRIS V. PETER GARVEY
[1982] ILRM 177 Henchy J. (nem. diss)

The respondents were building a block of flats otherwise than in accordance with a planning permission obtained in its behalf. In particular the gable wall and the front wall were being built in locations which breached conditions attaching to the permission. The applicant sought an order that the walls be removed. The High Court made an order requiring demolition of the building. This order was upheld by the Supreme Court.

Henchy J.:
. . . Under section 27(1), which deals with cases where required development permission has not been got and development is being carried out without the required permission, and with cases where an unauthorised use is being made of land, the Court is empowered to prohibit the continuance of the development or the unauthorised use. So much of the section is merely prohibitory. Its aim is merely to restrain a continuance of the illegality. Section 27(2), which is the relevant provision in this case, is in a different vein and of a wider scope. . . .

. . . Section 27(2) is one of the most important and least understood or used provisions of the planning code. The section expressly recognized for the first time that a member of the public (as well as the planning authority), regardless of his not satisfying any of the qualifications based on property or propinquity or the like (which are usually required to justify bringing proceedings), once he discovers that a permitted developer is not complying with, or has not complied with, the conditions of the relevant development permission, may apply in the High Court for an order compelling the developer 'to do or not to do, or to cease to do, as the case may be, anything which the Court considers necessary to ensure that the development is carried out in conformity with the permission and specifies in the order'.

The jurisdiction thus vested in the High Court is extremely wide. It recognizes the fact, which has been stressed in other decisions of this Court, that in all planning matters there are three parties: the developer, the planning authority (or the Planning Board, in the case of an appeal) and the members of the public. Compliance with the statutory conditions for development is expressly recognized in section 27(2) to be the legitimate concern of any member of the public. We are all, as users or enjoyers of the environment in which we live, given a standing to go to Court and to seek an order compelling those who have been given a development permission to carry out the development in accordance with the terms of that permission. And the Court is given a discretion sufficiently wide to make whatever order is necessary to achieve that object.

If section 27(2) were to be treated as merely giving the Court power to interdict a continuance of the development in an unauthorised manner, the new jurisdiction given by the subsection would be self-defeating and would run contrary to the expressed purpose of the subsection, which is, 'to ensure that the development is carried out in accordance with the permission'. This Court has judicial notice, from what it has known to have happened in other cases, that developers who have contravened the conditions of the development permission, have for motives which may be put down to expediency, avarice, thoughtlessness or disregard of the rights or amenities of neighbours or of the public generally, knowingly proceeded with an unauthorised development at such a speed and to such an extent as they hoped would enable them to submit successfuly that the Court's discretion should not be exercised against them under Section 27(2), on the ground that the undoing of the work done would cause them undue expense or trouble.

For my part, I would wish to make it clear that such conduct is not a good reason for not making an order requiring work carried out in such circumstances to be pulled down. When section 27(2) is invoked, the Court becomes the guardian and supervisor of the carrying out of the permitted development according to its limitation, and in carrying out that function it must balance the duty and benefit of the developer under the permission as granted against the environmental and ecological rights and amenities of the public, present and future, particularly those closely or immediately affected by the contravention of the permission. It would require exceptional circumstances (such as genuine mistake, acquiescence over a long period, the triviality or mere technicality of the infraction, gross or disproportionate hardship, or suchlike extenuating or excusing factors) before the Court should refrain from making whatever order (including an order of attachment for contempt in default of compliance) as is 'necessary to ensure that the development is carried out in conformity with the permission'. An order merely restraining the developer from proceeding with the unpermitted work would not alone fail to achieve that aim but would often make matters worse by producing a part-completed structure which would be offensive to the eye as well as having the effect of devaluing neighbouring property.

In the present case I wholeheartedly support the order of demolition made by Costello J. The demolition expenses which the respondent will incur will be substantial, but they were foreseeable and avoidable and the justice of the case requires that they should fall on the respondent. While I do not impute to the respondent any of the baser motives to which developers in breach of development permission in other cases have left themselves open, the fact is that after receiving due notice of his unpermitted building operations he carried on with them despite the threat of legal proceedings. It is true that an official of the planning department of the Dublin Corporation stated (no doubt in good faith) that he did not look on the unpermitted work as involving any material deviation from the terms of the permission. Having regard to the uncontroverted evidence as to the extent of that deviation and as to its effect, in particular on the amenities of Dr. Morris's home, Costello J. rightly refused to act on that opinion. The respondent, if he wished to retain the unpermitted walls, should have applied for a fresh development permission, thus enabling Dr. Morris, or any member of the public, to raise such objection as might be thought warranted. The opinion of a planning official, no matter how genuinely given, cannot in such circumstances be allowed to defeat the rights of the public, and in particular those of the next door neighbour.[98]

DUBLIN CORPORATION V. MAIDEN POSTER SITES
[1983] I.L.R.M. 48 Murphy J.

Without obtaining the required planning permission the respondents erected four hoardings on the outer wall of a building and began using them for the display of advertisements. An application for permission to retain the hoardings was refused and the respondents appealed to An Bord Pleanala. While the appeal was still pending the applicant brought proceedings under Section 27(1) of the 1976 Act in which they sought to have the unauthorised use restrained.

Murphy J.:
. . . Apart from the existence of the appeal, the only argument offered by the respondents as to why an order restraining the continued unauthorised development should not be granted was that the works – albeit unauthorised – represent a considerable improvement to the appearance and amenities of premises which had become badly dilapidated. The factual basis for that argument is indeed supported by the photograph put in evidence by the respondents.

It is proper to say that an important issue was raised as to whether the Court has power under section 27(1) of the 1976 Act – that is to say where no planning permission has been granted – to direct the removal of the unauthorised structure. It is certainly clear, having regard to the decision delivered by the Supreme Court on the 8th March 1982 in *Morris* v. *Garvey* (and as yet unreported)[99] that the Court does have power under section 27(2) of the 1976 Act – that is to say where permission has been granted but the developmnt is carried out without complying with the terms of that permission – to order the demolition of the offending works in a proper case.

Whilst it would be surprising if the powers of the Court were any less comprehensive in a case where no permission at all had been obtained than in the case where a permission was obtained and departed from in certain respects, it does appear that a question may have to be determined as to whether this is so. However, having regard to the view which I take of this case and the relief which should be granted it is not necessary for me to decide that issue at the present time.

In the present case it is clear that an unauthorised use is being made of the premises in question. The Court does have a discretion as to whether an injunction should be granted to restrain that use. As the purpose of the section is to secure compliance with the legislation and the proper planning it is designed to achieve I feel that this is an appropriate case to grant an injunction in the terms of paragraph (a) of the Notice of Notion. Certainly I feel that the Court should not facilitate the respondents in continuing to derive a substantial income from an unauthorised development. Moreover, as I say, I must assume that the respondents knew or

[98] See also *Dublin Corporation* v. *McGrath.*
[99] See page 364.

should have known of the need to obtain a planning permission for the development.

I will, however, provide that the injunction will not take effect from three weeks from today's date. Furthermore, it seems to me that if the appeal to the Planning Board is successful that the injunction should be lifted. . . .

NANCY STAFFORD & ANOR V. ROADSTONE LIMITED
The High Court (Unreported) Barrington J., 17 January 1980 (Ref. No. 1979 No. 7448P)

In proceedings brought pursuant to section 27 of the 1976 Act the Court held that the respondents had been carrying out unauthorised developments at a quarry. It was not mandatory on the Court, however, to issue an injunction solely because an unauthorised development has been proved.

Barrington J.:
. . .Section 27 sub-section 1 provides that:
'The High Court *may* on application of a planning authority or any other person, whether or not the person has an interest in the land, by order prohibit the continuance of the development or unauthorised use'.

A question arises as to whether the word 'may' as used here is mandatory in the sense that the High Court 'must' when an unauthorised use or unauthorised development is established, issue an injunction. Traditionally Courts of Equity have always retained a wide discretion in themselves as to whether they should or should not issue an injunction. They have always retained the right to refuse an injunction to a plaintiff who has not come into Court with clean hands or to accept an undertaking, in lieu of an injunction, in an appropriate case.

Sub-section 2 of the Section gives the Court jurisdiction to issue mandatory orders directing the carrying out of certain works. While the word 'injunction' is not used in this section it is clear that the section confers on the High Court jurisdiction to issue both restraining and mandatory injunctions. In these circumstnces it appears to me that the word 'may' allows to the High Court, at least the discretion which the High Court has traditionally held in relation to the issue of injunctions.

It seems all the more important that the High Court should have such a wide discretion because of another inovation introduced by the section. The section allows the application for an injunction to be made, not only by the Planning Authority, but also by a private citizen 'whether or not the person has an interest in the land'. The section therefore makes each citizen a watchdog for the public. Presumably the purpose of this position is to guard against the kind of case (of which the present case may possibly be an example) where the Planning Authority may not have been as vigilant in the protection of the public's interest as it should have been. But, it seems to me, that if a person who is not the Planning Authority and who has no interest in the lands can apply for an injunction under Section 27 then it is all the more important that the High Court should have a wide discretion on the question of whether or not to issue an injunction. It appears to me that the Oireachtas could not have intended that the High Court should have no discretion but to issue an injunction when the plaintiff has no interest in the lands and the breach of the planning law on the part of the defendant has been innocent or technical and can be put right by an application for planning permission.

The matter, however, appears to me to go further than this. In the normal case a Court of Equity, in deciding whether or not to issue an injunction, would be primarily concerned with the position as between the parties to the litigation. But it appears to me that if a private citizen comes forward under Section 27 as a watchdog of the public that the Court, in exercising its discretion, is entitled to look not only at the convenience of the parties but at the convenience of the public. Again it appears to me that the Oireachtas could hardly have intended that the High Court would be obliged on the application of a private citizen with no interest in the lands automatically to close down, e.g. an important factory, because of some technical breach of the planning law irrespective of the inconvenience to workers and the public generally.

In the present case I am satisfied, on the evidence . . . that the development of the quarry at Carrickfoyle is of importance, not only to the defendants, but also to the people of Wexford generally. I am also conscious of the interests of the workers employed by the defendants who might lose their jobs in the event of the quarry being closed or of the defendants finding it impracticable to continue it in operation. As previously noted those witnesses who complained of the way in which the quarry is presently being operated asked, not that it be closed, but that it be placed subject to conditions.

On the basis of the evidence at present before me I am not in a position to formulate conditions which I could be sure would be safe or practicable.

I should say also, with the exception of the building of the machinery depot . . . I do not think there was any conscious or deliberate violation of the Planning Acts in the present case. I think there was room for legitimate disagreement as to whether the intensification of the use on which the defendants embarked was of such a degree as to amount to a material change of use. . .

I would be disposed not to issue an injunction in the event of the defendants giving certain undertakings to the Court. These undertakings should include an undertaking to apply to the Planning Authority for permission for a change of use and for the retention of any structures built without planning permission. They should also include an undertaking to prosecute any such application and any appeal from any decision made therein as quickly as practicable.

But I feel that the undertaking should go further. In the light of the decision which I have made the existing use which the defendants are making of these lands is unauthorised. It therefore appears to me that if the Court is to refrain from issuing an injunction pending the outcome of the planning application that the applicant should take all possible steps to ensure that, in the interval, their activities do not cause a nuisance to the local residents including the plaintiffs, and that they should give an undertaking to that effect. This would obviate the need for an Interlocutory Injunction in the Nuisance action. . .

AVENUE PROPERTIES LIMITED V. FARRELL HOMES LIMITED
[1982] I.L.R.M. 21

In proceedings brought under section 27(2) the applicants sought to restrain the respondents from continuing to construct an office block otherwise than in conformity with a planning permission granted in its behalf and an Order requiring the respondents to demolish such portion of the building as was already built. The respondent argued that no Order should be made because the applicant has not suffered any damage as a result of the departures from the planning permission. The Court held that it was not necessary for the applicant to show that he suffered any damage peculiar to himself. In the circumstances of this case the Court declined to make an order under section 27.

Barrington J.:

. . . I am satisfied that an applicant for an order under section 27 of the 1976 Act does not have to show that he has suffered any damage peculiar to himself. The Section contains the following words:

'The High Court may, on the application of a Planning Authority or any other person, *whether or not the person has an interest in the land*, by order prohibit the continuance of the development or unauthorised use.'

The section does not on its face distinguish between an application by a Planning Authority and an application by 'any other person'. It seems clear therefore that the intention of the section is that the Act should be policed not only by the Planning Authority but also by the individual citizens whether or not they have an interest in the lands. Clearly the Planning Authority would not have to show that it had suffered any 'loss' in order to support an application for an injunction and, as previously stated, the section does not on its face make any distinction between an application brought by a Planning Authority and an application brought by any other person. It appears to me therefore that it is not a precondition of bringing an application under Section 27 that the applicant should have suffered or anticipated any loss peculiar to himself.

However, so far as the High Court is concerned the order is discretionary. The term 'injunction' is not used in Section 27 but it is clear that the order contemplated by the section is an order in the nature of an injunction whether restraining or mandatory. The reference to 'interim' and 'interlocutory' orders in Section 27 sub-section 3 appears to reinforce this interpretation. It seems to me therefore that the High Court in exercising its discretion under Section 27 should be influenced, in some measure, by the factors which would influence a Court of Equity in deciding to grant or withhold an injunction.

At the same time the jurisdiction under Section 27 is peculiar in that the applicant need have no interest in the land the subject matter of the application and, it would appear, need have suffered no damage beyond such damage as all citizens suffer when the Planning Act is broken and public amenities impaired. From the foregoing it would appear that applicants under Section 27 could range from a crank or busybody with no interest in the matter at one end of the scale to, on the other end of the scale, persons who have suffered real damage through the unauthorised development or who, though they have suffered no damage peculiar to themselves, bring to the attention of the Court outrageous breaches of the Planning Act which ought to be restrained in the public interest. In these circumstances it appears to me all the more important that the Court should have a wide discretion as to when it should and when it should not intervene. . . .

I must . . . decide the case on the basis of the evidence presented before me. From this I am satisfied that the respondents had placed themselves formally in the wrong in that the building as constructed differs from the building for which permission was given in 1957 in at least three respects. The line of the building has been moved some few feet towards Kingram House; the projections have been omitted and cannot now be added; and the basement has been omitted. But I cannot see that the applicants are in any way adversely affected by these divergencies between the building as constructed and the building as planned in 1957. Indeed the effect of the changes appears to have been to reduce the floor area of the building by some 8,000 square feet. Likewise while it seems probable that the Planning Authority would not today authorise the building of an office block of this size in this area in the event of a totally new planning application being brought, nevertheless I must accept that the respondents are entitled to the benefit of the planning permission of 1957 and I must attach weight to this factor notwithstanding the fact that they have placed themselves formally in the wrong by not adhering strictly to it. Again I cannot see that public amenities are in any way damaged by the difference between the building as constructed and the building as planned in 1957. . . .

In all the circumstances of this case I think it would be burdensome to grant an injunction notwithstanding the fact that the respondents are formally in the wrong. I think the fairest thing to do is to give them an opportunity to put themselves right with the Planning Authority. . . .

In all the circumstances of the case it appears to me that the fairest thing for me to do is to refuse to make any order under Section 27 now but to adjourn the application generally and give the applicants liberty to apply in the event of the respondent failing to obtain planning permission for what has been done.[1]

DUBLIN COUNTY COUNCIL V. SELLWOOD QUARRIES AND ORS.
[1981] ILRM 23 Gannon J.

The respondents began the extraction of rock by blasting from a site which had previously been used as a sand and gravel pit on a commercial basis. Following complaints by local residents the applicants served a warning notice in respect of unauthorised buildings and brought section 27 proceedings to restrain the carrying out of unauthorised development, and use on the land. The Court was reluctant to make an order prohibiting the continuance of works when such an order would have such damaging conseqences for the respondents, their employees and those they did business with. *Cf. Dublin County Council* v. *Tallaght Block Limited.*

Gannon J.:
. . . There remains the question of whether or not an order should not be made on this application to prohibit the continuance of the works on the land which constitute a development without prescribed permission. It seems to me that the failure to apply for permission was due to a *bona fide* belief that such permission would not be required and that no unlawful infringement of the requirements of the Local Government (Planning and Development) Acts would be involved. An order of the nature sought would have very damaging consequences for the respondents and for those in their employment and for those to whom they are bound in contracts. The interests of the applicants in relation to their planning duties and objectives have

[1] The respondents made a successful application for retention.

not shown in the evidence other than the aspect of complaints of nuisance by local residents. Nevertheless I cannot decline to make some form of restraining order unless some alternative course can be devised consistent with the proper implementation of the requirements of the Planning Acts on the part of both parties. On this I wish to hear further submissions before making or declining to make an order.

DUBLIN CORPORATION V. KEVANS AND ORS
The High Court (Unreported) Finlay P., 14th July 1980
(Ref. No. 1980 No. 53 MCA)

In February 1972 the first-named respondent began using premises with a residential user as offices without obtaining planning permission for the change of use. In July 1974 the premises were inspected by an official of the applicants and on the 31st July 1974 the applicants served a notice on the first-named respondent requiring him to discontinue the unauthorised use of the premises. The first-named respondent failed to comply with the notice and in May 1975 the applicants brought proceedings pursuant to section 24 of the 1963 Act. In July 1975 the first-named respondent was convicted and fined. He appealed his conviction but the appeal remained undetermined at the time of the hearing of the section 27 proceedings. The first-named respondent continued to occupy the premises as office until the summer of 1977. In August 1977 he advertised the premises for letting as office accommodation. The applications wrote to him and the estate agent objecting to the form of the advertisement on the grounds that the premises did not have permission for office use. On the 1st July 1978 the premises were let to the second-named respondent who used them as offices. In November 1978 the basement portion was sub-let to the third-named respondents who used them as offices until June 1980 when they vacated the premises. On the 9 November 1979 the applicants served the first and second-named defendants with warning notices. No further action was taken on foot of these notices. On the 29th March 1979 the applicants served a further warning notice on the third-named defendant who vacated the basement portion of the premises in June 1980. On the 9th June 1980 section 27 proceedings were served on the first and second-named respondents. Finlay P. distinguished the case from *Dublin Corporation* v. *Mulligan* on the ground that the delay in commencing proceedings had not been as long and the respondent had not continuously used the premises for his practise.

Finlay P.:
. . . On these facts the respondents in resisting the making of an Order under Section 27 do not dispute that the user of the premises is an unauthorised user but rely upon the length of time during which the premises have in fact been used for office purposes with what they submit was the substantial acquiescence of the Planning Authority. In particular Counsel on behalf of the respondents submitted that the deliberate choice by the Planning Authority in 1975 to proceed by way of prosecution under Section 24 of the Act of 1963 the result of which could only be a single conviction and monetary fine rather than to exercise the right which was then available to them of pursuing and enforcement proceedings under the provisions of the Act of 1963 should be interpreted by me as a substantial acquiescence by the Planning Authority in the change of user. Their attitude, it is said, being one in

which it was necessary to make the point that the first-named respondent who was then still in occupation of the premises should have applied for permission for a change of user but that the decision of the Planning Authority must have been that the change of user was not of such injury to the orderly planning and development of the area as to make necessary its discontinuance. Counsel on behalf of the respondents relied on my own judgment in the *Dublin Corporation* v. *Mulligan* delivered on the 6th of May 1980.[2] in which I held that whilst I had jurisdiction to make an order under Section 27 of the Act of 1976 in respect of an unauthorised user which had commenced more than five years before the bringing of the application that I would exercise my discretion and refuse the order in relation to a portion of the premises which had since 1972 been continuously occupied by the respondent in that case as a solicitor's office.

I am not satisfied that the considerations which arose in the case of the *Dublin Corporation* v. *Mulligan* and which led me to exercise my discretion in that fashion are present in this case nor that I should exercise a discretion in this case so as to refuse the application under Section 27. I emphasised in my judgment in *Mulligan's Case* that the question as to whether or not a significant delay between the commencement of an unauthorised user and an application to the Court under Section 27 was a grounds for refusing an order under the Section depended upon the facts of each particular case. In *Mulligan's Case* no activity of any description on the part of the Planning Authority was taken in regard to the user of the premises until 1978 although it had commenced in February of 1973. Furthermore the particular vested interest which I described in my judgment of the respondent in the portion of the premises which he had continuously used as a solicitor's office since that time was that he was occupying it for the purpose of his professional practice and had acquired and was continuing to enjoy the fruits of the goodwill arising from that practice in that particular location for a period of approximately seven years at the time the matter came before me.

I reject the submissions made on behalf of the respondents in this case that the conduct and action of the Planning Authority with regard to these premises should be interpreted by me as a partial or almost complete acquiescence by them in the change of user which occurred in 1972. In just under two years from the time that the first-named respondent commenced his unauthorised use of the premises the applicants called upon him to cease it. They pursued that to the extent of prosecuting him for a criminal offence in the following year of 1975. It is true that such a prosecution was the least draconian or stringent of the choices available to the Planning Authority at that time but it was a prosecution for a criminal offence and might, it seems to me, have been considered particularly in the case of a respondent solicitor as being sufficiently serious and important to determine the issue as to whether he should continue or not unlawfully to use the premises. . . . Whilst it could hardly be said that there was an air of either urgency or strictness in the subsequent attitude of the Planning Authority their conduct in continuing even if somewhat sporadically to pursue this matter and in particular their reaction to the advertisement of these premises as being available for letting for office purposes is quite inconsistent with either a complete or partial acquiesence on their part in the unauthorised use.

The respondent's interest in these premises which is of course a very material and

---

[2] See page 342.

definite one at present is solely that of an investment property and he does not have the particular merit which would arise were he still occupying them for his own professional purposes. If I were not to refuse to grant an injunction against either of the respondents I would effectively be re-zoning these premises from their present status as being zoned solely for residential purposes to being zoned for office purposes. I would it seems to me be thereby conferring upon the first-named respondent at least a substantial benefit not enjoyed by persons who may have purchased similar premises but in obedience to the law either continued to use them for residential purposes only or properly sought permission for an appropriate change of use.

The length of time during which the first-named respondent at least has used these premises or let them for use as office premises does however substantially affect on the merits the form of order which I intend to make. I am satisfied that this respondent is entitled to a susbtantial period during which to make alternative arrangements with regard to the user of this part of his property. I therefore will make an order that he should cease to use or permit to be used any portion of the premises for other than residential purposes within twelve months of the date of the making of this order.

The second-named respondent has not got the merit of a lengthy user which the first-named respondent has but he is a lessee of the first-named respondent and the first-named respondent presumably has in the period during which he must necessarily make decisions and alternative arrangements with regard to the uses of these premises an interest in continuing to receive an income from them and I would therefore make the order against the second-named respondent in precisely the same terms.

It is part of my intention in delaying the implementation of this order for a period as long as twelve months from today that I would give to the first-named respondent an opportunity of applying to the Planning Authority in the ordinary way for retention of the unauthorised use. Should he succeed in such application either at the originating hearing or upon appeal then this order would of course become ineffective. . . .

DUBLIN COUNTY COUNCIL V. TALLAGHT BLOCK COMPANY LTD.
The Supreme Court Hederman J., 17 May 1983 (Ref. No. 282/1981)
See p. 62 for facts.

. . . I further agree with the findings of Costello J. that 'if an occupier of land carries out development . . . .applies under Section 28 of the 1963 Act for permission to retain the unauthorised structure and is refused, then he cannot be heard to argue in proceedings instituted against him under Section 27 of the 1976 Act that permission for the development was required'.

With regard to the contention of the appellants relating to the application of Section 5 of the 1963 Act, this Court has held in the case of *Cork Corporation* v. *Christopher O'Connell*[3] [1982] I.L.R.M. p. 525 per Henchy J. –

'that section 27 of the 1976 Act amounts to a summary and self-contained

---
[3] See page 106.

procedure which should not be allowed to be frustrated or protracted by the utilization of the collateral procedures allowed by Section 5 of the 1963 Act.'

And per Griffin J. –

'The jurisdiction of the High Court pursuant to Section 27 is not ousted by the institution of proceedings by Section 5.'

In this case the trial judge held that the Court had a wide discretion under Section 27, and could if it thought fit, adjourn the Section 27 application so that an application under Section 5 could be brought or alternatively itself decide the issue. In his discretion he did not adjourn the Section 27 application but decided the issue himself in the interest of its expeditious determination. In my opinion this was a course that he was fully justified in adopting on the facts of this case and fully accords with the decision of this Court in *Cork Corporation* v. *O'Connell*. As in this case, where a planning authority gives due notice of its intention to proceed against an occupier of lands for alleged breaches of the Planning Acts, the onus is on the occupier to avail with all reasonable speed of the provisions of Section 5 of the 1963 Act if he claims that the development complained of is 'exempted development'.

DUBLIN COUNTY COUNCIL V. MATRA INVESTMENTS LIMITED
[1980] I.L.T.R., Finlay P.

Finlay P.:
(i) The provisions of Section 31(1) of the 1963 Act concerning the five year limit on prosecutions under that section cannot, by implication, be incorporated into section 27 of the 1976 Act. No canon of construction permits this – the section contains no express time limit, and as it was enacted subsequent to the 1963 Act, it cannot be implied that the time limit applies in the case of Section 27 proceedings. Section 27 gives a right to injunct an unauthorised use no matter how long it has been in operation, provided it commenced after the appointed day which was the 1st October 1964.

(ii) The length of time for which a use may have been continued may affect the granting of an injunction or the form the injunction takes.

Section 27 is designed to enforce urgently and in a powerful manner, the provisions of the Planning Acts. It was intended by the legislature to be ancillary to the enforcement procedures under the 1963 Act. The County Council have asked me to enforce the law against the respondents, not to penalise them. In my view the Order should be made if I am satisfied there is unauthorised use of the land, unless exceptional reasons are shown by the respondents. Such reasons might be a merely technical breach of the Planning Acts, unreasonable delay in bringing the application or it might be that the user was a mere inadvertence on the respondents.[4]

DUBLIN CORPORATION V. GARLAND & ORS
[1982] ILRM 104 Finlay P.

In November 1973 the respondents began using premises as offices which had

[4] See page 361

formerly been a doctor's residence and surgery. No planning permission was obtained. In January 1974 the unauthorised change of use came to the attention of the applicant planning authority who issued proceedings under section 24. Upon the receipt of the summons the respondents made a section 5 reference to the Minister for Local Government and the proceedings were adjourned pending the outcome of the reference. In April 1976 the Minister decided that a material change of use had been made and that permission was required. The proceedings under section 24 were heard in December 1976 and the respondents were convicted and fined. The respondents made an application for permission for change of use in October 1977 which was refused in January 1977. The respondents continued to use the premises as offices. Another application for change of use was made in April 1977 which was refused by the applicant planning authority in August 1978 and by An Bord Pleanala in February 1979. In January 1978 the applicant planning authority issued an Enforcement Notice pursuant to section 31 of the 1963 Act and upon the respondents failure to comply with this Notice proceedings were brought under section 31(8). These were dismissed on technical grounds. In March 1980 fresh proceedings were issued under section 31(8). These were dismissed because the District Justice was not satisfied that the change of user had been made within five years of the Enforcement Notice. In April 1981 the applicants brought section 27 proceedings. In granting the order the Court held (1) section 27 cannot be used to challenge a decision of the planning authority in repect of the granting or withholding of permission, (2) the planning authority were not estopped from bringing the proceedings by reason of the premises being rated as offices and (3) the respondents had not acquried a vested interest to justify withholding the order.

Finlay P.:

. . . It was contended by counsel on behalf of the respondents firstly that the applicants, the Corporation of Dublin, having caused the premises to be rated as used for office purposes during the years from 1976 up to the present were estopped from bringing this application under Section 27 of the Act of 1976. Secondly, that even if that were not so that I should exercise my discretion by refusing to make an order under Section 27 on the grounds that the evidence before me would indicate there was no reality in the objection put forward by the Planning Authority leading to the refusal of permission to change the use of the premises and thirdly, that I should exercise my discretion on the basis of the unique hardship which would be applied to these respondents and in the latter context reliance was placed on my own decision in the *Dublin Corporation* v. *Mulligan*.[5]

Having regard to the issues raised in this application it seems to me necessary again to clarify and identify the issues which appear to me to be before the court in the bringing of an application under Section 27 of the Act of 1976. There can, in my view, be no function in the court on the making of an application under this Section in any way to review, alter or set aside a decision of the Planning Authority with regard to the granting or withholding of permission. The entire scheme of the Planning Acts is that subject to the limited exceptions for the determination by the High Court of questions of law specifically referred to it that decisions as to the proper planning and development of any area are peculiarly the function of the Planning Authority in the first instance and of An Bord Pleanala on appeal from

[5] See page 342.

them. The matters material to an application under Section 27 and the manner in which it is to be brought by simple Notice of Motion based in the first instance and frequently disposed of on affidavit rather than on oral evidence is plainly and patently quite inappropriate to the determination of matters of planning decision. The court cannot therefore entertain in my view in regard to applications under Section 27 any question challenging the validity or correctness of a decision of the Planning Authority in regard to the granting of refusing of permission though it may be concerned within the broader limits of its discretion with the consequences of unauthorised use or illegal development.

With regard to the point of estoppel taken on behalf of the respondents, I am satisfied it must fail. The basic principle of the doctrine of estoppel is that conduct on the part of one party which has been acted upon by the other to his or her detriment and which is inconsistent with the claim subsequently made may defeat that claim. There appears to me in the first place to be absolutely no inconsistency between the exercise by the rating authority of its proper power to levy upon the users and occupiers of premises a rate appropriate and applicable to their *de facto* use and benefit from them and a contention contemporaneously or subsequently made that that user is a breach of the Planning Acts and should be appropriate proceedings be discontinued. The plea of estoppel must therefore fail at the first primary enquiry quite apart from the question as to whether it can properly be said that the Planning Authority and the Rating Authority are the one party.

On the broader issues of discretion, I have come to the conclusion that I must exercise it in favour of the applicants. This is not a case in which there has been any conceivable question of laches or delay on the part of the applicants nor of any inactivity on their party. From a very short time after the commencement of this unauthorised use the applicants pursued every remedy available to them to try and achieve its termination. The delays in the bringing of the various proceedings by the Planning Authority were in my view no more than a reasonable approach to permitting the respondents as a matter of concession to exercise their rights for the determination of all legal questions concerned with the change of user and to obtain properly arrived at decisions with regard to the planning status and user of these premises. More importantly still bearing in mind the reasons for my decision in the *Mulligan* case the respondents have not at any time since very shortly after they purchased these premises been under any conceivable misapprehension as to the fact that their continued user of them as office premises was dependent on the result of a number of different applications which they were making to the Planning Authority and to the Minister for Local Government. They were never lulled into a belief as was the respondent in *Mulligan's case* that his user of the premises for office purposes had become tolerated or accepted. There cannot be in my view therefore any question of a vested interest created in them which would justify the withholding by this Court of the applicant *prima facie* right to an injunction under Section 27. I appreciate that in *Mulligan's Case* I distinguished between the refusal with regard to part of the premises which I there decided upon of an injunction under Section 27 and the authorisation for all time of an unauthorised user of the premises. In this case, however, it seems to me that notwithstanding the fact that I have very considerable sympathy for the respondents in the problem which now faces them and in the difficulty in which on the evidence I am satisfied they have encountered and are encountering in obtaining alternative accommodation that if I were to refuse to grant an injunction under Section 27 that I would be refusing to lend the aid of the Court which was intended by the legislature by the enactment of Section 27 to the implementation of decisions of the Planning Authority. In a case such as this where there is no other possible planning application which the respondents can make which could result in the granting of a permission to them to use the premises as offices to refuse an injunction would, it seeems to me, be in effect to reverse the decision of the the Planning Authority.

I am therefore satisfied that an injunction must be made but I am also satisfied that on the merits of the case the respondents should obtain a very substantial stay on the implementation of that injunction so as to permit them to obtain alternative accommodation for their office purposes. On the evidence before me, the form of the injunction restraining the respondents and each of them from continuing the user of the premises . . . or any part thereof as offices and further restraining them from using the said premises or any part thereof otherwise than as part residence and part surgery for a medical practitioner or entirely as residential premises.

Both Orders to be stayed for a period of 12 months from this date.

DONEGAL COUNTY COUNCIL V. KIERAN O'DONNELL
The High Court (Unreported) O'Hanlon J., 25th June 1982, (Ref. No. 1982 No. 51 MCA)

In March 1979 the applicants made a decision to grant planning permission to the respondent for a dwellinghouse subject to *inter alia* condition (1) which required 'Dwelling to be located within the area outlined in blue on the attached plan.' This condition required the respondent to build the house in a part of the site, other than that for which he had applied. The copy of the decision sent to the respondent had a line through condition (1) which had been superimposed during photocopying. Further he was not supplied with the plan mentioned in Condition (1). The respondent did not inquire if condition (1) applied to the planning permission nor did he request a copy of the plan. On the 18th April 1979 the Grant of planning permission was made in the same terms as the decision to grant and a copy of the notification of grant and the plan were sent to the respondent.

In July 1979 the respondent made another application for planning permission seeking to build the dwelling in the site indicated in the original application. This application was refused. The respondent began construction of the dwellinghouse in the area applied for. The applicants brought Section 27 proceedings.

The respondent argued that condition (1) did not apply to the grant of planning permission dated the 18th day of April 1979 on the following grounds:

(1) Condition (1) was crossed out in his copy the decision to grant planning permission.

(2) The failure to send the respondent a copy of the plan referred to in Condition (1) prejudiced him in that he might have exercised his right of appeal against the condition had he realised that it required him to build in a different part of the site.

(3) If he did build in the area required the dwelling would encroach on the public road.[6]

The Court rejected these arguments and granted an order under section 27.

---

[6] The plan had been based on the map accompanying the application which incorrectly indicated the boundaries of the respondent's site.

O'Hanlon J.:

. . . The respondent claims that he should not be bound by a condition which was crossed out in the document he received, but does not state, by affidavit or otherwise, that he was deceived by what had happened and caused to believe that the condition was not to apply. It is clearly legible in the document, and having regard to the numbering of the conditions in proper sequence (1) to (4), I am of opinion tht it would have been apparent to a person receiving the document that the condition was intended to apply, or he would at least have been put upon further inquiry directed to the Planning Authority to clear up any doubt which might remain in his mind about the matter. Consequently I commence by rejecting the first submission made on behalf of the respondent, that he should not be regarded as having been bound by the said condition.

. . .The respondent has deposed on affidavit to the fact that he did not receive any map with the said notification, and it is contended on his behalf that he was prejudiced by this default on the part of the planning authority, in that he might have exercised a right of appeal against the condition had it come to his notice immediately on receipt of the notification that they were requiring him to build in a completely different part of the site to that referred to in his application and the documents which accompanied it. However, the same condition was contained in the Grant of Permission, dated 18th April 1979 and this time the relevant plan accompanied the document. Once again, I would hold that the terms of condition no. (1) put the respondent upon inquiry as to its effect, and it would have been an easy matter for himself or for his architect to ask for inspection of the plan which was referred to in the condition and to point out that it had not been received.

. . . By reason of the fact that the map which accompanied the application was incorrect, the alternative site so designated by the Planning Authority as the only location on which they would permit the dwellinghouse to be erected, now appears to be quite unsuitable for a number of reasons – one reason being that the building would actually encroach on the public road if built where the County Council have said it should be built.

These considerations are not sufficient, in my opinion, to entitle the respondent to disregard the requirements of the Planning Authority and to substitute for them his own decision as to the most appropriate part of this lands for the execution of the building works.

In these circumstances, his action in proceeding to build on the site originally designated by him without having obtained planning permission or approval for so doing, constitutes a breach by him of the provisions of the Planning Acts, and the applicants are, in my opinion, entitled to an Order as sought by them under Section 27 of the Act of 1976, restraining the respondents from continuing with the building works which have already been commenced by him on his lands. . .

Having regard to a number of unsatisfactory features in the way the Planning Authority have dealt with the application for permission from the outset, and the correspondence relating thereto, I propose to make no Order as to costs in the matter – each party to bear their own cost.

Chapter 6

COMPENSATION

INTRODUCTION

Compensation will normally arise under section 55 of the Act of 1963 and is payable by a planning authority when as a result of a refusal or a conditioned grant there is a consequential reduction in the value of any person's interest existing in the land at the time of the relevant decision. By section 68 such a claim is dealt with in default of agreement by arbitration under the Act of 1919 as if it were a claim arising from the compulsory acquisition of land: in the result some of the case law of the United Kingdom relating to compensation in compulsory acquisition cases have been held to apply generally to compensation claims made under the Irish Planning Acts.[1]

The second way in which a dissatisfied applicant for planning permission may realise the value of his land is to force the planning authority to acquire it under section 29 of the Act of 1963. Here again compulsory acquisition statutes and authorities are relevant.

Subject to two general qualifications the measure of compensation is to be the amount by which the value of any interest in the land has been reduced as a result of the relevant planning decision taken in the context of the general planning circumstances affecting the subject site. In measuring the compensation the arbitrator is required[2] to have regard to any development available to the subject site either pursuant to an existing planning permission, an effective undertaking to grant planning permission if applied for or the exemption provisions of the Acts and statutory instruments. There is provision[3] for the recovery by a planning authority of compensation paid if significant development occurs on the site within 14 years of the payment of compensation.

Two general exceptions to the above emerge from an analysis of many provisions which exclude the payment of compensation. In general, compensation will be either excluded or reduced when (a) a reasonable alternative form of development is available to the subject site either by way of an existing planning permission or an undertaking to grant one if applied for,[4] and (b) when the development proposed would involve some interference with the amenities of the community at large

---

[1] The Lands Clauses Consolidation Act of 1845 is nowhere formally incorporated into the Planning Acts. Sections 69–79 are so incorporated by Section 71(2). The rules made under the Act of 1919 are extended by Section 69 of the Act of 1963 and the additional rules are set out in the Fourth Schedule to that Act. In the *Owenabue* case the President accepted that the effect of Section 68 was to apply the assessment principles of the Act of 1919 to Planning cases.

[2] Section 55 (2).

[3] Section 73.

[4] See especially Section 57.

either so as to be wholly unacceptable (and warrant refusal, for example, in the case of traffic hazard or danger to health) or partly unacceptable (so as to warrant, for example, the imposition of conditions limiting the density or regulating the layout of a housing estate).[5] Subject to the foregoing the claimant is entitled to the reduction in the value of the land resulting from the decision.[6] A compensation claim, however, must not be self-contradictory:[7] for example, the owner of agricultural lands can claim development land prices if he can show that the land could be developed as a housing estate; however, he could not in addition claim disturbance of his farming operation as this would have had to be disturbed in order to realise the development potential. He may make his claim on one basis or the other but not both.

A claim for compensation under section 55 may be made by a simple letter addressed to the planning authority;[8] a claim requiring purchase under section 29 is initiated by a simple form of notice again served on the planning authority: in each case the claim must be made within six months of the relevant decision.

Compensation claims may include one or more of the following different elements:

(1) THE VALUE (REDUCTION IN THE VALUE) OF THE LAND:
Rule 2 which provides for market value is the governing rule. The English Authorities on the subject were reviewed and applied in the *Deansrath* case. The value is the value to the owner rather than the acquiring/planning authority but will not include a value such as sentimental value which cannot be expressed in money terms. The value is to be the value of the land immediately before the relevant decision;[9] however, it is not necessary that the claimant have retained his interest in the land at the time of the assessment of the compensation provided his interest existed at the time of the relevant decision.[10] The existance or possibility of development by a local authority is to be excluded from consideration.[11] But a distinction is made between reservation for a specific purpose in a development plan which by Rule 11 is to be disregarded for the purpose of assessing compensation and the general zoning included in the plan pursuant to Section 19 of the Act of 1963. A further distinction[12] is made between such a reservation and the development in question when almost completely constructed although not yet in use.

(2) DAMAGE TO TRADE, BUSINESS OR PROFESSION:
This head of damage is specifically recognised in section 55(1) of the Act of 1963. A claim under this head could arise in the following way. The owner of a fish and chip shop might apply to extend them into an adjoining premises. He might be granted permission for this on condition that the entire business would close at 11.00 p.m.

5 See Section 56 generally.
6 See S. 55(1) of the 1963 Act.
7 See *Horn* v. *Sunderland Corporation* [1941] 1 All E.R. 480.
8 See Article 49 of the General Regulations for what must be included.
9 *Kilbeggan Property Investment Company Limited* v. *Dublin County Council* (Unreported: Gannon J. 18th April, 1977) (p. 444).
10 *Dublin Corporation* v. *Smithwick and Others* (Unreported: Finlay P: 12th July, 1977)
11 *Re: Deansrath Investments Limited* [1974] I.R. 228 (p. 441).
12 *Holiday Motor Inns Limited* v. *Dublin County Council* (Unreported: McWilliam J.: 20th December, 1977).

He might then make the claim that as occupier of the premises containing the existing business the trade carried on therein had suffered damage as a result of the imposition of this condition.

(3) COSTS:

A claim for compensation should include a claim for the cost of presenting the claim itself. These costs may include the fees and expenses of a valuer and in an appropriate case of a planning consultant. It is important to note that these costs do not include the costs of being represented at the arbitration if there is one: these latter costs are awarded in the discretion of the arbitrator.[13]

NOTE ON INJURIOUS AFFECTION (INCLUDING SEVERANCE) CLAIMS IN PLANNING CASES:

In *McKone Estates Limited* v. *Kildare County Council* O'Hanlon J. decided in delivering judgment on the 24th June, 1983, that a claimant for compensation under section 55 of the Act of 1963 was not entitled to include a claim in respect of injurious affection to lands not comprised in the site of the application for planning permission. The trial judge acceded to the argument that the rules set out in section 2 of the Act of 1919 as extended by section 69 of the Act of 1963 comprised a procedure whereby compensation should be measured but did not themselves confer a right to compensation. Such a right must arise outside the rules under different statutory provisions, for example, under the provisions of the Lands Clauses Acts if incorporated. The Judge could not find in section 55 of the Act of 1963 or elsewhere that the provisions of the Lands Clauses Acts were to apply in relation to claims under section 55, therefore such a claimant was not entitled to claim for injurious affection as he would have been under section 63 of the Lands Clauses Consolidation Act, 1845 if it applied, which it did not.[13a]

Finally, it should be noted that the whole question of compensation is complex and tricky. Many of the principles which apply have been articulated in the context of compulsory acquisition. The possibility of making a compensation claim should be borne in mind at all times including when presenting an application for permission.[14] Expert advice should be taken in presenting a claim for compensation even in the most simple cases as the manner of presentation can often affect the amount, if any, of compensation payable.

LOCAL GOVERNMENT (PLANNING AND DEVELOPMENT) ACT, 1963

PART I

PRELIMINARY AND GENERAL

2. – (1) In this Act, save where the context otherwise requires –

---

[13] Under Section 5(4) of the Act of 1919.
[13a] The effect of Section 1 of the Lands Clauses Consolidation Act, 1845, seems not to have been considered.
[14] And also when in receipt of a decision. It is often thought that a right to claim compensation can be resurrected by re-submitting a Planning Application. The right may be lost however by failure to apply within six months of the first decision: see Section 56(1) (j) of the Act of 1963.

'the Act of 1919' means the Acquisition of Land (Assessment of Compensation) Act, 1919;

'the Act of 1934' means the Town and Regional Planning Act, 1934 (repealed by this Act).[15]

. . .

PART VI

COMPENSATION

55. – (1) If, on a claim made to the planning authority, it is shown that, as a result of a decision under Part IV of this Act involving a refusal of permission to develop land or a grant of such permission subject to conditions (other than any such condition as is referred to in paragraph (*e*), paragraph (*g*) or paragraph (*h*) of subsection (2) of section 26 of this Act) the value of an interest of any person existing in the land to which the decision relates at the time[16] of the decision is reduced, such person shall, subject to the provisions of this Part of this Act, be entitled to be paid by the planning authority by way of compensation the amount of such reduction in value and, in the case of the occupier of the land, the damage (if any) to his trade, business or profession carried on on the land.

(2) In determining reduction of value for the purposes of this section, regard shall be had –

(*a*) to any permission under this Act to develop the land existing at the time compensation is agreed or determined,[17]

(*b*) to any undertaking[18] that may be given to grant permission to develop the land in the event of application being made under this Act in that behalf, and

(*c*) to the fact that exempted development may be carried out on the land, and, in a case in which there has been a refusal of permission, the calculation shall be made on the basis that, if the permission had been granted, any condition which might reasonably have been imposed in relation to matters referred to in paragraphs (*e*), (*g*) and (*h*) of subsection (2) of section 26 and paragraph (*c*) of sub-section (1) of section 56 of this Act (but no other conditions) would have been imposed.

(3) In determining reduction of value for the purposes of this section in a case in which there has been a decision involving a refusal of permission, it shall be asumed that, after the decision, and apart from any such undertaking as is mentioned in subsection (2) of this section, permission under this Act would not be granted for any development.

(4) Where, under section 29 of this Act, it is the duty of a planning authority to acquire an interest in land, compensation in relation to that interest shall not be payable pursuant to this section.[19]

(6)[20] A claim under this section shall be made within (but not after) –

(*a*) six months after the notification of the decision by the planning authority,

---

[15] For a fuller list of definitions see p. 6).

[16] See *Dublin Corporation* v. *Smithwick and others* (p. 473).

[17] The words 'compensation is agreed or determined' substituted by S. 41(*a*) of the Act of 1976.

[18] See *Byrne* v. *Dublin County Council* (p. 447).

[19] See also Rule 16 which excludes any allowance for disturbance or severance in S. 29 cases.

[20] Sub.-s 5 repealed by S. 45 of the Act of 1976.

the Board or the Minister (as the case may be), or

(b) such longer period as the Circuit Court may allow if it appears to the Court that there are reasonable grounds for requiring a longer period and that it would be just and reasonable to extend the period.

56. – (1) Compensation under section 55 of this Act shall not be payable –

(a) in respect of the refusal of permission for any development that consists of or includes the making of any material change in the use of any structures or other land,[21]

(b) in respect of the refusal of permission to develop land if the reason or one of the reasons for the refusal is that development of the kind proposed would be premature[22]

  (i) by reference to any existing deficiency in the provision of water supplies or sewerage facilities and the period within which any such deficiency may reasonably be expected to be made good, or

  (ii) because a road layout for the area or part thereof has not been indicated in the development plan or has not been approved of by the planning authority or by the Minister on appeal.

(c) in respect of the imposition, on the granting of permission to develop land, of any condition relating to any of the following matters:

  (i) the matters set out in paragraphs 1, 2, 3, 4 and 6 of Part II of the Third Schedule to this Act,

  (ii) the matters set out in paragraph 5 of the said Part II so far as that paragraph relates to unauthorised structures,

  (iii) the matters set out in paragraphs 1 and 3 of Part III of that Schedule,

  (iv) the matters set out in paragraph 2, paragraph 6, paragraph 7, subparagraph (b) of paragraph 8 and paragraphs 9, 10, 11 and 13 of Part IV of that Schedule,

  (iva) measures to reduce or prevent air pollution or the emission or the intrusion of noise or vibration,[23]

  (v) matters in respect of which a requirement could have been imposed under any other Act, or under any order, regulation, rule or bye-law made under any other Act, without liability for compensation,

(d) in respect of the imposition, on the granting of permission to develop land, of any condition under paragraph (j) of subsection (2) of section 26 of this Act for requiring the removal of an advertisement structure or any condition under that paragraph in a case in which the relevant application for permission relates to a temporary structure,

(e) in respect of the refusal of permission for development if the reason or one of the reasons for the refusal is that the proposed development would endanger public safety by reason of traffic hazard or obstruction of road users or otherwise,

(f) in respect of the refusal of permission for the erection of any advertisement structure or for the use of land for the exhibition of any advertisement,

[21] See *Viscount Securities Limited* v. *Dublin County Council* (p. 453).
[22] The emphasis here is on prematurity: see McMahon J. in *Short* v. *Dublin County Council* [1982] I.L.R.M. 117 and 119. (See p. 423).
[23] Inserted by s. 41(c) of the Act of 1976.

(g) in respect of the refusal of permission for development if the reason or one of the reasons for the refusal is the necessity of preserving any view or prospect of special amenity value or special interest,[24]

(h) in respect of the refusal of permission for development in an area to which a special amenity area order relates,[25]

(i) in respect of the refusal of permission for development comprising any structure or any addition to or extension of a structure if the reason or one of the reasons for the refusal is that the structure, addition or extension –

  (i) would infringe an existing building line or, where none exists, a building line determined by the planning authority or by the Minister,

  (ii) would be under a public road,

  (iii) would seriously injure the amenities, or depreciate the value, of property in the vicinity,

  (iv) would tend to create any serious traffic congestion,

  (v) would endanger the health or safety of persons occupying or employed in the structure or any adjoining structure, or

  (vi) would be prejudicial to public health,

(j) in respect of the refusal of permission for development if the reason or one of the reasons for the refusal is that the development would contravene materially a condition attached to an existing permission for development.[26]

(2) Nothing contained in subsection (1) of this section shall prevent compensation being paid –

(a) in a case in which there has been a refusal of permission for the erection of a new structure substantially replacing a structure (other than an unauthorised structure) which has been demolished or destroyed by fire or otherwise within the two years preceding the date of application for permission or there has been imposed a condition in consequence of which such new structure may not be used for the purpose for which the demolished or destroyed structure was last used, or

(b) in a case in which there has been imposed a condition in consequence of which the new structure referred to in the foregoing paragraph or the front thereof, or the front of an existing structure (other than an unauthorised structure) which has been taken down in order to be re-erected or altered, is set back or forward.

(3) Every dispute and question whether a new structure would or does replace substantially within the meaning of the foregoing subsection a demolished or destroyed structure shall be determined by the Minister.[27]

---

[24] In two unreported cases (*Hayes* v. *Clare County Council* (1982: 114:S.S.) decided by Gannon J. and *Clifford* v. *Limerick County Council* (1982: 372: S.S.) decided by Barrington J. the High Court looked beyond the actual words used which were not those of sub-s. (g) to the true meaning of the ground of refusal and in both cases held that the true reason was for the purpose set out in this sub-section. The Court will not hold a Planning Authority to the actual words of the statute although the use of these words is more advisable.

[25] All words after 'relates' repealed by S. 45 of the Act of 1976.

[26] The condition contravened might however have warranted a claim for compensation if presented within six months of the notification of the relevant decision.

[27] To be construed as the Board by S.10(9)(c) of the Act of 1976.

57. – (1) Compensation under section 55 of this Act shall not be payable in respect of a decision whereby permission to develop land is refused if, notwithstanding that refusal, there is available with respect to that land permission for development to which this section applies or if compensation has already been paid under section 55 of this Act by reference to a previous decision under part IV of this Act involving a refusal of permission.

(2) Where permission for development to which this section applies is available with respect to part only of the land, this section shall have effect only in so far as the interest subsists in that part.

(3) Where a claim for compensation under this Part of this Act is made in respect of an interest in land, permission for development to which this section applies shall be taken for the purposes of this section to be available with respect to that land or a part thereof if there is in force with respect to that land or part a grant of, or an undertaking[28] to grant, permission under this Act for some such development, subject to no conditions other than conditions in relation to matters referred to in paragraphs (*e*), (*g*) and (*h*) of subsection (2) of section 26 and paragraph (*c*) of subsection (1) of section 56 of this Act.

(4) This section applies to any development of a residential, commercial or industrial character, if the development consists wholly or mainly of the construction of houses, flats, shops or office premises, hotels, garages, and petrol filling stations, theatres or structures for the purpose of entertainment, or industrial buildings (including warehouses), or any combination thereof.

58. – (1) Where, in a case determined on an appeal under Part IV of this Act, permission to develop any land has, save in a case referred to in subsection (2) of this section, been refused or has been granted subject to any condition relating to any of the matters set out in paragraphs 3 and 4 of Part II of the Third Schedule to this Act, nothing contained in subsection (1) of section 56 or section 57 of this Act shall prevent compensation being paid if, an application having been made in that behalf within (but not after) two months after the notification of the decision by the Minister or the Board, as the case may be,[29] the Minister makes an order declaring that he is satisfied that it would not be just and reasonable in the particular circumstances that payment of compensation should be prevented by the provisions of subsection (1) of section 56 or section 57 of this Act.[30]

(2) Subsection (1) of this section does not apply –

(*a*) where there has been a refusal of permission for the erection of any advertisement structure or for the use of any land for the exhibition of any advertisement,

(*b*) where there has been a refusal of permission for development comprising any structure or any addition to or extension of a structure if the reason or one of the reasons for the refusal is that the structure, addition or extension –

(i) would infringe an existing building line or, where none exists, a building line determined by the planning authority or by the Minister,

---

[28] See generally *Byrne* v. *Dublin County Council* (p. 447).
[29] The words 'or the Board, as the case may be' inserted by S. 41(*d*) of the Act of 1976.
[30] Such an order was made in *Dublin Corporation* v. *Smithwick and others* (p. 473).

(ii) would be under a public road,

(iii) would endanger the health or safety of persons occupying or employed in the structure or any adjoining structure, or

(iv) would be prejudicial to public health.

59. – (1) Where permission to develop land has been revoked or modified by a notice under section 30 of this Act –

(a) if, on a claim made to the planning authority, it is shown that any person interested in the land has incurred expenditure in carrying out works which are rendered abortive[31] by the revocation or modification, that authority shall pay to that person compensation in respect of that expenditure,

(b) the provisions of subsections (1) to (4) of section 55 and sections 56, 57 and 58[32] of this Act shall apply in relation to the notice where it revoked the permission or modifies it by the imposition of conditions –

(i) in case it revoked the permission, as they apply in relation to refusal of permission to develop land, and

(ii) in case it modifies the permission by the imposition of conditions, as they apply in relation to a grant of permission to develop land subject to conditions,

subject to the modifications that, in subsections (1) and (2) of the said section 55, a reference to the time when the notice takes effect shall be substituted for any reference to the time of a decision and in subsection (4) thereof, the reference to section 29 of this Act shall be construed as a reference to that section as applied by section 30 of this Act.

(2) A claim under this section or section 55 of this Act as applied by this section shall be made within (but not after) –

(a) six months after the time when the notice takes effect, or

(b) such longer period as the Circuit Court may allow if it appears to the Court that there are reasonable grounds for requiring a longer period and that it would be just and reasonable to extend the period.

(3) For the purposes of this section, any expenditure reasonably incurred in the preparation of plans for the purposes of any works or upon other similar matters preparatory thereto shall be deemed to be included in the expenditure incurred in carrying out those works but, except as aforesaid, no compensation shall be paid by virtue of this section in respect of any works carried out before the grant of the permission which is revoked or modified, or in respect of any other loss or damage arising out of anything done or omitted to be done before the grant of that permission.

60. – (1) If, on a claim made to the planning authority, it is shown that, as a result of the removal or alteration of any structure consequent upon a notice under section 36 of this Act, any person has suffered damage by the depreciation of any interest in the structure to which he is entitled, or by being disturbed in his enjoyment of the structure, such person shall, subject to the provisions of this Part

---

[31] There is a widespread misconception that revocation gives rise to an automatic right to compensation. The right is qualified and it is to be noted that Ss. 56 and 57 apply.

[32] Reference to S. 58 added by S. 41(e) of the Act of 1976.

of this Act, be entitled to be paid by the planning authority by way of compensation the amount of such damage.

(2) A claim under this section shall be made within (but not after) –

(a) six months after the removal or alteration of the structure, or

(b) such longer period as the Circuit Court may allow if it appears to the Court that there are reasonable grounds for requiring a longer period and that it would be just and reasonable to extend the period.

(3) Where, under section 29 of this Act as applied by subsection (9) of section 36 of this Act, it is the duty of the planning authority to acquire an interest in land, compensation in relation to that interest shall not be payable pursuant to this section.

(4) Rule (12) of the Rules set o... in section 2 of the Act of 1919 shall not apply in relation to any case in which a claim is made under this section.[33]

61. – (1) If, on a claim made to the planning authority, it is shown that, as a result of the discontinuance, or the compliance with conditions on the continuance, of any use of land consequent upon a notice under section 37 of this Act, any person has suffered damage by the depreciation of any interest in the land to which he is entitled, or by being disturbed in his enjoyment of the land, such person shall, subject to the provisions of this Part of this Act, be entitled to be paid by the planning authority by way of compensation the amount of such damage,[34] provided that unless an application having been made to him in that behalf, the Minister makes an order declaring that he is satisfied that it would not be just and reasonable in the particular circumstances that payment of compensation should be prevented by the provisions of this proviso, no compensation shall be paid under this section in relation to damage resulting from the imposition under section 37 of this Act of conditions on the continuance of the use of land, being conditions imposed in order to avoid or reduce serious air or water pollution or the danger of such pollution.

(2) Subsection (1) of this section shall not apply where the use of land is use for the exhibition of advertising unless at the time of such discontinuance or compliance the land had been used for the exhibition of advertising for less than five years, whether such use was continuous or intermittent or whether or not, while the land was being so used, advertising was exhibited at the same place on the land.[35]

(3) A claim under this section shall be made within (but not after) –

(a) six months after the discontinuance or compliance, or

(b) such longer period as the Circuit Court may allow if it appears to the Court that there are reasonable grounds for requiring a longer period and that it would be just and reasonable to extend the period.

(4) Where, under section 29 of this Act as applied by subsection (8) of section 37 of this Act, it is the duty of the planning authority to acquire an interest in land, compensation in relation to that interest shall not be payable pursuant to this section.

(5) Rule (12) of the Rules set out in section 2 of the Act of 1919 shall not apply in relation to any case in which a claim is made under this section.

---

[33] The effect is to enable account to be taken of unauthorised structures or unauthorised uses which have been in existence for more than 5 years.

[34] Words after 'damage' added by S. 41(f) of the Act of 1976.

[35] Sub.-s. (2) substituted by S. 41(g) of the Act of 1976.

62. – (1) If, on a claim made to the planning authority, it is shown that, as a result of the removal or alteration of any hedge consequent upon a notice under section 44 of this Act, any person has suffered damage by the depreciation of any interest in the land on which the hedge is situate to which he is entitled, or by being disturbed in his enjoyment of such land, such person shall, subject to the provisions of this Part of this Act, be entitled to be paid by the planning authority by way of compensation the amount of the damage.

(2) A claim under this section shall be made within (but not after) –

    (*a*) six months after the removal or alteration of the hedge, or

    (*b*) such longer period as the Circuit Court may allow if it appears to the Court that there are reasonable grounds for requiring a longer period and that it would be just and reasonable to extend the period.

63. – (1) If, on a claim made to the planning authority, it is shown that the value of an interest of any person in land, being land over which a public right of way has been created by an order under section 48 of this Act made by that authority, is depreciated, or that any person having an interest in such land has suffered damage by being disturbed in his enjoyment of the land, in consequence of the creation of the public right of way, that authority shall pay to that person compensation equal to the amount of the depreciation or damage.

(2) A claim under this section shall be made within (but not after) –

    (*a*) six months after the time when the order creating the public right of way commences to have effect, or

    (*b*) such longer period as the Circuit Court may allow if it appears to the Court that there are reasonable grounds for requiring a longer period and that it would be just and reasonable to extend the period.

64. – (1) If, on a claim made to the planning authority, it is shown that, as a result of anything done under section 83 of this Act, any person has suffered damage, such person shall, subject to the provisions of this Part of this Act, be entitled to be paid by the planning authority by way of compensation the amount of such damage.

(2) A claim under this section shall be made within (but not after) –

    (*a*) six months after the damage is suffered, or

    (*b*) such longer period as the Circuit Court may allow if it appears to the Court that there are reasonable grounds for requiring a longer period and that it would be just and reasonable to extend the period.

65. – (1) If, on a claim made to the planning authority, it is shown that, as a result of the action of such authority pursuant to section 85 of this Act in placing, renewing or removing any cable, wire or pipeline, attaching any bracket or fixture or affixing any notice, any person has suffered damage by the depreciation of any interest in the land or structure concerned to which he is entitled, or by being disturbed in his enjoyment of such land or structure, such person shall, subject to the provisions of this Part of this Act, be entitled to be paid by the planning authority by way of compensation the amount of the damage.

(2) A claim under this section shall be made within (but not after) –

    (*a*) six months after the action of the planning authority, or

    (*b*) such longer period as the Circuit Court may allow if it appears to the Court that there are reasonable grounds for requiring a longer period and that it would be just and reasonable to extend the period.

66. – (1) In this section –

'interim direction' means a direction to do or refrain from doing any act which was given under the Act of 1934 directly or by implication by refusing a general permission or special permission, by granting a general or special permission subject to conditions, or by making a special prohibition whether subject to conditions or not so subject, not being a direction in respect of which an order was made under section 14 of the Town and Regional Planning (Amendment) Act, 1939;

'general permission', 'special permission', 'special prohibition', 'planning scheme' and 'work' have the same meanings respectively as these expressions had in the Act of 1934.

(2)(*a*) Where an interim direction was given in respect of any property –

    (i) any person who, on the day before the appointed day, had any estate or interest in or right over or in respect of such property, shall, on making a claim to the planning authority within the period of twelve months beginning on the appointed day, be entitled to be paid compensation by that authority unless they decide that compensation would not have been payable to him by virtue of the Act of 1934 on the assumption of the relevant planning scheme having come into operation on the day before the appointed day and having contained a provision to the same effect as the interim direction and on the assumption of an application for compensation having been duly made under section 61 of the Act of 1934.

    (ii) the amount of the compensation shall be the like amount as, on the said assumptions, would have been appropriate to be paid in accordance with the Act of 1934.

(*b*) Where a decision is given under the foregoing paragraph, the applicant may, within one month after being notified of the decision, appeal to the Minister, and the Minister shall either refuse the appeal or annul such decision.

(*c*) In deciding an appeal under this subsection, the Minister shall, in particular, have regard to subsection (2) of section 30 of the Act of 1934 and, for that purpose, may make any determination referred to in subsection (3) of that section in accordance with that subsection.

(3)(*a*) Where –

    (i) any person has refrained from doing any particular work on account of an interim direction arising from the refusing of a special permission or the making of a special prohibition, and

    (ii) he has suffered loss by so refraining,

such person shall, on making a claim to the planning authority within the period of twelve months beginning on the appointed day, be entitled to be paid by that authority by way of compensation the amount of such loss unless the planning authority decide that the doing of such particular work would have prejudiced the efficient and economical execution of the relevant planning scheme on the assumption that that scheme had come into operation.

(*b*) Where –

> (i) any person has, in the doing of any particular work complied with a condition attached to a special permission or contained in a special prohibition, and
>
> (ii) he has by such compliance suffered loss (other than loss arising from the reduction in value of any property),

such person shall, on making a claim to the planning authority within the period of twelve months beginning on the appointed day, be entitled to be paid by that authority by way of compensation the amount of such loss unless the planning authority decide that the doing of such particular work without complying with such condition would have prejudiced the efficient and economical execution of the relevant planning scheme on the assumption that that scheme had come into operation.

> (*c*) Where a decision is given under either of the foregoing paragraphs, the applicant may, within one month after being notified of the decision, appeal to the Minister, and the Minister shall either refuse the appeal or annul such decision.

(4) The amendment of the Act of 1919 effected by this Act shall be disregarded in the case of any determination of compensation under this section.

67. – Regulations[36] may provide for –

> (*a*) the form in which claims for compensation are to be made,
>
> (*b*) the provision by a claimant of evidence in support of his claim and information as to his interest in the land to which the claim relates,
>
> (*c*) a statement by a claimant of the names and addresses of all other persons (so far as they are known to him) having an interest in the land to which the claim relates and, unless the claim is withdrawn, the notification by the planning authority or the claimant of every other person (if any) appearing to them or him to have an interest in the land,
>
> (*d*) the information and documents to be submitted with an application for an order under section 58 of this Act,
>
> (*e*) the information and documents to be submitted by a planning authority in relation to an application for an order under section 58 of this Act.

68. – A claim under this Act for payment of compensation shall, in default of agreement, be determined by arbitration under the Act of 1919 in the like manner in all respects as if such claim arose in relation to the compulsory acquisition of land, but subject to the proviso that the arbitrator shall have jurisdiction to make a nil award.

69. – (1) Section 2 of the Act of 1919 is hereby amended, in cases where any compensation assessed will be payable by a planning authority or any other local authority, by the insertion after Rule 6 of the Rules set out in the Fourth Schedule to this Act.

(2) Subparagraph (*b*) of paragraph 1 of Part I of the Second Schedule to the Housing (Miscellaneous Provisions) Act, 1931, is hereby amended by the insertion at the end of the subparagraph of 'and by the Property Values (Arbitrations and

---

[36] These are contained in Part VI of S.I. No. 65 of 1977. See p. 404.

Appeals) Act, 1960, and the Local Government (Planning and Development) Act, 1963'.

70. – Where a person would, but for this section, be entitled to compensation under this Act in respect of any matter or thing and also to compensation under any other enactment in respect of the same matter or thing, he shall not be entitled to compensation in respect of such matter or thing both under this Act and under the other enactment, and shall not be entitled to any greater amount of compensation under this Act in respect of such matter or thing than the amount of the compensation to which he would be entitled under the other enactment in respect of such matter or thing.

71. – (1) All compensation payable under this Part of this Act by the planning authority shall, when the amount thereof has been determined by agreement or by arbitration in accordance with this Act, be recoverable from that authority as a simple contract debt in any court of competent jurisdiction, and all costs and expenses of parties to an arbitration to determine the amount of any such compensation shall, in so far as such costs and expenses are payable by the planning authority, be likewise recoverable from that authority as a simple contract debt in any court of competent jurisdiction.

(2) Sections 69 to 79 of the Lands Clauses Consolidation Act, 1845, as amended or adapted by or under the Second Schedule to the Housing of the Working Classes Act, 1890, or any other Act, shall apply in relation to moneys by this section made recoverable as a simple contract debt as if such moneys were a price or compensation under the said Act as so amended or adapted.

(3) Where money is paid into Court under section 69 of the Lands Clauses Consolidation Acts, 1845, as applied by this section, by the planning authority, no costs shall be payable by that authority to any person in respect of any proceedings for the investment, payment of income, or payment of capital of such money.

72. – (1) Where, on a claim for compensation under section 55 of this Act, under that section as applied by section 59 of this Act or under subsection (2) of section 66 of this Act, compensation has become payable of an amount exceeding twenty pounds, the planning authority shall prepare and retain a statement of that fact, specifying the refusal of permission or grant of permission subject to conditions, the revocation or modification of permission or the interim direction (as the case may be), the land to which the claim for compensation relates, and the amount of the compensation.

(2)(*a*) A planning authority shall enter in the register particulars of the statements prepared by them under this section.

(*b*) Every such entry shall be made within the period of fourteen days beginning on the day of the preparation of the statement.

73. – (1) No person shall carry out any development to which this section applies, on land in respect of which a statement (in this section referred to as a compensation statement) has stood registered under the last preceding section for less than fourteen years, until such amount (if any) as is recoverable under this section in respect of the compensation specified in the statement has been paid or secured to the satisfaction of the planning authority.

(2) This section applies to any development (other than exempted development), being development –

   (*a*) to which section 57 of this Act applies, or

   (*b*) to which, having regard to the probable value of the development, it is in the opinion of the Minister reasonable that this section should apply:

Provided that –

   (i) this section shall not apply to any development by virtue of paragraph (*b*) of this subsection if, on an application made to him for the purpose, the Minister has certified that, having regard to the probable value of the development, it is not in his opinion reasonable that this section shall apply thereto, and

   (ii) in a case where the compensation specified in the statement became payable in respect of the imposition of conditions on the granting of permission to develop land, this section shall not apply to the development for which that permission was granted.

(3) Subject to the two next following subsections, the amount recoverable under this section in respect of the compensation specified in a compensation statement –

   (*a*) if the land on which the development is to be carried out (in this subsection referred to as the development area) is identical with, or includes (with other land) the whole of, the land comprised in the compensation statement, shall be the amount of compensation specified in that statement;

   (*b*) if the development area forms part of the land comprised in the compensation statement, or includes part of that land together with other land not comprised in that statement, shall be so much of the amount of compensation specified in that statement as is attributable to land comprised in that statement and falling within the development area.

(4) For the purposes of paragraph (*b*) of subsection (3) of this section, the following provisions shall have effect:

   (*a*) the planning authority shall (if it appears to them to be practicable to do so) apportion the amount of the compensation between the different parts of the land according to the way in which those parts appear to them to be differently affected by the refusal or permission or grant of permission subject to conditions;

   (*b*) if no apportionment is made, the amount of the compensation shall be treated as distributed rateably according to area over the land to which the statement relates;

   (*c*) if an apportionment is made, the compensation shall be treated as distributed in accordance with that apportionment as between the different parts of the land by reference to which the apportionment is made, and so much of the compensation as, in accordance with the apportionment, is attributed to a part of the land shall be treated as distributed rateably according to area over that part of the land;

   (*d*) if any person disputes an apportionment under this subsection, the dispute shall be submitted to and decided by a property arbitrator.

(5) Where, in the case of any land in respect of which a compensation statement has been registered, the Minister is satisfied that, having regard to the probable value of any proper development of that land, no such development is likely to be

carried out unless he exercises his powers under this subsection, he may, in the case of any particular development, remit the whole or part of any amount otherwise recoverable under this section; and where part only of any such amount has been remitted, he shall cause the compensation statement to be amended by substituting therein for the specification of the amount of the compensation, in so far as it is attributable to that land, a specification of the amount which has been remitted under this subsection.

(6) Where, in connection with the development of any land, an amount becomes recoverable under this section in respect of the compensation specified in a compensation statement, then, except where, and to the extent that, payment of that amount has been remitted under the last preceding subsection, no amount shall be recoverable, in so far as it is attributable to that land, in connection with any subsequent development thereof.

(7) An amount recoverable under this section in respect of any compensation shall be payable to the planning authority, and –

    (*a*) shall be so payable either as a single capital payment or as a series of instalments of capital and interest combined, or as a series of other annual or periodical paayments, of such amounts, and payable at such times, as the planning authority may direct, after taking into account any representations made by the person by whom the development is to be carried out, and

    (*b*) except where the amount is payable as a single capital payment, shall be secured by that person in such manner (whether by mortage, covenant or otherwise) as the planning authority may direct.

(8) If any person initiates any development to which this section applies in contravention of subsection (1) of this section, the planning authority may serve a notice upon him, specifying the amount appearing to them to be the amount recoverable under this section in respect of the compensation in question, and requiring him to pay that amount to them within such period, not being less than three months after the service of the notice, as may be specified in the notice, and, in default of the said amount being paid to the planning authority within the period specified in the notice, it shall be recoverable as a simple contract debt in any court of competent jurisdiction.

. . .

PART IV
CONTROL OF DEVELOPMENT AND OF RETENTION OF CERTAIN STRUCTURES, ETC.

29. – (1) Where, in a case determined on an appeal under this Part of this Act, permission to develop any land has been refused or has been granted subject to conditions, then, if the owner of the land claims –

    (*a*) that the land has become incapable of reasonably beneficial use in its existing state, and

    (*b*) that the land cannot be rendered capable of reasonably beneficial use by the carrying out of any other development for which permission has been granted under this Part of this Act, or for which the planning authority have undertaken to grant such permission, and

    (*c*) in a case where permission to develop the land was granted as aforesaid subject to conditions that the land cannot be rendered capable of reasonably beneficial use by the carrying out of the permitted development in accordance with those conditions,

he may, at any time within the period of six months after the decision (or such longer period as the Minister [37] may allow), serve on the planning authority a notice (hereafter in this section referred to as a purchase notice) requiring the planning authority to purchase his interest in the land in accordance with the provisions of this section.[38]

(2) The planning authority on whom a purchase notice is served under this section shall, before the end of the period of three months beginning with the date of the service of that notice, serve on the owner by whom the purchase notice was served a notice stating either –

(a) that the authority are willing to comply with the purchase notice, or

(b) that, for reasons specified in the notice under this subsection, the authority are not willing to comply with the purchase notice and that they have transmitted a copy of the purchase notice and a copy of the notice under this subsection to the Minister.

(3) Where the planning authority upon whom a purchase notice is served under this section have served on the owner by whom the purchase notice was served a notice in accordance with paragraph (a) of subsection (2) of this section, it shall be the duty of the authority to acquire the interest of the owner and, for that purpose, the latter notice shall have the like effect as if it were a compulsory purchase order in respect of that interest which, consequent upon a decision made by the planning authority pursuant to subsection (1) of section 10 of the Local Government (No. 2) Act, 1960, had been duly made and confirmed.[39]

(4) Where a purchase notice is served on a planning authority under this section and the authority propose to serve on the owner a notice in accordance with paragraph (b) of subsection (2) of this section, they shall transmit a copy of that notice and copy of the purchase notice to the Minister, and subject to the following provisions of this section the Minister shall, if he is satisfied[40] that the conditions specified in paragraphs (a) to (c) or paragraphs (a) and (b) (as may be appropriate) of subsection (1) of this section are fulfilled, confirm the purchase notice, and thereupon it shall be the duty of the planning authority to acquire the interest of the owner, and for that purpose, –

---

[37] All functions of the Minister are transferred to the Board by S. 14(5) of the Act of 1976.

[38] The right to serve the notice is not precluded by S. 56.

[39] In *Portland Estates Limited* v. *Limerick Corporation* the Supreme Court ruled that a Planning Authority is obliged to serve a Notice to Treat in such cases. See p. 479.

[40] There are no regulations governing the determination of this matter by the Board, yet the outcome will be of crucial importance to the owner. The words of McWilliam J. in *O'Callaghan* v. *The Commissioners of Public Works in Ireland and Others* [1983] I.L.R.M. 391 are relevant: '. . . In the latter case it would be the responsibility of the body effecting the interference to ensure that procedures were adopted which conformed to the principles of natural justice, and, if they did not, the validity of the interference, but not of the statute, could be challenged in the Courts.' At the very least the owner should be given a copy of all relevant documentation including any submissions made by them to the Board supporting their decision to refuse to purchase and the owner should also be given an opportunity of making his own submissions. See also *Nolan* v. *Irish Land Commission* [1981] I.R. 23.

(*a*) the planning authority shall serve on the owner a notice stating that they propose to comply with the purchase notice,

(*b*) the notice so served shall have the like effect as if it were a compulsory purchase order in respect of that interest which, consequent upon a decision by the planning authority pursuant to subsection (1) of Section 10 of the Local Government (No. 2) Act, 1960, had been duly made and confirmed:

Provided that –

    (i) if it appears to the Minister to be expedient so to do, he may, in lieu of confirming the purchase notice, grant permission for the development in respect of which the application was made or, where permission for that development was granted subject to conditions, revoke or amend the conditions so far as appears to him to be required in order to enable the land to be rendered capable of reasonably beneficial use by the carrying out of that development;

    (ii) if it appears to the Minister, that the land, or any part of the land, could be rendered capable of reasonably beneficial use within a reasonable time by the carrying out of any other development for which permission ought to be granted, he may, in lieu of confirming the notice, or in lieu of confirming it so far as it relates to that part of the land, as the case may be, direct that such permission shall, subject to the provisions of this Act, be granted in the event of an application being made in that behalf.

(5) If within the period of six months from the end of the period specified in subsection (2) of this section, or the date on which a copy of the purchase notice is transmitted to the Minister, whichever is the earlier, the Minister has neither confirmed the notice nor taken any such other action as is mentioned in paragraph (i) or paragraph (ii) of the proviso to subsection (4) of this section, nor notified the owner by whom the notice was served that he does not propose to confirm the notice, the notice shall be deemed to be confirmed at the expiration of that period, and it shall be the duty of the planning authority on whom the notice was served to acquire the interest of the owner and, for that purpose, –

(*a*) the planning authority shall serve on the owner a notice stating that they propose to comply with the purchase notice,

(*b*) the notice so served shall have the like effect as if it were a compulsory purchase order in respect of that interest which, consequent upon a decision made by the planning authority pursuant to subsection (1) of section 10 of the Local Government (No. 2) Act, 1960, had been duly made and confirmed.

(6) Where, for the purpose of determining whether the conditions specified in paragraphs (*a*) to (*c*) or paragraphs (*a*) and (*b*) (as may be appropriate) of subsection (1) of this section are fulfilled in relation to any land, any question arises as to what is or would in any particular circumstances be a reasonably beneficial use of that land, then, in determining that question for that purpose, no account shall be taken of any prospective use of that land which would involve the carrying out of development of any class which is not exempted development.

ACQUISITION OF LAND (ASSESSMENT OF COMPENSATION) ACT, 1919

AN ACT TO AMEND THE LAW AS TO THE ASSESSMENT OF COMPENSATION IN RESPECT OF LAND ACQUIRED COMPUL-SORILY FOR PUBLIC PURPOSES AND THE COSTS IN PROCEED-INGS THEREON.
[19th August, 1919]

1. – (1) Where by or under any statute (whether passed before or after the passing of this Act) land is authorised to be acquired compulsorily by any Government Department or any local or public authority, any question of disputed compensation, and, where any part of the land to be acquired is subject to a lease which comprises land not acquired, any question as to the apportionment of the rent payable under the lease, shall be referred to and determined by the arbitration of such one[41] of a panel of offical arbitrators to be appointed under this section as may be selected in accordance with rules made by the Reference Committee under this section.

(5) The Reference Committee –[42]

(c) for Ireland shall consist of the *Chief Justice, the President of the High Court, and the Chairman of the Surveyors' Institution (Irish Branch)*, or (if the *said Chairman* thinks fit) a person, being a member of the council of that institution and having special knowledge of valuation of land in Ireland appointed by him to act in his place.

2. – In assessing compensation, an official arbitrator shall act in accordance with the following rules[43]. . . .

3. – (1) In any proceedings before an official arbitrator, not more than one expert witness on either side shall be heard unless the official arbitrator otherwise directs:

Provided that, where the claim includes a claim for compensation in respect of minerals, or disturbance of business, as well as in respect of land, one additional expert witness on either side on the value of the minerals, or, as the case may be, on the damage suffered by reason of the disturbance, may be allowed.

(2) It shall not be necessary for an official arbitrator to make any declaration before entering into the consideration of any matter referred to him.

(3) The official arbitrator shall, on the application of either party, specify the amount awarded in respect of any particular matter the subject of the award.

(4) The official arbitrator shall be entitled to enter on and inspect any land which is the subject of proceedings before him.

---

[41] See S. 4 of Property Values (Arbitrations and Appeals) Act, 1960 (p. 399). Note that all references to an 'official arbitrator' shall be construed as references to a 'property arbitrator'.

[42] See the provisions of the Acquisition of Land (Reference Committee) Act, 1925 (S. 1). Sub.-ss. (2), (3) and (4) were repealed by s. 7 of Property Values (Arbitrations and Appeal) Act, 1960. See p. 401.

[43] These six rules were extended by the addition of a further ten by S. 69 of the Act of 1963. The entire 16 rules appear on p. 405.

(5) Proceedings under this Act shall be heard by an official arbitrator sitting in public.

(6) The fees to be charged in respect of proceedings before official arbitrators shall be such as the *Minister for Finance* may prescribe.

(7) Subject as aforesaid, the Reference Committee may make rules[44] regulating the procedure before official arbitrators.

4. – Where notices to treat have been served for the acquisition of the several interests in the land to be acquired, the claims of the persons entitled to such interests shall, so far as practicable, and so far as not agreed and if the acquiring authority so desire, be heard and determined by the same official arbitrator, and the Reference Committee may make rules providing that such claims shall be heard together,[45] but the value of the several interests in the land having a market value shall be separately assessed.

5. – (1) Where the acquiring authority has made an unconditional offer in writing of any sum as compensation to any claimant and the sum awarded by an official arbitrator to that claimant does not exceed the sum offered, the official arbitrator shall, unless for special reasons he thinks proper not to do so, order the claimant to bear his own costs and to pay the costs of the acquiring authority so far as such costs were incurred after the offer was made.

(2) If the official arbitrator is satisfied that a claimant has failed to deliver to the acquiring authority a notice in writing of the amount claimed by him giving sufficient particulars and in sufficient time to enable the acquiring authority to make a proper offer,[46] the foregoing provisions of this section shall apply as if an unconditional offer had been made by the acquiring authority at the time when in the opinion of the official arbitrator sufficient particulars should have been furnished and the claimant had been awarded a sum not exceeding the amount of such offer.

The notice of claim shall state the exact nature of the interest in respect of which compensation is claimed, and give details of the compensation claimed, distinguishing the amounts under separate heads[47] and showing how the amount claimed under each head is calculated, and when such a notice of claim has been delivered the acquiring authority may, at any time within six weeks after the delivery thereof, withdraw any notice to treat which has been served on the claimant or on any other person interested in the land authorised to be acquired, but shall be liable to pay compensation to any such claimant or other person for any loss or expenses occasioned by the notice to treat having been given to him and withdrawn, and the amount of such compensation shall, in default of agreement, be determined by an official arbitrator.

---

[44] These are the Acquisition of Land (Assessment of Compensation) Rules, 1920 (SRO No. 600 of 1921), as amended by Property Values (Arbitrations and Appeals) Rules, 1961 (S.I. No. 91 of 1961). See p. 405.

[45] See Rule 7 of SRO No. 600 of 1921. See p. 406.

[46] In practice the arbitrators require a claimant to furnish in advance to the Planning Authority details of valuation including valuations of any comparable premises intended to be put in evidence. Compare Regulation 51 of the General Compensation Regulations (p. 405).

[47] The award is a single sum, however. See *Horn* v. *Sunderland Corp.* [1941] 1 All E.R. 480.

(3) Where a claimant has made an unconditional offer in writing to accept any sum as compensation and has complied with the provisions of the last preceding sub-section, and the sum awarded is equal to or exceeds that sum, the official arbitrator shall, unless for special reasons he thinks proper not to do so, order the acquiring authority to bear their own costs and to pay the costs of the claimant so far as such costs were incurred after[48] the offer was made.

(4) Subject as aforesaid, the costs of an arbitration under this Act shall be in the discretion of the official arbitrator who may direct to and by whom and in what manner those costs or any part thereof shall be paid, and the official arbitrator may in any case disallow the cost of counsel.

(5) An official arbitrator may himself tax the amount of costs ordered to be paid, or may direct in what manner they are to be taxed.

(6) Where an official arbitrator orders the claimant to pay the costs, or any part of the costs, of the acquiring authority, the acquiring authority may deduct the amount so payable by the claimant from the amount of the compensation payable to him.

(7) Without prejudice to any other method of recovery, the amount of costs ordered to be paid by a claimant, or such part thereof as is not covered by such deduction as aforesaid shall be recoverable from him by the acquiring authority summarily as a civil debt.

(8) For the purposes of this section, costs include any fees, charges, and expenses of the arbitration or award.

6. – (1) The decision of an official arbitrator upon any question of fact, shall be final and binding on the parties, and the persons claiming under them respectively, but the official arbitrator may, and shall, if the High Court so directs, state at any stage of the proceedings, in the form of a special case for the opinion of the High Court, any question of law arising in the course of the proceedings, and may state his award as to the whole or part thereof in the form of a special case for the opinion of the High Court.

(2) The decision of the High Court upon any case so stated shall be final and conclusive, and shall not be subject to appeal to any other court.[49]

7. – (1) The provisions of the Act or order by which the land is authorised to be acquired, or of any Act incorporated therewith, shall, in relation to the matters dealt with in this Act, have effect subject to this Act, and so far as inconsistent with this Act those provisions shall cease to have or shall not have effect:

Provided that nothing in this Act relating to the rules for assessing compensation shall affect any special provisions as to the assessment of the value of land acquired for the purposes of Part I or Part II of the Housing of the Working Classes Act, 1890, or under the Defence of the Realm (Acquisition of Land) Act, 1916, and contained in those Acts respectively, or any Act amending those Acts, if and so far as the provisions in those Acts are inconsistent with the rules under this Act and the

---

[48] The costs incurred before the offer was made should form part of the claim for compensation itself as a head of claim included under Rule 6 ('. . . any other matter not directly based on the value of the land').

[49] In the *Deansrath* case (p. 409) the arbitrator stated a case to the High Court which was in turn appealed. No point was taken in the Supreme Court under S. 6 (2). The same happened in *Murphy's* case (p. 457).

provisions of the Second Schedule to the Housing of the Working Classes Act, 1890, as amended by any subsequent enactment (except paragraphs (4), (5), (29), and (31) thereof) shall apply to an official arbitrator as they apply to an arbitrator appointed under that schedule, and an official arbitrator may exercise all the powers conferred by those provisions on such arbitrator.

ACQUISITION OF LAND (REFERENCE COMMITTEE) ACT, 1925.

AN ACT TO MAKE PROVISION FOR THE RE-CONSTITUTION OF THE REFERENCE COMMITTEE ESTABLISHED BY THE ACQUI-SITION OF LAND (ASSESSMENT OF COMPENSATION) ACT, 1919. [*27th June, 1925*]

BE IT ENACTED BY THE OIREACHTAS OF SAORSTAT EIREANN AS FOLLOWS:–

1. – (1) The Reference Committee constituted by paragraph (*c*) of sub-section (5) of section 1 of the Acquisition of Land (Asessment of Compensation) Act, 1919, shall consist of the Chief Justice of the Irish Free State, the President of the High Court, and the Chairman of the Surveyors' Institution (Irish Branch) in lieu of the persons mentioned in that paragraph.

(2) Every mention of or reference to the Reference Committee contained in the Acquisition of Land (Assessment of Compensation) Act, 1919 (other than sub-section (5) of section 1 thereof) shall be construed and have effect as a mention of or reference to the Reference Committee constituted by this section.

2. – This Act may be cited as the Acquisition of Land (Reference Committee) Act, 1925.

PROPERTY VALUES (ARBITRATIONS AND APPEALS) ACT, 1960

AN ACT TO PROVIDE FOR THE APPOINTMENT OF PROPERTY ARBITRATORS TO EXERCISE THE POWERS AND PERFORM THE FUNCTIONS BOTH OF REFEREES IN RELATION TO APPEALS UNDER PART I OF THE FINANCE (1909–10) ACT, 1910, AND OF ARBITRATORS IN RELATION TO ARBITRATIONS UNDER THE ACQUISITION OF LAND (ASSESSMENT OF COMPENSATION) ACT, 1919, AND THE ARTERIAL DRAINAGE ACT, 1945, FOR THOSE AND OTHER PURPOSES TO AMEND THOSE ACTS AND TO PROVIDE FOR OTHER MATTERS CON-NECTED WITH THE MATTERS AFORESAID. [*21st December, 1960*]

BE IT ENACTED BY THE OIREACHTAS AS FOLLOWS:–

1. – In this Act –
'the Act of 1910' means the Finance (1909–10) Act, 1910;

'the Act of 1919' means the Acquisition of Land (Assessment of Compensation) Act, 1919;

'the Act of 1945' means the Arterial Drainage Act, 1945;

'the Reference Committee' means the Reference Committee established by section 1 of the Act of 1919 as amended by the Acquisition of Land (Reference Committee) Act, 1925.

2. – (1) The Reference Committee may appoint one or more persons having special knowledge of the valuation of land or having such other qualifications as the Reference Committee considers suitable to be an arbitrator or arbitrators for the purposes of Part I of the Act of 1910 and the Act of 1945 and a person so appointed shall be known, and is referred to in this Act, as a property arbitrator.

(2) A property arbitrator shall hold office on such terms and conditions, other than those provided for under subsection (3) of this section, as the Reference Committee may from time to time determine with the approval of the Minister for Finance.

(3) A property arbitrator shall be paid, out of moneys provided by the Oireachtas, such remuneraton and allowances for expenses as the Minister for Finance may from time to time determine.

(4) Where, immediately before the date of the passing of this Act, a person holds office as a member of the panel of official arbitrators under the Act of 1919 and is in receipt of an annual salary in respect of such office, that person shall be deemed to have been appointed under this section on such date to be a property arbitrator for the purposes of Part I of the Act of 1910, the Act of 1919 and the Act of 1945 and to hold office on terms and conditions (including terms and conditions relating to remuneration and allowances for expenses) not less favourable than those on which he held office as a member of the panel aforesaid.

3. – (1) An appeal under section 33 of the Act of 1910 shall be referred to a property arbitrator who shall be nominated by the Reference Committee for the purposes of such reference in accordance with rules made by the Reference Committee under this section and, accordingly –

(a) so much of subsection (2) of the said section 33 as provides for the reference of an appeal thereunder to such one of a panel of referees appointed under Part I of the Act of 1910 as may be selected in manner provided by rules under the said section 33 shall cease to have effect, and

(b) references in the said section 33 to a referee selected under that section shall be construed as references to a property arbitrator nominated under this section and the reference in the said section 33 to the Reference Committee, established under that section shall be construed as a reference to the Reference Committee.

(2) Where, in an appeal under the said section 33, the value of any minerals is relevant to the determination of the property arbitrator, the appellant and the Revenue commissioners may each, in addition to the persons, if any, nominated under subsection (3) of the said section 33, nominate one person having experience in the valuation of minerals to consult the property arbitrator and, in determining the appeal, the property arbitrator shall consult any person nominated under this subsection.

4. – The arbitration referred to in subsection (1) of section 1 of the Act of 1919 shall, in relation to the reference and determination under that subsection of any question, be the arbitration of a property arbitrator nominated for the purposes of such reference and determination by the Reference Committee in accordance with rules made by the Reference Committee under this section and accordingly –

(*a*) so much of the said subsection (1) as provides for the reference of questions to and their determination by such one of a panel of official arbitrators to be appointed under the said section 1 as may be selected as therein provided shall cease to have effect, and

(*b*) references in the Act of 1919 to an official arbitrator shall be construed as references to a property arbitrator nominated under this section.

5. – The arbitrator for any purpose for which an arbitrator is required under the Act of 1945 shall be a property arbitrator who shall be nominated for that purpose by the Reference Committee and, accordingly, references in the Act of 1945 to an arbitrator nominated or appointed by the Reference Committee from the Panel of Drainage Arbitrators shall be construed as references to a property arbitrator nominated by the Reference Committee under this section.

6. – (1) This Act, other than this section, shall not have effect in respect of –

(*a*) any appeal under section 33 of the Act of 1910 in relation to which a referee has been selected under that section before the date of the passing of this Act,

(*b*) any question in relation to which an official arbitrator has been selected under the Act of 1919 before the date of the passing of this Act, or

(*c*) any dispute, claim, objection or matter in relation to which an arbitrator has been nominated or appointed under the Act of 1945 before the date of the passing of this Act.

(2) For the purposes of the validity of –

(*a*) any decision of a referee under section 33 of the Act of 1910 in relation to an appeal referred to him under that section before the date of the passing of this Act,

(*b*) the reference of the appeal to the referee, and

(*c*) the selection of the referee for the determination of the appeal,

the referee shall be deemed to have been selected in accordance with the provisions of that section from a panel of referees appointed under Part I of the Act of 1910 and consisting of at least two persons.

(3) For the purposes of the validity of –

(*a*) any decisions or award of an official arbitrator under the Act of 1919 in relation to a question referred to arbitration under that Act before the date of the passing of this Act,

(*b*) the reference of the question to the official arbitrator, and

(*c*) the selection of the official arbitrator for the determination of the questions,

the official arbitrator shall be deemed to have been selected in accordance with the provisions of that Act from a panel of official arbitrators appointed under that Act and consisting of at least two persons.

7. – Each enactment mentioned in the second column of the Schedule to this Act is hereby repealed to the extent mentioned in the third column of that Schedule opposite the mention of that enactment.

8. – This Act may be cited as the Property Values (Arbitrations and Appeals) Act, 1960.

SCHEDULE

ENACTMENTS REPEALED

Chapter and Session or Number and Year	Title	Extent of Repeal
10 Edw. 7, c. 8.	Finance (1909–10) Act, 1910.	In subsection (5) of section 33, the words 'and with respect to the mode in which the referee to whom any reference is to be made is to be selected,' and the words from 'The Reference Committee for England' to the end of the subsection; section 34.
9 & 10 Geo. 5, c. 57.	Acquisition of Land (Assessment of Compensation) Act, 1919.	Subsections (2), (3) and (4) of section 1.
No. 10 of 1924.	Courts of Justice Act, 1924.	Section 20.
No. 3 of 1945.	Arterial Drainage Act, 1945.	In subsection (2) of section 14, the words from 'with and subject to' to the end of the subsection; in subsection (4) of section 14, the words from 'but with and subject to' to the end of the subsection; Part VII.

RULES FOR ASSESSMENT OF COMPENSATION

ACQUISITION OF LAND (ASSESSMENT OF COMPENSATION) ACT. 1919
As amended by Local Government (Planning and Development) Act, 1963, S. 69 and Fourth Schedule

2. – In assessing compensation, an official arbitrator shall act in accordance with the following rules:

(1) No allowance shall be made on account of the acquisition being compulsory.[50]

---

[50] Before this rule came into force the practice had grown up of awarding an extra ten per cent (in most cases) on account of the acquisition being compulsory. See *Athlone Rifle Range* [1902] 1 I.R. 433.

(2) The value of land shall, subject as hereinafter provided, be taken to be the amount which the land if sold in the open market by a willing seller might be expected to realise,[51] provided always that the arbitrator shall be entitled to consider all returns and assessments of capital value for taxation made or acquiesced in by the claimant.

(3) The special suitability or adaptability of the land for any purpose shall not be taken into account if that purpose is a purpose to which it could be applied only in pursuance of statutory powers, or for which there is no market apart from the special needs of a particular purchaser or the requirements of any Government Department or any local or public authority; provided that any *bona fide* offer for the purchase of the land made before the passing of this Act which may be brought to the notice of the arbitrator shall be taken into consideration.

(4) Where the value of the land is increased by reason of the use thereof or of any premises thereon in a manner which could be restrained by any court, or is contrary to law, or is detrimental to the health of the inmates of the premises or to the public health, the amount of that increase shall not be taken into account.

(5) Where land is, and but for the compulsory acquisition would continue to be, devoted to a purpose of such a nature that there is no general demand or market for land for that purpose, the compensation may, if the official arbitrator is satisfied that reinstatement in some other place is *bona fide* intended, be assessed on the basis of the reasonable cost of equivalent reinstatement:

(6) The provisions of rule (2) shall not affect the assessment of compensation for disturbance or any other matter[52] not directly based on the value of land.

(7) In the case of a compulsory acquisition of buildings, the reference in Rule (5) to the reasonable cost of equivalent reinstatement shall be taken as a reference to that cost not exceeding the estimated cost of buildings such as would be capable of serving an equivalent purpose over the same period of time as the buildings compulsorily acquired would have done, having regard to any structural depreciation in those buildings.

(8) The value of the land shall be calculated with due regard to any restrictive covenant entered into by the acquirer when the land is compulsorily acquired.

(9) Regard shall be had to any restriction on the development of the land in respect of which compensation has been paid under the Local Government (Planning and Development) Act, 1963.

(10) Regard shall be had to any restriction on the development of the land which could, without conferring a right to compensation, be imposed under any Act or under any order, regulation, rule or bye-law made under any Act.

(11) Regard shall not be had to any depreciation or increase in value attributable to –

   (a) the land, or any land in the vicinity thereof, being reserved for any particular purpose in a development plan,[53] or

   (b) inclusion of the land in a special amenity area order.

---

[51] See the *Deansrath* case at p. 409 and cases referred to therein.

[52] It is not clear what is included under 'Other Matter'. Rule 16 acknowledges (by excluding it in S. 29 cases) the relevance of severance claims in planning compensation cases. Severence is a sub-category of 'injurious affection' as defined by S. 63 of the Lands Clauses Consolidation Act, 1845. Only Ss. 69 to 79 (not S. 63 of that Act are incorporated into the planning code, however, (by S. 71 (2)). Is injurious affection generally included under 'any other matter not directly based on the value of the land' in Rule 6? But see *McKone*, p. 428.

[53] See *Short* v. *Dublin County Council* (p. 423).

(12) No account shall be taken of any value attributable to any unauthorised structure or unauthorised use.

(13) No account shall be taken of –

  (a) the existence of proposals for development of the land or any other land by a local authority, or

  (b) the possibility or probability of the land or other land becoming subject to a scheme of development undertaken by a local authority.[54]

(14) Regard shall be had to any contribution which a planning authority would have required as a condition precedent to the development of the land.

(15) In Rules (9), (10), (11), (12), (13) and (14) 'development', 'development plan', 'special amenity area order', 'unauthorised structure', 'unauthorised use', 'local authority' and 'the appointed day' have the same meanings respectively as in the Local Government (Planning and Development) Act, 1963.

(16) In the case of land incapable of reasonably beneficial use which is purchased by a planning authority under section 29[55] of the Local Government (Planning and Development) Act, 1963, the compensation shall be the value of the land exclusive of any allowance for disturbance or severance.

For the purposes of this section, an official arbitrator shall be entitled to be furnished with such returns and assessments as he may require.

LOCAL GOVERNMENT (PLANNING AND DEVELOPMENT) REGULATIONS, 1977
(S.I. No. 65 of 1977)

PART VI

COMPENSATION

49. – (1) Every claim for compensation under Part VI of the Act of 1963 shall include –

  (a) a statement of the matter in respect of which compensation is claimed and of the amount of such compensation,

  (b) a statement of the name and address of the claimant and of the interest held by him in the land to which the claim relates, and

  (c) a statement of the names and addresses of all other persons (so far as they are known to the claimant) having an interest in the land to which the claim relates, or, where the claimant does not know of any such persons, a statement to that effect.

(2) Where a planning authority receive a claim for compensation under Part VI of the Act of 1963 which fails to comply with any requirement of sub-article (1), the authority may, and if the failure relates to the requirements of paragraph (c) of that article shall, require the claimant to comply with such requirement and the planning authority may defer consideration of the claim until he has complied with such requirement.

50. – (1) Within one month of the receipt by a planning authority of a claim for compensation under the Act of 1963, or within one month of compliance with a

---

[54] See the *Deansrath case* (p. 409).
[55] See *Kilbeggan Investments Limited* v. *Dublin County Council* (p. 444).

requirement under article 49 (2), the planning authority shall give notice to every person, other than the claimant, appearing to them to have an interest in the land to which the claim relates.

(2) Every such notice shall state the name and address of the claimant, the matter in respect of which the claim is made, the land to which the claim relates and the date after which a further claim for compensation in relation to such matter cannot . be made or can be made only where the time for making such a claim is extended by the Circuit Court.[56]

(3) Where more than one claim for compensation under the Act of 1963 in respect of the same matter has been received by a planning authority, the provisions of sub-article (1) shall not apply in respect of such persons as are claimants or have already been given notice of a claim in respect of that matter under that sub-article.

51. – Where a claim for compensation under the Act of 1963 is made the planning authority may require the claimant to provide evidence in support of his claim and information as to his interest in the land to which the claim relates and may defer consideration of the claim until he has complied with such requirement.

52. – Where an application is made to the Minister under section 58 or section 61 of the Act of 1963 for an order declaring that he is satisfied that it would not be just and reasonable in the particular circumstances that payment of compensation should be prevented by the provisions of section 56(1) or section 57 of the Act of 1963 –

(*a*) the applicant shall submit to the Minister a statement of his interest in the land to which the application relates and of the reasons why in the particular circumstances such an order should be made,

(*b*) the planning authority shall send to the Minister such documents and information relevant to the application and in their possession or procurement as the Minister may require, and

(*c*) the applicant shall send to the Minister such documents and information relevant to the application and in his possession or procurement as the Minister may require.

ACQUISITION OF LAND (ASSESSMENT OF COMPENSATION) RULES, 1920
(S.R.O. No. 600 of 1921), as amended by Property Values (Arbitration and Appeals) Rules, 1961 (S.I. No. 91 of 1961)

In pursuance of the Acquisition of Land (Assessment of Compensation) Act, 1919, the Reference Committee for Ireland constituted under that Act hereby make the following Rules:–

1. – These Rules may be cited as the Acquisition of Land (Assessment of Compensation) Rules, 1920.

2. – (1) In these Rules, unless the context otherwise requires, the expression 'the Act' means the Acquisition of Land (Assessment of Compensation) Act, 1919: the expression 'question' means any question of disputed compensation, or any question of the apportionment of a rent, which is to be referred to and determined by arbitration in manner provided by the Act.

[56] Pursuant to S. 55 (6)(*b*) of the Act of 1963.

(2) The Interpretation Act, 1889, applies for the purpose of the interpretation of these Rules as it applies for the purpose of the interpretation of an Act of Parliament.

5. – (1) The arbitrator nominated shall, as soon as may be, proceed with the determination of the question in dispute and shall arrange with the acquiring authority and the claimant the time and place of the hearing.

(2) The Reference Committee shall send to the arbitrator a copy of the application for the nomination of an arbitrator, and the acquiring authority and the claimant shall furnish to the arbitrator on his request any document or other evidence which it is in their or his power to furnish and which the arbitrator may require for the purpose of considering and determining the case.

(3) Subject to the provisions of the Act and of these Rules the proceedings before an arbitrator shall be such as the arbitrator, subject to any special directions of the Reference Committee, may in his discretion think fit.

7. – (1) Where notices to treat have been served for the acquisition of the several interests in the land to be acquired and questions as to the amount of compensation have arisen in the case of any two or more of those interests, the acquiring authority may, subject as hereinafter provided, after the arbitrator has been nominated to hear the case, apply to the arbitrator for an order that all the claims shall be heard together.

(2) Notice of intention to apply for such an order as aforesaid shall be sent to each claimant and to the arbitrator.

(3) If any claimant objects to have his claim heard together with the other claims, he shall within seven days after the receipt of the notice aforesaid send notice of his objection to the acquiring authority and to the arbitrator.

(4) Where the acquiring authority applies for an order under this Rule the arbitrator after taking into consideration any objections made to the application shall make such order in the matter as he thinks proper having regard to all the circumstances of the case.

(5) On an application for an order under this Rule an order for consolidation may be made if the arbitrator thinks fit with respect to some only of the claims, and the order may in any case be made subject to such special directions as to costs, witnesses, method of procedure and otherwise as the arbitrator thinks proper.

8. – (1) The fees prescribed by the Treasury in pursuance of the powers conferred on them by subsection (6) of section 3 of the Act in respect of an application under these Rules and in respect of the hearing before the official arbitrator shall be collected by means of adhesive stamps affixed to or stamps impressed on the application and the award of the arbitrator respectively.

(2) Any application under these Rules which is not properly stamped in accordance with the foregoing provision shall be treated as invalid and the award of the arbitrator shall not be published unless and until it has been properly stamped in accordance with the said provision.

10. – Save as herein otherwise expressly provided, any failure on the part of any authority or any person to comply with the provisions of these Rules shall not render the proceedings, or anything done in pursuance thereof, invalid, unless the arbitrator so directs.

PROPERTY VALUES (ARBITRATIONS AND APPEALS) RULES, 1961
S.I. No. 91 of 1961

We, the Reference Committee, in exercise of the powers conferred on us by section 33 of the Finance (1909–10) Act, 1910, the Acquisition of Land (Assessment of Compensation Act, 1919, and sections 3 and 4 of the Property Values (Arbitrations and Appeals) Act, 1960 (No. 45 of 1960), hereby make the following Rules, with the approval of the Minister for Finance in so far as they are made under the said section 33:

1. – These Rules may be cited as the Property Values (Arbitrations and Appeals) Rules, 1961.

2. – The Interpretation Act, 1937 (No. 38 of 1937), applies to these Rules.

3. – (1) In these Rules –
'the Act of 1910' means the Finance (1909–10) Act, 1910;
'the Act of 1919' means the Acquisition of Land (Assessment of Compensation) Act, 1919;
'question' means a question referred to in section 1 of the Act of 1919;
'the Reference Committee' means the Reference Committee established by section 1 of the Act of 1919, as amended by the Acquisition of Land (Reference Committee) Act, 1925 (No. 22 of 1925);
'the Rules of 1911' means the Land Values (Referee) (Ireland) Rules, 1911;
'the Rules of 1920' means the Acquisition of Land (Assessment of Compensation) Rules, 1920.
(2) These Rules shall, in so far as they amend the Rules of 1911, be construed as one with the Rules of 1911 and shall, in so far as they amend the Rules of 1920, be construed as one with the Rules of 1920.

4. – (1) An appeal under section 33 of the Act of 1910 to a property arbitrator may be made by sending to the Reference Committee and to the Revenue Commissioners within the period provided for by the Rules of 1911 a notice of appeal in the appropriate form set out in the Schedule to the Rules of 1911 or in a form to the like effect specifying the matter to which the appeal relates and giving particulars of the grounds of the appeal.
(2) The Revenue Commissioners shall cause printed copies of the forms of notices of appeal set out in the Schedule to the Rules of 1911 to be furnished free of charge on application by any person to the Revenue Commissioners or to any person authorised by the Revenue Commissioners to furnish the forms.

5. – Whenever the Reference Committee receives, pursuant to Rule 4 of these Rules, a notice of appeal in writing, it shall, as soon as may be, nominate a property arbitrator for the purpose of the reference and determination of the appeal to which the notice relates, and shall, as soon as it has nominated the property arbitrator, inform the Revenue Commissioners and the appellant of his name and address.

6. – In the Rules of 1911 –

(*a*) references to the Reference Committee for Ireland constituted under section 33 of the Act of 1910 shall be construed as references to the Reference Committee.

(*b*) references to a referee and the reference in Rule 8 to the referee selected shall be construed as references to a property arbitrator nominated under these Rules, and

(*c*) Rules 3, 7, 11 and 14 shall be revoked.

7. – (1) Where a question has arisen, any party to or affected by the acquisition in relation to which the question has arisen –

(*a*) may, at any time after the expiration of fourteen days from the date on which notice to treat was served in relation to the acquisition, send to the Reference Committee an application in writing for the nomination of a property arbitrator for the purposes of the reference and determination of the question, and

(*b*) shall, if he sends the application specified in paragraph (*a*) of this Rule, as soon as may be after such sending, send a copy thereof to every other party to, or affected by, the acquisition aforesaid.

(2) An application under this Rule shall be in writing and shall specify the parties to, or affected by the acquisition, the land to be acquired, the nature of the question to which the application relates, the statutory provisions under which the question arises and, if compensation is claimed, the interest in respect of which it is claimed.

8. – Whenever the Reference Committee receives, pursuant to Rule 7 of these Rules, a valid application in writing for the appointment of a property arbitrator, it shall, as soon as may be, nominate a property arbitrator for the purpose of the reference and determination of the question to which the notices relates, and shall, as soon as it has nominated the property arbitrator, inform the parties to, or affected by, the acquisition in relation to which the question has arisen of his name and address.

9. – In the Rules of 1920 –

(*a*) the definition of 'arbitrator' in Rule 2 shall be deleted,

(*b*) 'nomination' shall be substituted for 'appointment' in each place where it occurs, and 'nominated' shall be substituted for 'appointed' in each place where it occurs.

(*c*) references to an official arbitrator shall be construed as references to a property arbitrator nominated under these Rules, and

(*d*) Rules 3, 4, 6 and 9 and the Schedule shall be revoked.

10. – The Reference Committee may, in the case of the death or incapacity of a property arbitrator nominated for the purposes of the reference and determination of an appeal under section 33 of the Act of 1910 or a question, or if it is shown to the Reference Committee that it is expedient so to do, in any other case, at any time before the determination of the appeal or question, as the case may be, revoke the nomination of the property arbitrator and nominate another property arbitrator for the purposes of the reference and determination of the appeal or question, as the case may be, and the Reference Committee shall, as soon as it has nominated

the other property arbitrator, inform –
  (a) in the case of an appeal, the Revenue Commissioners and the appellant, and
  (b) in the case of a question, every party to, or affected by, the acquisition to which the question relates,
of the name and address of the other property arbitrator.

11. – Any notice or other document required or authorised by the Rules of 1911, the Rules of 1920 or these Rules to be sent to the Reference Committee or any other person shall be deemed to be duly sent if sent by post –
  (a) in the case of the Reference Committee, to the Secretary of the Reference Committee, Four Courts, Dublin, and
  (b) in the case of any other person, to his usual address.

12. – These Rules shall not have effect in respect of –
  (a) any appeal under section 33 of the Act of 1910 in relation to which a referee has been selected under the Rules of 1911 before the 21st day of December, 1960, or
  (b) any question in relation to which an official arbitrator has been selected under the Rules of 1920 before the 21st day of December, 1960.

CASES

RE DEANSRATH INVESTMENTS LIMITED
[1974] I.R. 228

This is the leading Irish case on compensation. It arose in the context of compulsory acquisition but is of general importance because of the careful review and application of English Cases in both the High and Supreme Court judgments. The judgment of Pringle J. in the High Court comprises a most helpful and comprehensive review of the relevant English case law. It is reproduced here in full as it is not included in the official Irish report.

Portion of the lands at Deansrath, Clondalkin, Co. Dublin were acquired by Dublin County Council as the housing authority. The lands had been used at all material times as agricultural lands. A pre-compulsory purchase order contract price appeared to reflect a price above the agricultural value and there had been negotiations regarding possible planning permission, but none such existed. This showed, however, a potential future use for the lands for housing purposes which were the purposes for which they were being compulsorily acquired. The evidence further showed that the planning authority was not prepared to grant planning permission for housing development for a period of 5 to 7 years because of the non-availability of services[57] and because of difficulties regarding disposal of surface water.

The matter went to arbitration and the acquiring authority contended that the effect of the rules and especially of Rule 13 was that the arbitrator was precluded from taking into account any development potential[58] of these lands including

---

[57] A reason which would preclude compensation by S. 56 (1)(b)(i).
[58] The 'hope' value.

development by a non-local authority and that the correct measure of value was at agricultural prices as this was the only use to which the lands had been put up to the date of the service of the notice to treat. The land owner contended that Rule 2 which establishes the open market as the assessment criterion was the governing rule and that Rule 13 was merely a restriction on the operation of Rule 2.

The arbitrator agreed with the developer's contention and assessed compensation to include the development potential[61] of the lands for housing purposes at £450,000 instead of agricultural values which would have been £150,000. He stated a case, however, to the High Court for confirmation that this approach was the correct one. In the High Court Pringle J. agreed with him and the local authority appealed[59] to the Supreme Court. This Court agreed with the arbitrator's approach also and dismissed the appeal.

Budd J.[60] made several observations as follows:
(1) there were no Irish cases dealing with the application of the 1919 Act rules or before that of Section 63 of the Lands Clauses Act, 1845,
(2) there were pre-1919 English decision which had set out such principles,
(3) these cases set out fairly clearly the broad principles which included that the value was to be the value to the owner before the date of the taking and not the value to the taker; the value was to be the market value or full price of the land; every element of value and all advantages present and future are to be taken into account in assessing the value to the owner and it is the present value of such advantages and elements which is to be considered in arriving at the full market value of the land;
(4) these principles were applied in England after 1919;
(5) in the absence of Irish authority these principles should be applied in this country;
(6) there were certain refinements of these principles which had already been established in England and in particular –
    (a) no value which was entirely due to the scheme underlying the acquisition was to be taken into account,
    (b) no value which was due to local authority development of other land was to be taken into account;
(7) Rule 13 read in context intended to reflect the above position but extended it somewhat by further excluding from consideration the possibility or probability to the land or other land becoming the subject of a local authority scheme of development;
(8) Rule 13 relied upon by the local authority makes no reference to proposals for development by any person other than a local authority and as existing rights pertaining to property are not to be taken away or cut down save by clear wording, in the absence of such clear wording Rule 13 must be taken as limiting the scope of Rule 2 only to the extent clearly set out therein. 'I may add that the right to compensation at market value existed before the passing of the Act of 1963 and that existing rights pertaining to property are not to be taken away or cut down save by the clear wording of a statute or statutory rule.'[61]
(9) Accordingly the wording used in this rule does not restrict the value to the value

---

[59] No point was taken under S. 6 (2) of the Act of 1919.
[60] Fitzgerald C.J. and McLoughlin J. concurring.
[61] See similar observations of Finlay P. in *Viscount Securities Limited* v. *Dublin County Council* (p. 455), and Kenny J. in *Movie News Limited* v. *Galway County Council* (p. 44).

of the land as used on the date of the service of the notice to treat as claimed by the local authority and the arbitrator was correct in taking into account the 'hope' value of the land.

High Court
Pringle J.:[62]

This is a Case stated by Mr. Owen MacCarthy, the Arbitrator nominated by the Land Reference Committee by their Order dated the 6th day of October 1970 on the hearing of an arbitration between the County Council of the County of Dublin (hereinafter referred to as the acquiring authority) and Deansrath Investments Limited (hereinafter referred to as the claimants) to determine the compensation to be paid by the acquiring authority to the claimants for their interest in the lands acquired from them by the acquiring authority pursuant to the Dublin County Council Compulsory Purchase (Housing Act 1966) No. 1 Order 1968 which was made on 30th August 1968.

The property arbitrator made his award on 25th March 1971 and in this award it is recited that counsel for the acquiring authority submitted that the effect of rules 10 and 13 in the fourth schedule to the Local Government (Planning and Development) Act 1963 (hereinafter referred to as The Act of 1963) restricted the arbitrator, in determining the value of the lands, to the value of the said lands as agricultural land on the 16th day of April 1970 (the date of the notice to treat). It was also recited that the arbitrator held that what he was required to determine was the amount which the said lands if sold by a willing seller on the 16th day of April 1970 might have been expected to realise: provided that the purchaser was aware of any restrictions on the development of the said lands which could, without conferring a right to compensation, be imposed under any Act, or under any Order, regulation, rule or bye-law made under any Act, and provided that the purchaser took no account of the existence of proposals for the development of the land or any other land by a local authority, or the possibility or probability of the land or any other land becoming subject to a scheme of development undertaken by a local authority, and that a purchaser should have been aware of any contribution which a planning authority would have required, or would require, as a condition precedent to the development of such land.

The arbitrator then made his award in the following form. 'I do find, award, and determine that, if I have held correctly, then the sum to be paid by the acquiring authority to the claimants as the price of their interest in the lands acquired by them is four hundred and fifty thousand pounds sterling, but if I have not held correctly and the acquiring authority's submission is correct, then the sum to be paid by the acquiring authority to the claimants for their interest in the lands acquired from them is one hundred and fifty thousand pounds sterling.'

From the agreed addendum to the statement of facts it appears that there was before the arbitrator a conflict of evidence between the valuer called on behalf of the claimants and the valuer called on behalf of the acquiring authority as to the amount which the lands if sold by a willing seller on 16th April 1970 would have been expected to realise on the basis adopted by the arbitrator. The evidence on behalf of the claimants was that the lands on that basis, would be expected to realize £3000 per acre (which would have given a total figure of £698,325), whereas

---

[62] Delivered 16th July, 1971. The case is reported at [1974] I.R. 228. The judgment of Pringle J. does not appear in that report and is set out in full here for that reason.

the evidence on behalf of the acquiring authority as to the value of the lands on the same basis was £1750 per acre, so that it is clear that the arbitrator fixed a figure somewhere between these two valuations. In addition, it appears that the evidence on behalf of the acquiring authority was that the lands should be valued solely as agricultural land and that their value on that basis was at the rate of £750 per acre which appears to be approximately the figure fixed by the arbitrator as the value of the lands, if it is to be fixed on that basis.

The question of law for the decision of this Court is whether the arbitrator was correct in his opinion as to the basis upon which his award should be made and in fixing by his award the sum of £475,000 as the sum to be paid by the acquiring authority to the claimants for their interest in the lands.

The question for decision is therefore a very nett one, that is to say whether the arbitrator was bound, having regard to Rules 10 and 13 in the Fourth Schedule to the Act of 1963 to fix the figure to which the claimants are entitled solely on the basis of the value of the lands as agricultural lands, which was the only use to which they had been put up to the date of the notice to treat. This is the contention put forward before me by counsel for the acquiring authority and I do not think it was suggested that, if this contention was not correct, the basis upon which the arbitrator fixed the price was in any way open to question.

The basic section dealing with the assessment of compensation for lands compulsorily acquired is section 2 of the Acquisition of Land (Assessment of Compensation) act, 1919 (hereinafter referred to as the act of 1919). This section provides that in assessing compensation, an official arbitrator shall act in accordance with the following rules: '(1) No allowance shall be made on account of the acquisition being compulsory: (2) The value of land shall, subject as hereinafter provided, be taken to be the amount which the land if sold in the open market by a willing seller might be expected to realise: provided always that the arbitrator shall be entitled to consider all returns and assessments of capital value for taxation made or acquiesced in by the claimant.' Then there follow four further rules dealing with certain matters which are not to be, and others which may be, taken into account in arriving at the value of the land under Rule 2.

Section 69 of the Act of 1963 provided in subsection (1) that 'section 2 of the act of 1919 is hereby amended, in cases where any compensation assessed will be payable by a planning authority or any other local authority, by the insertion after Rule 6 of the rules set out in the Fourth Schedule to this Act.' The fourth schedule contains new rules (numbered 7 to 16). These new rules, for the most part, set out certain matters which are either to be regarded or not regarded, or to be taken into account and it is clear that they are intended to relate back to the words 'subject as hereinafter provided' in Rule 2, so that, in arriving at the amount which the land if sold in the open market by a willing seller might be expected to realize, the arbitrator is restricted by these rules as to certain matters to which he may either have regard or of which he must take no account. Rule 10 provides that 'Regard shall be had to any restriction on the development of the land which could, without conferring a right to compensation, be imposed under any act or under any order, regulation, rule or bye-law made under any Act.' In other words the arbitrator must assume that the hypothetical purchaser in the open market is conscious of the fact that restrictions could be imposed on the development of the land without the payment of compensation, the result of which would be to reduce the value of the land for potential development. In my opinion the arbitrator has correctly given effect to this rule in his award. Rule 13 provides as follows 'No account shall be taken of – (a) the existence of proposals for development of the land or any other land by a local authority, or (b) the possibility of probability of the land or other land becoming subject to a scheme of development undertaken by a local authority.' This is the rule upon which Mr. Ronan Keane has mainly relied for his contention that the arbitrator must confine the value of the land to its value as agricultural land. He argues that the effect of this rule is that all other potential uses of the lands (as for instance for development for building by a private developer) must be disregarded. The claimants on the other hand contend that the effect of the rule is that the arbitrator must eliminate any increase in the value of the land by reason of its potentiality for development *by a local authority*, or by reason of the potentiality of any other land being developed *by a local authority*, but that he is not bound to eliminate any potentiality which the land may have for being put to other uses which might be more profitable than using it for agricultural purposes, as for instance by its development for building by a private developer.

Certain principles to be applied by an arbitrator in giving effect to section 2 of the Act of 1919 and, before that Act and, before that Act, to Section 63 of the Lands Clauses Act 1845, were laid down in a long series of decisions in England, to the more important of which I have been referred. One of those principles was that the value must be the value to the owner from whom the lands are being taken and not to the purchaser by whom they are being taken. Lord Justice Fletcher Moulton in *Lucas and Chesterfield Gas and Water Board* [1909] 1 K.B. at page 29 said 'The owner receives for the lands he gives up their equivalent, i.e., that which they were worth to him in money. His property is therefore not diminished in amount, but to that extent it is compulsorily changed in form. But the equivalent is estimated on the value to him, and not on the value to the purchaser, and hence it has from the first been recognized as an absolute rule that this value is to be estimated as it stood before the grant of the compulsory powers. The owner is only to receive compensation based upon the market value of his lands as they stood before the scheme was authorised by which they are put to public uses. Subject to that he is entitled to be paid the full price for his lands, and any and every element of value which they possess must be taken into consideration insofar as they increase the value to him.' This case was referred to with approval by Lord Dunedin giving the judgement of the privy council in the case of *Cedars Rapids Manufacturing and Power Company* v. *Lacoste and Others* [1914] AC. 569 in which he said[63] 'For the present purposes it may be sufficient to state two brief propositions: 1. The value to be paid for is the value to the owner as it existed at the date of the taking, not the value to the taker. 2. The value to the owner consists in all advantages which the land possesses, present or future, but it is the present value alone of such advantages that falls to be determined'. In some of the later cases the value of the potential future advantages is described as 'the hope value'.

These two cases were decided before the passing of the 1919 Act, but the same principles were applied in a number of cases in which Section 2 of that Act was the governing section. For instance, Lord Justice Parker in giving the judgment of the Court of Appeal in *Lambe* v. *Secretary of State for War* [1955] 2 QB 612 said[64] 'It is well settled, as was said by Lord MacDermott in the *Pointe Gourde Case*[65] that 'Compensation for the compulsory purchase of land cannot include an increase in

[63] At p. 576.
[64] At p. 622.
[65] *Pointe Gourde Quarrying & Transport Co.* v. *Sub-Intendent of Crown Lands* [1947] A.C. 565.

value which is entirely due to the scheme underlying the acquisition'. In the later case in the House of Lords of *Davy* v. *Leeds Corporation* [1965] 1 All ER 753, Viscount Dilhorne said[66] that it seemed to him that section 9(2) of the Town and Country Planning Act 1959 in England gave statutory effect to this principle stated by Lord MacDermott. That section, while not worded in the same way as Rule 13, provided that 'no account shall be taken of any increase or diminution of the value of the relevant interest which is attributable-(a) to the carrying out of any such development as is mentioned in relation thereto in the second column of the table which followed[67], or (b) to the prospect that any such development will or may be carried out, insofar as any such development (whether actual or prospective) is or would be development arising from the circumstances of that case'. By the Land Compensation Act 1961 in England, the Act of 1919 was repealed, but section 5(2) of that Act re-enacted section 2(2) of the 1919 Act with the exception of the proviso, and section 6(1) of that Act contained somewhat similar provisions to those contained in the 1959 Act to which I have referred, but it went further and provided, in effect, that, in addition no account was to be taken of any development on other land than that being acquired.

Lord Denning M.R. in the case of *Camrose (Viscount) and Another v. Basingstoke Corporation* [1966] 1 W.L.R. at page 1107 explained the effect of this section as follows 'The legislature was aware of the general principle that, in assessing compensation for compulsory acquisition of a defined parcel of land, you do not take into account an increase in value of that parcel of land if the increase is entirely due to the scheme involving the acquisition. That was settled by *Pointe Gourde Quarrying and Tranport Co.* v. *Sub-Intendent of Crown Lands* where the Privy Council disallowed the $15,000 increase in value of the quarry (which was compulsorily acquired) which was due to the scheme for a naval base. That decision has since been approved by the House of Lords in *Davy* v. *Leeds Corporation*. It is left untouched by Section 6(1). But there might be some doubt as to its scope. So the legislature passed Section 6(1) and the First Schedule in order to make it clear that you were not to take into account any increase due to the development of the other land, namely land other than the claimed parcel. I think that the decision in the Pointe Gourde case covers one aspect and Section 6(1) covers the other; with the result that the tribunal is to ignore any increase in value due to the Town Development Act both on the relevant land and on the other land.'

Finally, I have been referred by counsel since the arguments concluded, to the most recent case in England of *Wilson and others* v. *Liverpool Corporation* [1971] 1 W.L.R. 302, in which the *Pointe-Gourde* case and the *Camrose* case were applied in the Court of Appeal.

I have referred at some length to these English cases as it seems to me that, in the absence of any Irish authority, the same principles should apply here. Furthermore, I am of opinion that Rule 13 was intended to give statutory effect to those principles, just as was done (although the wording is not identical) in the English Acts of 1955 and 1961 to which I have referred. But I think sub-paragraph (b) of that Rule went further when it provided that not only the existence of proposals for development of the land or any other land by the local authority, but also the possibility of probability of the land or other land becoming subject to a scheme of

---

[66] At p. 758.
[67] Annexed to S. 9 (2).

development undertaken by a local authority was not to be taken into account.

What is to be left out of account is, under (a) the existence of proposals for development *by a local authority* and, under (b), the possibility or probability of the lands or other lands becoming subject to a scheme of development undertaken by *a local authority*. Nothing is said about proposals for development, or the possibility or probability of a scheme of development being undertaken by any person or Body other than a local authority. Mr. Keane suggested that no such development could take place without the necessary services being supplied by a local authority, which would necessarily involve development either of the lands or of other lands by a local authority. I am not satisfied that this is so. In many parts of the country houses are built without the benefit of main drainage or water supply and it is not essential for the development of land that a local authority should be involved in supplying such services. Furthermore, I think that Rule 10 itself, referring to restrictions on development and Rule 14 which provides that regard shall be had to any contribution which a planning authority would have required as a condition precedent to the development of the land, show that *some* form of potential development of the land could be taken into account. If the legislature had intended that the value of the land was to be confined to its value as used on the date of notice to treat, it could quite easily have said so, but it has not done so. I think the purpose of Rule 13 was to ensure that a claimant would not attain an enhanced price for the lands being acquired by reason of the fact that a local authority might be proposing to expend the ratepayers', or public, money in developing the land or other land in the neighbourhood, or that there was a possibility or probability that a local authority might include the land or such other land in a scheme of development, again at the expense of the ratepayers or the public. It would appear that Mr. Keane is correct in saying that the Planning Acts do not use the words 'scheme of development', but of course the word 'development' occurs frequently and is defined in the 1963 Act, and I do not think that 'scheme of development' means any more than a plan by a local authority to exercise the wide powers of development which it has under the Acts (see for instance Section 77 of the Act of 1963).

In my opinion the Rules relied upon do not have the effect contended for by the acquiring authority and the arbitrator has applied the correct principles in arriving at the price to which the claimants are entitled and in awarding to them the sum of four hundred and fifty thousand pounds for their interest in the lands acquired. The question referred to the Court by the arbitrator will be answered accordingly.

Supreme Court
Budd J.:[68]

The learned judge took the view that the principles to be applied by an arbitrator in valuing land compulsorily acquired so as to give effect to s. 63 of the Act of 1845, and now to s. 2 of the Act of 1919, were laid down in a long series of cases in England and he referred to two of these in particular. Lord Justice Fletcher Moulton in *Lucas and Chesterfield Gas and Water Board*[69] said at p. 29 of the report: 'The owner receives for the lands he gives up their equivalent, i.e., that which they were worth to him in money. His property is therefore not diminished in amount, but to that extent it is compulsorily changed in form. But the equivalent is

---

[68] Fitzgerald C.J. and McLoughlin J. concurring.
[69] [1909] 1 K.B. 16.

estimated on the value to him, and not on the value to the purchaser, and hence it has from the first been recognized as an absolute rule that this value is to be estimated as it stood before the grant of the compulsory powers. The owner is only to receive compensation based upon the market value of his lands as they stood before the scheme was authorized by which they are put to public uses. Subject to that he is entitled to be paid the full price for his lands, and any and every element of value which they possess must be taken into consideration in so far as they increase the value to him.' This case was referred to with approval by Lord Dunedin giving the advice of the Privy Council in *Cedars Rapids Manufacturing and Power Company* v. *Lacoste*[70] in which, at p. 576 of the report, he said: 'For the present purpose it may be sufficient to state two brief propositions: (1) The value to be paid for is the value to the owner as it existed at the date of the taking, not the value to the taker. (2) The value to the owner consists in all advantages which the land possesses, present or future, but it is the present value alone of such advantages that falls to be determined.' In some of the later cases the value of the potential future advantages is described as 'the hope value.' However, there is nothing novel or unusual in the conception of lands or buildings having a potential value if put to a new use and indeed the potential development value of land is something which is well recognised nowadays.

What emerges from the portions of the two judgments above cited is reasonably clear. The value to be taken is the value to the owner before the date of the taking and not the value to the taker. The value to the owner is to be the market value or full price of the lands. Further, every element of value which the land has and all the advantages which that land possesses, present and future, are to be taken into consideration in assessing the value to the owner; but it is the present value of such advantages and elements of value to the owner that the land possesses as it stood before the acquisition that is to be taken into consideration and has to be determined in arriving at the full market value of the land. These two cases were decided before the passing of the Act of 1919 but the same principles were applied in a number of cases in which s. 2 of that Act was the governing section, that is to say, that the value of the land under rule 2 of s. 2 of the Act of 1919 should be taken to be (subject as thereinafter provided) the amount which the land, if sold in the open market, might be expected to realize with all the advantages the land possesses, but that it was the present value of such advantages that was to be taken into consideration in ascertaining the market value. It would seem to me that the broad principles upon which the valuation of lands compulsorily acquired is to be assessed were laid down correctly in these cases, and I would agree with the learned trial judge that in the absence of Irish authority they should be applied in this country. . . .

It is clear and, indeed, agreed that the basic rule for assessing the value of land taken compulsorily is rule 2 of s. 2 of the Act of 1919 which provides that, subject as therein, the value of land thus taken shall be the amount which the land, if sold in the open market by a willing seller might be expected to realize. One of the matters covered by the words 'as hereinafter provided' is rule 13 which contains an important restriction on the assessment of the valuation of such land and I shall now consider its true construction. It would appear to me that rule 13, in providing that 'no account shall be taken of – (*a*) the existence of proposals for development of

---

[70] [1914] A.C. 569.

the land or any other land by a local authority', is a modified adoption of the principle enunciated in the *Pointe Gourde Case*[71] as extended by s. 6, sub-s. 1, of the (English) Land Compensation Act, 1961, in the manner explained by Lord Denning in *Viscount Camrose* v. *Basingstoke Corporation*.[72] The principle is that, in assessing compensation for the compulsory acquisition of a defined portion of land, you do not take into account an increase in the value of that land or other land if the increase is due entirely to the scheme involving the acquisition of that land or the other land. Our legislation goes further than the *Pointe Gourde* decision or the provisions of the said s. 6, sub-s. 1, in that it provides in rule 13(*b*) that not only must you take no account of the existence of proposals for the development of the land or any other land by a local authority but that you must take no account of the possibility or probability of the land or other land becoming subject to a scheme of development undertaken by a local authority.

Rule 13, on its true construction in the context of the rules set out in s. 2 of the Act of 1919 (as amended), is but a restriction of the basic rule 2 which states that, in assessing compensation to be paid in respect of land to be acquired compulsorily, the value shall be taken to be the open market value of the land. In my view, that restriction is to be applied only to the extent stated in the rule which is that, in assessing compensation under s. 2 you are not to take into account the matters mentioned in paragraphs (*a*) and (*b*) of rule 13, which matters are the existence of proposals for development by a local authority and the possibility or probability of the land or other land becoming subject to a scheme of development undertaken by a local authority. The arbitrator, both in his award and in the Case Stated, has stated that in assessing compensation he took no account of the matters mentioned in those paragraphs. Although we know that the acquiring authority decided to acquire the lands, there is no mention in the statement of facts of the existence of any proposals for the development of the land or other land by a local authority, nor of the possibility or probability of the land or other land becoming subject to a scheme of development undertaken by a local authority.

It will be particularly noticed that rule 13, in stating what is not to be taken account of in the way of development of the land, is confined to proposals for development or the possibility or probability of the lands or other lands becoming subject to a scheme of development undertaken by a *local authority*. There is nothing in the rule which could be said to prohibit in any way the taking into consideration, for the purpose of the assessment of value, proposals for development or the possibility or probability of development by any person or body other than a local authority. On the contrary, it may properly be said that rule 10, referring to restrictions on development and rule 14, which provides that regard shall be had to any contribution which a planning authority would have required as a condition precedent to the development of the land, show that some form of potential development of the land could be taken into account. The only conclusion to be drawn from the wording and draftsmanship of the rule is that it was quite open to the arbitrator, in so far as rule 13 is concerned, to take into consideration the potential development value of the lands by any person or body other than a local authority. If the legislature had intended that the possibility of private development was not to be considered or that the value of the lands was to be

---

[71] [1947] A.C. 563.
[72] [1966] 1 W.L.R. 1100.

confined to its value as it was used on the date of the notice to treat, it would assuredly have said so. The legislature has not done so and the market value is left as the ruling factor, subject only to the restrictions imposed by rule 13 and by any subsequent rules.

The potential development possibility of the land is obviously one of the elements of value referred to by Fletcher Moulton L. J. in the *Lucas and Chesterfield Gas and Water Board*[73] case when he says that 'every element of value which they possess must be taken into consideration in so far as they increase the value to him'; it is also one of the advantages which the land possesses and which can be taken into consideration in arriving at the market value, as mentioned by Lord Dunedin in the *Cedars Rapids* case where he says:[74] – 'The value to the owner consists in all advantages which the land possesses, present or future . . .'

The reason for the restriction contained in rule 13 is easy to understand in that the expenditure of public money is involved in the development of land by a local authority, and it is quite understandable that it should be thought right not to permit the landowner to obtain an increase in the value of his land by reason of proposals for development by a local authority. Therefore, it may be said that rule 13 is not a method of preventing a claimant from obtaining the market value of his lands but rather a method of preventing him from getting more than the market value. Viewing the rule in the context in which it is used, it would seem to me that the wording of the rule entirely supports such a construction. I may add that the right to compensation at market value existed before the passing of the Act of 1963 and that existing rights pertaining to property are not to be taken away or cut down save by the clear wording of a statute or statutory rule. There is not in rule 13 any such clarity of wording as would show an intention to cut down the value of any person's property in land compulsorily acquired; the limited restriction contained in rule 13 could in no wise be said to curtail the assessment of the value to that of agricultural lands. So far I see nothing to suggest that the arbitrator applied rule 13 incorrectly in determining the amount of compensation to be paid by the acquiring authority to the claimants. In my view, the rule does not restrict the arbitrator to valuing the land as used on the date of the notice to treat.

It has been urged that an important factor with regard to the lack of services and the delay that must occur in supplying them was not taken into consideration, or not sufficiently considered, by the arbitrator in arriving at his valuation and, indeed, in determining whether or not the valuation of the land should be on the basis of the land being agricultural land. At the time of the service of the notice to treat, the acquiring authority were not prepared to grant permission for the development of the land for the erection of houses and would not have been prepared to grant such permission for a period of from five to seven years. That is stated in the agreed statement of facts. This was by reason of the non-availability of drainage and water services and the difficulty of disposing of surface water from the lands. I would point out, first, that all this information was before the arbitrator, as appears from the agreed statement of facts, and there is no reason whatsoever for supposing that he did not take it into consideration in his valuation, or in considering whether the land should be treated as agricultural land for valuation purposes. At most, the lack of the provision of services was a matter that might

[73] [1909] 1 K.B. 16 at p. 30.
[74] [1914] A.C. 569 at p. 576.

cause, or would cause, delay in the development. During the waiting period the owner of the land could use the land in a profitable fashion. The arbitrator could take that into consideration and there is nothing to show that he did not do so. Secondly, there is a fact that the acquiring authority obviously regarded this land as suitable for development for housing purposes as a matter, one might safely assume, of urgent policy; so that it might further be safely assumed that any delay in the provision of services would be of the shortest duration possible, and that is a further factor which the arbitrator might legitimately consider in arriving at his valuation. All these matters could properly be taken into consideration as against any deduction that it might be thought proper to make for the suggested delay that might occur in the provision of services.

It was also suggested that the arbitrator should have taken into consideration the fact that the development of the land could not be carried out without permission which might not be forthcoming, so that the land would not have a development potential to be considered for valuation purposes which would leave it to be valued as agricultural land. As it is implicit in the agreed statement of facts that planning permission would be given with a delay of from five to seven years, and since the acquiring authority have shown by their own action in acquiring the land that it is in their own view suitable for development, it is difficult to see how this factor could affect the valuation adversely from a practical point of view and, in any event, there is no reason to believe that the arbitrator did not consider this point for what it is worth.

A further point that has been argued on behalf of the acquiring authority is that under the relevant portion of rule 3 of s. 2 of the Act of 1919 the special suitability or adaptability of the land for any purpose shall not be taken into account if that purpose is a purpose to which it could be applied only in pursuance of statutory powers. Rule 3 must be read and construed in the light of the fact that rule 2 is admittedly the basic rule; accordingly, rule 3 should be construed in such fashion that it does not impinge on the wording of the basic rule 2 unless the wording of rule 3 and its clear intendment indicate otherwise. In that light I must consider the true meaning of rule 3. It would seem to me that, on their true construction, the words 'if that purpose is a purpose to which it could be applied only in pursuance of statutory powers' refer only to such purposes as actually require a particular purpose to be carried into effect – such as the making of a railway or the like. The development of land for housing purposes does not of itself require statutory powers to enable houses to be built. It is true that there are many restrictions and much statutory control of housing development; but you do not have to obtain a statutory enactment to enable you to build your home or to develop your land for housing purposes. For this reason I take the view that rule 3 does not apply in this case. Hence it was not a matter for the arbitrator to take into account by the arbitrator in fixing the amount of compensation. I have already dealt with the effect of rule 13 as to valuation in the case of land compulsorily acquired for housing purposes by a local authority.

Reliance was also placed upon the opening words of sub-s. 1 of s. 3 of the Act of 1963 which are: '"Development" in this Act means, save where the context otherwise requires, the carrying out of any works on, in or under land. . .' It was suggested that this would cover the provision of services by the local authority and that when such services were provided by the local authority it would then be developing the land and that would bring the building operations into the ambit of a development by the local authority so that, in effect, they would become subject to a scheme for development by the local authority. Since the services would have to be provided in this case, it was further suggested that the possibility or probability of the land becoming subject to a scheme of development undertaken by a local authority existed in this case and that therefore the possibility of development undertaken by a local authority existed in this case and that therefore, the possibility of development by private enterprise could not be taken into consideration. I gathered that it was contended that such a suggested development would bring this case within the ambit of the wording of rule 13(*b*) and, therefore, that the possibility or probability of the land becoming subject to such a scheme, being a scheme of development undertaken by a local authority, could not be taken into account for valuation purposes. Such an argument to my mind leaves altogether out of consideration the saving clause. The meaning assigned to 'development' under s. 3 of the Act of 1963 does not apply 'where the context otherwise requires'. It would seem to me that the words used in rule 13(*b*), taken in their context and in their literal meaning, can only be construed as having reference to a scheme for the development of the entire land. The provision of some service, which I think might physically go only as far as the site boundary, could scarcely be described correctly as a scheme for the development of the land. In any event the *prima facie* meaning of rule 13 is that it restricts the taking into account of the possibility or probability of the land becoming the subject matter of a scheme of development by a local authority in the full sense, that is to say, a housing development in all its operations and not merely the carrying out of some particular works of a subsidiary nature. In my view therefore, s. 3 of the Act of 1963 has no relevance to the matter or the valuation of the lands; it does not in any way hinder the arbitrator from taking into consideration the potential advantage that the land has for housing development by persons other than a local authority.

Having considered the able arguments addressed to us, and having regard to the views which I have stated, I have come to the conclusion that the learned trial judge was correct in his view that the rules relied upon did not have the effect for which the acquiring authority contended, and that the arbitrator has applied the correct principles in arriving at the price to which the claimants are entitled and in awarding to them the sum of £450,000 for their interest in the lands acquired. I agree that the question referred to the Court should be answered accordingly, and I would dismiss this appeal.

OWENABUE LIMITED V. THE COUNTY COUNCIL OF THE COUNTY OF DUBLIN
[1982] I.L.R.M. 150

The plaintiff owned more than 18 acres of land near Belgarde Road, Co. Dublin. Application was made for planning permission for three houses on this site. The proposal by no means represented the optimum development for the land; the background was that the owners were aware that the land was required for road construction and the application was brought anticipating a refusal. The application was brought to generate a right to claim compensation under Section 55 of the Act of 1963 as the alternative seemed to be to wait for a distant day when a compulsory purchase order would be made and ultimately compensation awarded. As expected the application for planning permission was refused and the issue as to the amount of compensation went to an arbitrator. At the hearing of the arbitration the planning authority contended that the amount of compensation must be assessed on the basis of a three-house development: the owners contended that the arbitrator should consider any probable development for the land. Finlay P. found in favour of the owners' contentions.

Finlay P.:

By reason of that refusal on those grounds, it is agreed that the claimants became entitled to compensation from the respondents pursuant to the provision of s. 55 of the Local Government Planning and Development Act, 1963. Mr. McDermott having been appointed as the arbitrator to assess that compensation, an issue as to the interpretation of the section arose before him as a preliminary matter and was stated by him for the opinion of the court in a manner which neatly summarises what apparently were the contentions made on behalf of the claimant and respondent before him and indeed before me as well. The question raised by the arbitrator is as follows:

1. Is the contention of the claimant that I may consider evidence of the probabilities of obtaining permission for schemes of development not limited to three houses correct?
2. Is the contention of the respondent that I may only consider evidence relating to the proposed development of three houses correct?

The material provisions of s. 55 of the Act of 1963 are as follows:

(i) If on a claim made to the planning authority it is shown that as a result of a decision under Part 4 of this Act involving a refusal of permission to develop land. . . the value of an interest of any person existing in the land to which the decision relates at the time of the decision is reduced, such person shall subject to the provisions of this part of this Act be entitled to be paid by the planning authority by way of compensation the amount of such reduction in value. . .

Sub-paragraph 2 provides:

In determining reduction of value for the purposes of this section regard shall be had,
(a) to any permission under this Act to develop the land existing at the time of the decision,
(b) to any undertaking that may be given to grant permission to develop the land in the event of application being made under this Act in that behalf and
(c) to the fact that exempted development may be carried out on the land. . .

Sub paragraph 3 provides as follows:

In determining reduction of value for the purposes of this section in a case in which there has been a decision involving a refusal of permission, it shall be assumed that after the decision . . . permission under this Act would not be granting for any development.

The respondents who sought this case stated submitted to me that the application of the claimants for three houses only as they stated strategically placed on an 18 acre holding was the cause under s. 55 and the origin of their right to compensation and that accordingly they the respondents should not have to meet any claim for compensation based on a refusal and therefore in a sense the loss of a permission other than one of the nature and extent of the application for permission. In support of this submission reliance was placed on the fact that whereas on the application made in this case, the members of the public who might have been concerned with the original application for permission would have been aware only of an application for the building of three houses, that the compensation eventually payable, if the claimants interpretation of s. 55 is upheld, could be based on a wholly different probable future development of which no notice had ever been given to the public. The claimants on the other hand contend that the clear meaning and proper interpretation of s. 55 is that once an application for permission to develop land has been refused under circumstances and for reasons which give rise to a claim for compensation that in the absence of an undertaking given by the planning authority to grant permission, if applied for, or the existence of some other permission to develop the land or the fact that exempted development may be carried out on the land, none of which features arise in this case that the arbitrator must proceed in accordance with sub-clause 3 of s. 55 on the assumption that permission under the Act would not be granted for any development on the land and that this immediately makes it open to the claimants to establish any form of development which they assert could probably have been made in accordance with the Planning Acts and which is now prevented. In support of those contentions, counsel on behalf of the claimant relied upon the provisions of s. 68 of the 1963 Act which equates a claim for compensation under the Act with the right of a person to compensation upon the compulsory acquisition of their land. The claimant freely admitted that the form of application concerning these lands seeking outline permission for three houses only on an 18 acre area of land was designed in the knowledge that all or practically all of the lands were required by the county council for the road schemes envisaged. It forced the county council to pay compensation by this procedure rather than leaving the claimants as owners of the land to be paid compensation at some far removed eventual date of compulsory acquisition.

I am satisfied that the interpretation sought to be put on this section by the claimants is correct and that I must reject the interpretation sought to be put upon it on behalf of the respondents. The provisions of s. 55 of the Act of 1963 seem to me to create a scheme and situation for the payment of compensation which is clear and unambiguous. Firstly, there is granted a general right to compensation if a refusal of permission has reduced the value of the interest of the claimant in the land. This is, of course, significantly cut down by the provisions of s. 56 of the same Act which exempt from compensation refusals of permission given for a number of different categories of reason.

Provided, however, that the reason given does not include one of these categories and that is the instant case before me, what the section appears to provide is that the totality of the reduction in the value of the interest in the land arising from such refusal will be awarded. And the possibility that a person who has suffered a refusal of one particular project for the development of the land would get an unjust enrichment or undue amount of compensation is protected against by the specific provision that regard may be had to any other existing permission to any exempted development of the land and by the further provisions that it is open to the planning authority who must pay for the compensation to give an undertaking to permit some form of development, if applied for. For a person to obtain compensation on the basis that the land cannot be developed at all, all these three matters must be excluded.

That general scheme for the assessment of compensation is expressly and it seems to me very clearly provided by sub-s. 3 of s. 55 which I have already quoted. I cannot see how, giving effect to the provision of that sub-section as they apply to this present case, there could be any conceivable grounds for confining the claiming in proving the probable reduction in the value of his interest to development of any particular type or in particular to the development in respect of which he sought the actual permission out of which his right to compensation arises.

The importance of s. 68 of the Act equating a claim for compensation under s. 55 with compensation for compulsory acquisition is of course that it is a fundamental principle of compensation for compulsory acquisition that only one amount of compensation can be awarded and only one claim for compensation can be entertained. Were these claimants to be confined as is contended on behalf of the respondents in this application for compensation to the probable development value of the land if permission had been given for the erection of three houses on it, although it seems to be conceded by the parties before me that this land cannot be developed under the Planning Acts at all since practically the entire of it is required for the road improvement schemes with which the respondents are involved, they could not ever obtain just compensation for their inability to develop any part of the land not involved in these specific three houses. Such a result would manifestly be unjust and in my view would be in the teeth of the unambiguous meaning of sub-s. 3 of s. 55.

I have carefully considered as to whether it could be suggested that the particular manner in which these claimants applied for an outline planning permission was an attempt to operate a section of the Act in a way in which was unjust and/or could be unlawful. I am satisfied however, that this is not so and could not be a ground for reaching any different conclusion than that which I have reached in regard to the construction of s. 55. It seems reasonable to me for them to say that since they are aware and were at all times aware of the probability that they are debarred by reason of the road improvement schemes which are pending from developing these lands that they should not be forced to wait, using them at a significant under-value until such time as a compulsory acquisition order was eventually made against them. I would accordingly answer the questions raised by the Arbitrator for my opinion that the contention of the claimant that he may consider evidence of the probabilities of obtaining permission for schemes of development not limited to three houses as being correct and correspondingly answer the contrary submission made to him on behalf of the respondent as incorrect.

I would only add one further comment which on the submissions made by counsel is probably not particularly relevant to this case. Having regard to my construction of s. 55 it seems clear to me that if in any particular case a claimant for compensation based his valuation on a probable development which was different in character from that for which he sought permission and in respect of the refusal of which his right to compensation arose the justice of the case would appear to require that the respondent planning authority should have an ample opportunity upon learning the full details of such probable other development to consider their position in relation to giving an undertaking pursuant to the provisions of s. 55.

SHORTT V. DUBLIN CO. CO.[74a]
[1982] I.L.R.M. 117

[74a] Followed by O'Hanlon J. in *Meenaghan* v. *Dublin County Council*, 4th Sept., 1983.

'Reservation for a particular purpose' within Rule 11 is not the same as 'General zoning' in a development plan. In assessing compensation by Rule 11 reservation for a particular purpose must be ignored: zoning cannot be.

An occupier of premises within the district of the sanitary authority has a statutory right[75] to connect the foul water sewer servicing a development which takes place on the land to the main sewer. It would not be a ground for objection by the sanitary authority that while the sewer had capacity to receive the effluent such capacity was required for future development on other lands.

A refusal of planning permission on the grounds that the capacity of the main sewer is pre-empted to provide for development on other lands is not within section 56(1)(b)(i) as there would be no 'existing deficiency' nor would the application be premature in the sense that it could be renewed after facilities were available.

High Court
McMahon J.:

At the date of the notice to treat, which is the relevant date for the purpose of determining the value of the land, the land was zoned under the County Dublin Development Plan 1972. The greater part of the land is in an area designated Q in the development plan. Under the plan this means that the objective for the area is 'to preserve an area of high amenity' and the permitted use of the land is stated as 'primarily agricultural use.' The remainder of the land is designated T, meaning that the objective is 'to provide for recreational open space and ancillary structures' and the permitted use of the land is stated as 'solely recreational use'.

The first two questions in the case are designed to obtain a decision as to whether these designations amount to a reservation for a particular purpose within the meaning of rule 11 of the statutory rules for the assessment of compensation. Rule 11 is one of the rules contained in the Fourth Schedule to the Local Government (Planning and Development) Act, 1963 and inserted into s. 2 of the Acquisition of Land (Assessment of Compensation) Act, 1919 by s. 69 of the 1963 Act. Rule 11 is in these terms:

> Regard shall not be had to any depreciation or increase in the value attributable to
> (a) the land or any land in the vicinity thereof being reserved for any particular purpose in a development plan or
> (b) inclusion of the land in a special amenity area order.

The acquiring authority contended that the objectives 'to preserve an area of high amenity' and 'to provide for recreational open space and ancillary structures' were not particular purposes but general objectives and that particular purposes referred to specific uses such as burial grounds set out at heads 2, 3 and 4 of Part IV of the Third Schedule to the Local Government (Planning and Development) Act, 1963. The claimant contended that a designation for a public purpose is a reservation for a particular purpose and that the limitation of use to uses for purposes compatible with the preservation of an area of high amenity or use as a recreational open space destroyed any market for the land and the Arbitrator must therefore be entitled to ignore the particular purpose and ascertain what the value would be if there were no reservation.

---

[75] S. 23 of the Public Health (Ireland) Act, 1878. Compare observations of Henchy J. in *State (Finglas Industrial Estates Limited)* v. *Dublin County Council* (p. 224).

In s. 19 of the Local Government (Planning and Development) Act, 1963 the words 'particular purpose' are used to mean purposes which are residential, commercial, industrial, agricultural or otherwise. The same words when used in Rule 11 clearly must be given a different meaning. If these words had the same meaning as they have in s. 19 it would mean that the Arbitrator should disregard all zoning with the result that his valuation would exceed the market value which is largely based on zoning.

In the context of Rule 11 the word 'reserved' means set apart and 'particular purpose' means a purpose distinct from the purpose for which the other land in the area is zoned. Rule 11 therefore refers to land which is set apart from the other land in the area and zoned for a different purpose and in valuing such land the Arbitrator is to disregard the setting apart and value the land at the value it would have had if it had not been so reserved, that is the value having regard to the purposes for which the land generally in the area is zoned. The intention of the rule is to protect the owner from the detrimental effect on the value of his land of the reservation of the land for the particular purpose for the benefit of the community and to ensure that owners of other land do not profit from it.

Questions 1 and 2 will therefore be answered in the affirmative. On the third question the decision in *Molloy* v. *Gray*,[76] which is in accord with numerous decisions in England on the corresponding section in the English Act, establishes that if a development took place on the lands the claimant as an occupier of premises within the district of the sanitary authority would have an absolute right to connect the foul water sewers to the Dodder Valley main sewer. It would not be a ground for objection by the sanitary authority that, while the sewer had capacity to receive the effluent, that capacity was required for future development on other lands.

The acquiring authority contended that s. 23 of the Public Health (Ireland) Act 1878 was inconsistent with the provisions of the Local Government (Planning and Development) Act, 1963 and consequently was impliedly repealed by the 1963 Act. It was said that it was impossible for the acquiring authority as Planning Authority to plan for the Tallaght area, for which the Dodder Valley main sewer was designed, if occupiers outside the Tallaght area are entitled to connect to the sewer. It should be observed that the problem is a hypothetical one in relation to the claimant since the development plan precludes her lands from being built on. The Act of 1878 is a particular Act and that of 1963 a general Act so that the maxim *generalia specialibus non derogant* applies. There can be repeal by implication only if the two enactments are incapable of standing together. I see no impossibility when the main sewer is being designed of making it big enough to take the effluent from all occupiers who will have a right to connect to it having regard to the number of potential occupiers who may be so entitled as a result of the development plan. The answer to the third question is therefore in the negative.

Question 4 raises the issue whether s. 56(1)(*b*)(i) of the 1963 Act would debar the claimant from recovering compensation under s. 55 of that Act if planning permission were refused on the grounds that the capacity of the Dodder Valley main sewer was pre-empted to provide capacity for schemes of development on other lands some of which might be undertaken by a local authority.

Under s. 56(1)(*b*) compensation is excluded where a reason for refusal is that the development would be premature by reference to an existing deficiency in the

---

[76] 24 L.R. (Ir) 258.

provision of sewerage facilities and the period within which such deficiency may reasonably be expected to be made good. The case visualised in this question would not involve any existing deficiency in sewerage services because the deficiency is prospective only and it would not be a case where the application was premature in the sense that it could be renewed after facilities were available. Question 4 is therefore answered in the affirmative.

Supreme Court
O'Higgins C.J.:[77]

. . . The subject land falls into two parts, each of which is designated on the County Dublin Development Plan 1972, which plan was operative on the 10th November 1979. This was the date of the service of the notice to treat and, therefore, the critical date so far as the assessment of compensation is concerned. The larger portion of the land was designated 'Q' on this plan which indicated an objective 'to preserve an area of high amenity'. The smaller portion is designated 'T' which in the plan indicated an objective 'to provide for recreational open space and ancillary structures'. The land is situated in an area in which there has been extensive residential development and apparently represents an open undeveloped space left after housing development in the vicinity had concluded. If this were developed for housing there would be no difficulty in providing water supply nor would there be any difficulty in connecting foul water sewers from such a development to the Dodder Valley main sewer, nor in discharging surface water to the Dodder river. In fact, however, the main sewer, although then under 50 per cent in use, was 'pre-empted for future development on other lands'. While it is not expressly stated in the case, there is an implication that it might not be capable of taking all the sewage involved in all such future development and, in addition taking the sewage of a new development in the subject lands.

The first two questions raised in the case seek a decision as to whether the designation accorded to the subject lands amounts to a reservation for a particular purpose within Rule 11 of the Statutory Rules for the Assessment of Compensation. Rule 11 is one of the rules contained in the Fourth Schedule to the Local Government (Planning and Development) Act 1963 and inserted into Section 2 of the Acquisition of Land (Assessment of Compensation) Act 1919 by Section 69 of the 1963 Act. It provides as follows in relation to the assessment of compensation:

'(11) Regard shall not be had to any depreciation or increase in value attributable to –
(a) the land, or any land in the vicinity thereof, being reserved for any particular purpose in a development plan, or
(b) inclusion of the land in a special amenity area order.'

In the High Court Mr. Justice McMahon in dealing with this Rule said as follows:

'In the context of Rule 11 the word 'reserved' means set apart and 'particular purpose' means a purpose distinct from the purpose for which the other land in the area is owned. Rule 11, therefore, refers to land which is set apart from the other land in the area and is zoned for a different purpose and in valuing such

[77] Henchy, Hederman JJ. concurring. Unreported judgment delivered 13th May, 1983.

land the arbitrator is to disregard the setting apart and value the land at the value it would have had if it had not been so reserved, that is, the value having regard to the purpose for which the land generally in the area is zoned.'

I think this is a correct interpretation of the Rule and I find it unnecessary to add anything to that which Mr. Justice McMahon said in his judgment. I agree with him, therefore, that Questions 1 and 2 should be answered in the affirmative.

On the basis that Rule 11 is to be interpreted in the manner indicated and that, accordingly, Questions 1 and 2 are to be answered in the affirmative, the arbitrator raises two further questions. These are asked in order to seek guidance as to a set of facts which might be supposed to have been possible, having regard to the evidence before him, had the lands not been so reserved. The planning and engineering witnesses called on behalf of the acquiring authority had stated that the Dodder Valley sewer to which a housing development on the subject lands would require connection, was 'pre-empted' for other housing development in the area which had not yet taken place. I assume that this means that the sewer had been constructed in the light of the development which the planning officers foresaw as probable in the area intended to be drained. In these circumstances the arbitrator asks two questions, the answers to which he hopes will assist him in considering the reality of valuing these lands as building lands. These questions are necessarily hypothetical since they have not arisen and cannot arise on the actual facts. Nevertheless I would be anxious, as was Mr. Justice McMahon, to give the arbitrator as much assistance as is possible. For this reason I now turn to the first of these questions. This is Question No. 3 in which, in effect, the arbitrator asks whether the County Council as the sanitary authority could, in the event of housing development taking place on the subject lands, refuse a connection for sewerage to its main sewer, such sewer then being capable of absorbing such sewerage. In my view, it could not so refuse. It seems to me that the Public Health (Ireland) Act 1878, particularly section 23 thereof, obliges the sanitary authority to receive into its sewers the sewerage of all premises within its district, provided proper notice is given and the appropriate regulations observed. I agree with Mr. Justice McMahon and for the reasons which he gave that this Section is not repealed by implication by the provisions of the Planning Act. This question should, therefore, in my view, be answered in the negative.

The second question raises the possibility, in the event of such a development being proposed, of the County Council as planning authority refusing permission under the provisions of Section 56(1)(b)(i) of the Planning Act. This provision refers to a refusal of a planning application on the basis that it is premature in that there is an existing deficiency in the provision of water supplies or sewerage facilities. If a refusal is properly made on such grounds, compensation under the provisions of Section 55 is not payable. Here, however, it is apparent that an existing deficiency could not be established. On the basis of such a supposed development in the subject lands in accordance with the evidence before the arbitrator the main sewer would have been capable, without any difficulty, in taking such sewerage. It seems to me, therefore, while this question is hypothetical and based on many suppositions, it should nevertheless, be answered in the affirmative because such a decision would not be within the provision of section 56(1)(b)(i) of the Planning Act. I would dismiss this appeal.

I only wish to add that I appreciate the problem which the last two questions were intended to highlight. Obviously it is one which is becoming increasingly complex and one which is causing growing concern to planning authorities. I cannot feel, however, that any solution to the problem raised can be found under existing legislation. It seems to me that a solution can only be found in amending legislation.

McKONE ESTATES LIMITED V. THE COUNTY COUNCIL OF THE COUNTY OF KILDARE
(1982 No. 592 SS.) Unreported judgment delivered by O'Hanlon J.
24 June, 1983

The plaintiff was at all material times the owner of approximately 60 acres ('Cooldrinagh') situate on the South (County Dublin) side of the River Liffey near Leixlip which had the benefit of a permission granted on the 14th March, 1977 by the Minister for Local Government subject, inter alia, to a condition requiring the discharge of the sewerage into the treatment works of Kildare County Council which were situate across the River Liffey in Leixlip in the functional area of Kildare County Council. In August, 1979, the owners of Cooldrinagh applied to both County Councils for permission to run a sewer pipe connecting the Cooldrinagh development to the Leixlip plant. Application was made to Dublin County Council because the pipe was intended to run on the side of the public road in that Council's functional area and application was made to Kildare County Council because it was intended to connect the pipe into that Council's public sewer connecting to the Leixlip plant. It was also intended to carry the pipe across the river attaching it to a weir bridge, half of which was owned by each Council.

These applications were refused by both planning authorities and also by An Bord Pleanala on appeal. The reason given by An Bord Pleanala was that as Kildare County Council had refused to accept the foul sewerage in question, no purpose could be served by laying the proposed pipeline which was the development applied for. It was established that if they were entitled so to do Kildare County Council would refuse connection to their public sewer.

The application for compensation under Section 55 of the Act of 1963 arose out of this refusal by An Bord Pleanala. Whilst the subject site of the relevant planning application was merely the portion of the private land through which the proposed sewer pipe was to run (some 0.3 acres of land owned by the owners of Cooldrinagh but situate on the opposite (North) side of the River Liffey) the claim was for £3m which clearly related to the reduction in value of the lands at Cooldrinagh because of the fact that the sewerage could not be connected to the public system in County Kildare. This was a claim for injurious affection to the lands at Cooldrinagh. A case was stated by the arbitrator in which a number of questions were asked. The trial Judge held (a) that despite the fact that the claim for compensation was not expressed as a claim for injurious affection to the lands at Cooldrinagh and could be criticised for non-compliance with the appropropriate regulations, the claim could be admitted by the arbitrator as a valid claim and dealt with as a claim for reduction in value to the small piece of land on the north of the river and for injurious affection (if allowable) to the lands at Cooldrinagh, (b) neither Section 55 of the Act of 1963 nor any other section conferred upon the claimant for compensation under Section 55 a right to claim injurious affection. The rules set out at Section 2 of the Act of 1919 (as extended by Section 69 of the Act of 1963) did not confer such a right: they merely set out a procedure whereby compensation could be measured but the right to that compensation was to be found, if at all, in other statutory provisions. No statutory provisions provided for a right to injurious affection. Specifically the Lands Clauses Acts were not incorporated as such into the Planning Acts and therefore a claimant did not have a right to claim injurious affection under Section 63 of the Lands Clauses Consolidation Act, 1845. (c) The owner or occupier of lands situate outside the functional area of a sanitary authority had a *prima facie* right under Section 24 of the Public Health (Ireland) Act, 1878 to connect any sewer or drain from such premises to communicate with the sewers of that sanitary authority on such terms and conditions as may be agreed or, in the event of dispute, settled at the option of the owner or occupier by a Court of Summary Jurisdiction or arbitration. The trial Judge held, however, that because the claimant in the instant case had not demanded such a connection in explicit reliance on its rights under Section 24 thereby allowing the Kildare County Council Sanitary Authority to decide whether or not it would agree to such a connection in principle and attach whatever conditions and terms it thought fit, it was therefore premature to bring a claim under Section 55 because if arising out of such an application a Court were to hold that the sanitary authority was not entitled to refuse such a connection, then the whole basis of the Planning Board's decision would disappear. The arbitrator could not at this stage determine either the validity of the claim for compensation or the amount thereof which should be awarded if a valid claim existed under the Act.

O'Hanlon J.:

On the 8th October, 1982, Mr. Sean McDermott, in his capacity as Arbitrator, referred by Case Stated, a number of questions of law to the High Court for determination. The Case Stated was in the following terms:

CASE STATED.

On the 30th day of October, 1981, I sat as property arbitrator at the County Council offices at Naas, in the County of Kildare, for the purpose of hearing and determining a claim for compensation brought by McKone Estates Ltd. (hereinafter referred to as 'the claimant') against the County Council of the County of Kildare (hereinafter referred to as 'the Kildare County Council') pursuant to the provisions of Section 55 of the Local Government (Planning and Development) Act, 1963 (hereinafter referred to as 'the Act of 1963') arising out of a decision of An Bord Pleanala refusing to grant permission for a development described as 'the laying of a sewage pipeline at Leixlip to serve proposed housing and ancilliary development at Cooldrinagh, County Dublin'.

At the commencement of the arbitration it was submitted by Mr. Hugh Geoghegan S.C. who appeared for the Kildare County Council instructed by Messrs. Brown and McCann, Solicitors, Naas, that I had no jurisdiction to entertain the claim for compensation for the following reasons:

A. There was no valid claim for compensation before me because the letter of the 23rd February, 1981, sent to the Kildare County Council by the Claimant's solicitors and which constituted the claim before me related only to the lands owned by the Claimant at Cooldrinagh, County Dublin and no other lands, or alternatively related to the said lands at Cooldrinagh aforesaid and the adjacent property of the claimant in the County Kildare hereinafter referred to but was not confined to the said property in County Kildare which was the subject of the applications for planning permission. A copy of the said letter of the 24th February, 1981 is annexed to this Case Stated and marked Exhibit A.

B. A claim for compensation is excluded by virtue of the provisions of Section 56(1)(*b*) of the Act of 1963.

After hearing the submissions of Mr. E. M. Walsh S.C. who appeared on behalf of the claimant, instructed by Messrs. Gerard J.Quinn & Co., Solicitors, I held that there was a valid claim for compensation before me which was not excluded by the said Section 56(1)(*b*) of the Act of 1963 and I proceeded to hear the evidence on behalf of the claimant and the Kildare County Council and the submissions of Counsel on the said 30th day of October, 1981, and on the 4th and 7th days of December, 1981.

The following facts were either agreed or proved to my satisfaction during the course of the hearing.

1. On the 14th day of March, 1977, the Minister for Local Government granted permission on Appeal for a development comprising 455 houses, a shopping site, a school site and open space on approximately sixty acres of land at Cooldrinagh in the County of Dublin, in close proximity to the treatment works on the Kildare side of the river Liffey. The said permission was granted subject to five conditions including a condition which would have required the discharge of sewage from the completed development to the said treatment works at Leixlip. Copies of the said permission and of the refusal by Dublin County Council appealed against are annexed hereto (Exhibit B).

2. The said lands at Cooldrinagh were subsequently acquired by the claimant in fee simple and the claimant was at all times material to the arbitration the owner of the said lands.

3. On the 18th day of May, 1979, the claimant purchased a property known as the Toll House at Leixlip, in the County of Kildare, comprising a dwellinghouse on 0.3 acres of land close to the said lands of Cooldrinagh but on the opposite side of the river Liffey in County Kildare. The claimant was at all times material to the arbitration the freehold owner of the Toll House.

4. On the 3rd and 7th days of August, 1979, the claimant applied to the Kildare County Council and to Dublin County Council respectively for permission to construct a foul sewer to connect the already conditionally approved development at Cooldrinagh with the treatment works at Leixlip and for a surface water drain from the development to the river Liffey in County Dublin. The application to Dublin County Council simply involved laying a pipe along the public road from the lands of Cooldrinagh to the Salmon Weir Bridge across the river Liffey. The line took a defined route as far as the bridge and it was then proposed to attach a pipe to the structure of the bridge. The application to the Kildare County Council involved three alternative pipe lines from the bridge to the treatment works. The first alternative involved a road excavation and the laying of a pipe on the grounds of Toll House where it would connect with the main County Kildare sewer leading to the treatment works. The second alternative proposed laying a pipe entirely on the public road to a point where it would connect with the said main sewer. The third alternative proposed laying a pipe until it connected with the main sewer in land not owned by the claimant. Both applications for planning permission proposed a temporary connection to the treatment works at Leixlip and an ultimate permanent connection to piped services in the County of Dublin on a date to be

agreed between the Kildare County Council and Dublin County Council. This was made clear in the letter of application and accompanying notes. The said letter and accompanying notes and extract from the drawings, i.e. the large scale enlargements of the drains to cross the bridge are marked Exhibit C.

5. The County boundary is the centre of the river Liffey and the Salmon Weir bridge is owned as to one half by the County Council of the County of Dublin and as to the other half by the Kildare County Council.

6. The Kildare County Council and the County Council of the County of Dublin issued notifications of decisions to refuse permission, copies whereof are annexed hereto (Exhibits D. & E).

7. The claimant apealed to An Bord Pleanala against both decisions and following an oral hearing at which both appeals were considered together An Bord Pleanala refused permission for the proposed development. Attached hereto is a copy of the letter of appeal to An Bord Pleanala and the decision of An Bord Pleanala in the case of the application to the Kildare County Council (Exhibit F). The decision of An Bord Pleanala on the application to the County Council of the County of Dublin was in identical terms.

8. The treatment works at Leixlip is designed for a population of 20,000 and in the view of the planning authority that capacity has been fully absorbed. As of March, 1977, and also as of October, 1979 the existing treatment works would not have been fully absorbed but the sewerage from the Cooldrinagh development could only have been taken in place of a corresponding reduction of projected development in the County of Kildare. It is proposed to carry out works which will increase the capacity of the treatment works at Leixlip to 45,000 at the next stage and ultimately to 93,000 beyond which figure the capacity cannot be increased because of the absorption capacity of the river Liffey. The planning authority accepts that the treatment works will have a spare capacity from 1984 to 1995 or at the latest to the year 2000, but the Kildare County Council has earmarked in its development plan that spare capacity for projected further development in the administrative County of Kildare which it anticipates will use up the entire capacity of the treatment works between 1995 and 2000. If so entitled, the Kildare County Council as sanitary authority would have refused to enter into an agreement with the claimant under Section 24 of the Public Health (Ireland) Act 1878.

9. It was established at the oral hearing hereinbefore referred to that the County Council of the County of Dublin was not prepared to extend its piped services at any future time so as to accommodate the proposed development at Cooldrinagh and that the development could only proceed on the basis of a permanent connection with the treatment works at Leixlip.

10. On the 24th day of June, 1981, in the course of an arbitration in which the present claimant claimed against it in the sum of three million pounds for reduction in value of the claimant's interest in the Cooldrinagh lands by reason of refusal of permission to lay the mains referred to at 4 above the County Council of the County of Dublin undertook to grant planning permission to the claimant to enable the sewage from the development at Cooldrinagh to be discharged into the treatment works at Leixlip subject to certain conditions and a copy of the said undertaking is annexed hereto (Exhibit G).

11. As a result of the decision of An Bord Pleanala to refuse permission for a connection from the proposed development at Cooldrinagh to the treatment works at Leixlip there was a diminution in the value of the said lands at Cooldrinagh.

On the application of counsel for Kildare County Council I agreed to state a consultative case for the opinion of the High Court and to adjourn the further hearing of the arbitration pending the decision of the High Court on the questions raised in the case stated. The questions which I respectively formulate for the opinion of the High Court are as follows:

1. Was I correct in law in refusing to accede to the argument of Counsel for the Kildare County Council that I should decline jurisdiction to hear and determine the claim on either or both of the grounds hereinbefore recited?

2. Is the claimant entitled to include as part of its claim a claim in respect of injurious affection to the lands of Cooldrinagh having regard to the diminution in value of the said lands arising as a result of the aforesaid decision of An Bord Pleanala?

3. Is the permission of the Minister for Local Government operative having regard to the provisions of Condition no. 1 of the said permission and to the foregoing facts?

4. Whether on the basis of the foregoing facts and having regard to the provisions of Section 24 of the Public Health (Ireland) Act 1878 it is open to me to find that the claimant might not have been entitled to discharge sewerage from the said development at Cooldrinagh to the treatment works at Leixlip?

5. If the answer to question no. 4 is in the affirmative am I obliged as a matter of law to make a finding that the claimant would not have been so entitled?

6. If it is open to me to find that the claimant would have been entitled to discharge sewerage from the proposed development at Cooldrinagh to the treatment works at Leixlip is it open to me to find that such entitlement would have been for a limited period only?

Dated the 8th day of October 1982.

Signed: Sean McDermott
          Property Arbitrator'.

Before proceeding to deal with the specific questions raised by the arbitrator in the case stated, it appears to me to be helpful to consider the legal position under Section 24 of the Public Health (Ireland) Act, 1878, as to the entitlement of owners or occupiers of premises to require the sanitary authority of an adjoining district to permit a connection of sewers or drains from such premises to the sewers of that sanitary authority.

Since the present case was first argued before the Court, a judgment of the Supreme Court has clarified the position under s. 23 of the Act of 1878. In *Dublin County Council* v. *Shortt*, the judgment of the Court was delivered by O'Higgins CJ, with whom the other members of the Court concurred. He said:

'The planning and engineering witnesses called on behalf of the acquiring authority had sated that the Dodder Valley sewer to which a housing development on the subject lands would require connection, was "pre-empted" for other housing development in the area which had not yet taken place. I assume that this means that the sewer had been constructed in the light of the development which the planning officers foresaw as probable in the area intended to be drained. . . . The arbitrator asks whether the County Council as the sanitary authority could, in the event of housing development taking place on the subject lands, refuse a connection for sewerage to its main sewer, such sewer than being caable of absorbing such sewerage. In my view, it could not so refuse. It seems to me that the Public Health (Ireland) Act, 1878, particularly Section 23 thereof, obliges the sanitary authority to receive into its sewers the seweage of all premises within its district, provided proper notice is given and the appropriate regulations observed. I agree with Mr. Justice McMahon and for the reasons which he gave that this Section is not repealed by implication by the provisions of the Planning Act. 'The second question raises the possibility, in the event of such a development being proposed, of the County Council as planning authority refusing permission under the provisions of Section 56(1)(*b*)(i) of the Planning Act. This provision refers to a refusal of a planning application on the basis that it is premature in that there is an existing deficiency in the provision of water supplies or sewerage facilities. If a refusal is properly made on such grounds, compensation under the provisions of Section 55 is not payable. Here, however, it is apparent that an existing deficiency could not be established. On the basis of such a supposed development in the subject lands in accordance with the evidence before the arbitrator the main sewer would have been capable, without any difficulty, of taking such sewerage. It seems to me, therefore . . . such a decision would not be within the provisions of Section 56(1)(*b*)(i) of the Planning Act.

'I only wish to add that I appreciate the problem which the last two questions were intended to highlight. Obviously it is one which is becoming increasingly complex and one which is causing growing concern to planning authorities. I cannot feel, however, that any solution to the problem raised can be found under existing legislation. It seems to me that a solution can only be found in amending legislation.'

That decision of the Supreme Court referred to the position at present obtaining under the provisions of Section 23 of the Public Health (Ireland) Act, 1878. What arises for consideration in the present case are the provisions of Section 24 of the Act, dealing with the possibility of securing connection of sewers or drains servicing premises in one district with the sewer of a sanitary authority in a different district. As the wording of the two Sections is different in some important respects it may be helpful to quote the relevant provisions at this stage. They are as follows:

'23. The owner or occupier of any premises within the district of a sanitary authority shall be entitled to cause his drains to empty into the sewers of that authority on condition of his giving such notice as may be required by that authority of his intention so to do, and of complying with the regulations of that authority in respect of the mode in which the communications between such drains and sewers are to be made, and subject to the control of any person who may be appointed to superintend the making of such communications.'
'24. The owner or occupier of any premises without the district of a sanitary authority may cause any sewer or drain from such premises to communicate with any sewer of the sanitary authority on such terms and conditions as may be agreed on between such owner or occupier and such sanitary authority, or as in case of dispute may be settled, at the option of the owner or occupier, by a court of summary jurisdiction or by arbitration in manner provided by this Act.'

The terms of Section 22 of the English Public Health Act, 1875, which are in identical terms to those used in Section 24 of the Irish Act of 1878, were considered by Malins V.-C. in the case of *Newington Local Board* v. *Cottingham Local Board*,

12 Ch.D. 725, where the proprietors of some 55 acres of land known as the Botanic Gardens were proceeding to lay them out for building ground, and sought a connection with a sewer in an adjoining district. The Vice-Chancellor said:

> 'I have paid great attention to the case, which has been ably argued and I feel bound to come to the conclusion that it is the right of every owner without the district to consider what will be most convenient to him. It cannot, I think, be better illustrated than by the case of the Botanic Garden, which lies immediately contiguous, so that nothing could be more advantageous to them, nothing more obvious to them when building upon their ground, than to do that which it would be their duty to do, and drain into the nearest sewer, and that sewer is the sewer of the Cottingham district.
>
> 'That is the right which they have proceeded to exercise, and that is the right which, according to my view, is clearly conferred upon them by the 22nd section of the Act of 1875.'

North J. reached a similar conclusion when considering the similar provisions of the English Public Health Act, 1848, s. 48, in the case of *Mayor of New Windsor* v. *Stovell*, (1884) 27 Ch. D. 665. The relevant part of his judgment reads as follows:

> 'The words of the section are: 'Be it enacted that any owner or occupier of premises adjoining or near to but beyond the limits of any district, may cause any sewer or drain of or from such premises to communicate with any sewer of the local board of health upon such terms and conditions as shall be agreed upon between such owner and occupier and such local board, or, in case of dispute, as shall be settled by arbitration in the manner provided by this Act.' It is said that this section conferred a discretionary power upon the board as trustees or quasi trustees, and that they could not exercise it as to the drainage of property, and could not agree as to communications to be made, or do anything, except with respect to what was actually in existence at the time; and it is said that after that arrangement a fresh bargain must be entered into with respect to every communication to be made after that date from a house not then existing with the sewer of the board, either mediately or immediately. As regards that section, it does not seem right to say that it is a case in which the board are acting as trustees in the sense in which it was put. No doubt it is left to them to settle the terms and conditions, and inasmuch as those terms and conditions did not affect them individually, but affected the ratepayers, they were so far acting on behalf of other persons. But the power given to them is to make an arrangement as to the terms and conditions of the work, and there is nothing which enables them to say that it shall not be done at all. Under this Act, in case the terms should not be agreed upon they might be settled by arbitration. Under the Public Health Act, 1866 (29 & 30 Vict. c. 90, s. 9), for the first time, an additional power is given of having disputes settled by two justices. That clause appears almost verbatim in the Public Health Act, 1875, except that instead of two justices, a court of summary jurisdiction, which means the same thing, is mentioned.
>
> 'This was a case in which, in my opinion, the owner of the adjoining property had a right to have the communication made, as was decided by Vice-Chancellor Malins in the similar case of *Newington Local Board* v. *Cottingham Local Board*. . . .
>
> 'If that is so, there was a right on the part of Mr. Vansittart to have the sewer made to communicate with his land, and on what terms? The terms, no doubt,

are to be settled, and if the parties cannot agree, the terms are to be settled by arbitration, and when so settled, notwithstanding any objection on the part of the board, they would be binding, and the right to connect with the sewer would arise. As soon as that has been done, everything contemplated by the section has been done, and I do not see how after that anything further remains to be done.

'It is said that the board would have a difficulty in knowing upon what terms to settle, because they could not know what would be done with the land, how many houses would be built upon it, or what burden might be cast on them. That is one of the difficulties with which they have to contend, and they must deal with it by taking care that the terms which are made limit the number of houses, or require a payment in respect of them which will be a fair remuneration. . . . Therefore Mr. Vansittart having a right to make this connection, and to have all the provisions of this section immediately carried out, the board must do the best they can for the purpose of fixing the terms, and must fix them fairly and reasonably. Unless the terms are complied with the connection cannot be made, but as soon as they have been complied with, the connection is to be made, and, as it seems to me, there is an end of the matter. Under these circumstances the section is, in my opinion, equivalent to a grant to the owner of the adjoining land of a right to have the connection made and to use the connection when made. There are not express words as to user, but I consider that the direction to make the communication carries with it the right to do what was the only purpose in contemplation when the terms were arranged.'

See also, Glenn, *Public Health*, 14th Edn. (1925), Vol. 1, p. 88n.:

'Section 21 gives the owner or occupier the right to drain into the sewers belonging to the local authority of his own district without any restriction except as regards the mode of making the communications between his drains and the sewers. The present section (Section 22) also gives a right of drainage into the sewers to which it applies and does not give the local authority the power to refuse to permit such drainage at their absolute discretion, if the owner or occupier is willing to abide by such terms and conditions as may be settled in the manner provided by the Act.'

Accordingly, it appears to me that notwithstanding the significant difference in wording as between Sections 23 and 24 of the Public Health (Ireland) Act, 1878, a right similar to that conferred by Section 23 of the Act is also conferred by Section 24 – in the latter case, to the owner or occupier of premises to secure connection to the sewer of an adjoining sanitary district, subject to compliance with such terms and conditions as may be agreed with the sanitary authority or as may be settled by a court of summary jurisdiction or by arbitration, in default of agreement.

When it comes to carrying out the necessary works to secure such connection, however, permission must be sought under the terms of the Local Government (Planning and Development) Act, 1963, (as amended), and it is clearly envisaged by that Act, that planning permission may be refused (inter alia) 'by reference to any existing deficiency in the provision of water supplies or sewerage facilities and the period within which any such deficiency may reasonably be expected to be made good.' If refused on this ground, compensation in respect of the refusal of permission under Section 55 of the Act shall not be payable. (Sec. 56).

In the present case, as in the case of *Dublin County Council* v. *Shortt*, what is concerning the sanitary authority is not so much an existing deficiency in the provision of sewerage facilities, as the fact that they have additional capacity for sewerage disposal available but that this has been provided for the future needs of their own sanitary district and they view with great concern the possible absorption of a large measure of that capacity by building works in a different county altogether.

Having regard to the decision of the Supreme Court in *Shortt's Case*, however, I feel compelled to hold that this situation cannot be regarded as one entitling the sanitary authority to refuse the connection sought, out of hand, or the planning authority to refuse planning permission on the basis of existing sewerage facilities being deficient.

In fact, the refusal of permission was couched in somewhat different terms. The decision of Kildare County Council gave four reasons for the refusal of permission. They were as follows:

1. Capacity of the sewage treatment plant at Leixlip is already committed to provide for the overall development and expansion of the county towns to be connected to this system in accordance with the policy and zoning provisions adopted in the County Development Plan, 2nd Revision, 1978, and the proposed development would, therefore, be contrary to the proper planning and development of the area.
2. The housing scheme which the proposal is designed to service was not part of the design considerations of the Leixlip Sewage Treatment Plant and this development, if permitted, would constitute an undesirable precedent.
3. The proposed development which would interfere with the structure of Leixlip Bridge is not acceptable as it could lead to structural deterioration of the bridge.
4. The proposed development involving the placing of a pipe on the external face of the bridge would seriously injure the visual amenities of the Bridge.

On appeal to An Bord Pleanala, permission for the laying of the proposed pipe-line to connect to the Kildare County Council main sewer north of the bridge at Leixlip was again refused. The Board gave only one reason for this refusal and did not refer to the manner in which the proposed development would affect Leixlip Bridge. The Order of the Board, dated the 5th September, 1980, recited as follows:

As Kildare County Council have refused to accept the foul sewage from the development in question into the treatment works at Leixlip, the Board does not consider that the laying of the proposed pipe-line would serve any purpose in the context of the proper planning and development of the area.

On the basis of this refusal the developers then submitted a claim for compensation under Section 55 of the Act of 1963, by letter dated the 24th February, 1981. In order to substantiate such a claim it is necessary for an applicant to establish that 'as a result of a decision . . . involving a refusal of permission to develop land . . . the value of an interest of any person existing in the land to which the decision relates at the time of the decision is reduced. . . '. (I am omitting those parts of the sub-section which have no bearing in the present case).

It appears to me that the applicants for compensation in the present case have a *prima facie* statutory right under the provisions of Section 24 of the Public Health (Ireland) Act, 1878, to seek a connection with the main sewer of the Kildare County Council, and until they have asserted and exhausted such right it is not possible for the arbitrator to determine whether, in fact, the value of their interest in the land to which the decision of An Bord Pleanala relates has been reduced, and if so, to what extent. The documentary evidence which has been placed before the Court in relation to the present case stated does not indicate that the developers have at any stage applied for permission to connect a foul sewer with the Kildare County Council main sewer, in express reliance on whatever statutory rights may be available to them under the provisions of Section 24 of the Act of 1878. If Kildare County Council rejected such an application out of hand and it was subsequently decided in legal proceedings that they were not entitled to do so, then the entire basis for the decision already given by An Bord Pleanala would disappear. As has already been decided by McMahon J. in the High Court in *Shortt's* case, and affirmed on appeal by the Supreme Court, Sec. 23 of the Public Health (Ireland) Act, 1878, cannot be regarded as having been repealed by implication by the provisions of the Planning Acts, and I reach the same conclusion in relation to Section 24.

Turning now to the specific questions raised for consideration in the case stated, I have reached the following conclusions in relation to same.

1. I conclude that the arbitrator was correct in law in refusing to accede to the argument of counsel for the Kildare County Council that he should decline jurisdiction to hear and determine the claim on either or both of the grounds put forward in support of this contention. I agree with the submission made by Mr. Geoghegan on behalf of the County Council that the claim for compensation is open to serious criticism insofar as compliance with the requirements of the relevant Regulations made under Section 67 of the Act of 1963 is concerned.

Regulations 49 of the Local Government (Planning and Development) Regulations, 1977 (N.I. No. 65 of 1977) requires that every claim for compensation under Part VI of the Act of 1963 shall be made to the planning authority in writing and shall include (inter alia) –

(a) a statement of the matter in respect of which compensation is claimed and of the amount of such compensation

(b) a statement of the name and address of the claimant and of the interest held by him in the land to which the claim relates.

A claim arises under Section 55 when, as a result of a decision involving a refusal of permission to develop land, the value of an interest of any person existing in the land to which the decision relates at the time of the decision is reduced. Subject to the other provisions of the Act, the claim is to be paid by way of compensation the amount of such reduction in value.   .

The application to Kildare County Council was for permission to carry out works of development on a small tract of land involving only the laying of a sewage pipe-line to link up with another pipe-line to be constructed on other extensive lands of the applicants in County Dublin, and to connect up with the main sewer at Leixlip, Co. Kildare at its other extremity. The 'land to which the decision relates' within the meaning of the Section was the lands of the applicants known as Toll House, Leixlip Bridge, County Kildare, comprising some 0.3 acres. If a claim for compensation arose against Kildare County Council under Section 55 of the Act of 1963, it was in relation to the reduction in value of those lands, subject to a possible additional claim for injurious affection to the other lands of the applicants at Cooldrinagh in the County of Dublin. The application for compensation should have been so expressed, but while it refers to the refusal of planning permission by An Bord Pleanala in respect of the applicants' lands in Co. Kildare, the claim for compensation is not expressed as relating to a reduction in value in the Co. Kildare lands, but as relating to the lands at Cooldrinagh, Co. Dublin. With a considerable degree of hesitation I would be prepared to regard it as a claim for compensation based on the refusal of planning permission in respect of the lands in County Kildare and as including claims for a reduction in value of the said lands, and for injurious affection in respect of other lands of the applicants at Cooldrinagh, Co. Dublin, (if allowable).

For reasons already indicated in the course of this judgement, I condiser that the arbitrator was correct in refusing to decline jurisdiction on the basis that a claim for compensation was excluded by the provisions of Section 56(1)(*b*) of the Act of 1963. I do not consider that the decision of An Bord Pleanala to refuse permission should be regarded as having been based on any existing deficiency in the provision of sewerage facilities and the period within which any such deficiency might reasonably be expected to be made good. It was based, rather, on the fact that Kildare County Council were unwilling to allow a connection from the Cooldrinagh development to the main sewer at Leixlip because the capacity of that sewer for the foreseeable future was required to be retained by them to service projected building development in their own area of jurisdiction.

2. Section 68 of the Act of 1963 provides as follows:

> '68. A claim under this Act for payment of compensation shall in default of agreement, be determined by arbitration under the Act of 1919 in the like manner in all respects as if such claim arose in relation to the compulsory acquisition of land, but subject to the proviso that the arbitrator shall have jurisdiction to make a nil award.'

Section 2 of the Acquisition of Land (Assessment of Compensation) Act, 1919, lays down a number of rules to be applied by an official arbitrator in assessing compensation under the Act. Rule (2) provides that the value of land shall, generally speaking, be taken to be the amount which a willing seller might expect to realise on the open market, but Rule (6) goes on to say that 'the provisions of Rule (2) shall not affect the assessment of compensation for disturbance or any other matter not directly based on the value of land.'

The Rules comprised in Section 2 of the Act of 1919 have been added to by Section 69 of the Planning Act of 1963 and the 4th Schedule of that Act. One of the added Rules is Rule (16) which provides that in the case of land incapable of reasonably beneficial use which is purchased by a planning authority under section 29 of the Act of 1963, the compensation shall be the value of the land exclusive of any allowance for disturbance or severance. The argument put forward on behalf of the developers was that as claims under section 29 were expressly deprived of a disturbance or severance factor, it should be inferred that it was to be included in respect of claims under Section 55; furthermore that Rule (6) in Section 2 of the Acquisition of Land (Assessment of Compensation) Act, 1919 enables such a claim to be brought in when compensation is to be assessed in accordance with the provisions of that Act.

The contrary argument put forward by Mr. Geoghegan was to the following effect. The Rules contained in Section 2 of the Act of 1919 do not confer any new right of compensation but merely provide the procedure for measuring the compensation to be awarded under the provisions of some other statute. Where a statutory provision for the award of compensation in respect of acquisition of land or diminution of an interest in land incorporates the provisions of the Lands Clauses Acts this, in turn, gives rise to an entitlement to claim for injurious affection to other lands, but unless the statute creating the right to receive compensation does so expressly or by incorporating other statutory provisions which do so, such right is not created merely by incorporating the procedures laid down by the Act of 1919.[77a]

It appears to me that this is a correct reading of the situation. The position is stated as follows in *Halsbury's Laws of England*, 3rd Edn. Vol. 10 at p. 147:

> 'When part of an owner's land is taken, he may suffer damage in consequence of the injury thereby caused to his remaining land. It may, for instance, be cut into two parts, as when a road is made through an estate, or the alteration in its size or shape may render it less suitable for the purposes to which it is or could be applied. . . .
> 'Whether the owner is entitled to compensation for this damage depends, as in the case of compensation under other heads, on the provisions of the special Act and other enactments incorporated therewith. Under the Lands Clauses Acts the owner of land taken is entitled to compensation for damage sustained by him by reason of such severing, or otherwise injuriously affecting his other lands.'

And at pp. 96–98, dealing with the purpose and effect of the Acquisition of Land (Assessment of Compensation) Act, 1919:

> 'That Act provided a set of rules for the assessment of compensation, which the official arbitrator was required to follow, whether the statute authorising the compulsory purchase was passed before or after 19th August, 1919.
> 'Rule 2 reversed the old sympathetic hypothesis of the unwilling seller and willing buyer which underlay judicial interpretation of the Lands Clauses Acts, and the purpose of rule 6 is generally to prevent misconception as to the scope of the alteration effected by rule 2 in the previous judicial basis for ascertaining the market value to the owner of the land sold and in particular to forestall the argument that a willing seller must in law be presumed to have moved out voluntarily to give vacant possession to the buyer. Rule 6 confers no new right to compensation nor does it purport to give statutory validity to every pre-1919 judicial determination on the subject of disturbance.'

I conclude, therefore, that when compensation for injurious affection of other land is claimed the jurisdiction to award compensation on such basis must be sought elsewhere than in the provisions of the Acquisition of Land (Assessment of Compensation) Act, 1919, and it does not appear to me that it arises in relation to a claim for compensation under Section 55 of the Act of 1963 as I can find no indication in that Section or elsewhere that the provisions of the Lands Clauses Acts are to apply in relation to any such claim. This means that, in my opinion, the second question in the Case Stated should be answered in the negative.

3. Having regard to the conclusions I have already reached in relation to the applicability of Section 24 of the Public Health (Ireland) Act, 1878, it cannot be said that the decision of the Minister for Local Government dated the 14th March, 1977 is inoperative, but the extent to which effect can be given to the development permission thereby granted has yet to be decided. If and when an application is made to Kildare County Council to permit a connection to be made between the proposed development at Cooldrinagh and the main sewer at Leixlip, in accordance with a

---

[77a] The effect of Section 1 of the Lands Clauses Consolidation Act, 1845, seems not to have been considered.

claim of right made by the developer under the provisions of Sec. 24 of the Act of 1878. Kildare County Council will have to decide whether they wish to dispute the existence of any such right, or whether they are prepared to concede its existence in principle, and to lay down terms and conditions on which it may be exercised. These, in turn, if considered unreasonable by the developer, could be made the subject of an application to Court, or to an arbitrator appointed under the Act, to achieve a settlement of such dispute. It was suggested by Vice-Chancellor Malins in the passage already cited from his judgment in the *Newington Local Board Case* that it would be open to a sanitary authority under similar circumstances to those obtaining in the present case to impose terms limiting the number of houses that could be permitted to connect to the system, as well as requiring payment in respect of whatever number were allowed the connection. I do not commit myself to saying that the imposition of such a condition would be permissible under the Section but it is obviously something that Kildare County Council would consider very seriously if faced with an application from a large-scale development in an adjoining county. While the position of the developers and of the County Council under Sec. 24 remains in this condition of relative obscurity it is only possible to answer Question 3 of the Case Stated with a qualified 'Yes'.

4. This question is framed in terms which are not completely clear to me. It may suffice to repeat what has already been decided in the course of this judgment, namely, that the Claimant has, in my opinion, a *prima facie* right under Section 24 of the Act of 1878 to require Kildare County Council to grant permission for the connecting up of the sewer from the Cooldrinagh development with the main sewer at Leixlip, subject to the imposition of such terms and conditions as may be agreed, or as may, in default of agreement, be determined by the Court or by arbitration.

An apparent difficulty which faces the developers stems from the fact that no houses have as yet been built at Cooldrinagh, nor has any part of the sewer leading from the development to the main sewer at Leixlip been constructed. In *Faber* v. *Gosforth UDC* (1903) 67 JP 197, a state of affairs very similar to that which has arisen in the present case existed. An owner of land proposed to lay out some of it for building and gave notice to the authority of an adjoining district of his intention to connect his proposed sewer with their sewer. The authority objected, and stated that if he insisted on arbitration, they would appoint an arbitrator under protest, and raise their objection at every stage of the proceedings. He thereupon commenced an action claiming a declaration of his right to connect. Eady J. expressed himself unwilling to make the order sought. He stated:

> 'Here the plaintiffs have not proceeded with the contemplated work, no portion of the estate is yet built on, and no drains or sewers have been constructed. I am asked to declare that no matter what the result may be of connecting the sewers shown on the plan with the defendants' sewers, the plaintiffs have the absolute right to connect. The scheme is extensive, and no doubt if it is carried out, a considerable volume of sewage will be sent down. But not a brick has been laid, and no step has been taken towards the construction of the sewers, and I am not prepared to make the declaration asked for under the circumstances. It is inexpedient to give a judgment which might hamper an arbitrator, or a court of summary jurisdiction, without any evidence as to what the effect would be of the work being carried out. It is suggested that the construction of a new sewer by the defendants might be necessary. It seems exceedingly difficult to make a declaration 'whatever the result may be, the plaintiff has this legal right to connect',

and to say that I must now so determine irrespective of consequences. I am of opinion that it is not proper in the present case that I should exercise the jurisdiction given by Order XXV, r. 5. It is still open to the plaintiffs to go to arbitration, or to apply to a court of summary jurisdiction as to the terms on which they can cause any sewer or drain they may construct to connect with the defendants' sewer, and if on any such occasion any question of law arises, it can be determined.'

Since that judgment was delivered, however, the usefulness of the declaratory judgment has been more widely recognised, and the Courts have been willing to entertain such claims where it was necessary to do justice between the parties. Certainly, in a case such as the present, I think it would be unreasonable to hold that a developer must develop his lands and go to the expense of building his houses before having his right of access to the sewage disposal system determined.

5. This question may also be answered by referring again to the finding already made of a *prima facie* entitlement on the part of the claimant to seek to discharge sewarage from the proposed development at Cooldrinagh to the treatment works at Leixlip.

6. The answer to this question would appear to be governed by the possible imposition of conditions by Kildare County Council if a connection with the Leixlip main sewer is permitted at any time in the future. If a condition were sought to be imposed limiting the period during which such connection could be allowed to continue, the validity of such condition and its reasonableness would initially fall for determination, in case of dispute, by a court of summary jurisdiction or by an arbitrator appointed in accordance with the provisions of Section 24 of the Act of 1878.

Conclusion

To summarise the foregoing, and by way of general guidance to the arbitrator who has submitted the Case Stated for the opinion of the High Court, it appears to me that the application for compensation which has been brought under Section 55 of the Planning Act of 1963 is premature by reason of the failure of the developers to assert and exhaust any rights which may be open to them, and which appear to be open to them, under the provisions of Section 24 of the Public Health (Ireland) Act, 1878, and that while this situation continues it is not possible to determine either the validity of the claim for compensation under Section 55 of the Act of 1963, or the amount of compensation which should be awarded if a valid claim exists under the Act.

HOLIDAY MOTOR INNS LIMITED V. DUBLIN COUNTY COUNCIL
(Unreported: Judgment of McWilliam J. delivered 20 December, 1977.
Record No. 1977 No. 336 S.S.)

Rule 11 was also considered in this case in the following way. The relevant lands were situate close to the new Stillorgan by-pass which at the time of the service of the Notice to Treat was almost complete but not in actual use. The planning authority argued that until the road was actually completed the land over which it was to run should be treated as subject to a reservation for a particular purpose in the Development Plan so that the assessment of the compensation should be on the basis that the arbitrator should by virtue of Rule 11 ignore the presence of the road.

On behalf of the claimant it was urged that once the work was completed or practically completed the reservation in the Development Plan was irrelevant and the assessment should be made in the light of the reality that the road was almost complete and about to be commissioned. Judge McWilliam held in favour of the claimant's contention.

A further argument was made to the effect that whilst there was a statutory rate of interest payable under the Housing Act, 1966, if as in this case, the rate was less than a commercial rate the difference represented an item of loss to the claimant in respect of which he was entitled to be compensated. The Judge held against this contention.

The claimant, thirdly, contended that it was entitled to be paid the costs of objecting to the confirmation of the Compulsory Purchase Order by the Minister. The Judge also rejected this proposition.

McWilliam J.:
Three questions are submitted for my opinion, they are as follows:
1. Whether, in determining the market value of the land acquired, regard should be had to the fact that the new Stillorgun By-pass was nearing completion at the time of service of the notice to treat.
2. Whether compensation should be awarded to the Claimants in respect of loss to them due to the rate of interest payable under the Housing Act, 1966, being less than the commercial rate of interest ruling at the date of entry on the lands.
3. Whether the Claimants are entitled to compensation in respect of costs and expenses incurred by them in objecting to the confirmation of the compulsory purchase order made in respect of the land.

The compensation to be awarded to the claimants must be assessed in accordance with the provisions of the Acquisition of Land (Assessment of Compensation) Act, 1919. Section 2 of that Act set out six rules to be observed by an arbitrator upon an assessment under the Act. Section 69 of the Local Government (Planning and Development) Act, 1963, added ten rules, numbered (7) to (16), to the six rules set out in section 2 of the 1919 Act. These ten additional rules are set out in the Fourth Schedule to the 1963 Act.

On the first question in the case stated, my attention has been directed to Rule (11) in section 2 of the 1919 Act. This rule provides that regard shall not be had to any depreciation or increase in value attributable to – (a) the land, or any land in the vicinity thereof, being reserved for any particular purpose in a development plan. Under section 84(1)(*b*) of the 1966 Act the value of the land is to be assessed as at the date of service of the notice to treat. The notice to treat was dated 14th April, 1975, and I assume that it was served on that date or shortly afterwards. At this time the adjoining new Stillorgan By-pass was almost completed although it had not yet been opened to the public. The land on which the By-pass was constructed had been reserved for that purpose in the 1972 Development Plan for County Dublin.

On behalf of the claimant it is urged that, once the work was completed or practically completed, it is irrelevant whether the land had been reserved for the purpose of that work in a development plan or not, and that the position must be examined at the time of the service of the notice to treat. On behalf of the County Council it is urged that, until the new road was actually completed the land on which it was to run must be treated as still subject to the reservation in the development plan. Various passages from the judgment of Budd, J., in the case of

Deansrath Investments [1974] I.R. 228 were cited to me in support of both arguments and I was referred to several of the decisions cited in that case.

The *Deansrath Case* was a decision on Rule (13) inserted in section 2 of the 1919 Act. This rule provides that no account shall be taken (in assessing compensation) of the existence of proposals for the development of the land acquired or any other land by a local authority, and the Supreme Court decided that this rule did not prevent account being taken of proposed or possible development by other persons. This and the other cases cited do not give very much assistance with regard to the point before me now, except that they emphasise that the compensation payable is intended to be the full value of the property to the claimant on all grounds except those specifically excluded by the statute.

Had the claimants' land not been acquired until long after the by-pass had been completed and opened to the public, it seems to me that Rule (11) could not have had any application as the development would have been completed and a situation would have arisen where the plan could have no further application to the land. It also appears to me that, had the land not been acquired for the by-pass or had work not been commenced on it, the land would still have been subject to the development plan so that the rule would apply. It is difficult to say at what exact point between these two extremes land would cease to become subject to a development plan but I am of opinion it would be at the earliest stage at which there was no reasonable possibility of the work being discontinued. The ascertainment of this stage must present considerable difficulty in many cases but, in the present case, the work was all but complete at the time of the notice to treat and I am of opinion that the claimants are entitled to have their compensation fixed on the basis that the road was there and not on the basis that land was reserved by the development plan for the purpose of a road.

On the second question submitted, I was referred again to a number of cases deciding that a claimant is entitled to full compensation for all loss resulting from the compulsory acquisition, and, in particular, to the cases of *Metropolitan Board of Works* v. *McCarthy* (1874) 7 H.L. 243 and *Harvey* v. *Crawley Development Corporation* [1957] 1 Q.B. 485. I was also referred to the judgments of the Supreme Court in the case of *Murphy* v. *Dublin Corporation*[78] delivered on the 29th July 1977, in which it was decided that the correct rate of interest was what is described as the 'floating rate' and not the statutory rate of 5%. It is accepted by the claimants that this is the correct rate of interest but it is claimed that the Arbitrator should have compensated the claimants for the difference between the 'floating rate' and the commercial rate of interest when making his award of compensation. None of the cases cited has given any support to such a claim and I cannot accept that, where the legislature has declared a rate of interest on purchase money, an arbitrator is entitled effectively to increase this rate to the commercial rate by increasing the amount of the purchase price for this purpose.

Finally, on the question of costs of opposing the compulsory purchase order, the case is made on behalf of the claimants that this is a loss flowing from the acquisition and that these costs should therefore be allowed. I agree that these costs would not have been incurred except for the compulsory acquisition but I do not accept that they are part of the costs of the acquisition. These costs were incurred in a form of litigation by a person opposing a claim on the basis of being entitled to succeed in the proceedings. In this case it was decided that the claimants were

---

[78] Now reported at [1979] I.R. 115.

wrong and had no sufficient grounds for opposing the acquisition and I cannot see any sound reason why the claimants should be allowed the costs of their mistaken course of action as part of the costs of the acquisition.

KILBEGGAN PROPERTY INVESTMENT COMPANY LIMITED V. DUBLIN COUNTY COUNCIL
(Unreported judgment of Gannon J. delivered 18th April, 1977)

In assessing compensation in a Section 29 (Compulsory Purchase) case no award is made on account of disturbance or severance (Rule 16).

The claimant owned some 29.8 acres adjoining a public road and applied for planning permission for the 19.8 acres nearest the road. He was refused. The remaining ten acres were cut off from access to the road by the lands the subject of the application. No compensation being allowable for severance, the claimant made the case that the front land enjoyed an increment of value over and above its market value in that it held the key to the development of the back land and that this increment of value should be taken into account in assessing the compensation payable. Gannon J. ruled against this argument, noting in the course of his judg-ment that it was the claimant who designated the area to be acquired in that the claimant selected the portion of land comprising the site in the planning application and also it seemed that all parts of the entire holding of 29.8 acres enjoyed unrestricted access to the road immediately before the relevant decision; the value to be taken is the value of the lands to the owner at the time of the relevant decision. No severance occurred before acquisition: the increment of value claimed arose only on severance of the land which did not exist before acquisition. The Judge also took into account that the claim was 'in reality an endeavour to recover indirectly compensation for disturbance or severance affecting the retained land by diminution of its value notwithstanding that such compensation is expressly pre-cluded by Rule 16 . . .'.

Gannon J.:

Upon these admitted facts it is submitted by the claimants that the value of the retained 10 acres and the potential for its development is dependant upon the co-operation of the owner of the 19.8 acres. It is contended that the 19.8 acres has a special value of interest to any intending purchaser, in the control that can be exercised over the use of the 10 acres by imposing conditions and requiring money payment for the granting of access over the 19.8 acres to the public road. The claimants expressly disclaim any compensation for diminution of the value of the retained 10 acres by reason of the deprivation of access to the public road upon the purchase or acquisition of the 19.8 acres.

Upon the admitted facts it is contended by the respondents, the County Council, that no such factor of control by one part of the claimants' lands over the other part exists in the lands unless and until the claimants make a division of a nature which creates the potential for such control. It is further contended that this division creating such potential does not and will not take effect unless or until such part of the lands are purchased or acquired as will cause a deprivation to the retained portion. It is submitted for the respondents that this additional value factor is not an element of value of the lands to the claimants though it may become an element of value to a purchaser after acquisition. It is further submitted that the claim is in reality an endeavour to recover indirectly compensation for disturbance or severance affecting the retained land by diminution of its value notwithstanding that such compensation is expressly precluded by Rule 16. . . .

When land is the subject of a compulsory purchase its area, location and limitations, are normally chosen and defined by the body or authority intending to acquire it. Unlike land the subject of a compulsory purchase under statutory powers the land being acquired by the respondents, of which the market value falls to be assessed for compensation by the arbitrator, in this case is a portion of land designated by the claimants. This situation arises under the provisions of section 29 of the Local Government (Planning and Development) Act 1963 which was invoked by the claimants subsequent to a refusal by the Minister on appeal of an application to the Planning Authority for outline planning permission. The sub-sections of section 29 most pertinent to the questions submitted appear to be sub-sections (1) and (4). Sub-section (1) of section 29 is as follows:

'Where, in a case determined on an appeal under this part of this Act, permission to develop any land has been refused or has been granted subject to conditions, then, if the owner of the land claims – (a) that the land has become incapable of reasonably beneficial use in its existing state, and (b) that the land cannot be rendered capable of reasonably beneficial use by the carrying out of any other development for which permission has been granted under this Part of this Act, or for which the planning authority have undertaken to grant such permission, and (c) in a case where permission to develop the land was granted as aforesaid subject to conditions that the land cannot be rendered capable of reasonably beneficial use by the carrying out of the permitted development in accordance with those conditions, he may, at any time within the period of six months after the decision (or such longer period as the Minister may allow), serve on the planning authority a notice (hereafter in this section referred to as a purchase notice) requiring the planning authority to purchase his interest in the land in accordance with the provisions of this section'.

Sub-section (4) of section 29 is as follows:

'Where a purchase notice is served on a planning authority under this section and the authority propose to serve on the owner a notice in accordance with paragraph (b) of subsection (2) of this section, they shall transmit a copy of that notice and copy of the purchase notice to the Minister, and subject to the following provisions of this section the Minister shall, if he is satisfied that the conditions specified in paragraphs (a) to (c) or paragraphs (a) and (b) (as may be appropriate) of sub-section (1) of this section are fulfilled, confirm the purchase notice, and thereupon it shall be the duty of the planning authority to acquire the interest of the owner, and for that purpose – (a) the planning authority shall serve on the owner a notice stating that they propose to comply with the purchase notice, (b) the notice so served shall have the like effect as if it were a compulsory purchase order in respect of that interest which, consequent upon a decision by the Planning Authority pursuant to sub-section (1) of section 10 of the Local Government (No. 2) Act 1960, had been duly made and confirmed.'

Sub-section (4) continues with certain provisos that are of no significance in regard to the question for consideration.

In the absence of agreement as to the compensation to be paid for the acquisition of the claimants' interest in the 19.8 acres of land the subject of the purchase notice the assessment of the amount of such compensation fell to be determined by the arbitrator by whom this case is stated. He has made an assessment of the amount of the compensation in respect of the claimants' interest in the 19.8 acres without regard to the factor of its position between the 10 acres retained and the public road to which there is no access from such 10 acres otherwise than through or over the 19.8 acres. He proposes to assess the amount of an additional sum in respect of the value factor as contended for by the claimants if advised by this Court that such factor is a valid and permissible element in assessing the market value of the claimants' interest in the lands to be acquired by the respondents.

It is evident from the terms of section 29 of the 1963 Act that in assessing the value of the claimants' interest in the lands the same principles which apply in cases of compulsory acquisition are to be applied. In this context it would be helpful to quote from the judgment of Mr. Justice Budd in *Deansrath Investments Limited* [1974] I.R. 228 giving the judgment of the Supreme Court in that matter which was concerned with a compulsory purchase. It is sufficient to refer to, without quoting, the extracts from Fletcher Moulton L.J. in *Lucas* v. *Chesterfield Gas and Water Board* [1909] 1 K.B. 16 and from Lord Dunedin expressing the advice of the Privy-Council in *Cedars Rapids Manufacturing and Power Company* v. *Lacoste* [1914] A.C. 569 which are quoted by Mr. Justice Budd in his judgment. By way of adopting these opinions and the application of the principles therein Mr. Justice Budd says at page 240:

'What emerges from the portions of the two judgments above cited is reasonably clear. The value to be taken is the value to the owner before the date of the taking and not the value to the taker. The value to the owner is to be the market value or full price of the lands. Further, every element of value which the land has and all the advantages which that land possesses, present and future, are to be taken into consideration in assessing the value to the owner; but it is the present value of such advantages and elements of value to the owner that the land possesses as it stood before the acquisition that is to be taken into consideration and has to be determined in arriving at the full market value of the land. These two cases were decided before the passing of the Act of 1919 but the same principles were applied in a number of cases in which section 2 of that Act was the governing section, that is to say, that the value of the land under Rule 2 of section 2 of the Act of 1919 should be taken to be (subject as thereinafter provided) the amount which the land, if sold in the open market, might be expected to realise with all the advantages the land possesses, but that it was the present value of such advantages that was to be taken into consideration in ascertaining the market value. It would seem to me that the broad principles upon which the valuation of lands compulsorily acquired is to be assessed were laid down correctly in these cases, and I would agree with the learned trial Judge that in the absence of Irish authority they should be applied in this country.'

In estimating market value regard must be had to the disadvantages as well as to the advantages and thus determine the value to the owner of the property at the time of acquisition. It seems to me that the difficulty encountered in the application of these principles to the present case derives from the nature of the interest of the claimant in the lands. Under section 29 of the 1963 Act the respondents must 'acquire the interest of the owner' and it is this interest which must be valued with all its advantages and disadvantages, which are elements of value as it stands before acquisition.

I am not aware of whether the lands retained, namely the 10 acres, and the land to be acquired, namely the 19.8 acres, are physically divided from each other or are of their nature clearly distinguishable as to their use and potential for development. But it seems to me to be a necessary inference from the admitted facts that in their ordinary and regular use the 10 acres enjoy free and uninterrupted access to the public road for all purposes without any limitation over and through the 19.8 acres. If the 29.8 acres are a single unit, as the admitted facts seem to imply, each and every part of it bears in relation to any other undivided part all the same advantages and disadvantages in the hands of the one owner. Every part of it under such ownership must submit to all the burdens necessarily incidental to the effective enjoyment of the advantages of every other part. No farmer or land owner having a holding of land to which he has ready access would so divide his holding and dispose of part of it in such a manner as would deprive himself of all access to a retained portion without expressly reserving rights of access over the part of which he might dispossess himself. In doing so he would not be creating something new in the characteristics of the land but he would, in the circumstances of separate titles to parts of an undivided unit, be making provision for the preservation of the existing characteristics by creating co-relative rights and duties.

It is such characteristics which determine the nature of the interest of the land owner at the time of any intended purchase or acquisition; and that is the interest which falls to be valued, not the interest which may be found to exist after the purchase or acquisition has reached completion. On the facts as admitted before me I am of opinion that the interest of the claimants in the 19.8 acres to be acquired is subject to the burden of all rights of access from the public road to the 10 acres intended to be retained which may be necessary or pertinent to the user and potential development of the retained lands in the ownership of the claimants. The extent and nature of the burdens relative to the 10 acres to which the 19.8 acres must submit as characteristic of the claimants' interest in the latter are matters on which the arbitrator may require to hear evidence.

It is my opinion that the contentions of the claimants in this Court are based on a misconception of the nature of the interest to be valued and are not well founded. My reply to the question submitted is that the interest to be valued includes every element of disadvantage as well as of advantage, and the value factor contended for on behalf of the claimants is inconsistent with the nature of their interest before acquisition in the 19.8 acres intended to be acquired. Nevertheless the arbitrator may, and if he considers it advisable should, hear evidence to determine the nature of the interest to be valued of the claimants as existing before acquisition in the light of the foregoing opinion which is based on the admitted facts. In particular he may require to determine all necessary facts pertinent to the question of the position of the area of land intended to be acquired relative to the other contiguous land in the ownership and possession of the claimants which other land is separated from the public road by the land being acquired and as also in the ownership and possession of the claimants.

IGNATIUS BYRNE V. DUBLIN COUNTY COUNCIL
[1983] I.L.R.M. 213

Despite the ineptitude of Section 57 of the 1963 Act (which provides for an undertaking by a planning authority to grant planning permission in the context of a compensation claim) and given that the function of the court is to give effect to statutory provisions in a sensible manner where the intent is clear, an undertaking given pursuant to Section 57 to grant permission for the 'construction of hotels, theatres or structures for the purpose of entertainment or any combination thereof. . .' in respect of 65 acres of land at Portmarnock, Co. Dublin was an effective undertaking for the purposes of the section in this case where outline planning permission for a housing development and car park had been refused. The purpose of the compensation provisions is to compensate for such loss as flows from the relevant decisions neither more nor less, and where an effective undertaking is given under Section 57 an alternative form of development is available for the lands and precludes the payment of compensation.

The court rejected an argument by the claimant to the effect that the undertaking to grant must have been in existence at the same time as the grant of permission for which it would provide an alternative, must have been preceded by a decision reached in accordance with prescribed procedures, must specify the land to which it relates, the development for which permission will be given and the person in response to whose application it has been given, and must be capable of being acted upon in terms and in a manner consistent with the (other) statutory requirements. Principles in *Owenabue Ltd.* v. *Dublin County Council*[79] applied.

Gannon J.:

. . . .Mr. Ignatius Byrne, to whom I will refer as the claimant, is a farmer and the lands to which this case stated refers have been and are being used by for farming and the permitted user is agricultural in character. The development he proposed, for which permission has been refused, is of a residential character and consists wholly or mainly of the construction of houses with extensive ancillary car parking area which could be capable of use of a commercial character. Following the refusal of the permission and the appeal he still has his land which presumably he continues to farm. He claims compensation by way of money payment as recompense for the loss or deprivation of a potential use of his land. He does not claim that he has been deprived of all use of his land. His claim is that the value of his land as an asset capable of being realised now or at some future date has been diminished by the restriction placed on its potential use by the effect of the refusal of a permission to develop it in a manner for which it has a capacity and potential. His claim is not a claim for permission to use his land in a particular manner. Having been refused the planning permission which he sought he does not now request an alternative permission for development; not does he seek a declaration as to what form of development would, as an alternative, be acceptable for a planning permission. He does not admit that any such alternative is available or obtainable. As claimant under Section 55 of the 1963 Act he maintains that his farm lands have a potential for use in the character and manner of development for which he sought and was refused planning permission, and that by reason of the refusal they now have no value other than as farm lands. The value he puts on the reduction of value from lands having a potential for a development of a residential character to lands of merely agricultural character is £2,437,000.

The Dublin County Council, to whom I shall refer as the planning authority, by whom the pertinent Development Plan has been adopted is the body upon whom is the obligation to pay compensation by way of recompense for any such loss of value of the land as may be determined in accordance with the Local Government

[79] See p. 420.

(Planning and Development) Acts. When presented with such a claim the planning authority are bound by their own decision that the land may not be developed in the manner for which planning permission has been refused. Subject to their development plan and the objectives indicated therein the planning authority are bound to accept that the land has the capacity and potential for use by a development of the character the subject of the refusal of permission which gives rise to the claim. They must also accept that the claimant will continue to retain the lands and to have the use thereof of the nature from which permitted change of user was sought on the planning permission application. They must also accept that the claimant does not request an alternative permission for development but they are not bound to, and do not, admit that the land has no other capacity or potential for use other than of an agricultural character. In opposing the claim for compensation the planning authority maintain that the value of the land is not confined solely to its use for agricultural purposes, but that it has a capacity and potential for development by change of use to use of a character for which planning permission is obtainable or available under the Local Government (Planning and Development) Acts. If the land has, as they contend, a capacity and potential for development of a character which is of the nature of or similar to that for which planning permission has been refused the value has not been diminished. On the basis that compensation is not payable as recompense for deprivation of one potential development if and when another reasonably similar potential development is available the planning authority has produced to the arbitrator the undertaking cited so as to show that such alternative potential development is available. They undertake to grant planning permission for 'some such development' as comes within the terms of Section 57 of the 1963 Act. They do not grant planning permission, nor do they place any obligation on the claimant to apply for planning permission. The undertaking to grant permission for some such development does not initiate a planning application, nor any of the procedures related to such an application. It arises only in the context of an assessment of the amount of alleged diminution of value occasioned by a refusal of planning permission.

As a matter of general principles it may be said that compensation by a money payment is a legal remedy by way of recompense for a loss sustained involuntarily, most usually by a wrongful act, but also, as in this case, by an act made lawful which otherwise might derogate from the constitutional protection of personal rights. No money payment may be made where there is no loss sustained, nor where the loss, if any, has not, or is not capable of having, a money value. Where the loss is not immediate, but can reasonably be expected to be sustained in some probable future time, and where money value on such anticipated loss can be assessed a payment may be made. When an immediate payment is made in recompense for an anticipated future loss allowance should be made for the acceleration of payment of money for a loss not yet incurred and also for the risk or possibility that the loss may never ocur.

Section 55, which provides that a person having an interest in land at the time when a decision was made refusing him permission to develop his land may recover as compensation the amount of the reduction in value of his interest in the land caused by the decision, is in accord with the general principles. In the following respects the section accords with the general principle that the loss must be ascertainable and the compensation must not exceed the value of the actual loss. The section provides that if the decision is to grant permission subject to conditions – other than stated excluded conditions – the claimant may be compensated in respect of what he has to the extent of the diminished value caused by the imposition of such conditions, but in valuing what he has allowance would have to be made for the permission granted. In determining the value of the land as retained following the decision regard must be had under Section 55(2) for the value of developments of the land for which no permission would be required (e.g. exempted developments) and of any development requiring permission for the grant of which if applied for an undertaking might be given. Sub-section (3) of Section 55 provides that in a case of refusal of permission (unlike a case of a grant subject to conditions) it must be assumed, in determining the value of the interest of the claimant in the land without permission (namely what he has), that no permission will be granted for any development. However, this provision is expressed to be subject to or 'apart from any such undertaking as is mentioned in sub-section (2)'. It would seem to follow from the provisions of sub-section (3) of Section 55 that, in ease of the claimant permission to develop whose land has been refused, in calculating the value of what he has after the decision no allowance may be made for any possible alternative future development. The undertaking mentioned in paragraph (b) of sub-section (2) of Section 55 would seem therefore to refer to a permission which could be given in relation to matters ancillary to the use of the land as retained following the decision. These provisions are expressed to be 'in determining reduction of value for the purposes of this section', and it seems unnecessary to prescribe in the statute that the reduction of value should be assessed by calculating the difference between the value of the affected interest in the land as it is after the decision and as it would have been had the decision been to grant the permission as sought. The foregoing is, I believe, in accord with and complementary to what was said by the President in relation to this section in *Owenabue Ltd.* v. *Dublin Co. Council.*[80]

Section 55 declares the fact and circumstances of entitlement to compensation, the person to whom it may be paid, the subject matter of the compensation and the factors for consideration in the calculation of the compensation. Section 57 is expressed in a mandatory form declaring that in the circumstances therein provided 'compensation under Section 55 of this Act shall not be payable'. The mandatory form of Section 57 suggests that no function of assessment or calculation of compensation under Section 55 arises in the circumstances (a) of a refusal of permission consequent upon which compensation has already been paid under Section 55, or (b) of the availability of alternative permission for any of a number of developments of a prescribed character. Accordingly a claimant whose application for planning permission for a development has been refused and who has retained his land and has been paid compensation for the reduction of the value of his interest nevertheless may make an application for planning permission for an alternative development, but may not receive further compensation in the event of a refusal thereof. A further consequential effect of Section 57 is that a claimant whose application for planning permission for a development of a character to which Section 57 applies who has been refused and who has retained his land but without compensation because of the availability of permission for a development to which Section 57 applies may make an application for an alternative develop-

---

[80] Now reported at [1982] I.L.R.M. 150 See p. 420.

ment of the nature for which permission is available. In the event of permission being granted upon such further application, but subject to conditions other than those excluded by Section 55, the claimant would not then be deprived by Section 57 of the compensation to which he may be entitled under section 55. The provisions that compensation may not be payable more than once (see also Section 70) and that none is payable when the claimed reduction in value can be avoided within the application of the Act are consistent with the general principle that recompense by a money payment of compensation will not be given where no actual loss has been sustained. The application of this principle appears to be the purpose of Section 57, and the mischief which is being guarded against is that of retaining the interest in the land with the benefit of and opportunity for development within the scope of the Act and at the same time receiving monetary compensation for loss of such opportunity and benefit.

The applicability of Section 57 to the facts and circumstances of the instant case has given rise to arguments before the arbitrator which induced him to submit the questions in the case stated. At sub-section (4) of Section 57 it is provided that the section applies only to any development which is of a residential character or of a commercial character, or of an industrial character or any combination of these. The sub-section further restricts the application to such development only if it consists wholly or mainly of the construction of houses, flats, shops or office premises, hotels, garages and petrol filling stations, theatres, or structures for the purpose of entertainment, or industrial buildings (including warehouses). The section may be invoked only in cases in which a claimant for compensation under Section 55 has been refused permission to develop his lands as a result of a decision under Part IV of the Act. The prohibition enjoined by Section 57 may be applied only in relation to claims where, notwithstanding the refusal, permission is available for a development of the subject lands of the character and nature mentioned in sub-section (4). In sub-section (3) of Section 57 there is contained what is in effect a purported definition of the expression in sub-section (1) 'there is available with respect to that land permission for development to which this section applies'. Sub-section (3) of Section 57 declares that for the purposes of Section 57 permission for development to which the section applies shall be taken to be available if there is in force a grant of permission or an undertaking to grant permission for some such development to which the section applies. The course of the argument on behalf of the claimant has been to demonstrate that such 'definition' is inept and incapable of being given a meaning consistent with the operation, provisions, and procedures of and prescribed by the Local Government (Planning and Development) Acts, and that consequently there can be no such thing as 'an undertaking' upon which to invoke the operation of Section 57.

The claimant's argument may be summarised as follows. Sections 55 and 57 derive from a 'decision under Part IV of the Act' involving a refusal of permission. A permission, if in existence or in force, must be preceded by a decision made by the Planning Authority in response to an application by a person having an interest in the land sought to be developed. The Planning Authority cannot initiate an application, nor make a decision to grant or refuse permission for which no application has been made. Before a decision can be made procedures must be followed which involve and protect the interests of third parties and proper planning considerations must be applied. Sub-section (3) of Section 57 prescribes as an alternative to a grant of permission an undertaking to grant permission and provides that either must be in force. It was argued that such undertaking to grant to be 'in force' (a) must have been in existence at the same time as the grant of permission for which it would provide an alternative, (b) must have been preceded by a decision reached in accordance with prescribed procedures, (c) must specify the land to which it relates, the development for which permission will be given, and the person in response to whose application it has been given, and (d) must be capable of being acted upon in terms and in a manner consistent with the statutory requirements.

These arguments were submitted with a preliminary admonition that the words of the statute should be given their ordinary meaning with an endeavour to give the statute a sensible construction consistent with its other provisions. It was clearly demonstrated that if the 'undertaking to grant permission' were to be equated to a grant of permission it would not be possible to give the expression a sensible construction consistent with the other provisions and regulations of the Planning Acts. On that basis it has been submitted that the statutory provision is so inept as to be ineffectual and no valid effective undertaking can be given and that the undertaking of the 23rd July, 1981 is ineffective to bring Section 57 into operation in this case.

The demonstration of the ineptitude of the statutory provision has been very impressive. However, I conceive the function of the Court when presented with the statutory requirements of the Oireachtas to be to accept them, inept though they may be, and so far as possible to give them effect in a sensible manner in accordance with the manifest intention of the statute as shown by its provisions. I accept that the application of Section 57 does not arise, as was argued for the Planning Authority, unless and until a claim for compensation under Section 55 has been made. This is clearly the intention of the opening phrase of sub-section (3) of Section 57. Unlike Section 55, which provides for the circumstances requiring and the matters for consideration at an enquiry under Section 68 of the Act, Section 57 is not concerned with enquiries or procedures. As submitted on behalf of the planning authority it is in my view declaratory only of a state of facts which do or do not exist when a claim for payment of compensation has been made. I do not think it is intended that the undertaking to grant permission is to be equated to a grant of permission, nor do I think it is necessary that they should be equated. It seems to me that the use in sub-section (3) of the phrase 'shall be taken to be available' is a means of prescribing the nature of information from which a factual circumstance will be inferred. It is a method of expression used on occasions to give to a hypothetical circumstance the same effect as a factual circumstance. But in this instance the inclusion of the expression 'if there is in force' as used in the sub-section prevents the use of a hypothetical circumstance and suffices to bring together the factual circumstances of a grant of permission previously given in the normal process and the intention expressed in a binding manner to give, if and when so requested, a decision to grant a permission within the limits specified in the sub-section. In my view Section 57 can be construed, despite the demonstrated weakness of expression, and can only be construed as meaning that Section 57 precludes an award of compensation to a claimant, such as in this case, who has land capable of being developed in a manner indicated in sub-section (4) of Section 57 if the Planning Authority expressly states that it undertakes that it will grant permission for some such development.

RE VISCOUNT SECURITIES LIMITED
112 I.L.T.R. 17.

Because of the artificial meaning to the word 'use' (which does not include the use of the land by the carrying out of any works thereon) the scope of Section 56(1)(a) of the 1963 Act is greatly restricted from what it would have been if the ordinary meaning of the word 'use' applied. A proposal to develop agricultural lands as a housing estate did not involve 'the making of any material change in the use of . . . land' within the meaning of the sub-section because of the artificial meaning of the word 'use'. Accordingly compensation was not excluded by the sub-section.

Finlay P.:
This is a special case stated by Owen McCarthy, B.E., B.Sc., C.E.N.G., M.I.E.I., the Property Arbitrator duly nominated to act as Arbitrator between Viscount Securities Limited whom I will hereinafter call the claimants and Dublin County Council whom I will hereinafter call the Planning Authority, to determine the amount of compensation, if any, which should be paid by the Planning Authority to the claimants pursuant to section 55 of the Local Government (Planning and Development) Act, 1963. The facts found on the case stated by the Arbitrator out of which the question for determination by this Court arises may be summarised as follows.

The claimants applied to the Planning Authority for permission to develop certain lands at Kingston, Ballinteer Road, County Dublin the description of the development being the erection of two hundred and eighty-eight four-bedroomed houses. In the planning application for the claimants answered query number 11, which was: 'If application is in respect of a material change of user state,
(a) the present use when last used and
(b) the proposed use'
as respectively 'agricultural' and 'residential'

By a decision dated the 16th of March, 1973, the Planning Authority refused the application for permission upon the following grounds:
(i) That the site was located in an area zoned in the development plan to provide for further development of agriculture and that the development proposed would be in conflict with that objective and would not be in accordance with the proper planning and development of the area.
(ii) The public piped services were not available to serve the proposal.
(iii) That the proposed development would be premature by reason of the existing deficiency in the provision of water supply and sewage facilities.
(iv) That portion of the site was seriously affected by the southern cross route motorway.

Against that decision of the Planning Authority the claimants appealed to the Minister and by a decision dated the 15th day of July 1974 the Minister refused planning permission upon the grounds
1. That the site of the proposed development was located in an area in which it is the policy of the Planning Authority as expressed in their development plan to provide for the further development of agriculture and to provide for recreational open space and ancillary structures and that that objective was considered reasonable and the proposed housing development would be in conflict with it.

2. That portion of the site was seriously affected by land reservations required for the proposed southern cross route motorway.

The claimants then applied to the arbitrator to determine the amount, if any, of compensation which should be paid to them by the Planning Authority pursuant to section 55 of the Local Government (Planning and Development) Act, 1963, by reason of the said refusal of planning permission.

At the hearing before the arbitrator the application for planning permission, the refusal, the appeal and its refusal were proved and it was established and not challenged by the Planning Authority that the value of the claimant's fee simple interest in the land the subject-matter of the application was reduced as a result of the decision of the Planning Authority and of the Minister on appeal. It was further established and agreed before the arbitrator that at the date of the refusal of permission by the Planning Authority the land and the subject-matters of the application was used for the purposes of one private residence and for agriculture. Arising out of these facts the net question submitted to the Court for its opinion at the request of the Planning Authority was whether the arbitrator was precluded from awarding compensation to the claimants for the reduction in value, pursuant to section 55 of the Act of 1963, by virtue of the provisions of sub-section 1(a) of section 56 of that Act.

Section 55 of the Act of 1963 provides that if on a claim made to the Planning Authority it is shown that as a result of a decision under Part IV of the Act involving a refusal of permission to develop land the value of an interest of any person existing in the land to which the decision relates is reduced such a person shall, subject to the provisions of that Part of the Act, be entitled to be paid by the Planning Authority by way of compensation the amount of such reduction in value.

Section 56, (1), (a) of the Act of 1963 provides as follows: 'Compensation under section 55 of this Act shall not be payable (a) in respect of the refusal of permission for any development that consists of or includes the making of any material change in the use of any structures or other land.'

By section 2 of the Act of 1963 use in relation to land does not include the use of the land for the carrying out of any works thereon and works includes any act or operation of construction, excavation, demolition, extension, alteration, repair or renewal. By section 3 of the Act of 1963 development in the Act means, save where the context otherwise requires, the carrying out of any works on, in or under the land or the making of any material change in the use of any structures or other land.

From the documents annexed to the case stated it appears that the area of land involved in the application was 47.55 acres and the simple contention of the Planning Authority is that if 47.55 acres of land which is used for agriculture and contains one single residence only is by reason of a development converted into an area containing two hundred and eighty-eight four-bedroomed houses that that necessarily consists of or at least includes the making of a material change in the use of that land and that it is by reason of that fact alone exempted from compensation by virtue of the provisions of section 56(1), (a). Briefly summarised the contention on behalf of the claimants is that since by virtue of section 2 of the Act of 1963 use in relation to land does not include the use of the land by the carrying out of any works thereon and since the development in respect of which permission was sought consisted of the erection of two hundred and eighty-eight houses all of which would necessarily consist of works then having regard to the artificial meaning of the word 'use' provided for in the Act of 1963 there was not within the meaning of section 56, (1), (a) a development consisting of or including the making of any material change in the use of the land and that accordingly their rights to compensation is not exempted or prohibited by virtue of the provisions of that sub-section. The precise point thus arising has not previously been decided in this country though some assistance towards its decision can be obtained from the judgment of Mr. Justice Kenny in *The Central Dublin Development Association Limited and Ors.* v. *The Attorney General* 109 I.L.T.R. 69.[81] That case, which was a declaratory action brought by the plaintiffs in effect challenging in a broad manner the constitutionality of a number of the provisions of the Act of 1963, involved *inter alia* a consideration of the provisions with regard to compensation contained in that Act. Dealing with that particular aspect of the case the learned Judge stated as follows:

'Part VI deals with compensation. Section 55 provides that the Planning Authority shall be liable to pay compensation to a person the value of whose interest in land has been reduced by a decision under Part IV of the Act refusing permission to develop or granting it subject to conditions. Section 56 excludes compensation in certain cases: Paragraph (a) of sub-section (1) seems at first reading to exclude compensation in almost all cases for it reads 'Compensation under section 55 of this Act shall not be payable (a) in respect of the refusal of permission for any development that consists of or includes the making of any material change in the use of any structures or other land.' But the definition section by providing that use in relation to land does not include the use of the land by the carrying out of any works thereon' limits the wide language of paragraph (a).'

I must construe this part of the judgment of Mr. Justice Kenny as clearly indicating a view that the apparently wide effect of section 56, (1) (a) is substantially restricted or narrowed by reason of the definition of use in section 2 and whilst the learned Judge did not, as it was not necessary for the matter in issue before him to do, decide the precise way in which that narrowing or restriction of the apparent effect of section 56, (1), (a) arose it is at least plausible that the view there expressed by him is a support for the contention of the claimants in this case. Two major questions of principle would appear to me to affect the issues arising before me. The first is that the provisions in general contained in the Act of 1963 entitling a Planning Authority to refuse permission and the Minister on appeal to confirm such refusal or issue in effect a new refusal for the development of land is an invasion or restriction of the full property rights of an owner of land. If, therefore, the legislature intended that such invasion, restriction or reduction of property rights should be enacted without providing compensation in the event of a reduction in value for damage suffered it is a necessary principle of the construction of statutes in accordance with the Constitution that they should have expressly and unambiguously so provided.

The second major question of principle which seems to me to affect this issue is the practical interpretation of sections 55, 56, and 57 of the Act of 1963. Section 55 of that Act constitutes what might be described as a blanket provision for compensation in the event of a refusal of permission to develop land where the owner can establish a diminution in the value of his interest in that land by reason

---

[81] See p. 45.

of the refusal. If the interpretation sought to be placed by the Planning Authority in section 56, (1), (*a*) were valid then combined with the other provisions of section 56 and with the provisions of section 57 (which exclude from the right to compensation owners of an interest in land who have, upon refusal of permission to develop in accordance with an application for permission, been granted, instead, permission for alternative developments) would have the overall effect of making the case in which an owner refused development and suffering a reduction in value in his interest by reason thereof was entitled to compensation a rare or unusual rather than the general case. Such an interpretation of the combined provisions of the three sections referred to would appear to be at variance with the very general nature of the provisions of section 55 providing a right to compensation.

It is clear that looked at from the practical point of view and employing the ordinary or common use of language there is much to be said for the contention of the Planning Authority that to change an area of some 47 acres of land from being used for agricultural purposes to be the site of two hundred and eighty-eight houses is a manifest material change in the user of that land and that a development which has that result must by definition either consist of or at least include a material change in the user of land. This contention seems to me however to ignore the particularly artificial meaning attached to 'use' or 'user' of land by virtue of the definition contained in section 2 which I have already quoted. If I am to give full meaning and effect to this definition as I am bound to do in respect of the provisions of section 56, (1), (*a*) in the same way as it must be given effect in relation to the employment of the word 'use' in any other provision in the Act, then it seems to me that I must, in the application of section 56 (1), (*a*), sharply distinguish between use in its ordinary sense and use which consists of the carrying out of any works on land. There can be no serious contest but that the development in respect of which permission was sought in this case consisted exclusively of the carrying out of works on the land having regard to the definition of works contained in section 2 of the Act. All that was sought to be done was to build two hundred and eighty-eight houses and the ancillary services attached to them and each and every act thus sought to be legitimised consisted either of an act or operation of construction, excavation, extension or demolition.

Although the provisions of section 101, (1) (*a*) of the Town and Country Planning Act, 1962, which is the applicable statute in the United Kingdom is in identical terms to those contained in section 56, (1) (*a*) of the Act of 1963, little assistance is to be obtained from decisions in English law applicable to this topic. The matter was considered in the case of *Overland and Others* v. *The Minister of Housing and Local Government* (1957) 8 P. & C.R. 389. From the report in that case however it would appear that the non-application of the excluding provision to cases where development consisted solely of buildings was conceded by the Minister and that accordingly whereas the decision proceeds upon the basis that that is the meaning of the section it was not something which was argued before the Court. Some of the learned authors dealing with the question of the Planning Law in England have expressed the view that this concession was, *prima facie* at variance with the meaning of the section and that it was desirable that the section should be amended so as to be made consistent with the administrative policy of the Ministry concerned. The decision to which I have referred, however, and the comments of the text books are of little real immediate assistance on the interpretation of the section with which I am concerned.

Whilst to an extent the construction of this sub-section contended for by the claimants is in apparent conflict with the phrase 'consists of or includes the making of any material change in the use' the construction contended for on behalf of the Planning Authority is at even more striking variance with the definition of use contained in section 2. Broadly speaking it seems to me possible to elucidate in particular from the provisions of section 3 of the Act, which defines development, and from the general provisions of the Act two broad categories of development. One consists of works in the sense as defined of building, demolition, extension, alteration, repair or renewal and the second category being a change of user excluding such change as emanates from the act of building, demolition, extension, alteration or repair.

If one accepts these two broad divisions of development, not necessarily always exclusive, and sometimes inevitably overlapping, it is reasonable and consistent with the general provisions of the Act to construe section 56(1), (*a*) as excluding from the right to compensation an owner of land whose development has been refused in respect of the second category namely in the artifical sense the material change of user in the land or structures. The practical effect of such a construction contained in section 55 would not be nullified or attenuated to a minimal extent as would arise if the narrower construction of section 56, (1), (*a*) were made. Furthermore such a construction is in a sense a strict application of a section and sub-section which greatly limits in any event the right of compensation associated with the compulsory deprivation of a right attached to the ownership of property and is accordingly consistent with the proper constitutional approach to the construction of a statute such as this.

I am, accordingly, satisfied that it is the proper construction to apply to this sub-section and that the true meaning of it is that it excludes only from compensation a development consisting of or including a material change in the use of a structure or land other than the carrying out of works on this land. Since it is clear from the documents before me that the only development in respect of which permission was sought in this case exclusively consisted as a matter of fact of the carrying out of works on the land I am satisfied that the answer to the question raised in the case stated before me is that the arbitrator is not precluded from awarding compensation for the reduction in the value of the interest of the claimant pursuant to section 55 of the Act of 1963 by the provisions of sub-section (1), (*a*) of section 56 of that Act.

IN RE MURPHY
[1977] I.R. 243

Two questions were raised by the property arbitrator on a case stated arising out of the assessment of compensation payable on a compulsory acquisition of Mr. Murphy's lands. The acquiring authority had served two Notices to Treat and the question was which one was the effective one? The first was served after the High Court had rejected a challenge by Mr. Murphy to the validity of the Compulsory Purchase Order itself. This decision was subsequently appealed to the Supreme Court and was upheld. Following the Supreme Court decision a second Notice to Treat was served. The relevant statutory provision[82] which applied when there was

---

[82] S. 78(3)(*a*)(ii) of the Housing Act, 1966.

an application to the High Court to quash the Compulsory Purchase Order authorised the service of a Notice to Treat 'on the date of the determination of the
application.' The question was whether the application was 'determined' after the
ruling in the High Court or only after the final ruling in the Supreme Court. On
appeal to the Supreme Court it was decided that the application was determined
once there was a ruling in the High Court.

On the second branch of the case the Supreme Court decided that it is not proper
for an arbitrator to rely on evidence given in other proceedings for the purpose of
proving facts relevant to the arbitration. The lands in question were zoned for the
development of agriculture in the relevant development plan: the Minister for
Local Government (as he then was) confirmed the C.P.O. of the lands for local
authority housing purposes. This would have involved a variation in the zoning of
the land. The report of the Inspector of the public enquiry into objections into the
confirmation of the C.P.O. would have indicated the likelihood of such a variation.
This, if allowable in evidence, would have affected the valuation of the land as it
could have been argued that in the absence of a C.P.O. there was an increased
possibility that the land owner might have succeeded on appeal in getting permission to develop the land for housing purposes. Apart from the general rule that
everything relevant must be proved before the arbitrator, Henchy J. in the Supreme Court held the above argument to be a non-sequitur. He also held that the
arbitrator was debarred by Rule 13 from taking into account any local authority
scheme on the lands whether existing, probable or possible.

Henchy J.:[83]

I. *THE ISSUES*

The land in question here was acquired compulsorily by Dublin Corporation
('the acquiring authority') under the Housing Act, 1966. The relevant compulsory
purchase order was confirmed by the Minister for Local Government on the 7th
January 1969. Thereupon the owner of the land ('the claimant') began proceedings
in the High Court seeking to have the Minister's confirmation of the compulsory
purchase order held bad. Those proceedings terminated in the High Court on the
1st March 1973 with an order holding the compulsory purchase order to have been
validly confirmed. The acquiring authority then served a notice to treat, on the 12th
March 1973, which is the step, required by s. 79(1) of the Housing Act, 1966,
'where a compulsory purchase order confirmed under this Act has become operative and the housing authority decide to acquire land to which the order relates.'

The progress of the compulsory acquisition was interrupted at this stage by the
service on behalf of the claimant on the 20th March 1973 of a notice of appeal to the
Supreme Court against the order of the High Court holding the compulsory
purchase order to have been validly confirmed. It was not until the 5th April 1974
that this appeal was finally determined, when an order was made dismissing the
appeal and thereby affirming the order of the High Court.

The acquiring authority then served another notice to treat on the 12th May
1974, thereby implying that they considered the one served on the 12th March 1973
to have been invalidly served. When the matter came before the arbitrator to fix
compensation for the compulsory acquisition, he stated a case for the High Court
seeking a ruling on two questions:

[83] O'Higgins C.J., Griffin J. concurring.

(1) which of the two notices to treat which were served was the effective one? and

(2) was the arbitrator entitled to have regard to the transcript of the proceedings at the local public inquiry held prior to the confirmation of the compulsory purchase order, for the purpose of assessing the potential value of the land?

The answer given in the High Court to the first question was that it was the second notice to treat that was the effective one. The answer given to the second question was that the arbitrator could have regard to the transcript, but only 'so far as it may indicate that in relation to a proposal by the acquiring authority to develop the lands for residential purposes the Minister was prepared to consent to a departure from the zoning of the lands for agricultural purpose.'

The claimant now appeals against the reply given to the first question, and the acquiring authority has served a notice to vary the reply given to the second question. So both questions are in issue in this appeal.

II. *THE FIRST QUESTION*

It is common ground that, whatever may be the position under other statutes allowing compulsory acquisition of land, the date on which compensation is to be assessed for land compulsorily acquired under the Housing Act, 1966 ('the Act') is the date of the service of the notice to treat: see s. 84(1) of the Act. That date may be of great importance if the market value of land has changed since the compulsory purchase order was confirmed. For example, in the present case because land values were falling, the arbitrator's assessment of the value of the land (without regard to considerations deriving from the transcript) would be £1,107,100 if the date of assessment is the 2nd May 1974 (the date of the second service), whereas it would be £379,400 more if the date of assessment is the 12th March 1974 (the date of the first service).

S. 79(1) of the Act prescribes that when an acquiring authority wish to go ahead with the compulsory acquisition of land, they must serve a notice to treat after the compulsory purchase order made and confirmed under the Act has become operative. If the compulsory purchase order has been confirmed by the Minister and no application is made to the High Court to quash it, it becomes operative twenty-one days after the publication of notice of its confirmation: s. 78(3)(*a*)(i) of the Act. But where, as in the present case, such an application is brought in the High Court, and is unsuccessful, it becomes operative 'on the date of the determination of the application': s. 78(3)(*a*)(ii) of the Act.

The argument on this aspect of the appeal has reduced itself to a debate as to the meaning of the words 'determination of the application' in s. 78(3)(*a*)(ii). Counsel for the acquiring authority says they refer to the final determination in the Supreme Court. If that is correct, the only notice to treat that was correctly served in this case was the second one. Counsel for the claimant, however, says the words 'determination of the application' necessarily refer to the determination in the High Court. If that is so, it follows that the effective notice to treat is the one served first.

The main thing to be noted about s. 78, which is the section that governs this point, is that it envisages two distinct considerations regulating when a notice to treat will have to be served:

(1) when no application is brought in the High Court to quash the compulsory purchase order, and

(2) when such an application is made.

We are concerned here only with (2). If the application so made is withdrawn, the compulsory purchase order becomes operative twenty-one days after the withdrawal: s. 78(3)(a)(i). If the application is not withdrawn, the compulsory purchase order becomes operative when the application is determined against the applicant: s. 78(3)(a)(ii).

In my opinion, that determination necessarily refers to a determination in the High Court. The only court referred to, expressly or by implication, in s. 78 is the High Court. S. 78(2)(a) empowers the High Court to make an interim order suspending the operation of a compulsory purchase order 'until the final determination of the proceedings'. But 'final' there is used in contrast to 'interim' and means simply the final determination of the application in the High Court. When 'final' is used with reference to a judgment, it does not mean a judgment which is not open to appeal, but final as distinguished from interlocutory: per Cozens-Hardy L.J. in *Huntley* v. *Gaskell*.[84] When 'determination of the application' is used in subs. (3)(b) it can have no wider connotation than 'final determination' has in subs. (2)(a), namely final determination in the High Court.

The practical consequences of a contrary conclusion confirm that interpretation. The statute makes no provision for the withdrawal of a notice to treat, or for the service of a second notice to treat. Counsel for the acquiring authority is therefore driven to argue – as logically follows from his interpretation of s. 79 – that where an application is unsuccessfully brought in the High Court to quash a compulsory purchase order, a notice to treat can never be served until, at the earliest, the period allowed for serving a notice of appeal to the Supreme Court has run out. Only then could it be said that the application has been finally determined.

This submission does not bear any close scrutiny. The 'date of the determination' referred to in subs. (3)(ii) must mean the date of a judicial determination. It cannot be equated with a date fixed by rules of court as representing the end of a period within which a notice of appeal may be served against a judicial determination. That is clearly not what the statute says. But even if 'the date of the determination' could be stretched so as to give that meaning, there would be an unworkable situation if an acquiring authority validly served a notice to treat after the period for appealing had expired, and if the claimant was then given an extension of time within which to appeal. Since there is no power given by the Act to undo the valid service of a notice to treat, and since equally there is no power to make a second service of a notice to treat, service of a notice to treat so as to comply with the Act could not be made in such a case after the determination of the appeal in the Supreme Court. Yet it is the contention of counsel for the acquiring authority that whenever an appeal is unsuccessfully taken in the Supreme Court against the disallowance of an application in the High Court to have a compulsory purchase order quashed (as happened here), the date of the determination of the application for the purpose of s. 78(3)(a)(ii) is the date of the determination in the Supreme Court. The example I have given shows that this cannot be so. But, apart from that, the wording of the section precludes such an interpretation.

I would therefore hold that the date of determination which makes a compulsory purchase order operative under s. 78(3)(a)(ii) is the date of the final determination of the proceedings in the High Court. This means that I would differ from the answer given in the High Court to the first question in the case stated. I consider that service of notice to treat in compliance with s. 79(1) was that effected on the 12th March 1973 and that the second service on the 10th May 1974 was invalid.

---

[84] [1905] 2 Ch. 656 at p. 667.

III. *THE SECOND QUESTION*

The second question in the case stated was put because the arbitrator wished for an authoratitive ruling as to whether he could refer to the transcript of the evidence given at the local public inquiry for guidance as to the proper assessment of the compensation to be awarded to the claimant.

The short answer to this question is that it is not competent for the arbitrator to consult the transcript for the purpose of establishing any fact necessary for the assessment of compensation. It is not proper in an arbitration to rely on evidence given in other proceedings for the purpose of proving facts relevant in the arbitration – any more than it would be permissible to prove facts at a trial by referring to a transcript of the evidence given at a previous trial. Statements made on previous occasions are receivable in evidence only under limited and well-defined conditions, and as a general rule acts required to be proved may not be established by such statements. As a source of factual proof, therefore, the transcript should not be consulted by the arbitrator. In any event, it is merely part of a report made by the inspector to the Minister. It just happens that it is a verbatim transcript. It was intended to be read by the Minister only. It is merely an accident of litigation that in this case, because of a successful application for discovery of documents, it came to light. In the normal case, such a transcript would not be available to an arbitrator. So, rules of evidence apart, it is no part of the intended pattern of the arbitration proceedings.

The short answer that, because of the rules of evidence, the arbitrator should not refer to the evidence recorded in the transcript, would leave unresolved the arbitrator's quandary as to whether, even if such evidence were correctly tendered, he could use it for the purpose of assessing the compensation. For that reason I am prepared to deal with the point on the basis that the matters in question may be deemed to have been properly adduced in evidence to the arbitrator.

As I understand the submission of counsel for the claimant, it is this. The land in question stands zoned, in the development plan, for the development of agriculture. The Minister has now confirmed a compulsory purchase order for its acquisition to attain a housing objective under the Housing Act, 1966. This necessarily implies a decision by the Minister to vary the zoning of this land in the development plan, for the carrying out of the desired housing objective would mean that the land would cease to be used for agricultural purposes. This attitude of the Minister has increased the possibility that, if there were no compulsory purchase order pending, the claimant or a transferee from him, might succeed, by way of appeal to the Minister in a development application, in getting permission to use the land for a non-agricultural purpose, such as a housing development. That being so, the Minister's approach in the present compulsory acquisition may be treated as an indication that the land has a potential for non-agricultural purposes, and the arbitrator should take that potential into account in fixing the compensation.

I am not persuaded by that argument. I think it is fundamentally unsound. In the first place, I think it would be a non sequitur to hold that because the Minister is prepared to change the zoning of the land for agriculture, so that it may be used to attain a housing objective under the Act, he would be any the more likely to change the zoning so as to permit a private development of the land for housing. The purposes of the Act of 1966 – for which purposes alone land may be compulsorily acquired under the Act – are so socially orientated, so exclusively within the province of a housing authority, and so much under the surveillance of the Minister, that the Minister's willingness to vary a development plan made under s. 19 of the Local Government (Planning and Development) Act, 1963, so as to effectuate a compulsory purchase order made for those purposes, could not be considered a pointer as to how the Minister might exercise his appellate powers if a development application were made in respect of the same lands by a private person. The determining considerations would be radically different. So the arbitrator, for that reason if no other, would be in error if he treated the Minister's confirmaton of the compulsory purchase order as casting any light on the development potential of the land if it remained in private house.

But there is a more fundamental reason why the arbitrator may not have regard to the Minister's confirmation of the compulsory purchase order for the purpose of determining the compensation. He is debarred by statute from doing so. The arbitrator, in assessing compensation, is bound by the Rules in s. 2 of the Acquisition of Land (Assessment of Compensation) Act, 1919. Rule (13) of those Rules (as amended in the fourth Schedule to the Local Government (Planning and Development) Act, 1963) says that in assessing compensation:

'No account shall be taken of –

(a) the existence of proposals for development of the land or any other land by a local authority, or

(b) the possibility of the land or other land becoming subject to a scheme of development undertaken by a local authority.'

Here it is not a question of there being a possibility of the land or other land becoming subject to a scheme of development by a local authority. There exists, in fact, a proposal for development of the land by a local authority – as the compulsory purchase order proves. So it is Rule 13(*a*) that applies. This means, as was held by this Court in *In re Deansrath Investments*[85] that while the basic rule is that the measure of compensation is to be the open market value of the land, the arbitrator must leave out of the reckoning of that value the existence of the proposed local authority development. The reason for that restriction is plain. It is to ensure that the acquiring authority will not have to pay more for the land than would an ordinary purchaser if a local authority development were not overshadowing this or other lands. In other words, local authority interest – actually existing or even possibly impending – in land, for development purpose, is not allowed to trigger off increased land values in compulsory acquisitions. Local authorities are assured that they will not inflate land values against themselves if they are assiduous in carrying out, or even in considering carrying out, the development of land. This, if one may say so, is a commonsense rule, for if it did not apply, the compulsory acquisition of land for housing and other socially desirable purposes would be cramped by the consequence that from the time a local authority showed an interest in developing a particular piece of land, they would as a result not only have to pay a higher price for the land than it was worth before they cast their eye on it, but as well they would have to pay a consequentially inflated price for any other land which could be said to be enhanced in value by the proposed development. Compulsory acquisition could be effected only on prohibitively high terms. This would not be in the public interest.

As to the present case, no matter how the submission on behalf of the claimant is couched, it breaches the prohibition in Rule (13)(*a*). It would be impossible for the

[85] [1974] I.R. 228.

arbitrator to take into account, as an indicator of the potential development possibility of the land, the fact that the Minister was prepared to change the zoning of the land for agricultural purposes so as to enable the proposed housing development to be carried out, without at the same time taking into account the existence of the proposal for that development. The Minister's attitude to the zoning arises only in the context of that proposal. Without that proposal, the Minister does not come into the matter. It would be quite impossible to take into account the Minister's attitude, or the consequences of the Minister's attitude, without taking into account the proposal for development. It follows, therefore, that the arbitrator is debarred from considering whether the Minister's attitude to the zoning of the land gives the land a potential it would not otherwise have. Since the very existence of the proposed development is ruled out of consideration, the Minister's attitude to that development, whether established in the proceedings at the local public inquiry or otherwise, is also ruled out.

IV. *CONCLUSIONS*

I would allow the claimant's appeal against the answer given in the High Court to the first question. I would also allow the acquiring authority's appeal against the answer given to the second question. In my judgment, the answers to those questions should be:

1. The time referred to in s. 84(1)(*b*) of the Housing Act, 1966, (as of which the value of the land is to be assessed) is the 12th March 1973 (which is the date on which notice to treat was served after the determination of the proceedings in the High Court) and not the 2nd May 1974 (which was the date on which notice to treat was served after the determination of the appeal in the Supreme Court).

2. The arbitrator should not take into account, by reference to the transcript of evidence at the local public inquiry or otherwise, the existence of the acquiring authority's proposal for development, or any matter, such as the Minister's attitude to the zoning of the land, which can arise only by taking into account the existence of that proposal.

GUNNING V. DUBLIN CORPORATION
[1983] I.L.R.M. 56

The relevance of this case to claims for compensation in planning cases is questionable in the light of the recent decision in *McKone* v. *Kildare County Council*, which decided, inter alia, that a claimant for compensation under Section 55 of the Act of 1963 was not entitled to injurious affection. The same reasoning would appear to apply to a claim for disturbance in such a case. However, there is a fairly close analysis between disturbance and the entitlement granted under Section 55(1) of the Act of 1963 – 'to be paid by the Planning Authority by way of compensation the amount of . . . in the case of the occupier of the land, the damage (if any) to his trade, business or profession, carried on on the land.' The judgment of Carroll J. is accordingly included in this book as it comprises a useful exposition of the principles regarding disturbance generally.

The claimant carried on a motor car repair business at 168, Richmond Road, Fairview. In 1974 he consulted the relevant map in the Corporation's offices and discovered that this part of Richmond Road was affected by road realignment proposals. He decided that it was essential in order to mitigate his loss to acquire alternative premises and to have them equipped before the Corporation took possession. This he did and moved to the new premises in March, 1978.

The Compulsory Purchase Order had been made by the Corporation in November of 1976; the Notice to Treat served on the claimant was dated 7th September, 1978 (that is after he had moved) and was followed by a Notice to Enter dated 19th September, 1978. The claim for compensation included several items of loss incurred before service of the Notice to Treat.

The Corporation claimed that they were not liable for such losses or for double overheads from the date of Notice to Treat to the date on which possession was taken by them since these losses were occasioned by the fact that the claimant had relocated his business prior to the service of the Notice to Treat. Judge Carroll held that where steps were taken in order to mitigate loss referrable to an anticipated Notice to Treat and where it is clearly demonstrated that inevitable loss had thereby been avoided and that the steps taken in mitigation were reasonable and prudent and that the amount claimed thereby did not exceed the amount which would been awarded if no such steps had been taken, then the arbitrator might properly award those expenses and losses incurred.

Carroll J.:[86]

This is a special case stated by Mr Owen McCarthy, as property arbitrator, in respect of compensation to be paid by Dublin Corporation ('The acquiring authority') to Mr Christopher Gunning ('The claimant') for the compulsory acquisition of his interest in possession of premises situate at 168 Richmond Road, Fairview in the City of Dublin under the Richmond Road Area Compulsory Purchase (Road Widening and Improvement) Order 1976.

The facts are set out in detail in the case stated and may be summarised as follows:

The compulsory purchase order was made on 18 November 1976, was confirmed on 20 January 1978 and became operative on 19 May 1978. The acquiring authority served a Notice to Treat, pursuant to s. 79 of the Housing Act, 1966, dated 7 September 1978 and a notice of intention to enter, pursuant to s. 80 of the Housing Act 1966, dated 19 September 1978 on the claimant.

After inspection of the relevant map in the acquiring authority's office in January 1974, confirming that the proposed realignment of Richmond Road would necessitate the acquisition of his premises where he carried on a motor car repair business, the claimant decided that it was essential for him to acquire alternative premises as near as possible to his existing premises, and to have them equipped and ready to operate before the acquiring authority took possession of the existing premises. This decision was taken to mitigate the loss which would be occasioned to him if the acquiring authority were to take possession of his premises before he was able to secure suitable alternative premises. There was grave danger that if he could not secure alternative premises he would suffer a grievous loss of goodwill, the loss of his skilled staff and possibly the complete extinguishment of goodwill.

The claimant entered into a contract to purchase other premises near his existing business premises on 1 August 1974, subject to planning permission which was granted in August 1975, and the sale was closed. He went into occupation of the

---

[86] Delivered 24th June, 1982.

alternative premises in September 1977 and commenced building operations. He removed equipment from the premises and installed it in the alternative premises together with new equipment to replace such equipment as could not be removed, and he also installed some extra equipment. This work was completed by March 1978 when the claimant went into occupation of the alternative premises.

In addition to the market value of his premises at the date of the service on him of the notice to treat, the claimant also seeks to be compensated for losses occasioned to him by the compulsory acquisition under the following heads:

(a) relocation costs

(b) temporary loss of business

(c) double overheads

(d) his time in seeking new premises and

(e) miscellaneous disturbance

all of which were incurred before service of the notice to treat on the claimant, and also for double overheads from the date of the notice to treat to the date on which possession of the claimant's premises was taken by the acquiring authority.

It was agreed that had the claimant waited until the notice to treat had been served before securing alternative premises and relocating his business, the expenses and losses occasioned by the relocation would not have been less than those occasioned by the actual relocation, and that if it had not been possible to secure alternative premises, the losses due to the extinction of the goodwill of his business and the payment of redundancy to his staff, would have been greater.

The acquiring authority submitted that they were not liable to compensate the claimant for losses occasioned before the service of the notice to treat. They also submitted that they were not liable to compensate him for double overheads from the date of the notice to treat to the date on which possession was taken by the acquiring authority because these losses arose from the fact that the claimant had relocated his business prior to the notice to treat.

It was submitted on behalf of the claimant that due to the nature of his business and the almost complete certainty that the acquiring authority would go ahead with their proposed works, it would not have been prudent for him to await the service of the notice to treat and the possible taking of his lands any time after fourteen days thereafter, and that it was reasonable to take all possible precautions to secure alternative premises as soon as he knew the compulsory purchase order had been made.

The net point for the consideration of the court is whether the acquiring authority are correct in claiming that they are not liable to pay compensation for any expenses or losses incurred before the service of the notice to treat or for double overheads from the date of the notice to treat in the date possession was taken by them.

There is a further question in the alternative as to whether the claimant is entitled to be paid compensation by the acquiring authority for expenses and losses incurred by the severance of the old premises from his new premises.

S. 84 of the Housing Act, 1966 applies to this acquisition, and it provides as follows:

(1) Where land is acquired compulsorily by a housing authority for the purpose of this Act the compensation payable in respect thereof shall be:

(a) in the case of land consisting of a house mentioned in article 3 of the Third Schedule to this Act – the value of the land at the time the relevant notice to treat is served assessed in accordance with part 1 of the Fourth Schedule to this Act,

(b) In the case of any other land – the value of the land at the time the relevant notice to treat is served assessed in accordance with Part II of the Fourth Schedule to this Act.

(2) Subject to sub-s. (1) of this section and to paragraph (1) of article 2 of the said Third Schedule, the compensation payable in respect of such land shall be assessed in accordance with the provisions of the Acquisition of Land (Assessment of Compensation) Act 1919.

Sub-paragraph (b) of sub-s. (1) is the relevant paragraph and none of the matters mentioned in Part II of the fourth Schedule to the Act have a bearing on the issues involved here.

There is no contest between the parties in respect of the date for the assessment of the market value of the land, i.e. the date of service of the notice to treat. The conflict arises over the assessment of compensation for disturbance.

In this respect rules 2 and 6 contained in s. 2 of the Acquisition of Land (Assessment of Compensation) Act, 1919 ('the 1919 Act') are relevant. They provide as follows:

> Rule 2. The value of the land shall, subject as hereinafter provided, be taken to be the amount which the land if sold in the open market by a willing seller might be expected to realise; provided always that the arbitrator shall be entitled to consider all returns and assessments of capital value for taxation purposes made or acquiesced in by the claimant.
>
> Rule 6. The provisions of Rule (2) shall not affect the assessment of compensation for disturbance or any other matter not directly based on the value of the land.

The leading case on compensation for disturbance is *Horn* v. *Sunderland Corporation*[87] which held that an owner of agricultural land could have his compensation calculated either at the agricultural land value together with compensation for disturbance, or its value as building land, but he could not claim for its value as building land together with compensation for disturbance.

It was held (*inter alia*) that it is a mistake to construe rules 2 and 6 as though they conferred two separate and independent rights, each ascertaining in isolation. The two figures are really elements which go to make up the global figure payable but the statutory compensation must never exceed the owner's total loss.

The judgment of Scott LJ reviews the effect of legislation and decided cases on the whole subject of compulsory acquisition going back to the Land Clauses (Consolidation) Act, 1845. The following passages are taken from his judgment;

> It [i.e. the Act of 1845] possesses two leading features. The first is that what it gives the owner compelled to sell is compensation – the right to be put, so far as money can do it, in the same position as if his land had not been taken from him. In other words, he gains the right to receive a money payment not less than the loss imposed on him in the public interest, but, on the other hand, no greater. The other is that the legislation recognises only two kinds of categories of compensation to the owner from whom the land is taken: (1) The fair value to him of the lands taken, and (2) the fair equivalent in money of the damage

[87] [1941] 2 K.B. 26.

sustained by him in respect of other lands of his, held with the lands taken, by reason of severance or injurious affection. . . As I have already indicated inferentially, there is in the Act of 1845 no express provision giving compensation for disturbance or for any of the similar matters to which s. 2, r. 6, of the Act of 1919 refers, which for brevity I will treat as included in the word 'disturbance', the more suitably so as the claim in issue in the appeal is for disturbance proper. If I am right in saying that the Act expressly grants only two kinds of compensation to an owner who has land taken, (1) for the value to him of the land, and (2) for the injurous affection to his other lands, it is plain that the judicial eye which has discerned that right in the Act must inevitably have found it in (1), that is, in the fair purchase price of the land taken. That conclusion is consonant with all the decisions, so far as I can discover.

The Act is very loosely drawn and there is little attention paid in it as to accuracy of language, but with regard to the scope and purpose of the grant of compensation for the value of the land taken or purchased from an owner, there is no ambiguity. It may parenthetically be noted that the words 'purchased' and 'taken' are used as synonyms. The owner is given a purchase price for the land taken which will 'compensate' him for the compulsory sale. 'Compensation' for 'damage sustained' is expressly conferred as a separate right and is conferred only in respect of the owner's other lands. No express provision is made anywhere in the Act about damage sustained by him in respect of his ownership or possession of the lands taken (at 42–3).

After referring to the relevant sections he says:

Those extracts from the only relevant sections show clearly that a claim for disturbance connected with the land taken must be made as part and parcel of the claim for purchase money. It cannot come under the head of compensation for severance or for injurous affection to the other lands of the owner, and the statute knows no *tertium quid* in the way of compensation. None the less, the owner in a proper case – that is, in a case where he really does incur a loss of money by disturbance due to the taking over and beyond the loss for which he is to be reimbursed in respect of the land taken – is entitled, because it has to do with the land, to have that element of personal loss taken into the reckoning of the fair price of the land, as has been held by the courts from a very early stage (at 45).

He continued:

In the case of a sale by private treaty or auction the seller cannot put in his pocket more than the net market value. He can recover no loss to which he is put by his decision to part with his land, but on a compulsory sale the principle of compensation will include in the price of the land, not only its market value, but also personal loss imposed on the owner by the forced sale, whether it be the cost of preparing the land for the best market then available, or incidental loss in connection with the business he has been carrying on, or the cost of reinstatement, because otherwise he will not be fully compensated. But here we come to the other side of the picture. The statutory compensation cannot, and must not, exceed the owner's total loss, for, if it does, it will put an unfair burden on the public authority or other promoters who on public grounds have been given the power of compulsory acquisition, and it will transgress the principle of equivalence which is at the root of statutory compensation, the principle that the owner shall be paid neither less nor more than his loss. The enunciation of this principle, the most fundamental of all, is easy enough. Its justice is self-evident, but its application to varying facts is apt to be difficult (at 49).

The case of *Birmingham Corporation* v. *West Midland Baptist (Trust) Assoc. (Inc.)*[88] is basically a case concerned with reinstatement (i.e. r. 5, s. 2, 1919 Act). It held that the relevant date for the assessment of the reasonable cost of equivalent reinstatement under rule 5 was the date on which the work of reinstatement might reasonably have been commenced and not the date of the service of the notice to treat.

There is however a relevant passage in the judgment of Reid LJ relating to rule 6.

Moreover this so called principle (*i.e. taking the date of the notice to treat as the relevant date to assess the value of the land*) does not appear to have been applied to every element of the value of the land to the owner. It has certainly been regarded as applying to that element which consists of the market value of the land taken. But there is little or no indication that it was regarded as applicable to the other elements in an owner's claim. These might include costs of removal, loss of profit or other consequential loss, and there appears to be no suggestion in the authorities that these elements in the value of the land to the owner must be valued as at the date of the notice to treat. The actual costs or losses following an actual dispossession have been taken and that appears to be the accepted practice today with regard to claims under rule 6 (at 896).

While this passage must be regarded as *obiter* it appears to me to state the position correctly.

Reid LJ also says:

It has always been recognised that the value of the land means its value to the owner and does not mean its value to the promotors or its value in the open market. If the owner is in occupation the value of the land to him may far exceed its value in the open market. If he wishes to continue his activities he will not only have to obtain other premises but he will have to pay costs of removal, and if he is carrying on business the move may cause loss of profits and other loss. He will not be fully compensated unless all this is taken into account (at 893).

I have quoted extensively because these passages set out clearly and authoritatively the various principles on which compensation for compulsory acquisition is based.

It seems to me that these judgments confirm the following propositions relevant to the present case:

1. The underlying principle is the principle of equivalence. The owner should be able to recover personal loss imposed on him by the forced sale – otherwise he will not be fully compensated – but he should recover neither more nor less than his total loss.

2. Where other lands of the owner are not affected by the compulsory acquisition only one price is paid, but the fair price to which the owner is entitled will include the market value of the land together with personal loss sustained in respect of his ownership or possession of the lands.

---

[88] [1970] A.C. 874.

3. Where the value of the land is to be ascertained on the date of service of the notice to treat, the element of compensation for disturbance is not ascertained by reference to estimated losses on that date but is acertained when the award is made by reference to actual losses already incurred, with estimated future losses where relevant.

Accordingly, s. 84 of the Housing Act, 1966 which provides that compensation payable for land acquired compulsorily should be the value of the land at the time of the service of the notice to treat, must, in my opinion, be interpreted as referring to the market value of the land at that time, leaving unaltered the practice of assessing the other elements which go to make up the entire compensation at the time of the award by reference to actual losses incurred, and estimated future losses (if any).

The corporation did not argue that the losses to be included as compensation for disturbance must be ascertained as of the date of the notice to treat. They argued that only the losses incurred after the date of the notice to treat (other than the double overheads already mentioned) could be included in the compensation price as being the natural and probable consequences of the compulsory acquisition.

The case of *Harvey* v. *Crawley Development Corporation*[89] held that any loss sustained by an owner which flowed from the compulsory acquisition could properly be the subject of compensation for disturbance provided:
(a) That it was not too remote and
(b) That it was the natural, direct and reasonable consequence of the dispossession.

In this case the claimant did incur expenses he would not otherwise have incurred as a result of the initiation of procedures for compulsory acquisition. He thereby avoided certain loss which might well have been greater than the expense incurred. This is not a case of compensation being claimed for loss never suffered. The claimant has suffered a loss, but he suffered it in anticipation rather than as a consequence of the notice to treat.

The only case in which mitigation in anticipation of a notice to treat arose, appears to be the case of *Bloom (Kosher) and Sons Ltd* v. *Tower Hamlets London Borough Council* which was brought before an arbitrator and reported in the Estates Gazette.[90]

The case of *Hunter* v. *Manchester City Council*[91] which was cited, does not deal with the question of mitigation as such. In that case the owner who had acquired alternative premises before a clearance order was made, was qualified under the wording of the relevant statutory provision to claim compensation over and above the site value.

The facts in the *Bloom (Kosher)* case are strikingly similar to the present case. The arbitrator found as a fact that the purchase by the owners of new factory premises was entirely attributable to the belief that the existing factory was to be compulsorily acquired, and their purpose in moving to it from their old factory was to facilitate the continuance of their business and preserve their ability to earn profits. The owners based their claim to be reimbursed expenses incurred by them before the date of the notice to treat on the principles of causation and of mitigation.

---

[89] [1957] 1 Q.B. 485.
[90] (1977) E.G. 1091; (1978) 35 P & C.R. 423.
[91] [1975] 1 Q.B. 877.

On the causation point, the arbitrator held that the loss claimed could not be decribed as a loss directly consequent upon, or the natural and reasonable consequence of, the compulsory acquisition, and therefore was not caused by the acquisition.

In relation to the question of mitigation, it was submitted on behalf of the owners that if an owner knows that the acquiring authority has a settled intention to purchase his property by compulsory purchase order, then while he is not bound to do anything at all until lawfully required to do so, if nevertheless he acts in a way which is referable only to the impending compulsory purchase order and his actions are reasonable, he can recover his expenditure reasonably incurred when the compulsory purchase order takes effect, albeit that he takes a risk that if no order in fact ensues his expenditure will not be compensatable.

The arbitrator held:

1. That loss directly attributable to reasonable mitigation may be recoverable but not unless it is the direct and natural consequence of the acquisition and
2. That loss which precedes an acquisition cannot be regarded as a consequence of it.

In order to decide the issue before the court it is necessary to examine these two propositions.

Compensation for disturbance payable to an owner under rule 6 is akin to but not identical with damages for breach of contract or damages for tort.

In breach of contract the test for quantum of damage is not *de facto* loss. The aggrieved party is only entitled to recover such part of the loss actually resulting as was at the time of the contract reasonably foreseeable as liable to result from the breach either in the ordinary course of things or due to special circumstances known to the offending party. In tort the tortfeasor takes his victim as he finds him. The test for quantum of damage is whether the damage is of a type to be foreseeable, in which case damages can be recovered even if the degree of damage is unforseeable.

But compulsory acquisition involves neither breach of contract nor commission of a tort. In the case of compulsory acquisition, there is no contract between the owner and the acquiring authority. There is an enforced sale with provision for compensation over and above the value of the land for loss to the owner where such loss occurs.

It cannot be said either that compulsory acquisition is a tortious act. It is a lawful act under statute which provides for payment of money over and above the market value of the land to compensate for disturbance. The analogy with the tort of trespass made by Earl CJ in *Ricket* v. *Metropolitan Railway Company*[92] to the effect that the principle of compensation is the same as in trespass for expulsion, was doubted by Scott LJ in *Horn* v. *Sunderland Corporation*.[93]

Compensation for disturbance over and above the value of the land is akin to damages paid to a successful plaintiff for breach of contract or in respect of tort in that it seeks to put the owner, in so far as money can do so, in the same position as if the compulsory acquisition had not taken place. It should cover his loss, neither more nor less. I do not think that comparison can be drawn further than that. However, the principles of law relating to mitigation of damage in cases of contract

[92] (1867) L.R. 2 H.L. 175 H.L. (E.).
[93] [1941] 2 K.B. 26 at 45.

or tort can be examined in connection with the claim based on mitigation in this case.

Since there was no duty on the claimant to mitigate, the nearest comparison appears to me to be the case where a plaintiff has taken more steps in mitigation than were required of him and has thereby reduced his loss, thus enabling a defendant to take advantage of the reduction unless the steps in mitigation were completely collateral to the original wrong.

It is stated in Halsbury's *Laws of England* (4th Edition) Volume 12:

The defendant may take advantage of steps which are a reasonable and prudent course naturally arising out of the circumstances in which the plaintiff was placed by the defendant's wrong but not those which are *res inter alios acta* or collateral to the wrong (at paragraph 1196).

and later:

Steps which a plaintiff has taken before the commission of the defendant's wrong and which have the effect of reducing the plaintiff's loss will generally be collateral matters and irrelevant to the assessment of damages.

This latter passage infers that steps which have been taken before the commission of a wrong which are not collateral and are clearly referable to an anticipated wrongful act, whether in relation to contract or tort, may be taken into account in reducing the defendant's liability.

It is only one step further to say that if an anticipated wrongful act will inevitably result in loss and that loss is totally or partially avoided by the plaintiff taking steps which he is not obliged to take and with no collateral purpose, then if the wrong does occur, the plaintiff should be entitled to recover the expenses of avoiding that certain loss provided those expenses do not exceed the avoided loss.

In this case the claimant anticipated the service of the notice to treat, acquired new premises and removed his business before the acquiring authority served the notice to treat. He seeks to recover the expenses and losses incurred in anticipation of the notice to treat as part of his compensation for disturbance. It is admitted that if he had not acquired the other premises and relocated his business, his expenses and losses would not have been less than if he had waited for the service of the notice to treat and might well have been more.

It is not claimed on behalf of the claimant that he was under any duty to mitigate his loss by acting in anticipation of a notice to treat. I am of opinion that this is correct. If the claimant had chosen not to make any move until after service of the notice to treat, the acquiring authority could not have resisted a claim for compensation for disturbance based on the cost of relocation of business, loss of profits, etc., incurred after the notice to treat.

It appears to me to be clear from the case stated that the steps taken by the claimant to aquire new premises and relocate his business prior to the service of the notice to treat are referable only to the compulsory purchase order and the threatened acquisition of his premises. Therefore, there does not appear to be any collateral reason for his actions.

It seems to me to be eminently practicable, reasonable and desirable in the public interest that land-owners should be encouraged to mitigate compensation for disturbance by reasonable and prudent steps taken in advance of service of the notice to treat thus avoiding a greater expense on the acquiring authority than if they sit back and do nothing.

It is however necessary to consider whether those views are in accord with the code of compensation for disturbance as contained in the relevant statutes and enunciated in the relevant decisions.

It cannot be said that the loss incurred was a natural and probable consequence of the compulsory acquisition from the owner by the acquiring authority (see *Harvey* v. *Crawley Development Corporation*[94]), but the losses avoided by the claimant's actions were inevitable and if they had occurred they would have been the natural and probable consequence of the compulsory acquisition. If the claimant cannot recover the expense of avoiding this inevitable loss it would in my opinion be a breach of the principle of equivalence on which the code of compensation is based.

Therefore I disagree with the conclusion reached by the arbitrator in the *Bloom (Kosher)* case in relation to mitigation. I disagree that loss incurred in mitigation must be the direct and natural consequence of the acquisition. The important factor to my mind is that the loss *avoided* must be a direct and natural consequence of the acquisition.

It seems to me that in a case such as the present one it is proper for the arbitrator to look at the whole of the facts and ascertain if the course taken was one which a reasonable and prudent person might properly have taken in the ordinary course of business.

If an arbitrator can hold:

(1) that the steps taken in mitigation are clearly referable to an anticipated notice to treat, and

(2) that it is possible to show that an inevitable loss consequent on the notice to treat has been avoided, and

(3) that the steps taken, while not obligatory, are reasonable and prudent and have not been taken for a collateral purpose (i.e. it must be possible for an arbitrator to say that but for the compulsory acquisition the owner would still be in his premises and would not have acquired the other premises), then in my opinion the arbitrator may properly award those expenses and losses incurred, provided the cost of the steps taken in mitigation, or losses resulting from those steps do not exceed the amount which could be awarded if no steps had been taken until after service of the notice to treat. Since there is no duty to mitigate, the acquiring authority should not be damnified by the cost of mitigation being greater than the loss avoided.

An owner by acting in anticipation takes the risk

(1) that the notice to treat will never be served, in which case he can make no claim in respect of costs incurred and,

(2) that the cost of mitigation may exceed the amount which could have been awarded if no steps were taken, in which case he cannot recover more than the amount of the anticipated loss which has been avoided.

The claimant is not looking to be compensated for a loss he never suffered. He suffered a loss (i.e. the expenses of acquiring premises and moving his business) at an early stage thereby avoiding certain loss if he had waited till after the notice to treat was served.

If the claimant recovers the expenses and losses he incurred before the notice to treat he has then been put in the same position as if his land had not been taken from him. He is neither better nor worse off.

---

[94] [1957] 1 Q.B. 485.

Since the losses cannot be recovered as being consequent on the acquisition, the principles of mitigation must be applied in the light of the fundamental underlying principle of equivalence. In my opinion the case law does not prevent me giving the interpretation I have outlined already.

Accordingly, I answer the questions in the case stated as follows:

Question 1:

Is the submission of the acquiring authority that they are not liable to pay compensation for any of the expenses or losses claimed in paragraph 8 correct? (i.e. expenses and losses incurred before the service of the notice to treat).,

Answer:

No.

Question 2:

Is the submission of the acquiring authority that they are not liable to p' compensation for the expenses and losses claimed in paragraph 11 correct? e. double overheads from the date of the notice to treat to the date on hich possession was taken by the acquiring authority).

Answer:

Double overheads can be claimed in so far as they are reasonable. I not been told the date when possession was actualy taken. If the claimant ated handing over possession followig the expiration of notice of intention claim double had already alternativ premises, it would not be reason. overheads beyond the date of expiration.

Question 3:

Does not arise.

DUBLIN CORPORATION V. SMITH K AND OTH 77)

(Unreported judgment of the Presid

The defendants applied for planning per ble with the then existing zoning in at Pembroke oad, Dublin to office use the planning authority intended[95] to the area but ere refused on the basis n appeal the Minister confirmed the re-zone the rea for residential use o made for compensation on foot of a decision ar the reasons. Applicatio at it would be unjust and unreasonable Ministeria Order pursuant to Sectio should be precluded. At that time it was in the cir mstances that compens 6(1) (which precluded compensation if the thought at the provisions of Sect of use) operated to exclude compensation in applicatn involved a material ch an Order some 8 years later. By then the such a ase.[96] The Minister m . The plaintiffs challenged the validity of the defendnts had sold their pre s, namely (a) the defendants no longer had an Minisr's Order on two gr was a necessary implication of the statutory provi-inter in the premises an context of a number of other provisions in the Act of sion when considered in t pensation should have retained his interest in the land 196 that a claimant for pensation was assessed and (b) by further implication up the time that the under Section 58 was subject to a reasonable time which th making of an Or

See S. 2(7)(a) of e Act of 1963.
See however the bsequent judgment of Finlay P. in *Viscount Securities Limited* v. *Dublin County Counci* p. 453.)

had been exceeded in the present case. The President rejected both these arguments. He held that he should not put a restriction on the right of a landowner to compensation by implication unless he was forced so to do and he was not forced to do merely because considerations of some other sections in the Act showed that it could (as distinct from must) be interpreted as indicating the intention contended for by the Corporation. Secondly he held that while he might consider it desirable that the Section 58 Order ought to be given within a reasonable time, this was not in fact provided for in an Act which did impose many strict time limits. A court could not construe an Act in the light of what it thought desirable. There was no time limit. Moreover, the effect of the passage in time was to reduce in real terms the amount of compensation payable.

Fray P.;

In his action the plaintiff claims a declaration that the first and second-named defendants are not entitled to compensation pursuant to Section 55 of the Local Government (Planning and Development) Act, 1963, and a declaration that a purported decision made by the third-named defendant[97] pursuant to the power vested in him under Section 58 of the same Act is invalid. The case was heard before me in evidence on the pleadings and on an agreed book of documents admitted as between introducing an agreed statement of the facts. The facts thus second-named defence parties can be summarised as follows: The first and Military Order of St. J. are the trustees of the Irish delegation of the Sovereign hereinafter described Jerusalem of Rhodes and of Malta, popularly known of a substantial dwelling as the Knights of Malta, and as such were in 1965 plaintiffs, as of October of house at 51 Pembroke Road.

the premises as office planning authorities they applied for planning permission from the refused that application upon accommodate the City of Dublin, for the development of which the house was situated would on the 1st of December, 1965, the plaintiff second-named defendants appealed that it was envisaged that the area in appeal was finally determined by a con for residential purpose. The first and it on the 20th of July, 1966. On the 15th that decision to the Minister and that compensation pursuant to Section 55 of on of the refusal and of the grounds of they applied to the Minister for Local Gov ust, 1966, the defendant applied for 58(1) of the Act declaring that it would not ct and on the 31st of August 1966, circumstances that payment of compensation nt for an order pursuant to Section one of Section 56. This last application was ne st and reasonable in the particular permission sought and refused would, of course, uld be prevented by sub-section user and by virtue of the provisions of Section ry by reason of the fact that the declaration under Section 58 by the Minister, ha involved a material change of compensation. The defendants, as trustees of the Kn 1) would, were it not for a of December of 1965, agreed to sell these premises su prevented the payment of planning permission they subsequently sought in Octob of Malta had, on the 17th ditional upon the obtaining of the planning permission, an t to the obtaining of the the Minister on appeal the contractual relationship betwe That contract was conon its final refusal by the parties ceased.

[97] The Minister.

Subsequently the defendants by agreement of the 14th of October, 1966, sold the premises and that sale, which was unconditional and not dependant on any planning permission, was completed.

On the facts it is clear that the Minister was well entitled on the merits if he saw fit to make a declaration under Section 58(1) for the position had been at the time of the purchase of these premises by the Knights of Malta that they were then, apparently, zoned for office use and that the change did not consist of a change arising from a development plan to which they might have had an opportunity of objecting but was a result of a decision of the Planning Authority to zone them for residential purposes only in the future and the merits, therefore, were certainly sufficient, if the Minister's discretion were so exercised, to permit him to make a declaration under Section 58. The facts display that upon receipt of the application to him on the 31st of August of 1966 he inquired from the plaintiffs, as the Planning Authority, for their views or submissions with regard to the application before him and a correspondence, to some extent delayed by the plaintiffs themselves, took place which ceased in 1969. Nothing more on the facts before me was communicated either between the first and second-named defendants and the third-named defendant, the Minister, or between the plaintiff and the Minister or between the plaintiffs and the first and second-named defendants until, on the 16th of July, 1974, the Minister made a declaration pursuant to Section 58(1).

On these facts the plaintiffs challenge the right of the trustees of the Knights of Malta to compensation and the validity of the necessary order of the Minister on two net points of law. The first may be summarised by saying that it is contended on behalf of the plaintiffs that no person can recover compensation under Section 55 unless (1) he has a legal estate or interest in the lands at the time of the decision to refuse a planning permission and (2) he retains that legal interest up to the time his compensation is assessed. The second net point of law on which the plaintiffs rely is that they assert that the minister's decision under Section 58 is invalid because it failed to comply with the condition which must be implied into Section 58, that the decision on an application under that Section should be given by the Minister within a reasonable time.

The material terms of Section 55 dealing with the first point may be quoted as follows, omitting irrelevant parts: 'If on a claim made to the Planning Authority it is shown that as a result a decision under Part IV of this Act involving a refusal of permission to develop land the value of an interest of any person existing in the land to which the decision relates at the time of the decision is reduced, such person shall, subject to the provisions of the Act, be entitled to be paid by the Planning Authority by way of compensation the amount of such reduction in value.' Firstly it is clear that neither in that sub-section nor in any other part of Section 55 nor in the Act in general is there any express proviso which makes it a condition of the recovery of compensation that the person who is applying should not only have had an interest which was reduced in value at the time of the decision but that he should retain or have retained, that interest up to the time of the assessment or payment of compensation. Furthermore it seems to me that on the terms of Section 55(1) itself that there is considerable force in the argument that it has nominated in a vital and express way what is the time at which the interest must exist and it is nominated as being the time of the decision to refuse.

The plaintiffs urge, however, that particularly because of sub-section 2 of Section

55 and because also of sub-section 2 of Section 55 and because also of sub-section 4 and certain other provisions in the Act, it is impossible to construe or work the Act unless one implies into Section 55 a condition that the person becoming entitled to compensation must retain his interest in the lands at least up to the time of its assessment. Under sub-section 2 of Section 55 it is provided that in determining reduction of value for the purposes of the Section regard should be had (a) to any permission under the Act to develop the land existing at the time of the decision[98] and, more importantly from the point of view of the plaintiffs' contention (b) to any undertaking that may be given to grant permission to develop the land in the event of application being made under this Act in that behalf. By virtue of Section 55(4) it is provided that where, under Section 29 of the Act it is the duty of a Planning Authority to acquire an interest in land, compensation in relation to that interest should not be payable pursuant to the section.

The argument based on these two provisions is, with regard to sub-section 2, that if the arbitrator in assessing the compensation and the reduction of value is to have regard to a permission under the Act or to an undertaking to grant a permission under the Act, that this would not become workable unless at the time when it fell to assess the compensation, the person applying for it was the owner of his interest in the land and therefore able to avail of, if he wishes, a permission or an undertaking to grant a permission. With regard to sub-section 4 the argument is that the prevention or prohibition of compensation is confined to the case where it is still the duty of a Planning Authority to acquire an interest in land under Section 29. Section 29 of the Act, of course, provides – in summarised form – that where no real beneficial use can be made of land by reason of a refusal of permission or the nature of the conditions attached to a permission, that having regard to certain procedures, the owner can force the planning authority to acquire the land and the contention is that if it were not assumed by the draftsmen of the Act that the person applying for compensation would still be the owner of his interest in the land the phrase 'it is the duty of a planning authority' would be wholly inappropriate because the anomaly would arise that whereas in a case where the Planning Authority was obliged or had the duty to acquire an interest but had not yet done so, that compensation would be prevented but that in a case where the interest had actually been acquired and the duty had been discharged, compensation would still technically be available.

The other provisions of the Act on which Mr. Keane relied for this interpretation are, firstly, Sections 72 and 73. Those sections provide firstly for the registration of the fact of the payment of compensation and then for the recovery of the compensation so paid in the event of any subsequent owner of the land obtaining a permission in respect of the refusal of which the original compensation has been paid. The point raised on this is that if land can be sold then subsequent to a sale or possibly to a re-sale, the original owner who has been refused a permission can have his compenation assessed but the new owner of the land might find himself, upon the subsequent development, with a liability to the Planning Authority which

---

[98]   Interestingly S. 55(2)(*a*) was amended by S. 41(*a*) of the Act of 1976 (which became law on 5th July, 1976) to read – 'In determining reduction of value for the purposes of this section, regard shall be had – (*a*) to any permission under this Act to develop the land existing at the time compensation is agreed or determined, . . .', instead of '. . . at the time of the decision.'

he could not have been aware of or could not have assessed at the time he originally purchased the land. The last provisions mainly relied upon with regard to this interpretation of the Act was Section 71(2) which incorporates in the compensation procedures sections of the Land Clauses Act[99] dealing largely with questions of title and the ascertainment of title and where difficulty in regard to title exists which Mr. Keane urged, is quite inappropriate if the Act did not envisage only the person still owning the interest in the land applying for the compensation.

On this argument I am firstly satisfied, as to the principle of interpretation of this Statute, that I should not put by implication a restriction or condition on a right to compensation unless I am forced to do so. To put the matter in another way it seems to me that the appropriate principle is that it is not sufficient that the other provisions of the Act could be construed as contemplating a retention of interest as a condition precedent to compensation but that they must be so construed. I am satisfied that with regard to sub-section 2 of Section 55, that the reduction could apply to either circumstance. The reduction to be made in the amount of compensation by reason of the availability of a permission or an undertaking to give a permission is, of necessity, in any case, a notional reduction and it does not depend upon the person, even if he is still the owner of the land, actually making use of the availability of such permission. In a case where land has been sold before the compensation comes to be assessed I can see no difficulty in still applying the provisions of Section 2. To take, for example, the instant case before me: if, it seems to me, it were established to the satisfaction of an arbitrator that having regard to the permission which undoubtedly was available and was availed of by the subsequent purchase from the trustees of the premises to make a residential development that the sum of £22,000 which was obtained was not the highest or fullest price that could then have been obtained, the arbitrator would be entitled to have regard to the availability of the permission to the subsequent purchase in assessing the amount of compensation which would be payable. With regard to sub-section 4 and the argument arising on that, it seems to me that the answer to that is to be found in the provisions of Section 70. Where an acquisition is forced upon the Planning Authority under Section 29 of the Act, they operate, having regard to the provisions of that section as if they had made a compulsory purchase order under Section 10 of the Local Government (No. 2) Act, 1960. That, of course, creates the liability to pay compensation on the acquisition. Section 70 of the Planning Act of 1963 prohibits by its terms the payment of double compensation and prohibits the payment of any compenstion under the Act of 1963 where, in respect of the same matter, a person is entitled to compensation under any other Statute. And it seems, therefore, proper and reasonable to construe sub-section 4 as dealing with a situation where there is a duty on the Planning Authority to acquire and they have not yet acquired because Section 70 combined with the provisions of Section 29 deals with a situation where the acquisition has actually taken place.

With regard to the point raised under Section 72 and Section 73 it seems to me, as Mr. Walsh urged on behalf of the first and second defendants, that it is entirely possible, practical and, I would have thought, almost a routine precaution for a purchaser to enquire at the time of his purchase, whether on an original purchase or

---

[99] Lands Clauses Consolidation Act, 1845.

on a re-sale, with regard to the position under the Planning Acts. The whole right to compensation can only arise if an application for permission has been made and has ultimately been refused. The fact of an application for permission and the fact of a refusal is easily ascertained from the Planning Register and there does not seem to me to be any injustice or difficulty in applying Section 72 and Section 73 while at the same time assuming that a person applying for compensation may, if he wishes, sell the premises between the time of the original refusal and the time when he applies for or has his compensation assessed. With regard to Section 72 it is sufficient to say the Lands Clauses Acts and the incorporated sections of them referred to in that section are necessary for the case which, of course, will arise as well when the applicant for compensation retains his interest in the land up to the time the compensation falls to be assessed and paid.

It seems to me in general that there would be considerable injustice in forcing upon a person who is the owner of land, who has applied for permission and has had it refused and is then entitled to apply for compensation, the additional burden that he is prevented in order to acquire his compensation from disposing of his land if that is the most immediate best way of saving his loss. Having regard to my view of the other sections of the Act I am not forced to interpret the Act in that way and I am satisfied I should not do so and the first point made by the plaintiff fails.

With regard to the second point, firstly it should be emphasised that on the facts there is no suggestion that the plaintiffs are in any way prejudiced by the delay of the Minister. In point of fact it is the first and second-named defendants who have lost because if they have a right to compensation it is now, in terms of the inflationary period, nearly nine years after their original loss and correspondingly the liability that exists of the planning authority is, in an inflationary way, much less than it would have been had there been an earlier decision by the Minister. The contention is not, therefore, one of prejudice or in any way an estoppel that the planning authority has done anything to worsen or alter their position upon an assumption that a decision was not being made, but rather the contention that I should construe the Section as necessarily carrying an implied term that the decision should be made in a reasonable time. The Planning Act of 1963 contains a very considerable number of time limits, some of them inflexible and most of them relatively strict. In Section 29(5) there is a fixed time limit of six months on the Minister to make a decision with regard to the compulsory purchase by a Planning Authority under that Section and if he does not make a decision within that six months he is deemed therefore to have confirmed the purchase order. In the absence of a similar express provision in Section 58 I cannot see any warrant for implying it.

There is no doubt that it would be very desirable that there should be a reasonable time limit upon the Minister in reaching a decision in this case. It is unnecessary for me to emphasise again that it is not my function to legislate and I am not entitled to interpret into an Act something which I consider to be desirable; I must interpret the Act and construe it and I can only interpret it by way of implication if there is something which is absolutely essential for its construction or working. I am not satisfied that the provision of a reasonable time for the making of the Minister's decision under Section 58 comes within that category and this point also fails. I am therefore satisfied that the plaintiffs are not entitled to any of the declarations sought.

PORTLAND ESTATES (LIMERICK) LIMITED V. LIMERICK CORPORATION
(Unreported judgment of Butler J. in the High Court delivered 31st July, 1979
Unreported judgment of the Supreme Court delivered 27th March, 1980)

The nett point decided in the Supreme Court was that where a planning authority indicate compliance with a notice requiring them to purchase lands under Section 29 of the 1963 Planning Act, they must follow up such notice of compliance with a notice to treat and that the compensation must be assessed as of the date of the notice to treat.

However, the judgments of both Courts are of interest in that they underline the principle that compensation must fairly reflect the open market value of the land. Butler J. in the High Court held that the date for assessment was the date of the making of the assessment[1] of compensation by the arbitrator. He rejected the planning authority's contention that the relevant date was the date of its notice of compliance with the Section 29 purchase notice. Coming to this conclusion he was particularly guided by the principles laid down by Lord Reid in the *Birmingham Corporation* v. *West Midland Baptist Trust*[2] case in which the House of Lords rejected the contention that the date of notice to treat was the relevant date, because to do so could produce substantial injustice to the landowner.

In the Supreme Court it was held that a planning authority was under an obligation to follow their notice of compliance with a notice to treat which established the date as of which the assessment of compensation should be made. This had not been done in the instant case and the Chief Justice held that justice required that the Court takes 'a point of time most advantageous to the owner' in the circumstance that the failure of the planning authority was in no way his fault. He therefore held that the assessment should have proceeded on the basis of a notice to treat being served immediately before the arbitration comenced as this produced a substantially higher valuation than an assessment based on the date of the service of notice of compliance.

High Court
Butler J.:

In the present case the claimants were the owner of lands for which development permission had been refused. On 26th February 1976 they served a purchase notice pursuant to the above section 29 on the planning authority. By notice dated 21st May 1976 the authority served a compliance notice on the claimants and, the parties having failed to agree on a price the question was duly referred to the arbitration of Mr. Owen MacCarthy, the Official Arbitrator. He commenced the arbitration on the 26th October 1977 and continued the hearing on the 24th and 25th November 1977 and the 5th and 6th January 1978.

At the hearing the claimants contended that the relevant date as of which the lands fell to be valued was the date on which the value was assessed, namely the last day of taking of evidence as to value at the arbitration. The planning authority on

---

[1] Compare S. 55(2)(a) of the Act of 1963.
[2] [1969] 3 All E.R. 172.

the other hand contended that the appropriate date was the date on which they accepted the purchase notice, namely the 21st May 1976. The arbitrator made a finding as to the value of the lands on each of the dates contended for and has referred to this Court by way of special case the question as to which is the date in reference to which the value is to be determined. His findings as to value were; £108,000 on the 21st May 1976 and £135,000 on the 6th January 1978.

The history of the assessment of the compensation to be paid to an owner whose lands have been acquired compulsorily goes back to the Lands Clauses Consolidation Act 1845 and has been the subject of numerous judicial decisions since that date. For long, and certainly down to 1919 when the Acquisition of Lands (Assessment of Compensation) Act was passed the relevant date for the assessment was taken to be the date of the notice to treat. This is the date on which the acquiring authority irrevocably commits itself to acquisition and thereupon either party may apply to have the price determined and paid. Under section 29 of the 1963 Act the acceptance of the purchase notice is of like effect as a compulsory purchase order and by the acceptance notice the planning authority irrevocably binds itself to purchase the lands. It is this analogy that is the basis for the contention that the date of the acceptance notice is to be regarded as the date of the service of a notice to treat under a compulsory purchase order and that the price is to be fixed with regard to that date. However, the only statutory requirement that the date of the notice to treat is the date as of which compensation is to be assessed is Section 84 of the Housing Act, 1966 which provides that where land is compulsorily acquired by a housing authority for the purposes of the Act compensation shall be the value of the land at the time the relevant notice to treat is served. That provision has of course no application to the present case and what is in question is whether there is in law a rule that where lands are compulsorily acquired compensation is to be assessed on the basis of their value as at the date of the notice to treat.

This precise question was answered in the negative by the House of Lords in England in the case of *Birmingham Corporation* v. *West Midland Baptist Trust*, affirming the decision of the Court of Appeal. Lord Reid in his opinion deals fully with the authorities from 1845 onwards and recognizes that these authorities do support the existence of the rule. He notes, however, that the same and other judicial and expert opinion and indeed the statutory requirements postulate a more fundamental principle, namely, that the owner is to be fully and fairly compensated for the value of lands to him at the date of the expropriation. He introduces his review of the authorities by stating at page 176 of the report

'In the nineteenth century the purchasing power of money remained fairly constant over long periods, otherwise consols would not have been held to be the safest possible investment. And there was seldom any long delay by promoters in completing the acquisition of land after notice to treat had been served. . . . So from a practical point of view it did not much matter which stage in the process of acquisition was taken as the time as at which compensation should be assessed. It was convenient to take the date of the notice to treat, and from at least 1870 onwards it was generally asumed that this was the right date to take.'

He goes on to review the authorities noting that what the cases were really at pains to establish was the obviously necessary rule that the value of the lands cannot be increased by the owner after the date of the notice to treat, and concludes by stating at page 178

'I can find no substantial reason given for taking the date of the notice to treat other than that it was so near to the date of the actual taking that assessment as at the date of the notice to treat would do no substantial injustice to either party.

Dealing with the principle that compensation must be the value at the date of expropriation and the rule that compensation is to be assessed as at the date of the notice to treat, he says at page 179

'The principle and the rule cannot be reconciled except on the basis that the total value to the owner at the date of the notice to treat is always substantially the same as the value at the date of the expulsion. For it cannot be said that the owner is in any way expelled from his land by the notice to treat'.

In the event it was decided that the rule was formulated based on an assumption of fact that this was true when the rule was formulated but which is no longer true and which now in many cases causes serious injustices and consequently that it could be re-examined. It was further decided that the correct date for the assessment was the date on which possession was actually taken if compensation had not then been assessed or if not the date of assessment. I was informed that the Official Arbitrator now applies this decision in cases other than Housing Act cases. It was followed in England in the case of a purchase under English legislation similar to our Section 29 – W & S (Long Eaton) Ltd. v. Derbyshire County Council[3] which is noted in the current supplement to the latest edition of Halsbury.

The substantial point made by counsel for the planning authority is that the date of the acceptance notice should be taken because in reaching a decision whether or not to purchase the authority should be able to have regard to the price they would have to pay. This submission is based on the assumption that the planning authority have an option. They have not. If the conditions laid down in the section are satisfied they must purchase and if they fail to do so the Minister must either direct them to purchase or himself grant the planning permission sought or some alternative permission acceptable to the owner. Furthermore, if this is a serious consideration to the planning authority they can secure a speedy determination of the price by referring the matter to arbitration.

I find the review of the law and the reasoning in the Birmingham Corporation case compelling. I agree with the decision and with the rule propounded in that case and accordingly would answer the special case by informing the arbitrator that the market value of the subject land is to be determined by him on the scale of values existing at the time of the termination of the hearing.

Supreme Court
O'Higgins C.J.[4] (Henchy, Parke JJ. concurring):

Section 29 of the Local Government (Planning and Development Act 1963 (which I will hereinafter refer to as 'the Planning Act') imposes an obligation on a planning authority in certain cases to purchase land in respect of which planning permission has been refused on appeal or granted subject to conditions. Where the Section applies the owner is empowered to serve on the planning authority a purchase notice requiring that authority to purchase his interest in the lands in accordance with the section. The authority has three months in which either to comply or to refuse to comply with the notice. If it refuses to comply the matter is automatically referred to the Minister who may (a) overrule the refusal and confirm

[3] Reported at [1968] 1 All E.R. 205.
[4] Judgment delivered 27th March, 1980.

the purchase notice or (b) grant the permission originally applied for or (c) grant permission for an alternative development. Sub-section (3) applies when the authority served on the owner a notice indicating its willingness to comply with the purchase notice. It provides as follows:

'Where the planning authority upon whom a purchase notice is served under this Section have served on the owner by whom the purchase notice was served a notice in accordance with paragraph (a) of sub-section (2) of this Section, it shall be the duty of the authority to acquire the interest of the owner and, for that purpose, the latter notice shall have the like effect as if it were a compulsory purchase order in respect of that interest which, consequent upon a decision made by the planning authority pursuant to sub-section (1) of Section 10 of the Local Government (No. 2) Act, 1960, had been duly made and confirmed.'

In this case the respondents were the owners of land for which development permission was refused by the Minister on appeal by deicision dated 27th August 1975. On the 16th February 1976 the respondents served a purchase notice on the appellants pursuant to Section 29 of the Planning Act. On the 21st May 1976 the appellants served on the respondents, as owners, a notice pursuant to Section 29(2)(*a*) of the Planning Act to the effect that they were willing to comply with the purchase notice. The parties, having failed to agree on a price, the respondents on the 23rd May 1977 applied to the Land Reference Committee for the nomination of an arbitrator to determine the price to be paid by the appellants for such acquisition, pursuant to the provisions of the Acquisition of Land (Assessment of Compensation) Act 1919. Mr. Owen MacCarthy was by order of the Committee dated the 10th June 1977 duly nominated as arbitrator. Mr. MacCarthy commenced the arbitration on the 26th October 1977 and continued the hearing on the 24th and 25th November and on the 5th and 6th June 1978. At the arbitration it was contended on behalf of the respondents that the relevant date as of which the land should be valued was the last day of taking evidence at the arbitration, namely, the 6th January 1978. It was contended on behalf of the appellants that the appropriate date was the date of the notice of compliance with the purchase notice, namely, the 21st May 1976. The arbitrator made a finding of the value of the lands on each of the dates contended for and sent a special case to the High Court to determine which date was correct.

This special case came on for hearing in the High Court before Mr. Justice Butler who decided the date in relation to which the value or price should be determined was the last day of the arbitration hearing. Against that decision this appeal has been brought.

In deciding as he did in the High Court Mr. Justice Butler was guided by and followed the decision of the English Court of Appeal in *Birmingham Corporation* v. *West Midland Baptist Trust*.[5] He did so on the basis that the statutory provision in the Housing Act 1966 (Section 84) under which a time is specified in relation to which the value of land is to be assessed did not apply in this case. In my view, he was in error in this respect.

The various Local Government Acts, the Housing Acts and the Planning Acts from a code of interrelated statutes in the drafting of which clarity of language is remarkably absent. The seeker for the true meaning of particular statutory provisions is often sent from one statute to another and is frequently misled and

[5] [1969] 3 All E.R. 172.

confused by the use of different terms having the same meaning according to a particular adaptation used in one statute which may be absent in another. These statutes are drafted for an elite cognoscenti – those who in either central or local government are accustomed to the exercise of the powers prescribed and the language used. For others the ascertainment of what is laid down involves an arduous journey into the obscure.

Both the Planning Act and the Housing Acts deal with 'Local Authorities' which term in both statutes has the meaning assigned to it in the Local Government Act 1941. Such Local Authorities as are given functions under the Planning Act are termed 'Planning Authorities' and in the same manner such 'Local Authorities' as are given functions under the Housing Act are termed 'Housing Authorities'. In irrespective of the particular functions imposed on them under these Acts these bodies remain 'Local Authorities'.

Before considering the effect of Section 29(3) of the Planning Act it is necessary to consider some provisions of the Housing Act 1966. This Act authorises the acquisition of land compulsorily for the purposes of the Act by a Housing Authority. By Section 76 the acquisition may be authorised by a compulsory purchase order made by the authority and submitted to and confirmed by the Minister. The making and confirmation of a compulsory purchase order merely empowers the Housing Authority to acquire but does not bind it to do so. However, where the Housing Authority decide to acquire it, it is bound to serve a notice, termed a notice to treat, on all persons interested in the land (Section 79). The service of this notice authorises the taking possession of the land (Section 80), the making of a vesting order (Section 81) and, in default of agreement, the fixing of compensation in accordance with the Acquisition of Land (Assessment of Compensation) Act 1919 (Section 84). By Section 84 is is also provided that the compensation which is payable shall be assessed as of the time the relevant notice to treat is served. These various provisions are, of course, only applicable in relation to land being acquired compulsorily for the purposes of the Housing Act 1966.

I turn now to the provisions of Section 29(3) of the Planning Act. This sub-section applies, as already indicated, where a Planning Authority has served a notice stating its willingness to comply with the purchase notice. The sub-section provides that in such circumstances 'it shall be the duty of the authority to acquire'. It goes on to provide that 'for that purpose', namely, the acquisition of the land, the notice of compliance 'shall have the like effect as if it were a compulsory purchase order which, consequent upon a decision made by the planning authority pursuant to sub-section (1) of Section 10 of the Local Government (No. 2) Act 1960 had been duly made and confirmed'. A new Section 10 of the Act of 1960 has been inserted by Section 86 of the Housing Act 1966. It is therefore necessary to look at this provision to see what effect is to be attached to the notice of compliance served by the planning authority under Section 29(2)(a) of the Planning Act.

Section 10(1) of the 1960 Act, as inserted by Section 86 of the 1966 Act, applies where 'a Local Authority' intends to acquire compulsorily land 'for the purpose for which they are capable of being authorised by law to acquire land compulsorily' even if 'those purposes are purposes other than the purposes of the Housing Act 1966 or are purposes some only of which are purposes of that Act' but 'the Local Authority consider that it would be convenient to effect the acquisition under that Act'.

In such circumstances, the sub-section provides that 'The Local Authority may decide so to effect the acquisition'. When such a decision has been made, subsection (3) (*a*) and (*b*) provide that the acquisition may be authorised by means of a compulsory purchase order made and confirmed as provided for by Section 76 of the Housing Act 1966. Sub-section (4) goes on to provide that various Sections of the Housing Act 1966, including Sections 79 and 84, 'shall apply in relation to an order made by virtue of this Section. . . . and any reference in the said Sections . . . as so applied to a Housing Authority or the Minister shall be construed as a reference as to the Local Authority or the appropriate Minister, respectively.' Section 79 as already mentioned provided for the obligation on the Housing Authority to serve a notice to treat when it decided to acquire, and Section 84 provides that the compensation payable shall be determined having regard to the value of the land at the date of the notice to treat. Having regard to these provisions, it seems to me that under Section 29(3) the notice of compliance served by the Planning Authority must be regarded as a compulsory purchase order made and confirmed following a decision made under Section 10(1) of the Act of 1960. To such a compulsory purchase order Section 79 is expressly made to apply and thereby obliges the Planning Authority, which is under a duty to acquire, to serve a notice to treat. The Planning Authority is so obliged as a Local Authority. Section 84 is also made to apply and has the effect of providing that compensation must be determined having regard to the date of the service of this notice to treat. This, in my view, is the effect which, by Section 29(3) of the Planning Act, is made to attach to a notice of compliance served under Section 29(2) of that Act.

In this case, therefore, in my opinion, the Planning Authority having served a notice of compliance were bound to follow it up with a notice to treat. This notice to treat, in default of agreement being reached on compensation constituted the sine qua non for the assessment of compensation under Section 84. This Section was expressly made to apply under Section 10 of the Act of 1960. By Section 84(2) the assessment of compensation under the 1919 Act was expressly authorised on the basis that it would be determined having regard to the date of the notice to treat as provided for in sub-section (1) of the Section. In fact the Planning Authority in this case did not serve this notice to treat. It nevertheless permitted the arbitrator to be appointed and the arbitration to proceed, resulting in the assessment of compensation as indicated in the special case. In these circumstances, in my view, justice requires that, what ought to have been done be regarded and taken as having been done. The situation was brought about and created by the default of the Planning Authority. In this respect the owner was in no way at fault. In my view, therefore, the deeming to be done of what ought to have been done should be taken in relation to a point of time most advantageous to the owner. As the arbitration could not proceed under Section 84 without the service of a notice to treat but did in fact proceed, I feel that it should be taken to have proceeded on the basis of a notice to treat being served immediately before it commenced. On this basis, therefore, in my view, the compensation should be determined on the basis of the value of the land at the commencement of the arbitration. I would assume that no real difference could exist between the value on that date and the value on the latest date found by the arbitrator. If such a difference, however, does exist a fresh finding of value would be necessary.

I would answer the special case in the manner indicated in this judgment. I would like to add that in my view, as indicated in this judgment, in similar cases Planning Authorities are under a statutory obligation to follow a notice of compliance by a notice to treat and should do so.

APPENDIX A

DEVELOPMENT CONTROL
ADVICE AND GUIDELINES

CONTENTS

PREFACE

1. This Memorandum contains advice and guidelines of a general nature to assist planning authorities in reviewing their approach to development control and the details of the practices and procedures followed by them in dealing with planning applications. The Memorandum does not claim to be exhaustive and some of the material it contains is not new; it is, in part, a consolidation of earlier circulars and should be regarded as superseding those listed in Appendix I insofar as they relate to development control. It is hoped that the Memorandum can be extended and supplemented in due course by the issue of additional material.

2. The Memorandum does not purport to be a binding legal interpretation of the law nor is it to be regarded, apart from the matter referred to in paragraph 3.13, as containing general policy directives of the kind which the Minister is empowered to issue under section 7 of the Local Government (Planning and Development) Act, 1982. It is, essentially, an advisory document which also contains, for the information and guidance of planning authorities, statements of the Minister's policy on various issues. The need for further formal directives as to policy in relation to planning and development will be considered in the light of developments.

3. The problems faced by local planning authorities in dealing with over 50,000 planning applications each year are fully appreciated. The fact that difficulties and delays are frequently caused by applicants themselves is also recognised. Aplications can, for example be inadequately researched and badly presented with poor quality plans and a minimum of supporting material. Planning authorities, presented with such applications, will often have no alternative but to insist on a proper application being made before coming to a decision. Nevertheless, if an effort is to be made to improve the operation of the control system, a headline must be set by the public authorities who have primary responsibility for the system. It is for this reason that so many of the suggestions contained in this Memorandum relate to possible action by planning authorities rather than by applicants.

4. While the scope of the present Memorandum is limited, it attempts to cover those matters which appear from representations to the Minister and experience at appeals level to cause frequent problems and difficulties. Not all of the matters dealt with have equal relevance for all authorities and indeed the Department is aware of the effort made in many instances by planning authorities to provide a satisfactory level of service. Each planning authority in carrying out the review requested will therefore have to consider the relevance of particular advice in their circumstances.

5. Appendix II contains tables (based on returns from planning authorities and An Bord Pleanala) giving details in relation to the applications and appeals made to planning authorities and the Board in recent years. The data should be of assistance to planning authorities in reviewing their own individual approaches to development control. It is realised, of course, that severe pressure for particular types of development is experienced by some authorities and that some, having regard to the nature of their areas, need to excercise a more firm control than would be appropriate elsewhere. For this reason, some variation in the rate of refusal at local level or in the proportion of cases which have to be determined on appeal is only to be expected. Each planning authority will, however, be able to make relevant comparisons, having regard to their particular circumstances, and to decide for themselves whether the statistics suggest that there is a *prima facie* case for changes in their own approach.

6. For ease of reference, Appendix III contains a list of the enactments and regulations which are directly relevant to physical planning and are now in force.

Department of the Environment
October, 1982

PART I – THE GENERAL APPROACH

1.1 The Planning Acts are designed 'to make provision, in the interests of the common good, for the proper planning and development of cities, towns and other areas, whether urban or rural. . . .'. Under section 26 of the 1963 Act, planning authorities are restricted to considering 'the proper planning and development of the area' in dealing with planning applications and they must interpret and apply this basic criterion for themselves, having regard to the provisions of the development plan. Section 19 and the Third Schedule to the 1963 Act mention the purposes for which objectives may be indicated in development plans and are a good guide to the scope of 'proper planning and development'. Mention should also be made of section 24 of the 1976 Act under which regard must be had, in certain circumstances, to the probable effect of a particular decision on any place or area that is not within the area of the planning authority and to other considerations relating to development outside the area.

1.2 Because the development control system is intended to regulate land use and development in the public interest, the provisions of the Acts should be used for this purpose only and not for any extraneous purpose. In principle, the control mechanism should not be used for enforcing, or securing compliance with, the provisions of other legislation and regulations; this aspect is dealt with further in Part V. As indicated above, section 19 and the Third Schedule to the 1963 Act may be taken as a guide to what may be regarded as 'planning purposes'. Moreover, it should be noted that section 26(11) of the 1963 Act makes it clear that the existence of a planning permission does not, of itself, entitle a person to carry out any development.

1.3 Planning authorities should attempt to secure that the control system is responsive to public needs and reflects public aspirations to the greatest possible extent. The community expects that good standards in relation to safety, health and amenity will be applied to new development. It is also entitled to expect that development proposals – whether large or small – will be dealt with reasonably and expeditiously and that employment opportunities will not be put at risk or deferred by reason of defects and avoidable delays in the planning system.

1.4 Restrictions and prohibitions are necessary if orderly development is to be secured. However, the general approach to development control should not be an unduly restrictive one and permission should be refused only where there are serious objections on important planning grounds. Planning objectives should not be applied rigidly without regard to the circumstances and to the merits of each case; the system should also take account of the practical and human problems which arise under any system which can affect the property and the aspirations of every indiviual and which are relevant to planning. A reasonable, flexible approach should therefore be adopted and, while consistency and equality of treatment must be secured, it does not follow that uniformity must also be the rule.

1.5 Decisions which may appear to be inconsistent with other decisions of the planning authority will obviously not improve the reputation of the system. It is equally important, however, that the individual planning authority's approach to development control and the work programmes of the authority in relation to housing and other development should be consistent. Given the large proportion of planning applications which relate to housing, it is essential that the same general principles which govern the control of private housing development should be applied also to the local authority's housing development. Such development should be consistent in every material respect with the standards and requirements to which development which is subject to control by the authority is expected to conform.

1.6 Where a development proposal which appears to have been seriously prepared and presented is considered to have inherent planning defects (without being fundamentally objectionable), every effort should be made to overcome these defects, either by granting permission subject to conditions, or by advising the applicant as to how the proposal might be made acceptable. In some cases, the best approach may be to arrange for discussions with the applicant with a view to having an unacceptable proposal withdrawn and a fresh application submitted. In other cases, the applicant may be prepared to submit revised plans (without altering the essential character of the development) while in other circumstances, formal use of the discretionary power to invite the submission of modified plans may be more appropriate. Where the time for consideration by the planning authority of an application is not long enough to permit of discussions with an applicant, or the submission of modified plans, the power to extend the appropriate period within the meaning of section 26(4)(*a*) of the 1963 Act could be used with the consent of the applicant.

1.7 It is undesirable that persons should have to submit repeat applications for permission to find out by a process of trial and error what development is permissible. In cases in which planning objectives preclude the granting of permission in respect of a particular site, the planning authority should, whenever possible, endeavour to facilitate the applicant by indicating any alternative locations in which the proposed development could be allowed without conflict with fundamental objectives. The emphasis at all times should be on guiding and encouraging planned development rather than on a rigid application of controls.

1.8 While third parties are entitled to make representations or objections to a planning authority in relation to a planning application, and to have such representations or objections considered, it should be borne in mind that it is not the purpose of the planning system to protect the private interests of individuals or to provide a mechanism for resolving disputes between individuals about such interests. The effect of a proposed development on owners and occupiers of adjoining land is a relevant consideration but the net question for resolution through the planning system is whether the public interest or the common good would suffer if a particular proposal were to go ahead. Part VI of this Memorandum deals in some detail with the treatment by planning authorities of objections and with questions about property rights which may arise when applications are made.

1.9 Planning applications must be dealt with on the basis of planning considerations and, while relevant considerations of a personal nature should be taken into account, a planning authority cannot overlook the fact that development works may well remain long after the circumstances on which compassionate arguments are based have ceased to exist. Fundamental planning objections cannot, therefore, be set aside on compassionate grounds. In some cases, however, a genuine personal circumstance may be enough to justify giving the applicant 'the benefit of the doubt'. In some cases, too, conditions limiting the duration of a permission or limiting the use of a proposed structure may help in dealing with special hardship pleas; such conditions should, however, be used sparingly as they give rise to enforcement and other difficulties at a later stage.

1.10 Since the basic criterion for dealing with a planning application is the proper planning and development of the area, applications relating to particular sites cannot be dealt with in isolation; instead, account must be taken not only of what exists on the ground in the vicinity of the site but also of existing and impending permissions in relation to nearby sites, as well as any other commitments and any plans the authority itself may have in relation to the area.

1.11 Permissions that may exist in respect of a site – whether granted locally or an appeal – are a relevant consideration and should always be taken into account in dealing with a fresh application. Even where such a permission has ceased to have effect, it might still be a relevant or material consideration in determining a fresh application; while a planning authority should not therefore regard itself as being bound by a previous planning permission which has ceased to have effect, neither should it ignore the planning history of the site.

1.12 The development control system should concern itself with the important basic dimensions of proposals and should not become bogged down because of excessive attention to detail or to matters which are not of material planning concern. For example, the system should not, in general, concern itself with detailed standards of design or construction unless there is special need e.g. in areas of high architectural quality or scenic amenity. In regard to development in amenity areas, see also paragraphs **2.9** and **3.20**.

1.13 Special care should be taken to secure that matters of personal preference or taste are not allowed to affect decisions on planning proposals, particularly where these are prepared by competent and qualified designers.

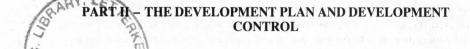

PART II – THE DEVELOPMENT PLAN AND DEVELOPMENT CONTROL

2.1 Under the 1934 and 1939 Planning Acts, a planning scheme was to have the force of law and its provisions were to regulate rigidly the future development of the area. By contrast, one of the objects of the 1963 act was to establish a more flexible planning system. Under the Act, the development plan does not itself confer any power to control development or impose controls as the pre-1963 Act schemes were intended to do. Instead, the plan indicates *development objectives* (section 19 of the 1963 Act) which provide a background against which decisions may be taken by planning authorities on particular development proposals. The control system is, therefore, a flexible one, allowing for reasonable discretion in its operation. Nevertheless, the plan is of fundamental importance in relation to development control. The planning authority, in exercising control, has to have regard to the provisions of the plan and must follow a special procedure before deciding to issue a control decision which contravenes materially the plan (see paragraph **2.5**). The importance of the plan in this regard relates to its more positive function of setting out a clear framework for the development of the area.

2.2 Development objectives stated in a plan must be realistic and within the technical and financial competence of the planning authority. Over-ambitious objectives will not only undermine confidence in the effectiveness of the planning process generally but also create serious problems in development control.

2.3 If a plan is basically sound and practical, clearly and concisely presented, understood by the public, and generally accepted as a fair and reasonable document, and if a plan is operated sensibly, major difficulties should not arise at local level in regard to development control and there should be less need to resort to the appeals machinery. The responsible developer will know where he stands and will be able to plan accordingly, while others will be deterred from pressing for permission for proposals which do not accord with proper planning principles. If the plan does not meet these criteria, especially in an area where pressure for development is strong, and if development control operates in what can be alleged to be a harsh or arbitrary way, difficulties will multiply: the number of appeals will increase, staff will have to be diverted from more positive work, development will be delayed and an atmosphere hostile to and cynical towards planning will be created.

2.4 Planning objectives – and the factors on which they are based – should be clearly stated in the development plan and regard must be had to the plan when applications are being considered. This does not mean, however, that planning authorities must always adhere rigidly to the provisions of the plan. It does not follow that development which is consistent with the provisions of the plan must necessarily be permitted or that a development proposal which contravenes the plan must be refused.

2.5 Planning authorities are not entitled to disregard the development plan and, where they decide to contravene it in operating the control system, there must be good reasons for doing so and these should be readily apparent. On the other hand, planning authorities should not adopt the view that, because a particular development proposal would contravene the development plan, there is no option but to refuse permission. This attitude is not in accordance with the law. In dealing with applications, planning authorities are restricted to considering the proper planning and development of the area but there is not prohibition in the Acts on the granting of permissions which contravene the plan. It is only where a *material contravention* is involved that the special procedure required by section 26(3) of the 1963 Act, as amended, must be operated before a permission can be granted. In deciding whether any development would contravene *materially* the development plan, an authority might consider whether there would be a departure from a fundamental provision of the plan or whether the development – alone or in conjunction with others – would seriously prejudice an objective of the plan.

2.6 If the relevant objectives of a development plan have been fully thought out and are carefully expressed and explained, the risk of conflict with the plan in the operation of development control will be minimised, and it must be the aim of all planning authorities to achieve this position. Practical experience in the operation of development control may, however, suggest that objectives are not fully appropriate or attainable or need to be developed or modified or replaced. Objectives may be expressed in terms which, though unobjectionable in themselves, lead to difficulties in development control or a clouding of the basic objectives which were in mind. A review of the relevant provisions of the plan may also be indicated where there is severe pressure for particular types of development, in order to make the planning authority's position more clear to potential applicants or to enable applications to be dealt with in a more flexible manner. Development plan defects of this kind should be remedied as soon as possible: there is no need to wait for the quinquennial review of a plan to make variations based on the practical lessons learned from experience of the operation of the development control system.

2.7 Much of what is said above is relevant to restrictive clauses in the development plan. It is important to ensure that essential restrictions, and the reasons for them, are clearly and fairly stated in the plan and that their significance is not lost sight of in less essential restrictions of a general nature. Such an approach could remove uncertainty from developers and save them and the public authorities time, effort and money in proceeding with applications and appeals which have little or no prospect of succeeding. The planning authority should, therefore, look at general clauses in the plan, in particular those of a prohibitory or restrictive nature, and consider whether, in the light of experience, they continue to be justified or need to be explained or refined and whether there is a need and scope for positive complementary provisions to provide for development affected.

2.8 Planning authorities are the principal guardians of scenic, recreational and amenity areas, in the mountains, in lakeland areas, along the coastline, and so on, and development plans generally reflect a concern to protect such areas. In many cases, however, there may be a particular need to clarify the relevant objectives in the plans. A general objective of attempting to preserve substantial areas can lead to serious difficulties in development control, particularly where the objective relates to the preservation of the rural amenity of large areas, the high amenity value of which may not be clear to the public. Such an approach may also add to the difficulty of conserving key locations where there is little or no room for compromise.

2.9 There are areas of very high amenity and recreational value, including the traditional beauty spots of national importance, where even well-designed residential or other development should not be allowed. There are, too, certain coastal and other areas where a restrictive approach to development will be essential to protect the attractiveness of the area. However, absolute restrictions should be avoided, unless they are considered to be absolutely essential; where possible, provision should be made for less stringent controls and the relevant provisions in the plan should be formulated in such a way that developers can see clearly where development may be permissible, the type of development, and the conditions to be complied with.

PART III – PARTICULAR CLASSES OF DEVELOPMENT

Introduction

3.1 The following paragraphs deal with some of the classes of development for which permission is frequently sought and with development which creates particular problems. It is hoped that more comprehensive guidance notes covering a wider range of topics can be developed at a later stage.

Housing development generally

3.2 The planning system must facilitate housing development generally. Every effort should be made by planniing authorities to enable overall housing requirements to be met and special consideration should be given to the desirability of a process of expansion in the smaller towns and villages. Such an approach would not only counteract over-rapid development of the larger urban areas (which can create heavy demands for infrastructure and other services) but would also assist in dealing with the problems arising from pressure for isolated housing development in rural areas, unrelated to any identifiable existing centre.

Housing estates

3.3 The development by the private sector of housing estates is an essential part of the housing programme and should be encouraged by planning authorities as far as possible. Much of what is stated elsewhere in this Memorandum about the approach to development proposals applies with special force to housing proposals. In addition, the drafting of permissions for such development needs special attention if the problem of unfinished estates is to be eliminated. In this regard, the advice contained in Part V about the use of conditions is of particular importance.

Non-estate type houses

3.4 A large proportion of total annual output of private houses in accounted for by the provision by private persons of non-estate type houses, many of them in villages, small towns and rural areas. Although it is an objective of many development plans that housing development should be concentrated in existing settlements which offer scope for the utilisation of existing physical and social infrastructure, this should not be taken as precluding in all cases proposals for single houses in other areas. In addition to keeping under review the implications of such objectives, the approach should be to examine each case on its merits and to determine whether there are in fact serious objections to the particular proposal on important planning grounds such as traffic safety, public health and amenity. While it is not easy to do so, planning authorities should also attempt to discriminate between the needs of members of the rural community and their families together with those whose occupations require them to reside in rural areas and, on the other hand, demands which arise merely from speculative pressure or a desire to artificially increase land values for bank borrowing purposes. Moreover, efforts should be made to differentiate between proposals which are likely to be of a 'one-off' nature and those which involve haphazard and disorderly siting of new groups of houses in rural areas.

Septic tanks

3.5 As a general rule, it should not be necessary, as part of the development control process, to go into detail on septic tank drainage arrangements, particularly in relation to single houses on large sites. Moreover, proposals for single houses drained by septic tanks should not be refused on the basis of objections stated in general terms nor should they be refused because the site is judged unsuitable for a septic tank following only a superficial examination. Care should be taken to ensure that refusals based on 'undue proliferation' or 'excessive concentration' of septic tanks are justified, having regard to site sizes, distance from other dwellings, topography, soil conditions, etc.

3.6 Where it is considered, following preliminary inspection, that there may be doubts about the suitability of a site for septic tank drainage, and there are no other major objections to the propose development, applicants might be asked, by way of the additional information system to provide evidence of suitability and to have trial holes dug and percolation tests carried out under supervision. Definite evidence of the unsuitability of the site for the treatment and effective disposal of septic tank effluent, or a clear risk of pollution of waters, or of contamination of water supplies, should be available before a refusal based wholly or mainly on septic tank reasons in contemplated. (See also paragraphs **4.4** and **6.22**).

3.7 Standards applied by planning authorities in relation to site sizes, etc., for septic tank purposes vary, having regard to local conditions Planning authorities will be aware of the I.I.R.S. Recommendations for Septic Tank Drainage Systems suitable for Single Houses (S.R. 6: 1975) which should be of assistance in operating development control. Attention is drawn to the foreword to that document (which sets out the spirit in which it should be used) and to Appendix C (which suggests possible methods of improving sites where ground conditions for the disposal of septic tank effluent are not ideal). Attention is also drawn to the emphasis on the location, etc., of the percolation area rather than that of the tank itself.

3.8 In general, it would seem to be preferable not to attempt to enforce rigid standards as regards minimum site sizes or road frontages, the location of septic tanks or percolation areas, distances from site boundaries, roads, wells or streams, or details of percolation areas and systems of distribution pipes: these are often matters which can best be decided in the particular circumstances of each case and on the basis of an assessment of actual site conditions. Local standards do have the merit of allowing control to be seen to operate in an even-handed and fair manner but, where it is decided to employ them, care should be taken to ensure that the standards are reasonable and that the reasoning behind them is clear.

3.9 Development proposals which involve the use of a combined or communal septic tank system for two or more houses, should generally be discouraged unless the local authority is itself prepared to undertake responsibility for the maintenance of the tank. Similar considerations apply in relation to development served by small treatment plants. Proposals which necessitate the location of a septic tank or percolation area outside a site (and particularly on the opposite side of a public road) should not, in general be favourably considered; where there are no other major objections, cases of this kind might be dealt with by inviting the applicant to submit modified plans to overcome the problem.

3.10 The objectionable features of excessive ribbon development are recognised in many development plans. In principle, such development is undesirable because of its disorderly nature, its effect on amenity and on agriculture, the difficulty and cost of providing services, the creation of traffic hazard and the reduction in the carrying capacity of roads. Ribboning tends to occur on the roads leading out of developed towns and villages because suitable housing and other sites are difficult to obtain within the development area; it can also occur on minor roads within commuting distance of an urban centre. Site cost may be a factor, particularly in the case of private housing, but a basic problem may also be scarcity or absence of serviced sites, the lack of access to suitable lands, including back-lands, or the reluctance of landowners to incur the expense of having plans prepared for development in depth.

3.11 In areas where ribboning is a problem, local planning authorities should attempt to devise a positive programme to deal with it. In some areas, it may be possible for the local authority itself to develop land for private building. Another approach would be to investigate the possibility of co-operating with landowners: assistance could be offered in the preparation of layouts, the provision of access or development roads, arrangements for temporary servicing, etc. This might be done on the basis of recoupment of the expenditure incurred, either from the landowner as sites are taken up, or from the individual developers. Again, where there is likely to be a substantial period before serviced sites in development areas are available, the planning authority should consider allowing minor development, on a phased basis, which would ultimately be consistent with an overall plan.

3.12 Unless positive steps to counteract, and provide alternatives to, ribbon development are being taken, the operation of development control must recognise the practical difficulties facing those seeking to house themselves in this way. Where serviced housing sites are not available in towns and villages at reasonable cost, a reasonably liberal approach to individual cases will be required, particularly where the roads concerned are not the principal routes radiating from the town and serious conflict with fundamental requirements such as amenity, health or traffic safety does not arise. In appropriate cases, a sterilisation clause, based on an agreement under section 38 of the 1963 Act, may help to regulate over-development.

Large retail shopping development
3.13 Attention is drawn to the general policy directive issued by the Minister pursuant to section 7 of the Local Government (Planning and Development) Act, 1982. Planning authorities are required to have regard to this directive in performing their functions, including their development control functions. The directive specifies that policy in relation to planning and development requires that the establishment of retail shopping development which would represent a large scale addition to the existing retail shopping capacity in a locality should be guided by the following considerations:-

(a) the adequacy of existing retail shopping outlets;

(b) the size and location of existing retail shopping outlets;

(c) the quality and convenience of existing retail shopping outlets;

(d) the effect on existing communities, including in particular the effect on established retail shopping outlets and on employment;

(e) the needs of elderly, infirm or disabled persons and of other persons who may be dependent on the availability of local retail shopping outlets;

(f) the need to counter urban decline and to promote urban renewal and to promote the utilisation of unused infrastructural facilities in urban areas.

Development along National Primary Roads

3.14 Most planning authorities already accept the need to restrict development alongside, or with access to, National Primary Roads. These roads account for only about 3% of the total mileage of public roads but they carry a high proportion of total traffic and are of vital importance to the development of the economy. The major road investment programme being carried out at present is designed to increase the capacity and safety of the national roads. It is essential that this investment is protected, as replacement will not be possible in this century. Any frontage development along the new roads should be prohibited and access to development should only be via a limited number of well planned access points. The cost of constructing the junctions involved will necessitate their limitation to absolutely essential locations.

3.15 Ribbon development is particularly undesirable on the national roads. It can create serious traffic hazards for both residents and road users and from a national investment point of view, it increases the length, and thereby the cost, of any by-pass facilities that will be required, and reduces the efficiency of existing by-passes. Service to the users of the National Primary Roads does not require that a proliferation of establishments such as taverns, motels, filling stations and shops, be sited indiscriminately along the network. Moreover, statistical analyses have shown that the accident rate on the routes increases with the number of access points.

3.16 As a general policy, the location of new means of access to the National Primary Roads, or residential, commercial, industrial or other development dependent on such means of access, should not be permitted except in areas where a speed limit of 30 – 40 m.p.h. applies, or in the case of infilling, in the existing built-up areas. It should also be borne in mind that where development adjoins a National Primary Road but has no direct vehicular access to it, hazardous situations can also arise because of the generation of parking, the opening of pedestrian routes, even of an informal nature, and so on.

3.17 Members of the farming community wishing to build houses for their own occupation on their land may have to be treated exceptionally but it is in the interest of the safety of these persons and their families that permission should not be granted for the provision of access to a National Primary Road if any other alternative is possible. In all cases, the onus should be put on the devleoper to show clearly that an exception is justified in his case.

3.18 Planning authorities should ensure that their development plans contain clear provisions regarding development along National Primary Roads. In addition, where permission is being refused for such development, it is important that the reason for refusal should fully reflect the policy and other considerations involved.

Brief statements, perhaps referring only to the creation of a traffic hazard, should be avoided. It would be desirable to attempt to bring out also such considerations as the need to preserve the carrying capacity of the road, to protect the public investment in its improvement to form a through-route for heavy traffic, and so on.

Development along National Secondary Roads

3.19 In general, the considerations set out above apply also to the National Secondary Roads. These account for a further 3% (approximately) of the total mileage of public roads and consist of medium-length through and semi-through routes serving as connecting links between principal towns and linking the National Primary Roads to form a homogeneous network. While the restriction of development alongside such roads is not of such critical national importance as in the case of the National Primary Roads, planning authorities will themselves appreciate the importance of the role of the National Secondary Roads in their own areas. In most cases, a restrictive policy will be justified with the onus on the applicant to show why an exception should be considered.

Development in amenity areas

3.20 There are areas of unspoilt natural beauty where a firm line must be taken and where a consistent approach is essential in operating development control. However, the amenity area objectives of development plans should not always be applied as blanket restrictions on development. For instance, an objective to preserve an area between a coastal road and the sea should operate as a complete prohibition on building only where that is the considered intention of the planning authority having regard to the particular topography, the scenic quality of the area, the needs of the planning authority area as a whole in relation to amenity, recreation and tourism, the desirability of not having beaches overlooked or polluted by sewage effluents, and other relevant considerations. In some cases, limited development should be permissible; for example, there may be no view of the sea from a particular section of road, or buildings may be unobtrusive because the site is sufficiently below the level of the road or is screened by hillocks or trees. Much the same considerations apply to lakeside and mountain areas. While the special beauty and attractiveness of many areas can be spoiled by the intrusion of a single badly located and unsuitably designed structure, care in siting and design (particularly in regard to finishes and roof colours) may often enable development to be carried out without serious injury to amenity. In other cases, additions to existing groups of houses or other buildings may not be harmful. Each case must, therefore, be considered on its merits and should not be dealt with solely by reference to general provisions in the plan.

Development in Gaeltacht Areas

3.21 Gaeltacht areas are, to a large extent, areas of scenic importance in which the physical features which may deter other forms of development repesent potential for tourist and holiday expansion. A basic need in the Gaeltacht is to encourage and facilitate suitable development of all kinds. In making and reviewing development plans, this will involve earmarking sites for all forms of development which it is reasonable to anticipate, or desirable to encourage, and the provision of whatever services are necessary to make the provision effective. It is particularly important that planning policies should be so designed that, while natural assets are protected against damaging development, no reasonable development opportunity is lost to a Gaeltacht area. Unreasonable or unneccessary restrictions or conditions on development are inimical to planning and are to be guarded against everywhere but specially in Gaeltacht areas because of the urgency and special nature of Gaeltacht problems.

Development where water and sewerage services are deficient

3.22 Lack of capacity in water supply systems or in sewers or sewage treatment systems, pending major improvement works, can lead to refusals of permission, even where there is an accepted need for new housing or other development. If improvement works are in progress and are likely to be completed within a reasonable time, it may be possible to give permission for housing or other projects subject to the phasing of completions. Where works are already in hands or about to commence, the planning authority should consider whether development can be permitted subject to appropriate conditions as to connection with the services or, in cases where planning of sewerage services is at an advanced stage, subject to temporary arrangements for sewage disposal and later connection to the public system.

3.23 Where there is pressure for scattered development in the rural environs of towns, limits may have to be imposed because of undue concentration of septic tanks or the need to protect roads from ribboning but, in that case, the possibility of providing serviced land in a suitable location should be examined. Where the planning authority are satisfied that such services can and will be made available quickly, they might consider deciding to grant a permission with a condition that the development shall not be occupied or used until it is linked up with the services.

Minor developments

3.24 The 1963 Act and Part III of the 1977 Regulations (as amended in 1981) exempt from development control a significant number of minor developments. Any blanket extension of the exempted development classes could give rise to serious problems and inequities in particular cases. There are however, a significant number of applications for permission for development of a minor nature which, in the particular circumstances, are likely to be unobjectionable. Planning authorities might therefore consider the adoption of special procedures for dealing expeditiously with such applications, especially those involving minor extensions of existing development. This may not always be justified, of course, especially in areas of high architectural quality or of special amenity. Where existing practice involves the circulation of all applications to a number of local authority departments (roads, water supply, drainage, fire, etc.,) consideration might be given to limiting the procedures in relation to specified minor developments.

Variations of permitted development

3.25 Applications which involve only minor variations of development proposals which have already been approved should be dealt with expeditiously. In addition, the making of such applications should not be used by the planning authority as an oportunity to revise conditions (including contribution conditions) in relation to matters which do not directly relate to, or arise from, the particular variations for which permission is being sought.

3.26 It is particularly important that a reasonable and co-operative attitude is adopted in relation to proposals for revised house types (either on single sites or within a housing estate). In some cases, such proposals can raise critical issues, for example, where an attractive and suitably designed house permitted in a high amenity area is to be replaced by a much inferior house, or where radical changes in house-types are proposed in a partially completed estate. Planning authorities should, however, make allowance for the fact that the housing market changes and that builders must be able to respond quickly. Accordingly, they should ensure that consideration of applications for revised house-types, which seem to be genuinely based, is confined to the essentials. They might also consider whether an abridged procedure might be employed to deal with such applications, in cases where no change in the already approved layout, etc., is involved. It should not be necessary, for example, to arrange to have such proposals examined *de novo* from the point of view of traffic safety, or from the drainage and water supply aspect.

Unauthorised structures or uses

3.27 Section 28 of the 1963 Act expressly provides that the power to grant a permission under section 26 includes power to grant permission for the retention of a structure which was erected without permission (or which was constructed with some variation from the approved plans) or for the continuance of a use which was instituted without permission. While it is essential to ensure that unauthorised development is discouraged and that the planning code is respected, it is for the planning authorities to use their enforcement powers to this end. When an application for permission for retention or continuance of a use is validly made, in an effort to regularise the position, it must be fairly dealt with in accordance with the criteria set out in section 26 of the 1963 Act and elsewhere in the legislation. The fact that an offence may have been committed, or the question of whether the person responsible should be prosecuted or penalised, should not affect the determination of such an application. The case must be dealt with on its merits, the only issue being whether permission should properly be granted or refused.

3.28 Applications relating to unauthorised structures or uses, especially if they succeed, can give rise to allegations that the law is being brought into disrepute and that encouragement is being given to developers who build first and seek permission afterwards. However, the appropriate response to such criticism lies in the proper use of the enforcement machinery rather than in the adoption of a different attitude to retention or continuance of use applications.

3.29 Requests for additional information under article 26 of the 1977 Regulations may be necessary in relation to an application for retention of a structure or for the continuance of a use. It is important, however, that such a request – and failure to respond to it – is not allowed to delay determination of such an application to an unreasonable extent. In this regard, attention is drawn to article 26(3) of the Regulations under which refusal or failure to comply within one month with an additional information request leave the way open to the planning authority to determine the application on the basis of the information available. Attention is also directed to article 21 of the Regulations in this regard.

PART IV – REFUSALS OF PERMISSION

Reasons for refusal generally

4.1 Formal refusals of permission will always be necessary in a proportion of cases – irrespective of what efforts are made by planning authorities to guide and assist developers – and it is in the interests of all that the same care and attention is devoted to the drafting of refusal decisions as is given to grants of permission.

4.2 Section 26(8) of the 1963 Act, as amended, requires that every decision to refuse a permission or approval must comprise a statement specifying the reasons for the refusal. This requirement is a fundamental one for it is essential that the applicant should know fully where he stands and that he should be in a position to assess properly the options open to him as a consequence of the refusal. Reasons for refusal should therefore be as informative and as helpful as possible, they should be self-contained statements and they should be related specifically to the particular development proposal.

Refusals arising from development plans

4.3 A statement of objectives in a plan should not be regarded as imposing a blanket prohibition on particular classes of development and does not relieve the planning authority of responsibility for considering the merits or otherwise of particular applications. A brief reference to an objective or policy statement is not, therefore, adequate as a reason for refusal if it is not made clear what the objective is, how it would be contravened by the proposed development and why that contravention would be contrary to the proper planning and development of the area. A reason for refusal must, as far as possible, bring out the reasonableness of applying the provisions of the plan in the particular case. Where there are other good reasons for refusal not explicitly based on the development plan, these should also be stated since it is the interests of intending developers to know all the fundamental objections to their proposals if they are considering amendment of their schemes, or the making of an appeal.

Number of reasons to be included

4.4 While it is not necessary that a statement of reasons for refusal should list every possible objection to a proposed development, all of the reasons which motivate the planning authority to refuse permission should be stated. The omission of a reason can, in some cases, be extremely misleading and can give rise to inconvenience and delay for an applicant, and at appeals level. An appropriate procedure would seem to be to list all of the fundamental objections to a proposed development or all of the objections which, even in isolation, would in the planning authority's view, warrant a refusal of permission. If this is not done, an applicant who has had a refusal of permission based, for example, on serious traffic hazard may submit revised plans to eliminate or mitigate the hazard only to find that a second refusal based on, say, inadequate drainage arrangements follows; the undesirability of such an eventuality does not need to be stressed. On the other hand, if reasons for refusal relating to matters of detail (for example, aspects of the design and layout of a housing estate) are included with fundamental objections based on considerations such as the need to reserve the land for some other purpose, deficiency of services, or inadequacy of the local road network, an applicant may be misled into thinking that the objections in principle are not considered by the authority to be very strong ones and he may wastefully revise his proposal to meet the minor objections. As a general guide, a matter which could be dealt with (if everything else were in order) by way of a condition, may not be an appropriate reason for a refusal.

Non-planning reasons

4.5 It follows from what has been stated earlier in this Memorandum that care must always be taken to avoid the use of 'non-planning' reasons to justify a refusal of permission or to attempt to strengthen the case for such a refusal.

Non-compensatable reasons

4.6 Section 56 of the 1963 Act provides that where permission is refused for particular reasons, compensation under section 55 will not normally be payable. Planning authorities will, naturally, be concerned to ensure that they will not incur a compensation liability in cases where the facts of the case are such that payment of compensation would clearly not be justified by reference to the provisions of section 56. There should be no question, however, of including or 'tailoring' reasons for refusal to obviate the possibility of successful compensation claims in cases where the facts of the case do not justify the reasons stated.

4.7 When reasons for refusal are being drafted, care should be taken to introduce expressions contained in section 56 where the facts justify their use, so that there can be no ambiguity about the compensation position. For example, where a site is on a dangerous bend leading to the conclusion that there would be a serious traffic hazard, the reason for refusal should read '*The proposed development would endanger public safety by reason of traffic hazard* because the site is located. . . , taking the words underlined from section 56(1)(*e*). Similarly, if it is concluded that a proposed development would be unacceptable because of its effects on the amenities of adjoining houses, the expression '*would seriously injure the amenities of property in the vicinity because*. . . .' contained in section 56(1)(*i*)(iii) should be used in the reason for refusal. It is important, of course, that the reason should contain, as well as the formal expressions referred to above, a clear statement as to why it is considered that the traffic hazard or serious injury to amenity would arise.

Premature development

4.8 Development which is premature having regard to water supply, sewerage or roads considerations can generally be refused without incurring a liability to pay compensation. Prematurity as a reason for refusal is not, however, the service in question will, in the future, be provided. To refuse, as premature, permission for the building of an isolated house in a rural area where there are no public water supply and sewerage services should not, for example, be contemplated unless there is a plan for servicing the area in the future or a reasonable prospect that such a plan will emerge. It should be borne in mind that for a compensation claim to succeed, a reduction in value must be shown to have occurred and that there are, therefore, many circumstances (other than those listed in sections 56 and 57 of the 1963 Act) which could have a bearing on the question of whether a liabilty to compensation is incurred.

4.9 Where it is proposed to reject a proposal as being premature pending the preparation of a detailed action area plan, or an overall road layout, or a comprehensive redevelopment plan, the planning authority should consider the provisions likely to be included in such a plan and satisfy itself that there is a real possibility that the proposed development would be likely to be incompatible with these provisions or to frustrate the implementation of the plan in some material respect. The absence of a plan, or the fact that a plan may not have been formally approved by the council, should not be used to justify a refusal based on prematurity in cases where, having regard to the situation on the ground, or previous planning decisions, the range of options available is so small as to enable an *ad hoc* assessment of the development proposal to be carried out without difficulty. It is particularly important that the absence of a comprehensive redevelopment plan should not stifle worthwhile proposals for new development or redevelopment in rundown inner urban areas.

PART V – CONDITIONS

Power to attach conditions

5.1 The power to attach conditions to a permission or an approval is, on the face of it, a very wide power but, to be valid, a condition must serve some genuine planning purpose in relation to the development permitted. It must be directed to securing the object for which the powers of the Act were given (regulating the development and use of land) and not to some totally extraneous object or some irrelevant purpose. The condition must also fairly and reasonably relate to the development permitted.

Conditions generally

5.2 Conditions proposed to be attached to permissions or approvals, and the reasons for them, should be carefully drafted so that their purpose and meaning are clear. Conditions must always be precise and unambiguous, particularly since the effectiveness of subsequent enforcement action may depend on the wording. Moreover, adequate reasons should be given by planning authorities to justify conditions; it is not, for example, generally acceptable to give as a reason 'in the interests of the proper planning and development of the area' since this affords the applicant no opportunity of informing himself as to the particular object of the condition.

The number of conditions

5.3 The number of conditions should be kept to the absolute minimum as the attempt to regulate details to an excessive extent may defeat its own ends. Moreover, difficulties can arise for developers and landowners generally at conveyancing and other stages in attempting to provide evidence of compliance with numerous conditions, especially those of a vague or general nature.

Standard conditions

5.4 Some planning authorities have devised standard conditions (and reasons) for use in relation to different types of applications. This practice is useful in the interests of consistency and can achieve time savings. Great care should be taken, however, to ensure that standard conditions are used only where they actually apply, that they are properly adapted to meet the needs of particular cases, and that the availability of sets of standard conditions does not lead to the automatic inclusion of unnecessary conditions in particular cases.

When conditions should be imposed

5.5 When it is desired to restrict or regulate proposed development in any way, it is necessary to impose a valid condition supported by good reasons. It is not sufficient to incorporate the requirement in the description contained in the decision order relating to the development being permitted. If, for example, it is intended that an office use should be ancillary to another use, a specific condition to that effect should be attached to the permission.

Basic criteria in regard to use of conditions

5.6 Certain basic criteria have often been suggested as a guide to deciding whether to impose a condition. These include the questions of whether the condition is –

    (a) necessary?
    (b) relevant to planning?
    (c) relevant to the development to be permitted?
    (d) enforceable?
    (e) precise?
    (f) reasonable?

In addition, it is useful before deciding to impose a condition to consider what specific reason can be given for it: if the only reason which can be framed is a vague, general one, the need for or relevance of the condition, or its validity, may be questionable.

Need for a condition

5.7 A useful test of need is whether, without the condition, permission for the proposed development would have to be refused. It is not enough to be able to say that a condition will do no harm: if it is to be justified, it ought to do some good in terms of achieving a satisfactory standard of development and in supporting objectives of the development plan. It should also be borne in mind that a condition is not necessary where what is sought by the condition is clearly provided for in the plans and particulars by reference to which the permission is being granted.

Relevance to planning

5.8 As the planning system is intended to be used for genuine planning purposes and not any extraneous purpose, it is obvious that a condition which has no relevance to 'the proper planning and development of the area' ought not to be attached to a planning permission. (As indicated earlier, section 19 and the Third Schedule to the 1963 Act, which mention the purposes for which objectives may be indicated in development plans, are a good guide to the scope of this term). In particular, matters which are the subject of other more specific statutory controls or are regulated by common law should not be dealt with by conditions. Further guidance on this aspect is contained in paragraphs **5.28**, **5.30** and **5.35**.

Relevance to permitted development

5.9 Unless the requirements of a condition are directly related to the development to be permitted, the condition may be *ultra vires*. Section 26(2)(a) of the 1963 Act gives power to impose a condition regulating the development or use of adjoining etc. land, but such land must be under the control of the applicant and the condition must be 'expedient for the purposes of or in connection with the development authorised by the permission'. Moreover, where a condition requires the carrying out of works, or regulates the use of land, its requirements must be connected with the development permitted on the land to which the planning application relates. For instance, it may be expedient that, on building a factory, a developer should be required to provide parking facilities for the factory workers on land which he owns adjoining the site and a condition to this effect would be in order. It would not be in order, however, to grant permission subject to a condition requiring the applicant to provide a car park to serve an existing factory which he owns at the other end of the town. Similarly, a condition requiring the removal of an existing building, whether on the factory site ot not, will be appropriate only if the need for that removal arises directly from the fact that a new building is to be erected – where for example, the site with both buildings on it, would be over-developed. Generally however, the grant of permission for a new building, or for a change of use, cannot properly be used to secure general tidying-up of existing structures by means of a condition attached to the permission.

Conditions should be enforceable

5.10 Clearly a condition should not be imposed if it cannot be made effective. In a case where any doubt arises, it may be useful, therefore, to consider how the enforcement provisions of the Acts could be operated to secure compliance with a proposed condition. To facilitate enforcement, the aim should be to frame conditions, where possible, so as to require some specific act to be done at or before a specified time, or to require some specific thing not to be done in carrying out the development.

Conditions should be precise

5.11 Every condition should be precise and clearly understandable. It must tell the developer from the outset exactly what he has to do, or must not do. A condition which requires the developer to take action if and when some other indefinite event takes place is unacceptable e.g. to improve an access 'if the growth of traffic makes it desirable'. A condition that requires that the site 'shall be kept tidy at all times' is clearly of little value as is a condition requiring that the permitted development 'shall not be used in any manner so as to cause nuisance to nearby residents'. In the one case, the condition is directed to matters which are controllable at common law, the question of whether or not a particular use constitutes a nuisance is left open. Conditions which can only be expressed in such vague general terms will often be found to be unnecessary or unenforceable.

Conditions should be reasonable

5.12 A condition may be so unreasonable that it would be in danger of rejection by the Courts. For example, it would normally be lawful to impose a continuing restriction on the hours during which an industrial or other use can be carried out, if the use of the premises outside these hours would seriously injure the amenities of property in the vicinity, but it would be unreasonable to restrict the hours of operation to such an extent as to nullify the permission. Again, it may be unreasonable to make a permission subject to a condition which has the effect of deferring the development for a very long period, by requiring, for example, that the permitted development shall not be carried out until a sewerage scheme for the area – which may only be at the preliminary design stage – has been completed. If the development is genuinely premature, the application ought to be refused. A condition which requires a developer to carry out additional works may be reasonable but the provisions of section 26(7) of the 1963 Act may come into play in some cases where such a condition is attached.

5.13 A useful test of reasonableness is some cases is to consider whether a proposed condition can be complied with by the developer without encroachment on land which he does not control, or without otherwise obtaining the consent of some other party whose interests may not coincide with those of the developer. It may be appropriate in some cases, before determining the application, to afford the developer an opportunity of either obtaining such consent or of revising or modifying the lodged plans to eliminate the need for it.

Time limits on the validity of permissions

5.14 Having regard to the specific statutory provisions governing the duration of planning permissions, a condition requiring that a development should either by commenced or completed within a specified period should never be imposed. It would be in order, however, to require by condition that a building is not to be occupied until it has been substantially completed in accordance with the approved plans, if this can be shown to be essential on planning grounds. Where a group of structures is proposed, it may occasionally be appropriate to regulate, by condition, the order in which the structures are to be completed or occupied.

5.15 Under section 3 of the Local Government (Planning and Development(Act, 1981, planning authorities have power, when deciding to grant a permission, to specify a period of duration longer than the standard five-year period. The operation of section 3 should not involve attaching conditions to permissions. Notes on the provisions of the 1982 Act which have already issued to planning authorities deal fully with this matter.

Temporary permissions

5.16 In deciding whether a temporary permission is appropriate, three main factors should be taken into account. First, the grant of a temporary permission will rarely be justified where an applicant wishes to carry out development of a permanent nature which conforms with the provisions of the development plan. Secondly, it is undesirable to impose a condition involving the demolition of a building that is clearly intended to be permanent. Lastly, it must be remembered that the material considerations to which regard must be had in dealing with applications are not limited or made different by a decision to make the permission a temporary one. Thus, the reason for a temporary permission can never be that a time limit is necessary because of the adverse effect of the development on the amenities of the area. If the development will certainly affect the amenities, they can only be safeguarded by ensuring that it does not take place.

5.17 An application for a temporary permission may, however, raise different material considerations from an application for permanent permission. Permission could reasonably be granted on an application for the erection of a temporary building to last seven years on land which will be required for road improvements in eight or more year's time, whereas permission would have to be refused on an application to erect a permanent building on the land. Similarly, an application for permission to erect an advertisement structure in a rundown area may warrant more favourable treatment if the structure is to be removed on the expiration of a specified period when redevelopment works are likely to be under way.

5.18 In the case of a use which may be a 'bad neighbour' to uses already existing in the immediate vicinity, it may sometimes be appropriate to grant a temporary permission in order to enable the impact of the development to be assessed, provided that such a permission would be reasonable having regard to the expenditure necessary to carry out the development. A second temporary permission should not normally be granted for that particular reason for it should have become clear by the expiration of the first permission whether permanent permission or a refusal is the right answer. In other circumstances, an application for a second temporary permission may be quite genuine and should be dealt with on its merits. For example, where a temporary permission has been granted for a structure which is inherently impermanent, an application for a permission for a further limited period could reasonably be made if the structure has been well maintained and there has been no other change in circumstances relating to the proper planning and development of the area concerned.

5.19 In all temporary permissions for structures, express provision should be made by condition requiring the removal of the structure and the carrying out of appropriate reinstatement works on the land at the expiration of the specified period. In addition, the condition should specify the period for which the permission is being granted by reference to some particular date and not by reference to the occurence of some indefinite future event. Use of expressions such as 'such longer period as the planning authority may allow' or 'on three months' notice. . . .' should be avoided.

Conditions appropriate to outline permissions

5.20 An outline permission is in every sense the permission required by the Acts and the subsequent approval of detailed plans does not constitute the granting of a further permission. The outline permission cannot be withdrawn except by revocation under section 30 of the 1963 Act. Any conditions relating to the development as a whole should therefore be imposed at the outline stage and any major restrictions should be determined at that stage. This aspect is dealt with in more detail in paragraph **6.5**.

Conditions restricting use of buildings and land

5.21 It is occasionally desirable on planning grounds to restrict the use of a building or other land to a single named activity where a change to other activities would not involve development. This may be done by way of a condition. In this regard, see also paragraph **6.47**.

Conditions about the occupation of buildings

5.22 The planning authority should not usually concern themselves with the question of who would occupy a proposed structure if they permitted it to be erected. While section 28(6) of the 1963 Act, as amended, allows for a condition limiting the use of a dwelling to use by persons of a particular class or description, this can have serious practical consequences. It could put a severe limitation on the freedom of the owner to dispose of his property and could make it difficult for the developer to finance the erection of the permitted dwelling by obtaining a mortgage loan. Generally, therefore, the use of such a condition should be avoided.

5.23 In exceptional cases, it may be necessary to impose an occupancy condition in the case of a house required for an agricultural worker, or a member of a farm family. Where such a house is proposed for a site on which a house would not normally be permitted, it may be a material planning consideration that the house would meet the particular need referred to in the application. If, in such a case, it is proposed to grant permission as an exception to the general planning policy for the area, it may be considered essential to ensure tht the house will be available to meet the need for which the exception was made, and a condition might be imposed for this purpose. However, a condition should never tie the house to occupation by a named individual or to the applicant or his family – these are much too limited to form 'persons of a particular class or description'.

Conditions requiring provision of lay-by, etc.

5.24 Planning authorities regularly attach conditions requiring the provision of a lay-by to enable vehicles to park clear of the carriageway. Such conditions should not, however, be framed to require the ceding of land for road purposes, or the carrying out of works wholly or partly on land which is not under the control of the applicant. It may be possible to achieve the desired effect in some cases by a condition requiring the provision of parking space for vehicles within the curtilage of the building and in cases where all that is needed is adequate sight lines, a splayed access may be sufficient.

Conditions relating to service roads

5.25 Conditions relating to service roads can present problems, particularly where a housing site is the subject of an outline permission and individual plots are sold to separate developers who obtain separate approvals for their houses. If the outline permission has been granted subject to a condition that a service road shall be provided as the means of access, it is important to ensure that any subsequent application for approval for the erection of single house takes account of the requirement. However, even then, it may be difficult to secure full and satisfactory compliance with the condition. The better course would appear to be to fix responsibility for compliance with a service road condition on the overall developer by specifying that the road (or the relevant sections of it) shall have been provided before construction of any house is commenced (or before some other appropriate date). If provision for a service road has not been made a condition of the outline permission, and does not form part of the proposals submitted at outline stage, it will not usually be possible, when an individual subsequently applies for approval in respect of a house on a single plot, to impose a condition requiring provision of part of a service road over his plot and over other land which he may not control.

Maintenance conditions

5.26 A condition requiring that some feature of the development permitted shall be maintained in a prescribed way is generally acceptable provided the development involves a continuing use of land, and the requirement to maintain arises from that. For example, where it is required that a tree-screen should be planted to conceal a refuse tip, it would be acceptable to require that the trees shall be maintained during the first few years (specifying the number of years) and that any which die shall be replaced. Where permission is granted for development consisting of a 'once for all' operation, such as the erection of a building, it would not be appropriate to impose a condition requiring the carrying out of subsequent works which might have to be executed at any time during the life of the building, such as a condition requiring that the building, or any particular feature of it, should be maintained in a prescribed way.

Conditions directly departing from the application

5.27 A condition which radically alters the nature of the development to which the application relates will usually be unacceptable. For example, a condition should not require the omission of a use which forms an essential part of a proposed development. If there is a fundamental objection to a significant part of a development proposal, and this cannot fairly be dealt with in isolation from the rest of the proposal, the proper course would seem to be to refuse permission for the whole.

Conditions related to other codes

5.28 There is a widespread tendency to attach to planning permissions conditions relating to matters which, though of concern in the exercise of development control, are the subject of more specific controls under other legislation or are directly regulated by other statues or by the common law. The aim, no doubt, is to seek to improve the operation of those other controls. or codes by the use of the enforcement provisions of the Planning Acts. It is inappropriate, however, in development control, to deal with matters which are the subject of other controls unless there are particular circumstances e.g. the matters are relevant to proper planning and development and there is good reason to believe that they cannot be dealt with effectively by other means. The existence of a planning condition, or its omission, will not free a developer from his responsibilities under other codes and it is entirely the wrong to use the development control process to attempt to force a developer to apply for some licence, approval, consent, etc., which his development would not otherwise need. At best, the imposition of conditions in relation to matters which are subject of other controls is an undesirable duplication. In practice, such an approach can give rise to conflict and confusion if the effect of a condition on a development is different from that of the specific control provision.
5.29 In view of the foregoing, planning authorities should not include in planning permissions –

  (i) conditions which require compliance with building bye-laws, or other bye-laws under the Public Health and Local Government Acts, or compliance with the Food Hygiene Regulations, the Conditions of Employment Acts, the Safety in Industry Acts, the Dangerous Substances act, and analagous legislation or regulations, or,
  (ii) conditions which relate to matters of detail covered by or under any such legislation.

Instead, where they consider it necessary to do so, a planning authority could, when notifying the grant of a permission, issue a clear warning about the requirement of other codes.

Fire conditions

5.30 While it is appropriate that the Planning Acts should be used to the full to ensure that all development meets adequate fire safety standards, it must be emphasised that when dealing with a planning application, fire safety can only be considered where it is relevant to the primary purpose of the Acts, namely the proper planning and development of the area. Part II of the Third Schedule to the 1963 Act is a good guide to the relevant considerations. It would be a relevant consideration if a proposed use were incompatible with that of neighbouring property, or if the layout, construction or material used precluded the possibility of reasonable fire safety measures being taken at a later stage, or if certain measures (for example, external escape stairs) could in themselves be unacceptable on some general planning grounds. The objectionable features must be an essential part of the proposal (and not something susceptible to later adjustment) before they could properly be dealt with by way of planning conditions. Conditions might properly be included to remove basic objections to a proposed development by requiring, for example, the relocation of a proposed building on its site, the improvement of access, the omission of certain uses, or the provision of adequate water supplies for fire fighting purposes (including static tanks where a public supply is unavailable or inadequate).

5.31 It is envisaged that Building Regulations will cover matters such as structural fire precautions, means of escape from fire, means of access for fire appliances, and assistance to the fire brigade in new buildings. The Regulations should therefore resolve many of the problems related to the use of fire conditions. Pending the making of the Regulations, it is open to planning authorities to request that consultation take place between the developer and the fire authority to ensure that the appropriate fire prevention devices, etc., are provided; moreover, planning authorities should have regard to relevant requirements of the Draft Regulations which were published in 1981, and should obtain from applicants an indication of the extent to which these requirements have been taken into account in the preparation of the proposals.

5.32 Where it is clear that a building is likely to be used by a large number of people, or that its use is likely to involve a particular fire hazard, or that an outbreak of fire there would have particularly serious consequences, conditions requiring the provision of emergency exits, fire escapes, or an appropriate layout would be in order, pending the coming into operation of Building Regulations. However, planning conditions should not require the provision of items such as fire-extinguishers, fire doors, sprinklers, etc., even though these may be desirable from a fire safety point of view. Such conditions would not be appropriate and would in effect anticipate the controls exercisable under the Fire Services Act, 1981, or the Safety in Industry Acts, 1955 and 1980, or under Building Regulations (when made).

5.33 While it is not normally necessary that notifications of favourable decisions on planning applications should state that the requirements of another code should be complied with, an exception to this may be justified in the case of matters related to fire. In appropriate cases, therefore, planning authorities should consider writing to an applicant at the time of the granting of a permission indicating that the grant does not relieve the developer of complying with any requirements of, or which may be imposed under, relevant legislation or regulations, including the Fire Services Act, 1981, the Safety in Industry Acts, 1955 and 1980, Regulations made under the Dangerous Substances Act, 1972, or Building Regulations (when made). Applicants might also be advised to consult the fire authority about the fire aspects (whether covered by Building Regulations or not) before commencing their development. These consultations would help avoid a situation arising where a fire authority might consider it necessary, after a development had been completed and occupiedf, to use its powers under other legislation to impose requirements involving works (such as the installation of a sprinkler system) which might best be done at the construction stage. It would be even more helpful if applicants could be advised of specific fire safety recommendations (other than conditions attached to the permission) at the same time as a permission was being issued.

5.34 Under no circumstances should a condition be included in a permission requiring that 'the developer shall consult with and comply with the requirements of the Fire Officer' (or other words to that effect), whether or not such requirements are known at the time the decision is made or are enclosed with the permission. This kind of condition is objectionable in principle and, probably, invalid. (See also paragraph **5.38**).

Water pollution and waste conditions

5.35 Prior to the coming into operation of the Local Government (Water Pollution) Act, 1977, the planning system was heavily relied on, in relation to the establishment of industry and other development, to control the discharge of effluents to waters, and to set standards for such effluents. The enactment of the separate water pollution legislation does not relieve the planning authority of the duty to consider the water pollution aspects entirely but they should do so only to the extent that such aspects could affect the land-use question in a fundamental way. In general, it is no longer appropriate that a planning permission should contain conditions setting out in detail the standards which effluents should meet; such standards can more appropriately be included in a licence under the 1977 Act and which, unlike planning conditions, is subject to periodic review. Similar considerations apply in the area of overlap between development control and the issue of permits under the Waste Regulations.

5.36 It is desirable that the planning and water pollution and waste disposal aspects of a major proposal are dealt with in a co-o..inated and consistent manner and, with this in view, planning authorities should encourage applicants for permission to make applications simultaneously for the necessary authorisations under the other codes.

Conditions requiring further approval

5.37 A condition attached to a permission or to an approval may require details of some aspects of the development concerned to be lodged with the planning authority for approval. Where this is done, the statutory procedure laid down in the Regulations must be followed in relation to any application for such approval; in particular, public notice must be given, a formal decision must be made by the planning authority, and the decision will be subject to appeal to An Bord Pleanala, including possible appeals by third parties. Accordingly, in framing conditions, planning authorities should be careful to avoid use of the word '*approval*' in cases where they do not intend that the formal approval process should be complied with.

Conditions requiring matters to be agreed

5.38 In some cases, it may be considered unreasonable when granting a permission or an approval to require the applicant to go through the statutory application procedure again in relation to some detail of the proposed development and, to obviate this, a practice has developed of using a form of condition which requires that the matter *shall be agreed* with the planning authority. In a judgement delivered on 12 November, 1976, in *Keleghan, Dodd and O'Brien* v. *Mary Hilary Corby and Dublin Corporation*, Mr. Justice McMahon expressed doubts about a condition which required that details of an access should be submitted for agreement and he saw serious difficulties about that kind of condition from the point of view of planning law. He stated:

'A planning authority is entitled to grant permission subject to conditions requiring work to be done but when that is done the planning permission must specify the work to be done and any person who thinks he is prejudiced by it can appeal because he has before him details of the work to be done, but in this case what was granted was permission for access subject to details to be submitted for agreement. The public would have no knowledge what details were in fact being agreed and no way of appealing against the details agreed on between the applicants and the planning authority'.

Although Mr. Justice McMahon found it unnecessary to decide the point, it seems prudent to have regard to his views as set out above. Accordingly, conditions requiring matters to be agreed with the planning authority should be avoided in cases where the matters involved are of a fundamental nature or such that third parties could be affected. A further reason for avoiding the use of such conditions as far as possible is the difficulty which can arise because of the absence of a mechanism for resolving disputes; in this connection it should be noted that An Bord Pleanala has not power to deal with such disputes, except those which arise under conditions of permissions or approvals granted on appeal. Conditions providing for determinations by the Board, in default of agreement at local level, should not therefore be used by planning authorities.

5.39 Planning authorities should make every effort to ensure that submissions from developers seeking agreements pursuant to conditions are dealt with expeditiously, and in a fair and reasonable manner.

5.40 Conditions requiring matters to be the subject of consultation with, or to be agreed with, a named officer of the planning authority, or with a particular section or branch of the local authority, or with another public authority, should not be attached to a permission or to an approval. Neither should an applicant be required by condition to ascertain and comply with the requirements of a particular officer or section of the local authority or to comply with some general requirements of the authority which are not clearly spelled out in the permission or elsewhere. If the matter in question is of genuine planning concern, it should be dealt with in the decision order, or be made the the subject of a further approval or an agreement *with the planning authority*; if the matter is not proper to planning, it should be omitted entirely from the decision.

5.41 Conditions requiring matters to be agreed prior to the commencement of any development should be used sparingly. Such conditions will sometimes be necessary and appropriate for enforcement purposes and otherwise but, where they are not absolutely necessary, their use should be avoided so as not to delay the commencement of a permitted development. For example, instead of requiring that a detailed landscaping scheme for a major housing development should be agreed prior to the commencement of development, a condition could require such a scheme to be submitted to the planning authority for their agreement not later than, say, six months after the commencement of the development, and require the site to be landscaped in accordance with the scheme as so agreed.

Conditions requiring the ceding of land, etc.,
5.42 Conditions should not be attached to planning permissions requiring land to be ceded to the local authority for road widening or other purposes nor should conditions require applicants to allow the creation of public rights-of-way, or to cede way-leaves over their land, or to agree to transfer part of their land to some third party as, say, the site for a school or a church. Conditions of this sort are not lawful. It is in order to require a developer to reserve land free of any development in order, for example, to permit the implementation of a road improvement proposal, or to reserve land as a site for a school or other community facility. It is not lawful, however, to require by condition a transfer or an interest in land to the local authority or otherwise.

Conditions requiring financial contributions
5.43 Section 26 of the 1963 Act empowers planning authorities to attach conditions requiring contributions towards expenditure incurred, or to be incurred, in respect of works which have facilitated or will facilitate the proposed development. It is a matter for each planning authority to determine in the first instance whether, and to what extent, such contributions would be warranted in the circumstances of its area. Information as to the operation of section 26 was sought from planning authorities some months ago with a view to enabling a review of the various systems of financial contributions to be carried out. This information has not yet been received from all authorities. The need for changes in the law, or for additional guidance for planning authorities in the matter, will be considered when the review has been completed.

Conditions relating to housing estates
5.44 If the problem of unfinished housing estates is to be eliminated, it is particularly important that special care is taken in devising and drafting the conditions attached to permissions for such estates. Much of what has already been stated in this Part applies fully in relation to the drafting of permissions for such estates. The following additional matters also arise:

(a) *Conditions requiring security for completion*: It is essential that permissions for the development of housing estates are subject to a condition under which an acceptable security it provided by way of bond, cash deposit or otherwise so as to secure the satisfactory completion of the estate. The amount of the security, and the terms on which it is required to be given, should enable the planning authority, without cost to themselves, to complete the necessary services (including roads, footpaths, water mains, sewers, lighting and open space) to a satisfactory standard in the event of default by the developer. The condition should require that the lodgment of the security should be coupled with an agreement which would empower the planning authority to realise the amount of the security at an appropriate time and apply it to meet the cost of completing the specified works. A security condition could also provide for the recalculation of the amount specified in the condition by reference to the House Building Cost Index (or other appropriate Index) if the development to which the permission relates is not commenced within a specified period after the granting of the permission.

(b) *Phasing*: In the case of large housing estates, it may be appropriate to attach a condition regarding the phasing of the development but it would be desirable that any such condition should be worked out in consultation with the developer. A phasing condition could include requirements relating to the completion of roads, public lighting, open spaces, etc., which are necessary for, or ancillary to, the completed houses in each phase. Such an arrangement would permit the security for satisfactory completion to be related to a particular phase or phases of the development and thus enable completion of section of the estate to be advanced while, at the same time, facilitating the developer by obviating the need for a very large security appropriate to the entire development. Care should be taken in devising any phasing arrangement to secure that main sewers, surface water drainage systems, main distributor roads, etc., are completed at an appropriate stage so that the first and each subsequent phase will, on completion, be fully serviced and independent in the event of other phases not proceeding.

(c) *Conditions at outline permission stage*: It is particularly important that conditions relating to basic services, financial contributions, security for completion, road reservations and other such fundamental matters are attached, where appropriate, to outline permissions for housing development. If this is not done, difficulties may arise at approval stage and an unsatisfactory development may result. Paragraph 6.5 deals in more detail with this aspect.

PART VI – PROCEDURAL MATTERS

General

6.1 A number of procedural matters which arise in the processing of planning applications can give rise to difficulty and the following notes deal with some of these.

Outline permission, permission and approval

6.2 The 1963 Act and the 1977 Regulations make provision for:

– *outline permission*, meaning a permission for development which is granted subject to the subsequent approval by the planning authority, (or on appeal) of detailed plans of the development; an application for an outline permission need be accompanied 'only by such plans and particulars as are necessary to identify the land to which the application relates and to enable the planning authority to determine the siting, layout or other proposals for development in respect of which a decision is sought'.

– *approval*, meaning an approval of detailed plans consequent on an outline permission or an approval of some details of a development which is required to be obtained under a condition subject to which a permission or an approval was granted, whether by a planning authority or on appeal.

– *permission*, (sometimes colloquially described as 'full' permission), which may be granted where detailed plans of the proposed development are lodged with an application.

6.3 An applicant should always state whether he is applying for an outline permission, a permission or an approval. Planning authorities should ensure that application forms are designed with this in mind and that any notes provided for applicants clearly indicate the difference between outline permission, permission and approval.

6.4 Whichever form of application is made, it must be dealt with as such, with one exception mentioned below. An application for an approval cannot be treated as an application for a permission or *vice versa*. Neither can an application for an outline permission, even if it is accompanied by detailed plans and particulars, be treated as an application for permission. The only exception permitted arises in relation to an application for a permission which is not accompanied by the prescribed plans and particulars; in such a case, the planning authority is expressly authorised to grant an outline permission 'if the application appears to them sufficient for that purpose only'. (Article 21 of the 1977 Regulations).

6.5 The grant of an outline permission amounts to a favourable decision as to the principle of a proposed development and, as stated in a High Court judgment, the 'whole procedure would be defeated if, at the approval stage, the planning authority could re-open the question of whether the development is acceptable in principle'. The outline permission sets the parameters within which the planning authority must consider an application for a subsequent approval and matters settled or permitted at outline stage may not be re-opened at approval stage. It follows from the foregoing that –

(a) by granting an outline permission, the planning authority are committing themselves to allowing the development to go ahead in some form provided, of course, the detailed plans submitted for approval are acceptable;

(b) an outline permission should not be granted unless the authority have sufficient information to enable them to assess all matters of principle involved;

(c) if the proposed development is considered acceptable subject to stringent or onerous conditions, these should be attached to the outline permission rather than leaving the matter to be settled at approval stage (examples of such conditions would be reductions in the height, scale or bulk of structures, or requirements to reserve parts of a site free of development); contribution conditions and security conditions should also be attached to the outline permission, rather than to the subsequent approval;

(d) an application for an approval consequent on an outline permission should not be refused for reasons of principle which imply that the development is not acceptable at all (for example, basic land-use considerations, unsuitability of the particular site for the proposed development, inadequacy of services, the effect on the site of a road reservation); neither should conditions of the kind referred to at (c) be introduced at approval stage;

(e) if there has been a change in planning circumstances since the grant of an outline permission, an application for an approval may raise the question of whether the outline permission should be revoked; approval could then validly be refused for the reason that the underlying outline permission has been revoked;

(f) while an application for an approval consequent on an outline permission may relate to part only of the development for which an outline permission was granted, such an application may not extend to development not covered by the outline permission or to land to which that permission did not relate;

(g) where an approval is granted pursuant to an outline permission, conditions inconsistent with those attached to the outline permission should not be attached;

(h) it is not necessary that the conditions attached at outline stage be repeated in the subsequent approval; however, if they consider it necessary, the planning authority may, in a covering letter, draw the attention of the developer to the need to comply with the conditions of the outline permission as well as those attached to the approval;

(i) where an outline permission has been granted and a permission (rather than an approval) is subsequently applied for, the conditions attached to the outline permission will not apply unless they are restated in the grant of permission.

6.6 The outline permission/approval procedure is provided in order to enable potential developers to obtain a decision in principle relatively quickly and without having to go to the expense of preparing fully detailed plans. Accordingly, while all essential matters of principle must be assessed in dealing with outline applications, applicants should not be subjected to unnecessary expense or delay by requests for information, or additional information, in relation to matters which do not affect the principle of the proposed development. On the other hand, a planning authority cannot be expected to write a blank cheque at outline permission stage. It follows that the plans and particulars submitted with an outline application should be sufficient to provide a clear picture of what is intended and to enable the planning authority to determine the intensity or quantity of use proposed, at least in general terms. For example, an outline application which is expressed to relate only to 'residential and ancillary development' on a large site and which is accompanied by little more than a site plan, will be difficult to process properly and, if granted, could give rise to serious difficulties at approval stage; in such a case, it would not be unreasonable (and would be consistent with the Regulations) to require the developer to specify whether houses or flats were intended, the number of units involved, the nature and extent of the ancillary development, and so on.

6.7 Attention is drawn to the fact that the provisions of the 1963 Act which exclude compensation in certain cases do not apply where an approval is refused or granted subject to conditions. Moreover, approvals cannot be revoked under section 30 of the 1963 Act, the appropriate procedure being to revoke the parent outline permission (where this course is warranted) and stated above about the relationship between outline permission and approval and the treatment of approval applications.

Public notice of planning applications
6.8 Complaints continue to be made about the inadequacy or misleading nature of the public notices given by some applicants in relation to the development they propose to undertake. It is the responsibility of the planning authority to ensure that proper notice of an application is given in accordance with Article 14 of the 1977 Regulations. The intention of the Acts and of the Regulations is that the notice should be such as would inform any person interested of the location and nature and extent of the proposed development. That aim can be secured either by erecting a suitable site notice or by publishing a notice in a newspaper circulating in the district in which the development is proposed.

6.9 Where a planning authority consider that proper notice of intention has not been given, they are entitled under the Regulations to require an applicant to publish further public notice, in such manner and in such terms as they think fit. If a notice erected on a site or published in a newspaper is misleading, or does not comply with the Regulations in other respects, it is prejudicial to the public interest and to the right of any aggrieved person to make submissions to the authority or to appeal to the Board. Arrangements should, accordingly, be made to ensure that when an application is being examined, the relevant notice is checked for compliance with the Regulations and that applicants are requested to give further notice where the planning authority consider this to be necessary.

6.10 The importance of ensuring that public notices are adequate and not misleading has been emphasised in a number of Supreme Court judgments. For example, in Monaghan U.D.C. v. Alf-a-Bet Promotions Ltd., Mr. Justice Henchy held

(24 March, 1980) that any deviation from the requirements of the Regulations in regard to notices must, before it can be overlooked, be so trivial, or so technical, or so peripheral or otherwise so insubstantial that, on the principle that it is the spirit rather than the letter of the law that matters, the prescribed obligation has been substantially, and therefore adequately, complied with. Mr. Justice Griffin, in the same context, stated that planning and development have become such an important feature of modern life that the Acts and the Regulations should be strictly applied by planning authorities and the Courts. In subsequent cases, the Courts have affirmed the view that a valid press advertisement or site notice is essential to a valid application (and, by extension, to a valid decision).

6.11 The requirement in the Regulations regarding newspaper notices provides for publication in a newspaper 'circulating in the district in which the relevant land or structure is situate'. It is a matter for each planning authority to decide, having regard to the circumstances prevailing in their area, whether any particular newspaper has sufficient circulation to warrant acceptance of a notice published in it as an adequate notice. The power to require a further notice to be published can be used in any case where it appears to the authority that the original notice was 'inadequate for the information of the public' by reason of the limited circulation in the district of the newspaper concerned.

6.12 The publication of notices in the Irish language is perfectly in order and is consistent with public policy in relation to the language. It is clear, however, that some applicants use, or attempt to use, the Irish language simply to minimise the effectiveness of a notice; for example, notices appear in the newspapers using words and phrases which would not be used by any genuine user of the language and which are so garbled as to be almost meaningless. This practice is repugnant to the spirit and to the letter of the Regulations (as well as bringing genuine use of the language into disrepute). It is open to an authority to require the applicant to publish a further notice, in terms specified by them, in any case in which the original notice appears to them, by reason of its content and incorrect use of the Irish language, to be misleading or inadequate.

6.13 Attention is drawn to the provisions of article 24 of the Regulations under which planning authorities are required to publish a weekly list of applications of which copies must be made available to the members of the authority and displayed in or at the offices of the authority for a period of not less than four weeks. The list may, where the council so resolves, be displayed in any other appropriate place and/or published by the authority in a newspaper circulating in the district and/or made available to any body, group or person likely to be interested.

Advice and assistance to applicants

6.14 While it is not a function of planning authorities to provide a free consultancy service, they should, where possible, be prepared to give advice and assistance to applicants, and potential applicants, for permission. The system as a whole must be objective, open and fair and, if it is to gain increased public acceptance, it must be seen to be so. A readiness to explain to applicants, and potential applicants, the planning authority's policies in relation to particular areas and the considerations taken into account in dealing with particular classes of applications, or with particular areas, is essential if this is to be achieved. In addition, planning authorities should be prepared to assist in identifying possible alternative locations when a particular proposal is considered to be unacceptable.

6.15 It seems likely that difficulties and delays for developers, and many appeals, could be avoided if developers had more precise information as to planning authorities' policies and objectives. It is also possible that fuller discussions with applicants on the types of development which would be permitted in different areas would avert an appeal in many cases and that objections to some development proposals could be overcome by alterations agreed in discussion with applicants and given effect by conditions attached to a permission.

6.16 Allegations are sometimes made that at preliminary discussions with the planning authority, applicants are faced with an objection which they succeed in meeting only to be told subsequently of a further unconnected objection. Another class of allegation is that verbal or other agreements or understandings reached in preliminary discussions with applicants and their agents are not subsequently honoured when a formal decision is being made. Every effort should be made to secure that the arrangements operated by planning authorities are such as to minimise the risk that such allegations will arise.

Objections in relation to applications

6.17 Neither the Acts nor the Regulations expressly give a right to interested parties to make submissions or observations or objections to a planning authority before an application is decided. The Supreme Court has however, confirmed that such a right exists: in Stanford and Others .v. Corporation of Dun Laoghaire, Mr. Justice Henchy held (20th February, 1981) that the tenor of the code suggests that interested parties were to be accorded an opportunity of making representations or objections in writing and that the purpose of the public notice of an application is to give them that opportunity. It follows from the foregoing that where objections or representations are made in regard to an application, the planning authority must consider them and, under article 32 of the Regulations, any person or body who has made such representations or objections in writing must, within seven days of the making of a decision on the application, be notifed of the decision by the planning authority. It is suggested that where a number of applications are made simultaneously in respect of the same site, persons or bodies who made representations or objections to the planning authority should be notified of the decision on each of the applications.

6.18 Persons who make representations or objections at local level may wish to pursue the matter. Accordingly, in order that such persons will be fully informed as to their right to appeal to An Bord Pleanala or to intervene in relation to an appeal made by another person, all notifications issued under article 32(2) of the Regulations should include a statement to the effect that any person may appeal against the relevant decision within the appropriate period and that, in the event of an appeal being made by a person other than the person to whom the notification is given, the latter may make such submissions or observations to An Bord Pleanala as he thinks fit.

6.19 An Bord Pleanala, when requesting from a planning authority documents relevant to an application which is the subject of an appeal, does not request that copies of representations or objections made at local level should be supplied to it: it is a matter for the persons concerned to contact the Board directly if they wish to maintain the position they adopted when the application was being considered locally or to amplify any case they may have made to the planning authority. Accordingly, when a planning authority is informed by An Bord Pleanala than an appeal has been made against a particular decision, the authority should inform those who made objections or representations at local level of the nature of the appeal so that they may, if they wish, pursue the matter through the appeals process. If, in an exceptional case, there are numerous individual objections, consideration could be given to notifying the appeal to a representative number.

6.20 As indicated above, the purpose of the public notice which applicants for planning permission must give is to inform persons, whose property or interests may be affected, of the development proposed. On being so informed, such persons are entitled to inspect the relevant plans, drawings, maps and particulars lodged with the planning application and to make representations or objections in writing to the authority in relation to the application. If, however, a planning authority were to decide an aplication very soon after the publication of the relevant notice (or of any further notice required by the authority), the rights of interested parties to make submissions (and to have them considered) would be infringed. In the case referred to in paragraph **6.17**, where a decision to grant permission was made on the day after the publication of an essential further notice of an application, the Supreme Court held that the action of the planning authority was calculated to deprive interested members of the public of a reasonable opportunity of submitting representations or objections in writing and that the planning authority thereby breached an essential pre-condition for the grant of a valid permission and acted *ultra vires*. Consideration will be given to the making of regulations to deal with this point. In the meantime, it is suggested that planning authorities should not determine an application until 14 days have elapsed after the publication of the notice of intention to make a planning application or, as the case may require, until 14 days after the publication of any further notice required under article 23 of the Regulations.

Further information

6.21 Where further information from an applicant in regard to a development proposal is essential for the proper consideration of an application, the information should be requested as soon as possible after receipt of the application. Such a request should indicate clearly all the infomation required. The Regulations do not permit a second request for further information to be made save where this is necessary to clarify the matters dealt with in the response to the first request.

6.22 It is a matter for concern that any impression should be given that the powers of planning authorities to seek further information are being abused in order effectively to extend the period for dealing with applications. To obviate this, serious efforts should be made to avoid eleventh hour requests for further information on one aspect of a proposal are not made in cases where there may be fundamental objections to the proposed development on other grounds. For example, applicants should not be asked to arrange for the carrying out of percolation tests to establish the suitability of a site for septic tank drainage if there is any risk that, after they have incurred expense and suffered delay in complying with the request, a refusal of permission on grounds of traffic hazard or amenity will issue. Situations like this should be avoided and, where necessary, internal arrangements should be reviewed with this in mind.

Revised plans

6.23 In some cases, discussions with applicants or requests for further information lead to the submission by an applicant of revised or additional plans. It is essential that such plans are examined to ensure that they can properly be taken into account in considering the applcation i.e. that they do not alter the essential character of the application and that there is no risk of adverse impact on third parties. If the plans are substantially different from those originally lodged with the authority, either a fresh application for permission or a further public notice may be required. On the other hand, if the revised plans are regarded as admissible and are acceptable, a permission or approval can be given by reference to them. (See also paragraph **6.46**).

Invitation to submit modified plans

6.24 Article 27 of the 1977 Regulations may be of assistance in cases where a planning authority is deposed to grant a permission or an approval but finds difficulty in framing the detailed types of conditions which might be required in certain circumstances. Under article 27, the planning authority may, in such circumstances, invite the applicant to submit plans etc., showing how his proposal can be modified to meet their requirements and they may then grant a permission or approval for the development on the basis of the modified plans etc., submitted at their invitation. (See also paragraph **6.46**). It should be emphasised that it is, in effect, necessary for the planning authority to have come to the conclusion that a permission could, in principle, be granted before use of the article 27 powers could be justified.

6.25 There is no specific provision in the Regulations requiring modified plans etc., submitted at the invitation of a planning authority to be sent to, or notified to, in interested parties, but such plans must be made available for inspection under article 29. In some cases where modified plans are received, it might be appropriate to seek to have appropriate public notice given by the applicant.

6.26 The power to seek modified plans cannot be used to seek plans which would change the essential nature or character of the scheme; the development proposal must remain basically the same as that to which the original application related. (A dictionary definition of 'modify' is 'to make minor changes in the form or structure of something or to alter something without transforming it').

Role of elected members

6.27 The elected members of planning authorities are entitled to become involved in the planning control process. The member's knowledge of local conditions and planning and development needs could in some cases assist in ironing out problems and difficulties and, consequently, reduce the number of decisions which cause dissatisfaction at local level and which lead to appeals.

6.28 Because circumstances vary from one area to another, different practices and procedures have evolved in different areas. Some authorities, for example, operate a system of consultation with elected members on major planning applications through committees of the planning authority – either formal planning committees, area committees, or informal committees. In other cases, councillors are kept informed by the circulation of lists of either applications or decisions (see article 24 of the Regulations) or they are informed where refusals are proposed and given an opportunity to present their views individually before decisions are made. Such arrangements might be reviewed, particularly in areas where the level of refusals and of appeals is high.

6.29 It should not be necessary for councillors to be involved in the consideration of all planning applications and, in any event, this would be impracticable having regard to the number of applications and the two month time-limit for deciding applications. The procedure most suited to any particular area can best be decided locally, having regard to local needs and circumstances.

Consultation with fire authority

6.30 It has already been indicated (paragraph **6.30**) that, in dealing with planning applications, fire safety should be considered where this relates to the proper planning and development of the area. In addition, attention is drawn to section 13 of the Fire Services Act, 1981, which empowers a fire authority to advise a planning authority on planning applications. It is a matter for each planning authority, in consultation with the fire authority, where appropriate, to make suitable arrangements for the examination, from the fire safety aspect, of planning applications. As a matter of course, those applications which relate to premises to whih the public have access, or which present special risks should be referred to fire service personnel in good time so that appropriate recommendations may be incorporated in the planning decision. A good guide to the type of premises involved is section 18 of the Fire Services Act, 1981, especially subsection (1) and paragraphs (b) to (e) of subsection (2).

6.31 It should not be necessary to refer all planning applications to fire service personnel, especially if this leads to delay on the planning side. This aspect should be carefully reviewed in consultation with appropriate fire service personnel and arrangements devised which will suit the particular circumstances of each area. However, it is suggested that fire service personnel concerned be provided with an appropriate list of all applications, including those for changes of use, thereby allowing them an opportunity to monitor applications generally.

Consultation with prescribed bodies

6.32 Planning authorities are reminded of the specific provisions of Article 25 of the 1977 Regulations in regard to consultation with the bodies prescribed in that article about applications involving amenity areas, tourist amenity works, national monuments, etc. Appropriate arrangements should be made to ensure that notices of relevant planning applications are sent to the appropriate bodies referred to in Article 25 and that the provisions of that article and of Article 32 are fully observed even in cases where doubt arises as to whether or not an application comes within the scope of Article 25. Notification of applications received should issue as soon as possible to give the prescribed bodies a reasonable time to transmit any observations and due consideration should be given by the planning authority to any comments or advice received. Greater co-operation with the prescribed bodies in this regard should result in more planning applications being decided at local level without giving rise to appeals.

Housing Act, 1969

6.33 The provisions of the Housing Act, 1969, must be fully complied with where a development proposal involves demolition or change of use of habitable accommodation. If they have not, the validity of any decision on the planning application may be called into question.

6.34 The 1969 Act is a temporary measure to prevent habitable houses from being demolished or converted to use other than for human habitation. Its provisions have been continued in force until 31 December, 1984. In general, the Act requires that any person who had not, prior to 15 July, 1969, obtained permission (including outline permssion) under the 1963 Act for development which involved the demolition of a habitable house, or a change to some other use, must obtain permission from the housing authority for the demolition or change.

6.35 Where planning permission is needed, as well as permission under the 1969 Act, application may be made at any time to the planning authority but the authority must not decide the planning application unless and until the Housing Act application has been fully determined, either locally or on appeal.

6.36 If permission is granted under the Housing Act, the planning authority has five weeks from the date of the decision on the housing application in which to decide the planning application (in lieu of the two months allowed under section 26(4) of the 1963 Act) but if the favourable housing decision is made within that two month period, no extension of time is allowed for the planning decision. Special internal arrangements may need to be made by planning authorities to ensure that compliance with these time limits is achieved and that claims for planning permission by default do not arise. Planning authorities should not, however, resort to refusing planning permission (even where there are good planning grounds for doing so) in advance of the Housing Act decision: any such refusal will be of no effect and can only create confusion for applicants and unnecessary work for An Bord Pleanala.

6.37 Where permission under the Housing act is refused (whether at local level or an appeal), the Act provides that a planning application, so far as it relates to the relevant house, shall not be considered and that the permission by default provisions of the 1963 Act will not apply. In some cases, a planning decision will have to be made in relation to the balance of the development applied for. Except in such cases, the practice of refusing planning permission, to copper-fasten the matter, should not be pursued as any such refusal will be of no effect and can only create confusion.

6.38 Where a Housing Act permission is granted subject to conditions, the planning authority, in dealing with a planning application, must have regard to the conditions. While this does not mean that the planning decision must slavishly follow the conditions of the permission under the Housing Act, or that such a permission pre-empts a decision on a planning application, every effort should be made to avoid creating a situation in which compliance with the conditions of one permission would involve non-compliance with the conditions of the other.

Questions relating to title to land

6.39 Although every planning application must give particulars of the interest held in the land or structure by the applicant, the Planning Acts are not designed for use as a mechanism for resolving disputes about title to land or premises or rights over land: these are ultimately matters for resolution in the Courts. In this regard, it should be noted that, under section 26(11) of the 1963 Act, a person is not entitled solely by reason of a permission or an approval to carry out any development.

6.40 In Frescati Estates Ltd. v. Walker (1975) I.R. 177, Mr. Justice Henchy of the Supreme Court, with whose judgment the other members of the Court agreed, held that –

'while the intention of the Act is that persons with no legal interest (such as would-be purchasers) may apply for development permission, the operation of the Act within the scope of its objects and the limits of constitutional requirements would be exceeded if the word 'applicant' in the relevant sections is not given a restricted connotation. The extent of that restriction must be determined by the need to avoid unnecessary or vexatious applications, with consequent intrusions into property rights and demands on the statutory functions of planning authorities beyond what could reasonably be said to be required, in the interests of the common good, for proper planning and development.

Applying that criterion I consider that an application for development permission, to be valid, must be made either by or with the approval of a person who is able to assert sufficient legal estate or interest to enable him to carry out the proposed development or so much of the proposed development as relates to the property in question. There will thus be sufficient privity between the applicant (if he is not a person entitled) and the person entitled, to enable the applicant to be treated, for practical purposes, as a person entitled'.

6.41 It appears to follow from the foregoing that a purported grant of permission to a person who is unable to assert sufficient legal estate or interest to enable him to carry out the proposed development, or who has not obtained the approval of a person with such an estate or interest, would be made in excess of jurisdiction. In such a case, the High Court, in *certiorari* proceedings or in an action for a declaration, could set aside the decision. Although it can hardly be said to follow from the Supreme Court decision that a planning authority should attempt to investigate and adjudicate on title in the case of every planning application, it is important that applicants should be required, when making their applications, to state what estate or interest they hold in the relevant land, and application forms should be drafted with this in mind. Where, in making an application, a person asserts that he has what appears to be a sufficient estate or interest, and there is nothing to cast doubt on the *bona fides* of that assertion or of the application, that should be the end of the matter as far as the planning authority is concerned. If, however, the terms of the application itself, or a submission made by a third party, or information which may otherwise reach the authority, raise doubts as to the sufficiency of the estate or interest, the matter may have to be taken further in order to avoid the risk of deciding to grant an invalid permission. The power to require further information under article 26 of the Regulations expressly provides for a requisition to submit further information 'as to any estate or interest in or right over land' and to produce any evidence required to verify any such information.

6.42 Where a question as to the sufficiency of an applicant's estate or interest is raised with a planning authority and the applicant has not satisfied the authority in relation to the matter, the proper course would seem to be to refuse to grant permission for the reason that 'the planning authority has not been satisfied that the applicant has sufficient estate or interest in the relevant land to enable him to carry out the proposed development'. If, of course, there is a definite admission by the applicant (or it if is clear from correspondence etc.,) that he does not have the necessary interest, the reason for refusal could be drafted in more confident terms, for example: 'The application has been made by a person who has neither sufficient estate or interest to enable him to carry out the proposed development of the relevant land nor the approval of a person who has such estate or interest.'

6.43 A particular application of the Frescati judgment arises in relation to land in the ownership of the local authority. Where a planning application is made to carry out development on land which is owned by the authority itself, or to retain a structure on, or continue a use of, such land, there would seem to be no point in dealing with the case on the planning merits unless the authority, *as landowner*, is prepared to allow the development. Particular examples of this arise in relation to advertising structures or signs in public car parks or on public roads or on poles erected by the roal authority to carry traffic signs. Irrespective of their planning merits, such applications are invalid (and should be dealt with as such) if, as landowner, the planning authority has not consented to the making of the application and has no intention of doing so.

Drafting of permissions

6.44 Section 28(5) of the 1963 Act provides that (except as may be otherwise provided by the permission) the grant of a permission shall ensure for the benefit of the land or structure and of all persons for the time being interested therein. The permission is not therefore personal to the applicant and can be a matter of concern to any propective purchaser of the land, or of adjoining land. In addition, the terms of a permission may be material when a claim for compensation is being adjudicated on and, of course, permissions will frequently have to be interpreted by the Courts. In these circumstances it is essential that permissions should be drafted in such a manner that persons other than the local planning authority and the particular applicant will be able to appreciate what exactly has been permitted.

6.45 When a planning application is made, the proposed development may not be adequately described or may be wrongly or incompletely described. This may give rise to questions as to whether the applicant should be required to publish an additional notice in relation to his application (in this regard, see paragraphs **6.8** and **6.9**) Moreover, in some cases, it may be necessary for the planning authority to seek information from the applicant as to what exactly the application is intended to cover and, where appropriate, to submit additional plans and particulars to clarify the matter. In all cases, however, whether a decision is being made to grant or to refuse permission, the planning authority itself should see to it that the description of the development used in the decision order, and in relevant notices and register entries, is accurate and complete even if this means departing somewhat from the description used in the application. For example, a planning application may be expressed to relate only to the alteration of a building whereas it may be clear from the plans and other particulars that a change of use if also involved. Similarly, an application which is expressed to relate to housing development may provide also for the construction of a number of shops and other community facilities. In such cases, the terms of a permission or of a decision to refuse should describe the development in appropriate terms.

6.46 In the normal case, it should be sufficient to relate a planning decision to the plans and other particulars lodged with the planning authority and, generally speaking, it should be possible to do this by appropriate drafting of the preamble to the decision, rather than by attaching a condition. Where revised plans have been submitted by an applicant, or where modified plans have been submitted, or where the original application contains alternative plans, it is however, essential that the decision should be drafted in such a way as to leave no room for dispute as to which set of plans it is related. Again, where a decision is being made in relation to the erection of a building or in relation to a change of use, the extent of the curtilage to be provided with the building or the extent of the area affected by the change of use should be quite clear. If the terms of the application and of the lodged plans leave any scope for dispute about such matters, a condition might be inserted in any permission to clarify the matter.

6.47 Section 28(6) of the 1963 Act provides that if the purpose for which a structure is to be used is not specified in a grant of permission, the permission shall be construed as including permission to use the structure for the purpose for which it is designed. In these circumstances, it should not normally be necessary to specify the use to which a building for which permission is being granted is to be put (for example, that a house of standard design be used as a single dwelling only). If, however, there is any room for doubt (where for example a building could be used for a variety of purposes), the planing authority should consider whether the permission should be framed in terms which allow only a specific use to be made of the building. Any such decision should, of course, be made by reference to the proper planning and development of the area (regard being had to the provisions of the development plan) and it does not follow that it will always be necessary to limit a permission to one of a number of possible alternative uses. For example, it may be quite acceptable in some situations and locations to permit the erection of a building which could be used either for warehousing purposes or for light industrial purposes.

APPENDIX I

CIRCULARS ETC. SUPERCEDED BY THIS MEMORANDUM IN SO FAR AS THEY RELATE TO DEVELOPMENT CONTROL

Reference No.	Date	Subject/Title
L 3/65	7 May, 1965	Examination of plans for building involving a fire risk.
PD 15	8 March, 1967	Planning Control
PA 2/67	20 Oct. 1967	Flexibility in Planning Control
PL 1/70	22 June, 1970	Publication of Planning Notices
RA 285/18	15 Jan. 1971	Roadside Development – Traffic and Safety on Arterial Roads
PD 140	15 Jan. 1971	Development Plan Reviews and Planning Control
PL 2/71	7 April 1971	Objections to Planning Applications
L 17/71	31 May 1971	Fire Precautions in Potentially Dangerous Buildings
L 33/71	22 Nov. 1971	do.
PL 257/2	30 Nov. 1972	Fire Precautions
PL 210/8	12 Nov. 1973	Planning Control Problems
—	30 Aug. 1974	Planning Appeals
PD 51/8	20 May, 1975	Planning Control/Appeals
ENV 2/76	9 Jan. 1976	Consideration of Fire Protection Matters in development proposals submitted under the Local Government (Planning and Development) Act, 1963.
PD 1/79; 126/3	30 Jan. 1979	National Monuments; Consultation with prescribed bodies
PD 2/80; 42/17	28 July 1980	Development of Smaller Towns and Villages.

APPENDIX II

Table A: Number of decisions made by each planning authority in each of the years 1977–1981 and percentage in which permission/approval was refused.

Table B: Breakdown on a county and county borough basis of appeals made to An Bord Pleanala in each of the years 1978–1981 and percentage of total attributable to each area.

Table C: Appeals made to An Bord Pleanala in each of the years 1978–1981 expressed as a percentage of total decisions made at county and county borough level.

Notes   1. In Tables B and C, the figures for urban districts and boroughs (excluding Dun Laoghaire) have had to be aggregated with those for the appropriate counties because the statistics in relation to appeals are maintained by An Bord Pleanala on that basis.
2. The statistics available in relation to appeals do not enable Tables B and C to cover 1977.

TABLE A

Area	Planning Decisions					% Refusals				
COUNTY	1977	1978	1979	1980	1981	1977	1978	1979	1980	1981
Carlow	312	394	543	398	406	2.56	2.28	6.62	9.79	4.92
Cavan	782	957	1134	958	918	11.89	10.44	9.61	10.54	14.92
Clare	1060	1184	1589	1384	1230	1.03	2.02	2.83	3.39	3.25
Cork	3578	4153	5303	4262	4674	13.24	17.48	17.10	17.03	22.20
Donegal	2345	2437	2626	2689	2299	8.57	6.48	8.49	6.91	7.65
Dublin	3103	3485	4446	3915	4050	19.14	17.67	15.87	18.95	19.14
Galway	2827	3504	4042	3302	3476	13.51	16.46	13.03	11.72	14.32
Kerry	1796	2243	2800	2318	2340	8.24	7.84	9.03	6.77	8.97
Kildare	956	1340	1553	1352	1408	9.93	16.71	23.11	19.60	19.31
Kilkenny	782	1093	1248	983	1029	3.45	3.11	4.40	4.78	7.96
Laois	573	732	1003	727	755	6.63	6.83	4.38	6.18	7.94
Leitrim	449	405	549	560	461	8.46	5.43	8.19	8.57	7.80
Limerick	1485	1718	1998	1566	1566	4.78	5.18	6.15	6.19	9.45
Longford	495	600	615	508	513	4.04	4.00	6.01	8.66	9.16
Louth	767	826	881	698	798	16.03	18.52	17.93	18.19	17.16
Mayo	1688	1926	2299	2032	1764	4.91	4.36	5.69	4.67	5.38
Meath	1688	1672	2199	1756	2274	10.84	8.91	10.14	16.51	22.42
Monaghan	653	781	795	665	662	7.19	8.45	7.67	10.07	14.95
Offaly	528	608	736	593	615	5.30	7.73	7.33	5.56	8.29
Roscommon	931	1008	1338	1135	1175	3.00	4.06	5.90	6.07	7.14
Sligo	719	821	859	744	868	18.63	14.85	15.36	19.89	14.63
Tipperary N.R.	593	815	881	768	818	4.72	5.76	7.83	8.59	11.24
Tipperary S.R.	537	761	882	687	646	2.04	5.51	5.21	4.94	6.19
Waterford	827	821	1125	787	744	11.97	15.46	19.11	16.01	i6.26
Westmeath	875	1015	1048	892	795	9.82	9.45	10.40	12.44	12.57
Wexford	1392	1533	1849	1562	1617	15.01	14.41	17.19	16.06	14.34
Wicklow	975	1127	1168	1131	1251	25.84	27.41	27.56	30.68	30.13
Sub-total	32716	37959	45509	38372	39152	10.73	11.41	11.83	12.23	14.31
COUNTY BOROUGH	1977	1978	1979	1980	1981	1977	1978	1979	1980	1981
Cork	620	741	846	610	656	13.70	14.17	15.72	11.63	15.09
Dublin	2611	2621	3116	3076	3004	18.07	21.17	20.31	20.38	23.56
Limerick	233	274	310	273	280	17.16	11.67	11.93	12.45	21.42
Waterford	175	203	240	311	354	9.14	10.83	5.00	11.89	7.90
Sub-Total	3639	3839	4512	4270	4294	16.84	18.59	18.06	18.00	20.84

BOROUGH URBAN DISTRICT	Planning Decisions					% Refusals				
	1977	1978	1979	1980	1981	1977	1978	1979	1980	1981
Arklow	63	91	81	79	59	11.11	5.49	6.17	17.72	6.78
Athlone	72	91	197	97	77	11.11	7.69	9.34	10.30	16.88
Athy	24	47	48	37	44	8.33	10.63	12.50	21.62	6.81
Ballina	45	41	52	75	54	6.66	12.19	15.38	10.66	22.22
Ballinasloe	53	64	89	44	68	1.88	6.25	12.35	9.09	16.18
Birt	20	26	45	27	38	5.00	3.84	8.88	11.11	7.89
Bray	126	157	208	215	222	16.66	15.28	10.09	15.81	21.17
Buncrana	52	48	49	43	55	15.38	16.66	2.04	18.60	9.09
Bundoran	32	56	58	58	34	12.50	21.42	15.51	13.79	20.58
Carlow	117	136	128	109	113	8.54	10.29	9.37	16.51	10.62
Carrickmacross	37	32	35	25	28	18.91	12.50	8.57	24.00	17.86
Carrick-on-Suir	51	39	29	26	24	5.88	2.56	3.44	3.84	8.33
Cashel	9	21	16	7	12	22.22	4.76	12.50	—	—
Castlebar	86	98	50	82	69	2.32	12.24	12.00	17.07	17.39
Castleblayney	31	36	79	23	18	9.67	8.33	2.53	13.04	16.66
Cavan	41	33	28	30	25	7.31	9.09	10.71	13.33	16.00
Ceanannus Mor	29	11	17	15	21	6.89	9.09	11.76	6.66	4.76
Clonakilty	14	37	39	20	21	14.28	13.51	2.56	5.00	4.76
Clones	19	21	18	8	13	15.78	9.52	16.66	—	15.38
Clonmel	83	71	109	70	95	7.22	11.26	15.59	10.00	21.05
Cobh	49	57	43	35	38	10.20	5.26	6.97	8.57	26.32
Drogheda	186	163	175	155	189	11.29	8.58	11.42	18.70	19.04
Dundalk	255	297	263	242	234	14.11	21.21	22.43	21.90	20.94
Dungarvan	44	59	54	55	68	—	1.69	9.25	7.27	2.94
Dun Laoghaire	392	431	408	497	580	18.62	10.67	13.72	22.93	25.51
Ennis	46	49	50	36	64	10.86	10.20	4.00	5.55	7.81
Enniscorthy	64	30	34	14	46	3.12	—	14.70	14.28	15.00
Fermoy	14	30	42	18	24	7.14	23.33	4.76	5.55	12.50
Galway	498	538	546	415	463	21.68	22.67	24.72	19.75	21.81
Kilkenny	98	126	127	125	113	17.34	15.87	5.51	11.20	14.15
Killarney	78	86	104	75	99	10.25	6.97	12.50	14.66	25.25
Kilrush	13	26	32	38	29	—	—	15.62	—	3.45
Kinsale	21	16	41	39	29	9.52	56.25	2.43	12.82	17.24
Letterkenny	61	89	106	78	87	8.19	6.74	9.43	7.69	6.89
Listowel	31	56	51	40	46	12.90	14.28	11.76	17.50	19.56
Longford	59	55	53	74	77	3.38	5.45	16.98	20.27	11.68

	Planning Decisions					% Refusals				
	1977	1978	1979	1980	1981	1977	1978	1979	1980	1981
Macroom	30	31	27	26	39	26.66	19.35	22.22	11.53	7.69
Mallow	57	62	67	42	58	12.28	11.29	22.38	2.38	24.13
Midleton	34	35	18	23	51	8.82	2.85	5.55	8.69	7.84
Monaghan	90	85	94	96	50	17.77	15.29	14.89	25.00	10.00
Naas	94	108	142	143	134	18.08	20.37	21.12	20.27	18.65
Navan	59	61	49	46	65	8.47	4.91	10.20	21.73	16.92
Nenagh	72	96	108	85	112	22.22	8.33	8.33	11.76	23.21
New Ross	32	37	59	34	43	—	—	6.77	5.88	13.95
Skibbereen	25	21	44	33	28	28.00	19.04	20.45	30.30	7.14
Sligo	127	121	163	161	150	21.25	14.87	21.47	26.70	28.00
Templemore	16	37	35	34	29	6.25	2.70	—	11.76	13.79
Thurles	36	64	60	49	37	8.33	9.37	8.33	2.04	13.51
Tipperary	33	33	34	31	26	12.12	—	2.94	12.90	3.85
Tralee	142	163	296	160	216	9.15	11.04	7.43	12.50	13.42
Trim	42	18	32	39	20	16.66	—	—	7.69	20.00
Tullamore	36	114	105	80	90	8.33	9.64	16.19	16.25	3.33
Westport	27	42	60	51	70	3.70	9.52	1.66	9.80	17.14
Wexford	145	141	134	129	143	9.65	9.21	8.20	3.87	3.14
Wicklow	60	43	73	67	54	11.66	25.58	8.21	7.46	5.56
Youghal	38	52	48	48	55	7.89	9.61	10.41	8.33	14.54
Sub Total	4108	4628	5062	4403	4736	13.35	12.72	13.05	15.85	17.27
Grand Total	40463	46426	55083	47045	48182	11.54	12.13	12.46	13.09	15.19

TABLE B

Area	Number of Appeals				Percentage of Total Appeals			
COUNTY	1978	1979	1980	1981	1978	1979	1980	1981
Carlow	17	28	38	26	0.48	0.74	0.96	0.57
Cavan	61	65	63	67	1.72	1.73	1.59	1.48
Clare	38	60	59	43	1.07	1.60	1.49	0.95
Cork	445	428	428	587	12.53	11.39	10.78	12.97
Donegal	84	70	97	63	2.37	1.86	2.44	1.39
Dublin	541	509	548	666	15.24	13.54	13.80	14.71
Galway	323	321	231	256	9.10	8.54	5.82	5.66
Kerry	101	125	126	150	2.84	3.32	3.17	3.32
Kildare	150	176	173	204	4.22	4.68	4.36	4.51
Kilkenny	28	38	39	38	0.79	1.01	0.98	0.84
Laois	26	37	31	38	0.73	0.98	0.78	0.84
Leitrim	17	16	28	22	0.48	0.42	0.70	0.48
Limerick	45	39	60	71	1.27	1.04	1.51	1.57
Longford	21	20	41	51	0.59	0.53	1.03	1.13
Louth	131	112	123	116	3.69	2.98	3.10	2.56
Mayo	57	85	82	106	1.61	2.26	2.06	2.34
Meath	96	144	164	205	2.70	3.83	4.13	4.53
Monaghan	43	57	53	70	1.21	1.52	1.34	1.55
Offaly	36	46	35	48	1.01	1.22	0.88	1.06
Roscommon	40	54	35	42	1.13	1.44	0.88	0.93
Sligo	68	62	80	75	1.92	1.65	2.01	1.66
Tipperary N.R.	36	52	53	92	1.01	1.38	1.33	2.03
Tipperary S.R.	38	31	28	34	1.07	0.82	0.71	0.75
Waterford	59	87	74	62	1.66	2.31	1.86	1.37
Westmeath	54	52	52	69	1.52	1.38	1.31	1.52
Wexford	97	99	109	103	2.73	2.63	2.75	2.28
Wicklow	252	209	294	302	7.10	5.56	7.41	6.67
County Borough/ Borough								
Cork	80	76	65	77	2.25	2.02	1.64	1.70
Dublin	451	526	577	621	12.70	13.99	14.54	13.72
Limerick	15	30	21	41	0.42	0.8	0.53	0.91
Waterford	11	8	30	31	0.31	0.21	0.76	0.68
Dun Laoghaire	90	99	133	150	2.53	2.63	3.35	3.32
Total	3551	3759	3970	4526	100	100	100	100

TABLE C

Area	Appeals as % of Decisions			
COUNTY	1978	1979	1980	1981
Carlow	3.21	4.17	7.50	5.01
Cavan	6.16	5.59	6.38	7.10
Clare	3.02	3.59	4.05	3.25
Cork	9.90	7.55	9.41	11.70
Donegal	3.19	2.47	3.38	2.55
Dublin	15.52	11.45	14.00	16.44
Galway	7.87	6.86	6.14	6.50
Kerry	3.96	3.84	4.86	5.55
Kildare	10.03	10.10	11.29	12.86
Kilkenny	2.30	2.76	3.52	3.33
Laois	3.55	3.35	4.26	5.03
Leitrim	4.20	2.91	5.00	4.77
Limerick	2.62	1.95	3.86	4.53
Longford	3.21	2.99	7.04	8.64
Louth	10.19	8.49	11.23	9.50
Mayo	2.71	3.45	3.66	5.41
Meath	5.45	6.27	8.84	8.61
Monaghan	4.50	5.58	6.41	9.08
Offaly	4.81	5.19	5.00	6.46
Roscommon	3.97	4.04	3.08	3.57
Sligo	7.22	6.07	8.84	7.37
Tipperary N.R.	3.48	4.73	5.62	9.13
Tipperary S.R.	4.20	2.94	3.44	4.30
Waterford	6.70	7.38	8.79	7.64
Westmeath	4.88	4.50	5.26	7.91
Wexford	5.57	4.77	6.27	5.57
Wicklow	17.77	13.66	19.71	19.04
County Borough/Borough				
Cork	10.80	8.98	10.66	11.74
Dublin	17.21	16.88	18.76	20.67
Limerick	5.47	9.68	7.69	14.64
Waterford	5.42	3.33	9.65	8.78
Dun Laoghaire	20.88	24.26	26.76	25.86
National Average	7.65	6.82	8.44	9.39

APPENDIX III

ENACTMENTS AND REGULATIONS DIRECTLY RELEVANT TO PHYSICAL PLANNING

Planning Acts
Local Government (Planning and Development) Act, 1963 (No. 28 of 1963).
Local Government (Planning and Development) Act, 1963 (No. 20 of 1976).
Local Government (Planning and Development) Act, 1963 (No. 21 of 1982).
Local Government (Planning and Development) Act, 1963 (No. 28 of 2963).

Regulations, Rules and Policy Directive
Rules of the Superior Courts (No. 1), 1976 (S.I. No. 286 of 1976).
Local Government (Planning and Development) Regulations, 1977 (S.I. No. 65 of 1977).
Local Government (Planning and Development) (Amendment) Regulations, 1980 (S.I. No. 231 of 1980)
Local Government (Planning and Development (Amendment) Regulations, 1981 (S.I. No. 154 of 1981)
Local Government (Planning and Development) General Policy Directive, 1982 (S.I. No. 264 of 1982).

Enactments which amend or affect the Planning Acts
Housing Act, 1969   (No. 16 of 1969) S. 10 and 12
Gas Act, 1976   (No. 30 of 1976) S. 42
Wildlife Act, 1976   (No. 39 of 1976) S. 21 (8)
Casual Trading Act, 1980   (No. 43 of 1980) S. 7 (3)
Fire Services Act, 1981   (No. 30 of 1981) S. 13
Litter Act, 1982   (No. 11 of 1982) S. 19.

APPENDIX B

LOCAL GOVERNMENT (PLANNING AND DEVELOPMENT) GENERAL POLICY DIRECTIVE, 1982
(S.I. No. 264 of 1982)

The Minister for the Environment, in exercise of the powers conferred on him by section 7 of the Local Government (Planning and Development) Act, 1982 (No. 21 of 1982), hereby issues the following general directive:

1. This Directive may be cited as the Local Government (Planning and Development) General Policy Directive, 1982.

2. Policy in relation to planning and development requires that the establishment of retail shopping development which would represent a large scale addition to the existing retail shopping capacity in a locality should be guided by the following considerations:

  (a) the adequacy of existing retail shopping outlets:
  (b) the size and location of existing retail shopping outlets;
  (c) the quality and convenience of existing retail shopping outlets;
  (d) the effect on existing communities, including in particular the effect on established retail shopping outlets and on employment;
  (e) the needs of elderly, infirm or disabled persons and of other persons who may be dependent on the availability of local retail shopping outlets;
  (f) the need to counter urban decline and to promote urban renewal and to promote the utilisation of unused infrastructural facilities in urban areas.

APPENDIX C

ADDITIONAL CASES

CHAPTER 1: ESTOPPEL AND PLANNING AUTHORITIES

STATE (DINO APRILE) v. NAAS URBAN DISTRICT COUNCIL
(1983: 347 S.S.)

A planning authority which confines itself to only one ground of refusal of planning permission does not thereby preclude itself from relying on other grounds of refusal on a similar application relating to the same lands. *Res judicata* applies only in the case of identical applications. *Mandamus* will be granted only as a remedy of last resort.

O'Hanlon J. (22nd November, 1983):
. . . Two legal issues arise for consideration in relation to the present application for relief by way of mandamus. The first concerns the Prosecutor's claim that a planning authority which has committed itself to particular grounds for refusing an application for development permission under the Planning Acts cannot resort to other grounds for refusing a similar application which is made after the applicant has incurred expense in eliminating the original grounds for objection to his proposal. Secondly, the respondent, while disputing this contention, makes the further submission that relief by way of mandamus should not, in any event, be granted in a case like the present where a statutory right of appeal to An Bord Pleanala is available to the prosecutor – an alternative remedy which may be regarded as being as convenient, beneficial and effective as the remedy by way of mandamus.

  With reference to the first of these two legal issues, the prosecutor relied strongly on the decision of Gavan Duffy J. in *Athlone Woollen Mills Co. Ltd.* v. *Athlone UDC,* [1950] I.R.1, which involved an examination of the provisions of the Town and Regional Planning Acts, 1934 and 1939. In that case the developer having made an application for planning permission which was granted in turn by the UDC and by the Minister, on appeal, but in each case subject to conditions which the developer claimed gave rise to a right to compensation under the Acts, sought to enforce this right of compensation. Having allowed the statutory period to go by without asserting this claim, the developer sought to revive it by resubmitting an identical claim for planning permission, which was rejected as being invalid by the planning authority and by the Minister. Gavan Duffy J. held that they were correct in coming to this concluson, and stated the law as follows (at p. 9):

> 'In my opinion, the grant of a special permission (with or without conditions) by a planning authority, or its grant as passed by the Minister on appeal, involves the exercise of limited powers of a judicial nature, so that the decision is properly described as a judicial decision pronounced by a judicial tribunal, as those terms

are understood in relation to the doctrine of *res judicata*. I am of opinion that the doctrine of *res judicata* with the consequent estoppel applies.'

I am unwilling to extend the application of that decision beyond the type of situation covered by the facts of that particular case. In the later case of *O'Dea* v. *Minister for Local Government and Dublin Co. Council*, 91 ILTR 169, Dixon J. distinguished it and declined to follow it in relation to a case where he held that the two planning applications could not be regarded as identical, and the prior refusal of special permission (under the former Planning Acts) was in respect of an application which was different in kind and not merely the same application in a different guise. Accordingly, he held that the doctrine of *res judicata* did not apply to the facts of that case.

Sec. 26 of the Local Government (Planning and Development) Act, 1963 deals with the obligations which are imposed on the planning authority where an application is made for permission for the development of land or for an approval required by the permission regulations. The authority must reach a decision which is based upon a consideration of the proper planning and development of the area of the authority, regard being had to a number of special matters referred to in subsection (1) of that Section.

If the planning authority sees fit to confine its grounds for refusal of an application to a single ground (as happened in the present case in relation to the first application), it does not, in my opinion, tie its hands and precluded itself from relying on other grounds if a similar application is made to it in relation to the same lands, after that first ground of objection has been successfully disposed of. I do not regard the Statement of grounds in refusing an application for planning permission as amounting to a representation by the planning authority to the developer that these are the only grounds upon which the proposed development conflicts with the proper planning and development of the area, and if a fresh application is later made in relation to the development of the same lands, there is an obligation on the planning authority, whenever it is called upon to deal with the new application, to consider it *de novo* and to have regard to all aspects of the proper planning and development of the area as of that time, in granting or refusing the application.

This may seem to be calculated to work hardship on developers who incur expense in meeting objections raised to their first application, only to be confronted with new grounds when they have done so and renewed their application for permission. This difficulty can be surmounted quite readily, however, by a process of consultation between developers and the officials of the planning authorities and I believe that this is the course which is usually adopted in such cicumstances.

I conclude, therefore, that the doctrine of *red judicata* does not apply in the present case, and that a situation has not arisen which would justify the granting of an order of mandamus to compel the respondent to grant the permission sought by the prosecutor for the continuance of the use of his premises as an Amusement Centre.

I would also support the view put forward on behalf of the respondents that relief by way of Mandamus should, in any event, be refused, having regard to the alternative remedy of the right of appeal to An Bord Pleanala which is available under the Planning Acts.

'Mandamus has always been regarded as an extraordinary, residuary and "sup-

pletory" remedy, to be granted only when there is no other means of obtaining justice. Even though all the other requirements for securing the remedy have been satisfied by the applicant, the court will decline to exercise its discretion in his favour if a specific alternative remedy "equally convenient, beneficial and effectual" is available.'
(de Smith, *Judicial Review of Administrative Action*, 1st edn. p. 452).

In *The State (Cagney)* v. *McCarthy D.J.* 75 ILTR 224, these principles were applied by a Divisional Court in refusing an application for mandamus to compel a District Justice to state and sign a case for the opinion of the High Court in a case where the prosecutor wished to appeal by way of case stated against the dismissal of two civil processes brought against a defendant in the District Court. Maguire P., delivering the judgment of the Court, held that the relief that was available to the prosecutor by way of an appeal to the Circuit Court was equally convenient, beneficial and effective with that sought by him in the mandamus proceedings, and held that relief by way of mandamus should be refused.

However, the High Court, and on appeal, the Supreme Court, did not hesitate to grant mandamus in a similar case of *The State (Turley)* v. *O Floinn D. J.* [1968] I.R. 245, where the District Justice refused to state a case for the opinion of the High Court where the prosecutor had been convicted of a criminal offence, nor was it argued in that case that the right of appeal to the Circuit Court would necessarily defeat the right to mandamus.

It was suggested in the present case that relief by order of mandamus would be much more expeditious than the prosecution of an appeal to An Bord Pleanala and it was pointed out that the appeals already lodged by the prosecutor against previous refusals of permission had not yet been processed notwithstanding the lapse of about one year since the lodgment of notice of appeal. There was no evidence put before the Court, however, to indicate that this delay was a constant and inevitable feature of appeals brought before An Bord Pleanala, and as a specific machainery is provided by the Planning Acts for testing the correctness of decisions made by the planning authorities, I am of opinion that this should generally be resorted to in preference to mandamus proceedings unless there has been an actual failure or refusal of the planning authorities to carry out their obligations under the Acts.

For the reasons already stated in the course of this judgment, I propose to refuse the application to make absolute the Conditional Order of Mandamus already granted and I discharge the Conditional Order.

CHAPTER 2: DEVELOPMENT.
Material Change of Use

DUBLIN CORPORATION v. MOORE
(Unreported), The Supreme Court, Griffin J., Hederman, J., McCarthy, J. 28 July 1983 (Ref. No. 138/1982)

The parking of commercial ice-cream vans within the curtilage of a dwelling-house is not a material change of use of the premises (Griffin J. dissenting).

Griffin J.:

'Development' is defined in s. 3(1) of the 1963 Act (in so far as it is relevant to this case) as meaning, save where the context otherwise requires, the making of any material change in the use of land. S. 4 provides for development which shall be exempted development for the purpose of the Act, and in subs. '(1)(*h*) includes development consisting of the use of land 'within the curtilage of a dwelling-house for any purpose incidental to the enjoyment of the dwelling-house *as such*' (emphasis added). Using the premises for parking of these ice cream vans, plugged in to the electrical current in the house, was clearly a change in the use of the premises, the real question then being whether such change was 'material'. Mr. Justice McMahon held that it was, and in my opinion he was correct in so holding.

The purpose of s. 4(1)(*h*) was to enable the curtilage of a dwelling-house (which would include the driveway) to be used for any purpose incidental to the enjoyment of the dwelling-house as such. This would include the parking of a private car, but the parking of two ice cream vans of the type owned by the appellants would not be a use of the premises for a purpose incidental to the enjoyment of the dwelling-house, but would, as Mr. Justice McMahon found, be use incidental to the carrying on of the ice cream business. In my opinion, parking these vans in a driveway, in a residential area, so designated in the Dublin Development Plan by Dublin Corporation and held to be reasonably zoned as such by An Bord Pleanala, clearly constituted an interference with the residential amenity of the area and was a material change in the use of the premises. It seems to me that a fair yardstick by which to measure the question of materiality in the change of use in a case like this is whether, in a residential area, the average resident would like to see the house next door occupied by a neighbour who is going to park two such large vans in his driveway; or whether a prospective purchaser of the house next door to the appellants' house when viewing it while the appellants' vans were absent would have the same interest in buying the house if, on a return visit, these two large vans were parked in the driveway. I think the answer is self-evident. If, in a residential area, vans of this type can be parked with impunity in the driveway of a dwelling-house, what is to prevent the parking of a large articulated container truck in like manner?

In my opinion, Mr. Justice McMahon was quite correct in making an Order under s. 27 of the 1976 Act and I would dismiss this appeal.

McCarthy J.:

. . . The learned trial judge held that the use of the front driveway of No. 144 as described was a development within s. 3, and appears, from his note, to have adverted in that regard to subs. 2(*b*)(i). In my view, the note must be mistaken; subs. 2(*b*)(i) in purporting to identify, without delimiting, 'material change' refers, so far as relevant here, to the placing or keeping of vans, not just as such, but for a particular purpose – here, the sale of goods. In my view, what the subsection contemplates is that the van is kept in the particular land and *there* used for the sale of goods. Such is not the case here; the vans are, as it were, 'parked' when not in use for the sale of goods. Counsel for the Corporation cited the Local Government (Planning and Development) Regulations 1977 with particular reference to the third Schedule providing for exempted development – general. Class 16 of the description of development refers to 'the keeping or storing of not more than one caravan or boat within the curtilage of a dwelling-house.' This is a reference, so far as relevant here, to a caravan, not to a van as such; of course, a caravan is a van, but, to state the obvious, a van is not, necessarily, a caravan; indeed, subs. 2(*b*)(i) of s. 3 of the 1963 Act recognises this distinction by stating one of the offending manners of placing or keeping of a van on land would be 'the purpose of caravanning'. In the circumstances, in my view, Class 16 is irrelevant.

The learned trial judge further and, in my opinion, correctly, held that the keeping of the vans as alleged did not constitute exempted development pursuant to s. 4(l)(*h*) of the 1963 Act. It has not been sought to argue the contrary in this Court. The 'fall back' position adopted by the Corporation has been to say that, in any event, the use complained of constitutes 'material change in the use of land' and is therefore to be prohibited. It is important to recognise that the consequences of breaches of the planning code are penal in nature and, therefore, the statutes enforcing them must be strictly construed. I do not need, however, the aid of any such rule of strict construction to hold that the conduct complained of does not constitute development within the definition of s. 3 of the 1963 Act. The driveway of a home is always intended for parking of vehicles; it would be difficult to find a driveway to a home in the City or County of Dublin where it was not so used; s. 3, subs 2. is clearly intended to prevent an alteration of that particular type of use to one where it is supplemented by a use 'in situ'. It may well be that a driveway is not the ordinary parking place for a caravan or a boat – ergo, the exemption by Class 16. If one were to extend the ban contended for by the Corporation, one would have to contemplate that the taxi-driver, the small grocer who has a van, the small building contractor, the artisan, the discotheque provider, the children's entertainer, indeed, the gas, electrical or like specialist employees of Dublin Corporation, may not, lawfully, keep the vehicle attached to such trade or profession parked at home. In my view, it is a complete shutting out of reality not to recognise that people of the kind I have mentioned and, no doubt, a great variety of others, keep the vehicles of their trade at home. To avail of the electricity supply does not, in my view, affect the situation any more than the overnight charging of the battery of a car. I can well understand the objection voiced by Mr. Heneghan in his affidavit, to which I have referred — the residents of a quiet suburb naturally resent the presence of what may well be out of keeping with what they conceive to be the standards appropriate to the neighbourhood. There cannot, however, be one law for Cabra and another for Clondalkin – yet others for Finglas and Foxrock. Considerations of this kind are not appropriate to planning law – if they were, they might well offend against rights of equality. The ordinary law of nuisance remains, if nuisance there be; I am far from suggesting that there is an actionable nuisance in the presence of what may be something of an eyesore in an area such as that in question. I point, however, to the simple fact that there is a large Petrol Filling Station immediately across the intersecting side road from the house in question.

In my opinion, this application is misconceived; the appeal should be allowed and the order of the High Court discharged.

Hederman J. also delivered a judgment allowing the appeal.

CHAPTER 2: DEVELOPMENT.
Exempted Development

TRALEE U.D.C. v. STACK
(Unreported), The High Court, Barrington J., 13 January 1984, (Ref. No. 1983 No. 48 MCA).

The respondent began to fill in a pond in order to reclaim it for agricultural use with planning permission. In section 27 proceedings the Court rejected the respondent's contention that the works were exempted under s. 4(1)(*a*) or 4(1)(*i*).

Barrington J.:
. . . It appears to me that the present case turns upon a net point as to whether the works carried out, or proposed to be carried out, by the respondent constitute 'development' within the meaning of the Planning Acts. It is common case that the respondent proposes to reclaim the lands for agricultural purposes and that he has no planning perm.'ssion to do this. The issue is whether he requires planning permission or whether he does not.

It also seems clear that the work carried out, or proposed to be carried out, by the respondent constitutes what the lay-man would call land reclamation for agricultural purposes. The issue is whether it is, as the respondent maintains, land reclamation within the meaning of the Land Reclamation Act 1949.

Section 3 of the Local Government (Planning and Development) Act 1963 provides generally that development, save where the context otherwise requires, means the carrying out of any works on, in or under land or the making of any material change in the use of any structures or other land. Section 4 provides that certain developments are to be 'exempted developments'. One of these is development consisting of the use of any land for the purposes of agriculture. I do not think that land reclamation of the kind contemplated in the present case would be regarded as the 'use' of land for the purposes of agriculture even though the objectives may be to use the reclaimed land for agricultural purposes.

But Section 4 also exempts (at sub-section 1 paragraph (i)) –

'Development consisting of the carrying out of any of the works referred to in the Land Reclamation Act 1949'.

But the Land Reclamation Act 1949 refers to itself in its long title as an Act 'to authorise the Minister for Agriculture to carry out land reclamation. . .'. It is clear from the body of the Act that the land reclamation contemplated by the Act is land reclamation carried out by the Minister either at the request of the occupier of the land or on the Minister's own initiative. I do not think that the respondent in the present case can rely on the reference to the Land Reclamation Act 1949 contained in Section 4 of the Local Government (Planning and Development) Act 1963.

It therefore appears to me that the development carried out or proposed to be carried out by the respondent in the present case is not exempted development and that he is not free to carry it out without planning permission.

Under these circumstances it appears to me that the applicants are entitled to relief.

CHAPTER 3: PLANNING AUTHORITY BOUND BY REGULATIONS

THOMAS GERARD O'NEILL v. CLARE COUNTY COUNCIL
[1983] I.L.R.M. 141

The plaintiff was held entitled in principle to damages for the defendant's delay in granting him planning permission to which he became entitled by default.

McWilliam J.:
Of the declarations claimed by the plaintiff, he is entitled to a declaration that a decision to grant permission should be regarded as having been given on the last day of the period of two months from the 6th day of October, 1978, and to a declaration that the purported notification of a decision to grant permission subject to certain conditions, dated the 28th day of February, 1979, is null and void.

The plaintiff also claims damages and, as particulars of special damage, claims interest on £150,000, the value of the lands, from 6th December, 1978, until the date of granting of permission.

It has been argued on behalf of the defendant that section 26(1) provides that a planning authority may decide to grant permission or approval or withhold it and, as it is not mandatory, there can be no claim to damages. This disregards the provisions of subsection (9) which are that the planning authority *shall* make the grant of permission so soon as may be after (in this case) the expiration of the period for the taking of an appeal otherwise than by the applicant. This is a mandatory provision and, from early in January until 31st July, 1979, the defendant was in default and, as it appears to me, deliberately so from receipt of the letter of 20th March, 1979. This being so, no argument has been addressed to me which persuades me that the plaintiff is not entitled to such damages as resulted from such default.

On the other hand, it is for the plaintiff to establish the amount of his loss and establish that this loss was due to the default of the defendant. The evidence in this respect was most unsatisfactory. . . .

It is clear that there was a slump in property sales from the end of July, 1979, and I am satisfied that the delay by the defendant probably caused the plaintiff some loss but I have not been given sufficient evidence to calculate this loss and I will award a nominal sum of £500 damages.

CHAPTER 3: INTERPRETATION

JACK BARRETT (BUILDERS) LIMITED v. DUBLIN COUNTY COUNCIL
(Supreme Court Ref. 148–1979)

In reaching the conclusion that on the true interpretation of a planning permission the plaintiff was obliged to construct a link road shown on the plans for a housing development (thereby reversing the trial judge) the Supreme Court reiterated the principles to be applied when construing a planning permission.

Hederman J. (Henchy, McCarthy JJ. concurring) on 28th July 1983:
. . . . I am satisfied that when one examines the lay-out on which the original application No. 778 was granted the plan speaks for itself and there is no ambiguity as to the work to be undertaken by the developer and the works to be undertaken by the Local Authority. Clearly the link road which goes through the centre of the development and would measure approximately 717 yards is part of the permission and conditions granted to the respondent in the erection of approximately 500 houses in this particular area.

The failure of the developer to put in the link road has resulted in the residents in part of the estate being obliged to use two unauthorised road connections made by the respondent, one of which gives access to Grange Road on the eastern side of the development and the other which has been provided by building a short link road to provide temporary access for residents in the south western portion of the estate across the land reserved for the link road and adjoining an estate road which gives access to Grange Road.

In the course of his judgment in *Readymix Eire Limited* v. *Dublin County Council and Minister for Local Government* (unreported) (with which Walsh J. agreed) given in this Court on the 30th July 1974, Henchy J. said at p. 4:

'When a permission issues in a case such as this, it enures for the benefit not alone of the person to whom it issues but also for the benefit of anyone who acquires an interest in the property: s. 28(5). A proper record of the permission is therefore necessary. This is provided for by s. 8, which prescribed that a planning authority shall keep a register of all land in their area affected by the Act. This register is the statutorily designated source of authoritative information as to what is covered by a permission. The Act does not in terms make the register the conclusive or exclusive record of the nature and extent of a permission, but the scheme of the Act indicates that anybody who acts on the basis of the correctness of the particulars in the register is entitled to do so. Where the permission recorded in the register is self-contained, it will not be permissible to go outside it in construing it. But where the permission incorporates other documents, it is the combined effect of the permission and such documents that must be looked at in determining the proper scope of the permission. This, because in the present case the permission incorporated by reference the application for permission together with the plans lodged with it, it is agreed that the decision so notified must be construed by reference not only to its direct content but also to the application and the plans lodged.

Since the permission notified to an applicant and entered in the register is a public document, it must be construed objectively as such, and not in the light of subjective considerations special to the applicant or those responsible for the grant of the permission. Because the permission is an appendage to the title to the property, it may possibly not arise for interpretation until the property has passed into the hands of those who have no knowledge of any special circumstances in which it was granted. Since s. 24(4) of the Act allows the production by a defendant of the permission to be a good defence in a prosecution for carrying out without permission development for which permission is required, it would be contrary to the fundamentals of justice as well as the canons of statutory interpretation to hold that a permission could have variable meanings, depending on whether special circumstances known only to certain persons are brought to light or not.'

I accept the reasoning as quoted in Mr. Justice Henchy's judgment as being the proper principles to be applied in this case and in applying these principles I am satisfied that the construction of the link road as set out in the original application is the exclusive responsibility of the respondent.

CHAPTER 3: APPLICATION REGULATIONS

THOMAS C. BURKE V. DROGHEDA CORPORATION
(1979 6699P)

The plaintiff's planning application did not specify whether full or outline permission was sought. No decision being notified within two months of receipt the plaintiff was held entitled to a default outline permission.

McWilliam J.:

If the application was for full permission it did not comply with the provisions of Article 4(1) in that the plan did not show any elevations or sections and did not comply with the provisions of Article 8(1) in that the plan did not show buildings and other features in the vicinity of the property, was not drawn to scale with an indication of the scale and did not indicate the north point. I have been referred to the judgments of the Supreme Court in the case of *Monaghan U.D.C.* v. *Alf-a-Bet Promotions Ltd.*, delivered on 24th March, 1980, in which it was held that compliance with the regulations was mandatory and that an application which does not comply with them is a nullity unless the deviation from the requirements is so trivial, so technical, so peripheral or otherwise so unsubstantial that the prescribed obligation has been substantially and therefore adequately complied with. Accordingly I am of opinion that the plaintiff's application of 17th September 1974, was not adequate as an application for full planning permission.

On the other hand I am of opinion that the plan furnished was sufficient to support an application for outline permission under the provisions of Article 5(1). This leads to the question whether the application was one for full permission or was or can be treated as having been an application for outline permission.

The plaintiff's application was not unequivocally expressed to be an outline application but left the matter at large as to whether he was applying for full permission or only for outline permission. But Article 6 of the Regulations gives four alternative courses which may be adopted by a planning authority where an application does not comply with the provisions of Article 4 and is not expressed to be an outline application. Of these, the course of refusing permission can only be adopted if it appears that there are adequate reasons for such decision. No argument has been advanced to me to suggest that this is not a decision which must be given within the time limited by section 26 of the Act, and, in default of such decision, it appears to me that at the end of the stipulated period outline permission must be regarded as having been granted if the application was sufficient for that purpose only.

If this is correct, the defendant raises the further pleading point that the claim is for a declaration that full planning permission has been obtained, the expression used in the Statement of Claim being 'planning permission'. I have not been referred to any definition in the Act which is relevant to this point and, in view of the definition in Article 2 of the Regulations that 'permission' includes outline permission, I do not consider that the pleading is bad although it could have been drafted more clearly.

Accordingly, I must hold that outline permission must be regarded as having been granted on 17th November 1974.

CHAPTER 4: APPEALS TO THE BOARD

THE STATE (FITZGERALD) V. AN BORD PLEANALA
(Unreported), The High Court, Carroll J., 4 November 1983,
(Ref. No. 1983 No. 379 SS)

The Board made a decision to grant permission to retain an unauthorised house giving the following reason for its decision:

'SCHEDULE: Having regard to the development on adjacent sites and Clyde Lane generally it is considered that the retention of this house would be in accordance with the proper planning and development of the area. The degree of injury and departure from original plan are not such as to warrant removal of structure.'

The Court held that the Board had taken into account the desirability of the removal or non-removal of the house in coming to its decision, which was not a proper consideration. An absolute Order of *Certiorari* was granted.

Carroll J.:
. . . Under Section 26 of the Local Government (Planning and Development) Act 1963 (the '1963 Act') it is provided that in dealing with any application for planning permission the Planning Authority 'shall be restricted to considering the proper planning and development of the area of the Authority (including the preservation and improvement of the amenities thereof), regard being had to the provisions of the development plan, the provision of any special amenity area order relating to the said area and the matters referred to in sub-section 2 of this section.' Sub-section 2 does not have relevance in this matter.

Under Section 26(5) of the 1963 Act (as amended by the 1976 Act) it is provided that where an appeal is brought from a decision of the Planning Authority, the Board shall determine the application as if it had been made to it in the first instance. Therefore the Board are restricted in the same way as a Planning Authority as to the matters they may consider in dealing with applications.

In deciding this matter I must construe the wording of the orders dated the 5th May, 1983 having regard to any explanations given in the affidavit filed on behalf of the Board.

In my opinion all the matters included in the Schedule must be construed as a composite reason for the decision. It follows that the conclusion of the Board that the retention of the house 15D would be in accordance with the proper planning and development of the area must have been preceded by the formation of their opinion that the degree of injury together with the departure from the original plan did not warrant the removal of the structure. It could not have formed part of the reason for the decision if the Board deliberated on the injury to amenity or departure from plans *vis à vis* the removal of the structure after they had decided that the retention was in accordance with proper planning and development.

The removal or non-removal of the structure should not have entered into their deliberations at all. It was entirely immaterial to good planning and development that there was an unauthorised development there. They should have decided without reference to the existing structure.

While they could decide that the injury to amenity was not sufficient to refuse permission, they could not decide that the injury to amenity was not sufficient to warrant removal. This is putting in the balance the injury to amenity on one hand and the removal of the structure on the other (which in this context must mean expense and inconvenience to the developer).

It also appears to me that the degree of departure from plans is not a proper planning reason either. There might be a very slight degree of departure from approved plans which would render a building unacceptable from the point of view of proper planning and development e.g. if windows were out of character with the neighbourhood. On the other hand there could be a large degree of departure from plans, yet the building might be completely acceptable from a planning point of view.

Undoubtedly if the Court were hearing an application under Section 27 of the 1976 Act where there was a question of demolition of an unauthorised development, the Court would take into consideration exceptional circumstances favouring the developer. These were outlined by Henchy J. in *Morris* v. *Garvey* [1982] I.L.R.M. 180 as 'genuine mistake, acquiescence over a long period, the triviality or mere technicality of the infraction, gross or disproportionate hardship or such like extenuating or excusing factors'. The Courts in exercising their judicial function must have regard to the justice of the case. But the Board in making a decision whether to grant permission on appeal is not concerned with the justice of the case. It is confined solely to considerations of good planning and development.

The Conditional Order of Certiorari will be made absolute.

CHAPTER 4: APPEALS
Appeals to the Board

THE STATE (BOYD) v. AN BORD PLEANALA
(Unreported) The High Court, Murphy J., 18th February 1983, (Ref. No. 1982 No. 609S.S.)

The prosecutrix appealed a decision to grant a permission for construction of a chemical plant. Her principal objection was that there was a danger that the drawing off of water required for the process to be carried out at the plant would cause subsidence damaging her house. The applicant for permission had a report prepared dealing with the effect of the pumping water on her house which the Board forwarded to her. The report as forwarded did not contain some of its sections nor the appendices. The prosecutrix through her solicitors wrote to the Board pointing out the omissions and asking it to forward these to her. The letter further indicated that she thought the report was inadequate and that further expert evidence was required. The Board determined the appeal without forwarding the omitted portions of the report. In the reasons it gave for its decision the Board expressed the opinion that the question of the damage it was alleged would result to the prosecutrix's house 'should not be permitted to govern its decision'. The Court granted Orders of Certiorari and Mandamus.

Murphy J.:
. . . . it does seem clear beyond dispute that at the end of August, 1982 the Board through their officers were aware that the prosecutrix was seeking to make a case on the appeal in which she had a bona fide belief and indeed which was suported at least to some extent by her professional advisers. Even more important is the fact that the prosecutrix herself believed and was entitled to believe that the Board recognised that the question of water withdrawal was material to their decision on the appeal. It is impossible not to conclude from the correspondence that the prosecutrix and her advisers were awaiting and expecting a reply to the letter of the 23rd August, 1982. Indeed a reminder was sent on the 21st September, 1982 repeating the request for the information already referred to. Unhappily that letter was not received by the Board until the 28th September on which date, by an unhappy coincidence, the Board issued their decision on the matter. Whilst the Board in their reasons explained that they were 'unable to determine on the evidence available to it whether or not development which has already taken place on the appeal site has caused serious structural damage to the appellant's adjoining property 'or' whether a continuance of activity on the appeal site would result in further damage to the appellant's property' they went on to grant the permission partly on the basis that the then existing permission related to substantially the same industrial process. The Board further expressed the view that the issue in relation to the alleged structural damage to the Glebe house should be resolved elsewhere 'and should not be permitted to govern its decision'.

Whilst it is true that planning permission does not confer a licence on the grantee relieving him from the obligation which he owes in tort to his neighbour not to cause unlawful damage to the premises which he owns or occupies, that does not mean that the possibility of such damage takes the matter out of the sphere of planning considerations. It may have been even in the particular circumstances of the present case – that a stronger, more detailed and more authoritatively supported submission on behalf of the prosecutrix would have led the Board to a different conclusion. I am not concerned as to whether or not that would have been the result but it seems to me that it must be accepted that such was a real possibility. Accordingly the failure – and I have no doubt that it was entirely unintentional – by the Board either to furnish the prosecutrix with the required information or to afford her an opportunity of making a final submission meant that the appeal was not conducted in accordance with the minimum standards of fair procedures granted by the Constitution.

In the circumstances it seems to me that the Conditional Order must be made absolute and the cause shown disallowed.

As to the consequences of the order made herein, I would propose to follow the procedure indicated by the President of the High Court in the *Genport Case* (unreported judgment dated the 1st February, 1982) and to direct the Board to make available for inspection by the prosecutrix the sections and appendices referred to in the Cullen report together with the environmental study supplied or commissioned by the Industrial Development Authority within one week from the date hereof and to allow the prosecutrix a fixed period – I would suggest a period of four weeks – within which the prosecutrix will make her full and final submission to the Board in relation to the subject matter of the appeal.

CHAPTER 5: THE ENFORCEMENT OF PLANNING CONTROL – SECTION 27.

DUBLIN COUNTY COUNCIL V. ELTON HOMES LTD. (IN LIQ.) AND ORS.
(Unreported) The High Court, Barrington J., 19 May 1983,
(Ref. No. 1982 No. 103 MCA)

A company in creditor's voluntary liquidation had failed to comply with the conditions attached to a planning permission for the construction of 21 houses insofar as they related to remedial works, public lighting, etc. The Applicants issued section 27 proceeding against the company, and its two directors. The Court held that while it could make an Order against the directors of a company, in the circumstances of the case it would not do so, the directors not having been guilty of any impropriety. Further no Order would be made against the liquidator who had undertaken to co-operate with the planning authority.

Barrington J.:
. . . The powers conferred on the High Court by the sub-section are very wide powers. It may require 'any person' specified in the order to do or not to do or to cease to do, as the case may be, anything which the Court considers necessary to ensure that the development is carried out in conformity with the permission.

One must assume that the sub-section was deliberately drafted in wide terms. At the same time the powers conferred on the High Court are not arbitrary powers but must be exercised in accordance with principles which are judicially acceptable.

If, in the present case, the company were solvent there would be no problem. Clearly an injunction could be granted against the company to ensure that it carried out the conditions attaching to the planning permissions. It would also appear that, in a proper case, an order could be made against the persons in control of the company (be they the directors or a liquidator) to ensure that the company fulfilled its obligations to the planning authority. The problem is that the company is insolvent. The liquidator says that his responsibility is to the creditors of the company who, as things stand, will only receive 25p in the pound. If the Court were not to make an order directing the company to complete the development in accordance with the conditions it would be penalising the creditors of the company who, presumably, traded with the company in good faith, and already stand to lose heavily.

It was a term of the planning permission that the company should take out a bond in the sum of £10,000 with an approved insurance company for the due completion of the work. Such a bond was in fact taken out but, unfortunately, the amount of the bond is now insufficient to secure the proper completion of the work. Resort has already been had to the bond in the sum of £5,325.00 and only the sum of £4,675.00 now remains. In the event of the Planning Authority finishing the work and claiming against the bond the liquidator is prepared to undertake to cooperate with the Planning Authority in recovering this sum of £4,675.00 on foot of the bond. In these circumstances I do not think I would be justified in making the Order against the liquidator or the company.

The question arises of whether the court can or ought to make an Order against Mr. Keogh and Mr. English personally as the former directors of the company. Let me say at once that I think it may be quite proper, in certain circumstances, to join the directors of a company as respondents when an application is made by a Planning Authority against a company pursuant to the provisions of Section 27. Mr. Gallagher, who appeared for the Planning Authority, referred me to a motion *Dublin County Council* v. *Crampton Builder Limited & Ors.* which came before the President on the 10th of March, 1980 in which directors of a building firm had been joined as respondents to the motion. The President did not in that case make an order against the directors but he apparently said that, in his view, section 27 was sufficient widely drafted to empower the joining of company directors as respondents, but that whether an order would or would not be made against them would depend on the facts of each individual case. There may be many cases, particularly in the case of small companies, where the most effective way of ensuring that the company complies with its obligations is to make an order against the directors as well as against the company itself. But in such a case the order against the directors would be a way of ensuring that the company carried out its obligations. A body corporate can only act through its agents and the most effective way of ensuring that it does in fact carry out its obligations might be to make an order against the persons in control of it.

What is sought against the second and third named respondents in the present case is very different. They are no longer in control of the company and it is not suggested that, through them, the company can be forced to carry out its obligations. What is suggested is that because they were directors of the company at the time when the company obtained planning permission that they should be ordered to complete the development at their own expense. I am not saying that there might not be cases where the Court would be justified in making such an order. If the case were one of fraud, or if the directors had syphoned off large sums of money out of the company, so as to leave it unable to fulfil its obligations, the Court might be justified in lifting the veil of incorporation and fixing the directors with personal responsibility. But that is not this case. The second and third named respondents appear to be fairly small men who, having failed in this particular enterprise, are now back working for others. The worst that can be imputed against them is mismanagement.

They gave personal guarantees to the insurance company which supplied the bond for £10,000.00 and to the company's bankers. They therefore stand to lose heavily arising out of the transaction. Moreover Mr. Noel Daly of the liquidator's office who gave evidence before me said that the liquidator and his officials entertain no suspicion that there has been any impropriety on the part of the directors in dealing with the assets of the company.

It appears to me that Mr. Keogh and Mr. English traded with the benefit of limited liability in this case and that, in the absence of an evidence of impropriety on their part, I would not be justified in attempting to make them personally responsible for the default of the company.

I am aware that the result is an unfortunate one for the Planning Authority and the local residents. Perhaps the moral is that the Planning Authority before granting planning permission, should be very careful, especially in these inflationary times, to ensure that the security demanded by it of a developer for completion of proposed works is realistic.

CHAPTER 5: THE ENFORCEMENT OF PLANNING CONTROL
Section 27

DUBLIN COUNTY COUNCIL v. LOUGHRAN
(Unreported) The High Court, Murphy J., 18 May 1983, (Ref. No. 1983 No. 3 MCA)

In section 27 proceedings the Court held:

(a) The reduction in value of the respondent's premises which will result from an order being made under S. 27 is not a relevant consideration for the Court in deciding whether to make an order.

(b) Where a respondent does not purport to carry out a development in accordance with a planning permission the appropriate order is an Order requiring a discontinuance of the unauthorised development and not an order requiring that the development be carried out in accordance with a planning permission outstanding.

Murphy J.:

. . . Whilst I accept that in general the owner of property fronting on a public highway has ordinarily the right of access to the highway from every part of his property it seems to me entirely within the competence of a planning authority to impose conditions restrictive of the exercise by an owner of his property or other rights as a term of granting the particular permission. In so far as the right of access was authorised by the 1956 permission this was appurtenant to or formed part of the permission to erect two semi-detached houses which were never built. Moreover the access as actually laid out does not accord with that provided for in the plans approved in 1956. It seems to me that in effect the respondent is seeking to establish something in the nature of a composite permissson by selecting the mode of access as provided for in 1956; the general type of house as approved by the Gallagher permissions and the particular house as ratified by the retention permission granted by the Planning Board. In my view such an approach is not warranted by the Planning Acts. There is no single permission authorising the existing house with an access from the Castleknock Road. Indeed logically the house itself – not having conformed with the 1956 permission – is unauthorised if and as long as the access to it is directly from the Castleknock Road as the only permission authorising its retention requires the access in the manner provided by the retention permission of 1978.

A further effort was made by the respondent to regularise the matter by applying to the Planning Board for a ruling to the effect that the entrance to his premises was an exempted development and that question was decided adversely to his contention on the 26th of February, 1980. In my view the Court has no function to go behind that decision at this stage having regard to the fact that the time for appealing from that decision has expired. The respondent is understandably concerned by the fact that the closure of the access to the Castleknock Road will reduce considerably the value of his premises and furthermore create serious practical problems in relation to alternative modes of access. At the present time a wall erected by the respondent himself separates his premises from the estate road and there is some doubt as to the existence of a right of way in favour of the respondent over that road which has not yet been taken in charge. It may take some time to resolve these problems but resolved they must be. The reduction in value of the respondent's premises, however, is not in my view a relevant consideration in these proceedings.

The applicants have claimed an Order in the nature of a mandatory injunction requiring the respondent to carry out the development at Tudor Lodge in accordance with the later of the Gallagher planning permissions. I do not see the basis for making such an Order accepting, as I do, that the respondent did not purport to develop in accordance with that permission. It seems to me that the appropriate order at this stage is to grant an Order requiring the respondent to discontinue the unauthorised use of the present entrance to the premises Tudor Lodge (formerly 126 Castleknock Park) but to put a stay on the Order until further Order. The matter may be re-entered as soon as the estate has been taken in charge. As soon as I am satisfied that that has been done I will lift the stay on the Order.

CHAPTER 5: THE ENFORCEMENT OF PLANNING CONTROL
Section 27

DROGHEDA CORPORATION v. GANTLEY AND ORS
(Unreported) The High Court, Gannan J., 28 July 1983, (Ref. No. 1982 No. 57 MCA)

The Court made an order pursuant to section 27 requiring the first-named respondent to carry out specified works within a specified time and in default of him doing so the third and fourth-named respondents were to carry out the works. The order against the third and fourth-named respondents was to take effect only if the Insurance Corporation of Ireland failed to carry out the works under a guarantee Bond made between the first-named respondent and the Insurance Corporation of Ireland jointly with Drogheda Corporation. Liberty to apply was given. The third and fourth-named respondents re-entered the matter and sought an Order compelling the Insurance Corporation of Ireland to pay the fine or penalty under the Bond to the Drogheda Corporation. The Court held that S. 27 could not be used to call upon the Court to construe and enforce private contractual agreements between other parties which are entirely collateral or ancillary to the permitted development.

Gannon J.:
. . . . Recourse to the Court for relief by any claimant, complainant, or aggrieved party must be regulated in an orderly manner. The procedures for recourse to the High Court are regulated by the rule-making authority of the Superior Courts and are set out in the Rules of Court adopted in 1960 and as amended. Section 27 of the 1976 Act by sub-section (3) prescribes that an application for relief in the circumstnces and by the persons indicated in that section shall be made to the High Court by motion. But that section does not thereby purport to prescribe a procedure different from or at variance with the procedures prescribed by the Rules of the Superior Courts. The sub-section designates one of the procedures prescribed in the Rules as available for the relief conferred by section 27 but without altering the mode or nature of that procedure. The procedure by motion is normally resorted to

as incidental to proceedings initiated by summons or in relation to matters within the administrative functions of the courts. The reference in sub-section (3) of section 27 to making interim or interlocutory orders confirms that procedure under section 27 may be supplementary to substantive proceedings brought by summons for oral hearing of evidence. It would appear therefore that a final order may be made under section 27 upon a determination only of the issues put before the Court on affidavit by motion on notice or an order of a temporary nature may be made pending resolution of disputed questions of fact or law submitted for adjudication by formal pleadings.

The order made by Costello J., on the 9th of July 1982 appears to be a final order which deals completely with all matters then before the Court for determination. The addition to an order of the expression 'liberty to apply' is made in practice to enable further application to be made to the Court for the implementation of its order by way of enforcement or variation or suspension. I do not think this formula may be used for the purpose of requiring the Court to revise its decision or to entertain and resolve further to other matters in dispute which the parties had omitted to submit to the Court. It is not in my view a formula which permits a party found in default to resort to a type of third party procedure for the purpose of obtaining contribution or of casting on some third party the burden of compliance with the order made upon the claim. The nature of the application now brought by the above named third and fourth respondents goes even further as they do not claim contribution from the party intended to be added but merely seek enforcement against that party of a claim which the applicants, the planning authority, did not and do not make against that party. The nature of the order sought does not put it in the category of an implementation of the order made.

Section 27 of the Local Government (Planning and Development) Act, 1976 is unusual in that it allows persons who may have no interest in a development to have recourse to the courts to enforce obligations imposed in the public interest on designated authorities and persons to ensure that a development be carried out in conformity with planning permission. But I do not think section 27 of the 1976 Act goes so far as to allow persons to call upon the Court to construe and enforce private contractual arrangements between other parties which are entirely collateral or merely ancillary to the permitted development. An order pursuant to sub-section (2) of section 27 must specify in it what the Court requires the person designated in the order to do or to not do or to cease to do and such matters should appear to be necessary to ensure that the development be carried out in conformity with the permission granted. I do not think that this Court could specify the payment of a fine or a penalty by a guarantor upon the default of the compliance with the planning permission by the developer as something which ensures the carrying out of the development in conformity with the permission granted. This is particularly so when the applicants themselves are held by the Court liable to carry out the development but without any guarantor for their default.

This present application by the above-named third and fourth respondents in the title hereof does not come within the range of application authorized by section 27 of the 1976 Act nor within the procedures prescribed in the Rules of Court and accordingly must be dismissed.

Index